THE HENRY LOUIS GATES, JR. READER

THE
HENRY
LOUIS
GATES, JR.
READER

Henry Louis Gates, Jr.

Edited by Abby Wolf

BASIC *CIVITAS*
A Member of the Perseus Books Group
New York

Many of the essays in this collection have been revised and updated by the author since their original publication.

Books published by Basic *Civitas* Books are available at special discounts for bulk purchases in the United States by corporations, institutions, and other organizations. For more information, please contact the Special Markets Department at the Perseus Books Group, 2300 Chestnut Street, Suite 200, Philadelphia, PA 19103, or call (800) 810-4145, ext. 5000, or e-mail special.markets@perseusbooks.com.

Designed by Trish Wilkinson
Set in 10 point Baskerville

Library of Congress Cataloging-in-Publication Data

Gates, Henry Louis.
    The Henry Louis Gates, Jr. reader / Henry Louis Gates, Jr. ; edited by Abby Wolf.
        p.   cm.
    Includes bibliographical references and index.
    ISBN 978-0-465-02831-3 (hardcover : alk. paper) — ISBN 978-0-465-02924-2 (e-book) 1. American literature—African American authors—History and criticism. 2. African Americans in literature. 3. Literature and society—United States. I. Wolf, Abby. II. Title.
PS153.N5G273 2012
810.9'896073—dc23   2011049179

10 9 8 7 6 5 4 3 2 1

Dedicated to Frank H. Pearl,
for fulfilling the dream of W. E. B. Du Bois's
Africana Encyclopedia

CONTENTS

INTRODUCTION

MY FATHER DIED shortly before we began putting this reader together. He was 97 and a half years old when he passed, and for most of his time on Earth he was telling stories. His stories were rich and warm and wickedly funny, and they certainly were a form of sustenance to me. But they also left me always wanting more, so I went looking to our literature and history. And I found a treasure trove.

When I entered the field of Afro-American Studies, as it was called then, there were a few trailblazers showing us the way—for instance, Charles T. Davis, John Blassingame, and John Hope Franklin, to name but three. But we were working within a larger culture that could not comprehend a literary history for a people who, for much of their time in this country, not only had been denied literacy but also had been deemed unworthy of it. What our teachers found, and what we continued to unearth under their instruction, was a long and complex history of writing, reading, and representation. Black men and black women have imitated, manipulated, complicated, and *created* forms of literary expression (oral or written) that were sufficient to tell their own stories—stories of individuals and stories of a people—for most of the five centuries we have been in this country.

As workers in this "new" field, we devoted ourselves not only to understanding the substance of these stories but also to enumerating and theorizing their formal elements. We were interested in what the stories *meant*, of course, but also in how they were constructed. By establishing the consciousness that went into making these works, we were able to talk about African American consciousness itself, about the multitude of ways in which blacks have reflected on their own lives and the lives of others. Black writing did not just happen; it was not simply a spontaneous and disorganized profusion of words and images. Rather, it was an art that displayed the same craft, skill, and method as Shakespeare, romantic poetry, the novel, or any other literary form that has been pronounced canonical and, more to the point, legitimate. It has been my great honor as a member of the literary critical profession to help bring these stories to public view. There is certainly a thrill of discovery in finding a buried manuscript, but there is an even more profound thrill in seeing that manuscript on a high school syllabus.

For my entire reading and writing life, I have been driven mainly by two questions: Where are we?, and How did we get here? These are the questions that unite all of the pieces contained in this reader. Implicit in both of those questions is, of course, Where are we going? But as a scholar of literature and of history, I have not been in the habit of predicting. A reader of this type may gesture toward the future by suggesting continuums, but it necessarily looks back. It shines a light—sometimes loving, sometimes harsh—on one's body of existing work.

The selections that make up this reader display the common threads that have bound together even the most disparate-seeming pieces of my writing. The chapter from *The Signifying Monkey*, for instance, traffics in the jargon of literary theory whereas an essay like "Family Matters" for *The New Yorker* takes a belletristic tone. But however different the sounds of the pieces may be, and whether I was writing about the African origins of literary signification or the narrative history of my family, I have been deeply concerned with and devoted to tracing roots.

Over the course of my career, I have moved from exploring the roots of our literature to exploring the literal roots of our people. Rather than interpreting our lives by deconstructing literary texts, I now more often attempt to reconstruct our past by interpreting genealogical and historical documents. But the same impulses are still there. I'm still fascinated by the stories that get told and how those stories are told. This love of stories is something I learned at home; it is, indeed, something that makes any place I am a home. I am proud to be a part of this African American literary and historical genealogy, and though, as I said, I am not in the habit of predicting the future, I imagine a rich and colorful one for people of African descent as we continue to make our way in the world through our words and stories.

A note on the text: We have chosen not to update the pieces in this book, and we have retained the style of each of the original publications.

Henry Louis Gates, Jr.
Cambridge, Mass.

PART I
GENEALOGIES

THE AFRICAN AMERICAN literary tradition gives a privileged place to stories of family and descent. Sometimes these are families bound by blood; other times these are families forged by necessity. This tradition is certainly not unique in its regard for genealogy. But often, and uniquely, these stories reflect the fractures that slavery wrought on the African American family, the currents of pain, and the burden of rebuilding that slavery left in its wake.

Gates's own family history is characterized less by fractures than solidity. Both sides of his family, the Colemans and the Gateses, lived in slavery and then in freedom in the same area of West Virginia and Western Maryland for 250 years. Still, there were stories to be uncovered, histories to be unearthed, and myths to be put to rest. While his genealogy films date only from 2006, his personal family history has been a subject of great interest since his childhood; it has been the source of some of his most lyrical writing since he published a memoir of his boyhood home, *Colored People*, in 1994.

This section ends with Gates's meditation on the election of President Barack Obama, which was a moment both of unmatched historical significance and of intensely personal—familial—reflection. Placed as it is here, it is difficult not to imagine how Obama's election would have been celebrated on the streets of Piedmont, West Virginia, and how it would have been marveled at and welcomed by ancestors such as Jane Gates and John Redman.

Abby Wolf

FAMILY MATTERS

MY FATHER'S FATHER, Edward St. Lawrence Gates—known to his children and grandchildren as Pop—had two hobbies. He was renowned for one of them in and around his hometown of Cumberland, Maryland: he grew tulips—"like a Dutchman," people said. He practically looked like a Dutchman, too—"light and bright and damned near white," as my father used to say. I learned about his second hobby only after his death, in 1960, when he was eighty-one and I was nine.

Pop Gates was buried at the Rose Hill Cemetery, where our forebears were among the very few Negroes allowed to disturb the eternal sleep of Cumberland's élite white Episcopal citizenry. The town's Episcopal churches had been segregated at least since the black St. Philips offered its first Communion, on June 19, 1910. That day, the church's records show, Pop, his mother, Maud, his wife, Gertrude Helen Redman, and about half a dozen other Gateses took the Sacrament, which was offered by the Diocese of Maryland's white bishop.

I was struck by how different Rose Hill was from Thorn Rose, the all-colored cemetery in Keyser, West Virginia, where my mother's relatives had been buried. The effect was one of unkempt, chaotic modesty, each plot separately maintained by the family of the deceased. The dead at Rose Hill, by contrast, looked almost prosperous, their graves immaculate, some even regnant, crowned with ornate granite memorials. Rose Hill had a full-time groundskeeper and a stone-clad gatehouse, where records of the dead were kept. It was locked at night, unlike Thorn Rose, where just about everyone went to make out. At Thorn Rose, records of the dead seemed to exist only in the collective memory of the families whose ancestors were buried there.

My brother and I had been made keenly aware, early in our childhood, that the Gateses had a certain status in Cumberland. No one ever explained whether it was because they had owned property for a very long time in what is still mostly a white neighborhood, or because of light-skin privilege,

3

or some combination of both. Being a Gates was somehow special, and not just within the black community in Cumberland.

After Pop's burial, my father took us back to the Gates family home, at 505 Green Street, a two-family house that my great-grandfather had bought in 1882. My brother and I followed my father up stairs that I had never climbed. As we walked in single file behind my dad, I noticed that the walls of the living room and staircase of my grandparents' house were lined with framed sets of blue, red, and yellow ribbons, which Pop had won for his tulips. My grandparents' bedroom was a cabinet of wonders, its walls decorated with only blue ribbons, along with photographs of family members I would never meet. My dad led my brother and me past the bedroom and onto a sun porch adjoining it. On the right was a trunk that was brimming with toys; it reminded me of something I'd recently seen in a Disney movie. My father turned left, though. Opening a closet door, he pulled out dozens of musty leather books: partially used bank ledgers. (Pop had once been a janitor at the First National Bank on Baltimore Street.) The books were about an inch thick, with big blue- and red-lined pages. A few had been tied with string where the red leather binding had lost its strength. Slowly and silently, he turned glue-stiffened pages that were covered, front and back, with newspaper clippings. So—Pop Gates had kept scrapbooks! That was his second hobby.

The clippings covered various news stories and human-interest items. There were hundreds of them, seemingly random, sharing only a macabre tenor: headlines about injuries and death, especially murders and fatal accidents; articles about war casualties, robberies, automobile accidents, and even plane crashes. Nestled among them were obituaries, funeral notices, funeral programs, and those laminated bookmarks noting the passing of the dead, complete with a bit of religious verse, a passage from the Bible, birth and death dates, and sometimes a photograph of the deceased. Those scrapbooks were like an archive, decade by decade, of Cumberland's colored dead, although plenty of dead white people poked their pale visages out of those pages as well, fighting for air among all those Negroes.

After a while, it occurred to me that the white and the colored denizens of the obituary notices were dressed alike, their sartorial equality reflecting the shared aesthetic of an Olan Mills photography parlor: three-piece suits and white starched collars, hair slicked down or pressed. I felt as if those scrapbooks were a portal into a world I did not know. I began to wonder: Who were these people?

"Look here, boy," Daddy said, startling me as he broke the silence. There, deep in those yellowing pages of newsprint, were two obituaries. One, dated Saturday, January 7, 1888, was from the Cumberland *Evening Times*. The headline read "DEATH OF 'AUNT JANE GATES'":

Last night at 11 o'clock 'Aunt Jane Gates,' colored, a family servant of the Stover's died in the 75th year of her age. She has lived for a long time on Green Street where her death occurred. Her remains will be interred at Rose Hill Cemetery to-morrow afternoon at 3 o'clock. Services will be held at her residence on Green Street.

I especially remember another article that called her "an estimable colored woman." Daddy then retrieved a framed photograph of this woman, who had lived just up the street from where we sat, and was buried steps away from Pop Gates's newly dug grave. "That woman was Pop's grandmother," Daddy said. "She is your great-great-grandmother. And she is the oldest Gates."

I stared at the picture until I had that face memorized, an image of the oldest colored woman I'd ever seen, etched indelibly into my nine-year-old head. In 1979, my great-aunt Pansy made a present to me of the original, which now hangs in my kitchen. What was most striking about the woman in the photograph, apart from the white nurse's hat and uniform she wore, was that she didn't look like a Gates. She was much darker than her grandson. I would have guessed that she was about my color, although the sepia patina that the photograph has acquired over a century and a quarter makes it hard to tell. But she had a long, straight nose, light eyes, high cheekbones, and an austere countenance. Her hair, poking out from under her nurse's bonnet, appeared to be a curly wave. She didn't look especially feminine; in fact, she could have been a man in drag, as my father pointed out years later with irreverent glee.

Finally, Daddy shut the album and slowly stood up. By the time we made our way downstairs, the house was teeming with family. Enough food to start a restaurant had been crowded onto the oak dining table. I headed for the fried chicken and the potato salad, hungry all of a sudden, not sure what had taken place upstairs. When I got home, I looked up the word "estimable."

My career as a historian began that afternoon in 1960. Soon after the funeral, I became obsessed with my family tree. I peppered my mother and father with questions about the names of their ancestors, their birthplaces and birthdays, their occupations, the places and dates of their deaths. My father was the storyteller of the family, and most of my conversations about our ancestors ended up being with him.

And, besides, I was far more concerned with my Gates lineage than I was with my mother's ancestors, as I was convinced that if any distinction was to be found on my family tree, it would be through the Gates branches, given the family members' skin color and the texture of their hair, and the fact that they had owned so much property for so long, including a two-hundred-acre farm, where my father was born, in 1913, at Patterson Creek, just across the West Virginia border. On more than one occasion, my father tried to tell me that my mother's family was more distinguished than his, but I thought that he was being modest. He never seemed to tire of these interrogations, even when I repeated questions that I had asked a year or two earlier. I dutifully began to write it all down, in a brown spiral notebook.

Sometimes I would grow bored and put the notebook away; then, after a few days or weeks had passed, I would be seized with a desire to learn more. Once, I took my notebook for a presentation before my fifth-grade class but found myself embarrassed that I was unable to explain, when asked, how my ancestors had come to be slaves, or where in Africa they had come from. The girl who asked was, like most of my classmates, white. As far as I knew, the only way to explore a black family's history was through family stories.

Eventually, as glossy magazines began to advertise that they could send you your family's "coat of arms," I longed to possess the knowledge that would allow me to claim one of these. What I really wanted, as much as the family tree detailing the identity of my African-American ancestors, was a family crest that would tie us to our white ancestors. History had allowed them to hide, to avoid responsibility for their progeny. Perhaps that crest could lead to a new set of ancestors and cousins whose identities had been reduced to whispers, gossip, and wishful thinking—the speculation, sometimes playful and sometimes maddened, that fuelled so many discussions among my father and his siblings.

When we studied American Colonial history in fourth grade, we learned that the first black slaves arrived on the James River in 1619, two hundred years before Jane Gates was born. Were there black people who could trace their families back that far? I couldn't bring myself to order the family tree of some other Gates line, though I did relish the idea that we were related, somehow, to Horatio Gates, the Revolutionary War general whom we had studied at school.

I was searching not just for the names of my ancestors to fill out my family tree but also for stories about them. Each new name that I was able to find and print in my notebook was another link to the colored past that had produced, by fits and starts, but also, inevitably, the person I had become and was becoming. On my mother's side, J. R. Clifford, my great-uncle, was, I learned, the first black man to be admitted to the bar in the state of West Virginia. Far more thrilling to me was the fact that, during the Civil War, he had served in the U.S. Colored Troops. He had also published his own newspaper, the *Pioneer Press*, in Martinsburg, West Virginia. Later, I learned that, in 1905, he had co-founded the Niagara Movement—the forerunner of the NAACP—with W. E. B. Du Bois. On my father's side, three generations of Jane Gates's descendants had graduated from Howard University, starting with my great-aunt Pansy, in 1910, and including two generations of dentists. My father's first cousin had graduated from Harvard Law School in 1949; there he had met his wife, who, in 1955, was the first black woman to earn a Ph.D. in comparative literature at Harvard. Kind of hard to top that, my father would argue, but J. R. Clifford knew Du Bois, and Du Bois was the ultimate trump card, black history's ace of spades.

With just a little effort, most African-Americans can trace at least one line of their family back to the 1870 federal census, which was the first taken after the Civil War and is therefore the first in which all our ancestors appear as citizens with two names, rather than as property. In the 1850 and 1860 censuses, there is a list of "Slave Inhabitants" held by each owner by age, gender, and color (black or mulatto), but not by name. Since many freedmen took their surnames from their masters, one part of the pre-1870 puzzle can sometimes be solved through a simple comparison: once you have found your ancestor in the 1870 census, you can examine the "Slave Inhabitants" list from the 1850 and 1860 censuses to see if a white person with the same surname and in the same geographical area owned a slave; then see whether a slave ten or twenty years younger than your ancestor is identified on those lists. Estate papers and property records can also be used to cobble together a history of slave ancestors. The 1870 census, which relied on the same door-to-door information gathering used when I was a boy, lists all the members of a particular household, by their full names, birth places, ages, and occupations.

Census data, despite their simplicity, can be surprisingly revealing. The entry for Jane Gates, for example, says the following, if I summarize the relevant columns: "Jane Gates, age 51, female, mulatto, laundress and nurse, owns real estate valued at $1,400, born in Maryland, cannot read or write." A mulatto? An illiterate mulatto at that? Nothing in the oral lore of the Gates family had prepared me for either of these facts. Who was Jane's father? And who was the father of her children? With her in the house are her daughter Alice, age twenty-two; her son Edward, age twelve; and two grandchildren (Jennie, age five, and David, age nine, both children of her daughter Laura). Edward and David are in school and can read and write. Alice can read but not write; she also works as a laundress and nurse.

As a child, I had been told with absolute certainty that the Gateses were descended from an Irishman named Samuel Brady, who supposedly owned Jane, fathered her children, and gave her the money to purchase her home.

Jane's son (and Pop's father), Edward, my great-grandfather, who was born into slavery in 1857, on Brady's farm, would, when questioned by his children, respond only that he and his siblings all shared the same father. It was his children—my grandfather's generation—who were the source of the Brady rumor. Had Jane given her son some clue that this was so? Did Edward the elder whisper it to Pop in a moment of speculation or confessional intimacy? Whatever the source of the rumor, it had become canon law by the time I was born.

The more I learned about Brady and the Gateses, the more likely it seemed that he had known Jane and, indeed, slept with her, as family lore held. Edward Gates was born—I learned from his obituary of 1945—"on Brady Farm near Cresaptown." According to extensive research by Jane Ailes, a genealogist (and Brady's third-great-granddaughter), Samuel Brady had a farm just outside Cresaptown, exactly as family legend had it. And between 1828 and 1865 Samuel Brady owned slaves, starting with one, and reaching a high point of forty-two in 1850, according to the federal census. Brady was a study in contradictions: three of his sons fought for the Confederacy, and one of them spent eighteen months in a Union prison; nevertheless, a year before the war ended, Brady signed deeds of manumission for four of his slaves so that they could enlist in the 30th Regiment of the U.S. Colored Troops and fight for the North.

Emboldened by these findings, I set out to prove or disprove the family story about the supposed father of Jane's children. In the past decade, developments in DNA testing and the retrieval and digitization of archival records have made it possible for black families to begin to trace their ancestry further back through American history and, ultimately, even across the Atlantic. In 2005, I placed an advertisement in the Cumberland *Times* and posted a message on a Brady family online forum asking for male descendants of Samuel Brady to identify themselves, hoping that one would submit a DNA sample for a belated paternity test.

One of Brady's direct male descendants and a direct male descendant of Brady's brother William agreed to take a DNA test. The tests established, without a doubt, that Samuel Brady was not the father of Jane Gates's children. When I told my father and his sister, Helen, what the tests had revealed, Aunt Helen summed up the reaction of just about all the Gates family members: "I've been a Brady eighty-nine years, and I am still a Brady, no matter what that test says."

I found myself pleased at Aunt Helen's defiance, as irrational as it might seem; I guess I had always thought of myself as a Brady, so being told that we weren't Bradys was a bit like being orphaned. For my cousin John Gates, there will always be two stories about our ancestry: the story that our genes tell, and the story that our ancestors told. And he wants both to be in play for his three sons and his grandchildren. The challenge of genealogy used to be the reconciliation of a family's oral memories with public written records, and in the search for one's ancestors nothing is as pleasing as having these two streams of testimony confirm each other. But genetics can now demolish or affirm a family's most cherished beliefs and stories with just a bit of saliva and a cotton swab.

What about the father of Jane's children, then? Well, given that all males with my Y-DNA marker (it's known as the Ui Neill haplotype) bear one of a few dozen surnames, a team of genealogists and I have begun to compile a list of all the men with those names in the 1850 and 1860 censuses for Allegany County, Maryland. We are advertising for their male descendants, and asking them to take a DNA test. With a little patience, and a lot of luck, perhaps DNA can solve the last remaining mystery in the Gates family line, the secret that Jane Gates took with her to her grave.

African-American history is a young discipline; restoring the branches of even one black family tree can profoundly change our understanding of the larger story of who the African-American people really are. By telling and retelling the stories of our own ancestors, we can move that history from our kitchens and parlors into the textbooks, ultimately changing the official narrative of American history itself.

My family tree hangs in my kitchen, just across from the photo of Jane Gates. But the graphic record of the entangled blood lines, impressive and gratifying though it is, does not fulfill my boyhood longing for a coat of arms. Of the scores of names neatly arrayed in those boxes, only one is that of a white ancestor, even though a "genetic admixture" test reveals me to be fifty percent "European." Until the family crest of the Irishman who fathered Jane Gates's children graces my family tree, along with his name and the names of his ancestors, my family story will remain a tale only half told.

Then again, I'm still amazed by the ancestral additions I've already gained. The genealogists, in the process of researching my family tree, found three sets of my fourth-great-grandparents, all free Negroes, including, on my mother's side, John Redman, who enlisted in the Continental Army, at Winchester, Virginia, in 1778, and served until 1782, seeing combat near Savannah, Georgia. So we had a patriot ancestor after all, even if his name wasn't Horatio and even if he wasn't a Gates. When I discovered that my mother had descended from seven lines of Negroes who had been freed by the eighteen-thirties—three of them by 1776—I felt chagrined that I hadn't spent more time interviewing her. She had an enigmatic reserve when it came to her family's past, an attitude that was in stark contrast to my father's fondness for vivid narratives. "We come from people," she liked to say.

I had long assumed that Pop Gates's scrapbooks had been discarded, perhaps after a spring cleaning, by someone who wasn't aware of their value or by someone who didn't wish to revisit the past. As part of the celebration of my father's ninety-fifth birthday, I decided to scan the photographs owned by the far-flung Gates family members, so that we could collect them in a book and present it to him. Amid my Aunt Helen's possessions, my cousin Bette found a red-and-black bank ledger, full of old news clippings and stamped with the logo of Cumberland's First National Bank. My grandfather was such a shadowy figure in my life that I can't even remember the sound of his voice. But the discovery of this scrapbook, covering the years 1943–46, allowed me to take a stroll through his mind.

I am tempted to call the scrapbook Pop Gates's Book of the Dead, just as I might have been when I was nine. Its interpretation of the grim theme is even more all-encompassing than I remembered, though. The book is full of statistics about war casualties but also contains intimate features about the individual dead. And tallies of Cumberland's wartime losses are mixed in with articles cataloguing the massacre of thousands of Jews and Serbs and reports about the starving population of India.

On April 5, 1943, an article reports that the governor of Alabama "Calls for Full Racial Segregation": "The two races are distinct. They occupy spheres in life that began in different origins, have continued in diverging channels and should remain separate, as they have always been since the creation. No influences from outside should or can change these fundamental safety principles." But the war was bringing hope for race relations, and Pop recorded that, too. While, early in the scrapbook, an AP article applauds "the first all-Negro division activated by the United States Army" because "at the outbreak of the war, the American Negro clamored for an active part in the nation's war effort," a feature near the book's end, datelined Paris, March 20, 1945, announces, "Negroes and Whites . . . Go Into Battle Side by Side for First Times in U.S. Army History." The pages of Pop's chronicle celebrate the appointment of Francis Ellis Rivers as a City Court judge in New York, as well as the first nine months of service of Hugh Mulzac, the "First Negro Captain of an American Ship."

Pop compiled these clippings about the wartime heroics of black servicemen while working as a janitor at the First National Bank. At sixty-three, he was too old to serve but was required to register. Pop's draft-registration card from 1942 contains the fullest description of him that has ever come to my attention: his height is five feet eight inches, his eyes are hazel, his weight is a hundred and sixty-two pounds, his hair is gray, and his complexion is "ruddy." (The choices for complexion were "sallow," "light," "ruddy," "dark," "freckled," "light brown," "dark brown," and "black.") Under the column for "Race," the "White" box had initially been checked; evidently, the registrar had taken him for a white man. In decisive black ink, the check mark was crossed out. The registrant must have demurred. (By contrast, Pop's brother Roscoe chose to take advantage of a similar error that year and pass for white.) Identity wasn't merely a matter of skin color; it was a matter of history. Pop knew himself to be an estimable colored man. The new check mark appeared beside "Negro."

SOURCE: *The New Yorker*, December 1, 2008.

MY YIDDISHE MAMA

SINCE 1977, WHEN I sat riveted every night for a week in front of my TV, I have had "Roots" envy. Even if scholars remain deeply skeptical about his methodology, Alex Haley went to his grave believing that he had found the ethnic group from which his African ancestors originated before surviving the dreaded Middle Passage.

Two years before, I proudly told a fellow student at Cambridge, an Anglo-Ghanaian, that I could trace my slave ancestors back to 1819, the birth date of Jane Gates, my paternal great-great-grandmother. I wondered if he could do better?

He invited me to accompany him to the University Library, where, buried deep in the stacks, he found a copy of Burke's Peerage, then walked me through his mother's English ancestry with certainty back to one Richard Crispe who died in 1575, and who, the book said "probably" descended from William Crispe, who had died in 1207. His father's side, members of the Asante people in Ghana, he could trace to the 17th century. The roots of my "Roots" envy?

After years of frustration, I determined to do something about it. So I decided to invite eight prominent African Americans to allow their DNA to be tested and their family histories to be researched for a documentary film. When the paper trail would end, inevitably, in the abyss of slavery, we would then try to find their African roots through science.

Having been involved in after-school programs, I was hoping to get inner-city school kids engaged by the wonders of both genetics and archival research.

But I had ulterior motives, too. I wanted to find my white patriarch, the father of Jane Gates's children. Maybe genetics could verify the family legend that the father of Jane's children was an Irish man from Cresaptown, Md., a slave-holder named Samuel Brady. Perhaps I could give Jane her Thomas Jefferson–Sally Hemings moment!

I also had hopes for my African origins. Throughout my adult life, I've always been drawn to Nigeria's Yoruba culture—to its cuisine, its legends, its rhythms and its songs. As a Fela Ransome-Kuti album played in my head, I wondered whether geneticists could determine that I had physical, not only spiritual, affinities to the Yoruba.

Our genealogists as well as our geneticists were given a tough assignment. Five generations ago, each of us has 32 ancestors, or two to the fifth power. If we go back 10 generations, or 300 years, each of us has 1,024 theoretical ancestors, or two to the 10th power. Even with genetics, we can only trace two of our family lines. The first African slaves arrived in Virginia in 1619; the slaves were freed in 1865, and appeared with two legal names for the first time in the 1870 census. Penetrating the name barrier of 1870 required detailed and imaginative sleuthing through the records of slave-holders, praying that they somehow mentioned one of their slaves by first name, in wills, tax records or estate division papers.

The stories that we found are not the sort found in textbooks, which tend either to recreate Black History through the narratives of great women and men, or else through broad social movements. We were able to find stirring stories of heretofore anonymous individuals who made heroic contributions against seemingly insurmountable odds. If the promise of America was the right to own land, very few blacks were able to do so before the middle of the 20th century. But some did.

Oprah Winfrey's great-great-grandfather, Constantine Winfrey, a farm worker in Mississippi, had the audacity to approach a white man, John Watson, in 1876, and make a wager: If he picked 10 bales of cotton in one year, Watson would give Winfrey 80 acres of his land in return. (In 1870, a bale of cotton weighed 500 pounds.) On June 21, 1881, a property deed recorded the land exchange between the two. Constantine is listed in the 1870 census as illiterate; 10 years later, he had learned to read and write. And when, in 1906, the local "colored school" was slated for destruction, Constantine arranged to save it by having it moved to this property.

Chris Tucker's great-great-grandfather, Theodore Arthur Bryant Sr., sold off parcels of his land to his black neighbors for below-market prices so that they would not join the Great Migration to the North, thereby saving the black community of Flat Rock, Ga.

Whoopi Goldberg's great-great-grandparents, William and Eisa Washington, in 1878 received 104.5 acres in Alachua County, Fla., under the Southern Homestead Act of 1866. Less than 10% of black petitioners in Florida received land. "My country 'tis of thee," Whoopi exclaimed, when she received this news. "My country."

In the case of the astronaut Mae Jemison, we were able, incredibly, to trace three of her family lines deep into slavery, including discovering both a fourth great-grandmother and a fourth or fifth great-grandfather. Four of our subjects are descended from people who owned property in the 1800s, two well before the Civil War, and two more by 1881. The latter two, freed in 1865, in effect got their 40 acres, if not the mule.

Our genetic research also yielded a rich panoply of results, and a few surprises. My subjects share common ancestry with, among others, members of the Mbundu of Angola, the Kpelle of Liberia, the Tikar of Cameroon, the Igbo of Nigeria, the Mandinka and the Pepel of Guinea-Bissau, the Makua of Mozambique, and the Bamileke of Cameroon. I had expected the revelation of their African roots to form the dramatic climax of our research. But our subjects' reactions to their putative genetic identities remained somewhat abstract.

What really stirred them was the light shed on their American heritage, their known world, as Edward Jones put it. It was a world they could touch and imagine, through the branches of their family trees. Genealogy trumped genetics. It was as if Africa, as the poet Langston Hughes wrote, was "so long, so far away." Roots, like charity, start at home.

Contrary to conventional wisdom, and contrary to those who worry about "the geneticization of identity," our sense of identity—in this case at least—seems to be more deeply rooted in the histories of family members we can name than in anonymous ancestors emerging out of the dense shadows of an African past, unveiled through a process admittedly still in its infancy. For my subjects, genealogy seems to have been a way of staking a claim on a richer American identity, an identity established through individual triumphs like the attainment of literacy and the purchasing of land.

What of my own case of "Roots" envy? We advertised for, and found, two male descendants of Samuel Brady, and compared their Y-DNA with mine. My haplotype, common in Western Ireland and the Netherlands, has as much in common genetically with Samuel Brady as it does, I suppose, with half of the males in Galway and Amsterdam. So much for that bit of family lore.

On the other hand, our genealogical research uncovered, to my astonishment, one of my fifth great-grandfathers and two fourth great-grandfathers, two born in the middle of the 18th century. I learned that one, John Redman, a Free Negro, even fought in the American Revolution. Despite the fact that we didn't find Jane Gates's children's father, we believe that we have found her mother, a slave, born circa 1799.

As for my mitochondrial DNA, my mother's mother's mother's lineage? Would it be Yoruba, as I fervently hoped? My Fela Ransome-Kuti fantasy was not exactly borne out. A number of exact matches turned up, leading straight back to that African Kingdom called Northern Europe, to the genes of (among others) a female Ashkenazi Jew. Maybe it was time to start listening to "My Yiddishe Mama."

SOURCE: *The Wall Street Journal,* February 1, 2006.

NATIVE SONS OF LIBERTY

ON JUNE 11, 1823, a man named John Redman walked into the courtroom of Judge Charles Lobb in Hardy County, Virginia, to apply for a pension, claiming to be a veteran of the Revolutionary War. Redman, more than 60 years old, testified that he had been in the First Virginia Regiment of Light Dragoons from Christmas 1778 through 1782, serving initially as a waiter to Lt. Vincent Howell.

The Light Dragoons fought mainly on horseback, using sabers, pistols, and light carbines. They marched from Winchester, Va., to Georgia, where, in the fall of 1779, they laid siege to Savannah. The following year, they fought in Charleston, S.C., narrowly escaping capture in a rout by the British. Redman's regiment fought the Creek Indians and the British early in 1782, ultimately triumphing over them in June at Sharon, Ga., near Savannah. After the war, Redman settled in Hardy County, where he and his wife kept a farm.

Four decades later, a neighbor and fellow veteran named John Jenkins affirmed Redman's court testimony. A few weeks later, Redman was granted his Certificate of Pension, receiving the tidy sum of $8 a month until his death in 1836.

Yet standing before Judge Lobb in his courtroom that morning in 1823, John Redman had every reason to be nervous, for his appeal was anything but ordinary. Redman was the rarest of breeds: not just a patriot, but a black patriot—both a free Negro in a nation of slaves and a black man who had fought in a white man's war.

In 1790, only 1.7 percent of Virginia's population consisted of free people of color; in the 13 former colonies and the territories of Kentucky, Maine and Vermont, the combined figure was even smaller. Historians estimate that only 5,000 black men served in the Continental Army, whereas tens of thousands fled slavery to join the British.

The story of John Redman is illuminating because it opens a window on an aspect of the Revolutionary War that remains too little known: the contributions and sacrifices of a band of black patriots. But it is particularly fascinating to me because, as I learned just recently, John Redman was my ancestor.

I have been obsessed with my family tree since I was a boy. My grandfather, Edward Gates, died in 1960, when I was 9. After his burial at Rose Hill Cemetery in Cumberland, Md.—Gateses have been buried there since 1888—my father showed me my grandfather's scrapbooks. There, buried in those yellowing pages of newsprint, was an obituary, the obituary, to my astonishment, of our matriarch, a midwife and former slave named Jane Gates. "An estimable colored woman," the obituary said.

I wanted to know how I got here from there, from the mysterious and shadowy preserve of slavery in the depths of the black past, to my life as a 10-year-old Negro boy living blissfully in a stable, loving family in Piedmont, W. Va., circa 1960, in the middle of the civil rights movement.

I peppered my father with questions about the names and dates of my ancestors, both black and white, and dutifully recorded the details in a notebook. I wanted to see my white ancestors' coat of arms. Eventually, I even allowed myself to dream of discovering which tribe we had come from in Africa.

More recently, in part to find my own roots, I started work on a documentary series on genetics and black genealogy. I especially wanted to find my white patriarch, the father of Jane Gates's children. The genealogical research into my family tree uncovered, to my great wonder, three of my fourth great-grandfathers on my mother's side: Isaac Clifford, Joe Bruce and John Redman.

All were black and born in the middle of the 18th century; two gained freedom by the beginning of the Revolutionary War. All three lived in the vicinity of Williamsport, a tiny town in the Potomac Valley in the Allegheny Mountains, in what is now West Virginia.

I am descended from these men through my maternal grandmother, Marguerite Howard, whom we affectionately called "Big Mom." When Jane Ailes, a genealogist, revealed these discoveries to me, I could scarcely keep my composure. In searching for a white ancestor, I had found—improbably—a black patriot instead.

Frankly, it had never occurred to me that I, or anyone in the many branches of my family—Gateses, Colemans, Howards, Bruces, Cliffords, and Redmans—had even the remotest relationship to the American Revolution, or to anyone who had fought in it. If anyone had told me a year ago that this summer I would be inducted into the Sons of the American Revolution as the descendant of a black patriot—183 years almost to the day after John

Redman proved his claim—I would have laughed. I had long supposed that slavery had robbed my ancestors of the privilege of fighting for the birth of this country.

Like most African-Americans of my generation, I had heard of the Daughters of the American Revolution, unfortunately, because of their refusal in 1939 to allow the great contralto, Marian Anderson, the right to perform at Constitution Hall. Anderson responded to the group's racism with sonorous defiance, holding her Easter Sunday concert on the steps of the Lincoln Memorial instead.

In part to make amends for their treatment of Anderson, the Daughters of the American Revolution have begun counting the number of black patriots; so far they have documented about 3,000. Harvard's Du Bois Institute and the Sons of the American Revolution are now researching the 80,000 pension and bounty land warrant applications of Revolutionary War veterans to compare these names to census records from 1790 to 1840.

Already, in just a few weeks, we have discovered almost a dozen African-Americans who served in the war and whose racial identity had been lost or undetected. With this systematic approach, we hope to expand substantially our knowledge of African-Americans who served in the Continental Army and, eventually, to reach a definitive number.

Once the research is completed, we will advertise for descendants of these individuals and encourage them to join the Sons or Daughters of the American Revolution, thus increasing the organizations' black memberships beyond the meager few dozen or so the two groups have now. (If all of my aunts, uncles and cousins who are also descended from John Redman join, we will quadruple the number of black members in both organizations!)

We want to establish the exact number of descendants of African-Americans who served in the Continental Army, great American patriots, defenders of liberty to which they themselves were not entitled.

Of course, it is perfectly irrelevant, in one sense, what one's ancestors did two centuries ago; but re-imagining our past, as Americans, can sometimes help us to re-imagine our future. In doing so, it may help to understand that the founding of this Republic was not only red, white and blue, it was also indelibly black.

SOURCE: *The New York Times Week in Review*, August 6, 2006.

IN THE KITCHEN

WE ALWAYS HAD a gas stove in the kitchen, though electric cooking became fashionable in Piedmont, like using Crest toothpaste rather than Colgate, or watching Huntley and Brinkley rather than Walter Cronkite. But for us it was gas, Colgate, and good ole Walter Cronkite, come what may. We used gas partly out of loyalty to Big Mom, Mama's mama, because she was mostly blind and still loved to cook, and she could feel her way better with gas than with electric.

But the most important thing about our gas-equipped kitchen was that Mama used to do hair there. She had a "hot comb"—a fine-toothed iron instrument with a long wooden handle—and a pair of iron curlers that opened and closed like scissors: Mama would put them into the gas fire until they glowed. You could smell those prongs heating up.

I liked what that smell meant for the shape of my day. There was an intimate warmth in the women's tones as they talked with my mama while she did their hair. I knew what the women had been through to get their hair ready to be "done," because I would watch Mama do it to herself. How that scorched kink could be transformed through grease and fire into a magnificent head of wavy hair was a miracle to me. Still is.

Mama would wash her hair over the sink, a towel wrapped round her shoulders, wearing just her half-slip and her white bra. (We had no shower until we moved down Rat Tail Road into Doc Wolverton's house, in 1954.) After she had dried it, she would grease her scalp thoroughly with blue Bergamot hair grease, which came in a short, fat jar with a picture of a beautiful colored lady on it. It's important to grease your scalp real good, my mama would explain, to keep from burning yourself.

Of course, her hair would return to its natural kink almost as soon as the hot water and shampoo hit it. To me, it was another miracle how hair so "straight" would so quickly become kinky again once it even approached some water.

My mama had only a few "clients" whose heads she "did"—and did, I think, because she enjoyed it, rather than for the few dollars it brought in. They would sit on one of our red plastic kitchen chairs, the kind with the shiny metal legs, and brace themselves for the process. Mama would stroke that red-hot iron, which by this time had been in the gas fire for half an hour or more, slowly but firmly through their hair, from scalp to strand's end. It made a scorching, crinkly sound, the hot iron did, as it burned its way through damp kink, leaving in its wake the straightest of hair strands, each of them standing up long and tall but drooping at the end, like the top of a heavy willow tree. Slowly, steadily, with deftness and grace, Mama's hands would transform a round mound of Odetta kink into a darkened swamp of everglades. The Bergamot made the hair shiny; the heat of the hot iron gave it a brownish-red cast. Once all the hair was as straight as God allows kink to get, Mama would take the well-heated curling iron and twirl the straightened strands into more or less loosely wrapped curls. She claimed that she owed her strength and skill as a hairdresser to her wrists, and her little finger would poke out the way it did when she sipped tea. Mama was a southpaw, who wrote upside down and backwards to produce the cleanest, roundest letters you've ever seen.

The "kitchen" she would all but remove from sight with a pair of shears bought for this purpose. Now, the *kitchen* was the room in which we were sitting, the room where Mama did hair and washed clothes, and where each of us bathed in a galvanized tub. But the word has another meaning, and the "kitchen" I'm speaking of now is the very kinky bit of hair at the back of the head, where the neck meets the shirt collar. If there ever was one part of our African past that resisted assimilation, it was the kitchen. No matter how hot the iron, no matter how powerful the chemical, no matter how stringent the mashed-potatoes-and-lye formula of a man's "process," neither God nor woman nor Sammy Davis, Jr., could straighten the kitchen. The kitchen was permanent, irredeemable, invincible kink. Unassimilably African. No matter what you did, no matter how hard you tried, nothing could dekink a person's kitchen. So you trimmed it off as best you could.

When hair had begun to "turn," as they'd say, or return to its natural kinky glory, it was the kitchen that turned first. When the kitchen started creeping up the back of the neck, it was time to get your hair done again. The kitchen around the back, and nappy edges at the temples.

Sometimes, after dark, Mr. Charlie Carroll would come to have his hair done. Mr. Charlie Carroll was very light-complected and had a ruddy nose, the kind of nose that made me think of Edmund Gwenn playing Kris Kringle in *Miracle on 34th Street*. At the beginning, they did it after Rocky and I had gone to sleep. It was only later that we found out he had come to our house so Mama could iron his hair—not with a hot comb and curling iron but with our very own Proctor-Silex steam iron. For some reason, Mr. Charlie would conceal his Frederick Douglass mane under a big white Stetson hat, which I never saw him take off. Except when he came to our house, late at night, to have his hair pressed.

(Later, Daddy would tell us about Mr. Charlie's most prized piece of knowledge, which the man would confide only after his hair had been pressed, as a token of intimacy. "Not many people know this," he'd say in a tone of circumspection, "but George Washington was Abraham Lincoln's daddy." Nodding solemnly, he'd add the clincher: "A white man told me." Though he was in dead earnest, this became a humorous refrain around the house—"a white man told me"—used to punctuate especially preposterous assertions.)

My mother furtively examined my daughters' kitchens whenever we went home for a visit in the early eighties. It became a game between us. I had told her not to do it, because I didn't like the politics it suggested of "good" and "bad" hair. "Good" hair was straight. "Bad" hair was kinky. Even in the late sixties, at the height of Black Power, most people could not bring themselves to say "bad" for "good" and "good" for "bad." They still said that hair like white hair was "good," even if they encapsulated it in a disclaimer like "what we used to call 'good.'"

Maggie would be seated in her high chair, throwing food this way and that, and Mama would be cooing about how cute it all was, remembering how I used to do the same thing, and wondering whether Maggie's flinging her food with her left hand meant that she was going to be a southpaw too. When my daughter was just about covered with Franco-American SpaghettiOs, Mama would seize the opportunity and wipe her clean, dipping her head, tilted to one side, down under the back of Maggie's neck. Sometimes, if she could get away with it, she'd even rub a curl between her fingers, just to make sure that her bifocals had not deceived her. Then she'd sigh with satisfaction and relief, thankful that her prayers had been answered. No kink . . . yet. "Mama!" I'd shout, pretending to be angry. (Every once in a while, if no one was looking, I'd peek too.)

I say "yet" because most black babies are born with soft, silken hair. Then, sooner or later, it begins to "turn," as inevitably as do the seasons or the leaves on a tree. And if it's meant to turn, it *turns,* no matter how hard you try to stop it. People once thought baby oil would stop it. They were wrong.

Everybody I knew as a child wanted to have good hair. You could be as ugly as homemade sin dipped in misery and still be thought attractive if you had good hair. Jesus Moss was what the girls at Camp Lee, Virginia, had called Daddy's hair during World War II. I know he played that thick head of hair for all it was worth, too. Still would, if he could.

My own hair was "not a bad grade," as barbers would tell me when they cut my head for the first time. It's like a doctor reporting the overall results of the first full physical that he has given you. "You're in good shape" or "Blood pressure's kind of high; better cut down on salt."

I spent much of my childhood and adolescence messing with my hair. I definitely wanted straight hair. Like Pop's.

When I was about three, I tried to stick a wad of Bazooka bubble gum to that straight hair of his. I suppose what fixed that memory for me is the spanking I got for doing so: he turned me upside down, holding me by my feet, the better to paddle my behind. Little *nigger,* he shouted, walloping away. I started to laugh about it two days later, when my behind stopped hurting.

When black people say "straight," of course, they don't usually mean "straight" literally, like, say, the hair of Peggy Lipton (the white girl on *The Mod Squad)* or Mary of Peter, Paul and Mary fame; black people call that "stringy" hair. No, "straight" just means not kinky, no matter what contours the curl might take. Because Daddy had straight hair, I would have done *anything* to have straight hair—and I used to try everything to make it straight, short of getting a process, which only riffraff were dumb enough to do.

Of the wide variety of techniques and methods I came to master in the great and challenging follicle prestidigitation, almost all had two things in common: a heavy, oil-based grease and evenly applied pressure. It's no accident that many of the biggest black companies in the fifties and sixties made hair products. Indeed, we do have a vast array of hair grease. And I have tried it all, in search of that certain silky touch, one that leaves neither the hand nor the pillow sullied by grease.

I always wondered what Frederick Douglass put on *his* hair, or Phillis Wheatley. Or why Wheatley has that rag on her head in the little engraving in the frontispiece of her book. One thing is for sure: you can bet that when Wheatley went to England to see the Countess of Huntington, she did not stop by the Queen's Coiffeur on the way. So many black people still get their hair straightened that it's a wonder we don't have a national holiday for Madame C. J. Walker, who invented the process for straightening kinky hair, rather than for Dr. King. Jheri-curled or "relaxed"—it's still fried hair.

I used all the greases, from sea-blue Bergamot, to creamy vanilla Duke (in its orange-and-white jar), to the godfather of grease, the formidable Murray's. Now, Murray's was some *serious* grease. Whereas Bergamot was like oily Jell-O and Duke was viscous and sickly sweet, Murray's was light brown and *hard*. Hard as lard and twice as greasy, Daddy used to say whenever the subject of Murray's came up. Murray's came in an orange can with a screw-on top. It was so hard that some people would put a match to the can, just to soften it and make it more manageable. In the late sixties, when Afros came into style, I'd use Afro-Sheen. From Murray's to Duke to Afro-Sheen: that was my progression in black consciousness.

We started putting hot towels or washrags over our greased-down Murray's-coated heads, in order to melt the wax into the scalp and follicles. Unfortunately, the wax had a curious habit of running down your neck, ears, and forehead. Not to mention your pillowcase.

Another problem was that if you put two palmfuls of Murray's on your head, your hair turned white. Duke did the same thing. It was a challenge: if you got rid of the white stuff, you had a magnificent head of wavy hair. Murray's turned kink into waves. Lots of waves. Frozen waves. A hurricane couldn't have blown those waves around.

That was the beauty of it. Murray's was so hard that it froze your hair into the wavy style you brushed it into. It looked really good if you wore a part. A lot of guys had parts *cut* into their hair by a barber, with clippers or a straight-edge razor. Especially if you had kinky hair—in which case you'd generally wear a short razor cut, or what we called a Quo Vadis.

Being obsessed with our hair, we tried to be as innovative as possible. Everyone knew about using a stocking cap, because your father or your uncle or the older guys wore them whenever something really big was about to happen, secular or sacred, a funeral or a dance, a wedding or a trip in which you confronted official white people, or when you were trying to look really sharp. When it was time to be clean, you wore a stocking cap. If the event was really a big one, you made a new cap for the occasion.

A stocking cap was made by asking your mother for one of her hose, and cutting it with a pair of scissors about six inches or so from the open end, where the elastic goes up to the top of the thigh. Then you'd knot the cut end, and behold—a conical-shaped hat or cap, with an elastic band that you pulled down low on your forehead and down around your neck in the back. A good stocking cap, to work well, had to fit tight and snug, like a press. And it had to fit that tightly because it *was* a press: it pressed your hair with the force of the hose's elastic. If you greased your hair down real good and left the stocking cap on long enough—*voilà:* you got a head of pressed-against-the-scalp waves. If you used Murray's, and if you wore a stocking cap to sleep, you got a *whole lot* of waves. (You also got a ring around your forehead when you woke up, but eventually that disappeared.)

And then you could enjoy your concrete 'do. Swore we were bad, too, with all that grease and those flat heads. My brother and I would brush it out a bit in the morning, so it would look—ahem—"natural."

Grown men still wear stocking caps, especially older men, who generally keep their caps in their top drawer, along with their cufflinks and their see-through silk socks, their Maverick tie, their silk handkerchief, and whatever else they prize most.

A Murrayed-down stocking cap was the respectable version of the process, which, by contrast, was most definitely not a cool thing to have, at least if you weren't an entertainer by trade.

Zeke and Keith and Poochie and a few other stars of the basketball team all used to get a process once or twice a year. It was expensive, and to get one you had to go to Pittsburgh or D.C. or Uniontown, someplace where there were enough colored people to support a business. They'd disappear, then reappear a day or two later, strutting like peacocks, their hair burned slightly red from the chemical lye base. They'd also wear "rags" or cloths or handkerchiefs around it when they slept or played basketball. Do-rags, they were called. But the result was *straight* hair, with a hint of wave. No curl. Do-it-yourselfers took their chances at home with a concoction of mashed potatoes and lye.

The most famous process, outside of what Malcolm X describes in his *Autobiography* and maybe that of Sammy Davis, Jr., was Nat King Cole's. Nat King Cole had patent-leather hair.

"That man's got the finest process money can buy." That's what Daddy said the night Cole's TV show aired on NBC, November 5, 1956. I remember the date because everyone came to our house to watch it and to celebrate one of Daddy's buddies' birthdays. Yeah, Uncle Joe chimed in, they can do shit to his hair that the average Negro can't even *think* about—secret shit.

Nat King Cole was *clean*. I've had an ongoing argument with a Nigerian friend about Nat King Cole for twenty years now. Not whether or not he could sing; any fool knows that he could sing. But whether or not he was a handkerchief-head for wearing that patent-leather process.

Sammy Davis's process I detested. It didn't look good on him. Worse still, he liked to have a fried strand dangling down the middle of his forehead, shaking it out from the crown when he sang. But Nat King Cole's hair was a thing unto itself, a beautifully sculpted work of art that he and he alone should have had the right to wear.

The only difference between a process and a stocking cap, really, was taste; yet Nat King Cole—unlike, say, Michael Jackson—looked *good* in his process. His head looked like Rudolph Valentino's in the twenties, and some say it was Valentino that the process imitated. But Nat King Cole wore a process because it suited his face, his demeanor, his name, his style. He was as clean as he wanted to be.

I had forgotten all about Nat King Cole and that patent-leather look until the day in 1971 when I was sitting in an Arab restaurant on the island of Zanzibar, surrounded by men in fezzes and white caftans, trying to learn how to eat curried goat and rice with the fingers of my right hand, feeling two million miles from home, when all of a sudden the old transistor radio sitting on top of a china cupboard stopped blaring out its Swahili music to play "Fly Me to the Moon" by Nat King Cole. The restaurant's din was not affected at all, not even by half a decibel. But in my mind's eye, I saw it: the King's sleek black magnificent tiara. I managed, barely, to blink back the tears.

SOURCE: Henry Louis Gates, Jr., *Colored People* (Alfred A. Knopf, 1994).

WALK THE LAST MILE

MAMA CAME TO believe early on that the key to wealth and comfort in America was owning property. She wanted a nice house for the same reason she liked nice things. But she wanted to own a piece of *earth* too. Because colored people were hindered from owning property in Piedmont throughout the years of my childhood, our houses were always rented.

So Mama always wanted to buy a house. She was possessed by the subject. The funny thing, though, is that up to the very end, she would say that her first home with Daddy was her favorite. And now that I have been married for two decades, I understand how a house for four people that was as big as a postage stamp could be re-created by imagination and memory as a château. She loved it because she was happy, and in love, and in love with her life there. This would not always be so. But none of that stopped her from moving.

Unfortunately for Mama, the only person in the Gates family I ever heard of who didn't care for owning property was Daddy. Just Mama's luck, and ours. Daddy was terrified of debt. So even in the late sixties, when her brother Earkie established a precedent by purchasing the Coleman family house, he still wasn't interested. And the inability to own became one of Mama's great frustrations.

Where Daddy shied from debt, Mama was intrepid, at least until the change. She could leverage Daddy's two salaries like a Wall Street financier. But Miss Pauline wanted a house, and that was tantalizingly out of reach.

She started buying house books and magazines. Dozens, for research. She and I would look at them, just as I would study the pages of the three or four mail order catalogues we'd regularly receive: Ward's, Sears, Roebuck, General Merchandise, Mayer's. (Almost all of our Christmas gifts came from General Merchandise.)

At one point, Mama's plan was to build a house, on land near her mother or brothers on Erin Street. The first time I ever saw Mama *really* angry at my father—much angrier than when she'd accuse him of flirting with Miss Noll or Miss Mary—was on the day when he killed the deal that would have let us build a sort of family complex with two or three of Mama's brothers. We had the plans, the land was picked out (just below Big Mom's, near where Miss Lizzy's dogs barked at night when the Sneakin' Deacon made his rounds visiting his parishioners), and Mama was all excited. Radiant, in fact. She loved to dream, like all the Colemans, and she loved to make things *happen,* which was more Gates than Coleman. (When it came to finance and risk, Daddy was more Coleman than Gates.)

"We're not going to do it," Daddy said.

"Why not?" Mama demanded.

"Because I'm not going to sign the papers."

That was it. The whole thing. I don't think Mama ever got over it. Not until they bought the old Thomas house on East Hampshire Street, if then.

Mrs. Thomas was an old white lady for whom Mama had worked when she was a little girl. I never met Mrs. Thomas, but I knew the name because Mama would mention her to Daddy once in a while. She and her husband had a son, Paul, who went off to college and became some sort of executive. He lived Elsewhere. "I used to call all colored women Dorothy," Paul told me later, "because Dorothy Coleman [Nemo's wife] was our maid, and I loved her so much." (Nemo was Mama's brother, James Coleman, Sr., the oldest of the nine Coleman siblings.)

I thought that was sweet. Racist cracker, Daddy would later say. Then he'd laugh: All niggers do *kinda* look alike.

Cut to 1960. I was all of ten years old and was sitting in the living room of Mrs. Thomas's house. She had just been buried, and her son was selling off their antiques. Mama knew the furniture, because she had cleaned it. She was very comfortable with Paul too. He treated her with a great deal of respect, even deference.

Mama had something on her mind, some goal in sight, and she was determined to achieve it. So we had bathed and put on our good clothes. She was dressed to kill.

I want those two bookcases, Paul, she said straightforwardly. And the desk in your room.

Paul hadn't wanted to sell that desk, I suspect. He looked sort of blankly at Mama.

They *are* a set, she said.

They stared at each other for a little bit, like two animals dancing for dominance.

Is twenty dollars too much? Paul finally asked. When Paul went to get the receipt book, Mama whispered that maybe we'd live in a nice house like this someday.

One case went for our reference books, the other went down to Aunt Marguerite's, and the desk went to me. Elmer Shaver—Daddy's boss at the telephone company—bought the house.

Owning furniture wasn't the same as owning a house, and as I grew up, I resolved to do something about it.

Our rented house had been plenty big enough, until Mama started collecting obsessively, canned food and bolts of cloth for a rainy day, as she'd said at first. You never know when you'll need these things, she'd said. One day next Tuesday, Daddy would mumble under his breath, by which he meant the twelfth of never. All of us, even Daddy, used to spend long hours praying that one day next Tuesday would come soon. She hoarded items like someone who was afraid of being poor again, and she was immune to reassurance. She had even taken to hiding her money in the drawer of her bureau.

I came home from college one summer and walked up the pavement. When Mama opened the door, I saw her as if for the first time: so old and tired and despondent. The years of having her hair done had damaged her hair so much that she was going bald. She'd taken to wearing a wig. I know I look bad, she said, wiping her forehead, where the sweat ran down from under her wig. I am just so tired.

Opportunely, Elmer Shaver had decided to retire and sell the Thomas house he'd bought when I was ten. My brother Rocky, Daddy and I pooled all our resources, including a few scholarship checks, and the deal was done.

The purchase of the Thomas house wasn't all I arranged at that time. I also prepared to go to court and change my name from Louis Smith Gates, as my birth certificate reads, to that of my father. Mama had promised her best friend, unmarried Miss Smith, that she'd pass her name on to the second-born, since the first-born was named for his grandfathers, Paul Coleman and Edward Gates. I had hated that name, Smith, felt deprived of my birthright. Finally, I got around to telling my parents. Then, oddly, I found myself climbing Up the Hill to tell my grandmother. "Thank the Lord," Big Mom said. "That name never made sense to me anyhow." A few days later, I was on the witness stand, responding to Judge Cuppett's questions about why I sought to do this thing after all this time. Because I love my father and because it is my true name, I said, in the presence of Mama and Daddy and my soon-to-be wife, Sharon, and a bailiff. We all cried and cried together at that courthouse in Keyser.

Completing the purchase of the Thomas house from the Shavers proved a more delicate affair. A year later, just after the closing, Mama decided she didn't want to move in. She preferred *this* house or *that* house. Even the Campbell house next door, which needed a complete renovation. She wasn't going to leave Erin Street. She didn't have enough furniture. The house was too big. It was too dark. Who'd cut the grass? The neighbors were racists.

Mama, what's wrong with you? I pleaded. We'll lose all our money.

It was a pitched battle, but Mama finally moved. Sharon and I bought a dining room set at Macy's—on a charge account that was soon canceled for nonpayment—rented a U-Haul, and drove it from New York City to the Valley. Mama's brothers unpacked it and carried it in. Rocky and his wife, Paula, and their two girls drove down from New Jersey. And we had one hell of a feast. Roast beef and brown potatoes; "baked baked beans"; baked corn; kale, well-seasoned, cooked for hours with a big piece of fatback. Then I asked Mama, in the quiet of the celebration's aftermath, just what all the rigmarole about not moving was all about.

"Skippy, you'll never know," she said.

Then, haltingly, she began to talk.

"Mrs. Thomas used to make me sit out in the kitchen, at a little wooden table, and eat the scraps. She was a mean woman. She used to leave money around, to see if I would steal it. She made me work on Thanksgiving and Christmas. She treated me bad. . . . The thought of moving into this house . . . I wanted to burn this house down."

Her eyes were glassy; she lowered her head, placing two fingers on the bridge of her nose. It was a gesture of resignation; she was angry that the memories still had that power.

Mama cried for a long time. And she almost *never* cried. But it was Mama's house now. And she had it a decent while before the onset of her final depression, when she would sit for most of the day in her big reclining chair, talking about death if she talked at all. I'll never know if we did the right thing by buying her that house, or whether our insistence on vindicating her was somehow misguided.

It was 1987 and I had been at an out-of-town conference, when I got the news. I'll never forget that slow walk down the corridor to the hotel door. From a distance, I could see the pink message slips taped all over my door. It had to be death or its imminence, I thought. It had to be Mama. Messages from the dean, from the police, from the department, from my wife, my father, from the hotel manager, from the police again, CALL HOME.

She had been in the hospital for a checkup, and she seemed to be doing fine. The white lady sharing the room with her said she was talking one minute and slumped over the next. They kept her alive on a machine.

She's up, she's down, she might not make it through the night. She's a little better? She's worse? She won't . . . not even through the night? I flew out to Pittsburgh, the nearest airport, at dawn, then rented a car from there, weeping all the way. Sharon and the kids drove from Ithaca.

At the hospital, Mama kept looking up at me, then at the big blue-gray machine, trying to ask something with her eyes. She'd be fully awake and conscious, then they'd have to jump-start her heart again. She'd come back as if she'd just been asleep, asking that same question again with her eyes. We'd go, we'd come, over the course of the day, till my family finally got there, at about nine that night. She'd waited to say goodbye.

It was about midnight when we agreed not to shock her heart anymore. Rocky, by now an oral surgeon, had assumed charge. I had told her how much I loved her, and she had smiled that deep-down smile, something to take with her on the road.

Nemo and Mama are buried near each other, in the new, highly esteemed, and otherwise white cemetery just outside Keyser, behind the hill overlooking Mr. Bump's trailer park. It probably bothers Mama to be looking down at Nemo every day, unless she has forgiven him for not calling her to say goodbye when Big Mom was dying.

It's the kind of cemetery that seems fake to me, with all the headstones bronze and flat, exactly the same size. We got the "deluxe" model and jazzed it up as best we could. It's got a little poem on it, and a bas-relief flower. Maybe it should have just said "Miss Pauline," because everybody'd know who that was.

I hate that cemetery. Not because of the lack of aesthetic appeal; not because it's integrated; but because what Nemo called the Power isn't there. When you go up on Radical Hill, up past where Sherry Lewis used to live, enter the gate, and take the dusty road to the colored cemetery . . . now, that's a *cemetery*. All the markers have different shapes, and the graves are laid out whopper-jawed. Upkeep varies, so some graves look pretty disheveled. Not Daddy Paul's, of course, and not Big Mom's, either.

This is where the old souls come to hide, resting till the Day of the Lord. Falling out over graves, like I once saw Mr. Bootsie do when I was a boy, listening to Mama perform her eulogy. Please, please—just one more look, don't take her yet, just one more look, was all he said, shouting and whooping and hollering and falling out all over his mother's grave.

You had a chance, in a colored funeral. You had a chance to work out your grief. You didn't have to be in a hurry with it, either. You could touch it, play with it, and talk to it, letting it work itself up in its own good time. Mama said she didn't want one of those tearjerkers, with crepe-hangers sitting in the mourners' pew and then crowding around her grave. She wanted a closed casket, ten minutes at the max, and don't let Nemo officiate. That was when she was younger. She'd pick out her dress and wig hat, the jewelry and the shoes, when she got old. By the time my mother died, at the worst of her dejection and alienation from herself, her family, the Colemans, seemed to me coolly distant, somewhat embarrassed by her eccentricities and depression. They were tired of her, it almost seemed, and she was tired of life. I think by the end she wanted to die. Nor did she believe in an afterlife. She just wanted release.

Instead of the modern Episcopal Milquetoast service we had for Mama, I passionately wish that her funeral had been like the one for Miss Minnie, or the one for Papa Charlie—or the one for Uncle Boke, which happened back when I was five. That was a nice one.

The sermon was long and loud, demanding that you break down. He's with the Lord today, walking in grandeur past brooks and fountains, hand in hand with his mother, Miss Lucy Clifford, and his kind old father, Mr. Samuel. I know you want him back, but the Lord had need of him up there. Maybe it was to sing the tenor parts of the spirituals, or maybe to tend the fires. Maybe to polish the silver up nice, or to keep the gold real shiny. I *know* you'll miss him; we'll miss him too. But we'll meet again soon at the Pearly Gates. On that Great Day of the Judgment, when we cross over, he'll be waiting there for us, welcoming us into the fold.

Oh, man, did those sermons feel *good,* sad-good, and hurting. And then they'd sing that killer song, people falling out all along.

When I'm gone the last mile of the way I will rest at the close of the day, And I know there are joys that await me When I've gone the last mile of the way.

Then Mama had risen to read her piece, looking all good and sounding all fine.

At Mama's funeral, I wanted to fall out like that, too. I wanted that blueblack preacher who had substituted that time for Reverend Mon-roe and had blown his tired ass away. I wanted him to get up on that pulpit and preach the Sermon of the Dry Bones, like he'd done for Uncle Boke. People *still* dated things by that sermon: Hey . . . that was two years, three months, fourteen days, seven hours, and five minutes after Brother Blue Gums preached the Sermon of the Dry Bones.

I wanted the Heavenly Gospel Choir to sing a lot of long, sad songs, and I wanted people to fall out. I wanted the church to be *hot,* with the windows closed, those paper-colored funeral home fans spreading the steam rather than cooling things down. I wanted starched collars to wilt and straightened hair to kink up and "go back," I wanted the kitchens crinkling up in that heat, crackling loud and long, before our very eyes. I wanted the whole world to know my mama's death and her glory while alive. I wanted to cry and cry and cry, so I could tell her how sorry I was for not being a good enough son. I wanted her to know that I could have tried to do more, I could have tried to understand better, I could have come home more. I wanted her to know that I had tried, and that I loved her like life itself, and that I would miss her now that she was gone. I wanted to be sad in that dark, holy place, and I wanted that sadness to last.

SOURCE: Henry Louis Gates, Jr., *Colored People* (Alfred A. Knopf, 1994).

THE LAST MILL PICNIC

SOME COLORED PEOPLE claimed that they welcomed the change, that it was progress, that it was what we had been working for for so very long, our own version of the civil rights movement and Dr. King. But nobody really believed that, I don't think. For who in their right mind wanted to attend the mill picnic with the white people, when it meant shutting the colored one down?

Just like they did Howard High School, Nemo's son, Little Jim, had said. I was only surprised that he said it out loud.

Everybody worked *so* hard to integrate the thing in the mid-sixties, Aunt Marguerite mused, because that was what we were supposed to do then, what with Dr. King and everything. But by the time those crackers made us join them, she added, we didn't want to go.

I wish I could say that the community rebelled, that everybody refused to budge, that we joined hands in a circle and sang "We Shall Not, We Shall Not Be Moved," followed by "We Shall Overcome." But we didn't. In fact, people preferred not to acknowledge the approaching end, as if a miracle could happen and this whole nightmare would go away.

It was the last colored mill picnic. Like the roll called up yonder, everybody was there, even Caldonia and Old Man Mose. But Freddie Taylor had brought his 45s and was playing the best of rhythm and blues like nobody could believe. "What Becomes of the Brokenhearted?" was the favorite oldie of the day, because Piedmont was a Jimmy Ruffin town. Mellow, and sad. A coffee-colored feeling, with lots of cream. Jerry Butler's "Hey, Western Union Man" and Marvin Gaye's "I Heard It Through the Grapevine" were the most requested recent songs.

We had all come back for it, the diaspora reversing itself. There was a gentle hum or rumble that kept the same pitch all through the day, a lazy sort of pace as we walked back and forth along the arc of parked cars and just-mowed grass at Carskadon's Farm. Timothy grass and raspberry, black-eyed Susans big as saucers, thistle and dandelion, and everywhere sumac.

The greensward was an allergist's nightmare, cow pies were a perpetual threat. Still, we walked.

They had tried to shut down Walden Methodist first, but Big Mom, the matriarch, had simply refused to stop attending her church of eight decades. And "the boys"—her sons, the Colemans—had of course supported her. Other than her doctor, Big Mom almost never saw white people. Nor did she care to be with or worship with them. People huddled together and lobbied her, then huddled together and lobbied her some more, to no avail. Big Mom wasn't going to stop attending Walden Methodist. And that was that. Since she had a weak heart and high blood pressure, had lost most of her sight because of a degenerating retina, couldn't hear unless you spoke in her ear—and had, above all else, a steely sense of resolve—*nobody* messed with Big Mom.

The white minister at the newly integrated United Methodist Church, over in the Orchard, would preach his normal sermon and then traipse over to Back Street and minister to Big Mom, Mr. Ozzie, Mr. Doug Twyman, Mr. Lynn Allen, and a Coleman son or two. Miss Toot and her daughters, Frieda and Eudie, would still sing gospel, including "The Prodigal Son." White people can't preach too good, was all that Big Mom would volunteer about her experience with integration. I know she thought that God was white: there were all those pictures hanging on her walls. But that was another matter.

They might have kept Walden Methodist, but there was no hope for the mill pic-a-nic. And what was worse was that nobody had known what to do to reverse it. The mill administration itself made the decision, it said, because the law forbade separate but equal everything, including picnics. So the last wave of the civil rights era finally came to the Potomac Valley, crashing down upon the colored world of Piedmont. When it did, its most beloved, and cementing, ritual was doomed to give way. Nobody wanted segregation, you understand; but nobody thought of this as segregation.

So much was the way I remembered these occasions from my earliest childhood, and yet a new age had plainly dawned, an age that made the institution of a segregated picnic seem an anachronism. All of the people under thirty-five or so sported newly coiffed Afros, neatly rounded and shiny with Afro-Sheen. There were red and black and green dashikis everywhere, blousing over bell-bottomed trousers. Gold peace symbols dangled over leather vests, bare nigger toes poked out of fine leather sandals. Soul handshakes filled the air, as did the curious vocatives "brother" and "sister." I found myself looking for silk socks and stocking-cap waves, sleeveless see-through T-shirts peeking over the open neck of an unbuttoned silk shirt, Eyetalian style. Like Uncle Joe liked to wear when he dressed up. For bottles of whiskey and cheap wine in brown paper bags, furtively shared behind the open trunks of newly waxed cars, cleaned for the occasion, like Mr. Bootsie and Jingles and Mr. Roebuck Johnson used to do. Even the gamblers didn't have much to say, as they laid their cards down one by one, rather than slapping them down in the bid whist way, talking shit, talking trash, the way it used to be, the way it always was. The way it was supposed to be.

Miss Sarah Russell was there, carrying that black Bible with the reddish-orange pages—the one that printed the Sacred Name of Jesus and His words in bold red letters—still warning everybody about the end of the world and reminding us that Jesus wasn't going to be sending us a postcard or a telegram when He returned to judge us for our sins. He'd be coming like a thief in the night. The signs of the times are near, she shouted, the signs of the times. Don't nobody know the season but for the blooming of the trees. There's war and then there's the rumors of wars. My God is a harsh master, and the Holy Ghost has unloosed the fire of the spirit, and we know that fire by the talking in tongues.

Whenever Miss Sarah came around, Mr. Bootsie, Mr. Johnson, and Mr. Jingles would never drink out of whatever it was they kept in those brown paper bags. She appreciated that.

Mr. Bootsie and Mr. Marshall were running their card game at its usual place in the arc of parked automobiles, hoping that Miss Sarah would just keep walking by, as she made the rounds, fulfilling her obligation to remind her friends about Jesus' imminent return, and sharing a cool glass of lemonade and maybe a crisp fried chicken leg as she paused to catch her breath. Miss Ezelle had on a bright-red dress—she always *did* look good in red—and she was telling Mr. Buddy Green to lower his voice and not talk about how much money he was losing at poker until Miss Sarah got out of the way.

Greg and I, spying Miss Sarah over by the gamblers' card table, made a beeline down to the river, figuring that Jeannie and Tanya Hollingsworth had probably decided to go swimming by now. And Miss Sarah Russell, despite all the symbolism of water in the Bible, would never have been caught dead down by the river, where all that bare brown flesh, glistening in the sunshine, could prove too distracting even to the saved.

No one was at the river yet, so we headed back up the bank, passed Nemo's cast-iron vat, where he boiled the corn, and headed over to watch the last softball game, the game that pitted the alumni of Howard High School against the alumni of Everyplace Else. Roebuck Johnson was there, standing next to Mr. Comby Curl, the latter's wavy hair shining even more brightly than usual and sliced neatly by the part that he had shaved himself with that same straight-edged razor that made the back of my neck break out in shaving bumps. Involuntarily, I rubbed the back of my neck with my left hand, to see if they had disappeared yet. They were still there from yesterday's haircut. Roebuck was watching the game because he loved sports and also to escape the prying eye of all of his competing interests and loyalties. But it was exhilarating to watch the Howard team, headed by Earkie and Raymond, beat the hell out of the team from Elsewhere, just like they did every year. Only this time, the beating seemed more relentless, Poochie Taylor—who many people thought was the best natural athlete in a kingdom of natural athletes—tore the leather off the softball. "Couldn't stand to be away from the Valley," was what they said when he came home from spring training in the big leagues. Everybody had wanted him to make it to the World Series, just to beat the racist Yankees. Instead, he went to work up at the mill and then got his own church as a pastor. Everybody said he was sincere, unlike some of the other born-agains.

I was surprised that no one made any speeches, that no one commemorated the passing of the era in a formal way. But it did seem that people were walking back and forth through Carskadon's field a lot more times than they normally did, storing up memories to last until the day when somebody, somehow, would figure out a way to trick the paper mill into sponsoring this thing again. Maybe that's why Miss Ezelle seemed to take extra care to make her lips as red as Sammy Amoruso's strawberries in late August, and why Uncle Joe had used an extra dab of Brylcreem that morning, to give his silver DA that extra bit of shine. And why Miss Toot's high-pitched laughter could be heard all over that field all the day long, as she and Mr. Marshall beat all comers in a "rise and fly" marathon match of bid whist. So everyone could remember. We would miss the crackle of the brown paper bag in which Mr. Terry Conway hid his bottle of whiskey, and the way he'd wet his lips just before he'd tilt his whole body backwards and swig it down. The way he'd make the nastiest face after he drank it, as if he had tasted poison itself. When the bottle ran out, Mr. Terry would sleep himself back to health in the cool dawn splendor of a West Virginia morning.

Nor were there any fights at the colored Legion that night, not even after Inez Jones, with George Mason's white handkerchief dangling between her legs, did the dirty dog to end all dirty dogs.

The colored mill picnic would finish its run peaceably, then, if with an air of wistful resignation. All I know is that Nemo's corn never tasted saltier, his coffee never smelled fresher, than when these hundreds of Negroes gathered to say goodbye to themselves, their heritage, and their sole link to each other, wiped out of existence by the newly enforced anti–Jim

Crow laws. The mill didn't want a lawsuit like the one brought against the Swordfish.

Yeah, even the Yankees had colored players now, Mr. Ozzie mumbled to Daddy, as they packed up Nemo's black cast-iron vat, hoping against hope to boil that corn another day.

SOURCE: Henry Louis Gates, Jr., *Colored People* (Alfred A. Knopf, 1994).

IN OUR LIFETIME

FROM TOILING AS White House slaves to President-elect Barack Obama, we have crossed the ultimate color line.

A new dawn of American leadership is at hand.

We have all heard stories about those few magical transformative moments in African-American history, extraordinary ritual occasions through which the geographically and socially diverse black community—a nation within a nation, really—molds itself into one united body, determined to achieve one great social purpose and to bear witness to the process by which this grand achievement occurs.

The first time was New Year's Day in 1863, when tens of thousands of black people huddled together all over the North waiting to see if Abraham Lincoln would sign the Emancipation Proclamation. The second was the night of June 22, 1938, the storied rematch between Joe Louis and Max Schmeling, when black families and friends crowded around radios to listen and cheer as the Brown Bomber knocked out Schmeling in the first round. The third, of course, was Aug. 28, 1963, when the Rev. Dr. Martin Luther King Jr. proclaimed to the world that he had a dream, in the shadow of a brooding Lincoln, peering down on the assembled throng, while those of us who couldn't be with him in Washington sat around our black-and-white television sets, bound together by King's melodious voice through our tears and with quickened-flesh.

But we have never seen anything like this. Nothing could have prepared any of us for the eruption (and, yes, that is the word) of spontaneous celebration that manifested itself in black homes, gathering places and the streets of our communities when Sen. Barack Obama was declared President-elect Obama. From Harlem to Harvard, from Maine to Hawaii— and even Alaska—from "the prodigious hilltops of New Hampshire . . . [to] Stone Mountain of Georgia," as Dr. King put it, each of us will always remember this moment, as will our children, whom we woke up to watch history being made.

My colleagues and I laughed and shouted, whooped and hollered, hugged each other and cried. My father waited 95 years to see this day happen, and when he called as results came in, I silently thanked God for allowing him to live long enough to cast his vote for the first black man to become president. And even he still can't quite believe it!

How many of our ancestors have given their lives—how many millions of slaves toiled in the fields in endlessly thankless and mindless labor—before this generation could live to see a black person become president? "How long, Lord?" the spiritual goes; "not long!" is the resounding response. What would Frederick Douglass and W. E. B. Du Bois say if they could know what our people had at long last achieved? What would Sojourner Truth and Harriet Tubman say? What would Dr. King himself say? Would they say that all those lost hours of brutalizing toil and labor leading to spent, half-fulfilled lives, all those humiliations that our ancestors had to suffer through each and every day, all those slights and rebuffs and recriminations, all those rapes and murders, lynchings and assassinations, all those Jim Crow laws and protest marches, those snarling dogs and bone-breaking water hoses, all of those beatings and all of those killings, all of those black collective dreams deferred—that the unbearable pain of all of those tragedies had, in the end, been assuaged at least somewhat through Barack Obama's election? This certainly doesn't wipe that bloody slate clean. His victory is not redemption for all of this suffering; rather, it is the symbolic culmination of the black freedom struggle, the grand achievement of a great, collective dream. Would they say that surviving these horrors, hope against hope, was the price we had to pay to become truly free, to live to see—exactly 389 years after the first African slaves landed on these shores—that "great gettin' up morning" in 2008 when a black man—Barack Hussein Obama—was elected the first African-American president of the United States?

I think they would, resoundingly and with one voice proclaim, "Yes! Yes! And yes, again!" I believe they would tell us that it had been worth the price that we, collectively, have had to pay—the price of President-elect Obama's ticket.

On that first transformative day, when the Emancipation Proclamation was signed, Frederick Douglass, the greatest black orator in our history before Martin Luther King Jr., said that the day was not a day for speeches and "scarcely a day for prose." Rather, he noted, "it is a day for poetry and song, a new song." Over 3,000 people, black and white abolitionists together, waited for the news all day in Tremont Temple, a Baptist church a block from Boston Common. When a messenger burst in, after 11 p.m., and shouted, "It is coming! It is on the wires," the church went mad; Douglass recalled that "I never saw enthusiasm before. I never saw joy." And then he spontaneously led the crowd in singing "Blow Ye the Trumpet, Blow," John Brown's favorite hymn:

> *Blow ye the trumpet, blow!*
> *The gladly solemn sound*
> *Let all the nations know,*
> *To earth's remotest bound:*
>
> *The year of jubilee is come!*
> *The year of jubilee is come!*
> *Return, ye ransomed sinners, home.*

At that moment, an entire race, one that in 1863 in the United States comprised 4.4 million souls, became a unified people, breathing with one heart, speaking with one voice, united in mind and spirit, all their aspirations concentrated into a laser beam of almost blind hope and desperate anticipation.

It is astounding to think that many of us today—myself included—can remember when it was a huge deal for a black man or woman to enter the White House through the front door, and not through the servants' entrance. Paul Cuffe, the wealthy sea captain, shipping merchant, and the earliest "Back to Africa" black colonist, will forever have the distinction of being the first black person to be invited to the White House for an audience with the president. Cuffe saw President James Madison at the White House on May 2, 1812, at precisely 11 a.m. and asked the president's intervention in recovering his famous brig *Traveller*, which had been impounded because officials said he had violated the embargo with Britain. Cuffe, after the Quaker fashion, called Madison "James"; "James," in turn, got Paul's brig back for him, probably because Cuffe and Madison both favored the emigration of freed slaves back to Africa. (Three years later, on Dec. 10, 1815, Cuffe used this ship to carry 38 black people from the United States to Sierra Leone.)

From Frederick Douglass, who visited Lincoln three times during his presidency (and every president thereafter until his death in 1895), to Sojourner Truth and Booker T. Washington, each prominent black visitor to the White House caused people to celebrate another "victory for the race." Blacks became frequent visitors to Franklin Roosevelt's White House; FDR even had a "Kitchen Cabinet" through which blacks could communicate the needs of their people. Because of the civil rights movement, Lyndon

Johnson had a slew of black visitors, as well. During Bill Clinton's presidency, I attended a White House reception with so many black political, academic and community leaders that it occurred to me that there hadn't been as many black people in the Executive Mansion perhaps since slavery. Everyone laughed at the joke, because they knew, painfully, that it was true.

Visiting the White House is one thing; occupying the White House is quite another. And yet, African-American aspirations to the White House date back generations. The first black man put forward on a ticket as a political party's nominee for U.S. president was George Edwin Taylor, on the National Liberty Party ticket in 1904. Portions of his campaign document could have been written by Barack Obama:

> . . . in the light of the history of the past four years, with a Republican president in the executive chair, and both branches of Congress and a majority of the Supreme Court of the same political faith, we are confronted with the amazing fact that more than one-fifth of the race are actually disfranchised, robbed of all the rights, powers and benefits of true citizenship, we are forced to lay aside our prejudices, indeed, our personal wishes, and consult the higher demands of our manhood, the true interests of the country and our posterity, and act while we yet live, 'ere the time when it shall be too late. No other race of our strength would have quietly submitted to what we have during the past four years without a rebellion, a revolution, or an uprising.

The revolution that Taylor goes on to propose, he says, is one "not by physical force, but by the ballot," with the ultimate sign of the success being the election of the nation's first black president.

But given all of the racism to which black people were subjected following Reconstruction and throughout the first half of the 20th century, no one could actually envision a Negro becoming president—"not in our lifetimes," as our ancestors used to say. When James Earl Jones became America's first black fictional president in the 1972 film, *The Man*, I remember thinking, "Imagine that!" His character, Douglass Dilman, the president pro tempore of the Senate, ascends to the presidency after the president and the speaker of the House are killed in a building collapse, and after the vice president declines the office due to advanced age and ill health. A fantasy if ever there was one, we thought. But that year, life would imitate art: Congresswoman Shirley Chisholm attempted to transform "The Man" into "The Woman," becoming the first black woman to run for president in the Democratic Party. She received 152 first-ballot votes at the Democratic National Convention. Then, in 1988, Jesse Jackson got 1,219 delegate votes at the

Democratic convention, 29 percent of the total, coming in second only to the nominee, Michael Dukakis.

The award for prescience, however, goes to Jacob K. Javits, the liberal Republican senator from New York who, incredibly, just a year after the integration of Central High School in Little Rock, predicted that the first black president would be elected in the year 2000. In an essay titled "Integration from the Top Down" printed in *Esquire* magazine in 1958, he wrote:

> What manner of man will this be, this possible Negro Presidential candidate of 2000? Undoubtedly, he will be well-educated. He will be well-traveled and have a keen grasp of his country's role in the world and its relationships. He will be a dedicated internationalist with working comprehension of the intricacies of foreign aid, technical assistance and reciprocal trade. . . . Assuredly, though, despite his other characteristics, he will have developed the fortitude to withstand the vicious smear attacks that came his way as he fought to the top in government and politics . . . those in the vanguard may expect to be the targets for scurrilous attacks, as the hate mongers, in the last ditch efforts, spew their verbal and written poison.

In the same essay, Javits predicted both the election of a black senator and the appointment of the first black Supreme Court justice by 1968. Edward Brooke was elected to the Senate by Massachusetts voters in 1966. Thurgood Marshall was confirmed in 1967. Javits also predicted that the House of Representatives would have "between thirty and forty qualified Negroes" in the 106th Congress in 2000. In fact, there were 37 black U.S. representatives, among them 12 women.

Sen. Javits was one very keen prognosticator. When we consider the characteristics that he insisted the first black president must possess—he must be well-educated, well-traveled, have a keen grasp of his country's role in the world, be a dedicated internationalist and have a very thick skin—it is astonishing how accurately he is describing the background and character of Barack Obama.

I wish we could say that Barack Obama's election will magically reduce the numbers of teenage pregnancies or the level of drug addiction in the black community. I wish we could say that what happened last night will suddenly make black children learn to read and write as if their lives depended on it, and that their high school completion rates will become the best in the country. I wish we could say that these things are about to happen, but I doubt that they will.

But there is one thing we can proclaim today, without question: that the election of Barack Obama as president of the United States of America means that "The Ultimate Color Line," as the subtitle of Javits' *Esquire* essay put it, has, at long last, been crossed. It has been crossed by our very first postmodern Race Man, a man who embraces his African cultural and genetic heritage so securely that he can transcend it, becoming the candidate of choice to tens of millions of Americans who do not look like him.

How does that make me feel? Like I've always imagined my father and his friends felt back in 1938, on the day that Joe Louis knocked out Max Schmeling. But ten thousand times better than that. All I can say is "Amazing Grace! How sweet the sound."

SOURCE: "In Our Lifetime," The Root, November 5, 2008, URL: http://www.theroot .com/views/our-lifetime.

PART II
EXCAVATION

ZORA NEALE HURSTON has been something of a touchstone for Gates throughout his career, and with good reason. She was a brilliant writer and a keen observer of black culture whose vivid tableaux and spicy vernacular jump off the page to create a living landscape of African American life. But it was Alice Walker's discovery of her unmarked grave and her subsequent recovery of a brilliant life and career that renders Hurston so potent a symbol for African American literature.

Hurston had hardly been obscure throughout much of her lifetime: her novels and stories were lauded for both their literary and anthropological contributions when they were published in the 1930s and 1940s. But she made no money, her fame faded, and her unmarked grave in Florida told a different story—or no story at all—until Walker found it and put a name to it.

Walker's discovery and Hurston's story are emblematic of the African American literary tradition. African American writing—by both men and women—has existed for centuries, but it has taken concerted acts of excavation and recovery to restore it to simple visibility and, in a great many cases, to prominence. Gates has been a participant in and a champion of this type of literary detective work for three decades. The works in this section present some of the fruits of those investigations.

Abby Wolf

INTRODUCTION, *OUR NIG; OR, SKETCHES FROM THE LIFE OF A FREE BLACK,* BY HARRIET E. WILSON

Though I've no home to call my own,
My heart shall not repine;
The saint may live on earth unknown,
And yet in glory shine.

When my Redeemer dwelt below,
He chose a lowly lot;
He came unto his own, but lo!
His own received him not.

> —HARRIET E. WILSON, CIRCA 1852

I sincerely appeal to my colored brethren
universally for patronage, hoping that they
will not condemn this attempt of their sister
to be erudite, but rally around me a faithful
band of supporters and defenders.

> —HARRIET E. WILSON, 1859

ON THE EIGHTEENTH day of August 1859, at the Clerk's office of the District Court of Massachusetts, Mrs. Harriet E. Wilson entered the copyright of her novel, a fictional third-person autobiography entitled *Our Nig; or, Sketches from the Life of a Free Black, In A Two-Story White House, North. Showing That Slavery's Shadows Fall Even There.* Printed for the author by the George C. Rand and Avery company, the novel first appeared on September 5, 1859.

In a disarmingly open preface Mrs. Wilson states her purpose for publishing *Our Nig:*

> In offering to the public the following pages, the writer confesses her inability to minister to the refined and cultivated, the pleasure supplied by abler pens. It is not for such these crude narrations appear. Deserted by kindred, disabled by failing health, I am forced to some experiment which shall aid me in maintaining myself and child without extinguishing this feeble life.

The experiment undertaken for financial reasons was a book whose central theme is white racism in the North as experienced by a free black indentured servant in antebellum days: a subject that might have been highly controversial among white abolitionists and free blacks who did not wish to antagonize their white benefactors. Nonetheless, Harriet E. Adams Wilson asked her "colored brethren" to "rally around me a faithful band of supporters and defenders," and to purchase her book so that she might support herself and her child.

Just five months and twenty-four days after the publication of *Our Nig,* the Amherst, New Hampshire, *Farmer's Cabinet* dated February 29, 1860, included among its obituaries the following item:

> In Milford, 13th inst[ant], George Mason, only son of H. E. Wilson, aged 7 yrs. and 8 mos.

According to his death certificate, George Mason Wilson succumbed to "Fever" on February 15, 1860. Described as the child of Thomas and Harriet E. Wilson, he was probably named in honor of George Mason, the prominent Revolutionary-era Virginia planter and statesman who opposed slavery. The "color" of the child is listed as "Black." The death certificate of George Mason Wilson establishes that "Mrs. H. E. Wilson"—the name that appears on the copyright page of the first edition of *Our Nig* and in the *Farmer's Cabinet* death notice—was a black woman, apparently the first to publish a novel in English. Ironically, George's death certificate helped to rescue his mother from literary oblivion. His mother wrote a sentimental novel, of all things, so that she might become self-sufficient and regain the right to care for her only son; six months later, her son died of that standard disease, "fever"; the *record* of his death, *alone,* proved sufficient to demonstrate his mother's racial identity and authorship of *Our Nig.* These curious historical events could easily have formed part of the plot of a sentimental novel. That Harriet Wilson, moreover, dared to entitle her text with the most feared and hated epithet by which the very humanity of black people had been demeaned adds to the list of ironies in her endeavor.

With this audacious act of entitlement, Harriet Wilson became most probably the first Afro-American to publish a novel in the United States, the fifth Afro-American to publish fiction in English (after Frederick Douglass, William Wells Brown, Frank J. Webb, and Martin R. Delany), and along with Maria F. dos Reis, who published a novel called *Ursula* in Brazil in 1859, one of the first two black women to publish a novel in any language. Despite their importance to the Afro-American literary tradition, however, Mrs. Wilson and her text seem to have been ignored or overlooked both by her "colored brethren universally" and by even the most scrupulous scholars during the next one hundred and twenty-three years, for reasons as curious and as puzzling as they are elusive, reasons about which we can venture rather little more than informed speculation.

Reconstructing the life and times of Harriet E. Wilson is as challenging as it is frustrating. While there remains no questions as to her race or her authorship of *Our Nig,* we have been able to account for her existence only from 1850 to 1860. Even her birthdate and date of death are unknown.

The first record of the woman who through marriage would become "Mrs. H. E. Wilson" is the 1850 federal census of the state of New Hampshire. This document lists one "Harriet Adams" (H. E. Wilson's maiden name) as living in Milford, New Hampshire. Her age is said to be "22" and her race is described as "Black" (the choices were "White," "Black," and "Mulatto"). Harriet Adams's birthplace is listed simply as "New Hampshire." If these statements are correct, then Miss Adams was born a free black in 1827 or 1828.

This birthplace and birth date, however, are problematic for several reasons. According to the 1860 Boston federal census, Mrs. Harriet E. Wilson was born in Fredericksburg, Virginia, in 1807 or 1808 (if the age of fifty-two recorded by the data collector was accurate). Again, as in the 1850 census, she is described as "Black." We have found no other black women listed in either Hillsborough County, New Hampshire (where Milford is located), or in Boston, where the author of *Our Nig* registered her copyright on August 18, 1859.

A strong reason for pursuing the leads in the 1860 federal census is that the novel itself asserts that its author lived in Massachusetts at the time it was written, namely 1859, as internal evidence suggests. In the final chapter of *Our Nig,* where the narrator abandons the mask of storyteller, and, in her own voice, appeals to the reader for sympathy and support, the text reads as follows: "She passed into the various towns of the State she lived in, then into Massachusetts."

If Harriet E. Adams Wilson's place and date of birth remain shaky, we are on firmer ground in the decade between 1850 and 1860. Harriet Adams, in 1850, lived with a white family in Milford, New Hampshire, the family of Samuel Boyles. (Boyles, a white fifty-year-old carpenter—according to the 1850 census—is fifty-two in the 1860 census; similarly, his birthplace has shifted from "Vermont" in 1850, to "Massachusetts," suggesting that discrepancies in census data were common even among stable and middle-class white Americans.) Since the Boyleses had four resident adult nonfamily members living with them, according to the 1860 census—three of whom are described as "Spinsters"—we can surmise that they rented rooms to boarders and possibly were remunerated by the county for sheltering the aged and disabled, probably on a regular basis.

One year later, in 1851, according to records at the Milford Town Clerk's Office, Harriet Adams married Thomas Wilson. This information was "returned by the Rev. E. N. Hidden" in April 1852, along with information about a dozen or so other marriages. The Reverend Hidden, a thirty-eight-year-old white Congregational clergyman, according to the 1850 census, dated the marriage as October 6, 1851, at Milford, New Hampshire. Thomas Wilson's "residence" is listed as "Virginia," and Harriet Adams's as "Milford." Incidentally, the church's marriage records, which could have provided more information, were destroyed by fire.

In late May, or early June 1852, George Mason Wilson was born, the first and apparently only child of Harriet E. Adams and Thomas Wilson. (Of Thomas Wilson, we know no vital statistics. A brief narrative of the escape of a 'Tom Wilson' from New Orleans to Liverpool was published in the Liverpool *Inquirer* on February 28, 1858. This narrative, however, does not overlap in any way with *Our Nig* or the three letters in its Appendix.) We know the child's birth date, his race, and his parents' identity from his 1860 death certificate. His birth date was approximately nine months after Thomas and Harriet married.

George Mason Wilson was born in Goffstown, New Hampshire, just a few miles from Milford, where his parents were married. In Goffstown was located the Hillsborough County Farm, which was established in 1849. One of the letters appended to *Our Nig* states that, abandoned by her husband, the author of *Our Nig* was forced—after "days passed; weeks passed"—to go to the "County House," where she gave birth to a child.

The 1855 *Boston City Directory* listed a "Harriet Wilson, Widow," at 7 Robinson Alley. Two "Harriet Wilsons" appeared in the *Boston City Directory* of 1856. One listing designates a "widow," who lived at 4 Webster Avenue, the other a "dressmaker," who lived or worked at 19 Joy Street. These "Harriet Wilsons" may, or may not, be the same person. In each successive *Boston City Directory,* an annual publication similar to contemporary telephone directories, only one Harriet Wilson appeared between 1857 and 1863: the widow who remained at Webster Avenue.

This widow, according to the 1860 Boston census, was born in Fredericksburg, Virginia, and is listed as "52" years of age. The census describes her as "Black," and living in the home of Daniel and Susan Jacobs, ages thirty-eight and thirty-one, respectively. The census lists Mr. Jacobs's profession as "mariner."

Harriet E. Wilson registered the copyright of *Our Nig* at the District Clerk's Office at Boston on August 18, 1859. Because New Hampshire had had its own District Clerk's Office since 1789, and because the office in Boston served most, if not all, of Massachusetts, it is reasonable to assume that Harriet E. Wilson was a resident of Massachusetts by 1859, and was separated from her son, whom she had been forced to foster to another family because of her desperate financial condition. Since the novel was printed for the author, rather than "published" by a commercial house, and since other Massachusetts printers would have been capable of producing *Our Nig,* the fact that she selected the George C. Rand and Avery company of Boston reinforces speculation that by 1859 Mrs. Wilson lived in or near that city.

Many of these facts about H. E. Wilson's life that have been drawn from public documents correspond dramatically to assertions about the life of the author of *Our Nig* that were made by three acquaintances who endorsed her novel, in the seven-page Appendix that follows Chapter XII. When brought together, these facts leave no doubt that the author of *Our Nig,* who signed her copyright as "Mrs. H. E. Wilson," and Harriet E. Adams Wilson, are the same person. But another source of confirmation is the plot of *Our Nig*—described as autobiographical by her supporters—which parallels major events of Mrs. Wilson's life that we have been able to verify.

Let us first analyze the statements found in the text's Appendix.

Margaretta Thorn, whose letter is entitled "To the Friends of Our Dark-Complexioned Brethren and Sisters, This Note Is Intended," is the source of the little that we know about the author's childhood. She has "known the writer of this book for a number of years," she testifies, and therefore is uniquely able to "add my testimony to the truth of her assertions." Harriet Wilson, "the writer of this books," she repeats as she concludes her first paragraph, "has seemed to be a child of misfortune." Harriet's childhood apparently was less than ideal: early on, she was "deprived of her parents, and all those endearing associations to which childhood clings." She was hired out to a family "calling themselves Christians," Margaretta Thorn continues, adding parenthetically that may "the good Lord deliver me from such." This family put her to work "both in the house and in the field," allegedly ruining her health by unduly difficult work. "She was indeed a slave, in every sense of the word," she continues, "and a lonely one, too."

Harriet's health had been impaired since she was "eighteen," Margaretta Thorn continues, and "a great deal of the time has been confined to her room and bed." This protracted illness forced some authorities, she suggests, to take her child to "the county farm, because she could not pay his board every week." Mrs. Wilson, however, was able to place her son in what we would call a foster home, where, Margaretta Thorn tells us, "he is contented and happy, and where he is considered as good as those he is with." From Margaretta Thorn's assertion that this unnamed foster family treated her son as their son and Harriet Wilson "as a daughter," and refused to maintain friendships with neighbors who did not do so as well, we may safely conclude that the foster family was white. She then concludes her pious epistle, as do both Allida and C.D.S., with an exhortation that those who call themselves friends of the blacks should purchase the novel and thereby enable its author to become self-sustaining and to retrieve her child:

> And now I would say, I hope those who call themselves friends of our dark-skinned brethren, will lend a helping hand, and assist our sister, not in giving, but in buying a book; the expense is trifling, and the reward of doing good is great.

The third appended letter, signed simply "C.D.S.," is dated "Milford, July 20th, 1859," two days short of one month before Mrs. Wilson registered her copyright at the District Court at Boston. The 1860 census for Milford, New Hampshire, listed two residents whose first names begin with "C" and whose surnames end in "S," but none is listed with "D" as a middle name or initial: Catherine Shannahan and Charles Shepard. But "C.D.S." was also a *legal* abbreviation for "Colored Indentured Servant." C.D.S.'s epistle is less informative than Margaretta Thorn's or Allida's, claiming only that he has "been acquainted with" the "writer of this book" for "several years" and knows her character to be "worthy the esteem of all friends of humanity; one whose soul is alive to the work to which she puts her hand." Appealing to "the sympathy of all Christians, and those who have a spark of humanity in their breasts," C.D.S. asks his readers to purchase the book, so "that its circulation will be extensive." C.D.S., we can deduce, is either, like Margaretta Thorn, a white citizen—since he adds the customary confirmation that "Although her complexion is a little darker than my own, I esteem it a privilege to associate with her, and assist her whenever an opportunity presents itself"—or a mulatto indentured servant. Closing by "bidding her God speed," the author signs "C.D.S."

Allida's long letter occupies most of the Appendix. It is an especially compelling document not only because of its length, but also because it contains scattered clues and suggestions about *Our Nig's* author, as well as three subtexts, including an excerpted letter from Harriet to a "Mrs. Walker," in whose household she lived in W——, Massachusetts, where she mastered the fine art of making straw hats; a poem written by Harriet; and a poem probably written by Allida.

Allida asserts that she has known "the author of this book" for "about eight years," or roughly since 1851, so she is able to verify the "truth" of this strange fiction, which she will later label "an Autobiography." The author was "brought to W——, Mass." by "an itinerant colored lecturer," she begins her testimony. This unnamed town, she continues, is "an ancient town," in which "mothers and daughters" work "willingly with their hands" with "straw," which Allida underscores as if to provide a clue to the town's identity. Of the numerous "W——, Massachusetts" towns, three present themselves as likely candidates for Harriet's temporary dwelling place. Walpole was "well-known" for its straw works between 1830 and 1842 or so; the "straw goods" industry began at Ware, Massachusetts, in 1832, and "straw sewing was done largely in the homes about town," just as Allida informs us Harriet did in Mrs. Walker's household. *The History of Westborough, Massachusetts* claims that the straw goods and millinery industries were "for a long time confined to this part of Massachusetts." From these facts we can conclude that Harriet most probably lived in the section of Massachusetts that includes Ware and Walpole, as well as Worcester, which is approximately fifteen miles from Westborough.

In this town Harriet boarded with "the family of Mrs. Walker," who "immediately succeeded in procuring work for her as a 'straw sewer.'" An ideal pupil, Allida continues, Harriet learned quickly "the art of making straw hats," yet was prevented by ill health ("on account of former hard treatment") from continuous employment, a condition that forced Mrs. Walker to nurse her in "a room joining her own chamber." Citing Harriet's direct speech about her maternal feelings toward Mrs. Walker, Allida reveals that Harriet called her "Aunt J——," confirming that the name "Allida" is a pseudonym. After a brief period of bliss, disaster strikes in the form of a black lover.

"One beautiful morning in the early spring of 1842" (surely a printer's error for 1852, since we know the marriage was *registered* in the spring of 1852), Allida's narrative proceeds, Harriet, out for a walk, met the "'lecturer'" who had brought her to W——, Mass. He was accompanied by "a fugitive slave," whom Allida characterizes as "Young, well-formed and very handsome," a self-described "*house*-servant, which seemed to account," she concludes, "in some measure for his gentlemanly manners and pleasing address." This "entirely accidental" meeting, Allida laments, "was a sad occurrence for poor Alfrado," the protagonist of *Our Nig* and the author herself: "Suffice it to say, an acquaintance and attachment was formed, which, in due time, resulted in marriage."

It must have been love at first sight because "in a few days, the couple left W——, and *all* her home comforts, and took up her abode in New Hampshire." After a blissful respite, Harriet's husband "left his young and trusting wife, and embarked for sea." Her husband failed to return, and Harriet's "heart failed her." Unable to sustain herself, with no friends other than "that class who are poor in the things of earth," Harriet was forced to seek refuge in "the 'County House;' *go she must.*" We recall that the Hillsborough County House, in Goffstown, New Hampshire, was George Mason Wilson's birthplace. Precisely at this point in her narrative Allida inserts a letter that Harriet purportedly wrote to "her mother Walker" about "her feelings on her way thither, and after her arrival," which, Allida assures us, "can be given better in her own language" than reported indirectly.

Harriet's letter serves as a confirmation of the fictional narrative's style, subtly reinforcing Allida's assertion of the veracity of the storyteller and her tale, as well as of her solitary authorship. Quite unlike the instance of Harriet Jacobs's *Incidents in the Life of a Slave Girl* (1861), whose prefatory authenticator, Lydia Maria Child, admits minimal "revision," "condensation," and "arrangement," not one of the three letters appended to *Our Nig* ever questions that Harriet Wilson wrote all the words in the text in their exact order. Her accomplishment is all the more astonishing because *Our Nig* reads so much more fluidly and its plot seems so much less contrived than *The Heroic Slave* (1853), *Clotel* (1853), *The Garies and Their Friends* (1857), or *Blake; or, The Huts of America* (partially serialized in 1859, then probably serialized fully in 1861), the fictions published before *Our Nig* in the Afro-American tradition; particularly since the authors of two of those novels, William Wells Brown and Martin R. Delany, traveled widely, published extensively, lectured regularly, and educated themselves diligently. Delany even studied medicine at Harvard.

Nevertheless, the "autobiographical" consistencies between the fragments of Harriet Wilson's life and the depiction of the calamities of Frado, the heroine of *Our Nig*, would suggest that Mrs. Wilson was able to gain control over her materials more readily than her fellow black novelists of that decade precisely by adhering closely to the painful details of suffering that were part of her experience. On "the portable inkstand, pens and paper" that Mrs. Walker and her friends at W—— presented to Harriet as wedding or farewell presents, Harriet wrote an epistle of lament to Mrs. Walker, which Allida quotes at length, including a five-stanza poem. Harriet's poetry is similar to the religious, sentimental stuff of the period; her letter, however, although suffused with melodrama, is characterized by the same attention to detail and event as is the text of *Our Nig*.

Her letter reads in part:

> ...just before nightfall, we halted at the institution, prepared for the *homeless*. With cold civility the matron received me, and bade one of the inmates shew me my room. She did so; and I followed up two flights of stairs. I crept as I was able; and when she said, 'Go in there,' I obeyed, asking for my trunk, which was soon placed by me. My room was furnished some like the 'prophet's chamber,' except there was no 'candlestick;' so when I could creep down I begged for a light, and it was granted. Then I flung myself on the bed and cried, until I could cry no longer.

George Plummer Hadley, in his *History of the Town of Goffstown, 1773–1920,* states that the Hillsborough County Farm was purchased in 1849 to house "the county poor, which at that time numbered eighty-eight." The "Farm" consisted of a large farm house, a barn, a "small dwelling-house near the oak tree," and some smaller buildings. The "paupers," as Hadley calls them, were "scattered through different buildings, which were heated by wood fires." Conditions there apparently were horrid: in 1853, some of the inmates "were stricken with smallpox, and it was necessary to build a pest-house" for their proper isolation and care. As Hadley concludes, "What tales of sorrow could some of the unfortunates unfold."

Allida proceeds to inform her readers that Harriet remained in this desolate institution "until after the birth of her babe," until both were rescued by the return of "her faithless husband," who "took her to some town in New Hampshire," where, to his credit, he supported his family "decently well." Then, he left again "as before—sudden and unexpectedly, and she saw him no more." Only "for a time" could Mrs. Wilson support herself and her son, then "her struggles with poverty and sickness were severe." Harriet and her infant escaped disaster only through the agency of "a kind gentleman and lady," who "took her little boy into their own family," providing for him well "without the hope of remuneration."

And what of the child's mother? Allida tells us: "As for the afflicted mother, she too has been remembered." Incredibly, "a stranger," one "moved by compassion," "bestowed a recipe upon her for restoring gray hair to its former color." The ingenious Harriet, who promptly "availed herself of this great help," apparently proved to be "quite successful" at this unusual trade, until her health, once again, failed her. Confined to bed, "she has felt herself obliged to resort to another method of procuring her bread—that of writing an Autobiography." Following a paragraph asking the reader to "purchase a volume," Allida ends her narrative of Harriet Wilson's life with an eight-stanza poem, "I will help thee, saith the Lord."

Mrs. Wilson's Preface to *Our Nig,* as unusual as it reads today, adds little to our reconstruction of the life of the author. Harriet Wilson's Preface begins with the expected apologia for all deficiencies in her text. "In offering to the public the following pages, the writer confesses her inability," Mrs. Wilson writes, "to minister to the refined and cultivated, the pleasure supplied by abler pens. It is not for such," she concludes with triumph and impressive control, "these crude narrations appear." She has been "forced to some experiment," she quickly adds, to maintain "myself and child without extinguishing this feeble life." The "experiment," of course, was the act of writing a fiction of her life. Here follows the attempt to anticipate the criticisms that such a book, published by a black one month before John Brown's raid on Harpers Ferry, might engender among those who had a vested interest in preserving the fiction that the stereotypic oppositions between North and South, freedom and slavery, black, as it were, and white allowed for no qualifications, no exceptions. For here, Harriet Wilson admits that her intention in writing this novel was to indict racism, whether it is found in the South or in the North.

> I would not from these motives even palliate slavery at the South, by disclosures of its appurtenances North. My mistress was wholly imbued with *southern* principles. I do not pretend to divulge every transaction in my own life, which the unprejudiced would declare unfavorable in comparison with treatment of legal bondmen; I have purposely omitted what would most provoke shame in our good anti-slavery friends at home.

Concluding that her "humble position" and "frank confession of errors" might possibly "shield me from severe criticism," Harriet Wilson then launches an appeal directly to "my colored brethren universally," asking of them their "patronage, hoping they will not condemn this attempt of their sister to be erudite, but rally around me a faithful band of supporters and defenders."

Although the direct appeal, for sympathy, patience, and financial support, was a standard feature of the apologia, not one other black author before Harriet Wilson felt compelled to anticipate the "severe" criticisms of even the Northern abolitionists. Mrs. Wilson, however, did, and wisely so. For Allida's letter erroneously, but rather self-consciously, attempts to direct the reader's attention away from the central subject of this novel, which is the brutality of a white woman racist who, against the wishes of all other members of her household—with the significant exception of the wicked mother's equally wicked daughter—enslaves the protagonist, Frado, in a prolonged indenture as brutal as any depicted in the autobiographical slave narratives. Lest the point of the narrative be mistaken, Mrs. Wilson's long subtitle of *Our Nig* confirms it:

SKETCHES FROM THE LIFE OF A FREE BLACK,
IN A TWO-STORY WHITE HOUSE, NORTH.
SHOWING THAT SLAVERY'S SHADOWS FALL EVEN THERE.
BY "OUR NIG."

The boldness and cleverness in the ironic use of "Nig" as title and pseudonym is, to say the least, impressive, standing certainly as one of the black tradition's earliest recorded usages. And if Allida's letter suggests that "Alfrado's tale" is that of love-betrayed, a glance at the text suggests the contrary. The subplot of love, marriage, childbirth, and betrayal only appears in the text's final chapter, Chapter XII, "The Winding Up of the Matter," which unfolds in scarcely five pages of a one-hundred-and-thirty-one-page novel. The chapter, headed by an epigraph from Solomon—"Nothing new under the sun"—recapitulates, almost as does a coda in a musical score, the themes of the text. It is this encounter with the racism of the white *petite bourgeoisie* of the North that Harriet Wilson squarely confronts. Frado's deserting husband, Samuel, dies an anonymous death of yellow fever in New Orleans; Frado's oppressor, Mrs. Bellmont, dies the slow, excruciatingly painful death that her sins, at least in the sentimental novel, have earned for her.

Perhaps another explanation for the obscurity of *Our Nig* was its unabashed representation of an interracial marriage, a liaison from which the novel's protagonist was an offspring. That relationship, which other writers in the decade of the 1850s called "amalgamation," had, it is true, been the subject of a few novels published before *Our Nig;* never, however, was miscegenation depicted with any degree of normality before *Our Nig.* The general attitude toward this controversial social matter was perhaps best articulated by Mrs. Mary Howard Schoolcraft in her novel, *The Black Gauntlet* (1860): "I believe a refined Anglo-Saxon lady would sooner be burned at the stake, than married to one of these black descendants of Ham."

Novels such as *The Ebony Idol* (1860) or *A Sojourn in the City of Amalgamation in the Year of Our Lord 19–* (1835) made the subject an object of bitter, racist satire. Interracial marriage, it is fair to say, was not a popular subject for representation in either antislavery or proslavery novels. As the omniscient narrator of *Our Nig* editorializes about the marriage of Jim, a black man, to "lonely Mag Smith":

> He prevailed; they married. You can philosophize, gentle reader, upon the impropriety of such unions, and preach dozens of sermons on the evils of amalgamation. Want is a more powerful philosopher and preacher. Poor Mag. She has sundered another bond which held her to her fellows. She has descended another step down the ladder of infamy.

Even this representation, obviously, was not without its ironies, and even demeaning aspects; Jim's proposal is not exactly rendered from a position of strength or from a sense of equality:

> "Well, Mag," said Jim, after a short pause, "you's down low enough. I don't see but I've got to take care of ye. 'Sposin' we marry!"
>   Mag raised her eyes, full of amazement, and uttered a sonorous "What?"
>   Jim felt abashed for a moment. He knew well what were her objections.
>   "You's had trial of white folks, any how. They run off an left ye, and now none of 'em come near ye to see if you's dead or alive. I's black outside, I know, but I's got a white heart inside. Which you rather have, a black heart in a white skin, or a white heart in a black one?"

Despite this less than noble stance, however, Jim and his reluctant bride, Mag Smith, live peacefully, productively, and fairly happily for three years, until Jim dies. Surely this "unproblematical" relationship, at least in the stereotypical social sense of that term, did nothing to aid the book's circulation in the North or the South.

We are free to speculate whether the oblivion into which Harriet Wilson disappeared for well over a century resulted from the boldness of her themes and from turning to that hated epithet, "nigger," both for title and authorial, if pseudonymous, identity. We can, unfortunately, only risk the most tentative speculation. But we can say that a systematic search of all extant copies of black and reform newspapers and magazines in circulation contemporaneously with the publication of *Our Nig* yielded not one notice or review, nor did searches through the Boston, Massachusetts, dailies and the Amherst, New Hampshire, *Farmer's Cabinet*.

How were other contemporary black novels reviewed? *Clotel* (1853), William Wells Brown's first novel of four, was reviewed in 1853 in the London *Eastern Star* (reprinted in the *National Anti-Slavery Standard* December 31), and in the Hereford (England) *Times* on December 17 (reprinted in the *Liberator* on January 20, 1854). On February 3, 1854, the *Liberator* reviewed *Clotel* itself. The serialized publication of Martin R. Delany's *Blake* was reviewed in the *Liberator* on April 15, 1859, as part of an advertisement. But neither Floyd J. Miller, in his edition of *Blake* (1970), nor Curtis W. Ellison and E. W. Metcalf, Jr., in their thorough reference guide, *William Wells Brown and Martin R. Delany,* could locate any other periodical reviews. Unlike the slave's narratives, we can see, black fiction was not popularly reviewed, but it was reviewed on occasion.

That such a significant novel, the very first written by a black woman, would remain unnoticed in Boston in 1859, a veritable center of abolitionist reform and passion, and by a growing black press eager to celebrate all black achievement in the arts and sciences, remains one of the troubling enigmas of Afro-American literary history. Encountering *Our Nig* anew, I can only offer the thematic "explanations" rendered above, as difficult as even I find them to accept or believe. To suppress a text by ignoring it because it depicts a "successful" interracial marriage, or a black man pretending to be an "escaped slave," only reinforces what the tradition must understand as the *difficulty* of reconstituting an act of language in its own milieu.

It is curious to trace the disappearance and reappearance of Harriet Wilson and her novel, *Our Nig.* It would be easier to imagine her presence in the tradition if we could identify some nineteenth-century reference to her, even an obscure reference, which then was overlooked or doubted; but we have found none. She does not even appear in Samuel May, Jr.'s 1863 *Catalogue of Anti-Slavery Publications in America, 1750–1863,* published just four years after Mrs. Wilson published *Our Nig.* Neither does she appear in the U.S. Bureau of Education Report of 1893–1894, which includes as its third section "Works by Negro Authors," nor in Robert M. Adger's *Catalogue of Rare Books and Pamphlets . . . upon Subjects relating to the Past Condition of the Colored Race and the Slavery Agitation in this Country* (1894) or his *Catalogue of Rare Books on Slavery and Negro Authors on Science, History, Poetry, Religion, Biography, eic.* (1904). Du Bois did not mention her in his three important bibliographies, published as part of his Atlanta University Studies, in 1900, 1905, and 1910. Daniel P. Murray, an Assistant Librarian at the Library of Congress, did not mention Mrs. Wilson or *Our Nig* in either his *Preliminary List of Books and Pamphlets by Negro Authors,* which he compiled for the American Negro Exhibit at the Paris Exhibition of

1900, or in the six-thousand-item bibliography that was to have been published as part of *Murrays Historical and Biographical Encyclopedia of the Colored
Race throughout the World*. Nor was she unearthed in any of the late nineteenth
and early twentieth-century black biographical dictionaries, such as W. J. Simmons's *Men of Mark* (1887) or J. L. Nichols and William H. Crogman's *Progress
of a Race; or the Remarkable Advancement of the American Negro* (1920).

If the historians, bibliophiles, and bibliographers overlooked Harriet Wilson, then the literary historians fared only a bit better. Benjamin Brawley, a
diligent scholar and critic, does not mention text or author in *The Negro in
Literature and Art in the United States* (1918; 1930), *Early Negro American Writers*
(1935), or in *The Negro Genius* (1937). Vernon Loggins, whose literary history
remains the most complete to date, makes no mention of her in *The Negro Author: His Development in America to 1900* (1931). Neither does Sterling A. Brown
refer to her in his critically sophisticated *The Negro in American Fiction* (1937).
Harriet E. Wilson's name is absent in Barbara Christian's *Black Women Novelists: The Development of a Tradition, 1892–1976* (1980); in Arlene A. Elder's *The
"Hindered Hand": Cultural Implications of Early African-American Fiction* (1978);
in Addison Gayle, Jr.'s *The Way of the New World: The Black Novel in America*
(1976); Richard Alan Yarborough's "The Depiction of Blacks in the Early
Afro-American Novel" (Ph.D. Dissertation, 1980); Nina Baym's *Woman's Fic-
tion: A Guide to Novels by and about Women in America, 1820–1870* (1978); and
Bert James Loewenberg and Ruth Bogin's *Black Women in Nineteenth-Century
American Life* (1976). The most complete bibliography of the Afro-American
novel, *Afro-American Fiction, 1853–1916,* edited by Edward Margolies and
David Bakish, does not include Mrs. Wilson; nor do Theressa Gunnels Rush,
Carol Fairbanks Myers, and Esther Spring Arata in their thorough *Black
American Writers, Past and Present: A Biographical and Bibliographical Dictionary*
(1975), or M. Thomas Inge, Maurice Duke, and Jackson R. Bryer in *Black
American Writers: Bibliographical Essays* (1978). Roger Whitlow's *Black American
Literature: A Critical History* (1974) and Maxwell Whiteman's *A Century of Fic-
tion by American Negroes, 1853–1952* (1955) are both silent about Mrs. Wilson's
existence. And so on.

I have, however, found five references to *Our Nig*. John Herbert Nelson
mentions in passing only the title in his 1926 study, *The Negro Character in
American Literature*. Herbert Ross Brown, in *The Sentimental Novel in America,
1789–1860* (1940), implies that H. E. Wilson is a white male, and says that
this novel is unusual within its genre because "The author of *Our Nig* dared
to treat with sympathetic understanding the marriage of Jim, a black, to a
white woman who had been seduced and deserted," an observation about
one of the themes of *Our Nig* that simply did not occur to me on a first reading. Monroe N. Work, in his monumental compilation, *A Bibliography of the*

Negro in Africa and America (1928), does indeed list both author and title, but under the category "Novels by White Authors Relating to the Negro." James Joseph McKinney's "The Theme of Miscegenation in the American Novel to World War I," a 1972 Ph.D. dissertation, discusses the novel's plot and suggests that the fiction is autobiographical. Both Mrs. Wilson and her novel are listed in Geraldine Matthews's bibliography, *Black Writers, 1713–1949* (1975), and in Carol Fairbanks and Eugene A. Engeldinger's *Black American Fiction: A Bibliography* (1978), but with no information beyond that found in the second volume of Lyle Wright's three-volume listing of American fiction (Wright II–2767). Curiously enough, the most complete entry for the title was made in a 1980 catalogue of the Howard S. Mott Company of Sheffield, Massachusetts, a company well-regarded among antiquarians. The listing, prepared by Daniel Mott, asserted that Mrs. H. E. Wilson's novel was the first by an Afro-American woman. Mott says he decided that Wilson was black because of the evidence presented in the text's appended letters. Perhaps it is appropriate that this second edition of *Our Nig* has been reprinted from Mott's extraordinarily rare first edition.

Let us, at last, read closely Harriet Wilson's novel. I propose, in the remainder of this essay, to describe the text's own mode of presentation, to gloss its echoes, to establish its plot structure and compare this to those details that we have been able to glean of Mrs. Wilson's biographical "facts," then to compare these elements of the plot of *Our Nig* to a typology of "Woman's Fiction" published in this country between 1820 and 1870, which Nina Baym has so carefully devised.

Harriet E. Wilson's Preface to *Our Nig,* as I have suggested, is an extraordinary document in the Afro-American literary tradition; it is, if not unique, certainly one of the rare instances in which a black author has openly anticipated a hostile reaction to her text from "our good anti-slavery friends at home." The author, moreover, confirms here both that her fiction is autobiographical, and that it has been crafted to minimize the potentially deleterious effects such a searing indictment of slavery's "appurtenances north" might well have upon the antislavery cause.

> I do not pretend to divulge every transaction in my own life, which the unprejudiced would declare unfavorable in comparison with treatment of legal bondmen; I have purposely omitted what would most provoke shame in our good anti-slavery friends at home.

There are darker horrors to my tale than even these I set forward here, Mrs. Wilson claims; these she has decided against drawing upon in her fiction for fear of wounding the fight against slavery, since these would be seen to be "unfavorable" even when compared to the treatment of the slave. Hers is not meant to be an attack on Northern whites at all; rather, "My mistress was imbued with *southern* principles."

Let us consider further this matter of the text's silences and lacunae. We may consider Mrs. Wilson's Preface and the three appended letters to comprise the documentary-biographical subsection of the text, while the novel itself comprises the text's fictional representation of Mrs. Wilson's experiences as an indentured servant in a Northern white household before 1850. What is curious about the relationship between these nonfictional and the fictional discourses, which together form the text of *Our Nig*, is this: the "closer" that the novel approaches the appended biographies, the less distance there is between "fact" and romance, between (auto)biography and fiction. This is one of the more curious aspects of this curious text: the fiction, or the *guise* of her fictional account of her life, tends to fall away the nearer her novel approaches its own ending, and the ending of her text, the composite biography written by Mrs. Wilson's friends. It is of considerable interest to outline the manner in which one discursive field "collapses," as it were, into quite another, of a different status than the other.

To be sure, there are tensions between autobiography and fiction early in the novel. This tension is evident in chapter titles. Chapter I, for example, Mrs. Wilson calls "Mag Smith, My Mother." The first-person pronoun would lead the reader to assume that the novel is narrated in the first person; it is not. Rather, a third-person narrator observes and interprets the thoughts and actions of all concerned. Clearly, however, the narrator is telling Frado's tale, a tale of abuse, neglect, betrayal, suffering consciousness, and certain death from that inevitable visitor of the sentimental novel, the dreaded "fever." These stock devices, employed with melodrama, direct appeal to the reader, and a certain florid, stilted diction in speech and thought, nevertheless function to reveal Frado's saga. But Frado's story, as these lapses into the first person would suggest, is Harriet E. Adams Wilson's tale as well. Chapter II, "My Father's Death," and Chapter III, "A New Home For Me," include other instances of the first-person shift. With Chapter IV and after, however, the chapter titles employ the third person, but are more often abstractions. These titles, in order, follow: "A Friend For Nig," "Departures," "Varieties," "Spiritual Condition of Nig," "Visitor and Departure," "Death," "Perplexities—Another Death," "Marriage Again," and "The Winding Up of the Matter."

What are we to make of the first-person lapses in the chapter titles? We can conclude, with Allida, that the novel is indeed "an Autobiography," of sorts, an autobiographical novel. Whether the lapses are the sign of an inexperienced author struggling with or *against* the received conventions of her form, or the result of the imposition of a life on the desires of a text to achieve the status of fiction, these first-person traces point to the complexities and tensions of basing fictional events upon the lived experiences of an author. The latter chapters of *Our Nig* contain events that parallel remarkably closely those experiences of Harriet Wilson's that we are able to document. Curiously enough, the first-person proprietary consciousness evinced in the titles of the early chapters does not parallel events that we have been able to document and that we probably shall not be able to document. Since these early chapters describe events far removed from the author's experiences closest in time to the period of writing, the first-person presences perhaps reveal the author's anxiety about identifying with events in the text that she cannot claim to recollect clearly, and some of which she cannot recollect at all, such as the courtship and marriage of her mother, and the protagonist's ultimate abandonment by her widowed parent. In later chapters Mrs. Wilson had no need to demonstrate or claim the direct relation between author and protagonist, since, as our research reveals, these two sets of events, the fictional and the biographical, overlap nicely. In Chapter XII, however, the narrator slips into the first person, in her first sentence, as if to reinforce the connection between narrator and protagonist.

In her Preface Mrs. Wilson explains away the text's lacunae, its silences and reticences, as does the disembodied narrative voice in the novel's final chapter. In the Preface, as I have suggested, Harriet Wilson argues that she has remained silent about those events in her life which, if depicted, could well result in an adverse reaction against Northern whites, and could thereby do harm to the anti-slavery movement. The novel's penultimate paragraph repeats that claim, but with a difference. This difference consists of a direct appeal to the reader to grant the author "your sympathy," rather than withholding it simply because more, critical details are not depicted in the text:

> Still an invalid, she asks your sympathy, gentle reader. Refuse not, because some part of her history is unknown, save by the Omnipresent God. Enough has been unrolled to demand your sympathy and aid.

She has revealed quite enough, the narrator tells us, for her readers to be convinced of the author's merit of their "sympathy and aid." To ask of her even more would be to ask too much. While the scholar wishes for more details of the life to have been named in the novel, details ideally transpiring between 1850 and 1860 in the author's life (Chapter XII of the text), even he must remain content to grant the author her plea.

What do we find in this ultimate chapter in the very space where these absent details of the author's life "should" be? We read, instead, one of the novel's few direct attacks upon white Northern racism:

> She passed into the various towns of the State [New Hampshire] she lived in, then into Massachusetts. Watched by kidnappers, maltreated by professed abolitionists, who did n't want slaves at the South, nor niggers in their own houses, North. Faugh! to lodge one; to eat with one; to admit one through the front door; to sit next one; awful!

It is clear that Harriet Wilson's anxieties about offending her Northern readers were not the idle uneasiness most authors feel about their "ideal" constituencies.

It is equally clear that the author of *Our Nig* was a broadly read constituent of nineteenth-century American and English literature. The text's epigraphs alone encourage speculation about the author's experiences with books. True, the structure of the novel would suggest that Mrs. Wilson not only read a number of popular, sentimental American novels but also patterned her fiction largely within the received confines of that once popular form. *Our Nig*'s plot even repeats a few crucial events found in Mattie Griffiths's novel, *The Autobiography of a Female Slave,* suggesting more than a passing acquaintance on H. E. Wilson's part with Griffiths's book. But *Our Nig*'s epigraphs, placed at the head of each of its twelve chapters and on its title page, reflect a certain eclecticism in Mrs. Wilson's reading habits, perhaps an eclecticism that reflects contact with the arbitrary titles to be found in a small middle-class American library, the "library" that might consist of one shelf of titles, or perhaps two. Josiah Gilbert Holland, Thomas Moore, Percy Bysshe Shelley, Eliza Cook, Lord Byron, Martin Farquhar Tupper, Henry Kirke White, perhaps Charlotte Elliott, and Solomon, are among the authors whom Harriet Wilson felt comfortable enough to quote.

Each epigraph is well-chosen, and each illustrates the predominant sentiment of the following chapter. Most, above all else, appeal directly to the sympathies of the reader, for love betrayed, hope trampled, dreams frustrated, or desire unconsummated. The epigraph to Chapter II, taken from Shelley's "Misery," is representative of Mrs. Wilson's tastes in poetry:

> *Misery! we have known each other,*
> *Like a sister and a brother,*
> *Living in the same lone home*
> *Many years—we must live some*
> *Hours or ages to come.*

The range of citation of American and English authors found in *Our Nig* is much greater than that generally found in the slave narratives or in other black nineteenth-century novels. Occasionally, however, we encounter belabored erudition and echoing in *Our Nig.* The five epigraphs that we have not been able to identify could well have been composed by Mrs. Wilson herself, especially since they often read like pastiches of other authors, or like lines from common Protestant hymns. At the least, we know that Harriet Wilson read rather widely and eclectically, and that she preferred the pious, direct appeal to the subtle or the ambiguous.

It is a rewarding exercise to compare the plot structure of *Our Nig* to the "overplot" of nineteenth-century women's fiction identified by Nina Baym in her study, *Woman's Fiction: A Guide to Novels by and about Women in America, 1820–1870.* Baym's overplot consists, in part, of the following characteristics:

1. The device of pairing heroines, or pairing a heroine and a villainess, is a central component of "some exemplary organizing principle in all this woman's fiction."

2. The heroine is initially "a poor and friendless child" who is either an orphan, or who "only thinks herself to be one, or has by necessity been separated from her parents for an indefinite time."

3. The heroine, at the conclusion of her story, "is no longer an underdog." Her "success in life [is] entirely a function of her own efforts and character."

4. There are two kinds of heroine in this kind of novel, the flawless and the flawed.

5. The self is depicted to be "a social product, firmly and irrevocably embedded in a social construct that could destroy it but that also shaped it, constrained it, encouraged it, and ultimately fulfilled it."

6. The heroine, as a child, is abused by those who have authority over her. In the realistic tradition of this kind of novel, a series of events represents "the daily wearing down of neglected and overworked orphans." The heroine's authority figures "exploit or neglect her," rather than "love and nurture her." The heroine's principal challenge "is to endure until she comes of age and at the same time to grow so that when she comes of age she will be able to leave the unfriendly environment and succeed on her own." The heroine must "strike a balance between total submission, . . . and an equally suicidal defiance."

7. The heroine is abused by one of several characters who "are the administrators or owners of the space within which the child is legally constrained. Least guilty are the mothers; often it is the loss of the mother that initiates the heroine's woes, and the memory of her mother that

permits her to endure them. Most guilty are aunts, . . . with whom many orphaned heroines are sent to live."

8. The heroine encounters people in her community who "support, advise, and befriend her," precisely as she is abandoned by her own family. They comprise a surrogate family.

9. The heroine's ultimate "domesticity" is not defined by her relations to her own children but to her surrogate family members; and, "although children may be necessary for a woman's happiness, they are not necessary for her identity—nor is a husband."

   A concluding, often happy, marriage "represents the institutionalizing of such families, for the heroine's new home includes not only her husband but all her other intimates as well."

10. The plot of woman's fiction has a tripartite structure: an unhappy childhood, "an interlude during which she must earn her own living," and the conclusion.

   Within this "interlude," the heroine's life is often influenced by strong, magnanimous, unmarried women, who mother her at a period when the heroine is unmarried and not being courted, and whose presence reinforces the idea that "relations with their own sex constituted the texture" of women's lives primarily.

11. In encounters "with a man, economic considerations predominated for these women. The women authors created stories in which, ultimately, male control and the money economy are simultaneously terminated."

12. Husbands and would-be lovers are less important to the heroine than "fathers, guardians, and brothers." The heroine "is canny in her judgment of men, and generally immune to the appeal of a dissolute suitor. When she feels such an attraction, she resists it."

13. The path to the Christian religion is unmediated by men, so that "faith is thus pried out of its patriarchal social setting."

14. The "woman's novel" contains "much explicit and implicit social commentary." Principal targets of this commentary were "the predominance of marketplace values in every area of American life," oppositions between the city and the country, and "the class divisions in American society." Slavery and intemperance also are themes, but secondary themes.

15. The novelists "abhorred and feared poverty."

Nina Baym's extraordinarily perceptive overplot, as I have summarized it here, enables us to compare the plot of *Our Nig* with that of the tradition into which Harriet E. Wilson's novel falls. Many of these fifteen elements of the

overplot of woman's fiction occur almost exactly in *Our Nig,* Frado, our heroine, most certainly is oppressed by her paired opposite, the evil Mrs. Bellmont. Also, Frado has been orphaned twice, once by the death of her loving,
black father, then again as she is abandoned by her desperate, yet unsym-
pathetic, white mother, who has now become the lover of her late husband's
friend and business partner.

Now left in the home of a white, lower middle-class family, the young mulatto child begins an extended period of harsh indenture. Her two torturers are
the evil female head of the household, and her daughter, equally evil, but in
miniature. *Our Nig,* too, shares the tripartite structure of other women's novels,
including an unhappy childhood, a seemingly endless period of indenture, and
the conclusion. During her interlude of abuse, one white woman character,
true to the received form, heavily influences Frado, comforts her, and becomes her only true confidant. Just as her torture is defined largely by two
women, so, too, is her principal source of succor afforded by her relationship
with this principal surrogate maternal figure, and a second, unnamed maternal
figure who expands her consciousness with books.

Our Nig does indeed share the "woman's novel's" use of fictional forms to
indict social injustice. As we might expect, racism, as visited upon the heroine
by another woman whose relationship to the heroine is defined *principally* by
an economic bond, is this novel's central concern. Curiously enough, it is the
complex interaction of race-*and*-class relationships, depicted in Frado's relation
to Mrs. Bellmont as inextricably intertwined, which *Our Nig* critiques for the
first time in American fiction. By dividing her white characters, of the same
family and the same class, into absolute categories of evil and good, Harriet E.
Wilson was allowing for more complexity in her analysis of the nature of oppression than generally did, or perhaps could have, those novelists who wrote
either to defend or to attack the institution of slavery.

In a sense, this narrative strategy can be read as a complex response to
Harriet Beecher Stowe's *Uncle Tom's Cabin.* Caroline E. Rush's response, for
example, was to attempt to enlist the new class of proslavery women writers
to turn away from slavery as subject and begin to write about "white, wearied, wornout" women protagonists. Rush, prime propagandist for the peculiar institution, is a dubious source of proto-feminist urgings. Writing in her
novel, *North and South, or Slavery and Its Contrasts* (1852), Rush first commands
her readers to cease crying for Uncle Tom—"a hardy, strong and powerful
Negro"—and start crying for pitiful, destitute children—"of the same color as
yourself." The freed blacks, of Philadelphia for example, Rush continues, lack
any "elegant degree of refinement and cultivation," thereby demonstrating
implicitly that blacks are incapable of 'elevation,' enslaved or free. Eschew
the profit motive, she concludes, and find a new subject:

Fine, profitable speculation may be made from negro fiction. Wrought up into touching pictures, they may, under the spell of genius, look like truth and have the semblance of reality, but where is the genius to paint the scenes that exist in our own cities?—to awaken a sympathy that shall give strength to the white, wearied, wornout daughters of toil?

It was to address this task, precisely seven years later, that Harriet E. Wilson published her novel, *Our Nig,* a novel written to demonstrate the suffering of a black, wearied, wornout daughter of toil. We see this clearly in the novel's characterization of men and women.

All the men in *Our Nig* befriend the heroine, except for one; all the principal women in this novel victimize the heroine, except for one. The exceptional male is a ne'er-do-well black "fugitive slave," who meets the heroine, seduces her, marries her, impregnates her, disappears, returns, disappears again, and succumbs to "Yellow Fever, in New Orleans," all in the novel's final six-page chapter, as if such matters deserved only an appendix. The great evil in this book is not love-betrayed, however, or the evils of the flesh; rather, it is poverty, both the desperation it inflicts as well as the evils it implicitly sanctions, which is *Our Nig*'s focus for social commentary. Even the six-page account of love, betrayal, deceit, and abandonment serves more to allow the text's narrator to appeal directly to the reader to purchase this book and to explain its writing than it does to develop the plot.

This treatment of the protagonist's marriage is an odd aspect of *Our Nig,* and is one of the crucial ways in which the plot structure of *Our Nig* diverges fundamentally from the overplot that Nina Baym so precisely defines as shared, repeated structures of white women's fiction in the mid-nineteenth century. These significant discrepancies of plot development suggest that the author of *Our Nig* created a novel that partakes of the received structure of American women's fiction, but often inverts that same structure, ironically enough, precisely at its most crucial points. Harriet E. Wilson used the plot structure of her contemporary white female novelists, yet abandoned that structure when it failed to satisfy the needs of her well-crafted tale. Mrs. Wilson, in other words, revised significantly the "white woman's novel," and thereby made the form her own. By this act of formal revision, she *created* the black woman's novel, not merely because she was the first black woman to write a novel in English, but because she *invented* her own plot structure through which to narrate the saga of her orphaned mulatto heroine. In this important way, therefore, Harriet Wilson's novel inaugurates the Afro-American literary tradition in a manner more fundamentally *formal* than did either William Wells Brown or Frank J. Webb, the two black Americans who published complete novels before her.

One major departure that *Our Nig* makes from the received structure of the fiction written by women is its conclusion. *Our Nig's* tale ends ambiguously, if it ends at all; the third-person narrator asks her readers directly for "your sympathy, gentle reader" for, the narrator continues, Frado remains "still an invalid," as she has remained since being abandoned by her mother. Although by the novel's conclusion, the villain, Mrs. Bellmont, has suffered "an agony in death unspeakable," and the good Aunt Abby has "entered heaven," the protagonist's status remains indeterminate, precisely because she has placed the conclusion of her "story," the burden of closure, upon her readers, who must purchase her book if the author-protagonist is to become self-sufficient. This "ending" is an anomalous one, and reinforces the "autobiographical" nature of the novel if only because the protagonist, the author, and the novel's narrator all merge explicitly into one voice to launch the text's advertisement for itself, for its status as a "worthy" fiction that should be purchased.

Our Nig does not share the respect for mothers that Baym identifies to be an important aspect in her overplot. While Frado's tale of sorrow and woe stems directly from her mother's absence, as is true of much of the contemporaneous woman's fiction, Mag Smith's absence is self-willed, and irresponsible. *Our Nig* questions profoundly the innocence of the mother-daughter relationship not only in Mag Smith and her daughter, but in Mrs. Bellmont's relation of identity with her evil daughter, both of whom conspire to make life miserable for their mulatto indentured servant. Only Aunt Abby relieves *Our Nig's* searching depictions of its principal white women characters.

Our Nig does not end either with a happy marriage or with the institutional consolidation, through this marriage, of the forces of good—Frado's surrogate family and the protagonist. On the contrary, *Our Nig* concludes with a marriage that ends in desertion and that forces the heroine to abandon her successful work as a milliner, and her first, and apparently liberating, encounters with books. The key members of the heroine's surrogate family are dead at the novel's conclusion, so her marriage to "Samuel" is an ironic, false resolution, one that exacerbates the heroine's condition and leaves her homeless with a newborn child. The desertion of her husband opens, rather than ends, the text, preventing the sort of closure we expect in this genre of the sentimental novel. Indeed, one of the few exercises of free will and desire by the heroine ends ironically and tragically. Frado's marriage to Samuel both obliterates the only independent, peaceful, relatively prosperous phase of her life, and serves as the incident that negates the novel's closure and forces the author of *Our Nig* to write, then attempt to sell, her story.

Similarly, the heroine's encounters with men depart significantly from her sister heroine's encounters in other novels written by women. Frado's relations with (white) men are remarkably free of economic considerations.

Rather, the men of the Bellmont household, all of whom ultimately die or move away, are sympathetic to Frado's sufferings and even conspire at times to help her to fight against Mrs. Bellmont's tyrannies. Frado's complex relationship to James, which intensifies as he lies slowly dying, is a curious blend of religion and displaced sexual desire. His economic status, however, does not come to bear directly upon his relations with Frado; however, Frado's dormant passion for religion initially awakes only insofar as she is able to associate being near to God with remaining near to James. While Aunt Abby and the local pastor seek to encourage her religious development, Frado's road to heaven is paved by her toils for James. Indeed, Frado never truly undergoes a religious transformation, merely the *appearance* of one; as the text emphasizes, "a devout and Christian exterior invited confidence from the villagers." Frado's innate innocence, outside of the respectability of the church, is one of the most subtle contrasts and social critiques of *Our Nig*. When the evil daughter, Mary, dies, well after Frado has "resolved to give over all thought of the future world" because "she did not wish to go" to a heaven that would allow Mrs. Bellmont entrance, Frado's innocent joy signifies her ironic rejection of Christian religion. Later, the narrator tells us that "It seemed a thanksgiving to Frado." As Frado tells Aunt Abby:

> "She got into the *river* again, Aunt Abby, did n't she; the Jordan is a big one to tumble into, any how. S'posen she goes to hell, she'll be as black as I am. Would n't mistress be mad to see her a nigger!" and others of a similar stamp, not at all acceptable to the pious, sympathetic dame; but she could not evade them.

This inversion of blackness and evil and good and whiteness is only one example of three, including Frado's lover, Samuel, and *Our Nig*'s title.

Frado, unlike most of her sister characters in other novels, succumbs to her attraction to a dissolute lover, a union that destroys her only period of independence and happiness. As the narrator relates, "There was a silent sympathy which Frado felt attracted her, and she opened her heart to the presence of love—that arbitrary and inexorable tyrant." Then, one paragraph later, "Here were Frado's first feelings of trust and repose on human arm. She realized, for the first time, the relief of looking to another for comfortable support. Occasionally," the narrator concludes anxiously, "he would leave her to 'lecture.'" Accordingly, husband Samuel

> left her to her fate—embarked at sea, with the disclosure that he had never seen the South, and that his illiterate harangues were humbugs for hungry abolitionists. Once more alone! Yet not alone.

Not alone, because husband Samuel leaves Frado in the early phase of a troubled pregnancy. The birth of the son, we know, motivates the author's creation of a text to contain her story and to provide sustenance for mother and child. This "professed fugitive from slavery," one of four black male characters in *Our Nig,* is the evil negation of Frado's father, Jim, "a kind-hearted African," a man she barely knew, since he died within "a few years" of marriage to "his treasure,—a white wife." He is also the negation of the long-suffering James. If *Our Nig* was a simple tale, or if it just conformed to the generic expectations of the sentimental, then black husband Samuel's portrayal would not have been so unremittingly negative, even if it had remained so brief.

Our Nig makes an even more important statement about the symbolic connotations of blackness in mid-nineteenth century America, and more especially of the epithet, "nigger." The book's title derives from the term of abuse that the heroine's antagonists 'rename her,' calling her "Our Nig," or simply "Nig." Harriet E. Wilson allows these racist characters to name her heroine, only to *invert* such racism by employing the name, in inverted commas, as her pseudonym of authorship. "By 'Our Nig'" forms in its entirety the last line of the book's title; its inverted commas underscore the use as an ironic one, one intended to reverse the power relation implicit in renaming-rituals which are primarily extensions of material relations. Transformed into an *object* of abuse and scorn by her enemies, the "object," the heroine of *Our Nig,* reverses this relationship by *renaming herself* not Our Nig but 'Our Nig,' thereby transforming herself into a *subject.*

She is now a subject who writes her own thinly veiled fictional account of her life in which *she* transforms her tormentors into objects, the stock, stereotypical objects of the sentimental novel. This, surely, is the most brilliant rhetorical strategy in black fiction before Charles Chesnutt's considerable talent manifests itself at the turn of the century. We may think of Mrs. Wilson's rhetorical strategy as a clever and subtle use of the trope of chiasmus, the trope which also is at the center of Frederick Douglass's rhetorical strategy in his *Narrative of the Life of Frederick Douglass, Written by Himself* (1845). Though related to Douglass's purposes, however, Harriet Wilson's employment of this device is unparalleled in representations of self-development in Afro-American fiction.

Wilson's achievement is that she combines the received conventions of the sentimental novel with certain key conventions of the slave narratives, then combines the two into *one new form,* of which *Our Nig* is the unique example. Had subsequent black authors had this text to draw upon, perhaps the black literary tradition would have developed more quickly and more resolutely than it did. For the subtleties of presentation of character are often lost in the fictions of Wilson's contemporaries, such as Frances E. W.

Harper, whose short story "The Two Offers" was also published in September 1859, and in the works of her literary "heirs."

Our Nig stands as a "missing link," as it were, between the sustained and well-developed tradition of black autobiography and the slow emergence of a distinctive black voice in fiction. That two black women published in the same month the first novel and short story in the black woman's literary tradition attests to larger shared cultural presuppositions at work within the black community than scholars have admitted before. The speaking black subject emerged on the printed page to declare himself or herself to be a human being of capacities equal to the whites. Writing, for black authors, was a mode of being, of self-creation with words. Harriet E. Wilson depicts this scene of instruction, central to the slave narratives, as the moment that Frado defies Mrs. Bellmont to hit her. The text reads:

> 'Stop!' shouted Frado, 'strike me, and I'll never work a mite more for you;' and throwing down what she had gathered, stood like one who feels the stirring of free and independent thoughts.

As had Frederick Douglass in his major battle with overseer Covey, Frado at last finds a voice with which to define her space. A physical space of one's own signifies the presence of a more subtle, if equally real, "metaphysical" space, within which one's thoughts are one's own. This space Frado finds by speaking, just as surely as Frances E. W. Harper's character, Chloe, finds hers while "Learning to Read":

> *So I got a pair of glasses,*
> *And straight to work I went,*
> *And never stopped till I could read*
> *The hymns and Testament.*
> *Then I got a little cabin,*
> *A place to call my own—*
> *And I felt as independent*
> *As the queen upon her throne.*

Reading, too, proved to be a major event in Frado's life. Shortly after finding her voice, Frado decided to recommence her early encounter with books, turning frequently, the text tells us, "from toil to soul refreshment":

> Frado had merged into womanhood, and, retaining what she had learned, in spite of the few privileges enjoyed formerly, was striving to enrich her mind. Her school-books were her constant companions, and every leisure moment

was applied to them. Susan was delighted to witness her progress, and some little book from her was a reward sufficient for any task imposed, however difficult. She had her book always fastened open near her, where she could glance from toil to soul refreshment.

In the penultimate chapter of *Our Nig,* the narrator tells us that along with mastering the needle, Frado learns to master the word:

> Expert with the needle, Frado soon equalled her instructress; and she sought to teach her the value of useful books; and while one read aloud to the other of deeds historic and names renowned, Frado experienced a *new impulse.* She felt herself capable of elevation; she felt that this book information supplied an *undefined dissatisfaction* she had long felt, but could not express. Every leisure moment was carefully applied to self-improvement, . . . [emphasis added]

In these final scenes of instruction, Harriet Wilson's text reflects upon its own creation, just as surely as Frado's awakened speaking voice signifies her consciousness of herself as a subject. With the act of speaking alone, Frado assumes a large measure of control over the choices she can possibly make each day. The "free and independent thoughts" she first feels upon speaking are repeated with variation in phrases such as "a new impulse," and "an undefined dissatisfaction," emotions she experiences while learning to read. "This book information," as the narrator tells us, enables Frado to *name things* by reading books. That such an apparently avid reader transformed the salient and tragic details of her life into the stuff of the novel—and was so daring in rendering the structures of fiction—is only one of the wonders of *Our Nig.*

What, finally, is the import of *Our Nig?* Its presence attests to a direct relation between the will and being of a sort rarely so explicit. Harriet E. Wilson's project, as bold and as unsure as it promised to be, failed to allow her to regain possession of her son. In this sense, Mrs. Wilson's project was a failure. Nevertheless, her legacy is an attestation of the will to power as the will to write. The transformation of the black-as-object into the black-as-subject: this is what Mrs. Harriet E. Wilson manifests for the first time in the writings of Afro-American women.

SOURCES: Harriet E. Wilson, *Our Nig; or, Sketches from the Life of a Free Black.* Preface, introduction and notes by Henry Louis Gates, Jr. (Orig. pub. Boston: G. C. Rand & Avery, 1859; New York: Vintage Books, 2002).

INTRODUCTION, *THE BONDWOMAN'S NARRATIVE: A NOVEL BY HANNAH CRAFTS*

THE SEARCH FOR FEMALE FUGITIVE SLAVE

EACH YEAR, SWANN Galleries conducts an auction of "Printed & Manuscript African-Americana" at its offices at 104 East Twenty-fifth Street in New York City. I have the pleasure of receiving Swann's annual mailing of the catalogue that it prepares for the auction. The catalogue consists of descriptions of starkly prosaic archival documents and artifacts that have managed, somehow, to surface from the depths of the black past. To many people, the idea of paging through such listings might seem as dry as dust. But to me, there is a certain poignancy to the fact that these artifacts, created by the disenfranchised, have managed to survive at all and have found their way, a century or two later, to a place where they can be preserved and made available to scholars, students, researchers and passionate readers.

The auction is held, appropriately enough, in February, the month chosen in 1926 by the renowned historian Carter G. Woodson to commemorate and encourage the preservation of African American history. (Woodson selected February for what was initially Negro History Week, because that month contained the birth dates of two presidents, George Washington and Abraham Lincoln, as well as that of Frederick Douglass, the great black abolitionist, author, and orator.)

For our generation of scholars of African American Studies, African American History Month is an intense period of annual conferences and commemorations, endowed lecture series and pageants, solemn candlelight remembrances of our ancestors' sacrifices for the freedom we now enjoy—especially the sacrifices of the Reverend Dr. Martin Luther King, Jr.—and dinners, concerts, and performances celebrating our people's triumphs over slavery and de jure and de facto segregation. We have survived, we have endured, indeed, we have thrived, Black History Month proclaims, and our job as Carter Woodson's legatees is, in part, to remind the country that "the struggle continues" despite how very far we, the descendants of African slaves, have come.

Because of time constraints, I usually participate in the auction by telephone, if at all, despite the fact that I devour the Swann catalogue, marking each item among its nearly four hundred lots that I would like to acquire for my collection of Afro-Americana (first editions, manuscripts, documents, posters, photographs, memorabilia) or for the library at my university.

This year's catalogue was no less full than last year's, reflecting a growing interest in seeking out this kind of material from dusty repositories in crowded attics, basements, and closets. I made my way through it leisurely, keeping my precious copy on the reading stand next to my bed, turning to it each night to fall asleep in wonder at the astonishing myriad array of artifacts that surface, so very mysteriously, from the discarded depths of the black past. Item number 20, for example, in this year's catalogue is a partially printed document "ordering several men to surrender a male slave to the sheriff against an unpaid debt." The slave's name was Aron, he was twenty-eight years of age, and this horrendous event occurred in Lawrence County, Alabama, on October 30, 1833. Lot 24 is a manuscript document that affirms the freed status of Elias Harding, "the son of Deborah, a 'coloured' woman manumitted by Richard Brook . . . [attesting] that he is free to the best of [the author's] knowledge and belief." Two female slaves, Rachel and Jane, mother and daughter, were sold for $500 in Amherst County, Virginia, on the thirteenth of October in 1812 (lot 13). The last will and testament (dated May 9, 1825) of one Daniel Juzan from Mobile, Alabama, leaves "a legacy for five children he fathered by 'Justine a free woman of color who, now, lives with me'" (lot 17). These documents are history-in-waiting, history in suspended animation; a deeply rich and various level of historical detail lies buried in the pages of catalogues such as this, listing the most obscure documents that some historian will one day, ideally, breathe awake into a lively, vivid prose narrative. Dozens of potential Ph.D. theses in African American history are buried in this catalogue.

Among this year's bounty of shards and fragments of the black past, one item struck me as especially interesting. It was lot 30 and its catalogue description reads as follows:

> Unpublished Original Manuscript. Offered by Emily Driscoll in her 1948 catalogue, with her description reading in part, "a fictionalized biography, written in an effusive style, purporting to be the story, of the early life and escape of one Hannah Crafts, a mulatto, born in Virginia." The manuscript consists of 21 chapters, each headed by an epigraph. The narrative is not only that of the mulatto Hannah, but also of her mistress who turns out to be

a light-skinned woman passing for white. It is uncertain that this work is written by a "negro." The work is written by someone intimately familiar with the areas in the South where the narrative takes place. Her escape route is one sometimes used by run-aways.

The author is listed as Hannah Crafts, and the title of the manuscript as "The Bondwoman's Narrative by Hannah Crafts, a Fugitive Slave, Recently Escaped from North Carolina." The manuscript consists of 301 pages bound in cloth. Its provenance was thought to be New Jersey, "circa 1850s." Most intriguing of all, the manuscript was being sold from "the library of historian/bibliographer Dorothy Porter Wesley."

Three things struck me immediately when I read the catalogue description of lot 30. The first was that this manuscript had emerged from the monumental private collection of Dorothy Porter Wesley (1905–95), the highly respected librarian and historian at the Moorland-Spingarn Research Center at Howard University. Porter Wesley was one of the most famous black librarians and bibliophiles of the twentieth century, second only, perhaps, to Arthur Schomburg, whose collection constituted the basis of the Harlem branch of the New York Public Library, which is now aptly named after him. Among her numerous honors was an honorary doctorate degree from Radcliffe; Harvard's W. E. B. Du Bois Institute for Afro-American Research annually offers a postdoctoral fellowship endowed in Porter Wesley's name. Her notes about the manuscript, if she had left any, would be crucial in establishing the racial identity of the author of this text.

The second fact that struck me was far more subtle: the statement that "it is uncertain that this work is written by a 'negro'" suggests that *someone*— either the authenticator for the Swann Galleries, who turns out to have been Wyatt Houston Day, a distinguished dealer in Afro-Americana, or Dorothy Porter Wesley herself—believed Hannah Crafts to have been black. Moreover, the catalogue reports that "the work is written by someone intimately familiar with the areas in the South where the narrative takes place." So familiar was she, in fact, with the geography of the region that, the description continues, "her escape route is one sometimes used by run-aways." This was the third and most telling fact, suggesting that the author had used this route herself. If the author was black, then this "fictionalized slave narrative"—an autobiographical novel apparently based upon a female fugitive slave's life in bondage in North Carolina and her escape to freedom in the North—would be a major discovery, possibly the first novel written by a black woman and definitely the first novel written by a woman who had been a slave. (Harriet E. Wilson's *Our Nig*, published in 1859, ignored for a century and a quarter, then rediscovered and authenticated in 1982, is the first novel published by a black woman. Unlike Hannah Crafts, however, Wilson had been born free in the North.)

Just as exciting was the fact that this three-hundred-page holograph manuscript was unpublished. Holograph, or handwritten, manuscripts by blacks in the nineteenth century are exceedingly rare, an especially surprising fact given that hundreds of African Americans published books—slave narratives, autobiographies, religious tracts, novels, books of poems, anti-slavery political tracts, scientific works, etc.—throughout the nineteenth century. Despite the survival of this large body of writing, to my knowledge no holograph manuscripts survive for belletristic works, such as novels, or for the slave narratives, even by such bestselling authors as Frederick Douglass, Frances Ellen Watkins Harper, or William Wells Brown. And because most of the slave narratives and works of fiction published before the end of the Civil War were edited, published, and distributed by members of the abolitionist movement, scholars have long debated the extent of authorship and degree of originality of many of these works. To find an unedited manuscript, written in an ex-slave's own hand, would give scholars an unprecedented opportunity to analyze the degree of literacy that at least one slave possessed before the sophisticated editorial hand of a printer or an abolitionist amanuensis performed the midwifery of copyediting. No, here we could encounter the unadulterated "voice" of the fugitive slave herself, exactly as she wrote and edited it.

One other thing struck me about Hannah Crafts's claim to authorship as "a fugitive slave," as she puts it in the subtitle of her manuscript. Fewer than a dozen white authors in the nineteenth century engaged in literary racial ventriloquism, adopting a black persona and claiming to be black. Why should they? Harriet Beecher Stowe had redefined the function—and the economic and political potential—of the entire genre of the novel by retaining her own identity and writing *about* blacks, rather than *as* a black. While it is well known that *Uncle Tom's Cabin* sold an unprecedented 300,000 copies between March 20, 1852, and the end of the year, even Stowe's next anti-slavery novel, *Dred,* sold more than 100,000 copies in one month alone in 1856.[1] There was no commercial advantage to be gained by a white author writing as a black one; Stowe sold hundreds of thousands more copies of *Uncle Tom's Cabin* and *Dred* than all of the black-authored slave narratives combined, despite the slave narrative's enormous popularity, and had no need to disguise herself as a black author.

The *artistic* challenge of creating a fictional slave narrative, purportedly narrated or edited by an amanuensis, did appeal to a few writers, however, as the scholars Jean Fagan Yellin and William L. Andrews have shown.[2] As early as 1815, Legh Richmond published a novel in Boston titled *The Negro Servant: An Authentic and Interesting Narrative,* which, Richmond claims in the novel's subtitle, had been "Communicated by a Clergyman of the Church of

England." Nevertheless, these fictionalized slave narratives were published with the identity of a white "editor's" or printer's presence signified on the title or copyright page, thereby undermining the ruse by drawing attention to the true author's identity as a white person. And even the most successful of these novels, Richard Hildreth's popular novel, *The Slave: or Memoirs of Archy Moore* (1836), was consistently questioned in reviews.[3]

Similarly, in the case of the sole example of a female fictionalized slave narrative—Mattie Griffith's *Autobiography of a Female Slave*, published anonymously in October 1856—"few readers seemed to credit the narrative voice as one that belonged to a former slave," as the editor of a recent edition, Joe Lockard, concludes from a careful examination of contemporary reviews. Accordingly, Griffith revealed her identity as a white woman within weeks of the book's publication, in part because reviews, such as one published in the *Boston Evening Transcript* on December 3, 1856, argued that the work could only be taken as the work of "some rabid abolitionist."[4]

Moreover, reading these ten slave narrative novels today reveals their authors often to be firmly in the grip of popular nineteenth-century racist views about the nature and capacities of their black characters that few black authors could possibly have shared, as in this example from Griffith's novel:

> Young master, with his pale, intellectual face, his classic head, his sun-bright curls, and his earnest blue eyes, sat in a half-lounging attitude, making no inappropriate picture of an angel of light, whilst the two little black faces seemed emblems of fallen, degraded humanity. [p. 113]

Griffith's passage—as Jean Yellin notes—echoes one from *Uncle Tom's Cabin.*

> There stood the two children, representatives of the two extremes of society. The fair, high-bred child, with her golden head, her deep eyes, her spiritual, noble brow and prince-like movements; and her black, keen, subtle, cringing, yet acute neighbor. They stood the representatives of their races. The Saxon, born of ages of cultivation, commands, education, physical and moral eminence; the Afric, born of ages of oppression, submission, ignorance, toil, and vice. (Chapter 20)[5]

Or this exchange purportedly between Griffith's mulatto heroine and the slave Aunt Polly:

> "Oh child," she begun [sic], "can you wid yer pretty yellow face kiss an old pitch-black nigger like me?"

"Why, yes, Aunt Polly, and love you too; if your face is dark I am sure your heart is fair." [p. 55]

Whereas several black authors of the slave narratives drew sharp class and intellectual distinctions between house and field slaves, and sometimes indicated these differences by color and dialect (I am thinking here of Frederick Douglass, Harriet Jacobs, William Wells Brown, among others), rarely did they allow themselves to be caught in the web of racist connotations associated with slaves, blackness, and the "natural capacities" of persons of African descent, as often did the handful of white authors in antebellum America attempting to adopt a black persona through a novel's narrator.

It occurred to me as I studied the Swann catalogue that another telling feature of this manuscript that would be essential to establishing the racial identity of its author would be the absence or presence of the names of real people—that is, people or characters who had actually existed and whom the author had known herself. Novels pretending to be actual autobiographical slave narratives rarely use anything but fictional names for their characters, just as Harriet Beecher Stowe does, even if Stowe had based her characters on historical sources, including authentic slave narratives, as she revealed in *The Key to Uncle Tom's Cabin; Presenting the Original Facts and Documents Upon Which the Story Is Founded* (1853). In other words, no white author had written a fictionalized slave narrative that used as the names of characters the real names of people who had actually existed. Nor had a white author created a fiction of black slave life that either did not read "like a novel," falling outside of the well-established conventions of the slave narrative as a genre, or did not unconsciously reflect racist assumptions about black people, flaws even more glaring because of the author's hatred of the institution of slavery.

Nor did a nineteenth-century white writer, attempting these acts of literary minstrelsy or ventriloquism, successfully "pass for black." Just as the minstrels in the nineteenth century—or Al Jolson, Mae West, Elvis Presley, and Eminem in the twentieth century—undertook the imitation of blackness to one degree or another, few of the contemporaries of these authors confused their fictional narrators with real black people. Whereas numerous black people have been taken for white, including the extremely popular twentieth-century historical novelist Frank Yerby or the critic Anatole Broyard, in acts of literary ventriloquism, virtually no white nineteenth-century author successfully passed for black for very long. My fundamental operating principle when engaged in this sort of historical research is that if someone *claimed* to have been black, then they most probably were, since there was very little incentive (financial or otherwise) for doing so.

Armed with these assumptions, I decided to attempt to obtain Hannah Crafts's manuscript. At the time of the auction—February 15, 2001—I was recovering from a series of hip-replacement surgeries and was forbidden to travel. I asked a colleague, Richard Newman, a well-known scholar, librarian, and bibliophile, and the Fellows Coordinator at the W. E. B. Du Bois Institute at Harvard, if he would go in my stead and bid on lot 30. He agreed. We discussed an upper limit on the bid.

The next day I waited expectantly for Dick's call, fearful that the bidding would far surpass my modest cap on the sale. When no phone call came by the end of office hours, I knew that we had failed to acquire the manuscript. Finally, late that night, Dick phoned. He had waited to call until the auction was complete. His first bid had been accepted, he reported, for far less than the floor proposed in the catalogue. No one else had bid on lot 30. I was astonished.

Dick also told me that he had spoken about the authenticity of the manuscript with Wyatt Houston Day, the only person who had read it in half a century other than Dorothy Porter Wesley. Day had told Dick that he had found "internal evidence that it was written by an African American." Moreover, he didn't think that Wesley would have bought it, as it turned out, in 1948—"if she didn't think it authentic." He also promised to send me the correspondence between Dorothy and the bookseller from whom she had purchased the manuscript. My suspicion about the curious line in the Swann catalogue description had been confirmed: Dorothy Porter Wesley had indeed believed Hannah Crafts to be black, and so did Wyatt Houston Day. Accordingly, I was even more eager to read the manuscript than I had been initially, and just as eager to read Porter's thoughts about its origins and her history of its provenance.

It turned out that Porter had purchased the manuscript in 1948 for $85 from Emily Driscoll, a manuscript and autograph dealer who kept a shop on Fifth Avenue. In her catalogue (no. 6, 1948), item number 9 reads as follows:

> A fictionalized biography, written in an effusive style, purporting to be the story of the early life and escape of one Hannah Crafts, a mulatto, born in Virginia, who lived there, in Washington, D.C., and Wilmington, North Carolina. From internal evidence it is apparent that the work is that of a Negro who had a narrative gift. Interesting for its content and implications. Believed to be unpublished.

Driscoll dated the manuscript's origin as "before 1860." (Wyatt Houston Day, judging from the appearance of the paper and ink as well as internal evidence, had dated it "circa 1850s.")

Dorothy Porter (she would marry the historian Charles Wesley later) wrote to Driscoll with her reactions to Hannah Crafts's text. Porter perceptively directed Driscoll's attention to two of the manuscript's most distinctive features: first, that it is "written in a sentimental and effusive style" and was "strongly influenced by the sentimental fiction of the mid-Nineteenth Century." At the same time, however, despite employing the standard conventions of the sentimental novel, which thrived in the 1850s as a genre dominated by women writers, this novel seems to be autobiographical, reflecting "first-hand knowledge of estate life in Virginia," unlike even those sentimental novels written about the South. Despite this autobiographical element, this text is a novel, replete with the conventions of the sentimental: "the best of the writer's mind was religious and emotional and in her handling of plot the long arm of coincidence is nowhere spared," Porter concludes with considerable understatement.

Most important of all, Porter strongly stresses to Driscoll that she is firmly convinced that Hannah Crafts was an African American woman:

> The most important thing about this fictionalized personal narrative is that, from internal evidence, it appears to be the work of a Negro and the time of composition was before the Civil War in the late forties and fifties.

Porter arrived at this conclusion not only because of Crafts's intimate knowledge of plantation life in Virginia but also—and this comment was the most striking of all—because of the subtle, "natural" manner in which she draws black characters.

> There is no doubt that she was a Negro because her approach to other Negroes is that they are people first of all. Only as the story unfolds, in most instances, does it become apparent that they are Negroes.

I was particularly intrigued by this observation. Although I had not thought much about it before, white writers of the 1850s (and well beyond) did tend to introduce Negro characters in their works in an awkward manner. Whereas black writers assumed the humanity of black characters as the default, as the baseline of characterization in their texts, white writers, operating on the reverse principle, used whiteness as the default for humanity, introducing even one-dimensional characters with the metaphorical equivalent of a bugle and drum. In *Uncle Tom's Cabin,* to take one example, white characters receive virtually no racial identification. Mr. Haley is described as "a short, thick-set man." Solomon is "a man in a leather apron." Tom Loker is "a muscular man." Whiteness is the default for Stowe. Blackness, by contrast, is almost always marked. For example, Mose and Pete, Uncle Tom's and Aunt Chloe's sons, are "a couple of wooly headed boys," similar in description to "wooly headed Mandy." Aunt Chloe surfaces in the text with a "round black shining face." Uncle Tom is "a full glossy black," possessing "a face [with] truly African features." At one point in the novel "little black Jake" appears. Black characters are almost always marked by their color or features when introduced into Stowe's novel. Thinking about Stowe's use of color when introducing black characters forced me to wonder what Porter had meant about Crafts's handling of the characterization of black people. Porter's observation was both acute and original.

In response to Porter's undated letter, Emily Driscoll wrote back on September 27, 1951. After saying she was "delighted" that Porter was keeping the manuscript for her personal collection, Driscoll reveals how she came upon it:

> I bought it from a scout in the trade (a man who wanders around with consignment goods from other dealers). Because of my own deep interest in the item as well as the price I paid him I often tried to find out from him where he bought it and all that I could learn was that he came upon it in Jersey!

"It's my belief," Driscoll concludes, "that it is based on a substratum of fact, considerably embroidered by a romantic imagination fed by reading those 19th Century novels it so much resembles." Driscoll, like Porter, believed the book to be an autobiographical novel based on the actual life of a female fugitive slave.

It is difficult to explain how excited I became as I read this exchange of letters. Dorothy Porter was one of the most sophisticated scholars of antebellum black writing; indeed, her work in this area, including both subtle critical commentary and the editing of an anthology that had defined the canon of antebellum black writing, was without peer in her generation of scholars. Because she thought Hannah Crafts to have been black, I wanted to learn more. But Dorothy Porter had apparently not attempted to locate the historical Hannah Crafts; she had, however, located a Wheeler family living in North Carolina "both before and after the war," the Wheelers being Hannah Crafts's masters. And, almost in passing, she mentioned to Driscoll that she had come across "one John Hill Wheeler (1806–1882)" who "held some government positions," presumably in Washington, D.C.

Curious about Dorothy Porter's report of her instincts, and filing away her observation about the Wheeler who had held government positions, I finally read the manuscript before embarking upon the arduous, detailed search through nineteenth-century U.S. census records for the characters in Crafts's novel and, indeed, for Crafts herself.

What I read is a fascinating novel about passing, set on plantations in Virginia and North Carolina and in a government official's residence in Washington, D.C. The novel is an unusual amalgam of conventions from gothic novels, sentimental novels, and the slave narratives. After several aborted attempts to escape, the heroine ends her journey in New Jersey, where she marries a Methodist minister and teaches schoolchildren in a free black community.

I found *The Bondwoman's Narrative* a captivating novel for several reasons. If indeed Hannah Crafts turned out to be black, this would be the first novel written by a female fugitive slave, and perhaps the first novel written by any black woman at all. Hannah Crafts's novel ends with the classic conclusion of a sentimental novel, which can be summarized as "and they lived happily ever after," unlike Wilson's novel, which ends with her direct appeal to the reader to purchase her book so that she can retrieve her son, who is in the care of a foster home. Crafts also uses the story of a fugitive slave's captivity and escape for the elements of her plot, as well as a subplot about passing, two other "firsts" for a black female author in the African American literary tradition.

The Bondwoman's Narrative contains one of the earliest examples of the topos of babies switched at birth—one black, one white—in African American literature.[6] The novel begins with the story of the mulatto mistress of the Lindendale plantation, who tries to pass but is trapped—appropriately enough—by one Mr. Trappe. Her story unfolds in chapter four, "A Mystery Unraveled." Crafts tells us that a nurse had placed her mistress "in her lady's bed, and by her lady's side, when that Lady was to[o] weak and sick and delirious to notice[, and] the dead was exchanged for the living." The natural mother is sold south, the child is reared as white, and Mr. Trappe, who eventually uncovers the truth through his position as the family's lawyer, uses his knowledge to blackmail Hannah's mulatto mistress. Mark Twain, among others, would employ a similar plot device in his novel *Pudd'nhead Wilson* (1894).

The costuming, or cross-dressing, of the character Ellen as a boy foreshadows Hannah's own method of escape and echoes the method of escape used in real life by the slave couple Ellen and William Craft in December 1848. The sensational story of Ellen's use of a disguise as a white male was first reported in Frederick Douglass's newspaper, *The North Star*, on July 20, 1849.[7] William Wells Brown's novel, *Clotel* (1853), employed this device, and William Still, in his book, *The Underground Railroad* (1872), reports similar uses of "male attire" by female slaves Clarissa Davis (in 1854) and Anna Maria Weems (alias Joe Wright) in 1855.[8] I wondered if Hannah's selection of the surname Crafts for her own name could possibly have been an homage to Ellen, as would have been the use of Ellen's name for the character in her novel.

⸺◦◦◦◦⸻

Hannah Crafts, as a narrator, is at pains to explain to her readers how she became literate. This is a signal feature of the slave narratives, and of Wilson's *Our Nig*. She also establishes herself as blessed with the key characteristics of a writer, as someone possessing "a silent unobtrusive way of observing things and events, and wishing to understand them better than I could."[9] "Instead of books," she continues modestly, "I studied faces and characters, and arrived at conclusions by a sort of sagacity" similar to "the unerring certainty of animal instinct." She then reveals how she was taught to read and write by the elderly white couple who ran afoul of the law because of their actions. Early in her novel, Crafts remembers that, even as a child, "while the other children of the house were amusing themselves I would quietly steal away from their company to ponder over the pages of some old book or newspaper that chance had thrown in [my] way. . . . I loved to look at them and think that some day I should probably understand them all."

Crafts is also remarkably open about her feelings toward other slaves. Her horror and disgust at moving from the Wheeler home to the "miserable" huts of the field slaves, whose lives are "vile, foul, filthy," her anger at her betrayal by the "dark mulatto" slave Maria with "black snaky eyes," and her description of Jo, are among the sort of observations, you will recall, that Dorothy Porter felt underscore the author's ethnic identity as an African American—that is, the very normality and ordinariness of her reactions, say, to the wretched conditions of slave life or to being betrayed by another black person. Rarely have African American class or color tensions—the tensions between house slaves and field slaves—been represented so openly and honestly as in this novel, foreshadowing similar comments made by writers such as Nella Larsen in the 1920s and 1930s, in another novel about a mulatto and passing:

> Here the inscrutability of the dozen or more brown faces, all cast from the same indefinite mold, and so like her own, seemed pressed forward against her. Abruptly it flashed upon her that the harrowing invitation of the past few weeks was a smoldering hatred. Then she was overcome by another, so actual, so sharp, so horribly painful, that forever afterwards she preferred to forget it. It was as if she were shut up, boxed up, with hundreds of her race, closed up with that something in the racial character which had always been,

to her, inexplicable, alien. Why, she demanded in fierce rebellion, should she be yoked to these despised black people? (*Quicksand,* chapter 10)

Often when reading black authors in the nineteenth century, one feels that the authors are censoring themselves. But Hannah Crafts writes the way we can imagine black people talked to—and about—one another when white auditors were not around, and not the way abolitionists *thought* they talked, or black authors thought they *should* talk or wanted white readers to believe they talked. This is a voice that we have rarely, if ever, heard before. Frederick Douglass, William Wells Brown, and Harriet Jacobs, for example, all drew these sort of class distinctions in their slave narratives and fictions (in the case of Douglass and Brown)—even contrasting slaves speaking dialect with those speaking standard English—but toned down, or edited, compared with Hannah Crafts's more raw version. This is the sort of thing Porter observed that led her initially to posit a black identity for Hannah Crafts.

Crafts, as Porter noted, tends to treat the blackness of her characters as the default, even on occasion signaling the whiteness of her characters, such as little Anna's "white beautiful arms." Often we realize the racial identity of her black characters only by context, in direct contrast to Stowe's direct method of accounting for race as the primary indication of a black character's identity. When the maid Lizzy is introduced in the novel, we learn that she was "much better educated than" Hannah was, that she was well traveled, and that she had "a great memory for dates and names" before we learn that she was "a Quadroon." When near the novel's end we meet Jacob and his sister, two fugitive slaves, Crafts describes them in the following manner: "Directly crossing . . . were the figures of two people. They were speaking, and the voices were those of a man and a woman." Only later does she reveal Jacob's race by reporting that "I opened my eyes to encounter those of a black man fixed on me," a description necessary to resolve the mystery of the identity of these two people who, it turns out, are fugitive slaves like Hannah. Crafts, a visual narrator who loves to use language to paint landscapes and portraits of her characters, in the most vivid manner, does distinguish among the colors and characteristics, the habits and foibles, of the black people in her novel—one woman, she tells us, has "a withered smoke-dried face, black as ebony"—but she tends to do so descriptively, as a keen if opinionated observer from within. Crafts even describes her fellow slave Charlotte as "one every way my equal, perhaps my superior," which would have been a remarkable leap for a white writer to make.

When she describes the wedding of Mrs. Henry's "favorite slave," she tells us about "[q]ueer looking old men," then adds a description of their "withered and puckered" black faces that "contrasted strangely with their white beards." Similarly, we see "fat portly dames" and then learn of their "ebony complexions" only as contrast to their "turbans of flaming red" and "gay clothes of rainbow colors." The color of her characters here is called upon to paint a picture; Stowe, by contrast, almost never uses a black character's color in this way. For Stowe, it is their defining marker of identity. For Crafts, slaves are always, first and last, human beings, "people" as she frequently puts it. Similarly, Crafts tells us that she was betrayed by a slave named Maria, "a wary, powerful, and unscrupulous enemy." It is only after describing Maria's attributes as an antagonist that Crafts thinks to tell us that she was "a dark mulatto, very quick motioned with black snaky eyes," physical characteristics rendered here as outward reflections of her inner personality. Even for a well-meaning abolitionist author such as Harriet Beecher Stowe, the reverse was often true: the sign of blackness or race predetermined the limited range of characteristics even possible for a black person to possess. The difference is a subtle one, but crucial. Occasionally, Crafts does not disclose the color or physical features of her black characters at all, as in her depiction of her mother and her husband in the final chapter of her novel. Few, if any, white novelists demonstrated this degree of ease or comfort with race in antebellum American literature.

As the scholar Augusta Rohrbach pointed out to me, Crafts's novel manifests a surprisingly sophisticated storytelling technique—such as the way she relinquishes her tale on two occasions to the character, Lizzy, only to reinsert herself after Lizzy's tale (which "made the blood run cold to hear") has finished.[10] But the novel also contains "all the clumsy plot structures, changing tenses, impossible coincidences and heterogeneous elements of the best" of the sentimental novels, as the critic Ann Fabian noted when I showed her the manuscript.[11] It is the combination, the unfinished blend of its clashing styles, that points to the untutored and self-educated level of the author's writing abilities, reflected in her vocabulary, in her spelling errors, in her uneven use of punctuation, in her narrative techniques, and in the clash of rhetorical devices borrowed from gothic and sentimental novels and the slave narratives.

Ann Fabian, the author of *The Unvarnished Truth*, a study of women's and blacks' narrative strategies in the nineteenth century, shared several telling observations with me about Crafts's mode of narration. The novel's plot elements, she writes,

> have subsets that she works in interesting ways. Her evangelical Protestantism gives the reader a glimpse of her own spiritual narrative, but she uses it as well to point out the hypocrisy of the slave-owning minister and the curious inconsistency of the absurd deathbed oath of the wife. She works her

abolitionist politics into a series of direct rhetorical appeals. She works pieces of travelogue into her forced migration to North Carolina. What was the city of Washington like in winter? (Gloom more symbolic than literal, perhaps, but interesting nonetheless.) She also uses her gothic scenes to play the role of detective. And her passing narratives run from the venal blackmailer to the Washington farce.[12]

Fabian also was struck by the way that Crafts establishes her authenticity as a storyteller:

> She is "a repository of secret." Mr. Trappe, the rival keeper of secrets, is un-
> done. By the end of the story, it's really the Bondwoman who could be the
> blackmailer. She knows the gossip, the secrets, the sins and sexual histories,
> the humiliations of everyone. ("A northern woman would have recoiled at
> the idea of communicating a private history to one of my race.") But she is,
> of course, too good a Christian to deploy those weapons of the weak she pos-
> sesses. A false accusation of gossip, of course, precipitates her escape from
> unwanted sex.[13]

Could Hannah Crafts, I wondered, be an example of what the novelist Ralph Ellison, describing the recovery of *Our Nig,* called the surprising degree of "free-floating literacy" among the black slaves of the nineteenth century? I decided to attempt to find out.

Authenticating the Text

Now that I had read the manuscript, I began to wonder if Dorothy Porter could have been correct: Could the person who had written this story have been a slave, judging by her text's intimacy of detail about her enslavement, especially her tracing of the complex power dynamics between master and slave? Was Porter correct that even the sharp distinctions that Crafts drew among black slaves, as Douglass and Jacobs had, rather than generalizing about them as a class or a group, reinforced the possibility of the author's identity as an African American female? Essentially, then, I decided to embark tentatively upon a slow and careful quest to examine Dorothy Porter's suspicions and claims, made a full half century before I obtained the manuscript and made with only a modicum of research.

How does one go about authenticating the racial identity of an author, and how does one date the composition of a manuscript? These two complex tasks stood in the way of verifying Dorothy Porter's thesis. I embarked on both simultaneously. But establishing the date of authorship, as precisely as possible, would, for reasons that shall become apparent below, make the search for the author and her ethnicity much simpler than would have casting about wildly through census records and other documents of the 1840s and 1850s. So I decided to consult with an array of experts to determine if we could date the manuscript and, if we could, what other facts might be uncovered in the process.

I have to confess that this aspect of my pursuit of Hannah Crafts proved to be the most illuminating. While I was quite familiar with the procedure for tracing historical figures using censuses and indices such as those created by the Church of Jesus Christ of Latter-Day Saints, which I had used to authenticate Harriet Wilson's *Our Nig* almost two decades ago, I had no experience with the depth of detail that a scientist could glean from what, to a layman at least, appeared to be faded brown ink on fragile, crumbling paper. Nothing prepared me for the subtlety or the depth of analysis that a historical-document examiner can force a holograph manuscript to yield.

I began the process of authentication by sharing the manuscript with Leslie A. Morris, the Curator of Manuscripts in the Harvard College Library. Morris concluded that "in its physical form, the manuscript is typically mid-nineteenth century, perhaps dating from 1850s or 1860s." A "date of 1855–1860," she concluded, "was certainly possible."[14] She encouraged me to approach a paper conservator.

I turned to Craigen W. Bowen, the Philip and Lynn Strauss Conservator of Works of Art on Paper and Deputy Director of Conservation at the Harvard University Art Museums. Bowen concurred with Morris's dating: "the characteristics of the paper, binding and ink," she wrote, "are commensurate with a mid-nineteenth-century date of origin."[15]

Next I asked Wyatt Houston Day, the bookseller and appraiser who had authenticated the manuscript for the Swann Galleries, to share his thoughts with me. Day, considering "the style of writing, the paper and the ink," concluded that the manuscript had been written "in the 1850s." Although he said that he could not be more precise about the date of origin, he was certain that it had been written before the start of the Civil War:

> I can say unequivocally that the manuscript was written before 1861, because had it been written afterward, it would have most certainly contained some mention of the war or at least secession.

Moreover, Day concluded, "given the style of the narrative, the handwriting and most important, the tone of the ink and type of paper," it was "probably [written in] the first half of the decade" of the 1850s.[16]

Laurence Kirshbaum, a friend and the chairman and CEO of AOL Time Warner Book Group, suggested that I have the manuscript examined by Kenneth W. Rendell, a well-known dealer in historical documents, to date the ink that Crafts had used to write her text. If, indeed, the manuscript had been written before the start of the Civil War, the author had to have used iron-gall ink. I drove the manuscript to Rendell's splendid offices, a converted Victorian mansion in South Natick, Massachusetts. If this manuscript was the first novel written by a female slave—and possibly the first novel written by a black woman—then identifying the kind of ink that she had used would be pivotal.

Rendell invited me to peer down the lens of his microscope before sharing his verdict with me. "What you are looking at, young man," he intoned, "is iron-gall ink," widely in use until 1860. Rendell thought it likely that the manuscript had been created as early as 1855. Rendell also demonstrated that this was Crafts's "composing copy" and not "a fair copy" (meaning a second or third draft). He also concluded that the manuscript had been bound much later than it had been written, possibly as late as 1880.[17] Rendell suggested that the services of Dr. Joe Nickell should be engaged to establish definitively the date of the manuscript. Kirshbaum agreed.

As I said, nothing in my experience as a graduate student of English literature or a professor of literature for the past twenty-five years had prepared me for the depth of detail of the results of Nickell's examination, nor for the sheer beauty of the rigors of his procedures and the subtleties of his conclusions.

Nickell describes himself as "an investigator and historical-document examiner." He has written seventeen books, including *Pen, Ink & Evidence: A Study of Writing and Writing Materials for the Penman, Collector, and Document Detective* (1990) and *Detecting Forgery: Forensic Investigation of Documents* (1996). He is an investigative writer for the *Skeptical Inquirer* magazine, based in Amherst, New York, where he is also Senior Research Fellow at the Center for Inquiry. Nickell also characterizes himself as an investigator of "fringe-science claims" and as an expert on "myths and mysteries, frauds, forgeries, and hoaxes." Nickell gained international notoriety when he exposed the fraud of the diary of Jack the Ripper. Picture John Steed in a bowler hat, driving Mrs. Peel in his Morgan to a grand estate in the English countryside: that was my image of Nickell.

Two paragraphs struck me in Nickell's report:

Considerable evidence indicates that *The Bondwoman's Narrative* is an authentic manuscript of circa 1853–1861. A specific mention of "the equestrian statue of Jackson" in Washington demonstrates that the work could not have been completed before 1853, and the omission of any reference to secession or the Civil War makes no logical sense unless it was written prior to those events. Other references in the text as well as indications from the language are also consistent with this period. No anachronisms were found to point to a later time of composition.

It was apparently written by a relatively young, African-American woman who was deeply religious and had obvious literary skills, although eccentric punctuation and occasional misspellings suggest someone who struggled to become educated. Her handwriting is a serviceable rendering of period-style script known as modified round hand (the fashion of ca. 1840–1865). She wrote more for legibility than speed, and was right handed.[18]

This summary fails to do justice to the elegance of Nickell's proof. Let me summarize his most telling observations. Nickell established that the author of the manuscript was probably a young woman who lacked a formal education, judging from her "serviceable" handwriting, her "relative slowness" in writing, and her "eccentric" punctuation, to say the least. Crafts never uses periods; she uses semicolons idiosyncratically, and she places both apostrophes and quotation marks "at the baseline (like commas)." All in all, these peculiarities amount to "a measure of unsophistication on the part of the writer," as we might expect of a self-educated former slave, whose encounters with reading and writing would be informal, interrupted, intermittent, and furtive. Nickell also draws attention to Crafts's style of handwriting, which is quite unlike "the minuscule script that was sometimes affected by Victorian ladies as an expression of femininity."[19] By contrast, Crafts's handwriting, he concludes, was "serviceable."

The fact that Crafts used a thimble to make "moistened paste wafers" bond more strongly to the page when she pasted over revisions, he concludes, argues persuasively that the author was a woman. Had Crafts been a white middle-class woman, he implies, her style of handwriting would quite possibly have been "elegant" and "diminutive."

Nickell pays close attention to Crafts's level of diction, the scope of her vocabulary, and, by implication, the degree of familiarity with other texts, or literacy, that she reflects in word choice, metaphors, analogies, epigraphs, and allusions to other words, concluding that she had the equivalent, by today's standards, of an eleventh-grade education. Slave authorship has been a vexed and contentious matter in American letters, one virtually as old as the slave narrative genre itself, which dates to 1760 but thrived as a weapon in the abolitionist movement between 1831 and 1865. Pro-slavery advocates—given the enormous popularity of the genre—scrutinized the writings of fugitive slaves in sustained attempts to find errors and thereby discredit the author's depictions of the horrors and abuses of slavery itself. Abolitionist amanuenses were sometimes accused of having written a slave's entire tale, as happened when Frederick Douglass, without question the most famous ex-slave author, published his classic 1845 *Narrative of the Life.* (His master wrote that he had known Douglass as a slave and that Douglass lacked the intelligence and ability to have written such a sophisticated narrative.) Occasionally, a slave's narrative was recalled when southerners questioned his veracity, as in the case of James Williams in 1838, who had dictated the powerful story of his bondage and escape to no less an auditor than John Greenleaf Whittier. Other slave authors, such as Harriet Jacobs (who used the pseudonym Linda Brent in her 1861 autobiography), were accepted as authors by their contemporaries, only to be discredited, erroneously, by historians a century later. Jacobs was rehabilitated by the careful research of Jean Fagan Yellin. To avoid the sort of profound embarrassment that the case of Williams's text generated within the abolitionist movement, slave authors were encouraged to be as precise and exact as possible, to name names and to embrace verisimilitude as a dominant mode of narrative development.

Considering that virtually none of these authors received a formal education, the degree of literacy found in the slave narratives is quite remarkable. It is little wonder that questions of authorship arose. Nevertheless, as scholars such as John W. Blassingame, Jean Fagan Yellin, and William L. Andrews have shown in great detail, the fugitive slaves were by and large the authors of their own tales, even if the editorial hand of an abolitionist corrected grammar or reshaped the flow of the narrative.

This is why Hannah Crafts's narrative, if authenticated, would have such great historical importance: to be able to study a manuscript written by a black woman or man, unedited, unaffected, unglossed, unaided by even the most well-intentioned or unobtrusive editorial hand, would help a new generation of scholars to gain access to the mind of a slave in an unmediated fashion heretofore not possible. Between us and them, between a twenty-first-century readership and the pre-edited consciousness of even *one* fugitive slave, often stands an editorial apparatus reflective of an abolitionist ideology, to some degree or another; here, on the other hand, perhaps for the first time, we could experience a pristine encounter. This is not to imply that the "written by himself" or "herself" subtitles to so many of the slave narratives should be questioned: it is only to say that never before have we been absolutely certain that we have enjoyed the pleasure of reading a text in the *exact* order of wording in which a fugitive slave constructed it.

Nickell points to Crafts's use of polysyllables—words such as *magnanimity, obsequious,* and *vicissitudes*—as proof that Crafts was not "an unread person."

Simultaneously, he continues, Crafts's misspellings are legion: "incumber" for *encumber*, "benumed" for *benumbed*, "meloncholy" for *melancholy*, "your" for *you're*. The curious combination of these two tendencies, moreover, is still another sign of the autodidact, "consistent with someone who struggled to learn." Crafts's progress from slavery to freedom overlaps precisely with her progress from "illiterate slave girl to keeper of 'a school for colored children.'" Her references to Byron, to "the law of the Medes and Persians," and the "lip of Heraclitus"—as well as her biblical epigraphs and other allusions—suggest the eclectic reading habits of a highly motivated person devouring the arbitrary selections in a small library in a middle-class, mid-century American home. Remarkably, Wheeler left a listing of the books in his private library, to which Crafts ostensibly would have had access. A list of these titles, compiled by Bryan Sinche, appears in Appendix C. In other words, Hannah Crafts wrote what she read, as is abundantly obvious from her uses of conventions from gothic and sentimental novels. In fact, no similar blend of genres exists in the antebellum tradition of African American writing.

Dorothy Porter's letter to Emily Driscoll in 1951 had referred to Crafts's text as a "manuscript novel" and as a "fictionalized personal narrative." Even without researching Crafts's life or any of the details of her narrative, it is obvious that, however true might have been the events upon which the episodes in her tale are based, Crafts sought to record her story squarely within the extremely popular tradition of the sentimental novel, replete with gothic elements.

If all of this were true, however—and all of these fictional elements are to be found in *The Bondwoman's Narrative*—then how could I ever find Hannah Crafts? That is to say, if her tale is a fiction, how could I verify that she had once been a slave, and was a fugitive, as her subtitle claims her to be, "recently escaped from North Carolina"? If I were lucky enough to find a black woman living in New Jersey (where she claims to be teaching "colored" children at novel's end) named Hannah Crafts—which I had become increasingly skeptical about being able to do, because of the text's references to Ellen Craft's cross-dressing, possibly pointing to "Crafts" as a protective pseudonym—how could I ever verify her claim to be an escaped slave? In other words, it occurred to me as I read Dr. Joe Nickell's amazingly detailed report that I possessed a manuscript that was written sometime between 1853 and 1861, that read like a novel despite its title and its internal claims to be a slave narrative, and that was in all probability written by a black woman who might not ever be found, which seemed to be the way that Hannah Crafts had wanted it. Nevertheless, this quasi-gothic, sentimental slave narrative—no matter how fictionalized I found it to read—rang true at times, especially in her account of the master-slave power relation; her depictions of life in Virginia, North Carolina, and Washington; and, as Wyatt Houston Day had suggested, her various passages about routes and methods of escape adopted by fugitive slaves. How was I to proceed with the search for Hannah Crafts?

As a rule, novels do not depict actual people by their real names. Slave narratives, by contrast, tend to depict all—or almost all—of their characters by their real names, to help to establish the veracity of the author's experiences with and indictment of the brutal excess implicit in the life of a slave. I write "almost all" because of an occasional change of name to protect the narrator's modesty or those who might be harmed back on the plantation by the revelation of the author's identity. Harriet Jacobs became "Linda Brent" and altered the names of characters, in large part because of her revelations about selecting a white lover out of wedlock and bearing his children. And indeed, Dickensian names such as the overseer in Frederick Douglass's *Narrative,* aptly named Mr. Severe, seem a bit too good to be true. (Actually, the overseer's name was Sevier, but Douglass's tale is so chock full of detail that an occasional allegorically named character is a relief!) But as a rule, fictions of slavery—whether *Uncle Tom's Cabin* or Mattie Griffith's *Autobiography*—tend not to contain characters named after the author's actual contemporaries, people who lived and breathed. (A historical novel like Frederick Douglass's *The Heroic Slave* is an obvious exception.) If I could find Crafts's characters in historical records, then, the possibility existed that she had known them as a slave.

I wrote earlier that I was pursuing the authentication of *The Bondwoman's Narrative* using two separate procedures. One was the scientific dating of the manuscript, using sophisticated techniques that could ascertain the approximate date of paper, ink, writing style, type of pen, even the use of thimbles to affix paste wafers, and the other mysterious processes that Dr. Joe Nickell used to date the manuscript between 1853 and 1861. The second method on which I had embarked simultaneously was the exploration of census indexes and records, using research tools developed by the Mormon Family Library, especially its Accelerated Indexing System (AIS), which is an alphabetical listing of the names recorded in each federal census since 1790.

I became familiar with this index when researching the identity of Harriet E. Wilson. When I found Mrs. Wilson's residence in Boston in 1860, using the *Boston City Directory* for that year (essentially the predecessor of a telephone book, without, of course, telephone numbers), I thought that it would be a straightforward matter to find Mrs. Wilson through AIS, but she was not listed. My colleague at Yale, the great historian John W. Blassingame, encouraged me to examine the actual manuscript record of the 1860 census for the street on which Wilson was reported to be living. Reluctantly, I agreed to do so, asking a research assistant to travel to the Boston Public Library, where the manuscript was held. I presumed that Mrs. Wilson had moved, or died, or been away from home on the day that the census taker knocked on her door. My research assistant, to her astonishment and my own, found that the bottom of the page on which Wilson's name appeared had been folded under. The photographer who had made the microfilm on which the AIS index was based had not realized this, hence lopping off an entire section of that neighborhood. Had not Blassingame insisted that I pursue my research to its original source, I could never have established Harriet E. Wilson's racial identity.

Numerous problems obtain with census records, not the least of which are human error, poor spelling, phonetic spelling, and the fact that some people will lie about their birth dates or birthplace, their ethnic identity, or their level of literacy. Not everyone wants to be located, locatable, or identified, especially if she has a reason for which to forge a new identity. Many former slaves never could be certain of their birth dates in the first place, and some even shifted this date (usually forward) decade by decade as a researcher tracks them through each successive census. Spellings can also be quite arbitrary, necessitating a broad approach to an array of phonetic possibilities for one's subject. Crafts, for example, can be written as Krafts, Croft, Kroft, Craff, etc. Census records can be a blessing for researchers, but they cannot be used uncritically. Just as important, indexes of census records are not entirely accurate, as I discovered when I used my great-great-grandmother Jane Gates as a control for the 1860, 1870, and 1880 census indexes, since I possessed copies of her listings in those records, which our family had made ourselves at the relevant county courthouses. Nevertheless, she did not appear in the AIS index. Electronic indexes—on CD-ROM and on-line, none of which existed, of course, when I went in search of Harriet Wilson—can be enormous time-savers but can never replace examination of an actual document. Human error in the replication of such an enormous database as the U.S. federal censuses is inevitable.

All of these caveats notwithstanding, I embarked upon a systematic examination of census records, using the Internet and a most efficient researcher at the Mormon Family Library in Salt Lake City, Tim Bingaman. Tim Bingaman was a godsend, not only because of his good humor and expertise with databases but because my travel was still restricted on account of my recuperation from hip-replacement surgery. I would phone Tim and request a search of this source or that, and back—by phone, fax, or mail—would come the result. Eventually, the search for Hannah Crafts would involve several archives: the Mormon Family History Library in Salt Lake City, the Library of Congress, the National Archives, Harvard, and the University of North Carolina, as well as family genealogy web sites and CD-ROM indexes, including the records of the Freedman's Bank, recently published by the Mormon Family History Library.

I began my research by compiling a list of all the proper names of the characters who appear in Hannah Crafts's manuscript. As I have written, if I could find at least one actual person named among her characters, then it would be clear that Crafts based her novel on some aspect of her own experience; that the novel was, to some extent, autobiographical; and that she, quite probably, knew the institution of slavery personally and may even have been a slave herself. The question would be one of degree.

By my count, thirty-one characters appear by name in *The Bondwoman's Narrative.* At least two characters—Mr. Trappe, Hannah's mulatto mistress's torturer, and Mr. Saddler, a slave trader—were certainly named allegorically. Then, too, the slaves listed by first name would be extremely difficult, if not impossible, to find, since the slave censuses listed slaves by age and gender under the name of slave owner rather than by the name of the slave. So I set the names of slaves such as Catherine, Lizzy, Bill, Jacob, Charlotte, and Jane aside. Then I began to pursue each name in alphabetical order, using the 1840, 1850, 1860, 1870, and 1880 federal census indexes.

I can only summarize the mountain of research that these searches produced and the frustrations, false starts, and dead ends attendant upon this kind of research. Let me say that the peaks and valleys of exhilaration and frustration when pursuing this sort of research are extreme, and not for those easily discouraged. Finding Harriet Wilson, as difficult as it was, by contrast was much simpler because it was more localized, confined initially to Boston. In this search, we cast our net wide, of necessity.

I was convinced that the success of the historical search for Crafts's characters would turn on locating her masters, especially Sir Clifford de Vincent. Either in Virginia or in the United Kingdom, I believed, Sir Clifford would be found. When he was not, I began to despair that Crafts's tale was entirely fabricated, or at least she had changed the names of all her characters—just as Harriet Wilson had done—and that this avenue of research would lead to a dead end. Even worse, no one named Hannah Crafts was listed in any census indexes that we initially searched. Still, she had located the first part of her narrative in Milton, Virginia—and the Milton that is found in Charles City County, on a bend in the James River, southeast of Richmond, fit her description of the region so very well. An extended, alphabetical search just might yield some clue about the real identity of perhaps one or two of her characters. So, rather than abandon this aspect of the search, I pressed on.

The first indication of a name in a census matching a name in the text was that of Charles Henry, the second of the novel's three characters having a first and last name. (Sir Clifford was the first.) Two Charles Henrys are listed in the 1850 Virginia census, and one in the 1860 census. "Charley" Henry, in the novel, was the son of "Mr. and Mrs. Henry," Hannah Crafts's kind new masters.

Crafts's characters Mr. and Mrs. Cosgrove, who took possession of the Lindendale plantation after the death of Mr. Vincent, would be difficult to trace, given the absence of a first name of either. But the 1840 Virginia census lists one Cosgrove, the 1850 Virginia census lists three Cosgroves, while the 1860s census lists four, all living in various parts of Virginia.

These similarities in surname were obviously too vague to be of much use, given the absence of first names. Only geographical proximity could help connect them in some way. The first promising association came with the location of Frederick Hawkins, the novel's third character with two names. The 1810 and 1820 Virginia censuses list a Frederick Hawkins living in Dinwiddie County. No Frederick Hawkins appears, however, in the censuses between 1830 and 1850. The distance between Milton and the closest northwest boundary of Dinwiddie County is about thirty kilometers, or 18.6 miles. When we recall that Hannah and her first mistress, the tragic mulatto, became lost on their way to Milton, it is at the home of Frederick Hawkins that they arrive. This was a very promising lead, seemingly too much of a correspondence to be entirely coincidental.

Once I had a location for Frederick Hawkins in Dinwiddie County, I could then return to the Virginia census listings in search of the Vincents, the Henrys, and the Cosgroves, to see if any lived near either Milton in Charles City County or in a nearby county, such as Dinwiddie. Nathan Vincent and Elisa Vincent lived in Dinwiddie County in 1830. Edward Vincent, Joseph Vincent, and William Vincent lived in Henrico County in 1840. In 1850 Nathan Vincent lived in Dinwiddie County and Jacob Vincent lived in Henrico County. Thomas Cosgrove lived in Henrico County in 1840, John Cosgrove lived there in 1850, and Frank Cosgrove lived there in 1860. Twenty kilometers separate Milton from the southeast border of Henrico County. Similarly, seven Henrys are listed as living in Henrico County in 1850, and one John H. Henry is even listed as a Presbyterian clergyman, age thirty-three, born in New York and living in Stafford County, which is eighty miles from Milton. It seemed possible to me that the Cosgrove, Henry, and Vincent families in the novel were named after these families living relatively close to Milton. The names of these characters, like the name of Frederick Hawkins, do not seem to have been arbitrary; the fact that the surnames of these characters matched real people who lived so closely together in one section of Virginia suggested that it was at least possible that Hannah Crafts had named her characters after people she had known in Virginia as a slave.

I wrote above that I had been pursuing Hannah Crafts along two parallel research paths. While I awaited the scientific analysis of the manuscript itself, I was gathering raw data from a variety of archives and sources. If Hannah Crafts had drawn upon her own experiences as a slave in Virginia and North Carolina as the basis of the events depicted in her novel, then sooner or later these two paths of research would have to overlap, or mirror each other, in their findings. Despite this expectation, nothing prepared me for the fascinating manner in which this mirroring would occur.

Joe Nickell had suggested near the end of his report that he felt that "the novel may be based on actual experiences." Why did he think this possible? Because of Crafts's peculiar handling of two of the characters' names:

> There are changes that may be due to fictionalization of real persons or events, such as the change of "Charlotte" to "Susan" [pp. 47 and 48]. More telling, perhaps, is the fact that the name "Wheeler" in the narrative was first written cryptically, for example as "Mr. Wh—r" and "Mrs. Wh—r," but then later was overwritten with the missing "eele" in each case to complete the name [pp. 152–156].[20]

What these manuscript changes imply is that Hannah Crafts most probably knew the Wheelers and that Wheeler was their actual name. Even more surprising is the fact that she has disguised their name initially, and then filled it in later, suggesting that the reasons she had wanted to veil their identity no longer obtained when she decided to fill in their names. Moreover, it is clear that she wanted to leave no doubt about the Wheelers' historical identity, about who they actually were.

When I read this paragraph in Nickell's report, I thought of Dorothy Porter's note to Emily Driscoll, pointing out that one John Hill Wheeler had held several government positions in the 1850s. Little did I know how important these clues would turn out to be.

John Hill Wheeler

I have no idea how Dorothy Porter identified John Hill Wheeler as a possible candidate for the Mr. Wheeler in *The Bondwoman's Narrative.* But she was correct. A painstaking search of federal census records for North Carolina and Washington, D.C., revealed that only one Wheeler in the entire United States lived in both North Carolina and Washington between 1850 and 1880. Every scholar embarked upon a search of this sort lives for a moment such as this. Not only had Wheeler served in a variety of governmental positions, he was also a slaveholder and an ardent and passionate defender of slavery, just as Crafts depicts him. But even more remarkably, John Hill Wheeler in 1855 became for a month or so perhaps the most famous slaveholder in the whole of America, and all because of an escaped female slave.

By this time, I had decided to share the manuscript with a few other scholars, namely William L. Andrews, Nina Baym, Rudolph Byrd, Ann Fabian, Frances Smith Foster, Nellie Y. McKay, Augusta Rohrbach, and Jean Fagan Yellin. The generous, encouraging but rigorous, and sobering responses of these other scholars of nineteenth-century American literature would be important to me as I struggled to gain my bearings in the choppy sea of raw research that my searches through various archives were producing.

One day William Andrews phoned to ask if I realized who Wheeler was. I told him what I had learned so far from several biographical entries, including that in the on-line *American National Biography* database, the most authoritative such listing of American lives yet compiled. In his searches, he replied, he had learned that John Hill Wheeler not only had been a slaveholder but was the petitioner in the infamous *Case of Passmore Williamson*, a fact that none of Wheeler's biographers had thought to mention. This case was one of the first challenges to the notorious Fugitive Slave Act of 1850, and it turned on Wheeler's attempt to regain his fugitive slave, Jane Johnson. This single observation would turn out to be the most important clue in establishing crucial details about Hannah Crafts's life as a slave.

John Hill Wheeler was born in Murfreesboro, North Carolina, in 1806, the son of John Wheeler (1771–1832), the postmaster of Murfreesboro, and Maria Elizabeth Jordan (1776–1810). He died in Washington, D.C., in 1882. Wheeler graduated from Columbian College of Washington, D.C. (now George Washington University) in 1826, then studied law under John L. Taylor, the chief justice of the North Carolina Supreme Court. In 1828 he received an A.M. degree from the University of North Carolina, a year after he was admitted to the bar. Between 1827 and 1852, he served for various periods in the North Carolina House of Commons, first between 1827 and 1830. From 1837 to 1841, he served as the superintendent of the branch mint of the United States at Charlotte. In 1832 Wheeler became the secretary of the French Spoilations Claims Commission. He served as state treasurer between 1842 and 1844.

In 1851 Wheeler published *Historical Sketches of North Carolina from 1584 to 1851*, then returned to the state legislature between 1852 and 1853. In 1854 he was named U.S. minister to Nicaragua, where he served until 1857, when he was forced to resign for contravening the instructions of Secretary of State William L. Marcy concerning the recognition of a new government. According to the historian Robert E. May, Wheeler was minister at the time that the American 'filibusterer' William Walker conquered Nicaragua. Walker eventually reestablished slavery in Nicaragua, in a bid to get southern support for his regime. Wheeler was extremely supportive of Walker's reestablishment of slavery, and earlier recognized Walker's regime prematurely, to the displeasure of the State Department.[21] He returned to Washington in 1857, visiting North Carolina several times before the Civil War began. Between 1859 and 1861, he worked in the statistical bureau. He returned to North Carolina during the Civil War, undertook research in England for a second edition of his history of North Carolina between 1863 and 1865, and returned to Washington in 1865. Wheeler also published *A Legislative Manual of North Carolina* (1874) and *Reminiscences and Memoirs of North Carolina and Eminent North Carolinians* (1884). He edited Colonel David Fanning's *Autobiography* (1861), and he left a diary, a Spanish edition of which (*Diario de John Hill Wheeler*) was published in 1974. Wheeler ran for Congress in 1830 but was defeated. He was married twice, first to Mary Elizabeth Brown between 1830 and 1836, and then after her death to Ellen Oldmixon Sully, whom he married in 1838. He had five children, three in his first marriage, two in his second.[22]

In 1842 Wheeler moved from Hertford County to Lincolnton in Lincoln County, where he ran a plantation. According to the *Dictionary of American Biography* (1999), Wheeler not only was "a plantation owner," he was also a "staunch advocate of slavery, and firm believer in American's manifest destiny to annex parts of Central America and the Caribbean." In fact, in 1831 Wheeler's brother raised a volunteer company from Hertford County that participated in the suppression of the famous Nat Turner rebellion in Virginia.[23] Wheeler was quite passionate not only about defending his own right to own slaves but also about defending and protecting the entire system of slavery.

According to the 1850 North Carolina census, Wheeler owned twenty-five slaves, ranging in age from one year to fifty. Fifteen were males and ten were females. Four of the female slaves were between the ages of twenty-one and twenty-five; one was twenty-one, while three were twenty-five. Could one of these four women have escaped to freedom in the North, and then, as Frederick Douglass and Harriet Jacobs had done, turned her pen against her master? I began to research Wheeler's role in *The Case of Passmore Williamson* in search of possible clues for Hannah Crafts, growing increasingly curious about this Jane Johnson.

THE CASE OF JANE JOHNSON

The case of Passmore Williamson—or, more properly, the case of Jane Johnson—became a cause célèbre in Philadelphia in 1855. According to a pamphlet published by the Pennsylvania Anti-Slavery Society in that year, and according to the black abolitionist William Still, who wrote about Jane Johnson's escape in his book, *The Underground Railroad* (1872), John Hill Wheeler arrived in Philadelphia on Wednesday, July 18, 1855, on his way from Washington, D.C., to Nicaragua, to take up his position as "the accredited Minister of the United States to Nicaragua."[24] Traveling with Wheeler were Jane Johnson, whom he had purchased in 1853 in Richmond, and her two sons, one six or seven, the other eleven or twelve.

When the foursome arrived in Philadelphia, Wheeler took them to Bloodgood's Hotel, located near the Walnut Street wharf. When Wheeler went to dinner in another part of the hotel, Johnson "spoke to a colored woman who was passing, and told her that she was a slave, and to a colored man she said the same thing, afterwards adding, that she wished to be free." William Still, chairman of the Acting Vigilant Committee of the Philadelphia Branch of the Underground Railroad, wrote in a letter published in the *New York Tribune* on July 30, 1855, that he was handed a note at 4:30 in the afternoon "by a colored boy whom I had never before seen, to my recollection." The note read as follows:

> M. Still—*Sir:* Will you come down to Bloodgood's Hotel as soon as possible—
> as there are three fugitive slaves here and they want liberty. Their master's
> here with them, on his way to New York.

Still, "without delay," ran to Passmore Williamson's office. Williamson was the secretary of "The Pennsylvania Society for Promoting the Abolition of Slavery, and for the Relief of Free Negroes unlawfully held in Bondage, and for improving the condition of the African Race." The society was incorporated in 1789, and Benjamin Franklin served as its first president. Williamson told Still to go to the slave and get the names of both the slaveholder and the slave; then he would telegraph this information to New York, where they would be arrested when they landed there by boat. By the time Still arrived at the hotel, however, he discovered that Williamson had changed his mind and decided to go himself.

Williamson and Still were told that the slaves and their master had left the hotel and had boarded a boat. Still interviewed one of the four black people who had seen them at the hotel, and was told that the slave "was a tall, dark woman, with two little boys." Still and Williamson rushed to the boat and found Wheeler and his slave, Jane Johnson, along with her two sons on the second deck; they then implored Jane to leave her master, flee with them, and seek her freedom in the courts. "If you prefer freedom to slavery, as we suppose everybody does," Still recalled saying to her, "you have the chance to accept it now. Act calmly—don't be frightened by your master—you are as much entitled to your freedom as we are, or as he is."

Wheeler kept interrupting Still and Williamson as they sought to persuade Johnson to flee with them, saying that she had no wish to leave. To the contrary, however, Still wrote, Jane "repeatedly said, distinctly and firmly, 'I am not freed, but I want my freedom—ALWAYS wanted to be free! But he holds me.'" According to Still, when Jane rose to leave, Wheeler attempted to interfere, taking "hold of the woman and Mr. Williamson." Williamson shook off Wheeler, and the party left the boat. Once rested, Jane was said to proclaim that she and her sons had been so "providentially delivered from the house of bondage." Still later informs us that Wheeler had instructed her twice not to speak to the hotel's colored waiters or listen to their "evil communication." If asked about her status, she should say that she was free. But Jane had said instead, "I and my children are slaves, and we want liberty." Still describes Johnson as "tall and well formed," with a "high and large forehead, of gentle manners, chestnut color, and seems to possess, naturally, uncommon good sense, though of course she has never been allowed to read."

Jane was spirited away, Williamson was sent to jail, and the "half dozen colored men" (including Still) who assisted with Jane's escape were accused of "riot," "forcible abduction," and "assault and battery" and were forced to stand trial. Accompanied by Lucretia Mott (and three other female antislavery sympathizers), Jane Johnson made a most dramatic, and surreptitious, appearance in court, in an attempt to provide testimony that would free the accused.

Still was acquitted; two of the other black men were found guilty of "assault and battery" and were forced to serve a week in jail. Williamson was found guilty of contempt of court and served a sentence between July 27 and November 3, 1855. Jane boarded a carriage immediately following her testimony, "without disturbance." Wheeler would complain in his diary that he was never able to recover her and her sons as his property.

I tried to locate Jane Johnson through the 1860 and 1880 censuses. In 1860 seventy Jane Johnsons were living in Pennsylvania alone, forty-seven of whom lived in Philadelphia. By 1880 more than one thousand black women named Jane Johnson were living in America. If Jane Johnson had wanted to blend facelessly into the African American community, she could have done no better than to select Johnson as her surname. In fact, Frederick Douglass tells us that he rejected the surname of Johnson when he escaped to the North precisely because it was so commonly used by other blacks.

As I read these accounts of the case, I recalled a passage in *The Bondwoman's Narrative* in which Mrs. Wheeler laments that her slave named Jane had run away, thus providing the motivation for acquiring Hannah. (Still reports that Jane had said that Wheeler had "sold all his slaves" within "the last two years" and had "purchased the present ones in that space of time," though I have not been able to find any record of these sales in Wheeler's papers or in the archives of Lincoln, North Carolina.) I suddenly realized that it was *this* Jane to whom Hannah Crafts refers in chapter 12 of her novel! Ironically, it was the character without a surname, Jane, whose identity I would most clearly be able to establish among all of Crafts's black characters, contrary to the laws of probability applicable to this sort of historical research. This means that Hannah Crafts could not have written her manuscript until after 1855. It also means that Hannah would have been purchased after Jane's escape, just as the novel claims. Jane, moreover, told the Philadelphia abolitionists that she had carefully planned her escape before she had left Washington on her trip with Wheeler: "I had made preparations before leaving Washington to get my freedom in New York; I made a suit to disguise myself in—they had never seen me wear it—to escape when I got to New York; Mr. Wheeler has that suit in his possession, in my trunk." Hannah Crafts would also avail herself of a disguise in a suit in her escape to freedom—at least as depicted in her novel. Armed with these new facts about Wheeler and Jane Johnson, I returned to the search for the elusive Hannah Crafts by examining John Hill Wheeler's diary.

THE DIARY OF JOHN HILL WHEELER

The biographies of John Hill Wheeler indicated that he kept a diary, now housed in his papers at the Library of Congress. Would this diary shed any light on Wheeler's feelings about Jane Johnson's escape and, even more important, about the identity of Jane's replacement, Hannah Crafts?

Wheeler wrote in his diary regularly from the time on his plantation located in Beattie's Ford in the county of Lincolnton, in North Carolina (about 250 miles from Wilmington), during his residency in Nicaragua, and all during his various periods of residence in Washington, D.C. The period covered in the diary housed at the Library of Congress is May 30, 1850, to his death in 1882. The diary is intact, except for the year 1858, much of which is damaged or illegible for the first half of the year. The latter half of his diary for 1856 is lost after May 23.

Wheeler lived in Nicaragua between 1855 and November 1856, according to a "Diary of Events" that he recorded in his diary. This chronology follows several pages of financial records, including that for the sale of a farm in Prince Georges County, Maryland, along with what appears to be the sales of three slaves, one named Joyce ($485.92), another named Gadis ($360.00), and finally Boker ($400.98). Wheeler moved from Washington to North Carolina during the Civil War, resettling in August 1861. He kept his permanent residence there until June 1865, when he moved to a farm near Washington. In 1873 he moved to a home in the city of Washington, apparently remaining there until he died. Even when he lived in Washington and Nicaragua, he returned to North Carolina several times, at least once accompanied by slaves.

Wheeler's diary for 1854 opens when he is assistant secretary to the president of the United States, Franklin Pierce. He reports a conversation with Pierce on June 2, 1854, during which Pierce was "delighted with the news from Boston that the slave [Anthony] Burns had been remanded by law to his master and that 'the only fear [that abolitionists] had was of lead and steel.'" Two months later Pierce appointed Wheeler "Minister Resident of the U.S. for the Republic of Nicaragua, Central America."

Wednesday, August 6, 1854, reports his return to his plantation: "much exhausted about 10—and went forthwith to bed." Wheeler complains, however, that he was unable to sleep "because my slumber much disturbed by the wake kept up by the Negroes over Captain Slade's servant—who died today—and who I hope has gone where the good Negroes go."

The following July, in 1855, Jane Johnson's escape occurs. Wheeler's diary entry for July 18 describes it as follows:

Left Washington City at 6 o'clock with Jane Daniel and Isaiah (my servants) for New York. D. Webster Esq. 6th Street Philadelphia in Co. Reached Philadelphia [a]t 1 1/2—went to Mr. Sully's to get Ellen's [i.e., Wheeler's wife] things—and hurried to the Warf [sic]. The Boat had just left—so we remained until 5 o'clock—took dinner at Bloodgood's hotel foot of Walnut Street. At 4 1/2 went on board of the Steamer Washington, and a few minutes before the boat started a gang of Negroes led on by Passmore Williamson an Abolitionist came up to us, and told Jane that [i]f she would go ashore she was free—On my remonstrating they seized me by the collar, threatened to cut my throat if I resisted, took the servants by force, they remonstrating and crying *murder*. Hurried them on shore—to a carriage which was waiting, and drove [stricken: "off"] them off.

Wheeler's diary for July 19:

I went to the Marshal's Office and with his Deputy, Mr. Mulloy, went to Judge Kane, who ordered a Habeas Corpus—returned to town about 10 o'clock, to M. J.C. Hazlitt the Deputy Clerk—took out the writ, then we went to the House of Williamson who had absconded. At 1 o'clock I left Philadelphia, and arrived at New York at 6—and put up at the Washington House.

Entries following, between July 19 and through much of August, refer to the trial of Passmore Williamson and that of the black men separately accused. Wheeler writes that Williamson had been confined to prison, "where he will stay until he gives up my property which he stole." (July 27, 1855) Jane—Wheeler never uses her surname—"has been induced to make an affidavit that she wished to be free—all stuff!" (August 3)

Wheeler reports that on August 15 he "engaged" two servants, Margaret Bina and Margaret Wood, both white, from the Protestant Servants Association in New York. In late August he returned to Philadelphia to testify in court, after which he reports attending a performance of "the Sanford Minstrels." A day later, on August 30, he reports that Jane—"escorted by Lucretia Mott and others"—had given her testimony, which he characterized as the "most barefaced perjury committed by her and her black confidantes." Wheeler's entry concludes with the report that he "went to see Judge Grier—to have her arrested." On August 31 he writes that a rumor had circulated that "the U.S. Officers would seize Jane—in Court at 10," causing "much excitement."

Wheeler was a religious person and saw absolutely nothing incompatible about being a good Christian and owning slaves. On the nineteenth anniversary of his first wife's death, Wheeler's diary entry of October 4, 1855, reads as follows:

This is the anniversary of the death of my Sainted Mary 19 years ago—In the stillness of midnight my mind reverted to this mysterious Providence—and tho I cannot know I shall know hereafter the reasons for so mournful a dispensation. May the Lord sanctify his acts and make me worthy to be with her in glory.

By 1857 Wheeler has returned from Nicaragua and has reestablished himself in Washington. Nine days after attending the inauguration of James Buchanan as president, Wheeler reports writing to his lawyers about the Passmore Williamson case once again. (March 13, 1857) On March 21 he leaves Washington for North Carolina. On April 2 Wheeler reports visiting his sons, then his cousin Mollie Mebane, accompanied by "Esther and John & James."[25] Given the fact that he gives no surnames for any of the three people accompanying him, it is highly likely that they are slaves. It is also possible that these slaves accompanied him when he left for his plantation at Lincolnton on April 7. On May 5 he returns to Washington.

Wheeler's diary for 1858 is severely damaged, and entries are missing between January and June, when he could have reported a slave escaping. The remainder of the diary is of interest to us indirectly for his anticipation and anxieties about the impending dissolution of the Union and the prospect of civil war. (On September 18, 1858, he reports seeing John Wilkes Booth in *The Robbers*, having seen him four days earlier in the role of Shylock: "a very promising actor," he writes.) Wheeler occasionally mentions his case against Williamson throughout 1858, hoping to receive compensation for Jane—or the return of Jane herself (February 18, 1859, March 31, 1859, and January 5, 1860). Along the way, he praises the hanging of John Brown:

> John Brown hung today at 11 o'clock at Charleston Va. For treason, murder
> & insurrection—large military force present—He died as he lived *game.* May
> such be the end of all traitors! (December 2, 1859)

As late as January 10, 1860, he wrote that he "engaged in preparations of memorial to the Legislature of Pennsylvania as to the forcible taking away of my Negroes at Philadelphia on 18 July 1855 by a mob for which I hope to be indemnified by the State." "This question [of slavery]," he had written on December 13, 1859, "is shaking the Union to the center." As Wheeler lamented in his own "Diary of Events," Jane Johnson and her sons got away: "the servants were never reclaimed."

On February 8, 1860, Wheeler reports that "one of our girls," Kate Dorsey, "took it into her head to commit matrimony last night," leaving "only one servant, Nora—which rather deranges matters." Wheeler's slaves have somehow disappeared, replaced by a series of white servants named Nora, Rosa Clark, and Mary Dorsey.

In terms of the search for Hannah Crafts, the most important fact that I learned from reading Wheeler's diary—other than that he loved minstrel shows almost as much as he loved slavery—was gleaned from his diary entry for November 28, 1857. It reads as follows:

> Visited Clark Mills, saw his equestrian Statue of Washington—on which he will be immortalized—as it is equal or superior to his Jackson.

When I read this, I remembered Dr. Joe Nickell's use of Crafts's reference to the construction of the equestrian statue of Jackson as a date before which *The Bondwoman's Narrative* could not have been written. It is a curious overlapping of references, suggesting perhaps Wheeler household discussions about Mills or Jackson's statue, which if true, underscore Crafts's proximity to the Wheelers as a house servant.

We do not know, however, from reading Wheeler's diary when Hannah Crafts escaped or whether she fled from the Wheeler home in Washington, or, like Jane, during one of Wheeler's trips, perhaps back home to North Carolina. If indeed she escaped from the Wheeler plantation, we can use Wheeler's diary to arrive at a reasonable date during which this could have occurred. The "window of opportunity" for Hannah's escape from the Wheeler plantation is established in John Hill Wheeler's diary by the earlier escape of Jane in July 1855, referred to by Hannah in her first meeting with Mrs. Wheeler, and the onset of the Civil War in 1861. Judging from the relevant information contained in Wheeler's diary, Hannah's escape would most likely have occurred between March 21 and May 4, 1857. This period corresponds not only with the Wheelers' recorded trip to the plantation from Washington but with several other unique events and circumstances in their lives during this time, such as Wheeler's recent dismissal from his government post. Negative evidence supporting the year 1857 for the escape is provided by the lack of known visits by the Wheelers to the plantation during the years 1855, 1856 (only the first half of the diary is extant, but Mr. Wheeler was still in Nicaragua until November of that year), and 1858 (only the last half of his diary survives). Trips were made by the Wheelers to North Carolina in 1859 (with President James Buchanan in early June), 1860 (in the latter half of December), and 1861 (about July, from which point Wheeler stayed in North Carolina). But Mr. Wheeler's continual employment as clerk of the Interior Department in Washington from 1857 would not have occasioned Hannah's reference to his recent dismissal from office during any of these years. Further, the relative proximity in time between the departure of Jane, a much-valued servant of Mrs. Wheeler, and the acquisition of Hannah as a competent replacement (less than two years) logically supports the year 1856 as the date of Hannah's service with the

Wheelers and her subsequent escape in the spring of 1857. Quite tellingly, Crafts writes that the Wheelers took her to North Carolina from Washington by boat. Wheeler's diary confirms that he did in fact travel to North Carolina by boat early in 1857.

What is clear is that the portrait Crafts draws of Wheeler and the portrait that Wheeler unwittingly sketches of himself are remarkably similar. In other words, there can be little doubt that the author of *The Bondwoman's Narrative,* as Dr. Nickell argues in his authentication report, was intimately familiar with Mr. and Mrs. John Hill Wheeler.

SEARCHING FOR HANNAH CRAFTS

In the U.S. census of 1860 for Washington, D.C., John Hill Wheeler is listed as the head of household, occupation "clerk." Wheeler has no slaves. What this means in our search for Hannah Crafts is that sometime between 1855, when Jane Johnson liberated herself in Philadelphia, and the taking of this census in Washington in 1860, the slave the Wheelers purchased after Jane escaped, like Jane, escaped to the North and wrote an autobiographical novel about her bondage and her freedom. Judging from evidence in Wheeler's diary, it seems reasonable to conclude that her escape occurred between March 21 and May 4, 1857. If these assumptions are correct, as I believe the manuscript and documentary evidence suggest, then Hannah Crafts was living in the gravest danger of being discovered by Wheeler and returned to her enslavement under the Fugitive Slave Act. Under this act, as David Brion Davis writes, "any citizen could be drafted into a posse and any free black person seized without a jury trial."[26]

Wheeler had sued to recover Jane, Daniel, and Isaiah Johnson under this act, which entitled slaveholders to retrieve fugitive slaves even in the North. The passage of the act led several well-known fugitive slaves— William and Ellen Craft, and Henry "Box" Brown, among them—to flee to Canada or England. (The Crafts went to both.) The Fugitive Slave Act effectively sought to cancel the states north of the Mason-Dixon Line as a sanctuary against human bondage; it meant that privileged fugitive slaves, such as Harriet Jacobs, were forced to allow friends to purchase their freedom from their former masters. But for most of the slaves who had managed to make their way by foot to the North, it meant a life of anxiety, fear, disguise, altered identity, changes of name, and fabricated pasts. The Fugitive Slave Act of 1850 made life in the northern free states—like freedom itself—a necessary tabula rasa for many fugitive slaves, and a state of being fundamentally imperiled.

I began this search for Hannah Crafts because I was intrigued by the notes left by the scholar and librarian Dorothy Porter concerning her belief that Crafts was both a black woman and a fugitive slave, all of which made me want to learn more. Although Porter purchased the manuscript in 1948 from a rare-book dealer in New York City, the manuscript had been located by a "book scout" in New Jersey. Since Crafts claims at the end of the tale to be living in a free colored community in New Jersey, it seemed reasonable to continue my search for her there.

The obvious name for which to search, as you might expect, was Hannah Crafts. But no Hannah Craftses are listed in the entire U.S. federal census between 1860 and 1880. Several women named Hannah Craft, however, are listed in the 1860 census index. As I would learn as my research progressed, much to my chagrin, Hannah Craft was a remarkably popular name by the middle of the nineteenth century. All of these Hannah Crafts were white, and none had lived in the South. But one Hannah Craft was indeed living in New Jersey in 1860. I eagerly searched for her in the census records. She was living in the town of Hillsborough, in Somerset County. She was thirty-four years of age and was married to Richard Craft. Both were white. This Hannah Craft was not living in New Jersey before 1860. And her entry listed no birthplace, the sole entry on this page of the census in which this information was lacking. I could not help but wonder if this Hannah Craft could be passing for white, "incognegro," as it were, given her imperiled and vulnerable status as a fugitive slave.

While I was trying to determine if the Hannah Craft living in New Jersey in 1860 could be passing, it suddenly occurred to me to broaden my search to 1880. After all, if Hannah Crafts had been in her mid to late twenties when she wrote her novel (Frederick Douglass was twenty-seven when he published his 1845 slave narrative), then she would be between fifty-five or so and sixty in 1880, assuming that she had survived. Perhaps I would find her there, living openly under her own name, now that slavery—and the Fugitive Slave Act—was long dead.

To my astonishment, one Hannah Kraft (spelled with a *k*) was listed as living in Baltimore County, Maryland, in 1880. She was married to Wesley Kraft. (How clever, I thought, to have rendered her husband, Wesley, metaphorically as a Methodist minister—after John Wesley—in her novel!) Both Wesley and Hannah were listed as black. What's more, Hannah claimed to have been born in Virginia, just as the author of *The Bondwoman's Narrative* had been! This had to be Hannah Crafts herself, at last. I was so ecstatic that I took my wife, Sharon Adams, and my best friend and colleague, Anthony Appiah, out to celebrate over a bit too much champagne shortly after ordering a copy of the actual census record for this long-lost author. We had a glorious celebration.

Three days later, the photocopy of the page in the 1880 census arrived from the Mormon Family History Library in Salt Lake City. I stared at the document in disbelief: not only was Hannah said to be thirty years of age—born in 1850, while the novel had been written between 1855 and 1861—but the record noted that this Hannah Kraft could neither read nor write! Despite all of the reasons that census data were chock full of errors, there were far too many discrepancies to explain away to be able to salvage this Hannah Kraft as the possible author of *The Bondwoman's Narrative.* My hangover returned.

In the midst of my growing frustration, I examined the Freedman's Bank records, made newly available on CD-ROM by the Mormon Family History Library. The Freedman's Bank was chartered by Congress on March 3, 1865. Founded by white abolitionists and businessmen, it absorbed black military banks and sought to provide a mutual savings bank for freed people. By 1874 there were 72,000 depositors with over $3 million. The bank's white trustees amended the charter to speculate in stocks, bonds, real estate, and unsecured loans. In the financial panic of 1873, the bank struggled to survive, and Frederick Douglass was named president in a futile attempt to maintain confidence. The bank collapsed on June 2, 1874, with most depositors losing their entire savings.

While no Hannah Craft or Crafts appears in the index of the bank's depositors, a Maria H. Crafts does. Her application, dated March 30, 1874, lists her as opening an account in a bank in New Orleans. Her birthplace is listed as either Massachusetts or Mississippi (the handwriting is not clear), and she identified herself as a schoolteacher. Her complexion is listed as "white," a designation meaning, as an official at the Mormon Library explained to me, that she could possibly have been white, but this was unlikely, given the fact that Freedman's was a bank for blacks.[27] A far more likely possibility is that she could have been a mulatto, perhaps an especially fair mulatto. Most interesting of all, she has signed the document herself.

I immediately sent a copy of this document to Dr. Joe Nickell for a comparison with the handwriting of the author of *The Bondwoman's Narrative.* Dr. Nickell reported that the results were inconclusive. According to Nickell, "the handwriting is a similar type, with some specific differences, notably the lack of the hook on the ending of the *s,* and a missing up-stroke on the capital *c.* But the matter is complicated by the fact that we don't actually have a signature for Hannah Crafts, we only have an instance of her name written in her handwriting on the novel's title page." "For some people," Nickell continued, "there is a marked difference. Because of the lapse of twenty years, during which time her handwriting may have changed, and because we are not comparing signature to signature, we cannot rule out the possibility that this is the handwriting of the same person."

With this cautiously promising assessment, I returned to the census records in search of Maria H. Crafts. Although twenty-three Mary H. Craftses are listed as "black" in the 1880 national index to the federal census, and six Mary Craftses are listed as mulatto, no Maria Craftses are listed. (Of these Mary Craftses, only one, listed as having been born in Virginia in 1840, could possibly be our author.) And in the case of Mary H. Crafts we have no record of what the initial *H* stands for. Still, the handwriting similarities are intriguing, as is the fact that this Maria H. Crafts was a schoolteacher, and hence a potential author.

I now decided to return to an early lead that had once seemed extremely promising. While typing the manuscript, my research assistant, Nina Kollars, suggested that I look for Hannah under the name of Vincent, since she was a slave of the Vincents' in Virginia, and could have taken Vincent as her surname. (My surname is Gates, I happen to know, because a farmer named Brady living in western Maryland purchased a small group of slaves from Horatio Gates in Berkeley Springs, Virginia, now West Virginia.) So I began to search for Hannah Vincent in the 1850 and 1860 censuses. To my great pleasure, I found Hannah Ann Vincent, age twenty-two, single, living in Burlington, New Jersey, in 1850 in a household that included another woman, named Mary Roberts. Vincent was twenty-two; Roberts, forty-seven. Roberts was black; Vincent was a mulatto, birthplace unknown. I was convinced that this Hannah Vincent was the author of *The Bondwoman's Narrative*—that is, until I received Dr. Nickell's conclusive report. I shelved this theory, since the author of the novel was a slave of the Wheelers' who had been purchased in 1855 or so because Jane Johnson had run away. Besides, no Hannah Vincent appears in the 1860 New Jersey census.

Because Hannah Crafts claims to be living in New Jersey at novel's end, in a community of free blacks, married to a Methodist clergyman, teaching schoolchildren, I decided in a last-ditch effort to research the history of black Methodists in New Jersey, taking Crafts at her word. (The obvious problem with an autobiographical novel is determining where fact stops and fiction starts. Still, the New Jersey provenance of the manuscript in 1948 supported this line of inquiry.) What is especially curious about Crafts's selection of New Jersey as her home in the North is that New Jersey "was the site of several Underground Railroad routes" and that "the region became a haven for slaves escaping the South," as Giles R. Wright puts it in his *Afro-Americans in New Jersey.*[28] Moreover "by 1870, New Jersey had several all-black communities," including Skunk Hollow in Bergen County; Guineatown, Lawnside, and Saddlerstown in Camden County; Timbuctoo in Burlington County; and Gouldtown and Springton in Cumberland County. In addition, Camden, Newton, Center, Burlington, Deptford, Mannington, Pilesgrove, and Fairfield also "had a sizeable number of Afro-Americans." It is, therefore, quite possible that Crafts was familiar with these communities and that she either lived in one or chose to end her novel there because of New Jersey's curious attraction for fugitive slaves. Yet, few, if any, authors of the slave narratives end their flight to freedom in New Jersey, making it difficult to imagine how Crafts knew about these free black communities as a safe haven from slavery if she did not indeed live in or near one. She did not, in other words, select New Jersey from a reading of slave narratives or abolitionist novels. Slave narrators such as Douglass, Brown, and Jacobs end their flight to the North in places such as Rochester, New Bedford, Boston, or New York.

Joseph H. Morgan's book, titled *Morgan's History of the New Jersey Conference of the A.M.E. Church,* published in Camden, New Jersey, in 1887, lists every pastor in each church within the conference since the church's founding, as well as each congregation's trustees, stewards, stewardesses, exhorters, leaders, organists, local preachers, officers, and Sunday school teachers.[29] Hannah Vincent was listed in the church at Burlington as a stewardess, church treasurer, and teacher. (The church was named the Bethel African Methodist Episcopal Church, located on East Pearl Street in Burlington, and was founded in 1830.) Could this Hannah Vincent be the person who was living in Burlington in 1850? I presumed so, but checked anyway.

I turned to the 1870 and 1880 federal census records from New Jersey. Hannah Vincent, age forty-six in 1870, was living in the household of Thomas Vincent, age forty-eight. He was listed as black, she as a mulatto. He was a porter in a liquor store, she was "keeping house." Both were said to have been born in Pennsylvania. Since the Hannah Vincent I had found in 1850 had been listed as twenty-two, single, and a mulatto, I presumed this Hannah Vincent (age forty-six) to be the same person, living with her brother, twenty years later. But in the 1880 census, Hannah—now claiming that her age was still forty-eight!—is listed as Thomas's wife, both now identified as having been born in New Jersey. Unless the 1850 Hannah Vincent had married a man also named Vincent, this Methodist Sunday school teacher was a different person from her 1850 namesake. To add to the confusion, a birth record for a Samuel Vincent, dated 1850, lists his parents as one Thomas and Hannah, despite the fact that our Hannah Vincent was single according to the 1850 census. Samuel Vincent's race is not identified. Only her marriage certificate could reveal her maiden name. But a search of the New Jersey marriage licenses stored in Trenton failed to uncover a record of Thomas's marriage to Hannah. Neither did a search of the tombstones at Bethel A.M.E. Church in Burlington found in the cemetery adjacent to the church uncover the graves of the Vincents.[30] Unless a marriage certificate, death records of their children, or some other document appears, we won't be able to ascertain the maiden name of this Hannah Vincent. But given the Methodist and Vincent connections, this person remains a candidate as the author of *The Bondwoman's Narrative.*

Why did Hannah Crafts fail to publish her novel? Publishing at any time is extraordinarily difficult, and was especially so for a woman in the nineteenth century. For an African American woman, publishing a book was virtually a miraculous event, as we learned from the case of Harriet Wilson. If Hannah Crafts had indeed passed for white and retained her own name once she arrived in New Jersey, then obviously she would not have wanted to reveal her identity or her whereabouts to John Hill Wheeler, who would have tried to track her down, just as he longed to do with Jane Johnson. Even if she changed her name and pretended to be simply writing a novel, the manuscript is so autobiographical that the copyright page would have revealed her new identity and would have led to her exposure.

Ann Fabian speculates that "perhaps she composed her narrative in the late 1850s and by the time" she finished it, saw she had missed the market as she watched a white abolitionist readership and the cultural infrastructure it supported dissolve and turn elsewhere. By the time the war was over, maybe she too was doing other things and never returned to a story "she had written in and for a cultural world of the 1840s and 1850s." The failure to publish is all the more puzzling, she continues, because the novel does not read as if she were "writing this for herself," since "it is not an internal sort of story (she doesn't grow or change) which makes me want to think of her imagining a public for it." Crafts obviously wanted the story of her life preserved at least for a future readership, because she preserved the manuscript so carefully, as apparently did several generations of her descendants. These facts make her inability to publish her manuscript all the more poignant.

Nina Baym suggests that her decision to write a first-person autobiographical novel could have made publication difficult in the intensely political climate of the anti-slavery movement of the 1850s. Veracity was every-thing in an ex-slave's tale, essential both to its critical and commercial success and to its political efficacy within the movement. As Baym argues:

> The first-person stance is also a possible explanation for her not trying to publish it. Given the public insistence on veracity in the handling of slave experiences (you know all those accusations about black fugitive speakers being frauds), she might well have hesitated after all to launch into the marketplace an experimental novel in the first person under her own name.[31]

As soon as pro-slavery advocates could discredit any part of it as a fiction, "the work and its author," Baym concludes, "would be discredited. But if she offered it as a fiction pure and simple, it would be ignored." Regardless of the reasons this book was never published, one thing seems certain: the person who wrote this book knew John Hill Wheeler and his wife personally, hated them both for their pro-slavery feelings and their racism, and wanted to leave a record of their hatred for posterity.

——⚬⚭⚬——

I have to confess that I was haunted throughout my search for Hannah Crafts by Dorothy Porter's claim that—judging from internal evidence—Hannah Crafts was a black woman because of her peculiar, or unusually natural, handling of black characters as they are introduced to the novel: "her approach to other Negroes," we recall that Porter wrote to Emily Driscoll, is "that they are people first of all." "Only as the story unfolds, in most instances," she concludes, "does it become apparent that they are Negroes." While speculation of this sort is risky, what can we ascertain about Hannah Crafts's racial identity from internal evidence more broadly defined?

It is important to remember that Hannah Crafts is a proto-type of the tragic mulatto figure in American and African American literature, which would become a stock character at the turn of the century. She is keenly aware of class differences within the slave community and makes no bones about describing the unsanitary living conditions of the field hands in their cramped quarters with far more honesty, earthiness, and bluntness than I have encountered in either the slave narratives or novels of the period. These descriptions are remarkably realistic and are quite shocking for being so rare in the literature. Whereas Crafts clings to her class orientation as an educated mulatto, as a literate house slave, she does not, on the other hand, reject intimate relationships with black people *tout court.* She is a snob, in other words, but she is not a racist.

Hannah decides to run away to protect herself from rape by a black man she finds loathsome and reprehensible, uneducated, uncouth, and unwashed and, as she freely admits, to avoid the squalor of life in the slave quarters. But throughout the novel, she bonds with a variety of black characters, starting with her unveiled mulatto mistress on the Lindendale plantation:

"And will you go with me?" she inquired.

"I will, my dear mistress."

"Call me mistress no longer. Henceforth you shall be to me as a very dear sister" she said embracing me again. "Oh: to be free, to be free."

Crafts clearly admires her fellow slave Lizzy, "a Quadroon" who, she tells us, "had passed through many hands, and experienced all the vicissitudes attendant on the life of a slave," from suffering "the extremes of a master's fondness" to his wife's "jealousy and their daughter's hate." (Crafts repeatedly stresses the sexual vulnerability of all female slaves, but especially that of house servants and mulattos.) Later, Crafts bonds with Jacob, a "black man" and a fugitive slave fleeing with his sister, as Crafts herself is fleeing near the end of the novel. And most important of all, she ends the novel by willingly selecting an identity as a black person, married to a free-born black Methodist minister, keeping "a school for colored children." This is all the more remarkable given the fact that she makes the final leg of her escape route in the disguise of a white woman, having been persuaded by Aunt Hetty to abandon her disguise as a white male. Crafts chooses her blackness willingly, in other words, just as she chooses her class identity. Breeding, education, morals, manners, hygiene—these are the values that Hannah Crafts embraces consistently throughout the novel, from her life as a slave to freedom within the colored middle class of New Jersey. In a sense Crafts seems determined to *unsanitize* depictions of the horrible conditions the slaves experienced, revealing the debilitating effects this brutal institution had upon the victims—the slaves—much as Richard Wright would later, in *Native Son* (1940), attempt to reveal the brutal effects of racism and capitalism on Bigger Thomas. That she makes no apologies for these attitudes is one of the most fascinating aspects of her narrative strategy, as if class trumps race when a choice is demanded. But class *and* race combined compose the ideal that Crafts valorizes throughout her text. That combination is the basis of the blissful life that she finds at the conclusion of her tale. Hannah Crafts can be thought of as the figurative grandmother of W. E. B. Du Bois's "talented tenth." Though other mixed-race narrators, such as Harriet Wilson or Harriet Jacobs, stress industry and hard work, none makes it a fetish in the way that Crafts does.

Throughout the novel, Crafts underscores the fact that the institution of slavery does not respect distinctions among the slaves. Class distinctions are irrelevant.

> He reck[on]ed not that she was a woman of delicate sensibilities and fine perfections—she was a slave, and that was all to him.

Elsewhere, Crafts rails against an irrational system that privileges "mere accident of birth, and what persons were the least capable of changing or modifying" over their capacity to "improve" themselves. It is native intelligence, diligence, and hard work that should be the ultimate measures of individual worth and success in a truly democratic society, she argues implicitly throughout her novel.

There can be little doubt that Crafts is intimately familiar with slavery, just as she is intimately familiar with the Wheeler family. Again and again she makes telling observations about the mind of both slaves and slave owners that are astonishingly perceptive, novel, and counterintuitive. For example, she writes that

> But those who think that the greatest evils of slavery are connected with physical suffering posses [sic] no just or rational ideas of human nature. The soul, the immortal soul must ever long and yearn for a thousand things inseperable [sic] to liberty. Then, too, the fear, the apprehension, the dread, and deep anxiety always attending that condition in a greater or less degree. There can be no certainty, no abiding confidence in the possession of any good thing.

Crafts repeatedly objects to slaves getting married, because their masters were not bound to honor the sanctity of this institution and because children of slaves were, by definition, slaves as well:

> Marriage like many other blessings I considered to be especially designed for the free, and something that all the victims of slavery should avoid as tending essentially to perpetuate that system. Hence to all overtures of that kind from whatever quarter they might come I had invariably turned a deaf ear. I had spurned domestic ties not because my heart was hard, but because it was my unalterable resolution never to entail slavery on any human being.

True marriage, she tells us earlier in the text, was an inconceivable idea for a slave:

. . . vows and responsibilities [were] strangely fearful when taken in connection with their servile condition. Did the future spread before them bright and cloudless? Did they anticipate domestic felicity, and long years of wedded love: when their lives, their limbs, their very souls were subject to the control of another's will; . . . and then might be decreed without a moment's warning to never meet again[?]

No, she concludes with the greatest finality, "The slave, if he or she desires to be content, should always remain in celibacy." "If it was my purpose," she continues, "I could bring many reasons to substantiate this view, but plain, practical common sense must teach every observer of mankind that any situation involving such responsibilities as marriage can only be filled with profit, and honor, and advantage by the free."

In her own case, it is Mrs. Wheeler's attempt to force her to "marry" a field slave—that is, to allow Bill to rape her and to force her to live in the squalor of the cabins ("most horrible of all doomed to association with the vile, foul, filthy inhabitants of the huts, and condemned to receive one of them for my husband")—that forces her to run away. As Crafts puts it, combining her concerns about the violation of her virtue and the integrity and sanctity of her sexuality with the violation of her sensibilities:

And now when I had voluntarily renounced the society of those I might have learned to love[,] should I be compelled to accept one, whose person, and speech, and manner could not fail to be ever regarded by me with loathing and disgust. Then to be driven in to the fields beneath the eye and lash of the brutal overseer, and those miserable huts, with their promiscuous crowds of dirty, obscene and degraded objects, for my home[,] I could not, I would not bear it.

Only this double violation—"a compulsory union with a man whom I could only hate and despise"—could force Hannah to flee: "it seemed that rebellion would be a virtue, that duty to myself and my God actually required" her to run away, she concludes. Rarely, if ever, in the literature created by ex-slaves has the prospect of rape, and the gap in living conditions between house and field, been put more explicitly and squarely. Obviously, Hannah Crafts had no fear about offending the sensibilities of northern abolitionists nor the tastes of her putative middle-class readership, or other black people. One is forced to wonder if her bluntness about these matters stood as an obstacle to her ability to publish her tale.

A final example of Crafts's intimate knowledge of slavery is a subtle one. It involves the degree of intimacy possible between a mistress and a female slave. Crafts's account reads as follows:

Those who suppose that southern ladies keep their attendants at a distance, scarcely speaking to them, or only to give commands have a very erroneous impression. Between the mistress and her slave a freedom exists probably not to be found elsewhere. A northern woman would have recoiled at the idea of communicating a private history to one of my race, and in my condition, whereas such a thought never occurred to Mrs. Wheeler. I was near her.

William Andrews (the author of the definitive study of the slave narratives) analyzes this passage as follows, relating it directly to a similar observation made in the slave narrative written by Elizabeth Keckley, titled *Behind the Scenes, or Thirty Years a Slave, and Four Years in the White House* (1868):

In chapter 14 of *Behind the Scenes* Keckley notes that soon after the war is over, her former mistress, Ann Garland, asks her to come back to see the family in Virginia. The idea that such a reunion would appeal to her former owners is incredible to Keckley's northern friends, who think that since Keckley was a slave she couldn't possibly care about the Garlands or they about her. Keckley goes on to recount her reunion with the Garlands to show that they think very highly of her even after the war.[32]

Andrews continues his fascinating line of reasoning as follows:

Of course, Mrs. Wheeler doesn't think highly of Hannah, but the fact that the narrator of that story is at pains to point out to her reader that female slaveholders treat their female slaves with a great deal more intimacy than standard abolitionist propaganda acknowledges allies the Crafts narrative to that of Keckley, who also insists to her northern white friends, equally convinced by antislavery propaganda that black women and white women couldn't possibly have any basis for communication after the war, that there was an intimate connection between her and her former mistress. In Keckley that intimacy is based on genuine mutual concern—at least that's the way she portrays it— whereas in Crafts's, Mrs. Wheeler cares nothing for Hannah as a person. The key similarity, however, is that in both texts, a black woman is trying to get her white readers to realize that the relationship between white and black women in slavery was not one of mere dictation, white to black, or mere subjugation of the black woman by the white woman. A white woman in the North in the antebellum era who wanted to preserve her antislavery credentials would have found it hard to make such a characterization of intimacy between women slaveholders and their female slaves. A white southern woman sympathetic to slavery might make such a claim, but she wouldn't suggest that Mrs. Wheeler is as shallow and self-interested in cultivating Hannah as Crafts makes her out to be. Thus only a black woman who had herself been a slave would be in a position of authority to make such a claim about this kind of intimacy between white and black women in slavery.

Andrews's observation convincingly reinforces Crafts's authenticity both as a black woman and former slave.

Given the extent of the circumstantial evidence, it seems reasonable to conclude that Dorothy Porter's intuition was correct. While we may not yet be certain of her name, we do know who Hannah Crafts is, that is, we know the central and defining facts about her life: that she was female, mulatto, a slave of John Hill Wheeler's, an autodidact, and a keen observer of the dynamics of slave life. Hannah Crafts has given us a black sentimental novel, one based closely on her experiences as a slave, but one at times written in a most unsentimental manner. As scholar Rudolph Byrd puts it, "*The Bondwoman's Narrative* is a text in which we have for the first time encountered the unmediated consciousness of a slave commenting upon the world of slavery."[33]

Did Hannah pass for white? Did she open a bank account at the Freedman's Bank in New Orleans in 1874 under the name of Maria H. Crafts? Or did Hannah marry Thomas Vincent, teach Sunday school in a black Methodist church in New Jersey, and use the unusual name of Crafts (plural) as an homage to Ellen and William Craft, to whose cross-dressing disguise Hannah refers twice in her novel? Only further research can determine the answer to these questions. To facilitate that process and to restore Hannah Crafts to her rightful place as the author of the first novel written by a female fugitive slave, I have decided to publish this fascinating novel, dedicated in memory of Dorothy Porter Wesley, who found it, to encourage other scholars to continue this search. Until that time, the life of the woman who just may have been the first female African American novelist will remain one of the most exciting mysteries of African American literature.

Henry Louis Gates, Jr.
Oak Bluffs, MA
August 24, 2001

NOTES

1. Joe Lockard, "Afterword," *Autobiography of a Female Slave* by Mattie Griffith (Jackson: University of Mississippi, 1998), pp. 407–08. The novel was first published

in 1856. On Stowe's sales, see Richard Newman, *Words Like Freedom* (Westport, Conn.: Locust Hill Press, 1996), p. 20.

2. See William L. Andrews, *To Tell a Free Story: The First Century of Afro-American Autobiography* (Urbana: University of Illinois, 1986), for the most sophisticated study of the various subgenres of the slave narratives and fictional slave narratives. See also Jean Fagan Yellin, *The Intricate Knot: Black Figures in American Literature, 1776–1863* (New York: New York University Press, 1992).

3. Although Hildreth published his novel anonymously, it was copyrighted under the name of the printer and publisher, John Eastburn. Hildreth's name, however, appears on the copyright page of the second edition (Boston, 1840), and on the title page as editor in the expanded 1852 edition, titled *The White Slave: or, Memoirs of a Fugitive* (London: Ingram, Cooke and Company, 1852). The review in *The Liberator* (March 31, 1837) defends the novel against those who doubted its authenticity, arguing that "it purports to have been written by a slave, and it is no more difficult to imagine this to be the case, than to imagine who could write it, if a slave did not." But reviews such as that published in *The Christian Examiner* in 1839 were far more typical: "We read, in what professes to be the language of a slave, that which we feel a slave could not have written" (quoted in Yellin, *The Intricate Knot,* p. 102).

4. Lockard, pp. 405, 408–09, 411.

5. Letter from Jean Fagan Yellin to Henry Louis Gates, Jr., November 21, 2001.

6. Letter from Werner Sollors to Henry Louis Gates, Jr., September 12, 2001.

7. See also *The North Star,* June 15, 1849; *The National Era,* November 7 and November 28, 1850; *Frederick Douglass's Paper,* January 1 and January 15, 1852.

8. William Still, *The Underground Railroad* (Philadelphia: Porter and Coates, 1872), pp. 60–61 and 177–89.

9. Letter from Augusta Rohrbach to Henry Louis Gates, Jr., July 23, 2001.

10. Ibid.

11. Letter from Ann Fabian to Henry Louis Gates, Jr., July 31, 2001.

12. Ibid.

13. Ibid.

14. Letter from Leslie A. Morris to Henry Louis Gates, Jr., April 5, 2001.

15. Letter from Craigen W. Bowen to Henry Louis Gates, Jr., April 5, 2001.

16. Letter from Wyatt Houston Day to Henry Louis Gates, Jr., April 6, 2001.

17. Letter from Kenneth Rendell to Laurence Kirshbaum, April 26, 2001.

18. Nickell's report, pp. 13–14.

19. Ibid., pp. 12–13.

20. Ibid., p. 27.

21. Letter to Henry Louis Gates, Jr., December 13, 2001. See also Robert E. May, *The Southern Dream of a Caribbean Empire, 1854–1861* (Gainesville: University Press of Florida, 2002), pp. 96–98 and 107.

22. On Wheeler, see S. Austin Allibone, editor, *Critical Dictionary of English Literature and British and American Authors* (Philadelphia: J. B. Lippincott, 1897), p. 1511; "Sally's Family Place" website (www2.txcyber.com/smkoestl/; John E. Findling, editor, *Dictionary of American Diplomatic History,* 2d ed., rev. and expanded (New York:

Greenwood Press, 1989), pp. 543–44; *Appleton's Cyclopaedia of American Biography*, ed. by James Grant Wilson and John Fiske (New York: Appleton, 1888), p. 453; *Dictionary of American Biography* (New York: Charles Scribner's Sons, 1928–58), vol. 22, p. 50; see also p. 139 of vol. 23 of the 1999 edition of the *ANB*.

23. Letter from Tom Parramore to Henry Louis Gates, Jr., November 16, 2001.

24. Bryan Sinche pointed this out to me.

25. See *The Case of Passmore Williamson* (Philadelphia: Pennsylvania Anti-Slavery Society, 1855), and Still, pp. 86–97. Two versions of Jane Johnson's testimony appear in Appendix B. See Still, pp. 94–95.

26. David Brion Davis, "The Enduring Legacy of the South's Civil War Victory," *New York Times*, August 26, 2001, section 4, p. 6.

27. Conversation with Tim Bingaman, Mormon Family History Library, May 15, 2001.

28. Giles R. Wright, *Afro-Americans in New Jersey* (Trenton: New Jersey Historical Commission, 1988), p. 39.

29. This book is reprinted in *The Black Biographical Dictionary Index*, ed. by Randall and Nancy Burkett and Henry Louis Gates, Jr. (Alexandria, Va.: Chadwyck Healy, 1985).

30. Elizabeth M. Perinchiet, *History of the Cemeteries in Burlington County, New Jersey, 1687–1975* (n.p. 1978), p. 30.

31. Letter from Nina Baym to Henry Louis Gates, Jr., May 9, 2001.

32. Letter to Henry Louis Gates, Jr., October 26, 2001.

33. Letter to Henry Louis Gates, Jr., November 2, 2001.

SOURCE: Hannah Crafts, *The Bondwoman's Narrative*. Edited by Henry Louis Gates, Jr. (New York: Warner Books, 2002).

IN HER OWN WRITE

Series Introduction, The Schomburg Library of
Nineteenth-Century Black Women Writers

*One muffled strain in the Silent South, a jarring chord and a vague and
uncomprehended cadenza has been and still is the Negro. And of that muffled
chord, the one mute and voiceless note has been the sadly expectant Black
Woman, . . .*

*The "other side" has not been represented by one who "lives there." And
not many can more sensibly realize and more accurately tell the weight and
the fret of the "long dull pain" than the open-eyed but hitherto voiceless
Black Woman of America.*

*As our Caucasian barristers are not to blame if they cannot quite put them-
selves in the dark man's place, neither should the dark man be wholly expected
fully and adequately to reproduce the exact Voice of the Black Woman.*

        —ANNA JULIA COOPER, *A VOICE FROM THE SOUTH* (1892)

THE BIRTH OF the Afro-American literary tradition occurred in 1773, when
Phillis Wheatley published a book of poetry. Despite the fact that her book
garnered for her a remarkable amount of attention, Wheatley's journey to the
printer had been a most arduous one. Sometime in 1772, a young African girl
walked demurely into a room at Boston to undergo an oral examination, the
results of which would determine the direction of her life and work. Perhaps
she was shocked upon entering the appointed room. For there, perhaps gathered in a semicircle, sat eighteen of Boston's most notable citizens. Among
them were John Erving, a prominent Boston merchant; the Reverend Charles
Chauncey, pastor of the Tenth Congregational Church; and John Hancock,
who would later gain fame for his signature on the Declaration of Independence. At the center of this group was His Excellency, Thomas Hutchinson,

governor of Massachusetts, with Andrew Oliver, his lieutenant governor, close by his side.

Why had this august group been assembled? Why had it seen fit to summon this young African girl, scarcely eighteen years old, before it? This group of "the most respectable Characters in *Boston*," as it would later define itself, had assembled to question closely the African adolescent on the slender sheaf of poems that she claimed to have written by herself. We can only speculate on the nature of the questions posed to the fledgling poet. Perhaps they asked her to identify and explain—for all to hear—exactly who were the Greek and Latin gods and poets alluded to so frequently in her work. Perhaps they asked her to conjugate a verb in Latin or even to translate randomly selected passages from the Latin, which she and her master, John Wheatley, claimed that she "had made some Progress in." Or perhaps they asked her to recite from memory key passages from the texts of John Milton and Alexander Pope, the two poets by whom the African claimed to be most directly influenced. We do not know.

We do know, however, that the African poet's responses were more than sufficient to prompt the eighteen august gentlemen to compose, sign, and publish a two-paragraph "Attestation," an open letter "To the Publick" that prefaces Phillis Wheatley's book and that reads in part:

> We whose Names are under-written, do assure the World, that the Poems specified in the following Page, were (as we verily believe) written by Phillis, a young Negro Girl, who was but a few Years since, brought an uncultivated Barbarian from *Africa*, and has ever since been, and now is, under the Disadvantage of serving as a Slave in a Family in this Town. She has been examined by some of the best Judges, and is thought qualified to write them.

So important was this document in securing a publisher for Wheatley's poems that it forms the signal element in the prefatory matter preceding her *Poems on Various Subjects, Religious and Moral,* published in London in 1773.

Without the published "Attestation," Wheatley's publisher claimed, few would believe that an African could possibly have written poetry all by herself. As the eighteen put the matter clearly in their letter, "Numbers would be ready to suspect they were not really the Writings of Phillis." Wheatley and her master, John Wheatley, had attempted to publish a similar volume in 1772 at Boston, but Boston publishers had been incredulous. Three years later, "Attestation" in hand, Phillis Wheatley and her master's son, Nathaniel Wheatley, sailed for England, where they completed arrangements for the publication of a volume of her poems with the aid of the Countess of Huntington and the Earl of Dartmouth.

This curious anecdote, surely one of the oddest oral examinations on record, is only a tiny part of a larger, and even more curious, episode in the Enlightenment. Since the beginning of the seventeenth century, Europeans had wondered aloud whether or not the African "species of men," as they were most commonly called, *could* ever create formal literature, could ever master "the arts and sciences." If they could, the argument ran, then the African variety of humanity was fundamentally related to the European variety. If not, then it seemed clear that the African was destined by nature to be a slave. This was the burden shouldered by Phillis Wheatley when she successfully defended herself and the authorship of her book against counterclaims and doubts.

Indeed, with her successful defense, Wheatley launched two traditions at once—the black American literary tradition *and* the black woman's literary tradition. If it is extraordinary that not just one but both of these traditions were founded simultaneously by a black woman—certainly an event unique in the history of literature—it is also ironic that this important fact of common, coterminous literary origins seems to have escaped most scholars.

That the progenitor of the black literary tradition was a woman means, in the most strictly literal sense, that all subsequent black writers have evolved in a matrilinear line of descent, and that each, consciously or unconsciously, has extended and revised a canon whose foundation was the poetry of a black woman. Early black writers seem to have been keenly aware of Wheatley's founding role, even if most of her white reviewers were more concerned with the implications of her race than her gender. Jupiter Hammon, for example, whose 1760 broadside "An Evening Thought. Salvation by Christ, With Penetential Cries" was the first individual poem published by a black American, acknowledged Wheatley's influence by selecting her as the subject of his second broadside, "An Address to Phillis Wheatley, Ethiopian Poetess, in Boston," which was published at Hanford in 1778. And George Moses Horton, the second Afro-American to publish a book of poetry in English (1829), brought out in 1838 an edition of his *Poems By A Slave* bound together with Wheatley's work. Indeed, for fifty-six years, between 1773 and 1829, when Horton published *The Hope of Liberty*, Wheatley was the only black person to have published a book of imaginative literature in English. So central was this black woman's role in the shaping of the Afro-American literary tradition that, as one historian has maintained, the history of the reception of Phillis Wheatley's poetry is the history of Afro-American literary criticism. Well into the nineteenth century, Wheatley and the black literary tradition were the same entity.

But Wheatley is not the only black woman writer who stands as a pioneering figure in Afro-American literature. Just as Wheatley gave birth to the genre of black poetry, Ann Plato was the first Afro-American to publish a book of essays (1841) and Harriet E. Wilson was the first black person to publish a novel in the United States (1859).

Despite this pioneering role of black women in the tradition, however, many of their contributions before this century have been all but lost or unrecognized. Wheatley, while certainly the most reprinted and discussed poet in the tradition, is also one of the least understood. Ann Plato's seminal work, *Essays* (which includes biographies and poems), has not been reprinted since it was published a century and a half ago. And Harriet Wilson's *Our Nig*, her compelling novel of a black woman's expanding consciousness in a racist northern antebellum environment, never received even one review or comment at a time when virtually *all* works written by black people were heralded by abolitionists as salient arguments against the existence of human slavery. We can only wonder how many other texts in the black woman's tradition have been lost to this generation of readers or remain unclassified or uncatalogued and, hence, unread.

This was not always so, however. Black women writers dominated the final decade of the nineteenth century, perhaps spurred to publish by an 1886 essay entitled "The Coming American Novelist," which was published in *Lippincott's Monthly Magazine* and written by "A Lady From Philadelphia." This anonymous essay argued that the "Great American Novel" would be written by a black person. Her argument is so curious that it deserves to be repeated:

> When we come to formulate our demands of the Coming American Novelist, we will agree that he must be native-born. His ancestors may come from where they will, but we must give him a birthplace and have the raising of him. Still, the longer his family has been here the better he will represent us. Suppose he should have no country but ours, no traditions but those he has learned here, no longings apart from us, no future except in our future—the orphan of the world, he finds with us his home. And with all this, suppose he refuses to be fused into that grand conglomerate we call the "American type." With us, he is not of us. He is original, he has humor, he is tender, he is passive and fiery, he has been taught what we call justice, and he has his own opinion about it. He has suffered everything a poet, a dramatist, a novelist need suffer before he comes to have his lips anointed. And with it all he is in one sense a spectator, a little out of the race. How would these conditions go towards forming an original development? In a word, suppose the coming novelist is of African origin? When one comes to consider the subject, there is no improbability in it. One thing is certain,—our great novel will not be written by the typical American.

An atypical American, indeed. Not only would the great American novel be written by an African-American, it would be written by an African-American *woman*:

> Yet farther: I have used the generic masculine pronoun because it is convenient; but Fate keeps revenge in store. It was a woman who, taking the wrongs of the African as her theme, wrote the novel that awakened the world to their reality, and why should not the coming novelist be a woman as well as an African? She—the woman of that race—has some claims on Fate which are not yet paid up.

This theme would be repeated by several black woman authors, most notably by Anna Julia Cooper, a prototypical black feminist whose 1892 *A Voice From the South* can be considered to be one of the original texts of the black feminist movement. It was Cooper who first analyzed the fallacy of referring to "the Black man" when speaking of black people and who argued that just as white men cannot speak through the consciousness of black men, neither can black *men* "fully and adequately reproduce the exact Voice of the Black Woman." Gender and race, she argues, cannot be conflated, except in the instance of a black woman's voice, and it is this voice which must be uttered and to which we must listen. As Cooper puts the matter so compellingly:

> It is not the intelligent woman vs. the ignorant woman; nor the white woman vs. the black, the brown, and the red,—it is not even the cause of woman vs. man. Nay, 'tis woman's strongest vindication for speaking that *the world needs to hear her voice*. It would be subversive of every human interest that the cry of one-half the human family be stifled. Woman in stepping from the pedestal of statue-like inactivity in the domestic shrine, and daring to think and move and speak,—to undertake to help shape, mold, and direct the thought of her age, is merely completing the circle of the world's vision. Hers is every interest that has lacked an interpreter and a defender. Her cause is linked with that of every agony that has been dumb—every wrong that needs a voice.
>
> It is no fault of man's that he has not been able to see truth from her standpoint. It does credit both to his head and heart that no greater mistakes have been committed or even wrongs perpetrated while she sat making tatting and snipping paper flowers. Man's own innate chivalry and the mutual interdependence of their interests have insured his treating her cause, in the main at least, as his own. And he is pardonably surprised and even a little chagrined, perhaps, to find his legislation not considered "perfectly lovely"

in every respect. But in any case his work is only impoverished by her re-maining dumb. The world has had to limp along with the wobbling gait and one-sided hesitancy of a man with one eye. Suddenly the bandage is re-moved from the other eye and the whole body is filled with light. It sees a circle where before it saw a segment. The darkened eye restored, every member rejoices with it.

The myopic sight of the darkened eye can only be restored when the full range of the black woman's voice, with its own special timbres and shadings, remains mute no longer.

SOURCE: This article is drawn from the series introduction by Henry Louis Gates, Jr. to *The Schomburg Library of Nineteenth-Century Black Women Writers* (New York: Oxford University Press, 1988).

INTRODUCTION, AFRICAN AMERICAN LIVES

WITH EVELYN BROOKS HIGGINBOTHAM

AFRICAN AMERICAN LIVES tells many stories and yet one. Its six hundred and eleven biographies span more than four centuries, presenting the lives of men and women whose backgrounds and achievements are as varied as their talents, skills, and knowledge. Taken together these lives of distinction attest to the integral character of African Americans to the life of this nation—to their abiding influence on American culture and institutions. *African American Lives* presents this history through a mosaic of individuals, some known throughout the world and others all but forgotten. We chose to include both familiar and unfamiliar names in the belief that history is more than the coherent account of important national events and social movements and that it is more than great ideas and works of art. The contours and content of history are shaped by people's lives, their personal choices and circumstances, individual uniqueness and creativity. Large events and small ones are brought about by ordinary people, for even the greatest of us is but an individual, while the least of us—as can be seen frequently in *African American Lives*—may have a profound effect on the course of world events.

African American Lives is the first publication of a much larger project, the *African American National Biography*, produced jointly by Harvard University's W. E. B. Du Bois Institute for African and African American Research and Oxford University Press. The project is modeled after the superb twenty-five volume *American National Biography* (1999), published by Oxford in collaboration with the American Council of Learned Societies—indeed, 257 entries in the current volume are reprinted from *ANB*. Taking *African American Lives* as its core, the *African American National Biography* will expand to eight volumes containing approximately 6,000 biographies and will thus illuminate the broad sweep of African American biography more fully than ever before, giving us an even greater appreciation of the roles played by African Americans in history.

The study of history itself has changed considerably since the 1970s when Rayford Logan and Michael R. Winston edited the *Dictionary of American Negro Biography* (1982), the first scholarly and comprehensive biographical reference work on African Americans. At the time of the *DANB*'s publication, African American women's history as well as the history of the civil rights and Black Power movements had just begun to emerge as vibrant fields of study. Attention to popular culture has provided greater insight into the lived experience of people who did not necessarily leave a written record. In the past three decades, historical methodology came increasingly to look upon new types of evidence, such as slave testimony and oral interviews, and to adopt interpretive frameworks that focused on indigenous movements, specifically the agency and social activism of local people rather than national leaders. The many changes in scholarship have brought to light an abundance of names remembered only by generations long gone.

Choosing some six hundred biographies to reflect so much history in a single volume proved a daunting task in itself. Our goal was to include not simply the greatest, the most deserving, or the most famous African Americans, but a selection that is representative of the broad range of African American experience. To accomplish this, we sifted through a database of over 11,000 names, solicited the advice of experts in many fields, and found ourselves in innumerable fascinating conversations. If the result of that process, as printed in this book, provokes further discussion among readers as to who should or should not be included, then it has served an important function already, because lively debate is an important tool for achieving understanding.

Reading through these biographies, one gets a sense of the interplay of the lives and careers of the subjects and of the breadth and depth of history behind their actions and ideas. As an example, let us follow through *African American Lives* the web of interconnections stemming from a single event— one that took place on 1 December 1955. Rosa Parks is rightly famed for refusing to give up her seat that day to a white rider on a bus in Alabama, but she did this neither on a whim nor alone. She was a protégé of the NAACP field secretary Ella Baker, and like Septima Clark, she had trained carefully to be an effective activist at the Highlander Folk School in Tennessee. Subsequent to her arrest, she worked with Jo Ann Robinson, E. D. Nixon, Martin Luther King Jr., and many others to organize the Montgomery bus boycott. Parks's refusal to give up her seat was itself no innovation, but rather drew upon a long history of similar protest. In 1947 Bayard Rustin was dragged from the front of a bus in Chapel Hill, North Carolina, and sentenced to thirty days on a chain gang; a few years earlier, before breaking the color barrier in major league baseball, Jackie Robinson was court-martialed—and acquitted—after refusing to move to the back of a segregated military bus. Benjamin Jefferson Davis Jr. was arrested in the early 1920s for sitting in the Jim Crow section of an Atlanta trolley car. The legality of the "separate but equal" doctrine itself was established by the infamous Supreme Court decision stemming from the arrest of Homer Plessy, who sat deliberately in a "whites only" railway coach in Louisiana in 1892 to challenge that principle. And there were similar protests before that: the career of Ida B. Wells-Barnett as both an activist and a journalist began in 1883 when she refused to leave a first-class ladies' car on the Chesapeake, Ohio, and Southwestern Railway; the Reconstruction congressman Robert Brown Elliott lobbied successfully for a bill to ban discrimination in public transportation in the 1870s; twice, in 1868 and 1866, Mary Ellen Pleasant sued a San Francisco streetcar company for not allowing her to ride; in 1866 in Philadelphia George Moses Horton protested with a poem entitled "Forbidden to Ride on the Street Cars"; in 1864 Sojourner Truth won in court the right to ride the streetcars in Washington, D.C. In 1855 James W. C. Pennington successfully challenged a New York City law prohibiting African Americans from riding inside a horse-drawn car. When Sarah Parker Remond was ejected from her seat in a place of public entertainment in Salem, Massachusetts, in 1853, she sued for reparations and won. There have been many others, but, as far as we know, the pioneer of such action was David Ruggles, who refused to give up his seat in a New Bedford, Massachusetts, railway car in 1841, only a year after the railway was established there. Of such connections is African American history made.

Like those named above, many of the subjects in *African American Lives* can be described as activists, but this book is not merely a collection of biographies of civil rights workers and politicians. *African American Lives* covers the full panoply of life for almost five centuries. In 1528, Esteban, the first African known to have stepped onto the North American continent, began his epic journeys across the South and Southwest, eventually becoming a Zuni deity after his death. African American history has continued ever since, and to represent that history in this book you will find at least the following:

- writers and journalists
- activists
- slaves

- politicians, government workers, judges, and lawyers
- musicians
- ministers, preachers, rabbis, and other religious workers
- educators
- athletes and sports figures
- actors, performers, directors, and filmmakers
- doctors, nurses, and medical workers
- artists and photographers
- business people and entrepreneurs
- military personnel
- scientists
- philanthropists
- dancers
- frontiersmen, pioneers, and cowboys
- inventors
- explorers
- aviators and astronauts
- legendary figures
- elephant hunter

If these numbers, incomplete as they are, add up to more than 611 (they actually add up to 918), that is because people are not easily classifiable and thus many must be included in more than one category. We all live varied, complex lives, and the subjects in *African American Lives* reflect that complexity to the fullest.

We have chosen to include in *African American Lives* the biographies of living subjects as well as dead. Many biographical dictionaries include only deceased subjects, and that certainly makes the writing, editing, and updating easier. However, much of importance has taken place in the past century, and the historical record would be seriously skewed if many undeniably significant people were left out of *African American Lives* simply because they are still alive. Martin Luther King Jr., Medgar Evers, and Eldridge Cleaver are gone, but James Meredith, Angela Davis, Jesse Jackson, and many others are still with us. The story of the struggle for civil rights in the latter half of the twentieth century is best appreciated through the lives of all of these and more. Alvin Ailey, too, has died, but Katherine Dunham, Arthur Mitchell, and Bill T. Jones have not; taken together, their careers brightly illuminate our understanding of the African American contribution to modern dance. Jimi Hendrix is dead, though many of those who paved the way for his success live on; perhaps we need mention only B. B. King, Chuck Berry, and Bo Diddley.

Every attempt has been made in *African American Lives* to include relevant family information. Typically, the first paragraph gives birth and death dates, the names and occupations of the parents, if these are known, and information about the subject's early life and education. The course of African American history, especially in earlier periods, has been such that in many cases dates, parentage, and family connections are difficult to determine. In order to make such connections explicit, the mother's maiden name has been given, where possible, so as to identify both sides of the family. This use of the maiden name is not meant to imply anything about the parents' marital status.

Cross-references throughout *African American Lives* make it easier to trace the web of contemporaneous and historical relationships that give structure to African American history. The first time anyone whose biography appears in *African American Lives* is named in the text of another biography, the name is printed in small capitals. For example, the biography of Malcolm X includes references to Marcus Garvey, Elijah Muhammad, Martin Luther King Jr., Muhammad Ali, Fannie Lou Hamer, Coretta Scott King, Adam Clayton Powell Jr., James Baldwin, Louis Farrakhan, Ossie Davis, Alex Haley, and Spike Lee. If any of these cross-references piques your interest or curiosity, you can simply turn to that entry to find out more about the person.

However, you do not necessarily need to know the name of a particular person in order to explore *African American Lives.* An index of subjects classified by category or area of renown will help you to find, for example, slaves and abolitionists, explorers and adventurers, civil rights workers, preachers and other religious figures, writers and journalists, artists and actors, dancers and musicians. A thematic index allows you to look up organizations, places of importance, and other significant topics. There you will find references to the NAACP, CORE, SNCC, SCLC, the Black Arts Movement, the Universal Negro Improvement Association (UNIA), the maritime underground railroad, and even the M Street School/Paul Laurence Dunbar High School, in Washington, D.C., where more than twenty of the subjects in *African American Lives* taught or were educated.

The biographies in *African American Lives* are also supplemented by several appendices. There are listings of all African American members of Congress and federal judges. There are also lists of winners of the NAACP Spingarn Medal, and all African American recipients of the Presidential Medal of Freedom, Nobel Prizes, Pulitzer Prizes, the National Medal of Arts, the National Humanities Medal, and the Congressional Medal of Honor. Names in boldface type in these appendices identify those for whom there is a biography in the book.

We are pleased to make available in a single volume these biographies of people who have significantly shaped our history. Some of them, like Jim Beckwourth and Mae Jemison, literally blazed trails to new frontiers. Others, like Moses Roper, Ellen and William Craft, and Henry "Box" Brown, found new pathways to freedom. Their successors labored long and hard to broaden those pathways, to pave them and make them smoother, as we see in the lives of Mary McLeod Bethune, Paul Robeson, and Gabrielle Kirk McDonald. Many others have taught us, lifted our spirits, entertained us, and even amazed us with their skills as educators, writers, artists, dancers, and athletes. We hope that *African American Lives* will serve as more than just a reference book—that it will provide its readers with the same insights, understanding, and pleasures that we have gained from editing it.

SOURCE: Henry Louis Gates, Jr., and Evelyn Brooks Higginbotham, eds., *African American Lives* (New York: Oxford University Press, 2004).

INTRODUCTION TO THE FIRST EDITION, FROM *AFRICANA: THE ENCYCLOPEDIA OF THE AFRICAN AND AFRICAN AMERICAN EXPERIENCE, SECOND EDITION*

WITH KWAME ANTHONY APPIAH

BETWEEN 1909 AND his death in 1963, W. E. B. Du Bois, the Harvard-trained historian, sociologist, journalist, and political activist, dreamed of editing an "Encyclopedia Africana." He envisioned a comprehensive compendium of "scientific" knowledge about the history, cultures, and social institutions of people of African descent: of Africans in the Old World, African Americans in the New World, and persons of African descent who had risen to prominence in Europe, the Middle East, and Asia. Du Bois sought to publish nothing less than the equivalent of a black *Encyclopaedia Britannica*, believing that such a broad assemblage of biography, interpretive essays, facts, and figures would do for the much denigrated black world of the twentieth century what *Britannica* and Denis Diderot's *Encyclopée* had done for the European world of the eighteenth century. These publications, which consolidated the scholarly knowledge accumulated by academics and intellectuals in the Age of Reason, served both as a tangible sign of the enlightened skepticism that characterized that era of scholarship, and as a basis upon which further scholarship could be constructed. These encyclopedias became monuments to "scientific" inquiry, bulwarks against superstition, myth, and what their authors viewed as the false solace of religious faith. An encyclopedia of the African diaspora in Du Bois's view would achieve these things for persons of African descent.

But a black encyclopedia would have an additional function. Its publication would, at least symbolically, unite the fragmented world of the African diaspora, a diaspora created by the European slave trade and the turn-of-the-century "scramble for Africa." Moreover, for Du Bois, marshalling the tools of "scientific knowledge," as he would put it in his landmark essay, "The Need for an Encyclopedia of the Negro" (1945), could also serve as a weapon in the war against racism: "There is need for young pupils and for mature students of a statement of the present condition of our knowledge concerning the darker races and especially concerning Negroes, which would make available our present scientific knowledge and set aside the vast accumulation of tradition and prejudice which makes such knowledge difficult now for the layman to obtain: A vade mecum for American schools, editors, libraries, for Europeans inquiring into the race status here, for South Americans, and Africans."

The publication of such an encyclopedia, Du Bois continued, would establish "a base for further advance and further study" of "questions affecting the Negro race." An encyclopedia of the Negro, he reasoned, would establish both social policy and "social thought and discussion upon a basis of accepted scientific conclusion."

Du Bois first announced his desire to edit an "Encyclopedia Africana" in a letter to Edward Wilmot Blyden, the Pan-Africanist intellectual, in Sierra Leone in 1909: "I am venturing to address you on the subject of a Negro Encyclopedia. In celebration of the 50th anniversary of the Emancipation of the American Negro, I am proposing to bring out an Encyclopedia Africana covering the chief points in the history and condition of the Negro race." Du Bois sent a similar letter to dozens of other scholars, white and black, including William James, Hugo Munsterberg, George Santayana, Albert Bushnell Hart (his professors at Harvard), President Charles William Eliot of Harvard, Sir Harry Johnston, Sir Flinders Petrie, Giuseppe Sergi, Franz Boas, J. E. Casely-Hayford, John Hope, Kelly Miller, Benjamin Brawley, Anna Jones, Richard Greener, Henry Ossawa Tanner, and several others, all of whom—with the sole exception of President Eliot—agreed to serve on his editorial board. Du Bois sought to create a board of "One Hundred Negro Americans, African and West Indian Scholars," as he put it in a letter, and a second board of white advisors. Du Bois, in other words, sought the collaboration of the very best scholars of what we would call today African Studies and African American Studies, as well as prominent American and European intellectuals such as James and Boas.

Nevertheless, as he put it to Blyden, "the real work I want done by Negroes." Du Bois, admitting that this plan was "still in embryo," created official stationery that projected a publication date of the first volume in 1913—"the Jubilee of Emancipation in America and the Tercentenary of the Landing of the Negro." The remaining four volumes would be published between 1913 and 1919.

Despite the nearly unanimous enthusiasm that greeted Du Bois's call for participation, he could not secure the necessary funding to mount the massive effort necessary to edit an encyclopedia of the black world. But he never abandoned the idea. At the height of the Great Depression, the idea would surface once again.

Anson Phelps Stokes, head of the Phelps-Stokes Association, a foundation dedicated to ameliorating race relations in America, called a meeting of 20 scholars and public figures at Howard University on November 7, 1931, to edit an "Encyclopedia of the Negro," a Pan-African encyclopedia similar to Du Bois's 1909 project. Incredibly, neither Du Bois nor Alain Locke, a Harvard-trained Ph.D. in philosophy and the dean of the Harlem Renaissance, nor Carter G. Woodson (like Du Bois, a Harvard Ph.D. in history and the founder of the Association for the Study of Negro Life and History) was invited to attend. Du Bois protested, angrily, to Phelps Stokes. A second meeting was convened on January 9, 1932, at which Du Bois was unanimously elected editor-in-chief. Between 1932 and 1946, Du Bois would serve as "Editor-in-Chief" of the second incarnation of his project, now named "The Encyclopedia of the Negro," and housed at 200 West 135th Street in New York City.

Du Bois planned a four-volume encyclopedia, each volume comprising 500,000 words. Just as he had done in 1909, he secured the cooperation of an impressive array of scholars, including Charles Beard, Franz Boas, John R. Connors, Edith Abbott, Felix Frankfurter, Otto Klineburg, Carl Van Doren, H. L. Mencken, Roscoe Pound, Robert E. Park, Sidney Hook, Harold Laski, Broadus Mitchell, "and scores of others," as Du Bois put it in a letter to the historian Charles Wesley. Du Bois's "Encyclopedia of the Negro" would require a budget of $225,000. It would be written by a staff of between "25 and 100 persons" hired to be "research aides," to be located in editorial offices to be established in New York, Chicago, Atlanta, and New Orleans. They would prepare bibliographies, collect books and manuscripts, and gather and write "special data" and shorter entries. Black and white scholars, primarily located in Europe, America, and Africa, would write longer interpretive entries.

Du Bois tells us that his project was interrupted by the Depression for three years. But by 1935, he was actively engaged in its planning full-time, time made available by his forced resignation from his position as editor of the *Crisis* magazine, the official organ of the National Association for the Advancement of Colored People, which Du Bois had held since its first publication in 1910. Du Bois had written an editorial advocating the development of independent Negro social and economic institutions, since the goal posts of the Civil Rights Movement appeared to be receding. The

NAACP's board of directors was outraged and demanded his resignation. Du Bois obliged. Du Bois sought funding virtually everywhere, including the Works Progress Administration and the Federal Writers' Project, to no avail, despite the fact that Phelps Stokes had pledged, on a matching basis, half of the needed funds. He continued to write to hundreds of scholars, soliciting their cooperation. E. Franklin Frazier, the great black sociologist, declined Du Bois's overture, citing in a letter dated November 7, 1936, the presence of too many "politicians," "statesmen," "big Negroes," and "whites of good will" on Du Bois's editorial board. Throw out the table of contents, fire the board of editors, replace them with scholars, Frazier wrote, and he would consider joining the project.

A few months before this exchange, Du Bois was viciously attacked by Carter G. Woodson in the black newspaper the *Baltimore Afro-American.* On May 30, 1936, a page-one headline blared the news that Woodson "Calls Du Bois a Traitor if He Accepts Post," with a subtitle adding for good measure: "He Told Ofays, We'd Write Own History." Woodson charged that Du Bois had stolen the idea of *The Encyclopedia of the Negro* from him and that his project was doomed to failure because Du Bois was financed by, and his editorial board included, white people. Du Bois was embarrassed and sought to defend himself in letters to potential contributors and board members. Between his enemies at the NAACP and his intellectual rivals such as Woodson and Frazier, Du Bois faced an enormous amount of opposition to his encyclopedia project. In this swirl of controversy, in the midst of the Depression, funding appeared increasingly elusive.

Du Bois's assistant editor, Rayford Logan, like Du Bois, Woodson, and Charles Wesley a Harvard-trained Ph.D. in history, told a poignant story about the failure of this project to receive funding. By 1937, Du Bois had secured a pledge of $125,000 from the Phelps-Stokes Fund to proceed with his project—half of the funds needed to complete it. He applied to the Carnegie Corporation for the remaining half of his budget, with the strong endorsement of Phelps Stokes and the president of the General Education Board, a group of four or five private foundations that included the Rockefeller Foundation. So convinced was Du Bois that his project would finally be funded, that he invited Logan to wait with him for the telephone call that he had been promised immediately following the Carnegie board meeting. A bottle of vintage champagne sat chilling on Du Bois's desk in a silver bucket, two cut crystal champagne flutes resting nearby.

The phone never rang. Persuaded that Du Bois was far too "radical" to serve as a model of disinterested scholarship, and lobbied by Du Bois's intellectual enemies, such as the anthropologist Melville J. Herskovits, the Carnegie Corporation rejected the project.

Nevertheless, Du Bois stubbornly persisted, even publishing two putative "entries" from the *Encyclopedia* in *Phylon* magazine in 1940, one on Robert Russa Moton, the principal of Tuskegee Institute between 1915 and 1935, the other on Alexander Pushkin. He even was able to publish two editions in 1945 and 1946 on a *Preparatory Volume with Reference Lists and Reports of the Encyclopedia of the Negro.* But the project itself never could secure adequate backing.

David Levering Lewis, Du Bois's biographer, tells us what happened to Du Bois's promised funding. The executive committee of the General Education Board rejected the proposal early in May 1937. "In his conference a few days later with Carnegie Corporation president Frederick Keppel, GEB's Jackson Davis paradoxically pleaded for favorable Carnegie consideration of the project. 'Dr. Du Bois is the most influential Negro in the United States,' Davis reminded Keppel. 'This project would keep him busy for the rest of his life.' Predictably, Carnegie declined. Within a remarkably short time, the study of the Negro (generously underwritten by the Carnegie Corporation) found a quite different direction under Gunnar Myrdal, a Swedish scholar then unknown in the field of race relations, one whose understanding of American race problems was to be distinctly more psychological and less economic than was Du Bois's. When the president of the Phelps Stokes Fund wrote Du Bois in 1944 at the time of the publication of *An American Dilemma: [The Negro Problem and Modern Democracy]* that 'there has been no one who has been quite so often quoted by [Gunnar] Myrdal than yourself,' Du Bois must have savored the irony."

Adding insult to injury, in 1948 the General Education Board, along with the Dodd Mead publishing company, approached Frederick Patterson, the president of Tuskegee Institute, to edit a new incarnation of the project, to be titled *The Negro: An Encyclopedia.* Then in 1950, the historian Charles Wesley wrote to Du Bois, informing him that in the wake of Carter Woodson's death, the Association for the Study of Negro Life and History had decided to resurrect the *Encyclopedia Africana* project, reminding him of Woodson's claims to have conceived of it in 1921. Du Bois wished him well, but cautioned him in a postscript that "there is no such thing as a cheap encyclopedia." Everyone, it seemed, wanted to claim title to the encyclopedia, but no one wanted Du Bois to serve as its editor. For black scholars, *Africana* had become the Grail. Its publication, as Du Bois put it, "would mark an epoch."

Long after Du Bois had abandoned all hope of realizing his great ambition, an offer of assistance would come quite unexpectedly from Africa. On September 26, 1960, Du Bois announced that Kwame Nkrumah, the president of the newly independent Republic of Ghana, had invited him to repatriate to Ghana, where he would serve as the editor-in-chief of *The Encyclopedia*

Africana. Du Bois accepted, moving in 1961. On December 15, 1962, in his last public speech before his death on the eve of the March on Washington in August 1963, Du Bois addressed a conference assembled expressly to launch—at last—his great project.

He wanted to edit "an *Encyclopedia Africana* based in Africa and compiled by Africans," he announced, an encyclopedia that is "long overdue," referring no doubt to his previously frustrated attempts. "Yet," he continued with a certain grim satisfaction, "it is logical that such a work had to wait for independent Africans to carry it out [because] the encyclopedia is concerned with Africa as a whole." Citing his own introductory essay in the *Preparatory Volume* of 1945, Du Bois justified this project by railing against "present thought and action" that "are all too often guided by old and discarded theories of race and heredity, by misleading emphasis and silence of former histories." After all of these centuries of slavery and colonialism, on the eve of the independence of the Continent, "it is African scholars themselves who will create the ultimate *Encyclopedia Africana.*" Eight months later Du Bois would be dead, and with him died his 54-year-old dream of shepherding a great black encyclopedia into print. Nevertheless, the Secretariat of the *Encyclopedia Africana,* based in Accra, Ghana, which Du Bois founded, eventually published three volumes of biographical dictionaries, in the late seventies and early eighties, and has recently announced plans to publish an encyclopedia about the African continent in 2009, which is welcome news.

We first became enamored of this project as students at the University of Cambridge. One of us, Henry Louis Gates, Jr., was a student of Wole Soyinka, the great playwright who in 1986 became the first African to receive the Nobel Prize for Literature. The other, Kwame Anthony Appiah, was an undergraduate studying philosophy. Though we came from very different backgrounds—in rural West Virginia and in urban Asante, in Ghana—we both already had, like Soyinka, a sense of the worlds of Africa and her diaspora as profoundly interconnected, even if, as we learned ourselves, there were risks of misunderstanding that arose from our different origins and experiences. The three of us represented three different places in the black world, and we vowed in 1973 to edit a Pan-African encyclopedia of the African diaspora, inspired by Du Bois's original objective formulated in 1909. Du Bois's later conception of the project was, we felt, too narrow in its scope, and too parochial in its stated desire to exclude the scholarly work of those who had not had the good fortune, by accident of birth, to have been born on the African continent. (Du Bois himself, had this rule been literally applied, would have been excluded from his own project!) Instead, we sought to edit a project that would produce a genuine compendium of "Africana."

Our own attempts to secure the necessary support were in vain, too, until four years ago when, first, Quincy Jones and Martin Payson, and then Sonny Mehta and Alberto Vitale at Random House, agreed to fund the preparation of a prototype of a CD-ROM encyclopedia of the African diaspora, to be edited by us, with Soyinka serving as the chair of an international and multiethnic board of editors. Two years later we secured the support for a 2-million-word encyclopedia from Frank Pearl, the CEO of a new publisher called Perseus Books, and from the Microsoft Corporation. Modifying the editorial structure that Du Bois planned to use to complete *The Encyclopedia of the Negro,* we deployed a staff of some three dozen writers and editors, and we solicited about 400 scholars to write longer, interpretive articles.

Du Bois's own idea, although he did not admit this, probably arose at least in part out of the publication of the *Encyclopedia Judaica* in 1907, as well as black encyclopedia antecedents such as James T. Holly's *The Afro-American Encyclopedia* (1895), Alexander W. Wayman's *Cyclopedia of African Methodism* (1882), Charles O. Boothe's *The Cyclopedia of the Colored Baptists of Alabama* (1895), and Revels Adams's *Cyclopedia of African Methodism in Mississippi* (1902). Other unpublished projects patterned after Du Bois's 1909 proposal included Daniel Murray's monumental "Historical and Biographical Encyclopedia of the Colored Race Throughout the World," which was to have been published in 1912 in six volumes and, later, Edward Garrett's self-written "A Negro Encyclopedia," consisting of 4000 entries, and completed on the eve of World War II. Both encyclopedias exist in manuscript form, but tragically were never published. All told, more than two dozen black encyclopedias have been published in the past century with limited distribution, but none has explored in a single compass both the African continent and the triumphs and the tragedies of Africa's people and their descendants around the globe.

That continent is where human prehistory begins. It was in Africa, as biologists now believe, that our species evolved, and so, in a literal sense, every modern human being is of African descent. Indeed, it was probably only about 100,000 years ago that the first members of our species left Africa, across the Suez Peninsula, and set out on an adventure that would lead to the peopling of the whole earth.

It is important to emphasize that Africa has never been separate from the rest of the human world. There have been long periods and many cultures that knew nothing of life in Africa. For much of African history, even in Africa, most Africans were unaware of other peoples in their own continent, unaware, in fact, that they shared a continent at all (just as most people in Europe, Asia, Australasia, and the Americas would have been astonished to learn that they were Europeans, Asians, Australasians, or Americans!). But the Straits of Gibraltar and the Suez Peninsula were always bridges more than obstacles to travel; the Mediterranean was already a system of trade long before the founding of Rome; the Sahara Desert, which so many people imagine as an impenetrable barrier, has a network of trade routes older than the Roman Empire. Starting some 2,000 or so years ago, in the area of modern day Cameroon, Bantu-speaking migrants fanned out south and east into tropical Africa, taking with them the knowledge of iron smelting and new forms of agriculture. And so, when Greek and Arab travelers explored the East Coast of Africa in the first millennium c.e., or European explorers began to travel down the West African coast toward the equator in the fifteenth century, they were making direct contact with cultures with which their ancestors had very often been in remote and indirect contact all along.

The first European scholars to write about Africa in the modern period, which begins with the European Age of Discovery, knew very little of Africa's history. They did not know that their ancestors, thousands of generations ago, had also lived in Africa. If they had read Herodotus, they might have noticed his brief discussion of the civilizations of the upper Nile, and so they might have realized that Egypt was in touch with other African societies. However, it probably would not have occurred to them that, since those societies were also in touch with still others, Egypt was in touch with Central Africa as well. So they thought of much of Africa as being outside the human historical narrative they already knew.

These first scholars were also obviously struck by the physical differences between Africans and themselves—especially of skin color and hair—and by the differences between the customs back home and the ones the European explorers found on the Guinea coast. And so they thought of Africans as different in kind from themselves, wondering, sometimes, whether they were really also descendants of Adam and Eve.

Attitudes like these already distorted Western understandings of Africa from the fifteenth century on. Worse yet, as the transatlantic slave trade developed, so did an increasingly negative set of ideas about African peoples and their capacities. It became normal to think of black Africans as inferior to Europeans, and many Europeans found in that inferiority a rationalization for the enslavement of Africans. As a result, much of the writing about Africans and about people of African descent in the New World was frankly derogatory. Because modern Africans were educated in European colonies, they too inherited a distorted and dismissive attitude toward Africa's past and African capacities, and one of the first tasks of modern African intellectuals has been to try to frame a sense of the world and our place in it that is freed from these sad legacies.

There have been many skirmishes in the battle to find a just representation of Africa and her peoples. But in the course of this century—and more especially in the last 30 or 40 years—a more objective knowledge of Africa has gradually emerged, both in Africa and elsewhere. Anthropologists began to describe the rich religious, artistic, and social life of African peoples. African historians have learned to interpret oral histories, passed down in Africa's many traditions, cross-checking them against archaeological and documentary evidence to produce a rich picture of the African past. Economists and political scientists, literary critics and philosophers, scholars of almost every discipline in the social sciences and the humanities have contributed to this new knowledge. And it has been the work of scholars on every continent, Africans prominent among them. Work in African American studies has led to new understandings of the culture of slaves and of the role of people of African descent in shaping the New World's language, religion, agriculture, architecture, music, and art. As a result, it is now possible to comb through a great library of material on African history and on the peoples of Africa and her diaspora, and to offer, in a single volume, a compendium of facts and interpretations.

An encyclopedia cannot include everything that is known about its subject matter, even everything that is important. So we have had to make choices. (And, alas, some of the most interesting questions are as yet unanswered.) But we have sought to provide a broad range of information and so to represent the full range of Africa and her diaspora. About two-fifths of the text of the encyclopedia has to do exclusively, or almost so, with the African continent: the history of each of the modern nations of Africa and what happened within their territories before those nations developed; the names of ethnic groups, including some that were formerly empires and nations, and their histories; biographies of eminent African men and women; major cities and geographical features: rivers, mountains, lakes, deserts; forms of culture: art, literature, music, religion; and some of Africa's diverse plant and animal life. Another third deals mostly with Latin America and the Caribbean, focusing on the influence of African cultures and people of African descent in shaping those portions of the New World. Slightly less than a third of the material deals with North America in the same way. And the rest is material of cross-cultural significance or has to do with the African presence in Europe, Asia, or the rest of the world.

Our main focus has been on history—political and social—and on literature and the arts, including music, to which African and African American contributions have been especially notable in modern times. Our aim has been to give a sense of the wide diversity of peoples, cultures, and traditions that we know about in Africa in historical times, a feel for the environment in which that history was lived, and a broad outline of the contributions of people of African descent, especially in the Americas, but, more generally, around the world.

It is natural, faced with a compendium of this sort, to go looking first for what we know already and to be especially pleased with ourselves if we find something missing! But in setting out to make an encyclopedia in a single volume, we had to make choices all the time about what to include, and we did so in the light of our own best judgments, in consultation with many scholars from around the world. It has been one of the great satisfactions of compiling a work with so many colleagues with so many different specialized areas of knowledge, that we have been able to fill in some of our own many areas of ignorance. That, we believe, is the great pleasure of this new encyclopedia: it not only answers many questions that you knew you wanted to ask, it invites you to ask questions that you had not dreamed of asking. We hope you will find, as we have, that the answers to these unfamiliar questions are as amazing and as varied as Africa, her peoples, and their descendants all around the globe.

We mentioned earlier some of the many encyclopedias of various aspects of African and African American life that have been published in the past. The publication of *Africana: The Encyclopedia of the African and African American Experience* as a one-volume print edition aspires to belong in the grand tradition of encyclopedia editing by scholars interested in the black world on both sides of the Atlantic. It also relies upon the work of thousands of scholars who have sought to gather and to analyze, according to the highest scholarly standards, the lives and the worlds of black people everywhere. We acknowledge our indebtedness to these traditions of scholarly endeavor—more than a century old—to which we are heirs, by dedicating our encyclopedia to the monumental contribution of W. E. B. Du Bois.

SOURCE: Kwame Anthony Appiah and Henry Louis Gates, Jr., eds., *Africana: The Encyclopedia of the African and African American Experience, Second Edition* (New York: Oxford University Press, 2005).

PREFATORY NOTES ON THE AFRICAN SLAVE TRADE

From *In Search of Our Roots: How 19 Extraordinary African Americans Reclaimed Their Past*

THIS BOOK IS in large measure about slavery and its aftermath, and the impact of that horrendous institution on generations of African American families and some of their more notable descendants, leading figures in the African American community today. Because the stories of these individuals and their ancestors are rooted in genealogical research, they are necessarily based on historical analysis and a few salient statistics about the origins of our ancestors forced into the slave ships and shipped to the United States between 1619 and the 1800s. Understanding this historical background will, I think, help you more fully to appreciate the stories in this book.

First and foremost, you need to understand who our slave ancestors were—that is, where they originated on the African continent. They were Africans of many different ethnic groups from many different regions, taken captive—often by other Africans—and sold to Europeans. They were then put on ships and transported to the New World. Many did not survive the dreadful journey: Historians estimate that 15 percent of those who boarded the slave ships along the African coast perished in the dreadful Middle Passage. Those who managed to survive endured a lifetime of unimaginable hardship, bound by people who carefully and willfully did all they could do in every possible way to strip away every aspect of their slaves' humanity.

All African Americans whose ancestors were born in the New World before the twentieth century are descended from these slaves, and every African American today—unless she or he is descended from a very recent African immigrant—can trace his or her lineage deep into the slave past. While some of our ancestors were fortunate enough to be freed by the Emancipation Proclamation—about 600,000 according to historian David

Blight—before the end of the Civil War (three of the individuals whose family lines are discussed in this book descend from slaves who were freed before 1800), about 87 percent of the 3,953,760 slaves in 1860 were freed from slavery only in 1865. But because of the way the slave system worked, few of us know much, if anything, about any of our ancestors from this period, even if they had been freed. We know even less about our African ancestors, of course. While it's not so likely, some may even have been members of royal families in Africa; many more would have been captured in battle, then sold to Europeans as the booty of war. Others were imprisoned because of debt; some were kidnapped. Regardless, however, of how they were enslaved in Africa, still they spoke their languages and knew their names. But here, on this side of the Atlantic, they soon lost those names.

Slavery poses enormous challenges to any scholar seeking to reconstruct its features. Though the practices of slave owners varied, sometimes significantly, in different eras and in different states and in different times, slavery was, almost everywhere, a systemic effort to rob black human beings of their very humanity itself—that is, of all the aspects of civilization that make a human being "human": names, birth dates, family ties, the freedom to be educated and to worship, and the most basic sense of self-knowledge and continuity of generations within one's direct family lines. With very few exceptions—and there were some, oddly enough—each slave had one name only, a first name, that the law and custom acknowledged. No matter what slaves called themselves within the confines of their own communities, within their sheltered and hidden lives as a veritable subcontinent of the plantation, and no matter what their family and friends knew them by, the American legal system did not generally acknowledge those names. (Slaves would usually be listed by first names in legal documents such as wills, estate papers of the deceased, and some tax records, for example. And, remarkably, in the schedules of the 1850 and 1860 federal censuses, eight counties— including Hampshire County, then in Virginia, now in West Virginia, where some of my own slave ancestors lived—listed the slaves owned there by a first name and a surname; but these were the exceptions, only eight counties among all the counties in all the states in America.) And sometimes, though very rarely, notices of slave auctions would list slaves to be sold by a first and a last name. (I own one of these advertisements.) How in the world can you reconstruct a family tree consisting of generations of people who had only one name, when even that name was not often listed in official, legal documents maintained by the state?

In my efforts to trace present-day African Americans back to their family roots in Africa, I frequently consult what I consider to be one of the most valuable and impressive historical research tools ever created: the Trans-

Atlantic Slave Trade Database. This database is a compilation of the records kept by shipping companies involved in the slave trade. It offers detailed information on 34,941 transatlantic slave-trading voyages that occurred between 1514 and 1866. Compiled under the direction of David Eltis, with the collaboration of Stephen D. Behrendt, Manolo Florentino, and David Richardson, it is the largest uniform, consolidated database of its kind in the world. The authors estimate that the assembled data cover at least two-thirds of the slaving voyages that crossed the Atlantic Ocean to the New World. Of especial interest to us are the voyages to the United States, either directly from Africa or via the Caribbean.

According to the database, before the slave trade ended in the United States, approximately 455,000 Africans were brought here against their will, 389,000 directly from Africa, and another 66,000 from the Caribbean, according to Greg O'Malley. Meaning that of the 12.5 million Africans taken from Africa and shipped across the Atlantic in slavery, only a tiny portion—less than 4 percent—were brought to this country (the remainder, of course, went to the Caribbean and Latin America). Of the 12.5 million Africans who left Africa, 10.7 million arrived in the Americas between 1501 and 1867. For most black Americans—about 90 percent of those of us living in the United States today—these 455,000 Africans are the basis of our ancestral gene pool. They are the core source of what are now more than 35 million African American citizens.

The vast majority of our African ancestors came to the United States as slaves between 1700 and 1820. Most, in fact, arrived in the final decades of the eighteenth century. David Eltis estimates that in 1700 only 4 percent of the original 455,000 had arrived here. By 1750 the figure is 41 percent; by 1800 it is 80 percent; and by 1820 it is 99.7 percent. This means that virtually all African American families had an ancestor here by 1820, if not much earlier. In fact, more than half of us had ancestors living in the United States by the signing of the Declaration of Independence. The black presence is as old as America itself.

In other words, if a room were full of black people and we gave each one a DNA test, we would learn that 23.0 percent of us are descended from people who were shipped from Congo or Angola, 17.5 percent of us from eastern Nigeria and the Cameroon Republic, 2.2 percent from Mozambique, 14.1 percent from Ghana, 2.4 percent from Benin and western Nigeria, and 40.8 percent from the countries that range from Senegal and Gambia to Liberia (known as Upper Guinea).

Within these regions there were scores of tribes or ethnic groups who were poured into the slave ships bound for America. Africa was, and remains, one of the most diverse continents, genetically and linguistically, on the face of the earth. Fifteen hundred languages are spoken on the African continent today. But the ancestors of the African American people are surprisingly localized. Linda Heywood and John Thornton have recently estimated that about fifty ethnic groups in Africa primarily made up the body of slaves who became the ancestors of the African American people. These ethnic groups have names today such as Mende, Igbo, Yoruba, and Fon, and these names refer to shared languages and cultural practices. Some of these names would have been used by Africans to describe themselves; others are of more recent vintage. As David Eltis explained to me, "There were some large ethnolinguistic groups such as Mende and Congo, but these were not necessarily part of people's self-identification. Identities would have been developed for much smaller units of people. From Upper Guinea, Mende, Koronko, Susu, Fula, and Mandingo would have been well represented. From the Bight of Biafra (in today's eastern Nigeria), more than half would likely have been Igbo." The slaves who commandeered the slave ship called the *Amistad*, for example, under the leadership of Cinque, identified themselves as members of the Mende people in a Bible they presented to their attorney, former president John Quincy Adams, in 1841. In other words, the names that Africans use to describe themselves today were not necessarily in use during slavery times as a form of self-identification, but many were. What this means is that if we could go back in time and meet our earliest enslaved ancestor, depending on the point in time, he or she may or may not think of him- or herself as "Mende," say, despite speaking a language that we call "Mende" and living in a "Mende" land. Such ancestors might think of themselves instead as belonging to a specific local group—a group whose name has been long ago lost. For the purposes of this book, and indeed for most work on slavery, we will not attempt to parse the local groups within the larger ethnic identities. If your ancestors shared genetic characteristics with a person who describes him- or herself as Mende today, I will call them Mende here. After all, just because Frederick Douglass thought of himself as "colored" doesn't mean that it would be incorrect to describe him today as an "African American."

Now, of course, once our ancestors came to this country, their ethnic identities were stripped from them, along with their names, religions, and family ties. They ceased to be Mende or Igbo or Kpelle and became Negro slaves, thrown together with people of other ethnicities without any consideration. Over the years the blending of their different ethnicities created the rich mixture—the pan-African identity—that is African American culture today. But it took time. And you can bet that there were some painful intra-African conflicts along the way. After all, what united these many different people of African descent was their color, the continent of their origin, and most especially their condition as the enslaved. There were also, of course, interracial mixtures with whites and with Native Americans—over half the African American people today have at least one European great-grandfather, while that figure for a Native American great-grandparent is much, much less, amounting to only about 5 percent—and all this intermixture contributes to who we are today when we describe ourselves as "African Americans."

I'll have more to say about our "admixture" throughout this book since this is one of the crucial tests that I administered to each of the individuals who participated in this project. In the broad picture, the geneticist Dr. Mark Shriver has advised me that African American DNA today breaks down something like this:

- 5 percent of African Americans have at least 12.5 percent Native American ancestry (equivalent of one great-grandparent).
- 58 percent of African Americans have at least 12.5 percent European ancestry (equivalent of one great-grandparent).
- 19.6 percent of African Americans have at least 25 percent European ancestry (equivalent of one grandparent).
- 1 percent of African Americans have at least 50 percent European ancestry (equivalent of one parent).

By contrast, Americans of predominantly white or European ancestry have the following mixtures:

- 2.7 percent of European Americans have at least 12.5 percent Native American ancestry (equivalent of one great-grandparent).
- Less than 1 percent of European Americans have at least 12.5 percent West African ancestry (equivalent of one great-grandparent).

These fascinating statistics should, I hope, give us all a better understanding of the genetic and geographical origins of the victims of the African slave trade to America.

Statistics are by their nature very broad and maddeningly vague and anonymous. It will always be so. We will never know even a tiny fraction of the names of our ancestors who were taken from Africa. We will never see their faces, never read their words. They are lost to us forever, because of the devastatingly effective way the slave trade worked in its attempt to erase the past from the present of a slave. Nevertheless, we can now, after all of these centuries, begin to get a sense of who our ancestors were, by analyzing the DNA of their descendants—and by re-creating the lines of the families they started in slavery, the families that against all odds now thrive in such great numbers today. After Nigeria and Brazil, the African Americans living in the United States constitute the third-largest group of black people in the world. Telling the story of their origins and their evolution from the seventeenth century to the present, from slavery to freedom, is precisely what this book attempts to do, through what I hope is a careful history of nineteen extraordinary individuals, individuals whose past—while unique, of course—is also most certainly representative of the world that our ancestors—your ancestors and mine, black and white—created out of the crucible of slavery and the centuries-long battle to become free and equal citizens in the great republic that America is still striving to be.

SOURCE: Henry Louis Gates, Jr., *In Search of Our Roots: How 19 Extraordinary African Americans Reclaimed Their Past* (New York: Crown Publishers, 2009).

PART III
CANONS

LITERARY CANONS DON'T just appear. The 1970s and 1980s saw numerous battles over the idea and content of the literary canon, not only in African American Studies, but also in fields like Women's Studies, Latino Studies, Jewish Studies, and other Ethnic Studies. Scholars working in the wake of the Civil Rights Movement and in the heat of feminism and academic post-structuralism deeply wanted to break canons, to reject the received wisdom that some works were inherently worth reading and some were irredeem-ably not. At the same time, many scholars—including Gates—saw a pressing need to reshape the literary canon to reflect the wide body of writing that actually existed, rather than the narrow stock of writing that made its way onto syllabi and into anthologies.

Eventually, through the labor of Gates and his colleagues, women writ-ers like Edith Wharton and black writers like Ralph Ellison—and black women writers like Toni Morrison—found a place at the canonical table and became vocal and admired presences there. As canon-breakers, Gates and his fellow critics exposed the stale notions of fixity and objective value that had determined and defined earlier bodies of knowledge as culturally deter-mined. At the same time, as canon-makers, they established new models of inclusion and valuation.

The pieces in this section address this fractious moment in literary and cultural studies in which Gates was a key player in the 1980s. The contra-dictions in the simultaneous work of canon-busting and canon-building are evident, especially as we look back on them from the more expansive van-tage point engendered by these debates.

Abby Wolf

THE MASTER'S PIECES

On Canon Formation and the African-American Tradition

WILLIAM BENNETT AND Allan Bloom, the dynamic duo of the new cultural right, have become the easy targets of the cultural left—which I am defining here loosely and generously, as that uneasy, shifting set of alliances formed by feminist critics, critics of so-called minority discourse, and Marxist and poststructuralist critics generally, the Rainbow Coalition of contemporary critical theory. These two men symbolize for us the nostalgic return to what I think of as the "antebellum aesthetic position," when men were men, and men were white, when scholar-critics were white men, and when women and persons of color were voiceless, faceless servants and laborers, pouring tea and filling brandy snifters in the boardrooms of old boys' clubs. Inevitably, these two men have come to play the roles for us that George Wallace and Orville Faubus played for the civil rights movement, or that Nixon and Kissinger played for us during Vietnam—the "feel good" targets, who, despite our internal differences and contradictions, we all love to hate.

And how tempting it is to juxtapose their "civilizing mission" to the racial violence that has swept through our campuses since 1986—at traditionally liberal northern institutions such as the University of Massachusetts at Amherst, Mount Holyoke College, Smith College, the University of Chicago, Columbia, and at southern institutions such as the University of Alabama, the University of Texas, and at The Citadel. Add to this the fact that affirmative action programs on campus have meanwhile become window-dressing operations, necessary "evils" maintained to preserve the fiction of racial fairness and openness, but deprived of the power to enforce their stated principles. When unemployment among black youth is 40 percent, when 44 percent of black Americans can't read the front page of a newspaper, when less than 4 percent of the faculty on campuses is black, well, you look for targets close at hand.

And yet there's a real danger of localizing our grievances, of the easy personification, assigning a celebrated face to the forces of reaction and so giving too much credit to a few men who are really symptomatic of a larger political current. Maybe our eagerness to do so reflects a certain vanity that academic cultural critics are prone to. We make dire predictions, and when they come true, we think we've changed the world.

It's a tendency that puts me in mind of my father's favorite story about Father Divine, that historic con-man of the cloth. In the 1930s he was put on trial for using the mails to defraud, I think, and was convicted. At sentencing, Father Divine stood up and told the judge: I'm warning you, you send me to jail, something terrible is going to happen to you. Father Divine, of course, was sent to prison, and a week later, by sheer coincidence, the judge had a heart attack and died. When the warden and the guards found out about it in the middle of the night, they raced to Father Divine's cell and woke him up. Father Divine, they said, your judge just dropped dead of a heart attack. Without missing a beat, Father Divine lifted his head and told them: "I *hated* to do it."

As writers, teachers, or intellectuals, most of us would like to claim greater efficacy for our labors than we're entitled to. These days, literary criticism likes to think of itself as "war by other means." But it should start to wonder: Have its victories come too easily? The recent move toward politics and history in literary studies has turned the analysis of texts into a marionette theater of the political, to which we bring all the passions of our real-world commitments. And that's why it is sometimes necessary to remind ourselves of the distance from the classroom to the streets. Academic critics write essays, "readings" of literature, where the bad guys (for example, racism or patriarchy) lose, where the forces of oppression are subverted by the boundless powers of irony and allegory that no prison can contain, and we glow with hard-won triumph. We pay homage to the marginalized and demonized, and it feels almost as if we've righted a real-world injustice. I always think of the folktale about the fellow who killed seven with one blow.

Ours was the generation that took over buildings in the late sixties and demanded the creation of black and women's studies programs, and now, like the return of the repressed, has come back to challenge the traditional curriculum. And some of us are even attempting to redefine the canon by editing anthologies. Yet it sometimes seems that blacks are doing better in the college curriculum than they are in the streets.

This is not a defeatist moan. Just an acknowledgment that the relation between our critical postures and the social struggles they reflect upon is far from transparent. That doesn't mean there's no relation, of course, only that it's a highly mediated one. In any event, I do think we should be clear about when we've swatted a fly and when we've toppled a giant.

In the swaddling clothes of our academic complacencies, few of us are prepared when we bump against something hard, and sooner or later, we do. One of the first talks I ever gave was to a packed audience at the Howard University Honors Seminar, and it was one of those mistakes you don't do twice. Fresh out of graduate school, immersed in the arcane technicalities of contemporary literary theory, I was going to deliver a crunchy structuralist analysis of a slave narrative by Frederick Douglass, tracing the intricate play of its "binary oppositions." Everything was neatly schematized, formalized, analyzed; this was my Sunday-best structuralism, crisp white shirt and shiny black shoes. And it wasn't playing. If you've seen an audience glaze over, this was double-glazing. Bravely, I finished my talk and, of course, asked for questions. Long silence. Finally, a young man in the very back of the room stands up and says, "Yeah, brother, all we want to know is, was Booker T. a Tom or not?"

The funny thing is, this happens to be an interesting question, a lot more interesting than my talk was. And while I didn't exactly appreciate it at the time, the exchange did draw my attention, a little rudely perhaps, to the yawning chasm between our critical discourse and the traditions they discourse on. You know—Is there a canon in this class? People often like to represent the high canonical texts as the reading matter of the power elite. I mean, you have to try to imagine James Baker curling up with the *Four Quartets,* Dan Quayle leafing through the *Princess Cassimassima.* I suppose this is the vision, anyway. What's wrong with this picture? Now, Louis L'Amour or Ian Fleming, possibly. But that carries us a ways from the high canonical.

When I think back to that Howard talk, I think back to why I went into the study of literature in the first place. I suppose the literary canon is, in no very grand sense, the commonplace book of our shared culture, in which we have written down the texts and titles that we want to remember, that had some special meaning for us. How else did those of us who teach literature fall in love with our subject than through our own commonplace books, in which we inscribed, secretly and privately, as we might do in a diary, those passages of books that named for us what we had for so long deeply felt, but could not say? I kept mine from the age of twelve, turning to it to repeat those marvelous passages that named myself in some private way. From H. H. Munro and O. Henry—I mean, some of the popular literature we had on the shelves at home—to Dickens and Austen, to Hugo and de Maupassant, I found resonant passages that I used to inscribe in my book. Finding James Baldwin and writing him down at an Episcopal church camp during the Watts riots in 1965 (I was fifteen) probably determined the direction of my intellectual life more than did any other single factor. I wrote and rewrote verbatim his elegantly framed paragraphs, full of sentences that were at once somehow Henry Jamesian and King Jamesian, yet clothed in the cadences and figures of the spirituals. I try to remind my graduate students that each of us turned to literature through literal or figurative commonplace books, a fact that we tend to forget once we adopt the alienating strategies of formal analysis. The passages in my commonplace book formed my own canon, just as I imagine each of yours did for you. And a canon, as it has functioned in every literary tradition, has served as the commonplace book of our shared culture.

But the question I want to turn to now is this: How does the debate over canon formation affect the development of African-American literature as a subject of instruction in the American academy?

Curiously enough, the first use of the word *canon* in relation to the African-American literary tradition occurs in 1846, in a speech delivered by Theodore Parker. Parker was a theologian, a Unitarian clergyman, and a publicist for ideas, whom Perry Miller described eloquently as "the man who next only to Emerson . . . was to give shape and meaning to the Transcendental movement in America." In a speech on "The Mercantile Classes" delivered in 1846, Parker laments the sad state of "American" letters:

> Literature, science, and art are mainly in [poor men's] hands, yet are controlled by the prevalent spirit of the nation. . . . In England, the national literature favors the church, the crown, the nobility, the prevailing class. Another literature is rising, but is not yet national, *still less canonized*. We have no American literature which is permanent. Our scholarly books are only an imitation of a foreign type: they do not reflect our morals, manners, politics, or religion, not even our rivers, mountains, sky. They have not the smell of our ground in their breath.

Parker, to say the least, was not especially pleased with American letters and their identity with the English tradition. Did Parker find any evidence of a truly American literature?

> The American literature is found only in newspapers and speeches, perhaps in some novel, hot, passionate, but poor and extemporaneous. That is our

national literature. Does that favor man—represent man? Certainly not. All is the reflection of this most powerful class. The truths that are told are for them, and the lies. Therein the prevailing sentiment is getting into the form of thoughts.

Parker's analysis, we see plainly, turns upon an implicit reflection theory of base and superstructure. It is the occasional literature, "poor and extemporaneous," wherein "American" literature dwells, but a literature, like English literature, which reflects the interests and ideologies of the upper classes.

Three years later, in his major oration on "The American Scholar," Parker had at last found an entirely original genre of American literature:

> Yet, there is one portion of our permanent literature, if literature it may be called, which is wholly indigenous and original . . . . [W]e have one series of literary productions that could be written by none but Americans, and only here; I mean the Lives of Fugitive Slaves. But as these are not the work of the men of superior culture they hardly help to pay the scholar's debt. Yet all the original romance of Americans is in them, not in the white man's novel.

Parker was right about the originality, the peculiarly *American* quality, of the slave narratives. But he was wrong about their inherent inability to "pay the scholar's debt"; scholars had only to learn to *read* the narratives for their debt to be paid in full. Parker was put off by the language of the slaves' narratives. He would have done well to heed the admonition that Emerson had made in his 1844 speech, "Emancipation in the British West Indies": "Language," Emerson wrote, "must be raked, the secrets of slaughter-houses and infamous holes that cannot front the day, must be ransacked, to tell what negro slavery has been." The narratives, for Parker, were not instances of great literature, but they were a prime site of America's "original romance." As Charles Sumner said in 1852, the fugitive slaves and their narratives "are among the heroes of our age. Romance has no storms of more thrilling interest than theirs. Classical antiquity has preserved no examples of adventurous trial more worthy of renown." Parker's and Sumner's divergent views reveal that the popularity of the narratives in antebellum America most certainly did not reflect any sort of common critical agreement about their nature and status as art. Still, the implications of these observations upon black canon formation would not be lost upon those who would soon seek to free the black slave, or to elevate the ex-slave, through the agency of literary production.

Johann Herder's ideas of the "living spirit of a language" were brought to bear with a vengeance upon eighteenth- and nineteenth-century considerations of the place in nature of the black. Indeed the relationship between the social and political subjectivity of the Negro and the production of art had been discussed by a host of commentators, including Hume, Hegel, and Kant, since Morgan Godwyn wondered aloud about it in 1684. But it was probably Emerson's comments that generated our earliest efforts at canon formation. As Emerson said, again in his speech on "Emancipation in the West Indies":

> If [racial groups] are rude and foolish, down they must go. When at last in a race a new principle appears, an idea—*that* conserves it; ideas only save races. If the black man is feeble and not important to the existing races, not on a parity with the best race, the black man must serve, and be exterminated. But if the black man carries in his bosom an indispensable element of a new and coming civilization; for the sake of that element, no wrong nor strength nor circumstance can hurt him; he will survive and play his part. . . . [N]ow let [the blacks] emerge, clothed and in their own form.

The forms in which they would be clothed would be registered in anthologies that established the canon of black American literature.

The first attempt to define a black canon that I have found is that by Armand Lanusse, who edited *Les Cenelles,* an anthology of black French verse published at New Orleans in 1845—the first black anthology, I believe, ever published. Lanusse's introduction is a defense of poetry as an enterprise for black people, in their larger efforts to defend the race against "the spiteful and calumnious arrows shot at us," at a target defined as the collective black intellect. Despite this stated political intention, these poems imitate the styles and themes of the French Romantics, and never engage directly the social and political experiences of black Creoles in New Orleans in the 1840s. *Les Cenelles* argues for a political effect—that is, the end of racism—by publishing apolitical poems, poems which share as silent second texts the poetry written by Frenchmen three thousand miles away. We are just like the French—so, treat us like Frenchmen, not like blacks. An apolitical art being put to uses most political.

Four years later, in 1849, William G. Allen published an anthology in which he canonized Phillis Wheatley and George Moses Horton. Like Lanusse, Allen sought to refute intellectual racism by the act of canon formation. "The African's called inferior," he wrote. "But what race has ever displayed intellect more exaltedly, or character more sublime?" Pointing to the achievements of Pushkin, Placido, and Augustine, as the great "African" tradition to which African-Americans were heir, Allen claimed Wheatley and Horton as the exemplars of this tradition, Horton being "decidedly the superior genius," no doubt because of his explicitly racial themes, a judgment quite unlike that which propelled Armand Lanusse into canon formation. As Allen put it, with the publication of their anthology:

> Who will now say that the African is incapable of attaining to intellectual or moral greatness? What he now is, degrading circumstances have made him. What he is capable of becoming, the past clearly evinces. The African is strong, tough and hardy. Hundreds of years of oppression have not subdued his spirit, and though Church and State have combined to enslave and degrade him, in spite of them all, he is increasing in strength and power, and in the respect of the entire world.

Here, then, we see the poles of black canon formation, established firmly by 1849: Is "black" poetry racial in theme, or is "black" poetry any sort of poetry written by black people? This quandary has been at play in the tradition ever since.

I won't trace in detail the history of this tension over definitions of the African-American canon, and the direct relation between the production of black poetry and the end of white racism. Suffice it to point to such seminal attempts at canon formation in the 1920s as James Weldon Johnson's *The Book of American Negro Poetry* (1922), Alain Locke's *The New Negro* (1925), and V. F. Calverton's *An Anthology of American Negro Literature* (1929), each of which defined as its goal the demonstration of the existence of the black tradition as a political defense of the racial self against racism. As Johnson put it so clearly:

> A people may be great through many means, but there is only one measure by which its greatness is recognized and acknowledged. The final measure of the greatness of all peoples is the amount and standard of the literature and art that they have produced. The world does not know that a people is great until that people produces great literature and art. No people that has produced great literature and art has ever been looked upon by the world as distinctly inferior.
>
> The status of the Negro in the United States is more a question of national mental attitude toward the race than of actual conditions. And nothing will do more to change that mental attitude and raise his status than a demonstration of intellectual parity by the Negro through the production of literature and art.

Johnson, here, was echoing racialist arguments that had been used against blacks since the eighteenth century, especially those by Hume, Kant, Jefferson, and Hegel, which equated our access to natural rights with our production of literary classics. The Harlem Renaissance, in fact, can be thought of as a sustained attempt to combat racism through the very *production* of black art and literature.

Johnson's and Calverton's anthologies "frame" the Renaissance period, making a comparison between their ideological concerns useful. Calverton's anthology made two significant departures from Johnson's model, both of which are worth considering, if only briefly. Calverton's was the first attempt at black canon formation to provide for the influence and presence of black vernacular literature in a major way. "Spirituals," "Blues," and "Labor Songs" each comprised a genre of black literature for him. We all understand the importance of this gesture and the influence it had upon Sterling Brown, Arthur Davis, and Ulysses Lee, the editors of *The Negro Caravan* (1941). Calverton, whose real name was George Goetz, announced in his introductory essay, "The Growth of Negro Literature," that his selection principles had been determined by his sense of the history of black literary *forms,* leading him to make selections because of their formal "representative value," as he put it. These forms, he continued, were *Negro* forms, virtually self-contained in a hermetic black tradition, especially in the vernacular tradition, where artistic American originality was to be found:

> . . . [I]t is no exaggeration whatsoever to contend that [the Negro's contributions to American art and literature] are more striking and singular in substance and structure than any contributions that have been made by the white man to American culture. In fact, they constitute America's chief claim to originality in its cultural history. . . . The white man in America has continued, and in an inferior manner, a culture of European origin. He has not developed a culture that is definitely and unequivocally American. In respect of originality, then, the Negro is more important in the growth of American culture than the white man. . . . While the white man has gone to Europe for his models, and is seeking still a European approval of his artistic endeavors, the Negro in his art forms has never sought the acclaim of any culture other than his own. This is particularly true of those forms of Negro art that come directly from the people.

And note that Calverton couched his argument in just that rhetoric of nationalism, of American exceptionalism, that had long been used to exclude, or anyway occlude, the contribution of the Negro. In an audacious reversal, it turns out that *only* the Negro is really American, the white man being a pale imitation of his European forebears.

If Calverton's stress upon the black vernacular heavily influenced the shaping of *The Negro Caravan*—certainly one of the most important anthologies in the tradition—his sense of the black canon as a formal self-contained entry most certainly did not. As the editors put it in the introduction to the volume:

> [We] . . . do not believe that the expression "Negro literature" is an accurate one, and . . . have avoided using it. "Negro literature" has no application if it means structural peculiarity, or a Negro school of writing. The Negro writes in the forms evolved in English and American literature. . . . The editors consider Negro writers to be American writers, and literature by American Negroes to be a segment of American literature. . . .
>
> The chief cause for objection to the term is that "Negro literature" is too easily placed by certain critics, white and Negro, in an alcove apart. The next step is a double standard of judgment, which is dangerous for the future of Negro writers. "A Negro novel," thought of as a separate form, is too often condoned as "good enough for a Negro." That Negroes in America have had a hard time, and that inside stories of Negro life often present unusual and attractive reading matter are incontrovertible facts; but when they enter literary criticism these facts do damage to both the critics and artists.

Yet immediately following this stern admonition, we're told the editors haven't been too concerned to maintain "an even level of literary excellence," because the tradition is defined by both form and content:

> Literature by Negro authors about Negro experience . . . must be considered as significant, not only because of a body of established masterpieces, but also because of the illumination it sheds upon a social reality.

And later, in the introduction to the section entitled "The Novel," the editors elaborate upon this idea by complaining about the relation of revision between *Iola Leroy* (1892) and *Clotel* (1853), a relation of the sort central to Calverton's canon, but here defined most disapprovingly: "There are repetitions of situations from Brown's *Clotel,* something of a forecast of a sort of literary inbreeding which causes Negro writers to be influenced by other Negroes more than should ordinarily be expected." The black canon, for these editors, was that literature which most eloquently refuted white racist stereotypes and which embodied the shared "theme of struggle that is present in so much Negro expression." Theirs, in other words, was a canon that was unified thematically by self-defense against racist literary conventions, and by the expression of what the editors called "strokes of freedom." The formal bond that Calverton had claimed was of no academic or political use to these editors, precisely because they wished to project an integrated canon of American literature. As the editors put it:

> [i]n spite of such unifying bonds as a common rejection of the popular stereotypes and a common "racial" cause, writings by Negroes do not seem to the editors to fall into a unique cultural pattern. Negro writers have adopted the literary traditions that seemed useful for their purposes. . . . While Frederick Douglass brought more personal knowledge and bitterness into his antislavery agitation than William Lloyd Garrison and Theodore Parker, he is much closer to them in spirit and in form than to Phillis Wheatley, his predecessor, and Booker T. Washington, his successor. . . . The bonds of literary tradition seem to be stronger than race.

Form, then, or the community of structure and sensibility, was called upon to reveal the sheer arbitrariness of American "racial" classifications, and their irrelevance to American canon formation. Above all else, these editors sought to expose the essentialism at the center of racialized subdivisions of the American literary tradition. If we recall that this anthology appeared just thirteen years before *Brown v. Board,* we should not be surprised by the "integrationist" thrust of the poetics espoused here. Ideological desire and artistic premise were one. African-American literature, then, was a misnomer; "American literature" written by Negroes more aptly designated this body of writing. So much for a definition of the African-American tradition based on formal relationships of revision, text to text.

At the opposite extreme in black canon formation is the canon defined by Amiri Baraka and Larry Neal in *Black Fire,* published in 1968, an anthology so very familiar to us all. This canon, the blackest canon of all, was defined both by formal innovations and by themes: formally, individual selections tend to aspire to the vernacular or to black music, or to performance; theoretically, each selection reinforces the urge toward black liberation, toward "freedom now" with an up-against-the-wall subtext. The hero, the valorized presence in this volume, is the black vernacular: no longer summoned or invoked through familiar and comfortable rubrics such as "The Spirituals" and "The Blues," but *embodied, assumed, presupposed* in a marvelous act of formal bonding often obscured by the stridency of the political message the anthology meant to announce. Absent completely was a desire to "prove" our common humanity with white people, by demonstrating our power of intellect. One mode of essentialism—"African" essentialism—was used to critique the essentialism implicit in notions of a common or universal American heritage. No, in *Black Fire,* art and act were one.

I have been thinking about these strains in black canon formation because a group of us will be editing still another anthology, which will constitute still another attempt at canon formation: W. W. Norton will be publishing the *Norton Anthology of African-American Literature.* The editing of this anthology has been a great dream of mine for a long time. After a year of readers' reports, market surveys, and draft proposals, Norton has enthusiastically embarked upon the publishing of our anthology.

I think that I am most excited about the fact that we will have at our disposal the means to edit an anthology that will define a canon of African-American literature for instructors and students at any institution which desires to teach a course in African-American literature. Once our anthology is published, no one will ever again be able to use the unavailability of black texts as an excuse not to teach our literature. A well-marked anthology functions in the academy to *create* a tradition, as well as to define and preserve it. A Norton anthology opens up a literary tradition as simply as opening the cover of a carefully edited and ample book.

I am not unaware of the politics and ironies of canon formation. The canon that we define will be "our" canon, one possible set of selections among several possible sets of selections. In part to be as eclectic and as democratically "representative" as possible, most other editors of black anthologies have tried to include as many authors and selections (especially excerpts) as possible, in order to preserve and "resurrect" the tradition. I call this the Sears and Roebuck approach, the "dream book" of black literature.

We have all benefited from this approach to collection. Indeed, many of our authors have managed to survive only because an enterprising editor was determined to marshal as much evidence as she or he could to show that the black literary tradition existed. While we must be deeply appreciative of that approach and its results, our task will be a different one.

Our task will be to bring together the "essential" texts of the canon, the "crucially central" authors, those whom we feel to be indispensable to an understanding of the shape, and shaping, of the tradition. A canon is often represented as the "essence" of the tradition, indeed, as the marrow of tradition: the connection between the texts of the canon is meant to reveal the tradition's inherent, or veiled, logic, its internal rationale.

None of us is naive enough to believe that "the canonical" is self-evident, absolute, or neutral. It is a commonplace of contemporary criticism to say that scholars make canons. But, just as often, writers make canons, too, both by critical revaluation and by reclamation through revision. Keenly aware of this—and, quite frankly, aware of my own biases—I have attempted to bring together a group of scholar-critics whose notions of the black canon might not necessarily agree with my own, or with each others'. I have tried to bring together a diverse array of ideological, methodological, and theoretical perspectives, so that we together might produce an anthology that most fully represents the various definitions of what it means to speak of an African-American literary tradition, and what it means to *teach* that tradition. And while we are at the earliest stages of organization, I can say that my own biases toward canon formation are to stress the formal relationships that obtain among texts in the black tradition—relations of revision, echo, call and response, antiphony, what have you—and to stress the vernacular roots of the tradition. For the vernacular, or oral literature, in our tradition, has a canon of its own.

But my pursuit of this project has required me to negotiate a position between, on the one hand, William Bennett, who claims that black people can have no canon, no masterpieces, and, on the other hand, those on the critical left who wonder why we want to establish the existence of a canon, any canon, in the first place. On the right hand, we face the outraged reactions of those custodians of Western culture who protest that the canon, that transparent decanter of Western values, may become—breathe the word—*politicized*. But the only way to answer the charge of "politics" is with an emphatic *tu quoque*. That people can maintain a straight face while they protest the irruption of politics into something that has always been political from the beginning—well, it says something about how remarkably successful official literary histories have been in presenting themselves as natural and neutral objects, untainted by worldly interests.

I agree with those conservatives who have raised the alarm about our students' ignorance of history. But part of the history we need to teach has to be the history of the idea of the "canon," which involves (though it's hardly exhausted by) the history of literary pedagogy and of the institution of the school. Once we understand how they arose, we no longer see literary canons as *objets trouvés* washed up on the beach of history. And we can begin to appreciate their ever-changing configuration in relation to a distinctive institutional history.

Universal education in this country was justified by the argument that schooling made good citizens, good American citizens; and when American literature started to be taught in our schools, part of the aim was to show what it was to be an American. As Richard Brodhead, a leading scholar of American literature, has observed, "no past lives without cultural mediation.

The past, however worthy, does not survive by its own intrinsic power." One function of "literary history" is, then, to disguise that mediation, to conceal all connections between institutionalized interests and the literature we remember. Pay no attention to the man behind the curtain, booms the Great Oz of literary history.

Cynthia Ozick once chastised feminists by warning that *strategies become institutions*. But isn't that really another way of warning that their strategies, heaven forfend, may *succeed?* Here we approach the scruples of those on the cultural left, who worry about, well, the price of success. "Who's co-opting whom?" might be their slogan. To them, the very idea of the canon is hierarchical, patriarchal, and otherwise politically suspect. They'd like us to disavow it altogether.

But history and its institutions are not just something we study, they're also something we live, and live through. And how effective and how durable our interventions in contemporary cultural politics will be depends upon our ability to mobilize the institutions that buttress and reproduce that culture. The choice isn't between institutions and no institutions. The choice is always: What kind of institutions shall there be? Fearing that our strategies will become institutions, we could seclude ourselves from the real world and keep our hands clean, free from the taint of history. But that is to pay obeisance to the status quo, to the entrenched arsenal of sexual and racial authority, to say that they shouldn't change, become something other, and, let's hope, better than they are now.

Indeed, this is one case where we've got to borrow a leaf from the right, which is exemplarily aware of the role of education in the reproduction of values. We must engage in this sort of canon deformation precisely because Mr. Bennett is correct: the teaching of literature *is* the teaching of values; not inherently, no, but contingently, yes; it is—it has become—the teaching of an aesthetic and political order, in which no women or people of color were ever able to discover the reflection or representation of their images, or hear the resonances of their cultural voices. The return of "the" canon, the high canon of Western masterpieces, represents the return of an order in which my people were the subjugated, the voiceless, the invisible, the unrepresented, and the unrepresentable. Who would return us to that medieval never-never land?

The classic critique of our attempts to reconstitute our own subjectivity, as women, as blacks, etc., is that of Jacques Derrida: "This is the risk. The effect of Law is to build a structure of the subject, and as soon as you say, 'well, the woman is a subject and this subject deserves equal rights,' and so on— then you are caught in the logic of phallocentricism and you have rebuilt the empire of Law." To expressions such as this, made by a critic whose stands on sexism and racism have been exemplary, we must respond that the Western male subject has long been constituted historically for himself and in himself. And, while we readily accept, acknowledge, and partake of the critique of *this* subject as transcendent, to deny us the process of exploring and reclaiming our subjectivity before we critique it is the critical version of the grandfather clause, the double privileging of categories that happen to be preconstituted. Such a position leaves us nowhere, invisible and voiceless in the republic of Western letters. Consider the irony: precisely when we (and other Third World peoples) obtain the complex wherewithal to define our black subjectivity in the republic of Western letters, our theoretical colleagues declare that there ain't no such thing as a subject, so why should we be bothered with that? In this way, those of us in feminist criticism or African-American criticism who are engaged in the necessary work of canon deformation and reformation confront the skepticism even of those who are allies on other fronts, over this matter of the death of the subject and our own discursive subjectivity.

So far I've been talking about social identity and political agency as if they were logically connected. I think they are. And that has a lot to do with what I think the task of the critic today must be.

Simone de Beauvoir wrote that one is not born a woman; no, and one is not born a Negro; but then, as Donna Haraway has pointed out, one isn't even born an organism. Lord knows that black art has been attacked for well over a century as being "not universal," though no one ever says quite what this might mean. If this means an attack against *self-identification,* then I must confess that I am opposed to "universality." This line of argument is an echo from the political right. As Allan Bloom wrote:

> . . . [T]he substantial human contact, indifferent to race, soul to soul, that prevails in all other aspects of student life simply does not usually exist between the two races. There are exceptions, perfectly integrated black students, but they are rare and in a difficult position. I do not believe this somber situation is the fault of the white students who are rather straightforward in such matters and frequently embarrassingly eager to prove their liberal credentials in the one area where Americans are especially sensitive to a history of past injustice. . . . Thus, just at the moment when everyone else has become "a person," blacks have become blacks. . . . "They stick together" was a phrase once used by the prejudiced, by this or that distinctive group, but it has become true by and large of the black students.

Self-identification proves a condition for agency, for social change. And to benefit from such collective agency, we need to construct ourselves, just as the nation was constructed, just as the class was, just as *all* the furniture in the social universe was. It's Utopian to think we can now disavow our social identities; there's not another one to take its place. You can't opt out of a Form of Life. We can't become one of those bodiless vapor trails of sentience portrayed on that "Star Trek" episode, though often it seems as if the universalists want us to be just that. You can't opt out of history. History may be a nightmare, as Joyce suggested, but it's time to stop pinching ourselves.

But there's a treacherous non sequitur here, from "socially constructed" to essentially unreal. I suppose there's a lurking positivism in the sentiment, in which social facts are unreal compared to putatively biological ones. We go from "constructed" to "unstable," which is one non sequitur; or to "changeable by will," which is a bigger problem still, since the "will" is yet another construction.

And theory is conducive to these slippages, however illegitimate, because of the real ascendancy of the paradigm of dismantlement. Reversals don't work, we're told; dismantle the scheme of difference altogether. And I don't deny the importance, on the level of theory, of the project; it's important to remember that "race" is *only* a sociopolitical category, nothing more. At the same time—in terms of its practical performative force—that doesn't help me when I'm trying to get a taxi on the corner of 125th and Lenox Avenue. ("Please sir, it's only a metaphor.")

Maybe the most important thing here is the tension between the imperatives of agency and the rhetoric of dismantlement. An example: Foucault says, and let's take him at his word, that the "homosexual" as life form was invented sometime in the mid-nineteenth century. Now, if there's no such thing as a homosexual, then homophobia, at least as directed toward people rather than acts, loses its rationale. But you can't respond to the discrimination against gay people by saying, "I'm sorry, I don't exist; you've got the wrong guy." The simple historical fact is, Stonewall was necessary, concerted action was necessary to take action against the very structures that, as it were, called the homosexual into being, that subjected certain people to this imaginary identity. To reverse Audre Lorde, *only* the master's tools will ever dismantle the master's house.

Let me be specific. Those of us working in my own tradition confront the hegemony of the Western tradition, generally, and of the larger American tradition, specifically, as we set about theorizing about our tradition, and engaging in attempts at canon formation. Long after white American literature has been anthologized and canonized, and recanonized, our attempts to define a black American canon, foregrounded on its own against a white backdrop, are often decried as racist, separatist, nationalist, or "essentialist." Attempts to derive theories about our literary tradition from the black tradition—a tradition, I might add, that must include black vernacular forms as well as written literary forms—are often greeted by our colleagues in traditional literature departments as misguided attempts to secede from a union which only recently, and with considerable kicking and screaming, has been forged. What is *wrong* with you people, our friends ask us in genuine passion and concern; after all, aren't we all just citizens of literature here?

Well, yes and no. It is clear that every black American text must confess to a complex ancestry, one high and low (literary and vernacular), but also one white and black. There can be no doubt that white texts inform and influence black texts (and vice versa), so that a thoroughly integrated canon of American literature is not only politically sound, it is *intellectually* sound as well. But the attempts of scholars such as Arnold Rampersad, Houston Baker, M. H. Washington, Nellie McKay, and others to define a black American canon, and to pursue literary interpretation from within this canon, are not meant to refute the soundness of these gestures of integration. Rather, it is a question of perspective, a question of emphasis. Just as we can and must cite a black text within the larger American tradition, we can and must cite it within its own tradition, a tradition not defined by a pseudoscience of racial biology, or a mystically shared essence called blackness, but by the repetition and revision of shared themes, topoi, and tropes, a process that binds the signal texts of the black tradition into a canon just as surely as separate links bind together into a chain. It is no more, or less, essentialist to make this claim than it is to claim the existence of French, English, German, Russian, or American literature—as long as we proceed inductively, from the texts to the theory. For nationalism has always been the dwarf in the critical, canonical chess machine. For anyone to deny us the right to engage in attempts to constitute ourselves as discursive subjects is for them to engage in the double privileging of categories that happen to be preconstituted.

In our attempts at canon formation we are demanding a return to history in a manner scarcely conceived of by the new historicists. Nor can we opt out of our own private histories, which Houston Baker calls the African-American autobiographical moment, and which I call the autocritography. Let me end, as I began, with an anecdote, one that I had forgotten for so long until just the other day.

Recently at Cornell, I was listening to Hortense Spillers, the great black feminist critic, read her important essay, "Mama's Baby, Papa's Maybe." Her delivery, as usual, was flawless, compelling, inimitable. And although I had read this essay as a manuscript, I had never before felt—or heard—the following lines:

The African-American male has been touched, therefore, by the *mother,* handled by her in ways that he cannot escape, and in ways that the white American male is allowed to temporize by a fatherly reprieve. This human and historic development—the text that has been inscribed on the benighted heart of the continent—takes us to the center of an inexorable difference in the depths of American women's community: the African-American woman, the mother, the daughter, becomes historically the powerful and shadowy evocation of a cultural synthesis long evaporated—the law of the Mother—only and precisely because legal enslavement removed the African-American male not so much from sight as from *mimetic* view as a partner in the prevailing social fiction of the Father's name, the Father's law.

Therefore, the female, in this order of things, breaks in upon the imagination with a forcefulness that marks both a denial and an "illegitimacy." Because of this peculiar American denial, the black American male embodies the *only* American community of males which has had the specific occasion to learn *who* the female is within itself, the infant child who bears the life against the could-be fateful gamble, against the odds of pulverization and murder, including her own. It is the heritage of the *mother* that the African-American male must regain as an aspect of his own person-hood—the power of "yes" to the "female" within.

How curious a figure—men, black men, gaining their voices through the black mother. Precisely when some committed feminists or some committed black nationalists would essentialize all "others" out of their critical endeavor, Hortense Spillers rejects that glib and easy solution, calling for a revoicing of the "master's" discourse in the cadences and timbres of the Black Mother's voice.

As I sat there before her, I recalled, to my own astonishment, my own first public performance, when I was a child of four years. My mom attended a small black Methodist Church in Piedmont, West Virginia, just as her mom had done for the past fifty years. I was a fat little kid, a condition that my mom defended as "plump." I remember that I had just been given a brand new gray suit for the occasion, and a black stringy-brim Dobbs hat, so it must have been Easter, because my brother and I always got new hats for Easter, just as my dad and mom did.

At any rate, the day came to deliver my Piece. What is a Piece? A Piece is what people in our church called a religious recitation. I don't know what the folk etymology might be, but I think it reflects the belief that each of the fragments of our praise songs, taken together, amounts to a Master Text. And each of us, during a religious program, was called upon to say our Piece. Mine, if you can believe it, was "Jesus was a boy like me, and like Him I want to be." That was it—I was only four. So, after weeks of practice in elocution, hair pressed and greased down, shirt starched and pants pressed, I was ready to give my Piece.

I remember skipping along to the church with all the other kids, driving everyone crazy, saying over and over, "Jesus was a boy like me, and like Him I want to be." "Will you shut up!" my friends demanded. Just jealous, I thought. They probably don't even know their Pieces.

Finally, we made it to the church, and it was packed—bulging and glistening with black people, eager to hear Pieces, despite the fact that they had heard all of the Pieces already, year after year, bits and fragments of a repeated Master Text.

Because I was the youngest child on the program, I was the first to go. Miss Sarah Russell (whom we called Sister Holy Ghost—behind her back, of course) started the program with a prayer, then asked if little Skippy Gates would step forward. I did so.

And then the worst happened: I completely forgot the words of my Piece. Standing there, pressed and starched, just as clean as I could be, in front of just about everybody in our part of town, I could not for the life of me remember one word of that Piece.

After standing there I don't know how long, struck dumb and captivated by all of those staring eyes, I heard a voice from near the back of the church proclaim, "Jesus was a boy like me, and like Him I want to be."

And my mother, having arisen to find my voice, smoothed her dress and sat down again. The congregation's applause lasted as long as its laughter as I crawled back to my seat.

For me, I realized as Hortense Spillers spoke, much of my scholarly and critical work has been an attempt to learn how to speak in the strong, compelling cadences of my mother's voice. To reform core curricula, to account for the comparable eloquence of the African, the Asian, and the Middle Eastern traditions, is to begin to prepare our students for their roles as citizens of a world culture, educated through a truly human notion of "the humanities," rather than—as Bennett and Bloom would have it—as guardians at the last frontier outpost of white male Western culture, the Keepers of the Master's Pieces. And for us as scholar-critics, learning to speak in the voice of the black female is perhaps the ultimate challenge of producing a discourse of the critical Other.

SOURCE: Henry Louis Gates, Jr., *Loose Canons: Notes on the Culture Wars* (New York: Oxford University Press, 1992).

INTRODUCTION, "TELL ME, SIR, . . . WHAT *IS* 'BLACK' LITERATURE?"

IN MEMORY OF JAMES A. SNEAD

. . . even today, it seems to me (possibly because I am black) very dangerous to model one's opposition to the arbitrary definition, the imposed ordeal, merely on the example supplied by one's oppressor.

The object of one's hatred is never, alas, conveniently outside but is seated in one's lap, stirring in one's bowels and dictating the beat of one's heart. And if one does not know this, one risks becoming an imitation—and, there-fore, a continuation—of principles one imagines oneself to despise.

—JAMES BALDWIN, "HERE BE DRAGONS"

FOR THOSE OF us who were students or professors of African or African American literature in the late sixties or through the seventies, it is a thing of wonder to behold the various ways in which our specialties and the works we explicate and teach have moved, if not exactly from the margins to the center of the profession of literature, at least from defensive postures to a po-sition of generally accepted validity. My own graduate students often greet with polite skepticism an anecdote I draw on in the introduction to my sem-inars. When I was a student at the University of Cambridge, Wole Soyinka, recently released from a two-year confinement in a Nigerian prison, was on campus to deliver a lecture series on African literature (collected and pub-lished by Cambridge in 1976 under the title *Myth, Literature, and the African World*). Soyinka had come to Cambridge in 1973 from Ghana, where he had been living in exile, ostensibly to assume a two-year lectureship in the fac-ulty of English. To his astonishment, as he told me in our first supervision, the faculty of English apparently did not recognize African literature as a le-gitimate area of study within the "English" tripos, so he had been forced to accept an appointment in social anthropology, of all things! (Much later, the distinguished Nigerian literary scholar Emmanuel Obiechina related a similar tale when I asked him why he had taken his Cambridge doctorate in social anthropology.) Shortly after I heard Soyinka's story, I asked the tutor in English at Clare College, Cambridge, why Soyinka had been treated this way, explaining as politely as I could that I would very much like to write a doctoral thesis on "black literature." To which the tutor replied with great disdain, "Tell me, sir, . . . what *is* black literature?" When I responded with a veritable bibliography of texts written by authors who were black, his evident irritation informed me that I had taken as a serious request for information what he had intended as a rhetorical question. Few, if any, students or scholars of African or African American literature encounter the sort of hostility, skepticism, or suspicion that Soyinka, Obiechina, and I did at the University of Cambridge. (To be perfectly fair, I should add that I was later able to find professors who, confessing their ignorance of my topic, were quite willing to allow me to work with them and to write the PhD thesis I chose. The faculty of English there is even trying to fund a chair in "Commonwealth literature.") At Oxford, meanwhile, a scholar of African American literature is to deliver the Clarendon Lectures in the spring of 1992. At Oxford, Cambridge, Sussex, Birmingham, and Kent—to list just a few institutions—sophisticated and innovative work in "postcolonial" literary criticism is defining this branch of study. Many of the younger scholars in the field are accepting teaching positions in Africa, India, Pakistan, and throughout the "Third World," attempting to wrestle control of pedagogy and scholarship from older conservative scholars, who are still under the spell of F. R. Leavis (whose influence on "Third World" literary pedagogy merits several doctoral dissertations) and who still believe in the possibility of a "pretheoretical" practical criticism.

In the United States, the status of black literatures within the academy has changed even more dramatically. Since 1985, according to the *MLA Job Information Lists,* few departments of English, for example, have not engaged in, or will not continue to engage in, searches for junior and senior professors of African American, African, or postcolonial literatures. Because of the sharp increase in demand, along with the scarcity of PhDs in these fields, scholars of African American literature commonly find themselves pursued by several departments competing to make imaginative job offers—especially at institutions that confuse the inclusion of black studies with affirmative action. Although nonminority job seekers in this area sometimes encounter difficulties reaching, or surviving, interviews at the MLA convention (if their ethnic identities have not been ascertained beforehand, often by phone calls to their referees), several of the major scholar-critics of African American and African literature are white. (Last year, I wrote *forty-nine* letters of recommendation for one talented white job candidate in African literature; all forty-nine applications were unsuccessful.) Despite such exceptional instances, however, African American and African literatures have never been more widely taught or analyzed in the academy than they are today. We have come a long way since the early twenties, when Charles Eaton Burch (1891–1941), as chairman of the department of English at Howard, introduced into the curriculum a course entitled Poetry and Prose of Negro Life, and a long way, too, from the middle thirties, when James Weldon Johnson, then the Adam K. Spence Professor of Creative Literature and Writing at Fisk University, became the first scholar to teach black literature at a white institution, New York University, where he delivered an annual lecture series on "Negro literature."

These larger changes, however, have yet to reach the high schools. As Arthur N. Applebee reports, Shakespeare, Steinbeck, Dickens, and Twain are the most frequently required authors, even in public schools with the highest proportion of minority students. In public schools overall, only Lorraine Hansberry and Richard Wright appear among the top fifty authors required in English classes between grades 7 and 12. In urban schools, they rank twenty-fifth and thirty-seventh. In schools with a fifty percent or higher minority enrollment, they rank only fourteenth and seventeenth(16). (Wright's *Black Boy,* in contrast, is among the three books most frequently banned from public schools.) These figures are still more surprising when we recall the extraordinarily large sales of the novels of Toni Morrison, Alice Walker, and Gloria Naylor. Clearly the opening of the canon in traditional university literature departments has not yet affected the pedagogical practices of high school teachers.

What has happened within the profession of literature at the college level to elevate the status of African American and other "minority" texts within the past decade and a half? It is difficult to be certain about the reasons for the heightened popularity of any area of study. Nevertheless, we can isolate several factors that, in retrospect, seem to bear directly both on the growth of student interest in these fields—an interest that has never been greater, if we can judge from the proliferation of titles being produced and the high sales figures—and on the vast increase in the number of teachers attempting to satisfy student demand.

One factor would seem to be the women's movement within African American and African literature. Since 1970, when Toni Morrison published *The Bluest Eye,* Alice Walker published *The Third Life of Granger Copeland,* and Toni Cade Bambara published her anthology, *The Black Woman,* black women writers have produced a remarkable number of novels and books of poetry. Morrison alone has published five novels, Walker four, and Gloria Naylor three. The list of black women writers with first and second novels is a very long one. Walker, Morrison, Naylor, and, in poetry, Rita Dove have won Pulitzer Prizes and National and American Book Awards; before 1970, Ralph Ellison and Gwendolyn Brooks were the only black writers who had been accorded these honors. The works by black women novelists, especially Walker and Morrison, are selling in record-breaking numbers, in part because of an expanded market that includes white and black feminists as well as the general black studies readership. What has happened, clearly, is that the feminist movement, in the form of women's studies on campus and the abandonment of quotas for the admission of women to heretofore elite male institutions, has had a direct impact on what we might think of as black women's studies. Indeed, black studies and women's studies have met on the common terrain of black women's studies, ensuring a larger audience for black women authors than ever before.

Scholars of women's studies have accepted the work and lives of black women as their subject matter in a manner unprecedented in the American academy. Perhaps only the Anglo-American abolitionist movement was as cosmopolitan as the women's movement has been in its concern for the literature of blacks. Certainly, Richard Wright, Ralph Ellison, and James Baldwin did not become the subjects of essays, reviews, books, and dissertations as quickly as Morrison and Walker have. Hurston, of course, attracted her largest following only after 1975, precisely when other black women authors rose to prominence. The women's studies movement in the academy has given new life to African American studies, broadly conceived. Forecasts of the death of African American studies abounded in 1975. Although the field had benefited from a great burst of interest in the late sixties, when student protests on its behalf were at their noisiest, it had begun to stagnate by the mid-seventies, as many ill-conceived, politically overt programs collapsed or were relegated to an even more marginal status than they had been before. American publishers, ever sensitive to their own predictions about market size, became reluctant to publish works in this field. Toni Morrison, however, herself an editor at Random House, continued to publish texts by black women and men, from Africa, the Caribbean, and the United States. The burgeoning sales of books by black women, for many of whom Morrison served as editor, began to reverse the trends that by 1975 had jeopardized the survival of black studies. Morrison's own novels, especially *Tar Baby* (1981), which led to a cover story in *Newsweek,* were pivotal in redefining the market for books in black studies. The popularity of—and the controversy surrounding—Michele Wallace's *Black Macho and the Myth of the Superwoman* (1978) and Ntozake Shange's *For Coloured Girls Who Have Considered Suicide* (1977) also generated a great amount of interest in the writings of black women.

Simultaneously, within the academy, scholars of black literature were undertaking important projects that would bear directly on the direction of their field. Whereas in the late sixties, when black studies formally entered the curriculum, history had been the predominant subject, a decade later, literary studies had become the "glamor" area of black studies. While the black arts movement of the mid-sixties had declared literature, and especially poetry, to be the cultural wing of the black power revolution, it had little effect on the curricula offered by traditional departments of English. As Kimberly Benston aptly characterizes the import of this movement, "the profound reorientation of energy and vision which took place among Afro-American thinkers, writers, performers, and their audiences during this period, centering on considerations of a nationalist, or *sui generis,* understanding of the 'black self,' took place through dynamic and complex *disputations* about the provenance, nature, and teleology of the sign of blackness." More than any other single factor, the black arts movement gave birth to the larger black studies movement, even if it did not have a direct impact on traditional university literature departments. This intervention would be dependent on the studies produced by a group of younger scholars—Donald Gibson, June Jordan, Houston Baker, Robert Stepto, Arnold Rampersad, Geneva Smitherman, Jerry Ward, Mary Helen Washington, Kimberly Benston, Addison Gayle, Werner Sollors, Stephen Henderson, Sherley Ann Williams, Carolyn Fowler, and others— many of whom had been trained by an older generation of African Americanists. That generation included such literary critics as Charles Davis, Charles Nilon, Michael Cooke, Charles Nichols, Richard Barksdale, Blyden Jackson, Darwin Turner, and J. Saunders Redding, many of whom had been recruited to previously segregated schools in response to student demands for the creation of black studies, as well as Arthur P. Davis, Hugh Gloster, Sterling Brown and others who remained at historically black colleges.

For a variety of reasons, and in a remarkable variety of ways, these scholars began to theorize about the nature and function of black literature and its criticism and, simultaneously, to train an even younger generation of students. While it is difficult, precisely, to characterize their concerns, it seems safe to say that they shared a concern with the "literariness" of African American works, as they wrestled to make these texts a "proper" object of analysis within traditional departments of English. Whereas black literature had generally been taught and analyzed through an interdisciplinary methodology, in which sociology and history (and, for African literature, anthropology) had virtually blocked out the "literariness" of the black text, these scholars, after 1975, began to argue for the explication of the formal properties of the writing. If the "blackness" of a text was to be found anywhere, they argued, it would be in the practical uses of language. So, at a time when theorists of European and Anglo-American literature were offering critiques of Anglo-American formalism, scholars of black literature, responding to the history of their own discipline, found it "radical" to teach formal methods of reading.

Of the several gestures that were of great importance to this movement, I can mention only three here. In chronological order, these are Dexter Fisher's *Minority Language and Literature* (1977), Dexter Fisher and Robert Stepto's *Afro-American Literature: The Reconstruction of Instruction* (1979), and Leslie Fiedler and Houston A. Baker, Jr.'s *Opening Up the Canon: Selected Papers from the English Institute, 1979* (1981). Conveniently, for my argument here, each of these anthologies, the published results of seminal conferences, expresses a different aspect of a larger movement.

The first two collections grew out of conferences sponsored by the Modern Language Association, while the third was sponsored by the English Institute. "In an effort to address the critical, philosophical, pedagogical, and curricular issues surrounding the teaching of minority literature," Dexter Fisher explains in her introduction to *Minority Language and Literature*, the MLA in 1972 formed the Commission on Minority Groups and the Study of Language and Literature. (Until the early seventies, black scholars did not find the MLA a welcoming institution; they formed instead the predominantly black College Language Association, which still thrives today. The commission's establishment was an attempt, in part, to redefine the MLA sufficiently to "open up" its membership to black and other minority professors.) Beginning in 1974, the commission, funded by the NEH, sponsored various colloquiums "to stimulate greater awareness and to encourage more equitable representation of minority literature in the mainstream of literary studies"(8). Fisher's book stemmed directly from a conference held in 1976, at which forty-four scholars, publishers, and foundation program officers came together to consider "the relationship of minority literature to the mainstream of American literary tradition":

> One of the major issues raised repeatedly at Commission-sponsored meetings is the relationship of minority literature to the mainstream of American literary tradition. The question of the "place" of minority literature in American literature raises a deeper, and perhaps more controversial, question: "In what ways does minority literature share the values and assumptions of the dominant culture, and in what ways does it express divergent perspectives?" This question has implications not only for curriculum development and critical theory, but also, and even more important, for the role of the humanities in bringing about a truly plural system of education.(9)

The conference's participants, including J. Lee Greene, Mary Helen Washington, Michael G. Cooke, Michael Harper, Geneva Smitherman, and Houston A. Baker, Jr., each a specialist in African American literature, explored the relations between "principles of criticism" and social contexts. As Fisher puts it nicely:

> The emergence of the Black Aesthetics Movement in the 1960s focused attention on the dilemma faced by minority writers trying to reconcile cultural dualism. Willingly or otherwise, minority writers inherit certain tenets of Western civilization through American society, though they often live alienated from that society. At the same time, they may write out of a cultural and linguistic tradition that sharply departs from the mainstream. Not only does this present constant social, political, and literary choices to minority writers, but it also challenges certain aesthetic principles of evaluation for the critic. When the cultural gap between writer and critic is too great, new critical approaches are needed.(11)

Above all else, the conference was concerned with "revising the canon of American literature," a matter that Fiedler and Baker would explore in even broader terms three years later at the English Institute.

In the same year that Fisher's volume appeared, she and Robert Stepto, a professor of English, American, and Afro-American studies at Yale, again with NEH funding, convened a two-week seminar at Yale entitled Afro-American Literature: From Critical Approach to Course Design. The five seminar leaders—Fisher, Stepto, Robert O'Meally, Sherley Anne Williams, and I—defined its purpose as "the reconstruction of instruction": "in this case," as Fisher and Stepto put it, "to design courses in, and to refine critical approaches to, Afro-American literature yielding a 'literary' understanding of the literature" (vii). The "literary," Stepto explains, is contrasted with the "sociological," the "ideological, etc." Noting that "many schools still do not teach Afro-American literature, while other institutions offering courses in the field seem to be caught in a lockstep of stale critical and pedagogical ideas, many of which are tattered hand-me-downs from disciplines other than literature" (1), Stepto and his colleagues, with all the zeal of reformers, sought to redefine African American literary study by introducing into its explication formalist and structuralist methods of reading and by providing a critique of the essentialism of black aesthetic criticism that had grown out of the black arts movement. These scholars were intent on defining a canon of both African American literature and its attendant formal critical practices.

As bold and as controversial as the Fisher-Stepto volume was within African American literary studies, the volume edited by Fiedler and Baker was perhaps even more daring, since it sought to explode the notion that English was, somehow, or could ever be, somehow, a neutral container for "world literature." Indeed, the institute's theme in 1979 was English as a World Language for Literature. The volume, featuring papers by Dennis Brutus and Edward Kamau Braithwaite on South African and Caribbean literature, respectively, carries a succinct yet seminal introduction by Baker that suggests something of the polemics generated by the notion that English might be anything but the most fertile and flexible language available to any writer for the fullest expression of literary sensibility. Baker's laconic remarks, made just a decade ago, suggest the heated responses of the institute's audience to the participants' critique of the "neocolonialism" of traditional English studies and to Baker's observations that "the conception of English as a 'world language' is rooted in Western economic history" and that we must juxtapose "the economic ascendancy of English and the historical correlation between this academy and processes of modern thought." English literature, Baker concludes, is not what it appears to be:

> The fact that a Sotho writer claims that he has chosen English because it guarantees a wide audience and ensures access to the literary reproduction systems of a world market may be less important as a literary consideration than what the writer has actually made of the English language as a literary agency. One might want to ask, for example, what summits of experience inaccessible to occupants of the heartland have been incorporated into the world of English literature? What literary strategies have been employed by the Sotho writer to preserve and communicate culturally-specific meanings? What codes of analysis and evaluation must be articulated in order to render accurate explanations for a Sotho or a Tewa or a Yoruba literary work written in English?(xiii)

These foundational volumes proved to be, each in its own way, enabling gestures for the growth of sophisticated theories and critical practices in African, Caribbean, and African American literatures. In the past decade, scores of books and hundreds of essays, reflecting structuralist, poststructuralist, gay, lesbian, Marxist, and feminist theories and practices, have been devoted to the study of black literature. Even the essentialism of race itself, long thought to be a sacrosanct concept within African American studies, has been extensively analyzed as a social construction rather than a thing. The black women's literary renaissance has found counterparts in Africa and the Caribbean. Since 1970 alone, fifty-six novels by black women have been published in the Caribbean. One scholar even declared recently that we are living in the age of the greatest African American novelist (Morrison), therefore the critical endeavor in black literary studies has a certain immediacy not found in other English studies. Derek Walcott's achievements in poetry and Soyinka's in the drama have had a similar effect on the study of Caribbean and African literature. That this generation of critics lives contemporaneously with the first black Nobel laureate is only one sign, albeit a large one, of the vibrancy and youth of the field today.

When the MLA's Executive Council and *PMLA*'s Editorial Board decided to introduce "special topics" into *PMLA*'s format, the unanimous choice for the first issue was African and African American literature. Despite the great activity in the field, the journal had published only three essays in this area. And despite the large number of sessions devoted to such topics at the annual convention, membership in the African, black American, and ethnic divisions remained surprisingly low. While the black American division had grown by a remarkable 93.3% between 1985 and 1987, there were still only 319 members. We hoped that our announcement of this special topic would attract new members in these divisions.

We were not to be disappointed. Since 1987, when the first advertisement for this special topic appeared, memberships in the three divisions have grown dramatically (I am grateful to David Cloyce Smith, of the MLA, for compiling the statistics):

	Change in Membership, %	
Division	**1985–87**	**1987–89**
African	+ 3.3	+39.4
Black American	+ 93.3[a]	+88.7
Ethnic	− 1.9	+30.4
Total MLA	+ 3.7	+11.7

[a]The black American division owes its initial increase in part to its newness; it was created in 1982. By 1987, however, enrollments had slowed. While the increase for 1985–86 was 48%, the increase for 1986–87 was only 30%.

The essays submitted reflected a variety of topics, including the following:

• African and Caribbean literature: Buchi Emecheta, Sembene Ousmane, Olaudah Equiano, Jacques Romain, Ngugi wa Thiongo, Aimé Césaire, Mongo Beti, Jose Luandino Vieira, Wole Soyinka, Francisco Jose Tenreiro, *mariage force* in francophone African theater, Orisa principle and African literary aesthetics

- Nineteenth-century African American: Frederick Douglass, slave narratives, Paul Laurence Dunbar
- Twentieth-century African American: James Baldwin, Ralph Ellison, Langston Hughes, Zora Neale Hurston, Gayl Jones, Martin Luther King, Jr., Nella Larsen, Paule Marshall, Toni Morrison, Ishmael Reed, Ntozake Shange, Melvin Tolson, Jean Toomer, Alice Walker, Richard Wright, Harlem Renaissance
- Performance/Music: blues, francophone African theater, jazz
- Theory: African American deconstruction, Africanist discourse, language theory, literary history, neocolonialism, Yoruba Ifa divination

This range of subjects suggests something of the breadth of work being undertaken in black studies today.

And what is the current state of the field? While one can be encouraged by the important institutional interventions that are serving to integrate African and African American literature into traditional literature departments and by the several editorial ventures that are making "lost" black texts available once again and generating sophisticated reference works and anthologies, black authors are still not well represented in many college curricula. (It is one of the paradoxes of pedagogic reform that the newfound prominence of black literature is still primarily a phenomenon of elite institutions.) Moreover, a large percentage of those who teach this literature are black, and such black scholars are themselves a diminishing presence in the profession. (In 1986, according to the National Research Council, blacks earned only seventy PhDs in all the humanities.) Thus we must conclude that the growth of the field within the academy depends in part on increasing the number of minority students in our graduate programs. The keen competition among literature departments for talented job candidates is based on scarcity; it is incumbent on the members of the MLA to develop viable recruitment mechanisms that will continue to diversify our graduate student population.

What, finally, has the experience of reading over a hundred submissions to this special issue revealed about the concerns of Africanists and African Americanists? Virtually no one, it seems clear, believes that the texts written by black authors cohere into a tradition because the authors share certain innate characteristics. Opposing the essentialism of European "universality" with a black essentialism—an approach that in various ways characterized a large component of black literary criticism since the black arts movement—has given way to more subtle questions. What is following the critique of the essentialist notions that cloaked the text in a mantle of "blackness," replete with the accretions of all sorts of sociological clichés, is a "postformal" resituation of texts, accounting for the social dynamism of subjection, incorporation, and marginalization in relation to the cultural dominant.

Black literature, recent critics seem to be saying, can no longer simply name "the margin." Close readings, of the sort gathered in this issue, are increasingly naming the specificity of black texts, revealing the depth and range of cultural details far beyond the economic exploitation of blacks by whites. This increased focus on the specificity of the text has enabled us to begin to chart the patterns of repetition and revision among texts by black authors. In *Notes of a Native Son* James Baldwin described his own obsession with "race" in his fiction: "I have not written about being a Negro at such length because I expect that to be my only subject, but only because it was the gate I had to unlock before I could hope to write about anything else" (8). One must *learn* to be "black" in this society, precisely because "blackness" is a socially produced category. Accordingly, many black authors read and revise one another, address similar themes, and repeat the cultural and linguistic codes of a common symbolic geography. For these reasons, we can think of them as forming literary traditions.

Richard Wright once argued, polemically, that if white racism did not exist, then black literature would not exist, and he predicted the demise of the latter with the cessation of the former. It is difficult to deny that certain elements of African American culture are the products of crosscultural encounters with white racism. But black culture, these close readings reveal, is a self-enclosed mythos, also existing apart from the social dynamism of white racism. While it is important to criticize nativistic essentialism, in doing so we can lose sight of the larger social dynamic, the things that make people come together into groups in the first place. Developments in African American studies have helped to reveal the factitious nature of an "American" identity; that which had been systematically excluded has now been revoiced as a mainstream concern.

We might think of the development of African American criticism over the past two decades in four distinct stages, beginning with the black arts movement of the mid and late sixties. The black arts movement, whose leading theoreticians were Amiri Baraka and Larry Neal, was a reaction against the New Criticism's formalism. The readings these critics advanced were broadly cultural and richly contextualized; they aimed to be "holistic" and based formal literature firmly on black urban vernacular, expressive culture. Art was a fundamental part of "the people"; "art for art's sake" was seen to be a concept alien to a "pan-African" sensibility, a sensibility that was whole, organic, and, of course, quite ahistorical. What was identified as European or Western essentialism—masked under the rubric of "universality"—was attacked by asserting an oppositional black or "neo-African" essentialism. In place of formalist notions about art, these critics promoted a poetics rooted in a social realism, indeed, on a sort of mimeticism; the relation between black art and black life was a direct one.

In response to what we might think of as the social organicism of the black arts movement, a formalist organicism emerged in the mid-seventies. This movement was concerned with redirecting the critic's attention toward the "literariness" of the black texts as autotelic artifacts, to their status as "acts of language" first and foremost. The use of formalist and structuralist theories and modes of reading characterized the criticism of this period. The formalists saw their work as a "corrective" to the social realism of the black arts critics.

In the third stage, critics of black literature began to retheorize social— and textual—boundaries. Drawing on poststructuralist theory as well as deriving theories from black expressive, vernacular culture, these critics were able to escape both the social organicism of the black arts movement and the formalist organicism of the "reconstructionists." Their work might be characterized as a "new black aesthetic" movement, though it problematizes the categories of both the "black" and the "aesthetic." An initial phase of theorizing has given way to the generation of close readings that attend to the "social text" as well. These critics use close readings to reveal cultural contradictions and the social aspects of literature, the larger dynamics of subjection and incorporation through which the subject is produced.

This aspect of contemporary African American literary studies is related directly to recent changes in critical approaches to American studies generally. Black studies has functioned as a strategic site for autocritique within American studies itself. No longer, for example, are the concepts of "black" and "white" thought to be preconstituted; rather, they are mutually constitutive and socially produced. The theoretical work of feminist critics of African and African American literature, moreover, has turned away from a naively additive notion of sexism and racism. Especially in this work, we have come to understand that critiques of "essentialism" are inadequate to explain the complex social dynamism of marginalized cultures.

WORKS CITED

Applebee, Arthur N. *A Study of Book-Length Works Taught in High School English Courses.* Albany: Center for the Learning and Teaching of Literature, 1989.

Baldwin, James. "Here Be Dragons." *The Price of the Ticket: Collected Nonfiction, 1948–1985*. New York: St. Martin's, 1985. 677–90.

——. *Notes of a Native Son*. Boston: Beacon, 1955.

Benston, Kimberly. Letter to the author. 16 Sept. 1989.

Fiedler, Leslie, and Houston A. Baker, Jr., eds. *English Literature: Opening Up the Canon; Selected Papers from the English Institute, 1979*. Baltimore: Johns Hopkins UP, 1981.

Fisher, Dexter, ed. *Minority Language and Literature: Retrospective and Perspective*. New York: MLA, 1977.

Fisher, Dexter, and Robert Stepto, eds. *Afro-American Literature: The Reconstruction of Instruction*. New York: MLA, 1979.

SOURCE: Henry Louis Gates, Jr., *PMLA*, Vol. 105, No. 1, Special Topic: African and African American Literature (January 1990).

PREFACE TO THE SECOND EDITION, *THE NORTON ANTHOLOGY OF AFRICAN AMERICAN LITERATURE*

With Nellie Y. McKay

In the fall of 1986, eleven scholars gathered on the campus of Cornell University to discuss the need for a *Norton Anthology of African American Literature* and to consider how best to execute the mammoth task of editing such a historic anthology, should we collectively decide to embark upon it. These scholars, chosen for their leadership in the field, represented a wide array of methodological approaches to the study of literature; each had a particular expertise in at least one historical period in the African American literary tradition. We were accompanied in our deliberations by M. H. Abrams, the "father" of Norton Anthologies, and John Benedict, vice president and editor at Norton, both of whom had championed our project during its two-year gestation period from proposal to approval.

Two things struck us all, we think it fair to say, about our discussions. First was a certain sense of history-in-the-making, in which we were participating by the act of editing this anthology. While anthologies of African American literature had been published at least since 1845, ours would be the first Norton Anthology, and Norton—along with just a few other publishers—had become synonymous to our generation with canon formation. Because of its scope and size, a Norton Anthology could serve as "a course in a book," as John Benedict was fond of saying. So, in spite of the existence of dozens of anthologies of black literature—a tradition of which we were keenly aware since we had closely studied the tables of contents and editorial introductions of each of these and photocopied and bound them for each of our prospective editors—none was ample enough to include between two covers the range of the texts necessary to satisfy the requirements of an entire survey course. To meet this need was our goal.

This was crucial if we were going to make the canon of African American literature as readily accessible to teachers and students as were, say, the canons of American or English literature. Too often, we had heard colleagues complain that they *would* teach African American literature "if only the texts were available" in a form affordable to their students, meaning in a one- or two-volume anthology, rather than in a half dozen or more individual volumes. Were we successful in our endeavor, we believed, then not only could teachers teach African American literature, but they would do so eagerly, and new courses would be created in four- and two-year institutions and at the high school level. A well-edited, affordable anthology democratizes access. And broader access was essential for the permanent institutionalization of the black literary tradition within departments of English, American Studies, and African American Studies.

The second surprise of our Ithaca meeting was how "un-theoretical" the process of editing would be. Many of us were deeply engaged in the passionate theoretical debates that would define "the canon wars," as they came to be called. It soon became apparent to us that editing an anthology is not primarily a process concerned with *theorizing* canon formation; rather, it is about *forming* a canon itself. If we were successful, we would be canon-makers, not canon-breakers. Our theories about the canon, no matter how intricately woven, were not as important as the actual practice of agreeing upon the periodization of African American literature published (principally in English) in England and the United States between 1746 and the present and then selecting the signal texts in the tradition that comprise its canon.

Ironically, we were embarking upon a process of canon formation precisely when many of our poststructuralist colleagues were questioning the value of a canon itself. Our argument was that the scholars of our literary tradition needed first to *construct* a canon before it could be deconstructed! And while the scores of anthologies of African American literature published since 1845 had each, in a way, made claims to canon formation, few, if any, had been widely embraced in the college curriculum. And that process of adoption for use in college courses is a necessary aspect of canon formation.

So, setting aside our individual passions for theorizing, we collectively got down to the nuts and bolts of editorial policymaking, addressing fundamental questions such as how many pages to devote to each period, where those periods should start and stop, and what principles of selection would lead us to the gathering of works that were essential both in the formation of our tradition and to its teaching and explication. Though readily available elsewhere, certain core texts, such as Frederick Douglass's 1845 slave narrative, we agreed, must be included, since our goal was to respond to our Norton editor's challenge to produce "a course in a book." Our task, then, was not primarily to bring lost or obscure texts back into print; rather, it was to make available in one representative anthology the major texts in the tradition and to construct a canon inductively, text by text, period by period, rather than deductively—that is, rather than through *a priori* ideological or thematic principles agreed upon in advance, which would function like a straitjacket for our selections. Further, through carefully edited introductions and headnotes, we wanted to help students see how these texts "speak to," or signify upon, each other, just as they had "spoken" to each other across time, space, and genre, as authors read and revised each other's representations of the experiences, feelings, and beliefs of persons of African descent pondering the ironies of being at once black, American, and human. We wanted the anthology to give full voice to the key tropes and topoi that repeat—are echoed and riffed and signified upon—so strikingly across the African American literary tradition, thereby allowing formal linkages to be foregrounded in the classroom. Most importantly, we agreed that each period editor would have the final say about the texts selected for her or his period. A full decade would follow our organizational meeting in Ithaca, but in 1997, the first edition of *The Norton Anthology of African American Literature* was born.

To our surprise, the anthology was widely reviewed in both trade and academic publications, commencing with a major feature in *The New York Times*. Perhaps even more surprising, the trade edition was purchased in great numbers by nonacademics, often members of the growing African American reading public, hungry for texts about themselves. Within the academy, 1,275 colleges and universities worldwide have adopted the anthology since publication in 1997. The first anthology to allow the oral tradition to "speak" for itself through the music and spoken-word performances on the Audio Companion CD, *The Norton Anthology of African American Literature* has proved popular with students and a helpful teaching tool to instructors. This innovation, now imitated by others, enabled us to make an important statement about the crucial role of the vernacular in shaping our written tradition.

We have attempted to reconstruct the African American literary heritage, at the turn of the twenty-first century, without pretending to completeness. Limitations of space and prohibitions on copyright have prevented us from including several authors whose texts are important to the canon and whose level of excellence warrants inclusion here. Despite these limitations, we believe that we have represented justly the African American literary tradition by reprinting many of its most historically important and aesthetically sophisticated works. The authors of these works (whose birth dates range from 1730 to 1969) have made the text of Western letters speak in voices and timbres resonant, resplendent, and variously "black." Taken together, they form a literary tradition in which African American authors collectively affirm that the will to power is the will to write and to testify eloquently in aesthetic forms never far removed from the language of music and the rhythmic resonance of the spoken word.

SOURCE: Henry Louis Gates, Jr., and Nellie Y. McKay, eds., *The Norton Anthology of African American Literature* (New York: W. W. Norton, 1996).

CANON CONFIDENTIAL

A Sam Slade Caper

HER NAME WAS Estelle. I should have known the broad spelled trouble when she came into my office and started talking about the canon. The literary canon.

I stubbed out my Lucky Strike and glanced up at her, taking in her brass-blond hair, all curled and stiff with spray. Like she had a still of Betty Grable taped to the corner of her mirror.

Turned out she'd been peddling her story for the past couple of years. Nobody would take it on; I shouldn't have either. But when I was a kid I used to write doggerel. Maybe that's why I didn't throw the babe out of my office.

"Tell me what I need to know, sugar." I splashed some bourbon in my coffee mug, put my feet on my desk and listened.

Seemed there was some kind of a setup that determined which authors get on this A list of great literature. Payout was all perks, so far as I could make out. If you're on this list, they teach your work in school and write critical essays on you. Waldenbooks moved you from the Fiction section to the Literature section. I couldn't figure where the percentage was, unless some big shot was getting a cut of the reprint royalties, but she didn't think that was it.

"So what are you saying? You want me to shut down this operation? Round up the bad guys?" "Nothing like that," she said huskily. "I got no beef with the canon as such. It serves a legit purpose." She looked around nervously and lowered her voice. "What I'm telling you is, it's fixed. It's not on the level." She paused. "What I'm telling you is, this is the biggest scam since the 1919 World Series."

I whistled softly. "We're talking thousands of books, right? The jewels of Western culture, right?"

She nodded. "You'll be going up against the big boys. Does that scare you?" I patted my shoulder holster. "I'm prepared." "You get 25 a day plus expenses," she said.

I said, "Fair enough." (It was all Philip Marlowe got in "Trouble Is My Business.") The first person I spoke to was Helen Vendler, and all she was sure of was I was wasting my time.

I found her at the Harvard Club, on 44th Street off Fifth Avenue, eating alone. She swore up and down I was being snookered.

"Oh, I hear the talk. But it's just a tabloid fantasy," she assured me, fastidiously squeezing a lemon section over her oysters. "There is no overlord, Slade. Nobody's fixing what we read—the whole idea's preposterous. If a book's good, people read it. If it's bad, people won't." She was smug about it. Too smug. "They've got something on you, don't they?" I said, thinking hard. "That's why they let you edit 'The Harvard Book of Contemporary American Poetry'—because they knew you'd do their dirty work for them."

She wasn't smiling anymore. "You won't get a thing out of me," she said. Then I saw her make eye contact with the bouncer. All 300 pounds of him. "Malloy," she said quietly, "get him out of here." Figured a walk would do me good anyway. I looked up a few of the writers I knew, but I didn't fare much better. It was like somebody had gotten to them first. Harold Brodkey told me he'd like to talk about it, only he'd grown too fond of his kneecaps. Toni Morrison was hiding out in South Nyack. And Cynthia Ozick slammed her front door on my thumb.

I was making the rounds at Columbia when a black Cadillac with tinted windows pulled up alongside me on Broadway at 115th Street. Two pugs came out and threw me in the back seat like a sack of potatoes.

"Let me be blunt, Mr. Slade. Do you know what happens to people who stick their noses into other people's business?"

On my left, Elizabeth Hardwick. On my right, one of her gorillas. I turned to the lady. "I seen 'Chinatown,'" I murmured. "A good film," she said. "But not a great one. The great ones are those taught in film classes, in universities around the country. For example, anything by Eisenstein." "I saw one of his films once. Bored me stiff." "As it does avid film students around the world. But that, my friend, is how canonization works. All the films you'd never see if it were just up to you, all the books you'd never read if you really had a choice—they are the very lifeblood of the canon." "You're losing me, Lizzy." "Come, come. The 19th-century American novels that go on for hundreds of mind-numbing pages about cetaceans. The endless Russian novels about theodicy, suffering and salvation, with an unpronounceable cast of thousands. Where would they be without the required reading list?" "Out of print?" I hazarded. "You see why we can't let you continue, then." She patted my knee consolingly. "There's simply too much at stake."

The car probably wasn't going much more than 20 miles an hour when they threw me out.

Fact was, I didn't much like being manhandled by literary mandarins. But now I had a pretty good hunch about where to look next. I caught up with Alfred Kazin in the New York Public Library; I figured he had to know something. Maybe he did, but when I mentioned the canon, he turned nasty. "Beat it," he growled. "I've got nothing to say to you." I grabbed him by the collar, lifted him a few inches off the floor and brought his face real close to mine. "Are we having a communication problem?"

"Please," he murmured, his head lolling against Edmund Wilson's "Letters on Literature and Politics." "You know I don't make the decisions."

"I've heard that tune more often than Pachelbel's Canon. Don't sweet-talk me, punk. Who's in on it?" His eyes glinted. "Look, it's an institutional configuration. It's societal. Everybody's in on it."

"Oh, get off it," I snapped. "Try telling that to the gals who never made it into the great American procession. Try telling that to Phillis Wheatley. Or Zora Neale Hurston. Or Charlotte Perkins Gilman." I poked him in the chest. "You guys really did a job on them. Kept them out in the cold."

"You still mad about that?" He rolled his eyes. "Hell, we made it up to them. Everybody's reading those broads today. Take a look at any freshman syllabus; they're practically compulsory." He mopped the sweat off his brow. "Look, better late than never, right?"

"That's not the point and you know it. Now tell me who supplies you."

His eyes darted around the stacks, and then he loosened up. That's when I knew something was wrong. "I believe the person you want is right behind you," he smirked. Something hard jabbed into my back. I turned around slowly, my hands held high. It was Jacques Barzun, a .38 Beretta resting comfortably in one hand. He was in black tie, looking like he'd just stepped out of a cocktail party.

"Big surprise," I said, trying to look more relaxed than I was. "Shoulda figured this one out myself." "There are a great many things you should have figured out, Mr. Slade." "Yeah? Gimme a for instance." "Standards, Mr. Slade. Do you know what standards are?" His menacing smile was perfect—probably practiced it in front of a mirror.

"No culture without norms, Mr. Slade. It's an elementary principle. History gives us no reason for optimism about the triumph of civilization over barbarity. Where we do not move forward, we regress. To be sure, it begins with slight lapses. Errors of usage—confusing 'disinterest' with 'uninterest,' using 'hopefully' for 'it is to be hoped.' And then, with astonishing swiftness, the rot sets in. With our sense of language dulled, who can appreciate the exquisite verbal precision of the very finest literature? We cease to judge, we join the relativist's party of mindless tolerance, we descend into the torpor of cultural egalitarianism." "Sounds ugly," I said. "It is." "Even so," I said levelly, "you wouldn't shoot me." "Wouldn't I?" He raised an eyebrow.

"You don't have a silencer," I pointed out, "and the sign says to be quiet in the library." I knew I had him there. There was one more lead I had to check out. Word on the street had it that a certain Harold Bloom was deeply involved in the whole business. He was a critic who taught at Yale and moonlighted at City College. I figured the time might be right to pay him a visit. I didn't talk conspiracy with him. Just said people around town thought he knew a lot about canon formation. Maybe even had something to do with it himself.

Bloom folded his hands together under his chin. "My dear, the strong poet will abide. The weak will not. All else is commentary. Politics has nothing to do with it." Something else was bothering me, and I decided to be up-front. "I noticed the cops paid you a visit before I came by. What'd they want?"

"I'm a suspect, if you can believe it." He looked at me wide-eyed. "Somebody killed off Thomas Stearns Eliot, and they think I had something to do with it. Imagine that. Little old me." Then he grinned, and I saw he could be a very dangerous man.

So Tommy was dead. That should have cheered me up, but it didn't. From a pay phone on the corner, I made a quick call to an old friend in the N.Y.P.D. Turned out Bloom had a rap sheet longer than a three-part New Yorker profile. They were after him for a whole series of murders, from Matthew Arnold to Robert Lowell. All of them savaged with bloody dispatch, often in a paragraph or less. So far, they couldn't pin anything on him.

The police were biding their time. Seems they had a decoy all set up. A young policewoman who wrote poetry in the style of Sylvia Plath, working undercover at *The New York Review of Books*. But that wasn't going to do me any good. Bloom was a small fish. I was angling for the biggest one of all.

Problem was, I was banging my head against a brick wall and it wasn't for sure which was going to give first. I didn't like to call in debts, but I couldn't put it off any longer. It was time to look up my old friend Jason Epstein. These days he was a big cheese at Random House, but I knew him back when he was a gumshoe at Pinkerton's.

When he showed up at the Royalton on West 44th Street, I could tell something was wrong. They had gotten to him. "You too, Jason?" It hurt; I couldn't hide that. "Just tell me why. What's in it for you?"

In reply, he dropped a book on my lap that made the Manhattan phone directory look like a pocket diary. "It's called 'The Reader's Catalog,'" he said, "and it's my baby. It lists every book worth reading." I was beginning to understand. He wouldn't meet my eyes. "Look, Slade, I can't afford to make up the 'Catalog' from scratch every week. We're talking stability. Critics talk about the literary canon, publishers talk about the importance of a strong backlist, but it comes to the same."

With the help of two waiters, I lifted "The Reader's Catalog" back onto the table. I thought about all the lives that had been ruined to make it possible. I thought about the most respected writers of our time acting like citizens of the Town That Dreaded Sundown. "You've got to give me a name, Jason," I said. There was anger in my voice; fear, too. I didn't care what they'd done to him, didn't care about the things he'd done. I just had to reach him somehow.

Jason didn't say anything for a long while, just watched the ice cubes dissolve in his Aqua Libra.

"I'm taking a big risk just being seen with you," he said, massaging his temples. But in the end, he came through. So that's what I was doing at 10 o'clock in the morning, my trench coat hunched over my head, tailing Susan Sontag down the rainy streets. Epstein told me she was scheduled to make a pickup that morning. If so, she'd lead me where I wanted to go.

My confidence was growing, and I didn't think twice when she strode under the 38th Street overpass on the East Side. Vandals had knocked out most of the lights. The darkness protected me, but I had a hard time making her out in the gloom.

Then somebody laid a blackjack to the back of my head and the lights went out completely.

When I came to, my head was throbbing and my eyes didn't want to focus. I made them.

Something told me I'd arrived at my destination. I was seated before an enormous desk, ornately carved with claw-and-ball feet. And an enormous tufted leather chair with its back to me. Slowly, it swiveled around. The old man was small, and the huge chair made him seem tiny. He winked at me. "Who are you?" I said. It came out like a croak. "It's not important," he said blandly. "The organization is what's important."

"Organization?" I was dimly aware of the floor vibrating beneath my feet. Meant we were probably in a factory of some sort.

"The literary canon—now that ain't chopped liver. Could be you don't understand how big this thing is. We've got people all over, wouldn't work otherwise. We've got the daily reviewers, we've got the head of the teachers' union. . . ." "Al Shanker? He's with you?" He seemed amused by my naivete. "We've got people in the teachers' training colleges. We got the literature profs at your colleges, they're all in on it. The guys who edit the anthologies—Norton, Oxford, you name it—they all work for us. Ever hear about the Trilateral Commission?" "Something to do with international trade?" His cheeks dimpled when he smiled. "That's the front. It's really about the literary canon. The usual hustle: we'll read Lady Murasaki if they let in James and Emerson. It's a tricky business, though, when you get into fair-trade issues. We got reports that the English are dumping. Some of our guys wanted to use the farm parity system for Anthony Burgess—you know, pay him not to write novels." He rolled his eyes. "Never works. They tried it over here with Joyce Carol Oates. She just sold the overage under a bunch of pseudonyms." I tried to cluck sympathetically, but it caught in my throat. "Sooner or later they'll come to me," he said. "And I'll take care of it, like I always do." "Sounds like a lot of responsibility." "You see why my boys didn't appreciate your sniffing around. There's too much at stake. You gotta play by the rules." He spread his brown-spotted hands on the desk. "Our rules."

"Who would've thought it? Literary immortality a protection racket."

He mouthed his cigar obscenely. "Come off it, kid. There's no immortality in this business. You want 20 years, even 40, we can arrange it. Beyond that, we'll have to renegotiate terms at the end of the period. Sooner or later there's going to be a, whaddaya call it, a reassessment. We send a guy down, he does an appraisal, figures the reputation's not really earned, and bingo, you're out. Maybe you'll get a call back in 50 years or so. Maybe not."

I shook my head. "You guys play hardball." I laughed, but I was scared. "You see what we did with James Gould Cozzens?" "Who?"

"Exactly. And 30 years ago, he was the hottest thing around. Then somebody got a little greedy, figured they could cut their own deal. . . . " The old man laughed, showed teeth like little yellow nubbins. "Something I want you to see."

He led me out of his office and onto an inside balcony overlooking a vast industrial atrium. I heard the din of machinery, felt the blast of hot factory air. And I saw the automatic conveyor belt below. At first I thought it was a moving slag heap, but it wasn't. All at once I felt sick and dizzy.

Heaped high on the conveyor belt, thousands and thousands of books were being fed into a belching, grinding mechanical maw. Turned into pulp. I could only make out some of the titles. There were fat novels by James Jones and Erskine Caldwell and Thomas Wolfe and James T. Farrell and Pearl Buck. Thin novels by Nelson Algren and William Saroyan. The old Brooks and Warren "Understanding Poetry" nestled beside the collected plays of Clifford Odets. I tried to look away, but my eyes were held by a sick fascination. "Butterfield 8" and "The Big Sky," "Young Lonigan" and "Manhattan

Transfer," "Darkness at Noon" and "On the Road"—the literary has-beens of our age, together at last, blended into a high-fiber gruel. The old man led me back into his office and closed the door. "Beginning to get the picture? You want to take care you don't end up on that pile, Mr. Slade." He squeezed my shoulder and said, "Of course there might be another way." I shook my head. "You're going to have to kill me," I said. He opened the left-hand drawer of his desk, removed a dogeared copy of a journal. "My boys came up with something interesting. It was in The Dalhousie Review, Spring 1947." He looked triumphant. "A sestina called 'Cadences of Flight.' Makes you a published poet yourself, doesn't it?"

"Jeepers," I said. My face was hot with embarrassment. "I was in high school."

That's when he made his proposal. I know, Dwight Macdonald said that people who sell out never really had anything to sell, but what did I care? Turned out Dwight was on their payroll from the beginning. Listening to the sound of untold literary tonnage being pulped, I had to admit there were worse things than being co-opted.

When I got to my apartment, I dialed Estelle's number and told her she might as well come over. She was at my door in a quarter of an hour, wearing a long gray trench coat with a belt, as heavily made-up as ever.

"Estelle," I said, "I'm off the case." I peeled $25 off my billfold. "You can have your money back."

"They turned you, didn't they?" she said, scarlet suffusing her beige pancake foundation.

I looked at her wistfully. The gal had spunk, and I admired that. I felt a sudden rush of warmth toward her. All these years of kicking around the city alone—maybe it was time to settle down with somebody. Sure, her cocka-mamie assignment had turned my life upside down, but right then her body looked inviting to my tired eyes. Maybe it was fate that brought us together, I was thinking. Maybe. I said, "Lookit, everyone's got a price." "Yeah? What was yours?"

"I'm in, sugar," I blurted. "You understand what I'm saying? They're going to put 'Cadences of Flight' in 'The Norton Anthology of Poetry,' fourth edition. It's gonna be deconstructed, reconstructed and historicized in PMLA. And there's going to be a couple of questions about it on the New York State Regents exam in English. It was a take-it-or-leave-it proposition, baby. How could I say no?" "You were going to blow the whistle on the whole outfit." "And they were going to feed me into a paper mill. Sometimes you don't know what's in your best interest till someone points it out to you." The look she gave me was smoldering, and not with passion. "But

Estelle"—and I gazed into her eyes soulfully—"I been thinking maybe we have the rest of our lives together for explanations."

Estelle stared at me for what seemed like a long time. Then she worked her fingers into her hair and started working it free. It was a wig. The eyelashes went next, then she ran a towel under the tap and scrubbed off her makeup. She fished out the stuffed brassiere last of all.

The transformation was astonishing. Before me stood a perfectly ordinary-looking man in his early 50's, his dark hair beginning to gray. I began to shake. "You're—you're. . . . " "Thomas Pynchon," he said in a baritone. Pulled off the white gloves and extended a meaty paw.

Thomas Pynchon. Now there was someone you never saw on "Oprah Winfrey."

My mind wanted to reel, but I pulled it in sharp. "So that's why you sent me on this mission impossible." "I knew you'd never take the case if you knew who I was." Mists were clearing. "Damn right I wouldn't. Being a famous recluse wasn't good enough for you. It was anonymity you were after. You didn't care if you had to bring down the whole system of dispensation to get it." I paused for breath. "I've got it right, haven't I? That's why you set me up, with this despicable Estelle act." Pynchon only shrugged. "So," I said, "you wanted out." The words came out through gritted teeth: "Out of the canon."

"Can you blame a guy for trying?" he asked, and walked out of my life.

Alone in my apartment, I poured myself a couple of fingers of Jack Daniel's and tried to make room on my shelves for the critical essays and Ph.D. dissertations about me they said would come flooding in. I was going to be explicated, which was good. I was going to be deconstructed, which wasn't so good. It was a tough job, being a canonical author.

But somebody had to do it.

SOURCE: *The New York Times Book Review*, March 25, 1990.

PART IV

"RACE," WRITING, AND READING

THE LAST SELECTION in this section, on the great Harlem Renaissance writer and innovator, Jean Toomer, was co-authored by Rudolph Byrd, a prominent scholar of African American literature and Gates's classmate at Yale, who died while we were putting this reader together. Much of what Gates and Byrd, along with other bright lights like Kimberly Benston and Barbara Johnson, learned in Yale's Deconstructionist heyday wasn't remote from what they would teach their undergraduate and graduate students (including me) a decade later: that race could be—and should be—unmoored from the fixed meanings attributed to it by our culture's binary thinking, that constructed significance trumped innate meaning, and that "scare quotes" around "race" could suggest the term's contingency and also the critic's own distance from a notion that was, in fact, a very real and inescapable fact of daily life. Hence, this section begins with Soyinka, whose masterwork dramatizes the very real difference race makes in the practice of power, and concludes with Toomer, whose own passing sheds light both on how race lives in literature and how we live with race.

One selection here deserves a special note. We have included the introduction to *The Image of the Black in Western Art*, the ten-book series based on the archive of nearly 30,000 images of black people in Western art, from classical Greece and Rome to the twenty-first century, of which Gates is a co-editor. The chief reason for its inclusion here—aside from its philosophical connection to the other pieces—is its debt to Dominique de Menil, who with her husband established this archive as a liberal humanist means to beat back racism in their adopted South. The seminal *Critical Inquiry* volume, *"Race," Writing, and Difference*, also excerpted in this section, is dedicated to de Menil. By placing the two pieces next to each other, we see that the spirit of the type of critical reading that dominated the academy in the 1980s is very much alive and in practice today, even if the writing has changed.

Abby Wolf

BEING, THE WILL, AND
THE SEMANTICS OF DEATH

Wole Soyinka's *Death and the King's Horseman*

> *Who would fardels bear,*
> *To grunt and sweat under a weary life,*
> *But that the dread of something after death,*
> *The undiscover'd country, from whose bourn*
> *No traveller returns, puzzles the will,*
> *And makes us rather bear those ills we have,*
> *Than fly to others we know not of?*
> *Thus conscience does make cowards of us all,*
> *And thus the native hue of resolution*
> *Is sicklied o'er with the pale cast of thought,*
> *And enterprises of great pitch and moment*
> *With this regard their currents turn awry,*
> *And lose the name of action.*

> —*Hamlet*, Act III, Scene I

NOT SINCE THE civil war in the Congo has a black African nation been so much in the consciousness of the United States as Nigeria is today. Perhaps it is not accidental that Wole Soyinka's play *Death and the King's Horseman* enjoyed its American premiere in October 1979, at Chicago's Goodman Theater, in the same week in which Nigeria transformed itself to a representative republic, becoming overnight, after thirteen years of military dictatorship, Africa's largest and most prosperous democracy.

Soyinka's public career as a writer dovetails somewhat ironically with modern Africa's anguished struggle for independence from colonial rule and

197

for a democratically elected government. Indeed, his fourth and most elaborate play, *A Dance of the Forests,* performed nineteen years ago at Nigeria's
Independence Day festivities, announced his presence as a major creative
writer. Yet, even then, the discordant relationship of Soyinka's art to his nation's image of itself was distinctly evident: the production was staged despite
its rejection by the Independence Day committee, rejected no doubt because
of its implicit refutation of a linear, naive, romantic idea of time and human
progress. Ironically, the play subsequently won the Encounter Drama Competition sponsored by London's *Observer.*

It is difficult to find exact analogues in the West for Soyinka's public role
in Nigeria and throughout Africa. Author of over a dozen plays, two novels,
and three books of poetry, he is perhaps the most widely read African writer,
both within and outside of Africa. In addition to this respect from African and
European audiences alike, Soyinka is also perceived as a force in the political
arena, embodying in a discreet way the moral authority of a disinterested
philosopher with the political authority of the *Times* of London's editorial
page. As an author he draws upon this public definition of his role—most recently as Secretary-General of the Union of African writers—both to protest
censorship and imprisonment of writers, especially by African and Latin
American governments, and to keep alive the dream of a unified Pan-African
continent governed by the democratic socialism he holds most dear. He has
no counterpart here: he is neither poet-turned-politician like Leopold Senghor, Aime Cesaire, or the late Augustino Neto; nor is he the artist-in-exile, demanding the mythical return to a federal never-never land, like Pound and
Solzhenitsyn; nor, finally is he, like the mutable Amiri Baraka, artist-become-
ideologue, determined to diminish that precious distance which irrevocably
separates art and shadow from act. On the contrary, Soyinka's stature as an
artist depends in part on his remarkable ability to avoid confusing art and
politics; never is he reductive, nor does he attempt to mirror reality in a
simple one-to-one relationship. He is a profoundly political writer in that
most subtle sense, in which Euripides was, or Lorca. Perhaps it is fair to say
that his most admirable characteristic as a writer and activist is the compelling
manner in which his art and his political acts have always assumed their
unique form—separate somehow, but equal.

Born in 1934 to a middle-class Nigerian family, Akinwande Oluwole
Soyinka was educated at University College at Ibadan and at the University
of Leeds, where he studied with G. Wilson Knight, the virtual dean of
Shakespeare critics, and with Arnold Kettle, a major practitioner of Marxist
criticism. As a Reader to London's Royal Court Theatre from 1957 to 1959,
he produced his one-act play, *The Invention,* a few months after two of his
plays, *The Lion and the Jewel* and *The Swamp Dwellers,* were first performed in

a "Soyinka Festival" at University College. A series of stunning artistic successes, commencing with the production of his play on Independence Day in 1960, seemed to guarantee for him an international reputation comparable to that of his fellow Nigerian, Chinua Achebe. As Penelope Gilliatt described his poetic diction in a review of *The Road* in the *Observer* in 1965, "Soyinka has done for our napping language what brigand dramatists from Ireland have done for centuries: booted it awake, rifled its pockets and scattered the loot into the middle of next week."[1] But it was precisely his status as a writer that compelled him to become the dark and foreboding voice for a certain moral order, much to the annoyance of various Nigerian governments. Soyinka has eschewed the familiar role of spokesman against colonialism and racism for the more difficult and politically dangerous role of spokesman against those forms of tyranny which black people practice against each other. "I knew from childhood," Soyinka says, "that independence in my country was inevitable. Freedom, I felt, should be as normal as breathing or eating, and I was interested then in what kind of society we were going to have. When I saw what was happening, I found it difficult to be silent to the point of criminality."[2]

Less than a month after *The Road* took first prize in London's 1965 Commonwealth Festival, Soyinka was imprisoned. On October 15, following the dubious elections in what was then Western Nigeria, the purported victor, Chief Akintola, taped a speech in which he announced that his party had officially won the elections. "What happened then," said the *Times* of London, "could variously be regarded as a serious crime or a riotous practical joke. Instead of the voice of Chief Akintola, the public heard a broadcast which began, 'This is the voice of free Nigeria,' and continued, in uncomplimentary terms, to advise Akintola to leave Nigeria, along with his 'crew of renegades.'"[3] Soyinka was incarcerated shortly thereafter. A host of American and British writers, including Lillian Hellman, Robert Lowell, Norman Mailer, Alfred Kazin, Lionel Trilling, William Styron, Norman Podhoretz, and Penelope Gilliatt, wired their protest to the Nigerian government. Not until late December was he released, with all charges dismissed.

He was incarcerated yet again in 1967. This occurred one year after he received the drama prize at the First World Festival of the Negro Arts at Dakar, where one critic called him "the most original man of letters in Africa,"[4] and less than one month after receiving, with Tom Stoppard, the John Whiting Drama Award, Soyinka was picked up for interrogation just outside the gates of Ibadan University shortly after returning from a writers' conference in Sweden. There he had wondered aloud about the African writer who felt he "must, for the moment at least (he persuades himself) postpone that unique reflection on experience and events which is what makes a writer"[5] and substitute a more directly political commitment. Eleven days before being arrested, Soyinka had held a clandestine meeting at Enugu, the capital of Biafra, with the secessionist leader, Lieutenant Colonel Odumegwu Ojukwu, to implore him to reconsider the Ibos' decision to secede from Nigeria.

This time, protests from Western writers would have no effect. For the next twenty-seven months, Soyinka languished in prison, where he spent some ten months in solitary confinement, in constant fear of his life under the most unbearable conditions. His cell measured four feet by eight: "Sixteen paces by twenty-three," as he writes in the prison poem, "Live Burial."[6] A Nigerian military government at war refused hundreds of pleas for Soyinka's release. Deprived of human contact, books, medical care, and writing implements, only the last-minute intervention of nameless informers saved him from murder. On the ninth anniversary of Independence and of his production of *A Dance of the Forests,* the victorious military government announced that Soyinka would be released in a general amnesty.

In his poignant prison notes, published in 1972 as *The Man Died,* Soyinka details the terror of his confinement, the torture and death, "the inhuman assault on the mind."[7] The book, whose name derives from a cable describing the brutal murder of Segun Sowemimo, a Nigerian journalist, for an imagined slight, has been called an African *J'accuse.* Cast in an artistic idiom which few have mastered, it chronicles the starvation of the human spirit, and the poet's struggle to survive through words. When at last he was allowed a few books in prison, including Radin's *Primitive Religion,* he "proceeded to cover the spaces between the lines with [his] own writing."[8] Soyinka survived by writing, secretly and in any matter he could. The only visit allowed his wife was announced with new clothes, haircut, a radio, typewriter, and paper, pen, and pencils, all of which were removed upon her departure. Aware of the coming raid, Soyinka allowed himself to enjoy only the luxury of the typing paper, which he stroked and caressed. Only narrowly did he escape murder; only through an act of enormous will did he remain sane. But Soyinka did not die; rather, he emerged from prison a great writer. As Angus Calder wrote in a review of *The Man Died,* "He seems to have accepted now, more fully even than his limitations let him, the weight of duty which that verdict implies. And I think he is, now, a great writer."[9]

"The Man Dies," Soyinka writes, "in all who keep silent in the face of tyranny."[10] Yet in Soyinka's writing, the protest against tyranny is as subtle as certain forms of tyranny. Just as the Caribbean Marxist, C. L. R. James, had written a full-length study of Melville twenty years earlier during an unlawful internment on Ellis Island, so too had Soyinka displaced his critique of tyranny. The play, *Madmen and Specialists,*[11] was rather a return to his earlier, ritual form. According to Mel Gussow in the *New York Times:*

Because of the genesis of *Madmen,* one might expect a political play, but in solitary confinement Soyinka obviously had more important, timeless concerns on his mind. The theme, as described by the author, is the corrupting effect of power on one's natural vocation. The central figure is a young doctor, a specialist who has given up medicine to become a tyrannical political force. The play is not at all topical and only peripherally political. The symbolic, ritualistic, and especially, the religious are of much interest in Soyinka.[12]

We can begin to understand such a complex artist, who refuses to allow his own horrendous prison experience to intrude in an obvious sense upon his play, by understanding something of his idea of tragedy and the nature of the tragedian. Two statements seem especially meaningful here, one excerpted from "The Fourth Stage," an essay written in honor of G. Wilson Knight and published while Soyinka was in prison,[13] the other a critique of the Western idea of tragedy, which oddly enough appears in *The Man Died.* Soyinka writes in "The Fourth Stage":

Nothing but the will . . . rescues being from annihilation within the abyss. . . . Only one who has himself undergone the experience of disintegration, whose spirit has been tested and whose psychic resources laid under stress by the forces most inimical to individual assertion, only he can understand and be the force of fusion between two contradictions. The resulting sensibility is also the sensibility of the artist, and he is a profound artist only to the degree to which he comprehends and expresses this principle of destruction and recreation.[14]

It is the human will, "the paradoxical truth of destructiveness and creativity in acting man,"[15] with which Soyinka the artist and Soyinka the activist are both concerned: the integrity of the will and a fundamental belief in its capacity to structure and restructure this world in which we live. Along with Gabriel Garcia Marquez and other politically committed writers, he never declaims this notion, nor becomes didactic. His critique of Western definitions of tragedy, along the lines of Brecht, written after his release from prison, and published in *The Man Died,* helps to explain why this is so:

History is too full of failed prometheans bathing their wounded spirits in their tragic stream. Destroy the tragic lure! Tragedy is possible solely because of the limitations of the human spirit. There are levels of despair from which the human spirit should not recover. To plunge to such a level is to be overwhelmed by the debris of all those anti-human barriers which are erected by jealous gods. The power of recovery is close to acquisition of superhuman energies, and the stagnation-loving human society must for self-preserving interest divert these colossal energies into relatively quiescent channels, for they constitute a force which, used as part of an individual's equipment in the normal human struggle, cannot be resisted by the normal human weapons. Thus the historic conspiracy, the literal brain-washing, that elevates tragedy far and above a regenerative continuance of the promethean struggle.[16]

It is this regard for the status of the will in the face of terror, combined with the unqualified rejection of the indulgence of pity, and a belief in the communality of individual struggle, that most characterizes Soyinka's metaphysics.

In response to the adage of Nietzsche's sage, Silenus, that it is an act of hubris to be born, Soyinka responds that "the answer of the Yoruba to this is just as clear: it is no less an act of hubris to die."[17] Not surprisingly, Soyinka's muse is his patron god Ogun, god of creativity and the Yoruba "proto-agonist," he who dared to cross the abyss of transition that separates the world of men from the world of the gods in the primal enactment of individual will.

I first confronted *Death and the King's Horseman* in 1973, two years before it was published. Soyinka, who was supervising my graduate work in English at the University of Cambridge, invited me to listen to the first reading of his new play. For three hours we listened as Oxford accents struggled to bring the metaphorical and lyrical Yoruba text to life. Although by now I had become accustomed to this densely figurative language of Soyinka's plays—indeed had begun to hear its peculiar music—I was stunned by the action of the play. That the plot was an adaptation of an actual historical event was even more stunning. And if the play's structure was classically Greek, the adaptation of a historical action at a royal court was compellingly Shakespearean. This, I thought, was a great tragedy.

Perhaps I should describe in outline the historical events before I recount the plot. In December 1944, Oba Siyenbola Oladigbolu, the Alaafin, or King of Oyo, an ancient Yoruba city in Nigeria, died. He was buried that night. As was the Yoruba tradition, the Horseman of the King, Olokun Esin Jinadu, was to commit ritual suicide and lead his Alaafin's favorite horse and dog through the transitional passage to the world of the ancestors. However, the British Colonial District Officer, Captain J. A. MacKenzie, decided that the custom was savage and intervened in January 1945 to prevent Olokun Esin Jinadu from completing his ritual act, the act for which his entire life had been lived. Faced with the anarchy this unconsummated

ritual would work upon the order of the Yoruba world, Olokun Esin Jinadu's last born son, Murana, in an unprecedented act, assumed his hereditary title of Olokun Esin, stood as surrogate for his father, and sacrificed his
own life. The incident, Soyinka told us following the reading, had intrigued
him ever since he had first heard of it. It had, he continued, already inspired a play in Yoruba by Duro Ladipo called *Oba Waja*.[18]

Soyinka adapted the historical event rather liberally in order to emphasize the metaphorical and mythical dimensions, outside of time, again reflecting implicitly the idea that an event is a sign and that a sign adumbrates
something other than itself by contiguity as well as by semblance. The relation that a fiction bears to reality is fundamentally related to the means by
which that relation and that fiction are represented. For Soyinka, a text me-
diates the distance between art and life, but in a profoundly ambiguous and
metaphorical manner. In that space between the structure of the historical
event and the literary event, that is to say, the somehow necessary or prob-
able event, one begins to understand Soyinka's idea of tragedy. The plot of
a play, certainly, can indicate what may happen as well as what did happen,
and this concern with what a protagonist will probably or necessarily do,
rather than what he did do, distinguishes Soyinka's universal and poetic art
from particular and prosaic Yoruba history. It is this central concern with
the philosophical import of human and black experience which so clearly
makes him unlike many other black writers. A summary of the play's plot
suggests this relation.

The Alaafin of Oyo is dead. To guide the Alaafin's horse through the narrow passage of transition, as tradition demands, the Horseman of the King,
Elesin Oba, must on the night of his King's burial, commit ritual suicide
through the sublime agency of the will. The action of the play occurs on the
day of his death. Death for Elesin is not a final contract; it is rather the rite
of passage to the larger world of the ancestors, a world linked in the continuous bond of Yoruba metaphysics to that of the living and the unborn. It is a
death which the Elesin seems willingly to embrace—but not before he pos-
sesses a beautiful market girl, a betrothed virgin whom he encounters as he
dances his farewell greeting before the ritual marketplace. Though Iyaloja,
the "mother" of the market, protests the Horseman's paradoxical selection,
she consents to and arranges this ritualistic union of life with death.

Revolted by the "barbarity" of the custom, a British Colonial Officer,
Pilkings, intervenes to prevent the death at the precise moment of the
Horseman's intended transition. Notified by his family, Olunde, the Horseman's eldest heir, has returned from medical school in England intending to
bury his father. Confronted with his father's failure of will, the son assumes

this hereditary title only to become his surrogate in death to complete the cosmic restoration of order. In a splendidly poignant climax to the action, the women of the market, led by Iyaloja, unmask the veiled corpse of the son and watch placidly as the Horseman of the King breaks his neck with his chains, fulfilling his covenant with tradition and the communal will, alas, too late. Two men have died rather than one.

As adapted by Soyinka, this is no mere drama of individual vacillation. Communal order and communal will are inextricable elements in the Elesin's tragedy, which not only reflect but amplify his own failure of will. In this sense, Soyinka's drama suggests Greek tragedy much more readily than Elizabethan tragedy, and is akin to the mythopoeic tragedies of Synge and Brecht and to Lorca's *Blood Wedding*. Nor is this merely a fable of the evils of colonialism or of white unblinking racism. *Death and the King's Horseman* is a classical tragedy, in which structure and metaphysics are inextricably intertwined.

Structurally, the play is divided into five acts and occurs almost exactly over twenty-four hours. Its basis is communal and ritualistic; its medium is richly metaphorical poetry which, accompanied continuously by music and dance and mime, creates an air of mystery and wonder. The cumulative effect defines a cosmos comprised at once of nature, of human society, and of the divine. The protagonist's bewilderment and vacillation, his courage and inevitable defeat, signify a crisis, confrontation, and transformation of values, transfixed in a time that oscillates perpetually in an antiphonal moment. Finally, the reversal of the *peripeteia* ("situation") and the *anagnorisis* ("recognition") occur at the same time, as they do in *Oedipus Rex*.

The characterization of Elesin, the protagonist, is also classically Greek. The play records the reciprocal relationship between his character and his fate. Elesin's grand flaw does not stem from vice or depravity, but from *hamartia* ("an error of judgment"), a sign of his weakness of will. Although not eminently good or just, he is loved. His will and his character are neither wholly determined nor wholly free. His character is at once noble and prone to error. The nine-member chorus again and again speaks against Elesin's special hubris, his unregenerate will. His, finally, is the great defeat, but suffered only after the great attempt. The play's action is timeless, as timeless as the child conceived by Elesin on the day of his death. Its plot unfolds in "the seething cauldron of the dark world will and psyche,"[19] where ambiguity and vacillation wreak havoc upon the individual.

Although self-sacrifice is a familiar motif in Soyinka's tragedies, Elesin's intended sacrifice is not meant to suggest the obliteration of an individual soul, but rather is an implicit confirmation of an order in which the self exists with all of its integrity but only as one small part of a larger whole. Elesin Oba, after all, is a conferred title, the importance of which derives from its context within the community and from its ritual function. The Elesin's character is determined in the play, not by any obvious material relationships, however, but rather by the plot itself, as the formal dramatic elements of any tragedy are determined by a silent structuring principle. Great tragic plots always determine the tragic character of their protagonists. To paraphrase Pilkings's servant, Joseph, the Elesin exists simply to die; he has no choice in the matter, despite the play's repeated reference to the ambiguity inherent in his role. And Pilkings's intervention, a kind of self-defense, challenges fundamentally the communal defense of self which this ritual embodies.

Elesin's dilemma is both individual and collective, both social and psychic, all at once. In the same way that Faust's hubristic transgression occurs within his consciousness—occurs, indeed, because of his deification of mind and will—so too is Elesin's tragic dilemma enacted internally, here within his will. As he suggests ominously early in *Death and the King's Horseman,* "My will has outlept the conscious act" (p. 18). His hubris is symbolized by the taking of a bride on the morning of his death in a ritual in which the thanatotic embraces the erotic; he chooses the satisfactions of the self over the exactions of the will. This is his tragic flaw. Elesin's inevitable fall results from a convergence of forces at work within the will and without, which conspire to reinforce those subliminal fears that confront all tragic heroes.

Not only is the Westernized Olunde's suicide a rejection of the relief of the resolution afforded by the Western philosophical tradition; it is also the ritual slaying of the father at the crossroads. Olunde's death leaves his father entrapped, penned outside of the rite of passage, for the fleeting moment of transition has passed, making ironic even an act as final as death. Iyaloja, perhaps the most powerful characterization of a woman in African literature, expresses the paradox: "We said, the dew on earth's surface was for you to wash your feet along the slopes of honor. You said No, I shall step in the vomit of cats and the droppings of mice; I shall fight them for the leftovers of the world" (p. 68). In the face of his son's slaying, the Elesin is poignantly "left-over." There will be no more Elesins, for the unbroken order of this world has now been rent asunder. As Iyaloja remarks acidly, "He is gone at last into the passage but oh, how late it all is. His son will feast on the meat and throw him bones. The passage is clogged with droppings from the King's stallion; he will arrive all stained in dung" (p. 76). To paraphrase the praise singer, the world has finally tilted from its groove (p. 10).

The ritual passage of the Horseman had served for centuries to retrace an invisible cultural circle, thereby reaffirming the order of this Yoruba world.

The ritual dress, the metaphorical language, the Praise-Singer's elegy, the Elesin's dance of death—these remain fundamentally unchanged as memory has recast them from generation to generation. The mixed symbols of semen and blood, implied in the hereditary relationship between succession and authority and reiterated in the deflowering of the virgin on the day of death, stand as signs of a deeper idea of transition and generation. But the role of the Horseman demands not only the acceptance of ambiguity, but also its embrace.

Although Elesin's is an individual dilemma and a failure of the human will, the dilemma is implicit in his role of the King's Horseman, a communal dilemma of preservation of order in the face of change. During the play, at a crucial moment, a traditional proverb is cited which reveals that doubt and ambiguity are not emotions uncharacteristic of the Elesin: "The elder grimly approaches heaven and you ask him to bear your greeting yonder; do you think he makes the journey willingly?" (p. 64). All myth, we know, reconciles two otherwise unreconcilable forces, or tensions, through the mediation of the mythic structure itself. The *Orestia* is a superb example of this. This trick of "structuration," as it were, is the most characteristic aspect of human mythology. Soyinka, in his "Director's Notes," in the *Playbill* of *Death and the King's Horseman* puts the matter this way: "At the heart of the lyric and the dance of transition in Yoruba tragic art, that core of ambivalence is always implanted. This is how society, even on its own, reveals and demonstrates its capacity for change."[20]

We do not need to know, as the Yoruba historian Samuel Johnson tells us, that at one time the reluctance of an Elesin to accompany a dead Alaafin engendered such disgrace that the Horseman's family often strangled him themselves, nor that the reluctance of the Elesins grew as contact with the British increased.[21] We do not need to know these historical facts simply because the Horseman's ambiguity over his choices is rendered apparent throughout Soyinka's text. And from *Hamlet* it is that sense of "conscience" as defined in the epigraph from Hamlet's soliloquy, implying self-consciousness and introspection, which is also the Horseman's fatal flaw—that which colors "the native hue of resolution . . . with the pale cast of thought."[22] As Elesin Oba puts it, in a splendid confession near the end of the play, he commits "the awful treachery of relief," and thinks "the unspeakable blasphemy of seeing the hand of the gods in this alien rupture of his world" (p. 69). This ambiguity of action, reflected in the ambiguity of figurative language and of mythic structure, allows this to remain a flexible metaphysical system. Formal and structured, it remains nonetheless fluid and malleable with a sophisticated and subtle internal logic.

Soyinka embodies perfectly the ambiguity of the Elesin's action in the ambiguity of the play's language. A play, among all the verbal arts, is most obviously an act of language. Soyinka allows the metaphorical and tonal Yoruba language to inform his use of English. Western metaphors for the nature of a metaphor, at least since I. A. Richards, are "vehicle" and "tenor," both of which suggest an action of meaning, a transfer through semantic space. The Yoruba, centuries before Richards, defined metaphor as the "horse" of words: "If a word is lost, a metaphor or proverb is used to find it."[23] As do tenor and vehicle, the horse metaphor implies a transfer or carriage of meaning, through intention and extension. It is just this aspect of the Yoruba language on which Soyinka relies. The extended use of such densely metaphorical utterances, searching for the lost or hidden meanings of words and events, serves to suggest music, dance, and myth, all aspects of *poeisis* long ago fragmented in Western tragic art.

In Soyinka's tragedies, languages and act mesh fundamentally. A superb example of this is the Praise-Singer's speech near the climax of the play, in which he denounces in the voice of his former King, the Elesin Oba:

> Elesin Oba! I call you by that name only this last time. Remember when I said, if you cannot come, tell my horse. What? I cannot hear you, I said, if you cannot come, whisper in the ears of my horse. Is your tongue severed from the roots Elesin? I can hear no response. I said, if there are boulders you cannot climb, mount my horse's back; this spotless black stallion, he'll bring you over them. Elesin Oba, once you had a path to me. My memory fails me but I think you replied: My feet have found the path, Alaafin. I said at the last, if evil hands hold you back, just tell my horse there is weight on the hem of your smock. I dare not wait too long. . . .
>
> . . . Oh my companion, if you had followed when you should, we would not say that the horse preceded its rider. If you had followed when it was time, he would not say the dog has raced beyond and left his master behind. If you had raised your will to cut the thread of life at the summons of the drums, we would not say your mere shadow fell across the gateway and took its owner's place at the banquet. But the hunter, laden with a slain buffalo, stayed to root in the cricket's hole with his toes. What now is left? If there is a dearth of bats, the pigeon must serve us for the offering. Speak the words over your shadow which must now serve in your place. (pp. 74–75)

In this stunning speech, the language of music and the music of language are one. In one sense, the music of the play gives it its force, the reciprocal displacement of the language of music with the music of language.

The antiphonal structure of Greek tragedy is also perhaps the most fundamental African aesthetic value, and is used as the play's internal structuring mechanism. As in music, the use of repetition, such as the *voudoun* ("voodoo") phrase, "Tell my horse," serves to create a simultaneity of action. The transitional passage before which the Elesin falters is inherent in all black musical forms. Soyinka's dances are darkly lyrical, uniting with the music of the drums and songs of the chorus to usher the audience into a self-contained, hermetic world, an effected reality. Soyinka's greatest achievement is just this: the creation of a compelling world through language, in language, and of language. He has mastered the power of language to create a reality, and not merely to reflect reality. But his mastery of spoken language is necessarily reinforced by mastery of a second language of music, and a third of the dance. "Where it is possible to capture through movements what words are saying," he says, "then I will use the movement instead of the words."[24] To evoke these languages, and to evoke the threnodic celebration of the meanings of death and the reciprocity of passage among the past, the present, and that state of being to be, and to escape the naive myths of Africa which persist in this country, Soyinka insists upon directing his tragedies himself, as he did the production at Chicago.

As a critic of silent literary texts, I was struck by the dynamic nature of the Chicago production, ever shifting, ever adapting itself toward an unspoken ideal, in a manner which in short space and time parallels what happens to a text when studied by a critic, but only over a much longer period. Soyinka, of course, knows what he wants a performance to say, and knows what combination of textures will suggest his meaning to an alien audience. Confronting an American audience's usual unease with, or condescension toward, an African setting no doubt reinforced whatever tendencies he had to adhere to a strict rendering of the play.

But is Soyinka's Yoruba world so very obscure? Is it any more obscure than the tribal world of the ancient Greeks, than Joyce's voices in *Ulysses* or the private linguistic circle of *Finnegan's Wake?* Footnotes to *The Waste Land,* topographies to Joyce, concordances to Shakespeare: we presume a familiarity with these texts which is made possible only by the academic industry of annotation. The fact of Soyinka's Africanness only makes visible an estranged relation which always stands between any text and its audience. As Shakespeare used Denmark, as Brecht used Chicago, Soyinka uses the Yoruba world as a setting for cosmic conflict, and never as an argument for the existence of African culture. Always in the language of his texts are ample clues for the decoding of his silent signs, since the relationship among character, setting, and language is always properly reinforcing. This is no mean achievement: it is the successful invocation of a hermetic universe.

It is for this reason that Soyinka is often compared favorably to his direct antecedents, Euripides and Shakespeare, Yeats and Synge, Brecht and Lorca. Statements such as this sound necessarily hyperbolic, no doubt. But it is impossible not to make such comparisons when one searches for a meaningful comparison of Soyinka's craft with Western writers. For so long, black Americans, especially, have had to claim more for our traditions than tact, restraint, and honesty might warrant, precisely to redress those claims that our traditions do not exist. But Soyinka's texts are superbly realized, complex meditations between the European dramatic tradition and the equally splendid Yoruba dramatic tradition. This form of verbal expression, uniquely his own, he uses to address the profoundest matters of human moral order and cosmic will.

What does remain obscure, nevertheless, is something else, a set of matters so much more subtle and profound than mere reference can ever be. And these matters involve an understanding of tragedy seemingly related to, yet fundamentally unlike, that notion of the tragedy of the individual first defined by Aristotle and, in essence, reiterated by Hegel, Nietzsche, and even Brecht. Set against the hubris, hamartia, and violent obliteration of a noble individual is Soyinka's evocation of a tragedy of the community, a tragic sense which turns upon a dialectic between retributive and restorative justice and order. The relation which the individual will bears to this process, the always problematic relation between the order of the community and the self-sacrifice of the protagonist, whose role is defined by his own intuition and will to act, forms the center of Soyinka's plays and of his conception of the role of the artist in society. Soyinka's protagonists are protagonists for the community; they stand as embodiments of the communal will, invested in the protagonist of the community's choice. Even the moment of most distinct individuation must always be a communal moment. He summarizes his own conception of this relationship in his art:

> Morality for the Yoruba is that which creates harmony in the cosmos, and reparation for disjunction within the individual psyche cannot be seen as compensation for the individual accident to that personality. Thus it is that good and evil are not measured in terms of offences against the individual or even the physical community, for . . . offences even against nature may in fact be part of the exaction by deeper nature from humanity of acts which alone can open up the deeper springs of man and bring about a constant rejuvenation of the human spirit. Nature in turn benefits by such broken taboos, just as the cosmos by the demand made upon its will by man's cosmic affronts. Such acts of hubris compel the cosmos to delve deeper into its essence to meet the human challenge. Penance and retribution are not therefore aspects of punishment for

crime but the first acts of a resumed awareness, an invocation of the principle of cosmic adjustment.[25]

It is this disintegration and subsequent retrieval of the protagonist's will which distinguishes Soyinka's tragic vision from its Western antecedents. His understanding of tragedy at long last gives some sense to what is meant by "the functional" and "the collective" in African aesthetics, two otherwise abused and misapprehended notions. Clearly, he reveals, these are relationships effected by the prototypic agonist, the acting individual will. Rightly, we look first to Soyinka's language to begin to understand his direct relation to Shakespeare's mastery of language. And Soyinka's language, always, is his own. Yet, it is this curious metaphysical structure of the tragic which most obviously remains unlike ideas of Western tragedy. Paradoxically, it is "African" certainly, but it is ultimately a Soyinka construct. Soyinka has invented a tragic form, and registered it in his own invented language, a fusion of English and Yoruba. Surely this is his greatest achievement. For, in the end, *Death and the King's Horseman* itself stands as a mythic structure, as a structure of reconciliation. As he concludes about the nature of tragedy:

> Great tragedy is a cleansing process for the health of the community. Tragic theatre is a literal development of ritual. It is necessary for balancing the aesthetic sensibilities of the community. Tragedy is a community event. It is the acting out of the neuroses, the recoveries, within a community. It does not just involve a single individual.[26]

NOTES

1. Penelope Gilliatt, "A Nigerian Original," *Observer,* 19 Sept. 1965, p. 25.

2. Personal interview with Wole Soyinka by Henry Louis Gates, Jr., 7 Oct. 1979.

3. John Mortimer, "Nigeria—Land of Law and Disorder," *Sunday Times,* London, 28 Nov. 1965, p. 5.

4. John Povey, "West African Drama in English," *Comparative Drama,* I, No. 2 (1967), 110.

5. Wole Soyinka, "The Writer in a Modern African State," in *The Writer in Modern Africa,* ed. Per Wasberg (New York: Africana Publishing, 1969), p. 15.

6. Wole Soyinka, "Live Burial," in his *A Shuttle in the Crypt* (London: Rex Collings/Eyre Methuen, 1972), p. 60.

7. Wole Soyinka, *The Man Died: Prison Notes of Wole Soyinka* (London: Rex Collings, 1972), p. 13.

8. Soyinka, *The Man Died,* p. 1.

9. Angus Calder, rev. of *The Man Died, New Statesman,* 8 Dec. 1972, p. 866.

10. Soyinka, *The Man Died,* p. 13.

11. Wole Soyinka, *Madmen and Specialists* (London: Eyre Methuen, 1971).

12. Mel Gussow, "Psychological Play from Nigeria," *New York Times,* 3 Aug. 1979, p. 38.

13. Wole Soyinka, "The Fourth Stage: Through the Mysteries of Ogun to the Origin of Yoruba Tragedy," in *Myth, Literature and the African World* (Cambridge, Eng.: Cambridge Univ. Press, 1976).

14. Soyinka, "The Fourth Stage," p. 150.

15. Soyinka, "The Fourth Stage," p. 150.

16. Soyinka, *The Man Died,* p. 88.

17. Soyinka, "The Fourth Stage," p. 158.

18. Duro Ladipo, *Oba Waja* in *Three Nigerian Plays,* ed. and trans. Ulli Beier (London: Longmans, 1967). Beier's translation captures almost nothing of the lyricism of the Yoruba.

19. Soyinka, "The Fourth Stage," p. 142.

20. Chicago, Goodman Theatre, 1979.

21. Samuel Johnson, *A History of the Yorubas: From the Earliest Times to the Beginning of the British Protectorate,* ed. O. Johnson (London: Routledge & Kegan Paul, 1969).

22. William Shakespeare, *Hamlet,* Act III, Scene I.

23. The Traditional Yoruba reads, "Owe l'esin oro, bi oro ba sonu owe ni a fi n wa a."

24. Personal interview with Wole Soyinka by Henry Louis Gates, Jr., 5 Oct. 1979.

25. Wole Soyinka, "Drama and the Revolutionary Ideal," in *In Person: Achebe, Awoonor, and Soyinka,* ed. Karen L. Morell (Seattle: Institute for Comparative and Foreign Area Studies, 1975), pp. 68–69.

26. Personal interview with Wole Soyinka by Nancy Marder, July 1979.

SOURCE: Henry Louis Gates, Jr., "Being, the Will, and the Semantics of Death." In *Perspectives on Wole Soyinka: Freedom and Complexity,* edited by Biodun Jeyifo (Jackson, MS: University Press of Mississippi, 2001), pp. 62–76.

INTRODUCTION, WRITING "RACE" AND THE DIFFERENCE IT MAKES

The truth is that, with the fading of the Renaissance ideal through progressive stages of specialism, leading to intellectual emptiness, we are left with a potentially suicidal movement among "leaders of the profession," while, at the same time, the profession sprawls, without its old center, in helpless disarray. One quickly cited example is the professional organization, the Modern Language Association. . . . A glance at its thick program for its last meeting shows a massive increase and fragmentation into more than 500 categories! I cite a few examples: . . . "The Trickster Figure in Chicano and Black Literature" . . . Naturally, the progressive trivialization of topics has made these meetings a laughingstock in the national press.

—W. JACKSON BATE, "THE CRISIS IN ENGLISH STUDIES"

Language, for the individual consciousness, lies on the borderline between oneself and the other. The word in language is half someone else's. It becomes "one's own" only when the speaker populates it with his own intention, his own accent, when he appropriates the word, adapting it to his own semantic and expressive intention. Prior to this moment of appropriation, the word does not exist in a neutral and impersonal language (it is not, after all, out of a dictionary that the speaker gets his words!), but rather it exists in other people's mouths, in other people's contexts, serving other people's intentions: it is from there that one must take the word, and make it one's own.

—MIKHAIL BAKHTIN, "DISCOURSE IN THE NOVEL"

They cannot represent themselves, they must be represented.

—KARL MARX, *THE EIGHTEENTH BRUMAIRE OF LOUIS BONAPARTE*

WHAT IMPORTANCE DOES "race" have as a meaningful category in the study of literature and the shaping of critical theory? If we attempt to answer this question by examining the history of Western literature and its criticism, our initial response would probably be "nothing" or, at the very least, "nothing explicitly." Indeed, until the past decade or so, even the most subtle and sensitive literary critics would most likely have argued that, except for aberrant moments in the history of criticism, race has not been brought to bear upon the study of literature in any apparent way. Since T. S. Eliot, after all, the canonical texts of the Western literary tradition have been defined as a more or less closed set of works that somehow speak to, or respond to, "the human condition" and to each other in formal patterns of repetition and revision. And while most critics acknowledge that judgment is not absolute and indeed reflects historically conditioned presuppositions, certain canonical works (the argument runs) do seem to transcend value judgments of the moment, speaking irresistibly to the human condition. The question of the place of texts written by the Other (be that odd metaphorical negation of the European defined as African, Arabic, Chinese, Latin American, Yiddish, or female authors) in the proper study of "literature," "Western literature," or "comparative literature" has, until recently, remained an unasked question, suspended or silenced by a discourse in which the canonical and the noncanonical stand as the ultimate opposition. In much of the thinking about the proper study of literature in this century, race has been an invisible quantity, a persistent yet implicit presence.

This was not always the case, we know. By mid-nineteenth century, "national spirit" and "historical period" had become widely accepted categories within theories of the nature and function of literature which argued that the principal value in a great work of literary art resided in the extent to which these categories were *reflected* in that work of art. Montesquieu's *De l'esprit des lois* considered a culture's formal social institution as the repository of its "guiding spirit," while Giambattista Vico's *Principi di una scienza nuova* read literature against a complex pattern of historical cycles. Friedrich and August von Schlegel managed rather deftly to bring "both national spirit and historical period" to bear upon the interpretation of literature, as W. Jackson Bate has shown. But it was Hippolyte-Adolphe Taine who made the implicit explicit by postulating "race, moment, and milieu" as positivistic criteria through which any work could be read and which, by definition, any work reflected. Taine's *History of English Literature* was the great foundation upon which subsequent nineteenth-century notions of "national literatures" would be constructed.

What Taine called "race" was the source of all structures of feeling and thought: to "track the root of man," he writes, is "to consider the race itself . . .

the structure of his character and mind, his general processes of thought and feeling, . . . the irregularity and revolutions of his conception, which arrest in him the birth of fair dispositions and harmonious forms, the disdain of appearances, the desire for truth, the attachment for bare and abstract ideas, which develop in him conscience, at the expense of all else." In race, Taine concludes, was predetermined "a particularity inseparable from all the motions of his intellect and his heart. Here lie the grand causes, for they are the universal and permanent causes, . . . indestructible, and finally infallibly supreme." "Poetries," as Taine puts it, and all other forms of social expression, "are in fact only the imprints stamped by their seal."[1]

Race, for Taine, was everything: "the first and richest source of these master faculties from which historical events take their rise"; it was a "community of blood and intellect which to this day binds its offshoots together." Lest we misunderstand the *naturally* determining role of race, Taine concludes that it is "no simple spring but a kind of lake, a deep reservoir wherein other springs have, for a multitude of centuries, discharged their several streams."[2]

Taine's originality lay not in his ideas about the nature and role of race but rather in their almost "scientific" application to the history of literature. These ideas about race were received from the Enlightenment, if not from the Renaissance. By 1850, ideas of irresistible racial differences were commonly held. When Abraham Lincoln invited a small group of black leaders to the White House in 1862 to present his ideas about returning all blacks in America to Africa, his argument turned upon these "natural" differences. "You and we are different races," he said. "We have between us a broader difference than exists between any other two races."[3] Since this sense of difference was never to be bridged, Lincoln concluded, the slaves and the ex-slaves should be returned to Africa. The growth of canonical national literatures[4] was coterminous with the shared assumption among intellectuals that race was a "thing," an ineffaceable quantity, which irresistibly determined the shape and contour of thought and feeling as surely as it did the shape and contour of human anatomy.

How did the pronounced concern for the language of the text, which defined the Practical Criticism and New Criticism movements, affect this category called race in the reading of literature? Race, along with all sorts of other "unseemly" or "untoward" notions about the composition of the literary work of art, was bracketed or suspended. Within these theories of literature to which we are all heir, texts were considered canonical insofar as they elevated the cultural; Eliot's simultaneous ordering of the texts that comprised the Western tradition rendered race implicit. History, milieu, and even moment were then brought to bear upon the interpretation of literature through philology and etymology: the dictionary (in the Anglo-American tradition, specifically the *Oxford English Dictionary*) was the castle in which Taine's criteria took refuge. Once the concept of value became encased in the belief in a canon of texts whose authors purportedly shared a common culture, inherited from *both* the Greco-Roman and the Judeo-Christian traditions, there was no need to speak of matters of race, since the race of these authors was "the same." One not heir to these traditions was, by definition, of another race.

Despite their beliefs in the unassailable primacy of language in the estimation of a literary work, however, both I. A. Richards and Allen Tate, in separate prefaces to books of poems by black authors, paused to wonder about the black faces of the authors and the importance of that blackness in the reading of their texts.[5] The racism often attributed to the Southern Agrarians, while an easily identifiable target, was only an extreme manifestation of the presuppositions forming much of the foundation upon which formalism was built. The citizens of the republic of literature, in other words, were all white, and mostly male. Difference, if difference obtained at all, was a difference obliterated by the simultaneity of Eliot's tradition. For the writer from a culture of color, Eliot's fiction of tradition was the literary equivalent of the "grandfather clause."[6] So, in response to the line in Robert Penn Warren's "Pondy Woods"—"Nigger, your breed ain't metaphysical"—Sterling Brown is fond of repeating, "Cracker, your breed ain't exegetical." This signifyin(g) pun deconstructs the "racialism" inherent in such claims of tradition.

———— ∞ ————

Race, as a meaningful criterion within the biological sciences, has long been recognized to be a fiction. When we speak of "the white race" or "the black race," "the Jewish race" or "the Aryan race," we speak in biological misnomers and, more generally, in metaphors. Nevertheless, our conversations are replete with usages of race which have their sources in the dubious pseudoscience of the eighteenth and nineteenth centuries. One need only flip through the pages of the *New York Times* to find headlines such as "Brown University President Sees School Racial Problems" or "Sensing Racism, Thousands March in Paris." In "The Lost White Tribe," a lead editorial in the 29 March 1985 issue, the *New York Times* notes that while "racism is not unique to South Africa," we must condemn that society because in "betraying the religious tenets underlying Western culture, it has made race the touchstone of political rights." The *Times* editorial echoes Eliot's "dissociation of sensibility," which he felt had been caused in large part by the fraternal atrocities of the First World War. (For many people with non-European origins, however, dissociation of sensibility resulted from colonialism and human slavery.) Race, in these usages, pretends to be an objective term of classification, when in fact it is a dangerous trope.

The sense of difference defined in popular usages of the term "race" has both described and *inscribed* differences of language, belief system, artistic tradition, and gene pool, as well as all sorts of supposedly natural attributes such as rhythm, athletic ability, cerebration, usury, fidelity, and so forth. The relation between "racial character" and these sorts of characteristics has been inscribed through tropes of race, lending the sanction of God, biology, or the natural order to even presumably unbiased descriptions of cultural tendencies and differences. "Race consciousness," Zora Neale Hurston wrote, "is a deadly explosive on the tongues of men."[7]

In 1973 I was amazed to hear a member of the House of Lords describe the differences between Irish Protestants and Catholics in terms of their "distinct and clearly definable differences of race." "You mean to say that you can tell them apart?" I asked incredulously. "Of course," responded the lord. "Any Englishman can."

Race has become a trope of ultimate, irreducible difference between cultures, linguistic groups, or adherents of specific belief systems which—more often than not—also have fundamentally opposed economic interests. Race is the ultimate trope of difference because it is so very arbitrary in its application. The biological criteria used to determine "difference" in sex simply do not hold when applied to "race." Yet we carelessly use language in such a way as to *will* this sense of *natural* difference into our formulations. To do so is to engage in a pernicious act of language, one which exacerbates the complex problem of cultural or ethnic difference, rather than to assuage or redress it. This is especially the case at a time when, once again, racism has become fashionable. The extreme "otherness" of the black African continues to surface as a matter of controversy even in such humanitarian and cosmopolitan institutions as the Roman Catholic Church. On a visit to west Africa in August, Pope John-Paul II sailed across Lake Togo to face Aveto, "supreme priest" of Togo's traditional African religion, on the edge of the sacred forest at Togoville, the historical meeting point of the Roman Catholic and traditional black religions. It was a confrontation of primal dimensions: the Pope, accompanied by the Vatican Secretary of State and other top officials, and Aveto, accompanied by five of his chief priests and priestesses, exchanged blessings and then discussed the compatibility of their belief systems. The Pope, however, a rather vocal critic of the creative African integration of traditional black ("animist") beliefs with those received from

Rome, emerged from his confrontation with the mystical black Other in the heart of darkness, still worried about "great confusions in ideas," "syncretistic mysticism incompatible with the Church," and customs "contrary to the will of God," thereby denying Africans the right to remake European religion in their own images, just as various Western cultures have done.[8]

Scores of people are killed every day in the name of differences ascribed only to race. This slaughter demands the gesture in which the contributors to this special issue of *Critical Inquiry* are collectively engaged: to deconstruct, if you will, the ideas of difference inscribed in the trope of race, to explicate discourse itself in order to reveal the hidden relations of power and knowledge inherent in popular and academic usages of "race." But when, on 31 March 1985, twenty-five thousand people felt compelled to gather on the rue de Rivoli in support of the antiracist "Ne touche pas à mon pote" movement, when thousands of people willingly risk death to protest apartheid, when Iran and Iraq each feel justified in murdering the other's citizens because of their "race," when Beirut stands as a monument of shards and ruins, the gesture that we make here seems local and tiny.

I have edited this special issue of *Critical Inquiry* to explore, from a variety of methodological perspectives and formal concerns, the curious dialectic between formal language use and the inscription of metaphorical racial differences. At times, as Nancy Stepan expertly shows in *The Idea of Race in Science,* these metaphors have sought a universal and transcendent sanction in biological science. Western writers in French, Spanish, German, Portuguese, and English have tried to mystify these rhetorical figures of race, to make them natural, absolute, essential. In doing so, they have *inscribed* these differences as fixed and finite categories which they merely report or draw upon for authority. It takes little reflection, however, to recognize that these pseudoscientific categories are themselves figures. Who has seen a black or red person, a white, yellow, or brown? These terms are arbitrary constructs, not reports of reality. But language is not only the medium of this often insidious tendency; it is its *sign.* Current language use signifies the difference between cultures and their possession of power, spelling out the distance between subordinate and superordinate, between bondsman and lord in terms of their "race." These usages develop simultaneously with the shaping of an economic order in which the cultures of color have been dominated in several important senses by Western Judeo-Christian, Greco-Roman cultures and their traditions. To use contemporary theories of criticism to explicate these modes of inscription is to demystify large and obscure ideological relations and, indeed, theory itself. Before discussing the essays gathered here, it would be useful to consider a typical example of Western culture's use of writing as a commodity to confine and delimit a culture of color. For literacy, as I hope to demonstrate, is the emblem that links racial alienation with economic alienation.

Where better to test this thesis than in the example of the black tradition's first poet in English, the African slave girl Phillis Wheatley, [as recounted in "In Her Own Write," from the second section of this book]. . . . Why was the creative writing of the African of such importance to the eighteenth century's debate over slavery? I can briefly outline one thesis: after Rene Descartes, *reason* was privileged, or valorized, above all other human characteristics. Writing, especially after the printing press became so widespread, was taken to be the *visible* sign of reason. Blacks were "reasonable," and hence "men," if—and only if—they demonstrated mastery of "the arts and sciences," the eighteenth century's formula for writing. So, while the Enlightenment is characterized by its foundation on man's ability to reason, it simultaneously used the absence and presence of reason to delimit and circumscribe the very humanity of the cultures and people of color which Europeans had been "discovering" since the Renaissance. The urge toward the systematization of all human knowledge (by which we characterize the Enlightenment) led directly to the relegation of black people to a lower place in the great chain of being, an ancient construct that arranged all of creation on a vertical scale from plants, insects, and animals through man to the angels and God himself.

By 1750, the chain had become minutely calibrated; the human scale rose from "the lowliest Hottentot" (black South Africans) to "glorious Milton and Newton." If blacks could write and publish imaginative literature, then they could, in effect, take a few "giant steps" up the chain of being in an evil game of "Mother, May I?" For example, scores of reviews of Wheatley's book argued that the publication of her poems meant that the African was indeed a human being and should not be enslaved. Indeed, Wheatley herself was manumitted soon after her poems were published. Without question, Wheatley's writing was learned, and its intellectual achievement was critical to the designation of her poetry as legitimate and her authorship as authentic. But implicit in her case was a hard economic fact, too. For Wheatley and other slave authors, writing was not an activity of mind; rather, it was a commodity which they could trade for their humanity.

Blacks and other people of color could not write.

Writing, many Europeans argued, stood alone among the fine arts as the most salient repository of "genius," the visible sign of reason itself. In this subordinate role, however, writing, although secondary to reason, is nevertheless the *medium* of reason's expression. We *know* reason by its writing, by its representations. Such representations could assume spoken or written form. And while several superb scholars give priority to the *spoken* as the privileged of the pair, most Europeans privileged *writing*–in their writings about Africans, at least–as the principal measure of the Africans' humanity, their capacity for progress, their very place in the great chain of being.

The direct correlation between economic and political alienation, on the one hand, and racial alienation, on the other, is epitomized in the following 1740 South Carolina statute that attempted to make it almost impossible for black slaves to acquire, let alone master, literacy:

> *And whereas* the having of slaves taught to write, or suffering them to be employed in writing, may be attending with great inconveniences;
>
> *Be it enacted,* that all and every person and persons whatsoever, who shall hereafter teach, or cause any slave or slaves to be taught to write, or shall use or employ any slave as a scribe in any manner of writing whatsoever, hereafter taught to write; every such person or persons shall, for every offense, forfeith the sum of one hundred pounds current money.

Learning to read and to write, then, was not only difficult, it was a violation of a law.

As early as 1705, a Dutch explorer, William Bosman, had encased the commodity function of writing and its relation to racial and economic alienation in a myth which the Africans he "discovered" had purportedly related to him. According to Bosman, the blacks

> tell us, that in the beginning God created Black as well as White men; thereby . . . giving the Blacks the first Election, who chose Gold, and left the Knowledge of Letters to the White. God granted their Request, but being incensed at their Avarice, resolved that the Whites should for ever be their masters, and they obliged to wait on them as their slaves.[9]

Bosman's fabrication, of course, was a claim of origins designed to sanction through mythology a political order created by Europeans. But it was Hume, writing midway through the eighteenth century, who gave to Bosman's myth the sanction of Enlightenment philosophical reasoning.

In a major essay, "Of National Characters" (1748), Hume discusses the "characteristics" of the world's major division of human beings. In a footnote added in 1753 to his original text (the margins of his discourse), Hume posited with all of the authority of philosophy the fundamental identity of complexion, character, and intellectual capacity:

> I am apt to suspect the negroes, and in general all the other species of men (for there are four or five different kinds) to be naturally inferior to the whites. There never was a civilized nation of any other complexion than white, nor even any individual eminent either in action or speculation. No ingenious manufactures amongst them, *no arts, no sciences* . . . Such a uniform and constant difference could not happen, in so many countries and ages, if *nature* had not made an original distinction betwixt these breeds of men. Not to mention our colonies, there are Negroe slaves dispersed all over Europe, of which none ever discovered any symptoms of ingenuity. . . . In Jamaica indeed they talk of one negroe as a man of parts and learning [Francis Williams, the Cambridge-educated poet who wrote verse in Latin]; but 'tis likely he is admired for very slender accomplishments, like a parrot, who speaks a few words plainly.[10]

Hume's opinion on the subject, as we might expect, became prescriptive.

In his *Observations on the Feeling of the Beautiful and Sublime* (1764), Kant elaborates on Hume's essay in section 4, entitled "Of National Characteristics, So Far as They Depend upon the Distinct Feeling of the Beautiful and Sublime." Kant first claims that "so fundamental is the difference between [the black and white] races of man, . . . it appears to be as great in regard to mental capacities as in color."[11] Kant, moreover, is one of the earliest major European philosophers to conflate color with intelligence, a determining relation he posits with dictatorial surety:

> Father Labat reports that a Negro carpenter, whom he reproached for haughty treatment toward his wives, answered: "You whites are indeed fools, for first you make great concessions to your wives, and afterward you complain when they drive you mad." And it to be considered; but in short, this fellow was *quite black* from head to foot, a clear proof that what he said was stupid.[12]

The correlation of "black" and "stupid" Kant posits as if it were self-evident.

Hegel, echoing Hume and Kant, claimed that Africans had no history, because they had developed no systems of writing and had not mastered the art of writing in European languages. In judging civilizations, Hegel's strictures with respect to the absence of written history presume a crucial role for *memory,* a collective, cultural memory. Metaphors of the childlike nature of the slaves, of the masked, puppet-like personality of the black, all share this assumption about the absence of memory. Mary Langdon, in her novel *Ida May: A Story of Things Actual and Possible* (1854), writes that "they *are* mere children. . . . You seldom hear them say much about anything that's past, if they only get enough to eat and drink at the present moment."[13] Without writing, no *repeatable* sign of the workings of reason, of mind, could exist. Without memory or mind, no history could exist. Without history, no humanity, as defined consistently from Vico to Hegel, could exist.

⸺⸙⸺

Ironically, Anglo-African writing arose as a response to allegations of its absence. Black people responded to these profoundly serious allegations about their "nature" as directly as they could: they wrote books, poetry, autobiographical narratives. Political and philosophical discourse were the predominant forms of writing. Among these, autobiographical "deliverance" narratives were the most common and the most accomplished. Accused of lacking a formal and collective history, blacks published individual histories which, taken together, were intended to narrate in segments the larger yet fragmented history of blacks in Africa, now dispersed throughout a cold New World. The narrated, descriptive "eye" was put into service as a literary form to posit both the individual "I" of the black author as well as the collective "I" of the race. Text created author; and black authors, it was hoped, would create, or re-create, the image of the race in European discourse. The very *face* of the race was contingent upon the recording of the black *voice*. Voice presupposed a face, but also seems to have been thought to determine the very contours of the black face.

The recording of an authentic black voice—a voice of deliverance from the deafening discursive silence which an enlightened Europe cited to prove the absence of the African's humanity—was the millennial instrument of transformation through which the African would become the European, the slave become the ex-slave, brute animal become the human being. So central was this idea to the birth of the black literary tradition in the eighteenth century that five of the earliest slave narratives draw upon the figure of the voice in the text—of the talking book—as crucial "scenes of instruction" in the development of the slave on the road to freedom.[14]

These five authors, linked by revision of a trope into the very first chain of black signifiers, implicitly signify upon another chain, the metaphorical great chain of being. Blacks were most commonly represented on the chain either as the lowest of the human races or as first cousin to the ape. Because writing, according to Hume, was the ultimate sign of difference between animal and human, these writers implicitly were signifyin(g) upon the figure of the chain itself. Simply by publishing autobiographies, they indicted the received order of Western culture, of which slavery was to them the most salient sign. The writings of James Gronniosaw, John Marrant, Olaudah Equiano, Ottabah Cugoano, and John Jea served to criticize the sign of the chain of being and the black person's figurative "place" on the chain. This chain of black signifiers, regardless of their intent or desire, made the first political gesture in the Anglo-African literary tradition "simply" by the act of writing. Their collective act gave birth to the black literary tradition and defined it as the "Other's chain," the chain of black being as black people themselves would have it. Making the book speak, then, constituted a motivated and political engagement with and condemnation of Europe's fundamental sign of domination, the commodity of writing, the text and technology of reason. We are justified, however, in wondering aloud if the sort of subjectivity which these writers seek through the act of writing can be realized through a process which is so very ironic from the outset: how can the black subject posit a full and sufficient self in a language in which blackness is a sign of absence? Can writing, with the very difference it makes and marks, mask the blackness of the black face that addresses the text of Western letters, in a voice that speaks English through an idiom which contains the irreducible element of cultural difference that will always separate the white voice from the black? Black people, we know, have not been liberated from racism by our writings. We accepted a false premise by assuming that racism would be destroyed once white racists became convinced that we were human, too. Writing stood as a complex "certificate of humanity," as Paulin Hountondji put it. Black writing, and especially the literature of the slave, served not to obliterate the difference of race; rather, the inscription of the black voice in Western literatures has preserved those very cultural differences to be repeated, imitated, and revised in a separate Western literary tradition, a tradition of black difference.

We black people tried to write ourselves out of slavery, a slavery even more profound than mere physical bondage. Accepting the challenge of the great white Western tradition, black writers wrote as if their lives depended upon it—and, in a curious sense, their lives did, the "life of the race" in Western discourse. But if blacks accepted this challenge, we also accepted its premises, premises which perhaps concealed a trap. What trap might this be? Let us recall the curious case of M. Edmond Laforest.

In 1915, Edmond Laforest, a prominent member of the Haitian literary movement called La Ronde, made his death a symbolic, if ironic, statement of the curious relation of the marginalized writer to the act of writing in a modern language. Laforest, with an inimitable, if fatal, flair for the grand gesture, stood upon a bridge, calmly tied a Larousse dictionary around his neck, then leapt to his death. While other black writers, before and after Laforest, have been drowned artistically by the weight of various modern languages, Laforest chose to make his death an emblem of this relation of overwhelming indenture.

It is the challenge of the black tradition to critique this relation of indenture, an indenture that obtains for our writers and for our critics. We must master, as Jacques Derrida writes in his essay in this collection, how "to speak the other's language without renouncing [our] own." When we attempt to appropriate, by inversion, "race" as a term for an essence—as did the négritude movement, for example ("We feel, therefore we are," as Leopold Senghor argued of the African)—we yield too much: the basis of a shared humanity. Such gestures, as Anthony Appiah observes in his essay, are futile and dangerous because of their further inscription of new and bizarre stereotypes. How do we meet Derrida's challenge in the discourse of criticism? The Western critical tradition has a canon, as the Western literary tradition does. I once thought it our most important gesture to *master* the canon of criticism, to *imitate* and *apply* it, but I now believe that we must turn to the black tradition itself to develop theories of criticism indigenous to our literatures. Alice Walker's revision of Rebecca Cox Jackson's parable of white interpretation (written in 1836) makes this point most tellingly. Jackson, a Shaker eldress and black visionary, claimed like Jea to have been taught to read by the Lord. She writes in her autobiography that she dreamed a white man came to her house to teach her how to *interpret* and understand the word of God, now that God had taught her to read:

> A white man took me by my right hand and led me on the north side of the room, where sat a square table. On it lay a book open. And he said to me. "Thou shall be instructed in this book, from Genesis to Revelations." And then he took me on the west side, where stood a table. And it looked like the first. And said, "Yea, thou shall be instructed from the beginning of creation to the end of time." And then he took me on the east side of the room also, where stood a table and book like the two first, and said, "I will instruct thee—yea, thou shall be instructed from the beginning of all things to the end of all things. Yea, thou shall be well instructed. I will instruct."
>
> And then I awoke, and I saw him as plain as I did in my dream. And after that he taught me daily. And when I would be reading and come to a hard word, I would see him standing by my side and he would teach me the word

right. And often, when I would be in meditation and looking into things which was hard to understand, I would find him by me, teaching and giving me understanding. And oh, his labor and care which he had with me often caused me to weep bitterly, when I would see my great ignorance and the great trouble he had to make me understand eternal things. For I was so buried in the depth of the tradition of my forefathers, that it did seem as if I never could be dug up.[15]

In response to Jackson's relation of interpretive indenture to "a white man," Walker, in *The Color Purple,* records an exchange between Celie and Shug about turning away from "the old white man" which soon turns into a conversation about the elimination of "man" as a mediator between a woman and "everything":

> You have to git man off your eyeball, before you can see anything a'tall. Man corrupt everything, say Shug. He on your box of grits, in your head, and all over the radio. He try to make you think he everywhere. Soon as you think he everywhere, you think he God. But he ain't. Whenever you trying to pray, and man plop himself on the other end of it, tell him to git lost, say Shug.[16]

Celie and Shug's omnipresent "man," of course, echoes the black tradition's epithet for the white power structure, "the man."

For non-Western, so-called noncanonical critics, getting the "man off your eyeball" means using the most sophisticated critical theories and methods available to reappropriate and to define our own "colonial" discourses. We must use these theories and methods insofar as they are relevant to the study of our own literatures. The danger in doing so, however, is best put by Anthony Appiah in his definition of what he calls "the Naipaul fallacy":

> It is not necessary to show that African literature is fundamentally the same as European literature in order to show that it can be treated with the same tools; . . . nor should we endorse a more sinister line. . . . the post-colonial legacy which requires us to show that African literature is worthy of study precisely (but only) because it is fundamentally the same as European literature.[17]

We *must* not, Appiah concludes, ask "the reader to understand Africa by embedding it in European culture" ("S," p. 146).

We must, I believe, analyze the ways in which writing relates to race, how attitudes toward racial differences generate and structure literary texts by us *and* about us. We must determine how critical methods can effectively disclose the traces of ethnic differences in literature. But we must also understand how certain forms of difference and the *languages* we employ to define those supposed differences not only reinforce each other but tend to create and maintain each other. Similarly, and as importantly, we must analyze the language of contemporary criticism itself, recognizing especially that hermeneutic systems are not universal, colorblind, apolitical, or neutral. Whereas some critics wonder aloud, as Appiah notes, about such matters as whether or not "a structuralist poetics is inapplicable in Africa because structuralism is European," the concern of the Third World critic should properly be to understand the ideological subtext which any critical theory reflects and embodies, and the relation which this subtext bears to the production of meaning. No critical theory—be it Marxist, feminist, post-structuralist, Kwame Nkrumah's "consciencism," or whatever—escapes the specificity of value and ideology, no matter how mediated these may be. To attempt to appropriate our own discourses by using Western critical theory uncritically is to substitute one mode of neocolonialism for another. To begin to do this in my own tradition, theorists have turned to the black vernacular tradition—to paraphrase Jackson, they have begun to dig into the depths of the tradition of our foreparents—to isolate the signifying black difference through which to theorize about the so-called discourse of the Other. . . .

———∞∞———

By allowing me to dedicate *"Race," Writing, and Difference* to Dominique de Menil, *Critical Inquiry* gracefully departs from previous practice. It does so for good reason. Dominique de Menil, born in Paris in 1908, has been for over five decades a central influence in the development of contemporary art. As the guiding force in assembling one of the world's great collections of art (soon to be housed in its own museum in Houston), as a highly regarded professor of the history of art, and as a patron of artists and scholars, Dominique de Menil has shaped, as much as has any individual, the direction of modern art and the lives of those who make it.

I wish to dedicate this special issue of *Critical Inquiry* to her, however, for still another reason. As the president of the Menil Foundation, for the past twenty-five years she has funded a project entitled "The Image of the Black in Western Art." This project, nearing completion, has produced three copious volumes of color reproduction and sophisticated historical commentary addressing the figure of the black person in Western art from 2500 B.C. to the twentieth century. Among other startling conclusions about the representation of the black Other in Western culture are the facts that black people and Europeans seem to have remained in fairly constant contact since Greco-Roman antiquity and that blacks were depicted in formal art in extraordinarily various ways—from gods, saints, and kings to devils, heathens, and slaves. Her support of liberal political causes, her early stand against racism and de jure segregation in the South, her antipathy toward apartheid, and her creation of the Truth and Freedom Awards for those whose humanitarian politics often led to imprisonment and death—all these are fitting analogues to her commitment to art.

It is for her consistent stand against those who would limit the human mind and spirit, for her concomitant affirmation of the nobility of the human spirit, for her philanthropic generosity, and for her example of the life of the mind well-lived that I dedicate *"Race," Writing, and Difference* to Dominique de Menil.

NOTES

1. Hippolyte-Adolphe Taine, intro. to *The History of English Literature,* in *Criticism: The Major Texts,* ed. Walter Jackson Bate, enlarged ed. (New York, 1970), pp. 503–4.

2. Ibid., pp. 504, 505.

3. Abraham Lincoln, quoted in Michael P. Banton, *The Idea of Race* (Boulder, Colo., 1978), p. 1.

4. See the special issue *Canons, Critical Inquiry* 10 (Sept. 1983).

5. See I. A. Richards, intro. to Claude McKay, *"Spring in New Hampshire" and Other Poems* (London, 1920), and Allen Tate, intro. to Melvin B. Tolson, *The Libretto for the Republic of Liberia* (New York, 1953).

6. The "grandfather clause" was a provision in several southern state constitutions designed to enfranchise poor whites and disfranchise blacks by waiving high voting requirements for descendants of men voting before 1867.

7. Zora Neale Hurston, *Dust Tracks on a Road: An Autobiography,* 2d ed. (Urbana, Ill., 1984), p. 326.

8. *New York Times,* 9 Aug. 1985, p. A3; *New York Times,* 14 Aug. 1985, p. A3; *Ithaca Journal,* 9 Aug. 1985, p. 9; *Ithaca Journal,* 10 Aug. 1985, p. 8.

9. William Bosman, *A New and Accurate Description of the Coast of Guinea* (1705; London, 1967), pp. 146, 147.

10. David Hume, "Of National Characters," *The Philosophical Works,* ed. Thomas Hill Green and Thomas Hodge Grose, 4 vols. (Darmstadt, 1964), 3:252 n. 1; my emphasis.

11. Immanuel Kant, *Observations on the Feeling of the Beautiful and Sublime,* trans. John T. Goldthwait (Berkeley and Los Angeles, 1960), p. 111.

12. Ibid., p. 113; my emphasis.

13. Mary Langdon, *Ida May: A Story of Things Actual and Possible* (Boston, 1854), p. 116.

14. See James Albert Ukawsaw Gronniosaw, *A Narrative of the Most Remarkable Particulars of Life of James Albert Ukawsaw Gronniosaw, An African Prince* (Bath, 1770); John Marrant, *Narrative of the Lord's Wonderful Dealings with John Marrant, A Black* (London, 1785); Ottabah Cugoano, *Thoughts and Sentiments on the Evil and Wicked Traffic of the Slavery and Commerce of the Human Species* (London, 1787); Olaudah Equiano, *The Interesting Narrative of the Life of Olaudah Equiano, or Gustavus Vassa, The African. Written by Himself* (London, 1789); and John Jea, *The Life and Sufferings of John Jea, An African Preacher* (Swansea, 1806).

15. Rebecca Cox Jackson, "A Dream of Three Books and a Holy One," *Gifts of Power: The Writings of Rebecca Jackson, Black Visionary, Shaker Eldress,* ed. Jean McMahon Humez (Amherst, Mass., 1981), pp. 146, 147.

16. Alice Walker, *The Color Purple* (New York, 1982), p. 179.

17. Anthony Appiah, "Strictures on Structures: The Prospects for a Structuralist Poetics of African Fiction," in *Black Literature and Literary Theory,* ed. Henry Louis Gates, Jr. (New York, 1984), pp. 146, 145; all further references to this work, abbreviated "S," will be included in the text.

SOURCE: "'Race,' Writing, and Difference." *Critical Inquiry* 12, no. 1 (1985): 1–20. Published by The University of Chicago Press. Stable URL: www.jstor.org/stable/1343459. Accessed 12/08/2011.

PREFACE, *THE IMAGE OF THE BLACK IN WESTERN ART*

WITH DAVID BINDMAN

THE IMAGE OF the Black in Western Art was conceived by the late Dominique Schlumberger de Menil (1908–1997) and her husband, John (1904–1973), fifty years ago. The de Menils were known internationally for their patronage of artists such as René Magritte and Max Ernst as early as the 1930s, and eventually for the size and range of their art collection. Their passion for art led them to set up, among many other things, the Menil Collection and the Rothko Chapel in Houston. They also were widely respected for their commitments to human rights. Dominique de Menil originated the idea of collecting images of persons of African descent in Western art at the height of the civil rights movement in the United States as a subtle bulwark and living testimony against antiblack racism. She also viewed this project as a way to counter, implicitly, the legion of all-too-familiar racist and stereotypical images of black people in American and European popular art by unveiling the fact that for centuries—indeed millennia—canonical Western arts had included black figures in positive, sometimes realistic, and often celebratory ways in virtually every medium.

In launching this extraordinary project, the de Menils knitted two strands of their family's passionate interests together into one unusual form. Dominique de Menil once said that she assumed the entire project would take about a year or so to complete, since no one at the time could have had any idea of the sheer scope and astonishing range of the presence of black images in the Western artistic tradition. A half century later, the project exists in the form of a photographic archive initially established in Houston by the Menil Foundation but now located in almost identical form at the W. E. B. Du Bois Institute for African and African American Research, Harvard University, and at the Warburg Institute, University of London. These twin archives remain the bedrock of the project and contain more than 30,000 images, far more than can be reproduced in a series of published volumes.[1] And the search for even more images of blacks in Western art continues.

The de Menils' idea in launching this project was based on their belief in the benevolent—indeed, transforming—power of art and their alarm at the stubborn persistence of racial segregation in the United States, to which they had both immigrated from France during World War II. It is no accident that the project was born in the heart of the South. After John de Menil's death, Dominique de Menil became even more actively involved in supervising the research and eventual publication of the initial volumes. In her preface to the first edition of Volume 1, she argues that works of art by master artists can reveal the common humanity of all people beyond the limits of conventional racial and social assumptions. Widely disseminated knowledge of and access to the beauty and range of these images could, she and her husband believed, be a source of pride and self-respect for Africans and African Americans, and might simultaneously promote greater tolerance and understanding of black people among white people. Art, in other words, could be drawn upon as another weapon in the fight against antiblack racism, both in America and throughout Europe. Black figures in great works of Western art might provide a window onto times in the past when, as Dominique de Menil put it a little wistfully, "ideals of fraternity blossomed" between Europeans and Africans, a time before the start of the African slave trade to Europe and the New World, a time when race-based slavery and Jim Crow segregation were not the basis of the dominant socioeconomic relationship between them or of the ways in which black people were "seen" and represented in Western culture. It was a noble idea, if perhaps characteristic of a more optimistic era than our own.

The de Menils were not the first to take a systematic interest in the representation of persons of African descent in European art. Grace Hadley Beardsley published a standard work, *The Negro in Greek and Roman Civilization: A Study of the Ethiopian Type*, in 1929, and she had noted that "the earliest important work on the subject" was J. Löwenherz's *Die Aetheiopen der altclassischen Kunst*, published in 1861, "an important year in negro history."[2] Beardsley makes the salient point that Löwenherz's study was undertaken precisely at the height of the abolition movement in the United States, in the first year of the Civil War. Similarly, publication of *The Image of the Black* was initiated at a turbulent time in the history of American race relations. Nonetheless, there is nothing explicit in the work of Löwenherz or Beardsley arguing that studying this subject might play a part in counteracting segregation or racial prejudice. At the other end of the scale from such works of scholarship were popular books like J. A. Rogers's *Sex and Race* (three volumes, 1940–1944), which used representations of blacks in the history of Western art as evidence, as its subtitle, *Negro Caucasian Mixing in All Ages and All Lands*, indicates, to argue against current theories of racial essentialism. Regardless of the intentions of these authors, it had become clear by the Harlem Renaissance in the 1920s that representations of black people in Western art could be drawn upon both as another front in the war against racism and to make the case for the inherent equality of freed slaves and their descendants.

The idea that a study of European images of blacks in art could be an antidote to prejudice was first adumbrated in its most sophisticated form by the great African American scholar and critic, Alain LeRoy Locke (1886–1954) in *The Negro in Art* of 1940.[3] Locke, upon graduating from Harvard College, became the first black Rhodes Scholar. After studying at Oxford University, he eventually returned to Harvard to become the first black person to earn a Ph.D. in philosophy there, in 1918. One of his areas of philosophical interest and expertise was aesthetics. He often wrote about art and its social uses, especially during the Harlem Renaissance, a cultural movement in part created by the massive anthology *The New Negro*, which he edited and published in 1925. In several of his own essays, in essays by others, such as the American inventor and art collector Alfred C. Barnes, and in lavish illustrations, many in color, Locke stressed the nature and function of art in society and its potential role in what he termed a necessary "reassessment" of the Negro, which he argued the Harlem Renaissance might effect. He brought various lines of his thought into a theory of art, race, and racial relations in *The Negro in Art*, the culmination of his thinking about Negro art and the Negro in art in the twenty years since he had completed his doctoral dissertation.

In this seminal book, Locke deepened his brief for the role of the arts in the Negro's attempt to gain social equality and equal treatment before the law, arguing that "the deep and sustained interest of artists generally in the Negro subject, amounting in some instances to preoccupation with this theme, runs counter to the barriers and limitations of social and racial prejudice, and evidences appreciative insights which, if better known, might prove one of the strongest antidotes for prejudice." Locke's claim rests on a belief in the artist as vanguard, the artist's superior aesthetic powers with the social hierarchy, and her or his ability to see beyond ordinary perceptions: "Here in this field, as in others, the eye of the artist vindicates its reputation for having in most instances broader, clear and deeper vision than ordinary." On the other hand, Locke argues, art could naturalize racial prejudice at the same time as mitigating it: "This is not to gainsay that art, too, has its limiting formula, or that in still other instances art reflects and even caters to its contemporary social conventions. But even in so doing, the net effect of art is to reveal the bias rather than to conceal it, while the usual course of the best art is to transcend it with a freshly original point of view."[4] In artistic depictions of black figures throughout the Western tradition, Locke was spurred by the formally transforming uses of African art by the cubists to create bold new ways of representing the human form, starting with Picasso's studies for *Les Demoiselles d'Avignon.* Locke maintained that ammunition could be found for deployment in the battle against antiblack racism where it had never occurred to anyone to look before: in the visual arts. As he had argued in *The New Negro,* if European artists could so fundamentally affect the world's attitudes toward and regard for traditionally benighted African masks, for example, just think of the implications of the creation of a truly resonant American Negro artistic tradition, and of the adoption of the Negro as a subject for art made by white Americans and Europeans. This is exemplified by the drawings of the German immigrant artist Winold Reiss that pepper the text of his canonical anthology. It was a complex argument, and a subtle one, uniquely Locke's own.

For Alain Locke, the sheer variety of physical types of blacks in European art acted as a solvent for the prevalent stereotypes that obtained in American society. He drew attention to the crucial importance of the fact that one of the Three Magi who visited the baby Jesus had since the late Middle Ages often been represented as a black man in paintings of *The Adoration of the Magi.* He pointed to paintings of blacks by Rembrandt, Velázquez, and Rubens, in which he discerned "a degree of virtuosity in technical expression and a penetration of emotional understanding." He also argued, in a sign that even he was embedded in and valorized certain racialist ideas of his time, that "they caught, in addition to the particular model, that indefinable but tangible something we feel as race." He saw something almost charming or engaging in paintings in which a great European gentleman or lady is accompanied by an adoring black slave: "even the late 17th and 18th Century tradition of the Negro page attendant, though grounded in slavery, still preserved something of the glamor of the exotic, investing that frequent figure with gaiety and charm."[5] While art could penetrate the superficial appearance of even a black person's social station or status, suggesting the universal human core beneath, he seemed unaware that it also had the potential to invest slavery with a certain glamour: a two-edged sword.

The de Menils certainly would have known Locke's book, if not Locke himself. However, there were more immediate influences on the generation of this research project, in particular the well-known Polish-French author and novelist Jean Malaquais (1908–1998), born Vladimir Malacki in Warsaw, who had been André Gide's secretary and who moved between Paris and the United States, where he held several academic posts. Malaquais, like Locke, had strong views about the efficacy of art to effect social change. The de Menils also knew the work of the African American scholar Frank M. Snowden, Jr. (1911–2007), like Locke a Harvard Ph.D. (in classics) and a colleague of Locke's at Howard University. Snowden's *Blacks in Antiquity: Ethiopians in the Greco-Roman Experience* (1970) and subsequent books on this topic made him an obvious choice as one of the authors for the first volume in this multivolume work, on black images in the ancient world.

The de Menils were insistent that the proposed volumes (initially three were envisaged, covering works of art from European antiquity to the early twentieth century) should contain illustrations of exceptional quality, for which they commissioned a number of campaigns by outstanding photographers. They also employed as director of the archive and editor of the proposed volumes, a young Paris-trained art historian, Ladislas Bugner, who produced a detailed chronological scheme for the volumes, which has remained the basis for the choice of images in the published books. Some of the volumes would be published in two large parts and all were originally produced in both English and French editions, a nod to the increasingly troubled politics of race on both sides of the Atlantic, to the provenance of so much of the art being reproduced and, of course, to the de Menils' native land. For various reasons, the volumes were not published in chronological order, leaving important historical gaps in the series' first incarnation. That unfortunate fact, combined with the two-part structure of two of the published volumes, often led to confusion among readers about the scope and organization of the project. The first volume, titled *From the Pharaohs to the Fall of the Roman Empire*, was published in 1976. Volume II, *From the Early Christian Era to the "Age of Discovery,"* was published in two parts in 1979, while Volume IV, *From the American Revolution to World War I*, came out, also in two parts, in 1989. Review of these publications was uniformly enthusiastic and unstintingly full of praise. We are pleased that we are now publishing, in three parts, the third chronological volume, *From the "Age of Discovery" to the Age of Abolition.*[6]

Sometime after the death of Dominique de Menil on the last day of 1997—but not before Harvard honored her with an honorary doctorate—the Menil Foundation decided to discontinue the publication of *The Image of the Black*, though authors had already been commissioned for the remaining volumes. Almost immediately, Henry Louis Gates, Jr., the director of the Du Bois Institute assumed responsibility for completing the project and fulfilling Dominique de Menil's original plan. In 1993 Madame de Menil had transferred the archive, under the direction of Karen C.C. Dalton, to the W. E. B. Du Bois Institute for African and African American Research at Harvard, where it was endowed through donations made by the Menil Foundation and various donors recruited by President Neil Rudenstine and by Gates. In 2005 the Du Bois Institute formally agreed to undertake the publication of the remaining volumes and to republish the existing volumes in the series, under the editorship of David Bindman and Professor Gates and the assistant editorship of Karen Dalton. This essay inaugurates this new series, [which will consist of ten books published with full color by Harvard University Press and] which includes texts written by a mixture of the original and newly commissioned authors. In addition to the original publishing scheme, a volume covering the twentieth century and a companion volume on the image of the black in African art are part of the Du Bois Institute's project.

ENDNOTES

1. Both archives can be consulted by the public by appointment, and the photographs can also be accessed on the Internet by subscription through ARTSTOR.

2. Grace Hadley Beardsley, *The Negro in Greek and Roman Civilization: A Study of the Ethiopian Type* (Baltimore, 1929), p. ix.

3. Alain LeRoy Locke, *The Negro in Art: A Pictorial Record of the Negro Artist and the Negro Theme in Art* (New York, 1968 [1940]).

4. Ibid., pp. 3, 138.

5. Ibid., p. 139.

6. As early as 1980, John Russell had, in commending "the exalted nature of [the project's] ambitions and . . . its beauty of presentation," already complained of "the august slowness of its fulfillment" (*New York Times,* 29 June 1980), p. 7.

SOURCE: David Bindman and Henry Louis Gates, Jr., eds., *The Image of the Black in Western Art* (Cambridge, MA: Belknap Press, 2010).

THE SIGNIFYING MONKEY AND THE LANGUAGE OF SIGNIFYIN(G)
Rhetorical Difference and the Orders of Meaning

> *Some of the best dozens players were girls ... before you can signify you got to be able to rap. .... Signifying allowed you a choice—you could either make a cat feel good or bad. If you had just destroyed someone or if they were down already, signifying could help them over. Signifying was also a way of expressing your own feelings. ... Signifying at its best can be heard when the brothers are exchanging tales.*
>
> —H. RAP BROWN

> *And they asked me right at Christmas*
> *If my blackness, would it rub off?*
> *I said, ask your Mama.*
>
> —LANGSTON HUGHES

I

If Esu-Elegbara stands as the central figure of the Ifa system of interpretation, then his Afro-American relative, the Signifying Monkey, stands as the rhetorical principle in Afro-American vernacular discourse. My concern in this chapter is to define a carefully structured system of rhetoric, traditional Afro-American figures of signification, and then to show how a curious figure becomes the trope of literary revision itself.

Thinking about the black concept of Signifyin(g) is a bit like stumbling unaware into a hall of mirrors: the sign itself appears to be doubled, at the very least, and (re)doubled upon ever closer examination. It is not the sign it-

234

self, however, which has multiplied. If orientation prevails over madness, we soon realize that only the signifier has been doubled and (re)doubled, a signifier in this instance that is silent, a "sound-image" as Saussure defines the signifier, but a "sound-image" *sans* the sound. The difficulty that we experience when thinking about the nature of the visual (re)doubling at work in a hall of mirrors is analogous to the difficulty we shall encounter in relating the black linguistic sign, "Signification," to the standard English sign, "signification." This level of conceptual difficulty stems from—indeed, seems to have been intentionally inscribed within—the selection of the signifier "Signification" to represent a concept remarkably distinct from that concept represented by the standard English signifier, "signification." For the standard English word is a homonym of the Afro-American vernacular word. And, to compound the dizziness and the giddiness that we must experience in the vertiginous movement between these two "identical" signifiers, these two homonyms have everything to do with each other and, then again, absolutely nothing.[1]

In the extraordinarily complex relationship between the two homonyms, we both enact and recapitulate the received, classic confrontation between Afro-American culture and American culture. This confrontation is both political and metaphysical. We might profit somewhat by thinking of the curiously ironic relationship between these signifiers as a confrontation defined by the politics of semantics, semantics here defined as the study of the classification of changes in the signification of words, and more especially the relationships between theories of denotation and naming, as well as connotation and ambiguity. The relationship that black "Signification" bears to the English "signification" is, paradoxically, a relation of difference inscribed within a relation of identity. That, it seems to me, is inherent in the nature of metaphorical substitution and the pun, particularly those rhetorical tropes dependent on the repetition of a word with a change denoted by a difference in sound or in a letter (agnominatio), and in homonymic puns (antanaclasis). These tropes luxuriate in the chaos of ambiguity that repetition and difference (be that apparent difference centered in the signifier or in the signified, in the "sound-image" or in the concept) yield in either an aural or a visual pun.

This dreaded, if playful, condition of ambiguity would, of course, disappear in the instance at hand if the two signs under examination did not bear the same signifier. If the two signs were designated by two different signifiers, we could escape our sense of vertigo handily. We cannot, however, precisely because the antanaclasis that I am describing turns upon the very identity of these signifiers, and the play of differences generated by the unrelated concepts (the signifieds) for which they stand.

What we are privileged to witness here is the (political, semantic) confrontation between two parallel discursive universes: the black American linguistic circle and the white. We see here the most subtle and perhaps the most profound trace of an extended engagement between two separate and distinct yet profoundly—even inextricably—related orders of meaning dependent precisely as much for their confrontation on relations of identity, manifested in the signifier, as on their relations of difference, manifested at the level of the signified. We bear witness here to a protracted argument over the nature of the sign itself, with the black vernacular discourse proffering its critique of the sign as the difference that blackness makes within the larger political culture and its historical unconscious.

"Signification" and "signification" create a noisy disturbance in silence, at the level of the signifier. Derrida's neologism, "differance," in its relation to "difference," is a marvelous example of agnominatio, or repetition of a word with an alteration of both one letter and a sound. In this clever manner, Derrida's term resists reduction to self-identical meaning. The curiously suspended relationship between the French verbs *to differ* and *to defer* both defines Derrida's revision of Saussure's notion of language as a relation of differences and embodies his revision which "in its own unstable meaning [is] a graphic example of the process at work."[2]

I have encountered great difficulty in arriving at a suitably similar gesture. I have decided to signify the difference between these two signifiers by writing the black signifier in upper case ("Signification") and the white signifier in lower case ("signification"). Similarly, I have selected to write the black term with a bracketed final *g* ("Signifyin(g)") and the white term as "signifying." The bracketed *g* enables me to connote the fact that this word is, more often than not, spoken by black people without the final *g* as "signifyin'." This arbitrary and idiosyncratic convention also enables me to recall the fact that whatever historical community of Afro-Americans coined this usage did so in the vernacular as spoken, in contradistinction to the literate written usages of the standard English "shadowed" term. The bracketed or aurally erased *g*, like the discourse of black English and dialect poetry generally, stands as the trace of black difference in a remarkably sophisticated and fascinating (re)naming ritual graphically in evidence here. Perhaps replacing with a visual sign the *g* erased in the black vernacular shall, like Derrida's neologism, serve both to avoid confusion and the reduction of these two distinct sets of homonyms to a false identity and to stand as the sign of a (black) Signifyin(g) difference itself. The absent *g* is a figure for the Signifyin(g) black difference.

Let me attempt to account for the complexities of this (re)naming ritual, which apparently took place anonymously and unrecorded in antebellum

America. Some black genius or a community of witty and sensitive speakers emptied the signifier "signification" of its received concepts and filled this empty signifier with their own concepts. By doing so, by supplanting the received, standard English concept associated by (white) convention with this particular signifier, they (un)wittingly disrupted the nature of the sign = *signified/signifier* equation itself. I bracket *wittingly* with a negation precisely because origins are always occasions for speculation. Nevertheless, I tend to think, or I wish to believe, that this guerrilla action occurred intentionally on this term, because of the very concept with which it is associated in standard English.

"Signification," in standard English, denotes the meaning that a term conveys, or is intended to convey. It is a fundamental term in the standard English semantic order. Since Saussure, at least, the three terms *signification, signifier, signified* have been fundamental to our thinking about general linguistics and, of late, about criticism specifically. These neologisms in the academic-critical community are homonyms of terms in the black vernacular tradition perhaps two centuries old. By supplanting the received term's associated concept, the black vernacular tradition created a homonymic pun of the profoundest sort, thereby marking its sense of difference from the rest of the English community of speakers. Their complex act of language Signifies upon both formal language use and its conventions, conventions established, at least officially, by middle-class white people.

This political offensive could have been mounted against all sorts of standard English terms—and, indeed, it was. I am thinking here of terms such as *down, nigger, baby,* and *cool,* which snobbishly tend to be written about as "dialect" words or "slang." There are scores of such revised words. But to revise the term *signification* is to select a term that represents the nature of the process of meaning-creation and its representation. Few other selections could have been so dramatic, or so meaningful. We are witnessing here a profound disruption at the level of the signifier, precisely because of the relationship of identity that obtains between the two apparently equivalent terms. This disturbance, of course, has been effected at the level of the conceptual, or the signified. How accidental, unconscious, or unintentional (or any other code-word substitution for the absence of reason) could such a brilliant challenge at the semantic level be? To revise the received sign (quotient) literally accounted for in the relation represented by *signified/signifier* at its most apparently denotative level is to critique the nature of (white) meaning itself, to challenge through a literal critique of the sign the meaning of meaning. What did/do black people signify in a society in which they were intentionally introduced as the subjugated, as the enslaved cipher? Nothing on the x axis of white signification, and everything on the y axis of blackness.[3]

It is not sufficient merely to reveal that black people colonized a white sign. A level of meta-discourse is at work in this process. If the signifier stands disrupted by the shift in concepts denoted and connoted, then we are engaged at the level of meaning itself, at the semantic register. Black people vacated this signifier, then—incredibly—substituted as its concept a signified that stands for the system of rhetorical strategies peculiar to their own vernacular tradition. Rhetoric, then, has supplanted semantics in this most literal meta-confrontation within the structure of the sign. Some historical black community of speakers most certainly struck directly at the heart of the matter, on the ground of the referent itself, thereby demonstrating that even (or especially) the concepts signified by the signifier are themselves arbitrary. By an act of will, some historically nameless community of remarkably self-conscious speakers of English defined their ontological status as one of profound difference vis-à-vis the rest of society. What's more, they undertook this act of self-definition, implicit in a (re)naming ritual, within the process of signification that the English language had inscribed for itself. Contrary to an assertion that Saussure makes in his *Course*, "the masses" did indeed "have [a] voice in the matter" and replaced the sign "chosen by language." We shall return to Saussure's discussion of the "Immutability and Mutability of the Sign" below.[4] . . .

The process of semantic appropriation in evidence in the relation of Signification to signification has been aptly described by Mikhail Bakhtin as a double-voiced word, that is, a word or utterance, in this context, decolonized for the black's purposes "by inserting a new semantic orientation into a word which already has—and retains—its own orientation." Although I shall return later in this chapter to a fuller consideration of this notion of double-voiced words and double-voiced discourse, Gary Saul Morson's elaboration on Bakhtin's concept helps to clarify what Bakhtin implies:

> The audience of a double-voiced word is therefore meant to hear both a version of the original utterance as the embodiment of its speaker's point of view (or "semantic position") *and* the second speaker's evaluation of that utterance from a different point of view. I find it helpful to picture a double-voiced word as a special sort of palimpsest in which the upper-most inscription is a commentary on the one beneath it, which the reader (or audience) can know only by reading through the commentary that obscures in the very process of evaluating.[5]

The motivated troping effect of the disruption of the semantic orientation of signification by the black vernacular depends on the homonymic relation of the white term to the black. The sign, in other words, has been demonstrated to be mutable.

Bakhtin's notion, then, implicitly critiques Saussure's position that

> the signifier . . . is fixed, not free, with respect to the linguistic community that uses it. The masses have no voice in the matter, and the signifier chosen by language could be replaced by no other. . . . [The] community itself cannot control so much as a single word; it is bound to the existing language.[6]

Saussure, of course, proceeds to account for "shift(s) in the relationship between the signified and the signifier," shifts in time that result directly from "the arbitrary nature of the sign." But, simultaneously, Saussure denies what he terms to be "arbitrary substitution": "A particular language-state is always the product of historical forces, and these forces explain why the sign is unchangeable, i.e. why it resists any arbitrary substitution." The double-voiced relation of the two terms under analysis here argues forcefully that "the masses," especially in a multiethnic society, draw on "arbitrary substitution" freely, to disrupt the signifier by displacing its signified in an intentional act of will. Signifyin(g) is black double-voicedness; because it always entails formal revision and an intertextual relation, and because of Esu's double-voiced representation in art, I find it an ideal metaphor for black literary criticism, for the formal manner in which texts seem concerned to address their antecedents. Repetition, with a signal difference, is fundamental to the nature of Signifyin(g), as we shall see.[7]

II

The Poetry of Signification

The literature or tales of the Signifying Monkey and his peculiar language, Signifyin(g), is both extensive and polemical, involving as it does assertions and counterassertions about the relationship that Signifyin(g) bears to several other black tropes. I am not interested in either recapitulating or contributing to this highly specialized debate over whether or not speech act *x* is an example of this black trope or that. On the contrary, I wish to argue that Signifyin(g) is the black trope of tropes, the figure for black rhetorical figures. I wish to do so because this represents my understanding of the value assigned to Signifyin(g) by the members of the Afro-American speech community, of which I have been a signifier for quite some time. While the role of a certain aspect of linguistics study is to discern the shape and function of each tree that stands in the verbal terrain, my role as a critic, in this book at least, is to define the contours of the discursive forest or, perhaps more appropriately, of the jungle.[8]

Tales of the Signifying Monkey seem to have had their origins in slavery. Hundreds of these have been recorded since the early twentieth century. In black music, Jazz Gillum, Count Basie, Oscar Peterson, the Big Three Trio, Oscar Brown, Jr., Little Willie Dixon, Snatch and the Poontang, Otis Redding, Wilson Pickett, Smokey Joe Whitfield, and Johnny Otis—among others—have recorded songs about either the Signifying Monkey or, simply, Signifyin(g). The theory of Signifyin(g) is arrived at by explicating these black cultural forms. Signifyin(g) in jazz performances and in the play of black language games is a mode of formal revision, it depends for its effects on troping, it is often characterized by pastiche, and, most crucially, it turns on repetition of formal structures and their differences. Learning how to Signify is often part of our adolescent education.

Of the many colorful figures that appear in black vernacular tales, perhaps only Tar Baby is as enigmatic and compelling as is that oxymoron, the Signifying Monkey.[9] The ironic reversal of a received racist image of the black is simianlike, the Signifying Monkey, he who dwells at the margins of discourse, ever punning, ever troping, ever embodying the ambiguities of language, is our trope for repetition and revision, indeed our trope of chiasmus, repeating and reversing simultaneously as he does in one deft discursive act. If Vico and Burke, or Nietzsche, de Man, and Bloom, are correct in identifying four and six "master tropes," then we might think of these as the "master's tropes," and of Signifyin(g) as the slave's trope, the trope of tropes, as Bloom characterizes metalepsis, "a trope-reversing trope, a figure of a figure." Signifyin(g) is a trope in which are subsumed several other rhetorical tropes, including metaphor, metonymy, synecdoche, and irony (the master tropes), and also hyperbole, litotes, and metalepsis (Bloom's supplement to Burke). To this list we could easily add aporia, chiasmus, and catechresis, all of which are used in the ritual of Signifyin(g).

Signifyin(g), it is clear, means in black discourse modes of figuration themselves. When one Signifies, as Kimberly W. Benston puns, one "tropes-a-dope." Indeed, the black tradition itself has its own subdivisions of Signifyin(g), which we could readily identify with the figures of signification received from classical and medieval rhetoric, as Bloom has done with his "map of misprision" and which we could, appropriately enough, label a "rap of misprision." The black rhetorical tropes, subsumed under Signifyin(g), would include marking, loud-talking, testifying, calling out (of one's name), sounding, rapping, playing the dozens, and so on.[10] [See Chart 2.]

The Esu figures, among the Yoruba systems of thought in Benin and Nigeria, Brazil and Cuba, Haiti and New Orleans, are divine: they are gods who function in sacred myths, as do characters in a narrative. Esu's functional equivalent in Afro-American profane discourse is the Signifying Monkey, a figure who would seem to be distinctly Afro-American, probably derived from Cuban mythology which generally depicts Echu-Elegua with a monkey at his side. Unlike his Pan-African Esu cousins, the Signifying Monkey exists not primarily as a character in a narrative but rather as a vehicle for narration itself. Like Esu, however, the Signifying Monkey stands as the figure of an oral writing within black vernacular language rituals. It is from the corpus of mythological narratives that Signifyin(g) derives. The Afro-American rhetorical strategy of Signifyin(g) is a rhetorical practice that is not engaged in the game of information-giving, as Wittgenstein said of poetry. Signifyin(g) turns on the play and chain of signifiers, and not on some supposedly transcendent signified. As anthropologists demonstrate, the Signifying Monkey is often called the Signifier, he who wreaks havoc upon the Signified. One is signified upon by the signifier. He is indeed the "signifier as such," in Kristeva's phrase, "a presence that precedes the signification of object or emotion."

Alan Dundes's suggestion that the origins of Signifyin(g) could "lie in African rhetoric" is not as far-fetched as one might think. I have argued for a consideration of a line of descent for the Signifying Monkey from his Pan-African cousin, Esu-Elegbara. I have done so not because I have unearthed archeological evidence of a transmission process, but because of their functional equivalency as figures of rhetorical strategies and of interpretation. Esu is the Yoruba figure of writing within an oral system. Like Esu, the Signifying Monkey exists, or is figured, in a densely structured discursive universe, one absolutely dependent on the play of differences. The poetry in which the Monkey's antics unfold is a signifying system: in marked contrast to the supposed transparency of normal speech, the poetry of these tales turns upon the free play of language itself, upon the displacement of meanings, precisely because it draws attention to its rhetorical structures and strategies and thereby draws attention to the force of the signifier.[11]

In opposition to the apparent transparency of speech, this poetry calls attention to itself as an extended linguistic sign, one composed of various forms of the signifiers peculiar to the black vernacular. Meaning, in these poems, is not proffered; it is deferred, and it is deferred because the relationship between intent and meaning, between the speech act and its comprehension, is skewed by the figures of rhetoric or signification of which these poems consist. This set of skewed relationships creates a measure of undecidability within the discourse, such that it must be interpreted or decoded by careful attention to its play of differences. Never can this interpretation be definitive, given the ambiguity at work in its rhetorical structures.

The speech of the Monkey exists as a sequence of signifiers, effecting meanings through their differential relation and calling attention to itself by rhyming, repetition, and several of the rhetorical figures used in larger cultural language games. Signifyin(g) epitomizes all of the rhetorical play in the black vernacular. Its self-consciously open rhetorical status, then, functions as a kind of writing, wherein rhetoric is the writing of speech, of oral discourse. If Esu is the figure of writing in Ifa, the Signifying Monkey is the figure of a black rhetoric in the Afro-American speech community. He exists to embody the figures of speech characteristic to the black vernacular. He is the principle of self-consciousness in the black vernacular, the meta-figure itself. Given the play of doubles at work in the black appropriation of the English-language term that denotes relations of meaning, the Signifying Monkey and his language of Signifyin(g) are extraordinary conventions, with Signification standing as the term for black rhetoric, the obscuring of apparent meaning.

Scholars have for some time commented on the peculiar use of the word *Signifyin(g)* in black discourse. Though sharing some connotations with the standard English-language word, *Signifyin(g)* has rather unique definitions in black discourse. While we shall consider these definitions later in this chapter, it is useful to look briefly at one suggested by Roger D. Abrahams:

> Signifying seems to be a Negro term, in use if not in origin. It can mean any of a number of things; in the case of the toast about the signifying monkey, it certainly refers to the trickster's ability to talk with great innuendo, to carp, cajole, needle, and lie. It can mean in other instances the propensity to talk around a subject, never quite coming to the point. It can mean making fun of a person or situation. Also it can denote speaking with the hands and eyes, and in this respect encompasses a whole complex of expressions and gestures. Thus it is signifying to stir up a fight between neighbors by telling stories; it is signifying to make fun of a policeman by parodying his motions behind his back; it is signifying to ask for a piece of cake by saying, "my brother needs a piece a cake."[12]

Essentially, Abrahams continues, Signifyin(g) is a "*technique* of indirect argument or persuasion," "a language of implication," "to imply, goad, beg, boast, by *indirect* verbal or gestural means." "The name 'signifying,'" he concludes, "shows the monkey to be a trickster, signifying being the language of trickery, that set of words or gestures achieving Hamlet's 'direction through indirection.'" The Monkey, in short, is not only a master of technique, as Abrahams concludes; he *is* technique, or style, or the literariness of literary language; he is the great Signifier. In this sense, one does not signify something; rather, one signifies in *some way.*[13]

The Signifying Monkey poems, like the *ese* of the Yoruba *Odu*, reward careful explication; this sort of extensive practical criticism, however, is outside the scope of this book, as fascinating as it might be. The stanzaic form of this poetry can vary a great deal. The most common structure is the rhyming couplet in an a-a-b-b pattern. Even within the same poem, however, this pattern can be modified, as in the stanzas cited below, where an a-a-b-c-b and an a-b-c-b pattern obtain (followed in the latter example by an a-b-a concluding "moral"). Rhyming is extraordinarily important in the production of the humorous effect that these poems have and has become the signal indication of expertise among the street poets who narrate them. The rhythm of the poems is also crucial to the desired effect, an effect in part reinforced by their quasi-musical nature of delivery.

The Monkey tales generally have been recorded from male poets, in predominantly male settings such as barrooms, pool halls, and street corners. Accordingly, given their nature as rituals of insult and naming, recorded versions have a phallocentric bias. As we shall see below, however, Signifyin(g) itself can be, and is, undertaken with equal facility and effect by women as well as men.[14] Whereas only a relatively small number of people are accomplished narrators of Signifying Monkey tales, a remarkably large number of Afro-Americans are familiar with, and practice, modes of Signifyin(g), defined in this instance as the rubric for various sorts of playful language games, some aimed at reconstituting the subject while others are aimed at demystifying a subject. The poems are of interest to my argument primarily in three ways: as the source of the rhetorical act of Signification, as examples of the black tropes subsumed within the trope of Signifyin(g), and, crucially, as evidence for the valorization of the signifier. One of these subsumed tropes is concerned with repetition and difference; it is this trope, that of naming, which I have drawn upon as a metaphor for black intertextuality and, therefore, for formal literary history. Before discussing this process of revision, however, it is useful to demonstrate the formulaic structure of the Monkey tales and then to compare several attempts by linguists to define the nature and function of Signifyin(g). While other scholars have interpreted the Monkey tales against the binary opposition between black and white in American society, to do so is to ignore the *trinary* forces of the Monkey, the Lion, and the Elephant. To read the Monkey tales as a simple allegory of the black's political oppression is to ignore the hulking presence of the Elephant, the crucial third term of the depicted action. To note this is not to argue that the tales are not allegorical or that their import is not political. Rather, this is to note that to reduce such complex structures of meaning to a simple two-term opposition (white versus black) is to fail to account for the strength of the Elephant.

There are many versions of the toasts of the Signifying Monkey, most of which commence with a variant of the following formulaic lines:

> *Deep down in the jungle so they say*
> *There's a signifying monkey down the way*
> *There hadn't been no disturbin' in the jungle for quite a bit,*
> *For up jumped the monkey in the tree one day and laughed*
> *"I guess I'll start some shit."*[15]

Endings, too, tend toward the formulaic, as in the following:

> *"Monkey," said the Lion*
> *Beat to his unbooted knees,*
> *"You and your signifying children*
> *Better stay up in the trees."*
> *Which is why today*
> *Monkey does his signifying*
> *A-way-up out of the way.*[16]

In the narrative poems, the Signifying Monkey invariably repeats to his friend, the Lion, some insult purportedly generated by their mutual friend, the Elephant. The Monkey, however, speaks figuratively. The Lion, indignant and outraged, demands an apology of the Elephant, who refuses and then trounces the Lion. The Lion, realizing that his mistake was to take the Monkey literally, returns to trounce the Monkey. It is this relationship between the literal and the figurative, and the dire consequences of their confusion, which is the most striking repeated element of these tales. The Monkey's trick depends on the Lion's inability to mediate between these two poles of signification, of meaning. There is a profound lesson about reading here. While we cannot undertake a full reading of the poetry of the Signifying Monkey, we can, however, identify the implications for black vernacular discourse that are encoded in this poetic diction.

Signifyin(g) as a rhetorical strategy emanates directly from the Signifying Monkey tales. The relationship between these poems and the related, but independent, mode of formal language use must be made clear. The action represented in Monkey tales turns upon the action of three stock characters—the Monkey, the Lion, and the Elephant—who are bound together in a trinary relationship. The Monkey—a trickster figure, like Esu, who is full of guile, who tells lies,[17] and who is a rhetorical genius—is intent on demystifying the Lion's self-imposed status as King of the Jungle. The Monkey, clearly, is no match for the Lion's physical prowess; the Elephant is, however. The Monkey's task, then, is to trick the Lion into tangling with the Elephant, who is the true King of the Jungle for everyone else in the animal kingdom. This the Monkey does with a rhetorical trick, a trick of mediation. Indeed, the Monkey is a term of (anti)mediation, as are all trickster figures, between two forces he seeks to oppose for his own contentious purposes, and then to reconcile.

The Monkey's trick of mediation—or, more properly, antimediation—is a play on language use. He succeeds in reversing the Lion's status by supposedly repeating a series of insults purportedly uttered by the Elephant about the Lion's closest relatives (his wife, his "mama," his "grandmamma, too!"). These intimations of sexual use, abuse, and violation constitute one well-known and commonly used mode of Signifyin(g).[18] The Lion, who perceives his shaky, self-imposed status as having been challenged, rushes off in outrage to find the Elephant so that he might redress his grievances and preserve appearances. The self-confident but unassuming Elephant, after politely suggesting to the Lion that he must be mistaken, proceeds to trounce the Lion firmly. The Lion, clearly defeated and dethroned from his self-claimed title, returns to find the Monkey so that he can at the very least exact some sort of physical satisfaction and thereby restore his image somewhat as the impregnable fortress-in-waiting that he so urgently wishes to be. The Monkey, absolutely ecstatic at the success of his deception, commences to Signify upon the Lion, as in the following exchange:

> *Now the Lion come back more dead than alive,*
> *that's when the Monkey started some more of his old signifying.*
> *He said, "King of the Jungles, ain't you a bitch,*
> *you look like someone with the seven-year itch."*
> *He said, "When you left [me earlier in the narrative] the lightnin'*
>   *flashed and the bells rung,*
> *you look like something been damn near hung."*
> *He said, "Whup! Motherfucker, don't you roar,*
> *I'll jump down on the ground and beat your funky ass some more."*
> *Say, "While I'm swinging around in my tree,"*
> *say, "I ought to swing over your chickenshit head and pee."*
> *Say, "Everytime me and my old lady be tryin' to get a little bit,*
> *here you come down through the jungle with that old 'Hi Ho' shit."*[19]

This is a salient example of Signifyin(g), wherein a verbal fusillade of insults spews forth in a structure of ritual rhetorical exchanges.

What happens next is also fascinating. The Monkey, at this point in the discourse deliriously pleased with himself, slips and falls to the ground:

> *Now the little old Monkey was dancing all around*
> *his feet slipped and his ass must have hit the ground.*

The startled Monkey, now vulnerable, seeks to repair his relationship with the Lion in the most urgent manner. So he begs initially:

> *Like a streak of lightning and a bolt of white heat,*
> *the Lion was on the Monkey with all four feet.*
> *Monkey looks up with tears in his eyes,*
> *he says, "I'm sorry, brother Lion," say, "I apologize."*
> *The Lion says, "Apologize, shit," say, "I'm gonna stop you from your*
> *signifyin'."* (p. 165)

The Lion now turns on the Monkey (only, incidentally, to be tricked rhetorically again), not because he has been severely beaten but because he has been beaten, then Signified upon. Another text substitutes the following direct speech of the Lion for that quoted immediately above:

> *[The Lion say], "I'm not gonna whip your ass 'cause that Elephant*
> *whipped mine,*
> *I'm gonna whip your ass for signifyin'."* (p. 168)

The Monkey's trick of Signification has been to convince the hapless Lion that he has spoken literally, when all along he has spoken figuratively. The Lion, though slow-witted enough to repeat his misreading through the eternity of discourse, realizes that his status has been deflated, not because of the Elephant's brutal self-defense but because he fundamentally misunderstood the status of the Monkey's statements. And still another poem represents this moment of clarity:

> *Said, "Monkey, I'm not kicking your ass for lyin',*
> *I'm kicking your hairy ass for signifyin'."* (p. 172)[20]

The black term *to lie*, as J. L. Dillard, Sterling A. Brown, and Zora Neale Hurston amply demonstrate, signifies tale-telling and constitutes a signal form of Signifyin(g).[21] But it is the naming ritual, in which the Monkey speaks aloud his editorial recapitulation of the previous events and their import, which even the dense Lion recognizes to be his most crucial threat, and against which he must defend himself, especially since the Lion returns to the Monkey's tree initially, at least, to impose *his* interpretation on his interchange with the Elephant:

> *Now the Lion looked up to the Monkey, "You know I didn't get beat."*
> *He said, "You're a lyin' motherfucker, I had a ringside seat."*
> *The Lion looked up out of his one good eye, said, "Lord, let that skinny*
>   *bastard fall out of that tree before I die."* (p. 172)

Which he, of course, does, only (in most cases) to escape once again, to return to Signify on another day:

> *He said, "You might as well stop, there ain't no use tryin'*
> *because no motherfucker is gonna stop me from signifyin'."* (p. 163)

While the insult aspect of the Monkey's discourse is important to the tales, linguists have often failed to recognize that insult is not at all central to the nature of Signifyin(g); it is merely one mode of a rhetorical strategy that has several other modes, all of which share the use of troping. They have, in other words, mistaken the trees for the forest. For Signifyin(g) constitutes all of the language games, the figurative substitutions, the free associations held in abeyance by Lacan's or Saussure's paradigmatic axis, which disturb the seemingly coherent linearity of the syntagmatic chain of signifiers, in a way analogous to Freud's notion of how the unconscious relates to the conscious. The black vernacular trope of Signifyin(g) exists on this vertical axis, wherein the materiality of the signifier (the use of words as things, in Freud's terms of the discourse of the unconscious) not only ceases to be disguised but comes to bear prominently as the dominant mode of discourse.

I do not cite Freud idly here. *Jokes and Their Relation to the Unconscious* and *The Interpretation of Dreams* have informed my reading of Signifyin(g), just as have Lacan's reading of Freud and Saussure, and Derrida's emphasis on the "graphematic" aspect of even oral discourse. Just as jokes often draw upon the sounds of words rather than their meanings, so do the poetry of the Signifying Monkey and his language of Signifyin(g). Directing, or redirecting, attention from the semantic to the rhetorical level defines the relationship, as we have seen, between signification and Signification. It is this redirection that allows us to bring the repressed meanings of a word, the meanings that lie in wait on the paradigmatic axis of discourse, to bear upon the syntagmatic axis. This redirection toward sound, without regard for the scrambling of sense that it entails, defines what is meant by the materiality of the signifier, its thingness. As Freud explained, there is nothing necessarily infantile about this, although infants, of course, engage in such paradigmatic substitutions gleefully. Similarly, there is absolutely nothing infantile about Signifyin(g) either, except perhaps that we learn to use language in this way in adolescence, despite the strangely compulsive repetition of this adjective as a pejorative in the writings of linguists about Signifyin(g).

If Freud's analysis of the joke mechanism is a useful analogue for Signifyin(g), then so too is his analysis of the "dream-work," which by now is so familiar as not to warrant summary here. The Signifying Monkey poems can usefully be thought of as quasi-dreams, or daydreams, dream narratives in which monkeys, lions, and elephants manifest their feelings in direct speech. Animals, of course, do not speak, except in dreams or in mythological discourse. As Freud puts it in *The Interpretation of Dreams*,

> this symbolism is not peculiar to dreams, but is characteristic of unconscious ideation, in particular among the people, and it is to be found in *folklore*, and in popular myths, legends, *linguistic idioms*, proverbial wisdom and current jokes, to a *more complete extent* than in dreams.[22] (emphasis added)

The Signifying Monkey tales, in this sense, can be thought of as versions of daydreams, the Daydream of the Black Other, chiastic fantasies of reversal of power relationships. One of the traditional Signifying poems names this relationship explicitly:

> *The Monkey laid up in a tree and he thought up a scheme,*
> *and thought he'd try one of his fantastic dreams.* (p. 167)

To dream the fantastic is to dream the dream of the Other.

Because these tales originated in slavery, we do not have to seek very far to find typological analogues for these three terms of an allegorical structure. Since to do so, inescapably, is to be reductive, is to redirect attention away from the materiality of the signifier toward its supposed signified, I shall avoid repeating what other scholars have done at such great length. For the importance of the Signifying Monkey poems is their repeated stress on the sheer materiality, and the willful play, of the signifier itself.

While I wrote earlier in this chapter that a close reading of the Monkey tales is outside the scope of a book whose intention is to define an indigenous black metaphor for intertextuality as configured in Afro-American formal literary discourse, I am tempted to write that, like this signal trickster, I have lied! While I am forced by the demands of this book to defer such a series of readings to another text, it is necessary for me to turn to the poems, if briefly, to explain what I mean about their emphasis on the signifier and its materiality. To do so, I have drawn upon William K. Wimsatt's well-known essay, "Rhyme and Reason," printed in *The Verbal Icon: Studies in the Meaning of Poetry* (1970), and Anthony Easthope's equally perceptive but less well-known essay, "The Feudal Ballad," printed in his *Poetry as Discourse* (1983).

Easthope's analysis of the structure of the English ballad dovetails nicely with my analysis of the structure of the Signifying Monkey tales. Because Easthope's crucial point of departure is a passage from Albert B. Lord's *The Singer of Tales*, let me repeat it here:

> The method of language is like that of oral poetry, substituting in the framework of the grammar. Without the metrical restrictions of verse, language substitutes one subject for another in the nominative case, keeping the same verb, or keeping the same noun, it substitutes one verb for another.[23]

Lord defines "substitutions," as Easthope explains, similarly to what Saussure identified as the paradigmatic axis, while Lord's "framework of the grammar" corresponds to the syntagmatic axis. Easthope's summary of the defining features of the "discourse exemplified in the ballad" reveals an identity with those of the discourse of the Monkey tales:

> [The] syntagmatic chain does not aim for tight closure and rigid subordination of elements in a linear development; rather it works through juxtaposition, addition and parallel, typically . . . in binary and trinary patterns.
>
> [Disruption] in the syntagmatic chain means that the discourse of the ballad does not offer transparent access to the enounced [*énoncé*, the narrated event, as opposed to enunciation (*enonciation*), the speech event], and so no fixed position is offered to the reader as subject of the enounced.[24]

Like the ballad, "vocabulary and phrasing" of the Monkey poem is "colloquial, monosyllabic and everyday." Even more important to our discussion of language use in the Monkey poems, however, are the three aspects that Easthope locates in the operation of the ballad's syntagmatic chain. These are intertextuality, stanzaic units, and incremental repetition.[25]

Intertextuality

As is apparent from even a cursory reading of the various Signifying Monkey poems, each poem refers to other poems of the same genre. The artistry of the oral narrator of these poems does not depend on his or her capacity to dream up new characters or events that define the actions depicted; rather, it depends on his or her display of the ability to group together two lines that end in words that sound alike, that bear a phonetic similarity to each other. This challenge is great when key terms are fixed, such as the three characters' identities and their received relationship to each other. Accordingly, all sorts of formulaic phrases recur across these poems, but (re)placed in distinct parts of a discrete poem.

One example demonstrates this clearly, especially if we recall that intertextuality represents a process of repetition and revision, by definition. A number of shared structural elements are repeated, with differences that suggest familiarity with other texts of the Monkey. For example, the placement of the figure "forty-four" is an instance of a formulaic phrase being repeated from poem to poem—because it has achieved a formulaic insistency—but repeated in distinct ways. For instance, the following lines in one poem:

> *The Lion jumped back with a mighty roar,*
> *his tail stuck out like a forty-four,*
> *he breezed down through the jungle in a hell of a breeze,*
> *knockin' giraffes to their knees.* (p. 162)

are refigured in another poem in this way:

> *And the Lion knew that he didn't play the Dozens*
> *and he knew the Elephant wasn't none of his cousins,*
> *so he went through the jungle with a mighty roar,*
> *poppin' his tail like a forty-four,*
> *knockin' giraffes to their knees*
> *and knockin' coconuts from the trees.* (p. 164)

and in another poem in this way:

> *The Lion got so mad he jump up trimmin' the trees,*
> *chopped baby giraffes, monkeys down on their knees.*
> *He went on down the jungle way a jumpin' and pawin'*
> *poppin' his tail worse in' a forty-four.* (p. 166)

It is as if a received structure of crucial elements provides a base for poeisis, and the narrator's technique, his or her craft, is to be gauged by the creative (re)placement of these expected or anticipated formulaic phrases and formulaic events, rendered anew in unexpected ways. Precisely because the concepts represented in the poem are shared, repeated, and familiar to the poet's audience, meaning is devalued while the signifier is valorized. Value, in this art of poeisis, lies in its foregrounding rather than in the invention of a novel signified. We shall see how the nature of the rhyme scheme also stresses the materiality and the priority of the signifier. Let me add first, however, that all other common structural elements are repeated with variations across the texts that, together, comprise the text of the Monkey. In other words, there is no fixed text of these poems; they exist as a play of differences.

Stanzaic Units

Every Signifying Monkey poem is characterized by at least two predominant features of stanzaic structure: an introductory formulaic frame and a concluding formulaic frame, as well as a progression of rhyming couplets, each of which usually relates to the next in a binary pattern of a-a-b-b rhyme, although occasionally a pattern of a-a-b-b-c or a-a-b-c-c appears, especially to include a particular vivid (visual) or startling (aural) combination of signifiers. The frame consists of a variation of the following:

> *Say deep down in the jungle in the coconut grove*
> *lay the Signifying Monkey in his one-button roll.*
> *Now the hat he wore was on the Esquire fold.*
> *his shoes was on a triple-A last.*
> *You could tell that he was a pimping motherfucker*
> *by the way his hair was gassed.* (p. 162)

> *He said, "Well, Brother Lion, the day have come at last,*
> *that I have found a limb to fit your ass."*
> *He said, "You might as well stop, there ain't no use tryin',*
> *because no motherfucker is gonna stop me from signifyin."* (p. 163)

I shall turn to the nature of the rhyme scheme and its import below.

Incremental Repetition

Incremental repetition in these poems assumes the form of the repeated binary structure of rhyming couplets, which function as narrative units in isolation or with a second or third set of couplets, and as larger narrative units in a tertiary relation that is contained within the binary frame described above. The frame defines a problem, the Monkey's irritation at the Lion's roaring, which disturbs the Monkey's connubial habits, and ends with some sort of resolution of that problem. The tertiary relation of the intervening narrative units turns upon the repetition of confrontation and engagement: the Monkey engages the Lion by repeating insults purportedly said by the Elephant;

next, the Lion rushes off helter-skelter and challenges the Elephant to a confrontation that the Lion loses; finally, the Lion returns to the scene of the crime, the Monkey's tree, and engages the Monkey, who insults the Lion, slips from his protective branch, then usually escapes certain defeat by tricking the Lion again with a Signifyin(g) challenge, such as the following:

> *The Monkey said, "I know you think you raisin' hell,*
> *but everybody seen me when I slipped and fell.*
> *But if you let me get my nuts up out of this sand*
> *I'll fight you just like a natural man."*

This tertiary repetition of confrontation-engagement-resolution occurs in representations of direct speech. The Lion's combat with the Elephant is balanced by the Lion's combat with the Monkey. Stasis is relieved by the Monkey's trick of mediation, his rhetorical play on the Lion's incapacity to read his utterance, a flaw that enables the Monkey to scramble back to his protective limb, only to continue to Signify.

The most important aspect of language use in these poems, however, is the nature of its rhymes. Here we can draw upon Wimsatt's analysis of the rhymes of Pope and Easthope's analysis of the feudal ballad to elucidate the import of the rhyme in the Monkey tales.

Wimsatt points out perceptively that Pope's rhyming words tend to be different parts of speech, while Chaucer's depend on the coincidence of parts of speech.

> Pope's rhymes are characterized by difference in parts of speech or in function of the same parts of speech, the difference in each case being accentuated by the tendency of his couplets to parallel structure.[26]

Easthope argues that "Such rhyming works to throw a stress upon the meaning so that meaning dominates sound and the rhyme is subordinated." Such a rhyme scheme, he continues, implicitly emphasizes the crucial role of the phonetic in the production of meaning: "relative to subordination, coincidence in rhyme emphasizes the phonetic, so acknowledging the dependence of signified [on] signifier." "Coincident rhyme," on the other hand, "foregrounds the signifier."[27]

While both coincidence and subordination occur in the Monkey tales, coincidence tends to occur more frequently, especially in the use of nouns to end a line. "Phonetic similarity," as Easthope maintains, links two words "at the level of the signifier." When rhymes of the same parts of speech coincide, as in Chaucer's poetry, the signifier and the signified are "in a relationship of equality" rather than subordination, such that "meaning is allowed to follow sound *as much as* sound does meaning." The dominance of rhymes of the same parts of speech in the Monkey poems, then, serves to italicize the role of the signifier, and its materiality, by flaunting, as it were, "the dependence of the signified on the signifier." As anyone who has heard these poems recited fully appreciates, they take their received meaning for granted and depend for their marvelous effect on the sheer play of the signifier.[28]

What does such a foregrounding of the signifier imply for black vernacular discourse? We must remember that the Signifying Monkey tales are the repositories of the black vernacular tradition's rhetorical principles, coded dictionaries of black tropes. First, the Monkey "tropes-a-dope," the Lion, by representing a figurative statement as a literal statement, depending on the Lion's thickness to misread the difference. Second, the ensuing depiction of action depends on the stress of phonetic similarity between signifiers. These poems flaunt the role of the signifier in relation to the signified, allowing it its full status as an equal in their relationship, if not the superior partner. Where meaning is constant, the (re)production of this fixed meaning, by definition, foregrounds the play of the signifier. Signifyin(g), then, is the sign of rule in the kingdom of Signification: neither the Lion nor the Elephant—both Signifieds, those Signified upon—is the King of the Jungle; rather, the Monkey is King, the Monkey as Signifier.

If the rhyme pattern of the poems depends on coincidence more often than subordination, then the Monkey's process of Signifyin(g) turns upon repetition and difference, or repetition and reversal. There are so many examples of Signifyin(g) in jazz that one could write a formal history of its development on this basis alone. One early example is relatively familiar: Jelly Roll Morton's 1938 recording entitled "Maple Leaf Rag (A Transformation)" Signifies upon Scott Joplin's signature composition, "Maple Leaf Rag," recorded in 1916. Whereas Joplin played its contrasting themes and their repetitions in the form of AABBACCDD, Morton "embellishes the piece two-handedly, with a swinging introduction (borrowed from the ending to A), followed by ABACCD (a hint of the tango here) D (a real New Orleans 'stomp' variation)," as Martin Williams observes. Morton's piano imitates "a trumpet-clarinet right hand and a trombone-rhythm left hand."[29] Morton's composition does not "surpass" or "destroy" Joplin's; it complexly *extends* and tropes figures present in the original. Morton's Signification is a gesture of admiration and respect. It is this aspect of Signifyin(g) that is inscribed in the black musical tradition in jazz compositions such as Oscar Peterson's "Signify" and Count Basie's "Signifyin'."

In these compositions, the formal history of solo piano styles in jazz is re-capitulated, delightfully, whereby one piano style follows its chronological predecessor in the composition itself, so that boogie-woogie, stride, and blues piano styles—and so on—are represented in one composition as histo-ries of the solo jazz piano, histories of its internal repetition and revision pro-cess. Improvisation, of course, so fundamental to the very idea of jazz, is "nothing more" than repetition and revision. In this sort of revision, again where meaning is fixed, it is the realignment of the signifier that is the signal trait of expressive genius. The more mundane the fixed text ("April in Paris" by Charlie Parker, "My Favorite Things" by John Coltrane), the more dra-matic is the Signifyin(g) revision. It is this principle of repetition and differ-ence, this practice of intertextuality, which has been so crucial to the black vernacular forms of Signifyin(g), jazz—and even its antecedents, the blues, the spirituals, and ragtime—and which is the source of my trope for black in-tertextuality in the Afro-American formal literary tradition.

III

Signifyin(g): Definitions

Signifyin(g) is so fundamentally black, that is, it is such a familiar rhetorical practice, that one encounters the great resistance of inertia when writing about it. By inertia I am thinking here of the difficulty of rendering the im-plications of a concept that is so shared in one's culture as to have long ago become second nature to its users. The critic is bound to encounter Ralph Ellison's "Little Man at Chehaw Station."[30]

Who is he? Ellison tells a marvelous story about himself when he was a student of music at Tuskegee. Having failed at an attempt to compensate for a lack of practice with a virtuoso style of performance, Ellison had sought some solace from the brilliant Hazel Harrison, one of his professors, with whom he had a sustained personal relationship. Instead of solace, however, his friend and mentor greeted his solicitation with a riddle. The exchange is relevant here:

> "All right," she said, "you must *always* play your best, even if it's only in the waiting room at Chehaw Station, because in this country there'll always be a little man hidden behind the stove."
>
> "A what?"
>
> She nodded. "That's right," she said, "there'll always be the little man whom you don't expect, and he'll know the *music*, and the *tradition*, and the standards of *musicianship* required for whatever you set out to perform!"[31]

This little man, who appears at such out-of-the-way places as the Chehaw Railroad Station, is, of course, a trickster figure surfacing when we least expect him, at a crossroads of destiny. This particular little man evokes Esu, the little man whose earthly dwelling place is the crossroads, as indicated in the following excerpts from a Yoruba poem:

> *Latopa, Esu little man*
> *Latopa, Esu little man*
> *Short, diminutive man*
> *Tiny, little man.*
>
> *He uses both hands to sniffle!*
> *We call him master*
> *He who sacrifices without inviting the manumitter*
> *Will find his sacrifice unacceptable*
> *Manumitter, I call on you.*
> *Man by the roadside, bear our sacrifice to heaven directly*
> *Master, and son of the owner of Idere*
> *Who came from Idere to found the town,*
> *The son of the energetic small fellow*
> *The little man who cleans the gates for the masquerade.*
> *Elderly spirit deity!*[32]

The "little man" or woman is bound to surface when the literary critic begins to translate a signal concept from the black vernacular milieu into the discourse of critical theory. While critics write for writers and other critics, they also write—in this instance—for "little" men and women who dwell at the crossroads.

The critic of comparative black literature also dwells at a sort of crossroads, a discursive crossroads at which two languages meet, be these languages Yoruba and English, or Spanish and French, or even (perhaps especially) the black vernacular and standard English. This sort of critic would seem, like Esu, to live at the intersection of these crossroads. When writing a book that lifts one concept from two discrete discursive realms, only to compare them, the role of the critic as the trickster of discourse seems obvious. The concept of Signification is such an instance.

What Ellison's professor did to him was a salient example of Signifyin(g). His professor, subtle and loving as she must have been, Signified upon her young protégé so that he would never allow himself to succumb to the lure of the temptation to skip the necessary gates placed in the apprentice's path, gates which must somehow be opened or hurdled. Ellison was Signified upon because his dilemma was resolved through an allegory. This mode of rhetorical indirection, as Roger D. Abrahams and Claudia Mitchell-Kernan have defined it, is a signal aspect of Signifyin(g). Despite its highly motivated, often phallocentric orientation, then, Signifyin(g), it is clear, can mean any number of modes of rhetorical play.

An article printed in the *New York Times* on April 17, 1983, entitled "Test on Street Language Says It's Not Grant in That Tomb," affords an opportunity to expand somewhat on received definitions of Signifyin(g). The test referred to in the story's title is one created by "some high school students" in Winston-Salem, North Carolina, "who were dismayed at [McGraw-Hill's] own standardized tests." The examination, a multiple-choice intelligence test, is entitled "The In Your Face Test of No Certain Skills." It was created shortly after the students told their teacher, Rob Slater, that "they had trouble relating to a standardized achievement test." As Slater explains, "They were taking one of these tests one day and one of my students looked up and asked what the reason for the test was, because all it did to him was make him feel academically inferior. After the test was over," Slater concludes, "I asked them if they wanted to get even. They took it from there."[33]

The students devised a test to measure vocabulary mastery in street language. They sent ten copies to McGraw-Hill, where eight employees took the test, only to score C's and D's. One of the test's questions, to which the *Times*'s article title refers, is an example of the most familiar mode of Signifyin(g). The question read, "Who is buried in Grant's tomb?" The proper response to this question is, "Your mama." It is difficult to explain why this response is so funny and why it is an example of Signifyin(g). "Your mama" jokes abound in black discourse, all the way from the field and the street to Langston Hughes's highly accomplished volume of poems, *Ask Your Mama*, from which an epigraph to this chapter has been taken. The presence in the students' test of this centuries-old black joke represents an inscription of the test's Signifyin(g) nature, because it serves as an echo of the significance of the test's title, "The In Your Face Test of No Certain Skills." The title Signifies in two ways. First, "In your face" is a standard Signifyin(g) retort, meaning that by which you intended to confine (or define) me I shall return to you squarely in your face. And second, the title is a parody (repetition motivated to underscore irony) of test titles such as "The Iowa Test of Basic Skills," which my generation was made to suffer through from the fourth grade through high school. The test itself, then, is an extended Signifyin(g) sign of repetition and reversal, a chiastic slaying at the crossroads where two discursive units meet. As the *Times* article observes, "The students' point was that they did not look at things in the same way as the people at McGraw-

Hill. The results of the 'In Your Face' test clearly show that McGraw-Hill and the ninth-graders at Hill High *do not speak the same language.*"[34]

The language of blackness encodes and names its sense of independence through a rhetorical process that we might think of as the Signifyin(g) black difference. As early as the eighteenth century, commentators recorded black usages of Signification. Nicholas Cresswell, writing between 1774 and 1777, made the following entry in his journal: "In [the blacks'] songs they generally relate the usage they have received from their Masters or Mistresses in a very satirical stile [sic] and manner."[35] Cresswell strikes at the heart of the matter when he makes explicit "the usage" that the black slaves "have received," for black people frequently "enounce" their sense of difference by repetition with a signal difference. The eighteenth century abounds in comments from philosophers such as David Hume in "Of National Characters" and statesmen such as Thomas Jefferson in *Notes on the State of Virginia*, who argued that blacks were "imitative" rather than "creative." All along, however, black people were merely Signifyin(g) through a motivated repetition.

Frederick Douglass, a masterful Signifier himself, discusses this use of troping in his *Narrative* of 1845. Douglass, writing some seventy years after Cresswell, was an even more acute observer. Writing about the genesis of the lyrics of black song, Douglass noted the crucial role of the signifier in the determination of meaning:

> [The slaves] would compose and sing as they went along, consulting neither time nor tune. The thought that came up, came out—if not in the *word*, in the *sound*;—and as frequently in the one as in the other . . . they would sing, as a chorus, to words which to many seem *unmeaning jargon*, but which, nevertheless, were *full of meaning* to themselves.[36]

Meaning, Douglass writes, was as determined by sound as by sense, whereby phonetic substitutions determined the shape of the songs. Moreover, the neologisms that Douglass's friends created, "unmeaning jargon" to standard English speakers, were "full of meaning" to the blacks, who were literally defining themselves in language, just as did Douglass and hundreds of other slave narrators. This, of course, is an example of both sorts of signification, black vernacular and standard English. Douglass continues his discussion by maintaining that his fellow slaves "would sing the most pathetic sentiment in the most rapturous tone, and the most rapturous sentiment in the most pathetic tone," a set of oppositions which led to the song's misreading by non-slaves. As Douglass admits,

> I have often been utterly astonished, since I came to the north, to find persons who could speak of the singing, among slaves, as evidence of their contentment and happiness. It is impossible to conceive of a greater mistake.[37]

This great mistake of interpretation occurred because the blacks were using antiphonal structures to reverse their apparent meaning, as a mode of encoding for self-preservation. Whereas black people under Cresswell's gaze Signified openly, those Douglass knew Signified protectively, leading to the misreading against which Douglass rails. As Douglass writes in his second autobiography, however, blacks often Signified directly, as in the following lyrics:

> *We raise de wheat,*
> *Dey gib us de corn;*
> *We bake de bread,*
> *Dey gib us de cruss;*
> *We sif de meal,*
> *Dey gib us de huss;*
> *We peal de meat,*
> *Dey gib us de skin*
> *And dat's de way*
> *Dey takes us in.*[38]

As William Faux wrote in 1819, slaves commonly used lyrics to Signify upon their oppressors: "Their verse was their own, and abounding either in praise or satire intended for kind and unkind masters."[39]

I cite these early references to motivated language use only to emphasize that black people have been Signifyin(g), without explicitly calling it that, since slavery, as we might expect. One ex-slave, Wash Wilson, in an interview he granted a member of the Federal Writers Project in the 1930s, implies that "sig'fication" was an especial term and practice for the slaves:

> When de niggers go round singin' "Steal Away to Jesus," dat mean dere gwine be a 'ligious meetin' dat night. Dat de *sig'fication* of a meetin'. De masters 'fore and after freedom didn't like dem 'ligious meetin's, so us natcherly slips off at night, down in de bottoms or somewheres. Sometimes us sing and pray all night.[40]

This usage, while close to its standard English shadow, recalls the sense of Signification as an indirect form of communication, as a troping. The report of Wilson's usage overlaps with Zora Neale Hurston's definition of *signify* in

Mules and Men, published in 1935. These two usages of the words are among the earliest recorded; Wilson's usage argues for an origin of "sig'fication" in slavery, as does the allegorical structure of the Monkey poems and the nature of their figuration, both of which suggest a nineteenth-century provenance. I wish to explore, in the remainder of this section of this chapter, received definitions of Signifyin(g) before elaborating my own use of this practice in literary criticism.

We can gain some appreciation of the complexity of Signifyin(g) by examining various definitions of the concept. Dictionary definitions give us an idea of how unstable the concepts are that can be signified by Signifyin(g). Clarence Major's *Dictionary of Afro-American Slang* says that "Signify" is the "same as the *Dirty Dozens*, to censure in 12 or fewer statements," and advises the reader to see "Cap on." The "Dirty Dozens" he defines as "a very elaborate game traditionally played by black boys, in which the participants insult each other's relatives, especially their mothers. The object of the game is to test emotional strength. The first person to give in to anger is the loser." To "Cap on" is "to censure," in the manner of the dozens. For Major, then, to Signify is to be engaged in a highly motivated rhetorical act, aimed at figurative, ritual insult.[41]

Hermese E. Roberts, writing in *The Third Ear: A Black Glossary*, combines Major's emphasis on insult and Roger D. Abrahams's emphasis on implication. Roberts defines "signifying," or "siggin(g)," as "language behavior that makes direct or indirect implications of baiting or boasting, the essence of which is making fun of another's appearance, relatives, or situation." For Roberts, then, a signal aspect of Signifyin(g) is "making fun of" as a mode of "baiting" or "boasting." It is curious to me how very many definitions of Signifyin(g) share this stress on what we might think of as the black person's symbolic aggression, enacted in language, rather than upon the play of language itself, the meta-rhetorical structures in evidence. "Making fun of" is a long way from "making fun," and it is the latter that defines Signifyin(g).[42]

Roberts lists as subcategories of Signifyin(g) the following figures: "joning, playing the dozens, screaming on, sounding." Under "joning" and "sounding," Roberts asks the reader to "See signifying." "Screaming on" is defined as "telling someone off; i.e. to get on someone's case," "case" meaning among other things "an imaginary region of the mind in which is centered one's vulnerable points, eccentricities, and sensitivities." "Screaming on" also means "embarrassing someone publicly." "Playing the dozens" Roberts defines as "making derogatory, often obscene, remarks about another's mother, parents, or family members. ('Yo' mama' is an expression used as retribution for previous vituperation.)" Roberts, in other words, consistently groups Signifyin(g) under those tropes of contention wherein aggression and conflict predominate.

Despite this refusal to transcend surface meaning to define its latent meaning, Roberts's decision to group joning, playing the dozens, screaming on, and sounding as synonyms of Signifyin(g) is exemplary for suggesting that Signifyin(g) is the trope of tropes in the black vernacular.

Mezz Mezzrow, the well-known jazz musician, defines "Signify" in the glossary of his autobiography, *Really the Blues*, as "hint, to put on an act, boast, make a gesture." In the body of his text, however, Mezzrow implicitly defines signifying as the homonymic pun. In an episode in which some black people in a bar let some white gangsters know that their identity as murderers is common knowledge, the blacks, apparently describing a musical performance, use homonyms such as "killer" and "murder" to Signify upon the criminals. As Mezzrow describes the event:

> He could have been talking about the music, but everybody in the room knew different. Right quick another cat spoke up real loud, saying, "That's *murder* man, really murder," and his eyes were *signifying* too. All these gunmen began to shift from foot to foot, fixing their ties and scratching their noses, faces red and Adam's apples jumping. Before we knew it they had gulped their drinks and beat it out the door, saying good-bye to the bartender with their hats way down over their eyebrows and their eyes gunning the ground. That's what Harlem thought of the white underworld.[43]

Signifying here connotes the play of language—both spoken and body language—drawn upon to name something figuratively.

Mezzrow's definitions are both perceptive and subtle. Signifyin(g) for him is one mode of "verbal horseplay," designed to train the subject "to think faster and be more nimble-witted." Mezzrow, then, is able to penetrate the content of this black verbal horseplay to analyze the significance of the rhetorical structures that transcend any fixed form of Signifyin(g), such as the verbal insult rituals called the dozens. Indeed, Mezzrow was one of the first commentators to recognize that Signifyin(g) as a structure of performance could apply equally to verbal texts and musical texts. As he summarizes:

> Through all these friendly but lively competitions you could see the Negro's appreciation of real talent and merit, his demand for fair play, and his ardor for the best man wins and don't you come around here with no jive. Boasting doesn't cut any ice; if you think you've got something, don't waste time talking yourself up, go to work and prove it. If you have the stuff the other cats will recognize it frankly, with solid admiration. That's especially true in the field of music, which has a double importance to the Negro because that's where he really shines, where his inventiveness and artistry come through in

full force. The colored boys prove their musical talents in those competitions called cutting contests, and there it really is the best man wins, because the Negro audience is extra critical when it comes to music and won't accept anything second-rate. These cutting contests are just a musical version of the verbal duels. They're staged to see which performer can snag and cap all the others *musically*. And by the way, these battles have helped to produce some of the race's greatest musicians.[44]

Signifyin(g) for Mezzrow is not what is played or said; it is rather a form of rhetorical training, an on-the-streets exercise in the use of troping, in which the play is the thing—not specifically what is said, but how. All definitions of Signifyin(g) that do not distinguish between manner and matter succumb, like the Lion, to serious misreading.

Malachi Andrews and Paul T. Owens, in *Black Language*, acutely recognize two crucial aspects of Signifyin(g): first, that the signifier invents a myth to commence the ritual and, second, that in the Monkey tales at least, trinary structure prevails over binary structure. "To Signify," they write,

> is to tease, to provoke into anger. The *signifier* creates a myth about someone and tells him a *third* person started it. The *signified* person is aroused and seeks that person. . . . Signifying is completely successful when the *signifier* convinces the chump he is working on, that what he is saying is true and that it gets him angered to wrath.[45]

Andrews and Owens's definition sticks fairly closely to the action of the Signifying Monkey tales. While Signifyin(g) can, and indeed does, occur between two people, the three terms of the traditional mythic structure serve to dispel a simple relation of identity between the allegorical figures of the poem and the binary political relationship, outside the text, between black and white. The third term both critiques the idea of the binary opposition and demonstrates that Signifyin(g) itself encompasses a larger domain than merely the political. It is a game of language, independent of reaction to white racism or even to collective black wish-fulfillment vis-à-vis white racism. I cannot stress too much the import of the presence of this third term, or in Hermese E. Roberts's extraordinarily suggestive phrase, "The Third Ear," an intraracial ear through which encoded vernacular language is deciphered.

J. L. Dillard, who along with William Labov and William A. Stewart is one of the most sensitive observers of black language use, defines Signifyin(g) as "a familiar discourse device from the inner city, [which] tends to mean 'communicating (often an obscene or ridiculing message) by indirection.'"[46] Dillard here is elaborating somewhat upon Zora Neale Hurston's gloss printed in *Mules and Men*, where she writes that to signify is to "show off."[47] This definition seems to be an anomalous one, unless we supply Hurston's missing, or implied, terms: to show off *with language use*. Dillard, however, is more concerned with the dozens than he is with Signifyin(g). In an especially perceptive chapter entitled "Discourse Distribution and Semantic Difference in Homophonous Items," Dillard ignores the homophone *signify* but suggests that so-called inner-city verbal rituals, such as the dozens, could well be contemporary revisions of "the 'lies' told by Florida Blacks studied by Hurston and the Anansi stories of the southern plantations," sans the "sex and scatology." "Put those elements back," Dillard continues, "and you have something like the rhymed 'toasts' of the inner city."[48] The "toasts," as Bruce Jackson has shown, include among their types the Signifying Monkey tales.[49] There can be little doubt that Signifyin(g) was found by linguists in the black urban neighborhoods in the fifties and sixties because black people from the South migrated there and passed the tradition along to subsequent generations.

We can see the extremes of dictionary and glossary definitions of *Signify* in two final examples, one taken from *The Psychology of Black Language*, by Jim Haskins and Hugh F. Butts, and the other from the *Dictionary of American Slang*, compiled by Harold Wentworth and Stuart Berg Flexner. Haskins and Butts, in a glossary appended to their text, define "to signify" as "To berate, degrade."[50] In their text, however, they define "signifying" as "a more humane form of verbal bantering" than the dozens, admitting, however, that Signifyin(g) "has many meanings," including meanings that contradict their own glossary listing: "It is, again, the clever and humorous use of words, but it can be used for many purposes—'putting down' another person, making another person feel better, or simply expressing one's feelings."[51] Haskins and Butts's longer definition seems to contradict their glossary listing—unless we recall that Signifyin(g) can mean all of these meanings, and more, precisely because so many black tropes are subsumed within it. Signifyin(g) does not, on the other hand, mean "To pretend to have knowledge; to pretend to be hip, esp. when such pretentions cause one to trifle with an important matter," as Wentworth and Flexner would have it.[52] Indeed, this definition sounds like a classic black Signification, in which a black informant, as it were, Signified upon either Wentworth or Flexner, or lexicographers in general who "pretend to have knowledge."

There are several other dictionary definitions that I could cite here. My intention, however, has been to suggest the various ways in which Signifyin(g) is (mis)understood, primarily because few scholars have succeeded in defining it as a full concept. Rather, they often have taken the part—one of its several tropes—as its whole. The delightfully "dirty" lines of the dozens seem to have generated far more interest from scholars than has Signifyin(g), and perhaps far more heat than light. The dozens are an especially compelling subset of Signifyin(g), and its name quite probably derives from an eighteenth-century meaning of the verb *dozen*, "to stun, stupefy, daze," in the black sense, through language.[53] Let us examine more substantive definitions of Signifyin(g) by H. Rap Brown, Roger D. Abrahams, Thomas Kochman, Claudia Mitchell-Kernan, Geneva Smitherman, and Ralph Ellison, before exploring examples of the definition of Signifyin(g) that I shall employ in the remainder of this book.

H. Rap Brown earned his byname because he was a master of black vernacular rhetorical games and their attendant well-defined rhetorical strategies. Brown's understanding of Signifyin(g) is unsurpassed by that of any scholar. In the second chapter of his autobiography, *Die Nigger Die!*, Brown represents the scenes of instruction by which he received his byname. "I learned to talk in the street," he writes, "not from reading about Dick and Jane going to the zoo and all that simple shit." Rather, Brown continues, "we exercised our minds," not by studying arithmetic but "by playing the Dozens":

> *I fucked your mama*
> *Till she went blind.*
> *Her breath smells bad,*
> *But she sure can grind.*
>
> *I fucked your mama*
> *For a solid hour.*
> *Baby came out*
> *Screaming, Black Power.*
>
> *Elephant and the Baboon*
> *Learning to screw.*
> *Baby came out looking*
> *Like Spiro Agnew.*

Brown argues that his teachers sought to teach him "poetry," meaning poems from the Western tradition, when he and his fellows were *making* poetry in the streets. "If anybody needed to study poetry," he maintains, "my teacher needed to study mine. We played the Dozens," he concludes, "like white folks play Scrabble." "[They] call me Rap," he writes humorously if tautologically, "'cause I could rap." To rap is to use the vernacular with great dexterity. Brown, judging from his poetry printed in this chapter of his autobiography, most certainly earned his byname.[54]

Brown's definitions and examples are as witty as they are telling. He insists, as does Claudia Mitchell-Kernan, that both men and women can play the dozens and Signify: "Some of the best Dozens players," he writes, "were girls." Whereas the dozens were an unrelentingly "mean game because what you try to do is totally destroy somebody else with words," Signifyin(g) was "more humane": "Instead of coming down on somebody's mother, you come down on them." Brown's account of the process of Signifyin(g) is especially accurate:

> *A session would start maybe by a brother*
> *saying, "Man, before you mess with me*
> *you'd rather run rabbits, eat shit and*
> *bark at the moon." Then, if he was talking*
> *to me, I'd tell him:*

> *Man, you must don't know who I am.*
> *I'm sweet peeter jeeter the womb beater*
> *The baby maker the cradle shaker*
> *The deerslayer the buckbinder the women finder*
> *Known from the Gold Coast to the rocky shores of Maine*
> *Rap is my name and love is my game.*
> *I'm the bed tucker the cock plucker the motherfucker*
> *The milkshaker the record breaker the population maker*
> *The gun-slinger the baby bringer*
> *The hum-dinger the pussy ringer*
> *The man with the terrible middle finger.*
> *The hard hitter the bullshitter the poly-nussy getter*
> *The beast from the East the Judge the sludge*
> *The women's pet the men's fret and the punks pin-up boy.*
> *They call me Rap the dicker the ass kicker*
> *The cherry picker the city slicker the titty licker*
> *And I ain't giving up nothing but bubble gum and hard times and*
> *   I'm fresh out of bubble gum.*
> *I'm giving up wooden nickels 'cause I know they won't spend*
> *And I got a pocketful of splinter change.*
> *I'm a member of the bathtub club: I'm seeing a whole lot of ass but*
> *   I ain't taking no shit.*
> *I'm the man who walked the water and tied the whale's tail in a knot*
> *Taught the little fishes how to swim*
> *Crossed the burning sands and shook the devil's hand*

Rode round the world on the back of a snail carrying a sack saying
   AIR MAIL.
Walked 49 miles of barbwire and used a Cobra snake for a necktie
And got a brand new house on the roadside made from a cracker's hide,
Got a brand new chimney setting on top made from the cracker's skull
Took a hammer and nail and built the world and called it "THE
   BUCKET OF BLOOD."
Yes, I'm hemp the demp the women's pimp
Women fight for my delight.
I'm a bad motherfucker. Rap the rip-saw the devil's brother'n law.
I roam the world I'm known to wander and this .45 is where I get
   my thunder.
I'm the only man in the world who knows why white milk makes
   yellow butter.
I know where the lights go when you cut the switch off.
I might not be the best in the world, but I'm in the top two and my
brother's getting old.
And ain't nothing bad 'bout you but your breath.

Whereas the dozens were structured to make one's subject feel bad, "Signifying allowed you a choice—you could either make a cat feel good or bad. If you had just destroyed someone [verbally] or if they were just down already, signifying could help them over."[55]

Few scholars have recognized this level of complexity in Signifyin(g), which Brown argues implicitly to be the rhetorical structures at work in the discourse, rather than a specific content uttered. In addition to making "a cat feel good or bad," Brown continues, "Signifying was also a way of expressing your own feelings," as in the following example:

Man, I can't win for losing.
If it wasn't for bad luck, I wouldn't have no luck at all.
I been having buzzard luck
Can't kill nothing and won't nothing die
I'm living on the welfare and things is stormy
They borrowing their shit from the Salvation Army
But things bound to get better 'cause they can't get no worse
I'm just like the blind man, standing by a broken window
I don't feel no pain.
But it's your world
You the man I pay rent to

If I had you hands I'd give 'way both my arms.
Cause I could do without them
I'm the man but you the main man
I read the books you write
You set the pace in the race I run
Why, you always in good form
You got more foam than Alka Seltzer . . . [56]

Signifyin(g), then, for Brown, is an especially expressive mode of discourse that turns upon forms of figuration rather than intent or content. Signifyin(g), to cite Brown, is "what the white folks call verbal skills. We learn how to throw them words together." Signifying, "at its best," Brown concludes, "can be heard when brothers are exchanging tales." It is this sense of storytelling, repeated and often shared (almost communal canonical stories, or on-the-spot recounting of current events) in which Signifyin(g) as a rhetorical strategy can most clearly be seen. We shall return to Brown's definition in the next section of this chapter.[57]

One of the most sustained attempts to define Signifyin(g) is that of Roger D. Abrahams, a well-known and highly regarded literary critic, linguist, and anthropologist. Abrahams's work in this area is seminal, as defined here as a work against which subsequent works must, in some way, react. Between 1962 and 1976, Abrahams published several significant studies of Signifyin(g). To track Abrahams's interpretative evolution helps us to understand the complexities of this rhetorical strategy but is outside the scope of this book.[58]

Abrahams in 1962 brilliantly defines Signifyin(g) in terms that he and other subsequent scholars shall repeat:

> The name "Signifying Monkey" shows [the hero] to be a trickster, "signify-
> ing" being the language of trickery, that set of words or gestures which ar-
> rives at "direction through indirection."[59]

Signifyin(g), Abrahams argues implicitly, is the black person's use of figurative modes of language use. The word *indirection* hereafter recurs in the literature with great, if often unacknowledged, frequency. Abrahams expanded on this theory of Signifyin(g) in two editions of *Deep Down in the Jungle* (1964, 1970). It is useful to list the signal aspects of his extensive definitions:

1. Signifyin(g) "can mean any number of things."
2. It is a black term and a black rhetorical device.
3. It can mean the "ability to talk with great innuendo."
4. It can mean "to carp, cajole, needle, and lie."

5. It can mean "the propensity to talk around a subject, never quite coming to the point."
6. It can mean "making fun of a person or situation."
7. It can "also denote speaking with the hands and eyes."
8. It is "the language of trickery, that set of words achieving Hamlet's 'direction through indirection.'"
9. The Monkey "is a 'signifier,' and the Lion, therefore, is the signified."

Finally, in his appended glossary of "Unusual Terms and Expressions," Abrahams defines "Signify" as "To imply, goad, beg, boast by indirect verbal or gestural means. A language of implication."[60]

These definitions are exemplary insofar as they emphasize "indirection" and "implication," which we can read as synonyms of *figurative*. Abrahams was the first scholar, to my knowledge, to define Signifyin(g) as a language, by which he means a particular rhetorical strategy. Whereas he writes that the Monkey is a master of this technique, it is even more accurate to write that he *is* technique, the literariness of language, the ultimate source for black people of the figures of signification. If we think of rhetoric as the "writing" of spoken discourse, then the Monkey's role as the source and encoded keeper of Signifyin(g) helps to reveal his functional equivalency with his Pan-African cousin, *Esu-Elegbara*, the figure of writing in Ifa.

Abrahams's work helps us to understand that Signifyin(g) is an adult ritual, which black people learn as adolescents, almost exactly like children learned the traditional figures of signification in classically structured Western primary and secondary schools, training one hopes shall be returned to contemporary education. As we shall see below, Claudia Mitchell-Kernan, an anthropologist-linguist, shares an anecdote that demonstrates, first, how Signifyin(g) truly is a conscious rhetorical strategy and, second, how adult black people implicitly instruct a mature child in its most profound and subtle uses by an indirect mode of narration only implicitly related in form to the Monkey tales, perhaps as extract relates to the vanilla bean, or as sand relates to the pearl, or, as Esu might add, as palm wine relates to the palm tree. Black adults teach their children this exceptionally complex system of rhetoric, almost exactly like Richard A. Lanham describes a generic portrait of the teaching of the rhetorical *paideia* to Western schoolchildren. The mastery of Signifyin(g) creates *homo rhetoricus Africanus*, allowing—through the manipulation of these classic black figures of Signification—the black person to move freely between two discursive universes. This is an excellent example of what I call linguistic masking, the verbal sign of the mask of blackness that demarcates the boundary between the white linguistic realm and the black, two domains that exist side by side in a homonymic relation signified by the very concept of Signification. To learn to manipulate language in such a way as to facilitate the smooth navigation between these two realms has been the challenge of black parenthood, and remains so even today. Teaching one's children the fine art of Signifyin(g) is to teach them about this mode of linguistic circumnavigation, to teach them a second language that they can share with other black people.[61] Black adolescents engaged in the dozens and in Signifyin(g) rituals to learn the classic black figures of Signification. As H. Rap Brown declares passionately, his true school was the street. Richard Lanham's wonderful depiction of the student passing through the rhetorical *paideia* reads like a description of vernacular black language training:

> Start your student young. Teach him a minute concentration on the word, how to write it, speak it, remember it. . . . From the beginning, stress behavior as performance, reading aloud, speaking with gesture, a full range of histrionic adornment. . . . Develop elaborate memory schemes to keep them readily at hand. Teach, as theory of personality, a corresponding set of accepted personality types, a taxonomy of impersonation. . . . Nourish an acute sense of social situation. . . . Stress, too, the need for improvisation, ad-lib quickness, the coaxing of chance. Hold always before the student rhetoric's practical purpose: to win, to persuade. But train for this purpose with continual verbal play, rehearsal for the sake of rehearsal.
>
> Use the "case" method. . . . Practice this re-creation always in an agonistic context. The aim is scoring. Urge the student to go into the world and observe its doings from this perspective. And urge him to continue his rehearsal method all his life, forever rehearsing a spontaneous real life. . . . Training in the word thus becomes a badge, as well as a diversion, of the leisure class.[62]

This reads very much like a black person's training in Signifyin(g). Lanham's key words—among which are "a taxonomy of impersonation," "improvisation," "ad-lib quickness," "to win," "to persuade," "continual verbal play," "the 'case' method," "the aim is scoring"—echo exactly the training of blacks to Signify. Even Lanham's concept of a "leisure" class applies ironically here, since blacks tend in capitalist societies to occupy a disproportionate part of the "idle" unemployed, a leisure-class with a difference. To Signify, then, is to master the figures of black Signification.

Few black adults can recite an entire Monkey tale; black adults, on the other hand, can—and do—Signify. The mastering of the Monkey tales corresponds to this early part of Lanham's account of Western rhetorical training. Words are looked at in the Monkey tales because the test of this form of *poeisis* is to arrive at a phonetic coincidence of similar parts of speech, as I have shown above. The splendid example of Signifyin(g) that I have cited in Ralph Ellison's anecdote about Hazel Harrison, and the anecdote of Claudia Mitchell-Kernan's that I shall discuss below, conform to Lanham's apt description of the mature capacity to look through words for their full meaning. Learning the Monkey tales, then, is somewhat akin to attending troping school, where one learns to "trope-a-dope."

The Monkey is a hero of black myth, a sign of the triumph of wit and reason, his language of Signifyin(g) standing as the linguistic sign of the ultimate triumph of self-consciously formal language use. The black person's capacity to create this rich poetry and to derive from these rituals a complex attitude toward attempts at domination, which can be transcended in and through language, is a sign of their originality, of their extreme consciousness of the metaphysical. Abrahams makes these matters clear.

In *Talking Black*, published in 1976, Abrahams's analysis of Signifyin(g) as an act of language is even more subtle than his earlier interpretations. Abrahams repeats his insightful definition that Signifyin(g) turns upon indirection. Black women, he maintains, and "to a certain extent children," utilize "more indirect methods of signifying." His examples are relevant ones:

> These range from the most obvious kinds of indirection, like using an unexpected pronoun in discourse ("Didn't we come to shine, today?" or "Who thinks his drawers don't stink?"), to the more subtle technique, of *louding* or *loud-talking* in a different sense from the one above. A person is loud-talking when he says something of someone just loud enough for that person to hear, but indirectly, so he cannot properly respond (Mitchell-Kernan). Another technique of signifying through indirection is making reference to a person or group not present, in order to start trouble between someone present and the ones who are not. An example of this technique is the famous toast, "The Signifying Monkey."[63]

These examples are salient for two reasons: first, because he has understood that adults use the modes of signification commonly, even if they cannot recite even one couplet from the Monkey tales, and, second, because he has realized that other tropes, such as loud-talking, are subtropes of Signifyin(g). His emphasis on the mature forms of Signifyin(g)—that is, the indirect modes—as more common among women and children does not agree with my observations. Indeed, I have found that black men and women use indirection with each other to the same degree.

Next, Abrahams states that Signifyin(g) can also be used "in recurrent black-white encounters as masking behavior." Since the full effectiveness of Signifyin(g) turns upon all speakers possessing the mastery of reading, what

Abrahams calls "intergroup" Signifyin(g) is difficult to effect, if only because the inherent irony of discourse most probably will not be understood. Still, Signifyin(g) is one significant mode of verbal masking or troping.[64]

Abrahams's most important contribution to the literature on Signifyin(g) is his discovery that Signifyin(g) is primarily a term for rhetorical strategies, which often is called by other names depending on which of its several forms it takes. As he concludes, "with *signifying* we have a term not only for a way of speaking but for a rhetorical strategy that may be characteristic of a number of other designated events."[65] I would add to this statement that, for black adults, Signifyin(g) is the name for the figures of rhetoric themselves, the figure of the figure. Abrahams lists the following terms as synonyms of Signifyin(g), as derived from several other scholars, and which I am defining to be black tropes as subsumed within the trope of Signifyin(g): *talking shit, woofing, spouting, muckty muck, boogerbang, beating your gums, talking smart, putting down, putting on, playing, sounding, telling lies, shag-lag, marking, shucking, jiving, jitterbugging, bugging, mounting, charging, cracking, harping, rapping, boo-kooing, low-rating, hoorawing, sweet-talking, smart-talking,* and no doubt a few others that I have omitted.[66] This is a crucial contribution to our understanding of this figure because it transcends the disagreements, among linguists, about whether trope x or y is evidenced by speech act a or b. What's more, Abrahams reveals, by listing its synonyms, that black people can mean at least twenty-eight figures when they call something Signifyin(g). He represents a few of the figures embedded in Signifyin(g) in Chart 1:

Chart 1. Roger D. Abrahams's Figure 1 in *Talking Black*, p. 46.

conversation on the streets; ways of speaking between equals		
informational; content focus *running it down*	aggressive, witty performance talk *signifying*	
	serious, clever conflict talk "me-and-you and no one else" focus *talking smart*	nonserious contest talk "any of us here" focus *talking shit*
	overtly aggressive talk *putting down* covertly aggressive, manipulative talk *putting on*	nondirective *playing* directive *sounding*
conversational (apparently spontaneous)	arises within conversational context, yet judged in performance (stylistic) terms	performance interaction, yet built on model of conversational back-and-forth

going deep; talking bad

He could have listed several others. When black people say that "Significa-tion is the Nigger's occupation," we can readily see what they mean, since mastering all of these figures of Signification is a lifetime's work!

When a black person speaks of Signifyin(g), he or she means a "style-focused message . . . styling which is *foregrounded* by the devices of making a point by indirection and wit." What is foregrounded, of course, is the signifier itself, as we have seen in the rhyme scheme of the Monkey tales. The Mon-key is called the signifier because he foregrounds the signifier in his use of language. Signifyin(g), in other words, turns on the sheer play of the signifier. It does not refer primarily to the signified; rather, it refers to the style of lan-guage, to that which transforms ordinary discourse into literature. Again, one does not Signify some thing; one Signifies in *some way*.[67]

The import of this observation for the study of black literature is manifold. When I wrote earlier that the black tradition theorized about itself in the ver-nacular, this is what I meant in part. Signifyin(g) is the black rhetorical differ-ence that negotiates the language user through several orders of meaning. In formal literature, what we commonly call figuration corresponds to Significa-tion. Again, the originality of so much of the black tradition emphasizes refigu-ration, or repetition and difference, or troping, underscoring the foregrounding of the chain of signifiers, rather than the mimetic representation of a novel con-tent. Critics of Afro-American, Caribbean, and African literatures, however, have far more often than not directed their attention to the signified, often at the expense of the signifier, as if the latter were transparent. This functions contrary to the principles of criticism inherent in the concept of Signifyin(g).

Thomas Kochman's contribution to the literature on Signifyin(g) is the recognition that the Monkey is the Signifier, and that one common form of this rhetorical practice turns upon repetition and difference. Kochman also draws an important distinction between directive and expressive modes of Signification. Directive Signifyin(g), paradoxically, turns upon an indirective strategy:

> . . . when the function of signifying is *directive*, and the *tactic* which is em-ployed is one of *indirection*—i.e., the signifier reports or repeats what someone has said about the listener; the "report" is couched in plausible language de-signed to compel belief and arouse feelings of anger and hostility.[68]

Kochman argues that the function of this sort of claim to repetition is to challenge and reverse the status quo:

> There is also the implication that if the listener fails to do anything about it—what has to be "done" is usually quite clear—his status will be seriously

compromised. Thus the lion is compelled to vindicate the honor of his family by fighting or else leave the impression that he is afraid, and that he is not "king of the jungle." When used to direct action, signifying is like shucking in also being deceptive and subtle in approach and depending for success on the naïvete or gullibility of the person being put on.[69]

Kochman's definition of expressive Signifyin(g), while useful, is less inclusive than that proposed by H. Rap Brown, including as it does only negative intentions: "to arouse feelings of embarrassment, shame, frustration, or futility, for the purpose of diminishing someone's status, but without directive implication." Expressive Signifyin(g), Kochman continues, employs "direct" speech tactics "in the form of a taunt, as in the . . . example where the monkey is making fun of the lion." For Kochman, Signifyin(g) implies an aggressive mode of rhetoric, a form of symbolic action that yields catharsis.[70]

While several other scholars have discussed the nature and function of Signifyin(g), the theories of Claudia Mitchell-Kernan and Geneva Smitherman are especially useful for the theory of revision that I am outlining in this chapter.[71] Mitchell-Kernan's theory of Signifyin(g) is among the most thorough and the most subtle in the linguistic literature, while Smitherman's work connects linguistic analysis with the Afro-American literary tradition.

Mitchell-Kernan is quick to demonstrate that Signifyin(g) has received most scholarly attention as "a tactic employed in game activity—verbal dueling—which is engaged in as an end in itself," as if this one aspect of the rhetorical concept amounted to its whole. In fact, however, "*Signifying* . . . also refers to a way of encoding messages or meanings which involves, in most cases, an element of indirection." This alternative definition amounts to nothing less than a polite critique of the linguistic studies of Signifyin(g), since the subtleties of this rhetorical strategy somehow escaped most other scholars before Mitchell-Kernan. As she expands her definition, "This kind of *signifying* might be best viewed as an alternative message form, selected for its artistic merit, and may occur embedded in a variety of discourse. Such *signifying* is not focal to the linguistic interaction in the sense that it does not define the entire speech event."[72]

I cannot stress too much the importance of this definition, for it shows that Signifyin(g) is a pervasive mode of language use rather than merely one specific verbal game, an observation that somehow escaped the notice of every other scholar before Mitchell-Kernan. This definition alone serves as a corrective to what I think of as the tendency among linguists who have fixed their gaze upon the aggressive ritual part and thereby avoided seeing the concept as a whole. What's more, Mitchell-Kernan's definition points to the implicit parallels between Signifyin(g) and the use of language that we broadly define to be figurative, by which I mean in this context an intentional deviation from the ordinary form or syntactical relation of words.[73]

Signifyin(g), in other words, is synonymous with figuration. Mitchell-Kernan's work is so rich because she studied the language behavior of adults as well as adolescents, and of women as well as men. Whereas her colleagues studied lower-class male language use, then generalized from this strictly limited sample, Mitchell-Kernan's data are derived from a sample more representative of the black speech community. Hers is a sample that does not undermine her data because it accounts for the role of age and sex as variables in language use. In addition, Mitchell-Kernan refused to be captivated by the verbal insult rituals, such as sounding, playing the dozens, and Signifyin(g), as ritual speech events, unlike other linguists whose work suffers from an undue attention to the use of words such as *motherfucker*, to insults that turn on sexual assertions about someone's mama, and to supposed Oedipal complexes that arise in the literature only because the linguist is reading the figurative as a literal statement, like our friend, the Signified Lion.

These scholars, unlike Mitchell-Kernan, have mistaken the language games of adolescents as an end rather than as the drills common to classical rhetorical study as suggested in Lanham's hypothetical synopsis quoted earlier in this chapter. As Mitchell-Kernan concludes, both the sex and the age of the linguist's informants "may slant interpretation, particularly because the insult dimension [of Signifyin(g)] looms large in contexts where verbal dueling is focal." In the neighborhood in which she was raised, she argues, whereas "*Sounding* and *Playing the Dozens* categorically involved verbal insult (typically joking behavior); *signifying* did not." Mitchell-Kernan is declaring, most unobtrusively, that, for whatever reasons, linguists have misunderstood what Signifyin(g) means to black people who practice it. While she admits that one relatively minor aspect of this rhetorical principle involves the ritual of insult, the concept is much more profound than merely this. Indeed, Signifyin(g) alone serves to underscore the uniqueness of the black community's use of language: "the terminological use of *signifying* to refer to a particular kind of language specialization defines the Black community as a speech community in contrast to non-Black communities." Mitchell-Kernan here both critiques the work of other linguists who have wrestled unsuccessfully with this difficult concept (specifically Abrahams and Kochman), and provides an urgently needed corrective by defining Signifyin(g) as a way of figuring language. Mitchell-Kernan's penetrating work enables Signifyin(g) to be even further elaborated upon for use in literary theory.[74]

Because it is difficult to arrive at a consensus of definitions of Signifyin(g), as this chapter already has made clear, Mitchell-Kernan proceeds "by way of

analogy to inform the reader of its various meanings as applied in interpretation." This difficulty of definition is a direct result of the fact that Signifyin(g)
is the black term for what in classical European rhetoric are called the figures
of signification. Because to Signify is to be figurative, to define it in practice is
to define it through any number of its embedded tropes. No wonder even
Mitchell-Kernan could not arrive at a consensus among her informants—
except for what turns out to be the most crucial shared aspects of all figures
of speech, an indirect use of words that changes the meaning of a word or
words. Or, as Quintilian put it, figuration turns on some sort of "change in
signification." While linguists who disagree about what it means to Signify all
repeat the role of indirection in this rhetorical strategy, none of them seems
to have understood that the ensuing alteration or deviation of meaning
makes Signifyin(g) the black trope for all other tropes, the trope of tropes, the
figure of figures. Signifyin(g) *is* troping.[75]

Mitchell-Kernan begins her elaboration of the concept by pointing to
the unique usage of the word in black discourse:

> What is unique in Black English usage is the way in which signifying is ex-
> tended to cover a range of meanings and events which are not covered in its
> Standard English usage. In the Black community it is possible to say, "He
> is signifying" and "Stop signifying"—sentences which would be anomalous
> elsewhere.[76]

Because in standard English signification denotes meaning and in the black
tradition it denotes ways of meaning, Mitchell-Kernan argues for discrepancies between meanings of the same term in two distinct discourses:

> The Black concept of *signifying* incorporates essentially a folk notion that dic-
> tionary entries for words are not always sufficient for interpreting meanings
> or messages, or that meaning goes beyond such interpretations. Complimen-
> tary remarks may be delivered in a left-handed fashion. A particular utter-
> ance may be an insult in one context and not another. What pretends to be
> informative may intend to be persuasive. The hearer is thus constrained to
> attend to all potential meaning carrying symbolic systems in speech events—
> the total universe of discourse.[77]

Signifyin(g), in other words, is the figurative difference between the literal
and the metaphorical, between surface and latent meaning. Mitchell-Kernan
calls this feature of discourse an "implicit content or function, which is potentially obscured by the surface content or function." Finally, Signifyin(g) pre-
supposes an "encoded" intention to say one thing but to mean quite another.[78]

Mitchell-Kernan presents several examples of Signifyin(g), as she is defining it. Her first example is a conversation among three women about the meal to be served at dinner. One woman asks the other two to join her for dinner, that is, if they are willing to eat "chit'lins." She ends her invitation with a pointed rhetorical question: "Or are you one of those Negroes who don't eat chit'lins?" The third person, the woman not addressed, responds with a long defense of why she prefers "prime rib and T-bone" to "chit'lins," ending with a traditional ultimate appeal to special pleading, a call to unity within the ranks to defeat white racism. Then she leaves. After she has gone, the initial speaker replies to her original addressee in this fashion: "Well, I wasn't signifying at her, but like I always say, if the shoe fits wear it." Mitchell-Kernan concludes that while the manifest subject of this exchange was dinner, the latent subject was the political orientation of two black people vis-à-vis cultural assimilation or cultural nationalism, since many middle-class blacks refuse to eat this item from the traditional black cuisine. Mitchell-Kernan labels this form of Signifyin(g) "allegory," because "the significance or meaning of the words must be derived from known symbolic values."[79]

This mode of Signifyin(g) is commonly practiced by Afro-American adults. It is functionally equivalent to one of its embedded tropes, often called louding or loud-talking, which as we might expect connotes exactly the opposite of that which it denotes: one successfully loud-talks by speaking to a second person remarks in fact directed to a third person, at a level just audible to the third person. A sign of the success of this practice is an indignant "What?" from the third person, to which the speaker responds, "I wasn't talking to you." Of course, the speaker was, yet simultaneously was not. Loud-talking is related to Mitchell-Kernan's second figure of Signification, which she calls "obscuring the addressee" and which I shall call naming. Her example is one commonly used in the tradition, in which "the remark is, on the surface, directed toward no one in particular":

> I saw a woman the other day in a pair of stretch pants, she must have weighed 300 pounds. If she knew how she looked she would burn those things.[80]

If a member of the speaker's audience is overweight and frequently wears stretch pants, then this message could well be intended for her. If she protests, the speaker is free to maintain that she was speaking about someone else and to ask why her auditor is so paranoid. Alternatively, the speaker can say, "if the shoe fits. . . ." Mitchell-Kernan says that a characteristic of this form of Signifyin(g) is the selection of a subject that is "selectively relevant to the speaker's audience."[81] I once heard a black minister name the illicit behavior of specific members of his congregation by performing a magnificent reading of "The Text of the Dry Bones," which is reading or gloss upon Ezekiel 37:1–14. Following this sermon, a prayer was offered by Lin Allen. As "Mr. Lin," as we called him, said, "Dear Lord, go with the gambling man . . . not forgetting the gambling woman," the little church's eerie silence was shattered by the loud-talking voice of one of my father's friends (Ben Fisher, rest his soul), whom the congregation "overheard" saying, "Got *you* that time, Gates, got *you* that time, Newtsy!" My father and one of our neighbors, Miss Newtsy, had been Signified upon.

Mitchell-Kernan presents several examples of Signifyin(g) that elaborate on its subtypes.[82] Her conclusion is crucial to the place of her research in the literature on Signification. "*Signifying,*" she declares as conclusion, "does not . . . always have negative valuations attached to it; it is clearly thought of as a kind of art—a clever way of conveying messages."[83] A literary critic might call this troping, an interpretation or mis-taking of meaning, to paraphrase Harold Bloom, because, as Mitchell-Kernan maintains, "*signifying* . . . alludes to and implies things which are never made explicit."[84] Let me cite two brief examples. In the first, "Grace" introduces the exchange by defining its context:

> (After I had my little boy, I swore I was not having any more babies. I thought four kids was a nice-sized family. But it didn't turn out that way. I was a little bit disgusted and didn't tell anybody when I discovered I was pregnant. My sister came over one day and I had started to show by that time.) . . .
> Rochelle: Girl, you sure do need to join the Metrecal for lunch bunch.
> Grace: (non-committally) Yes, I guess I am putting on a little weight.
> Rochelle: Now look here, girl, we both standing here soaking wet and you still trying to tell me it ain't raining.[85]

This form of Signifyin(g) is obviously a long way from the sort usually defined by scholars. One final example of the amusing, troping exchange follows, again cited by Mitchell-Kernan:

> I: Man, when you gon pay me my five dollars?
> II. Soon as I get it.
> I: (to audience) Anybody want to buy a five dollar nigger? I got one to sell.
> II: Man, if I gave you your five dollars, you wouldn't have nothing to signify about.
> I: Nigger, long as you don't change, I'll always have me a subject.[86]

This sort of exchange is common in the black community and represents Signifyin(g) at its more evolved levels than the more obvious examples (characterized by confrontation and insult) discussed by linguists other than Mitchell-Kernan.

The highly evolved form of Signifyin(g) that H. Rap Brown defines and that Ralph Ellison's anecdote about Hazel Harrison epitomizes is represented in a wonderful anecdote that Mitchell-Kernan narrates. This tale bears repeating to demonstrate how black adults teach their children to "hold a conversation":

> At the age of seven or eight I encountered what I believe was a version of the tale of the "Signifying Monkey." In this story a monkey reports to a lion that an elephant has been maligning the lion and his family. This stirs the lion into attempting to impose sanctions against the elephant. A battle ensues in which the elephant is victor and the lion returns extremely chafed at the monkey. In this instance, the recounting of this story is a case of signifying for directive purposes. I was sitting on the stoop of a neighbor who was telling me about his adventures as a big game hunter in Africa, a favorite tall-tale topic, unrecognized by me as tall-tale at the time. A neighboring woman called to me from her porch and asked me to go to the store for her. I refused, saying that my mother had told me not to, a lie which Mr. Waters recognized and asked me about. Rather than simply saying I wanted to listen to his stories, I replied that I had refused to go because I hated the woman. Being pressured for a reason for my dislike, and sensing Mr. Waters's disapproval, I countered with another lie, "I hate her because she say you were lazy," attempting, I suppose, to regain his favor by arousing ire toward someone else. Although I had heard someone say that he was lazy, it had not been this woman. He explained to me that he was not lazy and that he didn't work because he had been laid-off from his job and couldn't find work elsewhere, and that if the lady had said what I reported, she had not done so out of meanness but because she didn't understand. Guilt-ridden, I went to fetch the can of Milnot milk. Upon returning, the tale of the "Signifying Monkey" was told to me, a censored prose version in which the monkey is rather brutally beaten by the lion after having suffered a similar fate in the hands of the elephant. I liked the story very much and righteously approved of its ending, not realizing at the time that he was *signifying* at me. Mr. Waters reacted to my response with a great deal of amusement. It was several days later in the context of retelling the tale to another child that I understood its timely telling. My apology and admission of lying were met by affectionate humor, and I was told that I was finally getting to the age where I could "hold a conversation," i.e., understand and appreciate implications.[87]

Black people call this kind of lesson "schooling," and this label denotes its function. The child must learn to hold a conversation. We cannot but recall

Richard Lanham's ideal presentation of rhetorical training and conclude that what Mr. Waters says to the child, Claudia, is analogous to an adult teacher of rhetoric attempting to show his pupils how to employ the tropes that they have memorized in an act of communication and its interpretation. This subtle process of instruction in the levels of Signification is related to, but far removed from, adolescent males insulting each other with the Signifying Monkey tales. The language of Signifyin(g), in other words, is a strategy of black figurative language use.

I have been drawing a distinction between the ritual of Signifyin(g), epitomized in the Monkey tales, and the language of Signifyin(g), which is the vernacular term for the figurative use of language. These terms correspond to what Mitchell-Kernan calls "third-party signifying" and "metaphorical signifying." Mitchell-Kernan defines their distinction as follows:

> In the metaphorical type of *signifying*, the speaker attempts to transmit his message indirectly and it is only by virtue of the hearers defining the utterance as *signifying* that the speaker's intent (to convey a particular message) is realized. In third-party signifying, the speaker may realize his aim only when the converse is true, that is, if the addressee fails to recognize the speech act as *signifying*. In [the Signifying Monkey toast] the monkey succeeds in goading the lion into a rash act because the lion does not define the monkey's message as *signifying*.[88]

In other words, these two dominant modes of Signification function conversely, another sign of the maturation process demanded to move, as it were, from the repetition of tropes to their application.

The Monkey tales inscribe a dictum about interpretation, whereas the language of Signifyin(g) addresses the nature and application of rhetoric. The import of the Monkey tales for the interpretation of literature is that the Monkey dethrones the Lion only because the Lion cannot read the nature of his discourse. As Mitchell-Kernan argues cogently, "There seems something of symbolic relevance from the perspective of language in this poem. The monkey and lion do not speak the same language; the lion is not able to interpret the monkey's use of language, he is an outsider, un-hip, in a word." In other words, the monkey speaks figuratively, while the Lion reads his discourse literally. For his act of misinterpretation, he suffers grave consequences. This valorization of the figurative is perhaps the most important moral of these poems, although the Monkey's mastery of figuration has made him one of the canonical heroes in the Afro-American mythic tradition, a point underscored by Mitchell-Kernan.[89]

Mitchell-Kernan's summary of the defining characteristics of "Signifying as a Form of Verbal Art" helps to clarify this most difficult, and elusive, mode of rhetoric. We can outline these characteristics for convenience. The most important defining features of Signifyin(g) are "indirect intent" and "metaphorical reference." This aspect of indirection is a formal device, and "appears to be almost purely stylistic"; moreover, "its art characteristics remain in the forefront." Signifyin(g), in other words, turns upon the foregrounding of the Signifier. By "indirection" Mitchell-Kernan means

> that the correct semantic (referential interpretation) or signification of the utterance cannot be arrived at by a consideration of the dictionary meaning of the lexical items involved and the syntactic rules for their combination alone. The apparent significance of the message differs from its real significance. *The apparent meaning of the sentence signifies its actual meaning.*[90]

The relationship between latent and manifest meaning is a curious one, as determined by the formal properties of the Signifyin(g) utterance. In one of several ways, manifest meaning directs attention away from itself to another, latent level of meaning. We might compare this relationship to that which obtains between the two parts of a metaphor, tenor (the inner meaning) and vehicle (the outer meaning).

Signifyin(g), according to Mitchell-Kernan, operates so delightfully because "apparent meaning serves as a key which directs hearers to some shared knowledge, attitudes, and values or signals that reference must be produced metaphorically." The decoding of the figurative, she continues, depends "upon shared knowledge . . . and this shared knowledge operates on two levels." One of these two levels is that the speaker and his audience realize that "*signifying* is occurring and that the dictionary-syntactical meaning of the utterance is to be ignored." In addition, a silent second text, as it were, which corresponds rightly to what Mitchell-Kernan is calling "shared knowledge," must be brought to bear upon the manifest content of the speech act and "employed in the reinterpretation of the utterance." Indeed, this element is of the utmost importance in the esthetics of Signifyin(g), for "it is the cleverness used in directing the attention of the hearer and audience to this shared knowledge upon which a speaker's artistic talent is judged." Signifyin(g), in other words, depends on the success of the signifier at invoking an absent meaning ambiguously "present" in a carefully wrought statement.[91]

As I have attempted to show, there is much confusion and disagreement among linguists about the names and functions of the classical black tropes. While the specific terminology may vary from scholar to scholar, city to city, or generation to generation, however, the rhetorical functions of these tropes remain consistent. It is a fairly straightforward exercise to compare the black slave tropes to the master tropes identified by Vico, Nietzsche, Burke, and

Bloom, and to map a black speech act, such as Signifyin(g), into its component Western tropes. Chart 2 is intended to Signify upon Harold Bloom's
"map of misprision."[92] I echo the essence of this map here, adding columns
that list the Yoruba and Afro-American tropes that correspond to their Western counterparts.

We can, furthermore, chart our own map, in which we graph the separate lines of a "Signifyin(g) Riff," as follows:[93]

Slave Trope of Tropes, Signifyin(g)

Your mama's a man	(metaphor)
Your daddy's one too	(irony)
They live in a tin can	(metonymy)
That smells like a zoo	(synecdoche)

The fact that the street rhymes of blacks and their received rhetorical tropes
configure into the categories of classical Western rhetoric should come as no
surprise. Indeed, this aspect of black language use recalls Montaigne's statement, in "Of the Vanity of Words," that "When you hear people talk about
metonymy, metaphor, allegory, and other such names in grammar, doesn't
it seem that they mean some rare and exotic form of language?" Rather,
Montaigne concludes, "They are terms that apply to the babble of your
chambermaid."[94] We can add that these terms also apply to the rapping of
black kids on street corners, who recite and thereby preserve the classical
black rhetorical structures.

Signification is a complex rhetorical device that has elicited various,
even contradictory, definitions from linguists, as should be apparent from
this summary of its various definitions. While many of its manifestations
and possibilities are figured in the tales of the Signifying Monkey, most
people who Signify do not engage in the narration of these tales. Rather, the
Monkey tales stand as the canonical poems from which what I am calling
the language of Signifyin(g) extends. The degree to which the figure of the
Monkey is anthropologically related to the figure of the Pan-African trickster, Esu-Elegbara, shall most probably remain a matter of speculation.

Nevertheless, the two figures are related as functional equivalents because
each in its own way stands as a moment of consciousness of black formal language use, of rhetorical structures and their appropriate modes of interpretation. As I have argued, both figures connote what we might think of as the
writing implicit in an oral literature, and both figures function as repositories
for a tradition's declarations about how and why formal literary language
departs from ordinary language use. The metaphor of a double-voiced Esu-
Elegbara corresponds to the double-voiced nature of the Signifyin(g) utterance.

Chart 2. The Figures of Signification

Rhetorical Trope	Bloom's Revisionary Ratio	Afro-American Signifyin(g) Trope	Classical Yoruba	Lexically Borrowed Yoruba
Irony	Clinamen	Signifyin(g) ("Nigger business" in the West Indies)	Ríràn (èràn)	Àìróni
Synecdoche	Tessera	Calling out of one's name		Mètònimì
Metonymy	Kenosis			
Hyperbole, litotes	Daemonization	Stylin' or woofing ("Flash" in the West Indies)	Ìhàlè (Èpón)	
Metaphor	Askesis	Naming	À fiwé (elétóó) / À fiwé gaan	Mètáfò (indirect "naming")* Simili (direct "naming")*
Metalepsis	Apophrades	Capping	A fikàn; Àjàmó; Èni	

* N.B. "Naming" is an especially rich trope in Yoruba. Positive naming is call Oriki, while negative naming is called Inagije. Naming is also an especially luxurious (if potentially volatile) trope in the Afro-American vernacular tradition. "Naming" someone and "Calling [someone] Out of [his] name" are among the most commonly used tropes in Afro-American vernacular discourse. Scores of proverbs and epigrams in the black tradition turn upon figures for naming.

When one text Signifies upon another text, by tropological revision or repetition and difference, the double-voiced utterance allows us to chart discrete formal relationships in Afro-American literary history. Signifyin(g), then, is a metaphor for textual revision.

NOTES

1. Ferdinand de Saussure, *Course in General Linguistics*, ed. Charles Bally and Albert Sechehaye, trans. Wade Baskin (New York: McGraw-Hill, 1966), p. 66ff.

2. For a superbly lucid discussion, see Christopher Norris, *Deconstruction: Theory and Practice* (New York: Methuen, 1982), p. 32.

3. See my discussion of the word "down" in *Figures in Black: Words, Signs, and the Racial Self* (New York: Oxford University Press, 1986).

4. Saussure, Course, p. 71.

5. Quoted in Gary Saul Morson, *The Boundaries of Genre: Dostoevsky's "Diary of a Writer" and the Traditions of Literary Utopia* (Austin: University of Texas Press, 1981), p. 108.

6. Saussure, *Course*, p. 71.

7. Ibid., pp. 75, 72.

8. See, for example, Claudia Mitchell-Kernan, *Language Behavior in a Black Urban Community* (Monographs of the Language-Behavior Laboratory, University of California, Berkeley, No. 2), pp. 88–90; and Roger D. Abrahams, *Talking Black* (Rowley, Mass.: Newbury House Publishers, 1976), pp. 50–51.

9. On Tar Baby, see Ralph Ellison, "Hidden Name and Complex Fate: A Writer's Experience in the United States," *Shadow and Act* (New York: Random House, 1964), p. 147; and Toni Morrison, *Tar Baby* (New York: Knopf, 1981).

10. Geneva Smitherman defines these and other black tropes, then traces their use in several black texts. Smitherman's work, like that of Mitchell-Kernan and Abrahams, is especially significant for literary theory. See Geneva Smitherman, *Talkin' and Testifyin': The Language of Black America* (Boston: Houghton Mifflin, 1977), pp. 101–67. And on signifying as a rhetorical trope, see Smitherman, *Talkin' and Testifyin'*, pp. 101–67; Thomas Kochman, *Rappin' and Stylin' Out: Communication in Urban Black America* (Urbana: University of Illinois Press, 1972); Thomas Kochman, "'Rappin' in the Black Ghetto," *Trans-Action* 6 (February 1969): 32; Alan Dundes, *Mother Wit from the Laughing Barrel: Readings in the Interpretation of Afro-American Folklore* (Englewood Cliffs: Prentice-Hall, 1973), p. 310; Ethen M. Albert, "'Rhetoric,' 'Logic,' and 'Poetics' in Burundi: Culture Patterning of Speech Behavior," in John J. Gumperz and Dell Hymes, eds., *The Ethnography of Communication, American Anthropologist* 66 (1964): 35–54. One example of signifying can be gleaned from the following anecdote. While writing this essay, I asked a colleague, Dwight Andrews, if he had heard of the Signifying Monkey as a child. "Why, no," he replied intently. "I never heard of the Signifying Monkey until I came to Yale and read about him in a book." I had been signified upon. If I had responded to Andrews, "I know what you mean; your Mama

read to me from that same book the last time I was in Detroit," I would have signified upon him in return.

11. Julia Kristeva, *Desire in Language: A Semiotic Approach to Literature and Art* (New York: Columbia University Press, 1980), p. 31; Dundes, editor's note, *Mother Wit from the Laughing Barrel*, p. 310.

12. Roger D. Abrahams, *Deep Down in the Jungle: Negro Narrative Folklore from the Streets of Philadelphia* (Chicago: Aldine Publishing, 1970), pp. 51–52, 66–67, 264. Abrahams's awareness of the need to define uniquely black significations is exemplary. As early as 1964, when he published the first edition of *Deep Down in the Jungle*, he saw fit to add a glossary, as an appendix of "Unusual Terms and Expressions," a title which unfortunately suggests the social scientist's apologia.

13. Ibid., pp. 66–67, 264. (Emphasis added.)

14. Gloria Hall is a well-known professional storyteller, and she includes in her repertoire the Signifying Monkey poems.

15. Ibid., p. 113. In the second line of the stanza, "motherfucker" is often substituted for "monkey."

16. "The Signifying Monkey," *Book of Negro Folklore*, ed. Langston Hughes and Arna Bontemps (New York: Dodd, Mead, 1958), pp. 365–66.

17. Lies is a traditional Afro-American word for figurative discourse, tales, or stories.

18. Also known as "the dozens."

19. See Bruce Jackson, *"Get Your Ass in the Water and Swim Like Me": Narrative Poetry from the Black Oral Tradition* (Cambridge: Harvard University Press, 1974), esp. pp. 164–65. Subsequent references to tales collected by Jackson will be given in the text. Jackson's collection of "Toasts" is definitive.

20. A clear example of paradigmatic contiguity is the addition of the metonym "hairy" as an adjective for "ass" in the second quoted line.

21. J. L. Dillard, *Lexicon of Black English* (New York: Continuum, 1977), pp. 130–41; Zora Neale Hurston, *Mules and Men* (Philadelphia: J. B. Lippincott, 1935), p. 37; Sterling A. Brown, "Folk Literature," in *The Negro Caravan* (1941; New York: Arno, 1969), p. 433.

22. Sigmund Freud, *The Interpretation of Dreams*, trans. James Strachey (1953; New York: Avon, 1965), p. 386.

23. Quoted in Easthope, *Poetry as Discourse*, p. 82.

24. Ibid., pp. 82–83, 42.

25. Ibid., pp. 84–86.

26. Quoted in Easthope, *Poetry as Discourse*, p. 90. For a nineteenth-century commentary on black rhyme schemes in music, see James Hungerford, *The Old Plantation and What I Gathered There in an Autumn Month* [of 1832] (New York, 1859), reprinted in Eileen Southern, ed., *Readings in Black American Music* (New York: Norton, 1971), pp. 71–81, esp. p. 73.

27. Easthope, *Poetry as Discourse*, pp. 90–91.

28. Ibid., pp. 89–90, 93. (Emphasis added.)

29. Martin Williams, *The Smithsonian Collection of Classic Jazz* (Washington, D.C.: Smithsonian Institution, 1973), p. 16.

30. Houston A. Baker's reading of Ellison's essay suggested the alternative reading that I am giving it here. See Baker, *Blues, Ideology, and Afro-American Literature: A Vernacular Theory*, pp. 12–13, 64, 66.

31. Ralph Ellison, "The Little Man at Chehaw Station," *The American Scholar* (Winter 1977–78): 26.

32. Oriki Esu, quoted by Ayodele Ogundipe, *Esu Elegbara, the Yoruba God of Chance and Uncertainty: A Study in Yoruba Mythology*, 2 vols. Ph.D. dissertation, Indiana University, 1978, Vol. II, pp. 12, 77.

33. "Test on Street Language Says It's Not Grant in That Tomb," *New York Times*, April 17, 1983, p. 30.

34. Langston Hughes, *Ask Your Mama: 12 Moods for Jazz* (New York: Knopf, 1971), p. 8; "Test on Street Language," p. 30. (Emphasis added.)

35. *Journal of Nicholas Cresswell, 1774–1777*, ed. L. MacVeigh (New York: Dial Press, 1924), pp. 17–19.

36. Frederick Douglass, *Narrative of the Life of Frederick Douglass, An American Slave, Written by Himself* (1845; New York: Doubleday, 1963), pp. 13–14. (Emphasis added.)

37. Ibid., pp. 13, 15.

38. Frederick Douglass, *My Bondage and My Freedom* (New York: Orton & Mulligan, 1855), p. 253.

39. William Faux, *Memorable Days in America* (London: W. Simpkins and R. Marshall, 1823), pp. 77–78. See also John Dixon Long, *Pictures of Slavery in Church and State* (Philadelphia: the author, 1857), pp. 197–98.

40. George P. Rawick, ed., *The American Slave: A Composite Autobiography*, Vol. 5, Part 4, p. 198.

41. Clarence Major, *Dictionary of Afro-American Slang* (New York: International Publisher, 1970), pp. 104, 46, 34.

42. Hermese E. Roberts, *The Third Ear: A Black Glossary*, entry on signifying.

43. Mezz Mezzrow and Bernard Wolfe, *Really the Blues* (New York: Random House, 1946), pp. 378, 230.

44. Ibid., pp. 230–31.

45. Malachi Andrews and Paul T. Owens, *Black Language* (West Los Angeles: Seymour-Smith, 1973), p. 95. (Emphasis added.) See also their entry on "Wolf," p. 106.

46. Dillard, *Lexicon of Black English*, pp. 154, 177.

47. Hurston, *Mules and Men*, p. 161. See also C. Merton Babcock, "A Word List from Zora Neale Hurston," *Publications of the American Dialect Society*, No. 40 (University, Ala.: University of Alabama Press, 1963), pp. 1–12. I analyze Hurston's uses of Signifyin(g) in Chapter 5 herein.

48. Dillard, *Lexicon of Black English*, p. 134.

49. See Jackson, *"Get Your Ass in the Water,"* esp. pp. 161–80.

50. Jim Haskins and Hugh F. Butts, *The Psychology of Black Language* (New York: Barnes & Noble, 1973), p. 86.

51. Ibid., p. 51.

52. Harold Wentworth and Stuart Berg Flexner, comp. and ed., *Dictionary of American Slang, Second Supplemental Edition* (New York: Thomas Y. Crowell, 1975), p. 477.

53. Peter Tamary, quoted in Robert S. Gold, *Jazz Talk* (New York: Bobbs-Merrill, 1975), p. 76.

54. H. Rap Brown, *Die Nigger Die!* (New York: Dial Press, 1969), pp. 25–26.

55. Ibid., pp. 26–29.

56. Ibid., pp. 29–30.

57. Ibid.

58. See Roger D. Abrahams, "The Changing Concept of the Negro Hero," in *The Golden Log*, ed. Mody C. Boatright, Wilson M. Hudson, and Allen Maxwell (Dallas: Southern Methodist University Press, 1962), pp. 119–34; Abrahams, *Deep Down in the Jungle*, esp. "Introduction to the Second Edition" (1970).

59. Abrahams, "The Changing Concept," p. 125.

60. Abrahams, *Deep Down in the Jungle*, pp. 51–53, 66–70, 113–19, 142–47, 153–56, 264.

61. Richard A. Lanham, *The Motives of Eloquence: Literary Rhetoric in the Renaissance* (New Haven: Yale University Press, 1976), pp. 2–3. See also Abrahams, Deep Down in the Jungle, p. 17; and Edith A. Folb, *Runnin' Down Some Lines: The Language and Culture of Black Teenagers* (Cambridge: Harvard University Press, 1980), p. 90: "Young people growing up in the black community play endless verbal games with one another, much as their mainstream white counterparts play games of war, cops and robbers, or cowboys and Indians. Like skilled musicians, children early on learn to refine their verbal skills, to develop their instrument so that it can play a variety of songs."

62. Lanham, *The Motives of Eloquence*, pp. 2–3.

63. Roger D. Abrahams, *Talking Black* (Rawley, Mass.: Newbury House, 1976), p. 19.

64. Ibid., p. 33.

65. Ibid., p. 51.

66. Ibid., pp. 49, 46, 53, 56, 73–76, 50. See also Roger D. Abrahams, *The Man-of-Words in the West Indies: Performance and the Emergence of Creole Culture* (Baltimore: Johns Hopkins University Press, 1983), pp. 56–57.

67. Abrahams, *Talking Black*, p. 52. (Emphasis added.) "Duke Ellington and John Coltrane," Impulse Records, AS–30.

68. Thomas Kochman, "Towards an Ethnography of Black American Speech Behavior," in *Rappin' and Stylin' Out: Communication in Urban Black America* (Urbana: University of Illinois Press, 1972), p. 257. See also Kochman's "'Rappin' in the Black Ghetto," *Transaction* 6 (February 1969): 26–35. Kochman's "Towards an Ethnography" was originally published in *Afro-American Anthropology: Contemporary Perspectives*, ed. Norman E. Whitten, Jr., and John F. Szwed (New York: Free Press, 1970), pp. 145–63.

69. Kochman, "Ethnography," p. 257.

70. Ibid., p. 258.

71. See also Herbert L. Foster, *Ribbin', Jivin', and Playin' the Dozens: The Unrecognized Dilemma of Inner City Schools* (Cambridge: Ballinger, 1974), pp. 203–10; and Edith A. Folb, *Runnin' Down Some Lines; The Language and Culture of Black Teenagers* (Cambridge: Harvard University Press, 1980), esp. pp. 69–131.

72. See Claudia Mitchell-Kernan, *Language Behavior in a Black Urban Community*, Monographs of the Language-Behavior Laboratory, University of California, Berkeley, No. 2 (February 1971), esp. pp. 87–129, reprinted as "Signifying as a Form of Verbal Art" in *Mother Wit from the Laughing Barrel: Readings in the Interpretation of Afro-American Folklore*, ed. Alan Dundes (Englewood Cliffs: Prentice-Hall, 1973), pp. 310–28; and Kochman, *Rappin' and Stylin' Out*, pp. 315–36. These quotations appear on p. 311 of the Dundes reprint. All subsequent page numbers refer to this volume.

73. Mitchell-Kernan, "Signifying," p. 311.

74. Ibid., pp. 312–13, 311–12, 322–23.

75. Ibid., p. 313. See Richard A. Lanham, *A Handlist of Rhetorical Terms* (Berkeley: University of California Press, 1969), pp. 101–3, 52.

76. Mitchell-Kernan, "Signifying," p. 313.

77. Ibid., p. 314.

78. Ibid.

79. Ibid., pp. 314–15.

80. Ibid.

81. Ibid., p. 316.

82. Ibid., pp. 316–21.

83. Ibid., p. 318.

84. Harold Bloom, *A Map of Misreading* (New York: Oxford University Press, 1975), p. 93, esp. pp. 83–105; Mitchell-Kernan, "Signifying," p. 319.

85. Mitchell-Kernan, "Signifying," pp. 318–19.

86. Ibid., pp. 320–21.

87. Ibid., pp. 321–22.

88. Ibid., p. 322.

89. See ibid., pp. 322–23.

90. Ibid., p. 325. (Emphasis added.)

91. Ibid. For an excellent summary of the literature of Signifyin(g), see Lawrence W. Levine, *Black Culture and Black Consciousness: Afro-American Folk Thought from Slavery to Freedom* (New York: Oxford University Press, 1977), pp. 346, 378–80, 483, 498–99.

92. Harold Bloom, *A Map of Misreading*, p. 84.

93. The source for this riff and its analysis is a personal conversation with Kimberly W. Benston.

94. Montaigne, "Of the Vanity of Words," in *The Complete Essays of Montaigne*, trans. Donald M. Frame (Stanford: University Press, 1965), p. 223.

SOURCE: Henry Louis Gates, Jr., *The Signifying Monkey: A Theory of Afro-American Literary Criticism* (New York: Oxford University Press, 1988).

READING "RACE," WRITING, AND DIFFERENCE

"RACE," WRITING, AND DIFFERENCE was published as a special issue of *Critical Inquiry* in autumn 1985 (12.1). Responses to the essays in the special issue appeared in the journal's autumn 1986 number (13.1). The University of Chicago Press published both parts as a book in 1986. Since then, it has become the best-selling book version of a special issue of *Critical Inquiry* in the history of that splendid publication. And I believe that this occurred because its contributions simultaneously reflected and defined a certain pivotal moment in the history of both literary studies and the larger discourse on race, bringing the two fields together in a way that had not been done before. At least, that was the goal of editing it in the first place.

I conceived of this special issue soon after receiving my copy of the book version of the special issue of *Critical Inquiry* entitled *Writing and Sexual Difference*, edited by Elizabeth Abel and published in the winter of 1981. (The book was published in 1982.) "The 'Blackness of Blackness': A Critique of the Sign and the Signifying Monkey"—an essay of mine that would be published in June 1983—had just been accepted by the journal, so I picked up the phone and called the editor, W. J. T. Mitchell, and floated the idea. He encouraged me to develop it and make a tentative table of contents, which I did, not having any idea if scholars such as Anthony Appiah, Edward Said, Homi Bhabha, Hazel Carby, Mary Louise Pratt, Gayatri Spivak, Bernard Lewis, and Jacques Derrida (of all people) would feel compelled to write on this topic or even agree to be published in a collection of essays edited by an assistant professor who had received his PhD just three years earlier, in 1979. Next I flew to Chicago and presented my proposal to the editorial board. To my astonishment, it was enthusiastically accepted.

It seemed to me that Abel's strategically edited collection could be a model for those of us who cared about race and ethnicity, African and African American literature, the figure of the black in Western discourse, literary theory, and postmodernism to meet on some sort of common ground.

And that, I believe, is what was novel about our special issue of *Critical Inquiry*. Although it may seem somewhat naive and simplistic two full decades later, my goal was to publish essays that inserted the study of African American literature and what I think of as a broader discourse of the black into a larger theoretical discourse on race and various forms of difference as social constructs, while simultaneously inserting contemporary literary theory into the discourse on race, blackness, difference, and the criticism of African American literature. If that sounds like belabored reasoning, it was! But I believed it to be necessary at the time, if African American literature was ever to assume a central place as a canonical literature in English departments in the academy. And helping to achieve this goal—a goal that my colleagues in African American literary studies shared—was foremost in my mind back then. I saw the editing of this special issue as just one of several possible interventions—along, say, with editing a Norton anthology of African American literature, at one extreme, and publishing books on black literary theory, at the other—that could help us to move the study of African and African American literature from the margins of literature departments to the vital center.

Why did I think all this necessary? Today when I attempt to historicize the development of contemporary African American literary criticism to my students, who take the canonical status of black literature for granted, the expressions on their faces suggest that they think I am exaggerating, telling tall tales about a mythical version of Jim Crow in the academy. But the truth is that very few English departments back then thought of African American literature as canonical. Graduate students who wanted to teach it as a career were "encouraged" to demonstrate their "mastery" of the field by writing about white, canonical figures as the subjects of their dissertations and, somehow, to establish expertise in African American literature outside their thesis, on their own. Of course, since the black studies revolution introduced subjects such as black literature into the curriculum in the late sixties, these courses had begun to appear in English and American studies departments and programs, but they were often seen as marginal, subsets at best of the canon of American literature. Our graduate students back then were told that if they wanted a job at a major research institution, they would have to write about subjects that were, well, white. This was certainly true at Yale, where I was teaching at the time, and at Cambridge, where I had been a graduate student. And I, for one, thought this outrageous. One of my senior colleagues at Yale showed me a draft of an essay that he was about to submit to the journal *American Literature*. It began, "Writing about the slave narratives in a journal dedicated to explicating the canon of American literature is a bit like writing about hamburger in the pages of *Gourmet* magazine." (I persuaded him to strike that line.)

At Yale theory was the rage, and *Critical Inquiry* was the font of all cutting-edge wisdom about postmodernism and deconstruction. And at Yale Jacques Derrida—who conducted a special six-week graduate seminar every spring for students and faculty members alike—was regarded as some sort of demigod, so persuading him to write for this special issue was seen as nothing short of devilish trickery by some of my senior English department colleagues, who were desperately trying to impress the master of deconstruction themselves, in part by pretending, in a bizarre reversal of that perverse tradition of American expatriates in Paris, that black people and race didn't exist or, if they did, that never would they sully the purity of thought that was contemporary poststructuralist literary theory at Mother Yale. Please!

At a dinner for four at the home of Barbara Johnson and Shoshana Feldman, Derrida had told me that he had supervised the work of African students in African philosophy, such as Paulin Hountondji, and indeed thought of himself as "an African," having been born in Algeria, and wondered why no one at Yale ever asked him about that. I almost fell off my chair. Derrida was a brother all this time, and who knew? That was all of the opening I needed. I invited him on the spot to join me in seeing the latest Richard Pryor movie, out at Cinema One to Infiniti in Milford, Connecticut, just outside New Haven. Derrida laughed more than I did. Who could have imagined, reading those massively dense tomes of his, that Jacques Derrida himself would love him some Richard Pryor? Bemused at what I had just witnessed in the movie theater, I asked him if he would write something for the special issue. He said he would be delighted, that it would give him a chance to testify to an identity that he never had sought to hide.

For all these reasons, and especially because of the support and encouragement of the visionary editor, Tom Mitchell, who in the process of creating *"Race," Writing, and Difference* taught me how to edit a journal, I could think of no venue better than *Critical Inquiry* in which to enlist a wide array of brilliant colleagues to intervene in what—as Farah Jasmine Griffin points out—would become a new field. Editing that special issue was not the only way to help move the study of "minority literatures," race, and the politics of difference into the canon and move the canon of literary theory into these discourses, but I hoped it would be one way. It certainly never occurred to me that twenty years later *PMLA* would be pondering its historical significance.

I would like to thank my colleagues Farah Jasmine Griffin, Valerie Smith, and Eric Lott for taking the time to reread the volume of essays and to share their reflections on the book's possible legacies. I am gratified that Griffin believes that it "helped transform the academy. And this transformation was in response to the work's intellectual legitimization as well as to political pressure."

As I have argued above, I had hoped that the "volume and others like it provided the basis on which these concerns could enter the academy as an intellectual project that those outside African American, women's, and ethnic studies would take seriously." "Race," she concludes insightfully, it seems to me, "while still undermined as an essential category, nonetheless became an object of investigation considered worthy of attention even by those who were not racially marked."

Similarly, Valerie Smith points to profound transformations in the place of race and of what used to be called race literature in the academy today. Almost thirty years after she began her career in the profession, she writes, "the study of race has assumed a more prominent role in academic life. Not only is it increasingly common to find clusters of scholars working on race in English departments, but scholars of all races and ethnicities are engaged in the study of race." Just as important, "scholars of color are no longer assumed to focus on works of literature and culture produced by people of their own racial or ethnic backgrounds. Generally speaking, we have moved beyond the expectation that academic specialization follows phenotype." In other words, we have deracialized the study of race and of literatures created by people of color. I applaud this development and am deeply appreciative to Smith for suggesting that this publication made even a small contribution to this happy state of affairs.

Smith and Griffin also suggest, rightly, that my recent work as a producer of documentary films is a direct extension of the essays in *"Race," Writing, and Difference*, and this work began at the University of Cambridge in my PhD thesis, on pseudoscientific theories of race in creative and philosophical writings in the Enlightenment in Europe. For Smith, my "television documentaries—such as *Wonders of the African World* and *African American Lives*—have brought research about black culture, and about the scientific basis of race, into mainstream discourse." And for Griffin, "*African American Lives* might be seen as part of this larger project as well in that it demonstrates the fiction of race through scientific evidence without denying its power to determine the lived experience of those identified as black in the United States." I could not agree more.

Yet this exploration in these documentary films of "race" as a social construct and of biologically based genetic differences that can be sorted by social categories or constructions of race is deeply troubling to Eric Lott. In fact, he questions the connection between my recent films and the special issue of *Critical Inquiry* that we are reconsidering here. But if I were to choose an epigraph that explains the connection among *"Race," Writing, and Difference*, my three most recent documentary films, and my latest two books, nothing would be more appropriate than these words from Smith's essay, which speak directly to Lott's concerns: "Race may be a fiction, but it is the source of some of our deepest wounds. The desire to forget, move on, or transcend only dooms us to traumatic returns. The rush to transcend race propels us into acts of forgetting or misremembering that we can ill afford. From the spaces of difference into which blacks and other people of color have been written have emerged powerful strategies of resistance and wellsprings of creativity that have shaped every aspect of our shared humanity."

I believe that some of the most important contributions to scholarship that our generation has made in the discipline of African American studies have been large-scale, old-fashioned recovery or editing projects that have made available to new generations of readers canonical works by black writers who celebrated and defined their sense of black racial or ethnic and sexual difference. Why this should be troublesome to anyone is deeply puzzling to me. If nothing else, canon formation is a prelude to deconstruction, necessarily. But it is so much more than that: canon formation is our generation's tribute to the creators of the tradition that we study, teach, and explicate and our gift of ready availability to future generations of students, teachers, and others who wish to celebrate the myriad manifestations of the human spirit in forms created by persons of African descent. Who could possibly be disturbed by that?

Eric Lott worries that "what began . . . as the legitimation of African American literary study by way of canons of anti-essentialist theory should have eventuated in the certification of black roots using the latest in genetic science." Lott wonders about the "recrudescence of racial biologism" in these documentary film series, which explore and critique the role of biology in the creation of difference. While I edited the proposal that I would submit to the editorial board of *Critical Inquiry*, my second daughter, Elizabeth, was born. Just as we had done when her older sister, Maude, was born, in 1980, we had her doctor administer a test for the sickle cell trait. Fortunately, both tests were negative. And why did we do this? Precisely because there is a biological basis to inheriting the sickle cell trait that often tracks along socially understood racial lines. I pondered the irony of editing a special issue of a journal of criticism and theory that was about to deconstruct the concept of "race" yet willingly—eagerly—accepting the significance of biology and ethnicity in the heritability of this trait. (I fully realize that people who are not of African descent also have the sickle cell trait, but those of West African ancestry, and African Americans in the United States, have a disproportionate share of it too.) Was there a tension there? Only if you deny histories of evolution and migration that have resulted in Africans' having higher rates of the sickle cell trait than do most populations in Europe (with the exception of some Greeks and Italians).

Toni Morrison once asked me about this tension on another register. Didn't I think it was ironic, she asked me, that we were determined to put scare quotes around "race" precisely when our presence in the academy, and the strength of our literary tradition, had never been stronger and more central? Indeed, both *Playing in the Dark*, by Morrison, and Cornel West's *Race Matters* can be seen as critiques—valid critiques—of *"Race," Writing, and Difference*, reminding all of us who wanted to declare "race" nothing more or less than socially constructed that surely the matter was far more complicated than that. And Morrison and West were right. With the mapping of the genome, we are witnessing the massive exploration of interindividual genetic difference, which will profoundly influence our understandings of virtually every aspect of the human condition, directly or indirectly. We need to probe the limits of social-constructionist frameworks to account for physical realities—such as physiology—while we also need to interrogate the limits of genetic constructions, or models, to account for their social valences.

As Griffin and Smith (and a host of geneticists and social scientists who serve as consultants on the films) have recognized, *African American Lives* introduces the received categories of four or five races, inherited from the Enlightenment, but does so to deconstruct them. This is how deconstruction must work; this is the irony, the trap, of language use. For this reason, I am not sure that we had a choice, for example, but to place scare quotes around the word "race" in the title of the volume. And this process of deconstructing the typological categories of racial purity occurs ideally through the results of the genetic-admixture tests that we administer to the subjects in the series, even if these tests are in their infancy and even if their precision may only increase after more individual genomes are sequenced. As the molecular anthropologist Mark Shriver puts it, "Then, of course, there is also the possibility that with many more markers from many more of the world's populations considered, individuals from all continental groups would seem to bleed genetically into each other to varying degrees." Today the model is fashioned to reflect—and to project—realities of America's history by focusing on the encounter of Europeans, Africans, and Native Americans.

Lott mistakenly contends that these documentary film series only explore "black celebrities' racial genealogies," whatever a "racial genealogy" is supposed to be. The series explore the family trees of subjects from various professions, on this side of the Atlantic, and then use highly reliable y-DNA and mitochondrial DNA tests to trace the haplotypes of the subjects' fathers' fathers' fathers and mothers' mothers' mothers. If the database reveals an exact match with a person of, let's say, Yoruba descent, then the subject—indisputably—shares a common ancestor with that person. This is not an opinion; it is a fact.

What this means is enormously fascinating and complicated, since multiple exact matches are often found in different parts of the world. We explore these relations, raising questions of identity and identity formation just as surely as the contributors to *"Race," Writing, and Difference* tried to do, but in another way. My roots films use genetic types much like fingerprints or fossil records, enabling us to trace the movements of our indomitable ancestors beyond the veil of our literate past. It is an archeology that is inscribed—and is now increasingly legible—within the individual human genome itself. Let's consider just one example: in twenty-five percent of the tests administered to African American males, their y-DNA (again, their fathers' fathers' fathers' line) traces to Europe. According to Shriver, no less than fifty-eight percent of the African American people have a significant amount of European ancestry, the equivalent of one great-grandparent. In the series, we use the admixture tests to potentially deconstruct the series's own four or five received categories of so-called races, showing how fluid they are and have always been. My own admixture test revealed a fifty-fifty split between European ancestral markers and African ancestral markers. It is astonishing that none of the nineteen subjects studied in my documentary films has tested one hundred percent of anything. Large numbers of marker loci or alleles differ in frequency among source populations. When you average over a large number of loci and compare the frequency of one of these alleles among populations, you estimate admixture with some accuracy. And the reason for these differences in ancestral markers in the gene is an important question.

What *African American Lives* has tried to show is that genetic ancestry must be measured on a continuous scale, not divided up according to the typological race categories that we sought to deconstruct in *"Race," Writing, and Difference*. If anything, instead of reifying the racist categories received from the Enlightenment, ancestry tracing can show the fuzziness, the arbitrariness, the social constructedness, of what have appeared to be clear "racial" divides. The problem arises when someone associates individual genetic differences (which, of course, exist) with ethnic variation (which is sociocultural and malleable). But recognizing the arbitrariness of typological categories of "race" does not mean that genetic differences are not real; to paraphrase Cornel West, biology matters. The question that confronts us in the academy today (in an era of the new genetics, the sequencing of the genome, and the recuperation of biology for identity mapping, health-disparities research, and increasingly forensics) is how biology matters, and to whom? Neither essentialist sinners nor social-constructionist saints will have a monopoly on how these differences will be parsed. Humanists need to engage these questions. Accordingly, perhaps the most fitting sequel to *"Race," Writing, and Difference* would be a special issue of *Critical Inquiry* entitled *"Race," Science, and Difference.* Given all the developments in cultural studies and genetics over the past two decades, what could be more timely?

WORK CITED

Shriver, Mark. Letter to the author. 5 Apr. 2008.

SOURCE: *PMLA* 124, no. 5 (October 2008).

JEAN TOOMER'S CONFLICTED RACIAL IDENTITY

WITH RUDOLPH P. BYRD

ON AUGUST 4, 1922, about a year before he published his first book, *Cane,* Jean Toomer, age 27, wrote to his first love, a black teenager named Mae Wright, confessing his ambivalence about the dogged pursuit by African-Americans of Anglo-American cultural ideals: "We who have Negro blood in our veins, who are culturally and emotionally the most removed from Puritan tradition, are its most tenacious supporters." That would be one of the last times he admitted his own Negro ancestry, either publicly or privately. Six years later, Georgia O'Keeffe—Toomer's friend and later lover—wrote to her husband, Alfred Stieglitz, describing the way Toomer, then living in Chicago, was identifying himself: "It seems that in Chicago they do not know that he has Negro blood—he seems to claim French extraction."

When we were working on a new Norton critical edition of *Cane,* a masterpiece of modernism composed of fiction, poetry, and drama, we confronted the question of Toomer's race. Literary critics and biographers have long speculated about how he identified himself, but too often they have chosen not to conduct research into public documents about the topic. Was Toomer—a central figure in two faces of American modernism, the New Negro (or Harlem Renaissance) Movement and the Lost Generation—a Negro who, following the publication of *Cane,* passed for white?

Toomer is known for proclaiming a new, mixed racial identity, which he called "American." In an era of de jure segregation, such a claim was defiantly transgressive. But he may have been far more conflicted about his identity than his noble attempt to question American received categories of "race" might suggest.

Given the importance of the subject, we commissioned some original biographical research by the genealogist Megan Smolenyak. We can now understand more fully than ever conflicts within Toomer's thinking about his

295

race, as he expressed them in public documents, including the federal census, two draft registrations, his marriage license to the white writer Margery Latimer, and in statements to the news media.

In June 1917, Nathan Eugene Pinchback Toomer registered for the draft in Washington. He is recorded as an unemployed student, single, having an unspecified disability (two of his biographers have suggested "bad eyes and a hernia gotten in a basketball game"). He is listed as a "Negro." The 1920 census shows Toomer boarding with other lodgers in the home of an Italian couple on East Ninth Street in Manhattan. The census enumerator inaccurately listed his birthplace as New York, suggesting that Toomer may not have provided the information himself. His race is listed as "white."

In the 1930 census, Toomer is listed as a resident, with many others, at 11 Fifth Avenue. Because of the accuracy of the other data contained in the document—including his birthplace, his parents' states of birth, and his occupation as a freelance writer—it is likely that he furnished the details himself. The enumerator listed him as "white." At the very least, if we are right, Toomer did not correct the designation.

A year later, on October 30, 1931, Toomer married Latimer in Portage, Wis. Both the bride and groom are identified as "white" on the marriage license. According to Cynthia Earl Kerman and Richard Elridge, Toomer biographers, Latimer was aware of what she termed "the racial thing": that is, that Toomer was a Negro. Though she shared Toomer's vision of a new race in America, probably neither she nor he was prepared for headlines like the one published regarding the marriage: "Negro Who Wed White Writer Sees New Race." While Toomer proclaimed that his union was evidence of a "new race in America, . . . neither white nor black nor in-between," and that it was simply one between "two Americans," the news media chose to focus upon only the most sensational aspects of the nuptials.

In 1942, Toomer registered once again for the draft. He identified himself as Nathan Jean Toomer, married to Marjorie C. Toomer. She was his second wife, the white daughter of a wealthy stockbroker whom he had married in Taos, N.M., after his first wife died in childbirth. He is described as 5-foot-10, 178 pounds, with black hair and eyes, and a "dark brown complexion." He is identified as a "Negro."

It is clear from these documents that Toomer self-identified as Negro in 1917, when he first registered for the draft. Then either he or a roommate decided to give his identity as "white" on the census of 1920. Similarly, Toomer either self-identified as "white" to the enumerator of the 1930 census or failed to say that he was, in fact, born a Negro (at that time, enumerators had the sole authority to determine the race of a resident). A year later, on his marriage license, he self-identified as "white." He is identified as a "Negro" again, however, on his World War II draft registration—perhaps because the registrar, Edith Rider, who was black, according to the 1930 census, would have known from news-media accounts of his two interracial marriages.

In the course of the 25 years between his 1917 and 1942 draft registrations, it seems that Toomer was endlessly deconstructing his Negro ancestry. During his childhood and adolescence in Washington, as a member of the mulatto elite, he lived in both the white and the black worlds. At times he resided in white neighborhoods, but he was educated in all-black schools. Toomer would write that it was his experience in that special world, "midway between the white and Negro worlds," that led him to develop his novel "racial position" as early as 1914, at the age of 20, when he defined himself as an "American, neither white nor black."

Toomer may, indeed, have arrived at that definition as a young man, but as a young artist, he wrestled with the question of racial identity through various protagonists bearing uncanny resemblances to himself. The first short story he wrote, the autobiographical "Bona and Paul," composed in 1918, takes passing for white as its central theme. Equally important, his assertion that "Kabnis is me"—in his December 1922 letter to the novelist and social critic Waldo Frank, concerning his relationship to a character of mixed-race ancestry deeply conflicted about his Negro past—is another salient example of how Toomer's ambivalence about race manifested itself in *Cane*. Further, in a comment to a reporter in 1934 and in the manuscript of his unpublished autobiography, Toomer made the highly unlikely suggestion (given all extant documentation) that his grandfather P.B.S. Pinchback, the most famous black politician in the Reconstruction era, opportunistically passed for black to gain political advantage from the freedmen in New Orleans.

Toomer's deeply conflicted position on his black ancestry is also reflected in the publication of *Cane*. Indeed, his angry reaction to Frank's introduction, with its matter-of-fact identification of the author as a Negro, and later his refusal to cooperate with Horace Liveright, the publisher, in "featuring Negro" in the marketing of *Cane* in fall 1923, reflect that conflict. He all but said to Liveright: "I was not a Negro." However, according to the pioneering literary critic Darwin Turner, Toomer, in his correspondence with the writer Sherwood Anderson just a year before the publication of *Cane*, "never opposed Anderson's obvious assumption that he was 'Negro.' In fact, Anderson began the correspondence because Toomer had been identified to him as a 'Negro.'" Toomer's contradictory stances vis-à-vis Liveright and Anderson reveal the depth of his ambivalence in the weeks before the publication of the work that would link him to a literary tradition from which he would spend the rest of his life attempting to flee.

Toomer became angry with Alain Locke, one of the architects of the Harlem Renaissance, for reprinting excerpts of *Cane* in the *The New Negro* in 1925 (he was silent regarding Locke's decision to reprint the poem "Song of the Son" in the 1925 issue of the white magazine *Survey Graphic*). Toomer's attitude smacks of denial and ingratitude, given Locke's early and consistent support.

And then in 1934, almost 10 years after the publication of *The New Negro*, Toomer refused to contribute to Nancy Cunard's 1934 anthology *The Negro*, stating that "though I am interested in and deeply value the Negro, I am not a Negro." In that same year, following the announcement of his marriage to Marjorie Content, Toomer, most improbably, observed to the newspaper the *Baltimore Afro-American* that "I would not consider it libelous for anyone to refer to me as a colored man, but I have not lived as one, nor do I really know whether there is colored blood in me or not." Toomer then went on to make his claim that his grandfather was a white man who passed for black, saying that "my maternal grandfather . . . referred to himself as having Negro blood in order to get Negro votes." But note, the death certificate of Toomer's grandfather, including details provided by his son, Toomer's "beloved uncle Bismarck," lists Pinchback's race as "colored."

By that time, Walter Pinchback, Toomer's uncle, was the only living relative who could challenge Toomer's public denials of his Negro ancestry. In a conciliatory gesture toward his nephew (who was the only member of his family to pass), Walter (whom the *Baltimore Afro-American* carefully says identified himself his entire life as "colored," adding that his mother, father, and grandfather did as well) said that "Toomer had a right to belong to either race he desired." In a series of three articles about Toomer and his race, the newspaper, after repeatedly underscoring Toomer's Negro identity and pointing out that he graduated from all-black Dunbar High School and "has always been referred to as a colored writer and was known in colored circles here and in New York some years ago," said it supported Toomer's decision, but as a blow against segregation and anti-miscegenation laws: "Every time the races are scrambled, by legal marriage, we set an example for thousands of white residents in Dixie who believe in social equality only after dark."

Toomer's claims stand out as particularly disingenuous in light of facts like his weeklong sojourn with Frank in 1922 in Spartanburg, S.C., where they masqueraded as (in Toomer's words) "blood brothers," that is, as Negroes. After serving as Frank's "host in a black world," Toomer returned to Washington, and for two weeks worked as an assistant to the manager of the Howard Theatre, which served the capital's African-American community, and where he gathered material for such stories as "Box Seat" and "Theater," published in *Cane*.

Why is it so important, as we read *Cane,* to understand Toomer's conflicts over his racial identity? What light does it shine on scholarship about his work, about African-American literature, and the way our society has dealt with race? The first reason is the simple, or rather complicated, fact that Toomer himself thought it was important. Important? Toomer obsessed over it, endlessly circling back upon it in the comfortable isolation of his upper-middle-class home in Bucks County, Pa.

In our effort to map the genealogy of both academic and popular conceptions of race, Toomer's conflicts also help us distinguish between what we might think of as one's biological or genetic identity and one's cultural or ethnic identity. Biological identity is registered in one's genes and measured today through alleles and haplogroups, but cultural identity is, to a large degree, what scholars call socially constructed—arbitrary, fluid, contingent, and socially specific. Genetically, Jean Toomer was a light-complexioned Negro, descended from a long line of mulattoes. He was raised as a Negro American, in a family that identified as black. Like many African-Americans (one of us, for example, happens to be 50 percent European and 50 percent African, genetically), he had a significant amount of European ancestry. But not culturally. None of Toomer's direct ancestors chose to live or self-identify as white.

That is a matter about which there is a tremendous amount of confusion. Does it mean much to discover, as a mature adult, that one is as white as she or he is black, genetically? That would be to presuppose that genetic ancestry, or biology, has some inherently determining characteristics of personality formation. It does not.

The fact that Toomer's family tree consisted of a lot of light-skinned mulattoes who, for whatever reasons, married one another, is not exceptional. Many African-Americans' family trees are shaded in the very same way. Toomer was very much like the novelist Charles W. Chesnutt or the civil-rights leader Walter White or the many people who most certainly had to self-identify to a census enumerator to set the social or cultural record straight. (How else would a hapless census taker even begin to comprehend the nuances of Negritude that have so markedly defined the complex "black" identity in the United States?)

Toomer was right to declare that he was of mixed ancestry, and that the opposition between "white" and "black" was too simplistic. But he was wrong to say that he had never lived as a Negro. He lived as a Negro while growing up. And then he decided to live as an ex-Negro almost as soon as the print was dry on *Cane.*

In part—to his credit—Toomer did so as a rebellion against a racist form of racial classification. But clearly Toomer the artist had other reasons in choosing to reinvent himself precisely when he published his first book: as a tactic to enable his upward social and artistic mobility. It was important to flee his cultural identity when he became a published writer, we believe, because of all of the circumscriptions placed upon Negroes and Negro writers in America in the early 1920s, when he began his career.

Like the protagonist in James Weldon Johnson's novel *The Autobiography of an Ex-Coloured Man*, Toomer probably wanted to live as he pleased outside the strictures of segregation and Jim Crow laws; to be judged as a writer for his talents alone, on their terms; to be free to chase the dreams about which he fantasized; to love the women he loved, without concern about the law—to live freely. And who can blame him? The philosopher Kwame Anthony Appiah once wrote that "Race disables us." The more that we, as scholars, understand the full weight of race's burdens, the more understandable Toomer's admittedly imaginative denials become. Still . . .

We hope that the documents that we share in our new edition will provoke discussion and debate among students and colleagues about those twin pillars of postmodern studies, the social construction of race and our society's essentialization of race, born in the pseudoscience of the Enlightenment.

As to interpretations of *Cane,* the new contextual information takes nothing away from the splendid complexity of this marvelously compelling text, our most sublime rendering of the moment of transition of the first great migration, the migration of the ex-slave from the plantation to the city, from feudalism to modernity, from the South to the North, and of all that was lost and all that was gained in that marvelously complex process.

Toomer, more than any other New Negro writer (from whom he so desperately wished to stand apart), saw and felt that moment, and found lyrical registers of language to record it. Rather than confine his imagination to that of a "Negro writer," he seized upon the critical success of *Cane* to attempt to escape the confines of race in America.

Jean Toomer—to draw upon a famous metaphor of W. E. B. Du Bois—did not want to ride in the Jim Crow car of American literary culture or of American social life. But Du Bois's point in coining the metaphor was that the Negro should be allowed to ride in the proverbial "white" section of the American social train as a Negro, and not as a Negro in whiteface, or as a Negro who had left his sisters and brothers back in the smelly, cinder-covered Jim Crow car at the rear of the train.

Confronting the long history of speculation about Toomer's race, we confronted again the role of race not just in the construction of identity, but also in the creation of a literary tradition. We felt that it was vital to add clarity to an often ambiguous, contradictory portrait of Toomer. In the process, we grew to appreciate more deeply the tragic pattern of ambivalence and denial that is part of his legacy as one of the most gifted imaginative artists of the 20th century.

Certainly, Toomer's choices make it clear that we are long past the point of accepting uncritically what a writer says about himself or herself. We should subject all claims to the same critical analysis that we bring to the text itself. They, too, make clear the many issues about race to be confronted in our teaching.

So we come back to our carefully considered judgment, based upon an analysis of genealogical evidence previously overlooked, that Jean Toomer— for all of his pioneering theorizing about what today we might call multicultural or mixed-raced ancestry—was a Negro who decided to pass for white.

The poet Elizabeth Alexander's "Toomer" evokes her subject's shifting, complex, contradictory stance on race: "I made up a language in which to exist." That line captures not only Toomer's pioneering position on race as a social construction, but also his effort to liberate himself through language from his life-long ambivalence about his black ancestry.

SOURCE: *The Chronicle of Higher Education,* February 6, 2011.

PART V
READING PEOPLE

GATES HAS BEEN quoted as saying there are 35 million black people in this country, and there are 35 million ways of being black. The individuals profiled in this section, through their work and their words, have pushed us in their own varied ways to understand blackness as multiplicity and singularity, as performance and nature, as imitation and originality. Some have told us what black people *should* be; some have told us what black people *could* be; some would rather not tell us anything at all about black people. What they have in common is that they all dispel the myth of authenticity—that there is one "real" black identity—that too often is deployed to conceal limitless variation.

Abby Wolf

BOTH SIDES NOW

W. E. B. Du Bois

ONE HUNDRED YEARS AGO last month, a 35-year-old scholar and budding political activist named William Edward Burghardt Du Bois published "The Souls of Black Folk." Subtitled "Essays and Sketches," Du Bois's 265-page book consisted of 13 essays and one short story, addressing a wide range of topics including the story of the freedmen in Reconstruction, the political ascendancy of Booker T. Washington, the sublimity of spirituals, the death of Du Bois's only son, Burghardt. Hailed as a classic by his contemporaries, the book has been republished in no fewer than 119 editions since 1903.

Despite its fragmentary structure, the book's disparate parts contribute to a sense of a whole, like movements in a symphony. Each chapter is pointedly "bicultural," prefaced by both an excerpt from a white poet and a bar of what Du Bois calls the Sorrow Songs ("some echo of haunting melody from the only American music which welled up from black souls in the dark past").

Du Bois's subject was, in no small part, the largely unarticulated beliefs and practices of American Negroes, who were impatient to burst out of the cotton fields and take their rightful place as Americans. As he saw it, African-American culture in 1903 was at once vibrant and disjointed, rooted in an almost medieval agrarian past and yet fiercely restive. Born in the chaos of slavery, the culture had begun to generate a richly variegated body of plots, stories, melodies and rhythms. In "The Souls of Black Folk," Du Bois peered closely at the culture of his kin, and saw the face of black America. Or rather, he saw two faces.

"One ever feels his two-ness—an American, a Negro," Du Bois wrote. "Two souls, two thoughts, two unreconciled strivings; two warring ideals in one dark body, whose dogged strength alone keeps it from being torn asunder." He described this condition as "double consciousness," and his emphasis on a fractured psyche made "The Souls of Black Folk" a harbinger of the modernist movement that would begin to flower a decade or so later in Europe and in America.

Scholars, including Werner Sollors, Dickson Bruce and David Levering Lewis, have debated the origins of Du Bois's use of the concept of "double consciousness," but what's clear is that its roots are multiple, which is appropriate enough. Du Bois had studied in Berlin during a Hegel revival, and Hegel, famously, had written on the relationship between master and bondsman, whereby each defines himself through the recognition of the other. But the concept comes up, too, in Emerson, who wrote in 1842 of the split between our reflective self, which wanders through the realm of ideas, and the active self, which dwells in the here and now. ("The worst feature of this double consciousness is that the two lives, of the understanding and of the soul, which we lead, really show very little relation to each other.") Even closer to hand was the term's appearance in late-19th-century psychology. The French psychologist Alfred Binet, writing in his 1896 book "On Double Consciousness," discusses "bipartition," or "the duplication of consciousness": "Each of the consciousnesses occupies a more narrow and more limited field than if there existed one single consciousness containing all the ideas of the subject." William James, who taught Du Bois at Harvard, talked about a "second personality" that characterized "the hypnotic trance."

When Du Bois transposed this concept from the realm of the psyche to the social predicament of the American Negro, he did not leave it unchanged. But he shared with the psychologists the notion that double consciousness was essentially an affliction. "This American world," he complained, yields the Negro "no true self-consciousness, but only lets him see himself through the revelation of the other world. It is a peculiar sensation, this double-consciousness, this sense of always looking at one's self through the eyes of others, of measuring one's soul by the tape of a world that looks on in amused contempt and pity." Sadly, "the double life every American Negro must live, as a Negro and as an American," leads inevitably to "a painful self-consciousness, an almost morbid sense of personality and a moral hesitancy which is fatal to self-confidence." The result is "a double life, with double thoughts, double duties and double social classes," and worse, "double words and double ideas," which "tempt the mind to pretense or to revolt, hypocrisy or to radicalism." Accordingly, Du Bois wanted to make the American Negro whole; and he believed that only desegregation and full equality could make this psychic integration possible.

And yet for subsequent generations of writers, what Du Bois cast as a problem was taken to be the defining condition of modernity itself. The diagnosis, you could say, outlasted the disease. Although Du Bois would publish 22 books and thousands of essays and reviews, no work of his has done more to shape an African-American literary tradition than "The Souls of Black Folk," and no metaphor in this intricately layered book has proved more enduring than that of double consciousness.

Like all powerful metaphors, Du Bois's came to have a life of its own. For Carl Jung, who visited the United States in the heyday of the "separate but equal" doctrine, the shocking thing wasn't that black culture was not equal, it was that it was not separate. "The naïve European," he wrote, "thinks of America as a white nation. It is not wholly white, if you please; it is partly colored," and this explained "the slightly Negroid mannerisms of the American." "Since the Negro lives within your cities and even within your houses," Jung continued, "he also lives within your skin, subconsciously." It wasn't just that the Negro was an American, as Du Bois wrote, but that the American was Negro. The bondsman and the slave find their identity in each other's gaze: "two-ness" wasn't just a black thing any longer. As James Baldwin would put it, "Each of us, helplessly and forever, contains the other—male in female, female in male, white in black and black in white."

Today, talk about the fragmentation of culture and consciousness is a commonplace. We know all about the vigorous intermixing of black culture and white, high culture and low—from the Jazz Age freneticism of what Ann Douglas calls "mongrel Manhattan" to hip-hop's hegemony over American youth. Du Bois yearned to make the American Negro one, and lamented that he was two. Today, the ideal of wholeness has largely been retired. And cultural multiplicity is no longer seen as the problem, but as a solution—a solution to the confines of identity itself. Double consciousness, once a disorder, is now the cure. Indeed, the only complaint we moderns have is that Du Bois was too cautious in his accounting. He'd conjured "two souls, two thoughts, two unreconciled strivings." Just two, Dr. Du Bois? Keep counting.

SOURCE: *The New York Times*, May, 4, 2003.

THE PRINCE WHO REFUSED THE KINGDOM

John Hope Franklin

WHEN I WAS twenty, I decided to hitchhike across the African continent, more or less following the line of the Equator, from the Indian Ocean to the Atlantic. I packed only one pair of sandals and one pair of jeans to make room for the three hefty books I had decided to read from cover to cover: *Don Quixote*, *Moby Dick*, and *From Slavery to Freedom*, by John Hope Franklin. I read the latter—the black and white bound third edition of the book—while recovering from a severe bout of amoebic dysentery sailing down the Congo River. It became such a valued reference for me that I kept it, for years, in the bookcase at my bedside.

Like just about every Black student at Yale in 1969, I enrolled in the Introduction to Afro-American History survey course, taught quite ably by the Pulitzer Prize–winning historian, William McFeely. At the end of each class, someone would find a way to bring up the fact that while our subject matter was Black, McFeely was quite White, and hadn't he better find a way to remedy that fact? With the patience of Job, McFeely would graciously grant his accuser the point and add that he hoped to put himself out of a job just as soon as a Black historian could be found to take his place. He would then remind us that the textbook around which our course was structured, *From Slavery to Freedom*, had been written by a Black man—a Black man who had been trained at Harvard.

John Hope Franklin was the last of the great generation of Black historians to graduate from Harvard in the first half of the twentieth century. W. E. B. Du Bois, who graduated in 1895, paved the way for Carter G. Woodson (the father of Black History Month!) in 1912, Charles Wesley in 1925, Rayford W. Logan in 1936, and Franklin in 1941. Both because he was the youngest member of this academic royal family and because he was lean and elegant, poised and cosmopolitan, many of us in the younger generation came to refer to Franklin as "The Prince."

Despite all of the important work published by his four predecessors at Harvard, Franklin was the first to publish a comprehensive and popular story of the Negro's place in American life. *From Slavery to Freedom* was not just the first of its genre, it was canon-forming. It gave to the Black historical tradition a self-contained form through which it could be institutionalized—parsed, divided into fifteen weeks, packaged and taught—from Harlem to Harvard, and even, or especially, in those places where almost no Black people actually lived. Every scholar of my generation studied Franklin's book; in this sense, we are all his godchildren.

But Franklin's relationship with Harvard was a complicated and tense one. Because Harvard had trained him as an historian, Franklin aspired to become the college's first Black history professor. By the late 1960s, that dream certainly seemed to be in his grasp, especially after he had integrated the history department at Brooklyn College in 1956, then moved to the Midwest in 1964 to integrate the history department at the University of Chicago, just a year after Dr. King's March on Washington.

While my classmates and I down in New Haven were busy busting William McFeely's chops for being White, Harvard had the good sense to invite John Hope Franklin to become the first chair of its fledgling academic Afro-American studies department, which it started in 1969 along with Yale and most other research universities.

But Franklin had an understandably principled opposition to academic segregation or "ghettoization" of any kind. He was suspicious about the uneven and troubled origins and stated intentions of the nascent field of Afro-American studies. He agreed to hold his breath if the faculty hired to teach in the new department were jointly appointed in the departments in which they had taken their degrees. With Franklin's pedigree, a joint appointment should have been an obvious move.

But the tenured faculty of history at Harvard, including some of the classmates with whom he had studied while pursuing the Ph.D., refused. His appointment, were he to accept the offer of Chairman, would be solely in the Department of Afro-American Studies. Franklin angrily rejected the offer, calling it the most egregious insult of his academic career. Although he would accept an honorary doctorate from Harvard in 1981, in large part as a snub to the history department, Franklin never forgave his professional colleagues for the insult. In fact, he took a certain perverse pleasure in talking Black scholars out of accepting tenured professorships at Harvard, including most famously William Julius Wilson and Cornel West in the 1980s. When Drew Faust was inaugurated as Harvard's first female president two years ago, one of the few featured speakers was John Hope, who spoke "on behalf of the History profession." This painful history, of which only a few of us were aware, made President Faust's gesture all the more poignant.

The experience with Harvard's history department also deepened his initial skepticism about the entire field of Black Studies, making him, until the 1990s, an ardent foe if it was a subject area set apart from and not integrated with the traditional disciplines. I once heard a Black nationalist assistant professor at Yale in the late 1970s refer to him derogatorily as "John Hopeless Franklin." But for Franklin, there could be no Black History without "History," as it were, and on this point he was unequivocal. For most of his career, Franklin saw Black Studies as the unfortunate correlative of Jim Crow segregation, self-imposed by well-meaning but naive Black students and complicit Black professors eager to get lucrative jobs at historically White institutions.

John Hope and I had met at Yale in the early 1980s, over a small dinner attended by the great historians David Brion Davis and John W. Blassingame, following Franklin's lecture. Davis turned to me during dinner and asked if I had ever discovered how I had been selected in the first group of MacArthur Fellows. As I attempted to say no, John Hope, from the far end of the table, thundered out that he knew precisely how I had been selected, because he had done the selecting! It was a bit like winning the fellowship all over again; I blinked back tears.

I told him how influenced I had been by *From Slavery to Freedom*, and that I had carried my copy of the third edition, published in 1967, with me across the African continent, reading it from cover to cover. (I didn't tell him that I felt the third edition was his best, and that subsequent editions, perhaps responding to the pressures from publishers to make textbooks more "readable," more accessible, seemed dumbed down—a long way in style from the densely rich narrative blend of documented facts with philosophical speculation and musings that characterized the black and white edition.) We stayed in touch after that, mostly by phone. One day he called to ask me to accept an offer that had just been extended by Stanley Fish in Duke's English Department.

My tenure at Duke was regrettably brief. Still, it gave me time to get to know John Hope better, to listen to his stories about school and segregation, about the academic life before *Brown v. Board* and his role in and perceptions of the Civil Rights Movement. Best of all, I loved his anecdotes. His favorite story was about the day he met W. E. B. Du Bois. Franklin was a graduate student at Harvard, doing research in North Carolina for his thesis on the Free Negro in North Carolina before the Civil War. John Hope, taking his evening meal in the segregated Arcade Hotel in the spring of 1939 spotted the great Du Bois dining alone in a corner. Cautiously, tentatively, he approached his hero. Du Bois' gaze was riveted on a book. John Hope loved describing what happened next:

> Seeing Dr. Du Bois dining alone and reading, I decided that this was an opportunity that I would not let pass. Crossing the dining room, I approached his table and spoke to him, giving him my full name. Surely he would recognize the fact that I was named for one of his closest friends and hearing it would embrace me. He did not even look up. Then I told him that I was a graduate of Fisk University, class of 1935. That, I assumed, would bring him to his feet singing 'Gold and Blue.' Again, he continued to read and eat, without looking up. Finally, as a last resort, I told him that I was a graduate student in history at Harvard and was in Raleigh doing research for my dissertation. Without looking up from his book or plate, he said, 'How do you do.' Dejected, I retreated, completed my dinner, and withdrew from the dining room (Franklin 2005, p. 117).

John Hope loved to tell that story, always ending it with, "Of course we became close friends later, when he and his wife, Shirley, lived in Brooklyn and I was teaching at the College." He told the story as a way of explaining why he was so very generous with younger colleagues. Myself included.

In April of 2007, Butler University invited us both to campus for a dialogue. I agreed, but only if I could play the role of interviewer, and if we could talk with no strict time limit attached. John Hope regaled a standing-room-only crowd for over two hours with stories about his family, his education, his political beliefs, his triumphs and disappointments. And as we dined together, sharing a bottle of Margaux, followed by a cognac, he congratulated me on recruiting Bill Wilson and Cornel West to Harvard despite his best efforts to dissuade them from coming. I congratulated him on receiving the Presidential Medal of Freedom; he returned the compliment about my receipt of the National Medal of the Humanities.

I congratulated him on Duke University's creation of the John Hope Franklin Research Center, and the forthcoming edition of *From Slavery to Freedom*, being revised by my colleague Evelyn Brooks Higginbotham, the first Black professor ever to receive tenure in Harvard's history department. I told him how much I valued the old third edition, the one with the black and white cover, and that I deeply regretted that it had gotten misplaced somehow. He told me he was proud of what we had created at Harvard. I shared with him the faculty's decision to co-name the library at the Du Bois Institute in his honor. He promised to visit, which he did following his speech at Drew Faust's inauguration. He seemed touched by the gesture.

A few days later, a FedEx envelope arrived at my house in Cambridge. Inside was another package, carefully wrapped in brown paper, the way antiquarians in England wrap books that they mail. When I give books as Christmas presents, I wrap them the same way. There is something wonderful about that brown wrapping paper. Inside the paper was a signed copy of *From Slavery to Freedom*, the black and white paperback edition, dated 1967, the same one that Professor McFeely had assigned us back at Yale. It was signed, "With affectionate best wishes." It sits in the bookshelf by my bedside.

REFERENCES

Franklin, John Hope (1947). *From Slavery to Freedom: A History of African Americans* New York: A.A. Knopf. Reprint, 3ed. (1967). New York: Knopf.

Franklin, John Hope (2005). *Mirror to America: The Autobiography of John Hope Franklin.* New York: Farrar, Straus and Giroux.

SOURCE: *Du Bois Review: Social Science Research on Race* 7, no. 1 (Spring 2010): 5–8. Copyright © 2010 W. E. B. Du Bois Institute for African and African American Research. Reprinted with permission of Cambridge University Press.

KING OF CATS

Albert Murray

IN THE LATE seventies, I used to take the train from New Haven to New York on Saturdays, to spend afternoons with Albert Murray at Books & Company, on Madison Avenue. We would roam—often joined by the artist Romare Bearden—through fiction, criticism, philosophy, music. Murray always seemed to wind up fingering densely printed paperbacks by Joyce, Mann, Proust, or Faulkner; Bearden, typically, would pick up a copy of something daunting like Rilke's "Letters on Cézanne" and then insist that I read it on the train home that night.

In those days, Murray was writing Count Basie's autobiography—a project that he didn't finish until 1985. ("For years," he has remarked more than once, "when I wrote the word 'I,' it meant Basie.") But he had already published most of the books that would secure his reputation as a cultural critic—perhaps most notably, his début collection, "The Omni-Americans" (1970), which brought together his ferocious attacks on black separatism, on protest literature, and on what he called "the social science-fiction monster." Commanding as he could be on the page, Murray was an equally impressive figure in the flesh: a lithe and dapper man with an astonishing gift of verbal fluency, by turns grandiloquent and earthy. I loved to listen to his voice—grave but insinuating, with more than a hint of a jazz singer's rasp. Murray had been a schoolmate of the novelist Ralph Ellison at the Tuskegee Institute, and the friendship of the two men over the years seemed a focal point of black literary culture in the ensuing decades. Ellison's one novel, "Invisible Man," was among the few unequivocal masterpieces of American literature in the postwar era, satirizing with equal aplomb Garveyites, Communists, and white racists in both their Southern-agrarian and their Northern-liberal guises. Murray's works of critique and cultural exploration seemed wholly in the same spirit. Both men were militant integrationists, and they shared an almost messianic view of the importance of art. In their ardent belief that Negro culture was a constitutive part of American culture, they had defied an entrenched literary mainstream, which preferred to regard black culture as so much exotica—amusing, perhaps, but eminently dispensable. Now they were also defying a new black vanguard, which regarded authentic black culture as separate from the rest of American culture—something that was created, and could be appreciated, in splendid isolation. While many of their peers liked to speak of wrath and resistance, Murray and Ellison liked to speak of complexity and craft, and for that reason they championed the art of Romare Bearden.

In terms of both critical regard and artistic fecundity, these were good days for Bearden, a large, light-skinned man with a basketball roundness to his head. (I could never get over how much he looked like Nikita Khrushchev.) He, like Murray, was working at the height of his powers—he was completing his famous "Jazz" series of collages—and his stature and influence were greater than those which any other African-American artist had so far enjoyed. The collages combined the visual conventions of black American folk culture with the techniques of modernism—fulfilling what Murray called "the vernacular imperative" to transmute tradition into art.

After a couple of hours at the bookstore, we'd go next door to the Madison Cafe, where Romie, as Murray called him, always ordered the same item: the largest fruit salad that I had ever seen in public. He claimed that he chose the fruit salad because he was watching his weight, but I was convinced that he chose it in order to devour the colors, like an artist dipping his brush into his palette. He'd start laying the ground with the off-white of the apples and the bananas, and follow them with the pinkish orange of the grapefruit, the red of strawberries, the speckled green of kiwifruit; the blueberries and purple grapes he'd save for last. While Romie was consuming his colors, Murray would talk almost non-stop, his marvelous ternary sentences punctuated only by the occasional bite of a B.L.T. or a tuna fish on rye. Murray was then, as now, a man with definite preoccupations, and among the touchstones of his conversation were terms like "discipline," "craft," "tradition," "the aesthetic," and "the Negro idiom." And names like Thomas Mann, André Malraux, Kenneth Burke, and Lord Raglan. There was also another name—a name that never weighed more heavily than when it was unspoken—which sometimes took longer to come up.

"Heard from Ralph lately?" Bearden would almost whisper as the waitress brought the check.

"Still grieving, I guess," Murray would rasp back, shaking his head slowly. He was referring to the fire, about a decade earlier, that had destroyed Ellison's Massachusetts farmhouse and, with it, many months of revisions on his long-awaited second novel. "That fire was a terrible thing." Then Murray, who was so rarely at a loss for words, would fall silent.

Later, when Bearden and I were alone in his Canal Street loft, he'd return to the subject in hushed tones: "Ralph is mad at Al. No one seems to know why. And it's killed Al. He's not sure what he did."

The rift, or whatever it amounted to, used to vex and puzzle me. It was a great mistake to regard Murray simply as Ellison's sidekick, the way many people did, but he was without question the most fervent and articulate champion of Ellison's art. The two were, in a sense, part of a single project: few figures on the scene shared as many presuppositions and preoccupations as they did. Theirs was a sect far too small for schismatics. At the very least, the rift made things awkward for would-be postulants like me.

When "The Omni-Americans" came out, in 1970, I was in college, majoring in history but pursuing extracurricular studies in how to be black. Those were days when the Black Power movement smoldered, when militancy was the mode and rage de rigueur. Just two years before, the poets Larry Neal and Amiri Baraka had edited "Black Fire," the book that launched the so-called Black Arts movement—in effect, the cultural wing of the Black Power movement. Maybe it was hard to hold a pen with a clenched fist, but you did what you could: the revolution wasn't about niceties of style anyway. On the occasions when Ralph Ellison, an avatar of elegance, was invited to college campuses, blacks invariably denounced him for his failure to involve himself in the civil-rights struggle, for his evident disdain of the posturings of Black Power. For me, though, the era was epitomized by a reading that the poet Nikki Giovanni gave in a university lecture hall, to a standing-room-only crowd—a sea of colorful dashikis and planetary Afros. Her words seemed incandescent with racial rage, and each poem was greeted with a Black Power salute. "Right on! Right on!" we shouted, in the deepest voices we could manage, each time Giovanni made another grand claim about the blackness of blackness. Those were days when violence (or, anyway, talk of violence) had acquired a Fanonist glamour; when the black bourgeoisie—kulaks of color, nothing more—was reviled as an obstacle on the road to revolution; when the arts were seen as merely an instrumentality for a larger cause.

Such was the milieu in which Murray published "The Omni-Americans," and you couldn't imagine a more foolhardy act. This was a book in which the very language of the black nationalists was subjected to a strip search. Ever since Malcolm X, for instance, the epithet "house Negro" had been a staple of militant invective; yet here was Murray arguing that if only we got our history straight we'd realize that those house Negros were practically race patriots. ("The house slave seems to have brought infinitely more tactical information from the big house to the cabins than any information about subversive plans he ever took back.") And while radicals mocked their bourgeois brethren as "black Anglo-Saxons," Murray defiantly declared, "Not only is it the so-called middle class Negro who challenges the status quo in schools, housing, voting practices, and so on, he is also the one who is most likely to challenge total social structures and value systems." Celebrated chroniclers of black America, including Claude Brown, Gordon Parks, and James Baldwin, were shown by Murray to be tainted by the ethnographic fallacy, the pretense that one writer's peculiar experiences can represent a social genus. "This whole thing about somebody revealing what it is really like to be black has long since gotten out of hand anyway," he wrote. "Does anybody actually believe that, say, Mary McCarthy reveals what it is really like to be a U.S. white woman, or even a Vassar girl?" But he reserved his heaviest artillery for the whole social-science approach to black life, whether in the hands of the psychologist Kenneth Clark (of *Brown v. Board of Education* fame) or in those of the novelist Richard Wright, who had spent too much time reading his sociologist friends. What was needed wasn't more sociological inquiry, Murray declared; what was needed was cultural creativity, nourished by the folkways and traditions of black America but transcending them. And the work of literature that best met that challenge, he said, was Ellison's "Invisible Man."

The contrarian held his own simply by matching outrage with outrage—by writing a book that was so pissed-off, jaw-jutting, and unapologetic that it demanded to be taken seriously. Nobody had to tell this veteran about black fire: in Murray the bullies of blackness had met their most formidable opponent. And a great many blacks—who, suborned by "solidarity," had trained themselves to suppress any heretical thoughts—found Murray's book oddly thrilling: it had the transgressive frisson of samizdat under Stalinism. You'd read it greedily, though you just might want to switch dust jackets with "The Wretched of the Earth" before wandering around with it in public. "Very early on, he was saying stuff that could get him killed," the African-American novelist David Bradley says. "And he did not seem to care." The power of his example lingers. "One February, I had just delivered the usual black-history line, and I was beginning to feel that I was selling snake oil," Bradley recalls. "And right here was this man who has said this stuff. And I'm thinking, Well, *he* ain't dead yet."

As if to remove any doubts, Murray has just published two books simultaneously, both with Pantheon. One, "The Seven League Boots," is his third novel, and completes a trilogy about a bright young fellow named Scooter, his fictional alter ego; the other, "The Blue Devils of Nada," is a collection of critical essays, analyzing some favorite artists (Ellington, Hemingway, Bearden) and expatiating upon some favorite tenets (the "blues idiom" as an aesthetic substrate, the essentially fluid nature of American culture). Both are books that will be discussed and debated for years to come; both are vintage Murray.

The most outrageous theorist of American culture lives, as he has lived for three decades, in a modest apartment in Lenox Terrace, in Harlem. When I visit him there, everything is pretty much as I remembered it. The public rooms look like yet another Harlem branch of the New York Public Library. Legal pads and magnifying glasses perch beside his two or three favorite chairs, along with numerous ball-point pens, his weapons of choice. His shelves record a lifetime of enthusiasms; James, Tolstoy, Hemingway, Proust, and Faulkner are among the authors most heavily represented. Close at hand are volumes by favored explicants, such as Joseph Campbell, Kenneth Burke, Carl Jung, Rudolph Arnheim, Bruno Bettelheim, Constance Rourke. On his writing desk sits a more intimate canon. There's Thomas Mann's four-volume "Joseph and His Brothers"—the saga, after all, of a slave who gains the power to decide the fate of a people. There's André Malraux's "Man's Fate," which represented for Ellison and Murray a more rarefied mode of engagé writing than anything their compeers had to offer. There's Joel Chandler Harris's "The Complete Tales of Uncle Remus," a mother lode of African-American folklore. One wall is filled with his famously compendious collection of jazz recordings; a matte-black CD-player was a gift from his protégé Wynton Marsalis. You will not, however, see the sort of framed awards that festooned Ellison's apartment. "I have received few of those honors," he says, pulling on his arthritic right leg. "No American Academy, few honorary degrees."

A quarter of a century has passed since Murray's literary début, and time has mellowed him not at all. His arthritis may have worsened over the past few years, and there is always an aluminum walker close by, but as he talks he sprouts wings. Murray likes to elaborate on his points and elaborate on his elaborations, until you find that you have circumnavigated the globe and raced through the whole of post-Homeric literary history—and this is what he calls "vamping till ready." In his conversation, outrages alternate with insights, and often the insights are the outrages. Every literary culture has its superego and its id; Albert Murray has the odd distinction of being both. The contradictions of human nature are, fittingly, a favorite topic of Murray's. He talks about how Thomas Jefferson was a slaveholder but how he also helped to establish a country whose founding creed was liberty. "Every time I think about it," he says, "I want to wake him up and give him ten more slaves." He's less indulgent of the conflicting impulses of Malcolm X. Dr. King's strategy of nonviolence was "one of the most magnificent things that anybody ever invented in the civil-rights movement," he maintains. "And this guy came up and started thumbing his nose at it, and, to my utter amazement, he's treated as if he were a civil-rights leader. He didn't lead anything. He was in Selma laughing at these guys. God *damn*, nigger!"

Albert Murray is a teacher by temperament, and as he explains a point he'll often say that he wants to be sure to "work it into your consciousness." The twentieth century has worked a great deal into Murray's consciousness. He was fifteen when the Scottsboro trial began, twenty-two when Marian Anderson sang at the Lincoln Memorial. He joined the Air Force when it was segregated and rejoined shortly after it had been desegregated. He was in his late thirties when *Brown v. Board of Education* was decided, when the conflict in Korea was concluded, when Rosa Parks was arrested. He was in his forties when the Civil Rights Act was passed, when SNCC was founded, when John F. Kennedy was killed. And he was in his fifties when the Black Panther Party was formed, when King was shot, when Black Power was proclaimed. Such are the lineaments of public history—the sort of grainy national drama that newsreels used to record. For him, though, the figures of history are as vivid as drinking companions, and, on the whole, no more sacrosanct.

He is equally unabashed about taking on contemporary figures of veneration, even in the presence of a venerator. Thus, about the novelist Toni Morrison, we agree to disagree. "I do think it's tainted with do-goodism," he says of her Nobel Prize, rejecting what he considers the special pleading of contemporary feminism. "I think it's redressing wrongs. You don't have to condescend to no goddam Jane Austen. Or the Brontës, or George Eliot and George Sand. These chicks are tough. You think you'll get your fastball by Jane Austen? So we don't need special pleading for anything. And the same goes for blackness." He bridles at the phenomenon of Terry McMillan, the best-selling author of "Waiting to Exhale"—or, more precisely, at the nature of the attention she has received. "I think it's a mistake to try to read some profound political significance into everything, like as soon as a Negro writes it's got to be some civil-rights thing," he says. "It's just Jackie Collins stuff."

At times, his pans somehow edge into panegyrics, the result being what might be called a backhanded insult. About Maya Angelou's much discussed Inaugural poem he says, "It's like the reaction to 'Porgy and Bess.' Man, you put a bunch of brown-skinned people onstage, with footlights and curtains, and they make *anything* work. White people have no resistance to Negro performers: they charm the pants off anything. Black people make you listen up. They're singing 'Old Man River'—'Tote that barge, lift that bale'? What the fuck is that? Everybody responded like 'This is great.' That type of fantastic charm means that black performers can redeem almost any type of pop fare."

Since discipline and craft are his by-words, however, he distrusts staged spontaneity. "He plays the same note that he perfected twenty-five years ago, and he acts like he's got to sweat to get the note out of the goddam guitar," Murray says of the contemporary blues musician B. B. King. "He's got to shake his head and frown, and it's just going to be the same goddam note he already played twenty-five years ago." Murray himself doesn't mind returning to notes he played twenty-five years ago—his nonfiction books explore the same set of issues, and can be read as chapters of a single ongoing opus. Indeed, from all accounts the fashioning of this particular cultural hero began long before the start of his writing career.

In Murray's case, heroism was a matter both of circumstance and of will. Certainly he has long been an avid student of the subject. Lord Raglan's classic "The Hero: A Study in Tradition, Myth, and Drama" (1936) is among the books most frequently cited in his writing, and it remains a part of his personal canon. Moreover, the mythic patterns that Lord Raglan parsed turn out to have had resonances for Murray beyond the strictly literary. According to Raglan's exhaustively researched generalizations, the hero is highborn, but "the circumstances of his conception are unusual," and he is "spirited away" to be "reared by foster-parents in a far country." Then, "on reaching manhood," he "returns or goes to his future kingdom," confronts and defeats the king, or a dragon, or some such, and starts being heroic in earnest. So it was, more or less, with Oedipus, Theseus, Romulus, Joseph, Moses, Siegfried, Arthur, Robin Hood, and—oh, yes—Albert Murray.

Murray was born in 1916 and grew up in Magazine Point, a hamlet not far from Mobile, Alabama. His mother was a housewife, and his father, Murray says, was a "common laborer," who sometimes helped lay railroad tracks as a cross-tie cutter and at other times harvested timber in the Turpentine woods. "As far as the Murrays were concerned, it was a fantastic thing that I finished the ninth grade," he recalls, "or that I could read the newspaper." But he had already decided that he was bound for college. Everyone in the village knew that there was something special about him. And he knew it, too.

He had known it ever since an all-night wake—he was around eleven at the time—when he had fallen asleep in the living room, his head cradled in his mother's lap. At one point, he surfaced to hear himself being discussed, but, with a child's cunning, he pretended he was still asleep.

"Tell me something," a relative was saying. "Is it true that Miss Graham is really his mama?"

"She's the one brought him into the world," Mrs. Murray replied. "But I'm his mama. She gave him to me when he was no bigger than a minute, and he was so little I had to put him on a pillow to take him home. I didn't think he was going to make it. I laid him out for God to take him two or three times. And I said, 'Lord this child is here for something, so I'm going to feed this child and he's going to make it.'" It was a moment that Al Murray likens to finding out the truth about Santa Claus.

Murray's birth parents were, as he slowly learned, well educated and securely middle class—people who belonged to an entirely different social stratum from that of his adoptive parents. His natural father, John Young, came from a well-established family in town. His natural mother had been attending Tuskegee as a boarding student and working part time for John Young's aunt and uncle, who were in the real-estate business. When she learned that a close encounter with John Young had left her pregnant, she had to leave town—"because of the disgrace," Murray explains. As luck would have it, a cousin of hers knew a married woman who, unable to bear a child of her own, was interested in adopting one. Murray doesn't have to be prodded to make the fairy-tale connection. "It's just like the prince left among the paupers," he says cheerfully. (In "The Omni-Americans" he wrote, apropos of the 1965 Moynihan report on the breakdown of the black-family structure, "How many epic heroes issue from conventional families?")

As a freshman at the Tuskegee Institute—the ancestral kingdom he was fated to enter—Murray became aware of a junior whose reading habits were alarmingly similar to his. He was a music major from Oklahoma named Ralph Waldo Ellison, and what first impressed Murray about him was his wardrobe. "Joe College, right out of *Esquire*—he had fine contrasting slacks, gray tweed jacket. He would be wearing bow ties and two-tone shoes," Murray recalls. "In those days, when you checked out a book from the library you had a little slip in the back where you would write your name, and then they would stamp the due date." Consequently, when Murray took out a book by, say, T. S. Eliot or Robinson Jeffers, he could see who had previously borrowed the book. Time and again, it was that music major with the two-tone shoes.

Ellison left Tuskegee for New York before completing his senior year: his absence was meant to be temporary, a means of saving some money, but he never went back. Murray earned his B.A. at Tuskegee in 1939, and stayed on to teach. In 1941, he married Mozelle Menefee, who was a student there. He spent the last two years of the Second World War on active duty in the Air

Force. "I was just hoping I'd live long enough for Thomas Mann to finish the last volume of 'Joseph and His Brothers,'" he says. Two years after his discharge, he moved to New York, where, on the G.I. bill, he got a master's degree in literature from New York University. It was also in New York that the friendship between him and Ellison took off. Ellison read passages to Murray from a manuscript that would turn into "Invisible Man." The two men explored the streets and the sounds of Harlem together; over meals and over drinks, they hashed out ideas about improvisation, the blues, and literary modernism. Even then, Murray had a reputation as a "great explainer."

The prominent black religious and literary scholar Nathan A. Scott, who was a graduate student in New York in the forties and had become a friend of Ellison's, tells about being in the Gotham Book Mart one day and noticing another black man there. "I was somewhat surprised to find this slight, dark man there, because I'd never bumped into a Negro there," Scott recounts. "And some young white chap came in, and they knew each other and immediately plunged into a spirited conversation, and at a certain point I overheard this chap say to the black man, 'Well, what are you working on these days?' To which the black chap replied, 'Oh, I am doing an essay in self-definition.'" (And Scott laughs loudly.) Later, at a dinner at Ellison's apartment, Ellison introduced Scott to his friend Albert Murray: "Immediately, I thought, By God, here is the chap who was doing that essay in self-definition! Inwardly, I laughed all over again."

If it was clear that the young man was interested in trying to write, it wasn't so clear what the results were. In the early fifties, Saul Bellow and Ralph Ellison shared a house in Dutchess County, and Bellow recalls seeing Murray from time to time down in the city. "I think he agreed with Ralph, in simply assuming that they were deeply installed in the whole American picture," Bellow says. He adds that Ellison talked about Murray's writing in those days, but that he himself never saw any of it. In 1952, Ellison published "Invisible Man." The book was a best-seller for several months, and garnered some of the most enthusiastic critical responses anyone could remember. It was soon a classroom staple, the subject of books and dissertations. It was read and reread. Ellison, in short, had become an immortal. And Murray? With a wife and a daughter to support, he was pursuing a more conventional career—in the Air Force, which he rejoined in 1951.

As a military officer, Murray taught courses in geopolitics in the Air Force R.O.T.C. program at Tuskegee, where he was based for much of the fifties, and he oversaw the administration of large-scale technical operations both in North Africa and in the United States. While his military career has remained oddly isolated from his creative work—a matter of regret, in the opinion of some of his friends—the experience would leave him impatient with the pretensions of the by-any-means-necessary brigade. He says, in that distinctively Murrayesque tone of zestful exasperation, "Let's talk about 'the fire next time.' You know damn well they can put out the fire by Wednesday."

When Murray retired from the military, in 1962, he moved to New York, and soon his articles began to appear in periodicals (*Life, The New Leader*) and collections ("Anger, and Beyond"). In 1964, Ellison wrote a letter about his old friend to one Jacob Cohen, who was planning to start a magazine. "Actually I find it very difficult to write about him," the letter began. "I suppose because I have known him since our days at Tuskegee, and because our contacts since that time have been so constant and our assumptions about so many matters in such close agreement that I really don't have the proper sense of perspective." Ellison went on to say of Murray, "He has the imagination which allows him to project himself into the centers of power, and he uses his imagination to deal with serious problems seriously and as though he were a responsible participant in the affairs of our nation and our time." The following year, a panel of book critics, authors, and editors found "Invisible Man" to be the most widely admired novel published since the Second World War. Meanwhile, Albert Murray, then two years out of the Air Force, was scarcely known outside the circle of his acquaintances.

However asymmetric the public stature of the pair, people who spent time with Murray and Ellison in those days were impressed by the ease and intimacy of their friendship. In the late sixties, Willie Morris, then the editor of *Harper's*, eagerly sought their company: they provided him with a refreshing contrast to what he found a suffocating literary climate. He recalls, "In every way, they were like brothers—you know, soul brothers and fellow-writers—but Ellison's star was so bright, and Al was just really getting started." Soul brothers they may have been; they were also brothers-in-arms. When Murray rose to do battle with the rising ranks of black nationalism, he knew he shared a foxhole with Ralph Ellison, and there must have been comfort in that.

It may seem ironic that the person who first urged "The Omni-Americans" on me was Larry Neal, one of the Black Arts founders. But Neal was a man of far greater subtlety than the movement he spawned, and he understood Albert Murray's larger enterprise—the one that he shared with Ellison—better than most. People who may not read Murray but like the *idea* of him reflexively label him an "integrationist"; seldom do they take in the term's full complexity. In Murray's hands, integration wasn't an act of accommodation but an act of introjections. Indeed, at the heart of Murray and Ellison's joint enterprise was perhaps the most breathtaking act of cultural chutzpah this land had witnessed since Columbus blithely claimed it all for Isabella.

In its bluntest form, their assertion was that the truest Americans were black Americans. For much of what was truly distinctive about America's "national character" was rooted in the improvisatory prehistory of the blues. The very sound of American English "is derived from the timbre of the African voice and the listening habits of the African ear," Ellison maintained. "If there is such a thing as a Yale accent, there is a Negro wail in it." This is the lesson that the protagonist of Ellison's novel learns while working at a paint factory: the whitest white is made by adding a drop of black. For generations, the word "American" had tacitly connoted "white." Murray inverted the cultural assumptions and the verbal conventions: in his discourse, "American," roughly speaking, means "black." So, even as the clenched-fist crowd was scrambling for cultural crumbs, Murray was declaring the entire harvest board of American civilization to be his birthright. In a sense, Murray was the ultimate black nationalist. And the fact that people so easily mistook his vision for its opposite proved how radical it was.

But why stop with matters American? What did the European savants of Existentialism understand about *la condition humaine* that Ma Rainey did not? In later works, most notably "Stomping the Blues" (1976), Murray took the blues to places undreamed-of by its originators. It has long been a commonplace that the achievements of black music have far outstripped those of black literature—that no black writer has produced work of an aesthetic complexity comparable to Duke Ellington's, Count Basie's, or Charlie Parker's. This much, for Murray, was a point of departure: he sought to process the blues into a self-conscious aesthetic, to translate the deep structure of the black vernacular into prose. Arguably, LeRoi Jones attempted something similar in his celebrated "Blues People" (1963), but there sociology gained the upper hand over art. (Ellison, writing in *The New York Review of Books*, complained that Jones's approach was enough to "give even the blues the blues.") To Murray, the blues stood in opposition to all such reductionism. "What it all represents is an attitude toward the nature of human experience (and the alternatives of human adjustment) that is both elemental and comprehensive," he wrote in "Stomping the Blues," and he continued:

> It is a statement about confronting the complexities inherent in the human situation and about improvising or experimenting or riffing or otherwise playing with (or even gambling with) such possibilities as are also inherent in the obstacles, the disjunctures, and the jeopardy. It is also a statement about

perseverance and about resilience and thus also about the maintenance of equilibrium despite precarious circumstances and about achieving elegance in the very process of coping with the rudiments of subsistence.

Though Murray's salvific conception of the blues may seem fantastical, it represented precisely the alternative that Larry Neal and others were searching for. In truth, you could no more capture the sublimity of music in earthbound prose than you could trap the moon's silvery reflection in a barrel of rainwater, but there was heroism, surely, in the effort.

Nor was it only literature that could be revivified by jazz and the blues. That was where Bearden came in, and that was why his friendship with Murray had to be understood also as an artistic alliance. Bearden's mixed-media works could serve as a cultural paradigm for the kind of bricolage and hybridity that Murray favored.

In recent stanzas entitled "Omni-Albert Murray" the young African-American poet Elizabeth Alexander writes, "In my mind and in his I think a painting is a poem/A tambourine's a hip shake and train whistle a guitar." Certainly Murray proved an authoritative exponent of Bearden's works, the titles of which were frequently of his devising. The literary scholar Robert O'Meally remembers being with Bearden and Murray in Books & Company when the two were trying to decide on a name for whatever picture Bearden had brought along that day. O'Meally recalls, "It might be that Al Murray's eye was caught by the figure of a woman in one corner of the image. And he'd say, 'Who's that?' And Bearden would be looking embarrassed, because the woman in question had been an old girlfriend of his. Maybe Bearden would say, 'Oh, she's just a woman I once knew from North Carolina.' And then Murray would say, 'I've got it. Let's call it "Red-Headed Woman from North Carolina."' Or, 'I know, call it "Red-Headed Woman from North Carolina with Rooster."' And Bearden would go and write that on the back of his painting."

Murray stood ready to assist in other ways, too. When, in 1978, I asked Bearden if he would conduct a seminar on Afro-American art at Yale, where I was teaching, his immediate response was "Why don't you ask Al?" But this particular appointment called for an artist, and Bearden finally did accept, though with genuine reluctance and vehement protestations of pedagogic incompetence. So reluctant was he that I was astonished by the remarkably well-organized and cogent weekly lectures he had prepared—always neatly double-spaced and fifty minutes in duration, the precise length of the academic lecturer's hour. Comprehension soon dawned. Bearden, taking matters into his own hands, had found a way to bring Murray along to New Haven: the critic had ghostwritten Professor Bearden's erudite lectures.

But did Murray have debts of his own to acknowledge—in particular, to his Tuskegee schoolmate? The very similarity of their preoccupations proved a source of friction. Now it was Murray—here, there, and everywhere—spreading the glad word about the literary theorist Kenneth Burke, about Lord Raglan, about the luminous blending of craft and meta-physics represented by André Malraux and by Thomas Mann. Ellison's claim, at least to Kenneth Burke and Lord Raglan, seems clear: they were part of the swirl of ideas at Bennington College in the early fifties, when Ellison was living nearby and socializing with the faculty. One writer who had been friendly with both Murray and Ellison since the forties assures me that he has no doubt as to who was the exegete and who the originator: "This is not to say that Al was simply some sort of epigone. But *all* the fundamental ideas that are part of 'The Omni-Americans' came from Ellison. Al made his own music out of those ideas, but *I* know where they came from. The course of thought that Murray began to follow in the sixties was a result of Ralph's influence, I think there is no doubt about this at all."

That has become something of a consensus view. In a recent appreciation of Murray, the jazz critic Gene Seymour writes that on such subjects as improvisation, discipline, and tradition Murray (and, by extension, disciples of his like Stanley Crouch and Wynton Marsalis) sounds "like an echo." He maintains that the recently published volume of Ellison's collected essays "makes clear [that] Ellison was the wellspring for the ideals advanced by Murray, Crouch, and Marsalis."

It's a thorny subject. At one point, Murray tells me about V. S. Naipaul's visit with him in the late eighties—a visit that was recorded in Naipaul's "A Turn in the South." Naipaul wrote, "He was a man of enthusiasms, easy to be with, easy to listen to. His life seemed to have been a series of happy discoveries." At the same time, Naipaul identified Murray as a writer who "was, or had been, a protégé of Ralph Ellison's." Murray makes it clear that this gloss does not sit well with him. He counters by quoting something that Robert Bone, a pioneering scholar of African-American literature, told him: "I've been trying to figure out *who* is the protégé of *whom*."

Bone, an acquaintance of both principals, suggests beginning with a different set of premises. "On Murray's part, it must have been a terribly difficult thing for him to have been overshadowed by Ralph in terms of the timing of their two careers," he says. "In a way, they started out together at Tuskegee, and then they cemented that friendship in New York, but Murray got such a later start in his career as a writer. So when he came on the scene Ralph was, of course, a celebrity." What escapes us, Bone says, is that many of the positions with which Ellison was associated were ones the two had mulled over together and corresponded about—especially "the link between Afro-American writing and Afro-American music." Reverse all your assumptions, though, and one thing remains constant: "Murray, I think, naturally must have felt a good deal of envy and resentment." Where others see Darwin and Huxley, Bone sees Watson and Crick. Of Ellison and Murray he says, "There was a time when they were both young and aspiring writers, and they shared these ideas and they worked on them together, but Ralph got into print with them first, by a kind of accident." Speaking like a true literary historian, he adds, "I think these matters will be resolved when Murray leaves his papers—he has a box full of correspondence with Ellison. I think that that correspondence is going to bring out the mutuality of these explorations and discoveries."

It's clear that, beneath Ellison's unfailingly courtly demeanor, his own internal struggles may have taken their toll. The fire, in the fall of 1967, is often mentioned as a watershed moment for him, one whose symbolic freight would only increase over the years. He had been busy that summer in his Massachusetts farmhouse, making extensive revisions on his novel in progress—Murray recalls seeing a manuscript thick with interlinear emendations during a visit there. At times, Ellison had called Murray to read him some of the new material. The fire occurred on the very evening that the Ellisons had decided to return to New York. Murray says, "He packed up all his stuff and got everything together, put it all in the hallway leading out, with some of his cameras and some of his shooting equipment. Then they went out to dinner with Richard Wilbur. On the way home, when they got to a certain point, they saw this fire reflection on the skyline, and, the nearer they got, the more it seemed like it was their place. And as they turned in, they saw their house going up in flames." Ellison had a copy of the manuscript in New York, but the rewriting and rethinking that had occupied him for months were lost. "So he went into shock, really. He just closed off from everybody." Murray didn't hear from him until Christmas. In the months that followed, Ellison would sometimes call Murray up and read him passages—trying to jog Murray's memory so that he would jog Ellison's. "It took him years to recover," Murray says. Meanwhile, Murray's career was following an opposite trajectory. As if making up for lost time, he spent the first half of the seventies averaging a book a year; during the same period, Ellison's block as a novelist had grown to mythic proportions. Bellow says, "Ralph was suffering very deeply from his hangup, and it was very hard to have any connection with him. He got into a very strange state, I think."

Did Ellison feel betrayed? It seems clear that he did. ("Romie used to call it 'Oklahoma paranoia,'" Murray says, musing on the froideur that settled between them.) Did Ellison have reason to? That's harder to answer. The African-American poet Michael S. Harper, an Ellison stalwart, says, "The most important word I ever heard Ralph say was the word 'honor.' I happen to know some of the difficulties they went through when Albert was in a phase of making appearances in white literary salons, and reports came back from various people." Theories of the estrangement abound. One writer acquainted with the two men says that Ellison had learned that Murray was bad-mouthing him; another suggests that Ellison simply felt crowded, that Murray was presenting himself as Ellison's confidant—"as the man to see if you want to know"—in a way that Ellison found unseemly. The chill could make things awkward for acquaintances. One of them says, "I remember on one occasion Ralph and I were lunching at the Century Club, when Al saw me in the downstairs lobby. He came up immediately and we chatted briefly, and as we were talking to each other Ralph walked away and would have nothing to do with Al. Theirs had become a difficult relationship."

Murray, for his part, is inclined to see the matter in almost anthropological terms, as falling into the behavior patterns of out-group representatives amid an in-group: "Here's a guy who figures that he's got *his* white folks over here, and he got them all hoodwinked, so he don't want anybody coming in messing things up." In anthropological terms, the native informant never relishes competition. "Hell, it was probably inevitable," Willie Morris says of the estrangement.

For all their similarities in background, education, sensibility, even dress (they shared a tailor, Charlie Davidson, himself something of a legend in sartorial circles), the two men inclined toward rather contrasting styles of public presentation. A private man who in later years grew intensely aware of being a public figure, Ellison had contrived a persona designed to defeat white expectations of black brutishness. Hence the same words come up again and again when people try to write about him—words like "patrician," "formal," "aristocratic," "mandarin," "civilized," "dignified." James Baldwin once observed, shrewdly, that Ellison was "as angry as anybody can be and still *live.*" It was this banked anger that kept his back so straight in public settings, his manners so impeccable; even his spoken sentences wore spats and suspenders. Murray, who enjoyed verbal sparring as much as anybody, lacked that gift of anger, and as a conversationalist he had always taken delight in the saltier idioms of the street. (Imagine Redd Foxx with a graduate degree in literature.) The writer Reynolds Price, a friend of both Ellison and Murray, says, "Ralph had a kind of saturnine, slightly bemused quality. I thought Al always seemed the more buoyant person."

Writing is at once a solitary and a sociable act, and literary relationships are similarly compounded of opposites. So it was with Ellison and Murray, two country cousins. Many people speak of Ellison's eightieth-birthday party—to which Murray had been invited and at which he delivered a moving tribute to his old schoolmate—as a significant moment of reconciliation. "I think it was Ellison's way of reaching out to Murray," a friend of Ellison's says.

Then, too, for all his companionability, Murray's literary inclinations ran strongly toward the paternal. He takes deep satisfaction in that role, and there are many who can attest to his capacity for nurturance. James Alan McPherson, one of the fiction writers who have most often been likened to Ellison, recalls a time in the late seventies when he was in Rhode Island with Michael Harper, the poet, and Ernest J. Gaines, whose novels include "The Autobiography of Miss Jane Pittman." In a moment of mad enthusiasm, they hit on the idea of going to New York and letting Ellison know how much they admired him. When they phoned him, he told them, to their unbounded joy, that they should come right down. And so, after an almost mythic trek, these young black writers arrived at Riverside Drive to pay a visit to their hero.

"Mr. Ellison can't see you," they were told at the door. "He's busy working."

They were crushed. They were also adrift: with the destination of their pilgrimage closed to them, they had no place to go. "So we called Al Murray, and he picked up the slack," McPherson recounts. "He brought us to his apartment, where he had some apples and some bourbon and some fancy French cheese. And he said, 'Have you ever met Duke Ellington's sister?' We said no, so he took us over to meet Duke Ellington's sister. And he said, 'Do you want to see the Bearden retrospective?'" He took them to the Brooklyn Museum and on to the Cordier and Ekstrom gallery, where Bearden was then showing his work. "And I'll always remember Al for that," McPherson says. (Murray tells me, "Most guys forget that I'm just two years younger than Ralph, but they feel closer to me because I'm more accessible. They kid with me all the time.") Perhaps, in the end, Ellison was the better student of Lord Raglan: he knew that patricide, or some variant of it, was a staple of heroic literature. McPherson says, quietly, "Ellison didn't want any sons."

For McPherson, what crystallized things was a ceremony that City College held in 1984 to honor Ellison. McPherson and Harper were both there to give tributes. At the luncheon, Harper tapped on his glass and handed Ellison a wrapped box, saying, "Ralph, here's a gift from your sons."

"Then you'd better open it yourself," Ellison replied dryly. "I'm afraid it might explode."

Albert Murray has now reached the age where his progeny have progeny, two of the most prominent in his line being, of course, Stanley Crouch and Wynton Marsalis. Both are frequent guests at Lenox Terrace, and Marsalis tells me of dinner-table conversations that roam from Homer to Galileo, from the commedia dell'arte to Faulkner and Neruda. "Murray has given me a first-class education," he says. And he speaks eloquently about the impact that "Stomping the Blues," and Murray's very notion of jazz as an art form, had on him; he speaks about tradition, blues idioms, a poetics of inclusion. As he puts it, "I'm a Murrayite." Crouch, whose writing has brilliantly championed Murray's difficult aesthetic and emulated his pugnacious style of critique, says, "I think he's one of the foremost thinkers to appear in American letters over the last twenty-five years." (He also suggests that Murray would have been a far worthier candidate for a Nobel Prize than Toni Morrison.) "The last of the giants," McPherson calls him.

There is much to be said for having descendants. They spread the insights you have given them. They worry about why you are not better known. (Crouch has a simple explanation for Murray's relative obscurity: "It's because he spent all that time on the Basie book—there was that very long silence. I think what happened was that his career lost momentum.") They remind you, fetchingly, of your own callow youth. And they take inspiration from your fearless style of analysis and critique, and apply it to your own work—though this can be a mixed blessing.

No doubt it's the ultimate tribute to Murray's legacy of combative candor that his most fervid admirers are quite free in expressing their critical reservations—notably with regard to the new novel. "The Seven League Boots" has the distinction of being the least autobiographical of Murray's three novels: its protagonist leaves Alabama with his bass and joins up with a legendary jazz band—one not unlike Ellington's. The band is blissfully free of quarrels and petty jealousies, and Murray's alter ego, Scooter, inspires only affection in those he encounters. Indeed, this is, in no small part, a novel about friendships, about literary and intellectual conversations and correspondences, including those between Scooter and his old college roommate. On a trip across the Mississippi River Bridge, Scooter finds himself thinking about

> my old roommate again. But this time the writer he brought to mind was not Rilke but Walt Whitman, about whom he had said in response to my letter about joining the band for a while. . . . *According to my old roommate, old Walt*

Whitman, barnstorming troubadour par excellence that he was, could only have been completely delighted with the interplay of aesthetic and pragmatic considerations evidenced in the maps and mileage charts and always tentative itineraries. . . . It was Ralph Waldo Emerson who spoke of "melodies that ascend and leap and pierce into the deeps of infinite time," my roommate also wrote, which, by the way, would make a very fine blurb for a Louis Armstrong solo such as the one on "Potato Head Blues."

In the next few pages, there are allusions to, among others, Melville, James Joyce, Van Wyck Brooks, Lewis Mumford, Constance Rourke, Frederick Douglass, Paul Laurence Dunbar, and Antonin Dvorák. Perhaps the critic's library overstocks his novelistic imagination. In the *Times Book Review*, the novelist and critic Charles Johnson—who must be counted among Murray's heirs, and is certainly among his most heartfelt admirers—described it as "a novel without tension." It may well be that the pleasures this novel affords are more discursive than dramatic, more essayistic than narrative. Murray tells me, "I write hoping that the most sophisticated readers of my time will think that I'm worth reading." They do, and he is.

The poet Elizabeth Alexander writes:

> *Albert Murray do they call you Al*
> *or Bert or Murray or "Tuskegee Boy"?*
> *Who are the Omni-Ones who help me feel?*
> *I'm born after so much. Nostalgia hurts.*

You could say of him what he said of Gordon Parks: "Sometimes it is as if he himself doesn't quite know what to make of what he has in fact *already* made of himself." Sometimes I don't quite, either. On the one hand, I cherish the vernacular; on the other, I've always distrusted the notion of "myth" as something deliberately added to literature, like the prize in a box of Cracker Jack. And though my first two books can be read as footnotes to "The Omni-Americans," I, like most in the demoralized profession of literary studies, have less faith in the cultural power of criticism than he has. All the same, I find his company immensely cheering.

We live in an age of irony—an age when passionate intensity is hard to find outside a freshman dining hall, and when even the mediocre lack all conviction. But Murray was produced by another age, in which intelligence expressed itself in ardor. He has spent a career *believing* in things, like the gospel according to Ma Rainey and Jimmy Rushing and Duke Ellington. More broadly, he believes in the sublimity of art, and he has never been afraid of risking bathos to get to it. (I think the reason he took so long to write Basie's life story is that he wanted to step *inside* a great black artist, to see for himself how improvisation and formal complexity could produce high art.)

The last time I visited him at his apartment, I sat in the chair next to his writing desk as he talked me through the years of his life and his formation, and made clear much that had been unclear to me about cultural modernity. "Let me begin by saying that Romie frequently got me into trouble," Ralph Ellison told mourners at a 1988 memorial service for Bearden. "Nothing physical, mind you, but difficulties arising out of our attempts to make some practical sense of the relationship between art and living, between ideas and the complex details of consciousness and experience." In this sense, Murray, too, has always spelled trouble—for critics and artists of every description, for icon-breakers and icon-makers, for friends and foes. You learn a great many things when you sit with him in his apartment, but, summed up, they amount to a larger vision: this is Albert Murray's century; we just live in it.

SOURCE: *The New Yorker*, April 8, 1996, pp. 70–81.

WHITE LIKE ME

Anatole Broyard

IN 1982, AN investment banker named Richard Grand-Jean took a summer's lease on an eighteenth-century farmhouse in Fairfield, Connecticut; its owner, Anatole Broyard, spent his summers in Martha's Vineyard. The house was handsomely furnished with period antiques, and the surrounding acreage included a swimming pool and a pond. But the property had another attraction, too. Grand-Jean, a managing director of Salomon Brothers, was an avid reader, and he took satisfaction in renting from so illustrious a figure. Anatole Broyard had by then been a daily book reviewer for the *Times* for more than a decade, and that meant that he was one of literary America's foremost gate-keepers. Grand-Jean might turn to the business pages of the *Times* first, out of professional obligation, but he turned to the book page next, out of a sense of self. In his Walter Mittyish moments, he sometimes imagined what it might be like to be someone who read and wrote about books for a living—someone to whom millions of readers looked for guidance.

Broyard's columns were suffused with both worldliness and high culture. Wry, mandarin, even self-amused at times, he wrote like a man about town, but one who just happened to have all of Western literature at his fingertips. Always, he radiated an air of soigné self-confidence: he could be amiable in his opinions or waspish, but he never betrayed a flicker of doubt about what he thought. This was a man who knew that his judgment would never falter and his sentences never fail him.

Grand-Jean knew little about Broyard's earlier career, but as he rummaged through Broyard's bookshelves he came across old copies of intellectual journals like *Partisan Review* and *Commentary*, to which Broyard had contributed a few pieces in the late forties and early fifties. One day, Grand-Jean found himself leafing through a magazine that contained an early article by Broyard. What caught his eye, though, was the contributor's note for the article—or, rather, its absence. It had been neatly cut out, as if with a razor.

A few years later, Grand-Jean happened on another copy of that magazine, and decided to look up the Broyard article again. This time, the note on the contributor was intact. It offered a few humdrum details—that Broyard was born in New Orleans, attended Brooklyn College and the New School for Social Research, and taught at New York University's Division of General Education. It also offered a less humdrum one: the situation of the American Negro, the note asserted, was a subject that the author "knows at first hand." It was an elliptical formulation, to be sure, but for Anatole Broyard it may not have been elliptical enough.

Broyard was born black and became white, and his story is compounded of equal parts pragmatism and principle. He knew that the world was filled with such snippets and scraps of paper, all conspiring to reduce him to an identity that other people had invented and he had no say in. Broyard responded with X-Acto knives and evasions, with distance and denials and half denials and cunning half-truths. Over the years, he became a virtuoso of ambiguity and equivocation. Some of his acquaintances knew the truth; many more had heard rumors about "distant" black ancestry (wasn't there a grandfather who was black? a great-grandfather?). But most were entirely unaware, and that was as he preferred it. He kept the truth even from his own children. Society had decreed race to be a matter of natural law, but he wanted race to be an elective affinity, and it was never going to be a fair fight. A penalty was exacted. He shed a past and an identity to become a writer—a writer who wrote endlessly about the act of shedding a past and an identity.

Anatole Paul Broyard was born on July 16, 1920, in New Orleans to Paul Broyard and Edna Miller. His father was a carpenter and worked as a builder, along with his brothers; neither parent had graduated from elementary school. Anatole spent his early years in a modest house on St. Ann Street, in a colored neighborhood in the French Quarter. Documents in the Louisiana state archives show all Anatole's ancestors, on both sides, to have been Negroes, at least since the late eighteenth century. The rumor about a distant black ancestor was, in a sense, the reverse of the truth: he may have had one distant white ancestor. Of course, the conventions of color stratification within black America—nowhere more pronounced than in New Orleans—meant that light-skinned blacks often intermarried with other light-skinned blacks, and this was the case with Paul and his "high yellow" wife, Edna. Anatole was the second of three children; he and his sister Lorraine, two years older, were light-skinned, while Shirley, two years younger, was not so light-skinned. (The inheritance of melanin is an uneven business.) In any event, the family was identified as Negro, and identified itself as Negro.

It was not the most interesting thing about them. But in America it was not a negligible social fact. The year before Anatole's birth, for example, close to a hundred blacks were lynched in the South and anti-black race riots claimed the lives of hundreds more.

While Anatole was still a child, the family moved to the Bedford-Stuyvesant area of Brooklyn, thus joining the great migration that took hundreds of thousands of Southern blacks to Northern cities during the twenties. In the French Quarter, Paul Broyard had been a legendary dancer, beau, and *galant*; in the French Quarter, the Broyards—Paul was one of ten siblings—were known for their craftsmanship. Brooklyn was a less welcoming environment. "He should never have left New Orleans, but my mother nagged him into it," Broyard recalled years later. Though Paul Broyard arrived there a master carpenter, he soon discovered that the carpenters' union was not favorably inclined toward colored applicants. A stranger in a strange city, Paul decided to pass as white in order to join the union and get work. It was strictly a professional decision, which affected his work and nothing else.

For Paul, being colored was a banal fact of life, which might be disguised when convenient; it was not a creed or something to take pride in. Paul did take pride in his craft, and he liked to boast of rescuing projects from know-nothing architects. He filled his home with furniture he had made himself—flawlessly professional, if a little too sturdily built to be stylish. He also took pride in his long legs and his dance-hall agility (an agility Anatole would share). It was a challenge to be a Brooklyn *galant*, but he did his best.

"Family life was very congenial, it was nice and warm and cozy, but we just didn't have any sort of cultural or intellectual nourishment at home," Shirley, who was the only member of the family to graduate from college, recalls. "My parents had no idea even what the New York *Times* was, let alone being able to imagine that Anatole might write for it." She says, "Anatole was different from the beginning." There was a sense, early on, that Anatole Broyard—or Buddy, as he was called then—was not entirely comfortable being a Broyard.

Shirley has a photograph, taken when Anatole was around four or five, of a family visit back to New Orleans. In it you can see Edna and her two daughters, and you can make out Anatole, down the street, facing in the opposite direction. The configuration was, Shirley says, pretty representative.

After graduating from Boys High School, in the late thirties, he enrolled in Brooklyn College. Already, he had a passion for modern culture—for European cinema and European literature. The idea that meaning could operate on several levels seemed to appeal to him. Shirley recalls exasperating conversations along those lines: "He'd ask me about a Kafka story I'd read or a French film I'd seen and say, 'Well, you see that on more than one level, don't you?' I felt like saying 'Oh, get off it.' Brothers don't say that to their sisters."

Just after the war began, he got married, to a black Puerto Rican woman, Aida, and they soon had a daughter. (He named her Gala, after Salvador Dali's wife.) Shirley recalls, "He got married and had a child on purpose—the purpose being to stay out of the Army. Then Anatole goes in the Army anyway, in spite of this child." And his wife and child moved in with the Broyard family.

Though his military records were apparently destroyed in a fire, some people who knew him at this time say that he entered the segregated Army as a white man. If so, he must have relished the irony that after attending officers' training school he was made the captain of an all-black stevedore battalion. Even then, his thoughts were not far from the new life he envisioned for himself. He said that he joined the Army with a copy of Wallace Stevens in his back pocket; now he was sending money home to his wife and asking her to save it so that he could open a bookstore in the Village when he got back. "She had other ideas," Shirley notes. "She wanted him to get a nice job, nine to five."

Between Aida and the allure of a literary life there was not much competition. Soon after his discharge from the Army, at war's end, he found an apartment in the Village, and he took advantage of the G.I. Bill to attend evening classes at the New School for Social Research, on Twelfth Street. His new life had no room for Aida and Gala. (Aida, with the child, later moved to California and remarried.) He left other things behind, too. The black scholar and dramatist W. F. Lucas, who knew Buddy Broyard from Bed-Stuy, says, "He was black when he got into the subway in Brooklyn, but as soon as he got out at West Fourth Street he became white."

He told his sister Lorraine that he had resolved to pass so that he could be a writer, rather than a Negro writer. His darker-skinned younger sister, Shirley, represented a possible snag, of course, but then he and Shirley had never been particularly close, and anyway she was busy with her own life and her own friends. (Shirley graduated Phi Beta Kappa from Hunter College, and went on to marry Franklin Williams, who helped organize the Peace Corps and served as Ambassador to Ghana.) They had drifted apart: it was just a matter of drifting farther apart. Besides, wasn't that why everybody came to New York—to run away from the confines of family, from places where people thought they knew who and what you were? Whose family *wasn't* in some way unsuitable? In a *Times* column in 1979 Broyard wrote, "My mother and father were too folksy for me, too colorful. . . . Eventually, I ran away to Greenwich Village, where no one had been born of a mother and father, where the people I met had sprung from their own brows, or from the pages of a bad novel. . . . Orphans of the avant-garde, we out-distanced our history and our humanity." Like so much of what he wrote in this vein, it meant more than it said; like the modernist culture he loved, it had levels.

In the Village, where Broyard started a bookstore on Cornelia Street, the salient thing about him wasn't that he was black but that he was beautiful, charming, and erudite. In those days, the Village was crowded with ambitious and talented young writers and artists, and Broyard—known for calling men "Sport" and girls "Slim"—was never more at home. He could hang out at the San Remo bar with Dwight Macdonald and Delmore Schwartz, and with a younger set who yearned to be the next Macdonalds and the next Schwartzes. Vincent Livelli, a friend of Broyard's since Brooklyn College days, recalls, "Everybody was so brilliant around us—we kept dueling with each other. But he was the guy that set the pace in the Village." His conversation sparkled—everybody said so. The sentences came out perfectly formed, festooned with the most apposite literary allusions. His high-beam charm could inspire worship but also resentment. Livelli says, "Anatole had a sort of dancing attitude toward life—he'd dance away from you. He had people understand that he was brilliant and therefore you couldn't hold him if you weren't worthy of his attention."

The novelist and editor Gordon Lish says, "Photographs don't suggest in any wise the enormous power he had in person. No part of him was ever for a moment at rest." He adds, "I adored him as a man. I mean, he was really in a league with Neal Cassady as a kind of presence." But there was, he says, a fundamental difference between Broyard and Kerouac's inspiration and muse: "Unlike Cassady, who was out of control, Anatole was *exorbitantly* in control. He was fastidious about managing things."

Except, perhaps, the sorts of things you're supposed to manage. His bookstore provided him with entrée to Village intellectuals—and them with entrée to Anatole—yet it was not run as a business, exactly. Its offerings were few but choice: Céline, Kafka, other hard-to-find translations. The critic Richard Gilman, who was one of its patrons, recalls that Broyard had a hard time parting with the inventory: "He had these books on the shelf, and someone would want to buy one, and he would snatch it back."

Around 1948, Broyard started to attract notice not merely for his charm, his looks, and his conversation but for his published writings. The early pieces, as often as not, were about a subject to which he had privileged access: blacks and black culture. *Commentary*, in his third appearance in its pages, dubbed him an "anatomist of the Negro personality in a white world." But was he merely an anthropologist or was he a native informant? It wasn't an ambiguity that he was in any hurry to resolve. Still, if all criticism is a form of autobiography (as Oscar Wilde would have it), one might look to these pieces for clues to his preoccupations at the time. In a 1950 *Commentary* article entitled "Portrait of the Inauthentic Negro," he wrote that the Negro's embarrassment over blackness should be banished by the realization that "thousands of Negroes with 'typical' features are accepted as whites merely because of light complexion." He continued:

> The inauthentic Negro is not only estranged from whites—he is also estranged from his own group and from himself. Since his companions are a mirror in which he sees himself as ugly, he must reject them; and since his own self is mainly a tension between an accusation and a denial, he can hardly find it, much less live in it. . . . He is adrift without a role in a world predicated on roles.

A year later, in "Keep Cool, Man: The Negro Rejection of Jazz," he wrote, just as despairingly, that the Negro's

> contact with white society has opened new vistas, new ideals in his imagination, and these he defends by repression, freezing up against the desire to be white, to have normal social intercourse with whites, to behave like them. . . . But in coolness he evades the issue . . . he becomes a pacifist in the struggle between social groups—not a conscientious objector, but a draft-dodger.

These are words that could be read as self-indictment, if anybody chose to do so. Certainly they reveal a ticklish sense of the perplexities he found himself in, and a degree of self-interrogation (as opposed to self-examination) he seldom displayed again.

In 1950, in a bar near Sheridan Square, Broyard met Anne Bernays, a Barnard junior and the daughter of Edward L. Bernays, who is considered the father of public relations. "There was this guy who was the handsomest man I have ever seen in my life, and I fell madly in love with him," Bernays, who is best known for such novels as "Growing Up Rich" and "Professor Romeo," recalls. "He was physically irresistible, and he had this dominating personality, and I guess I needed to be dominated. His hair was so short that you couldn't tell whether it was curly or straight. He had high cheekbones and very smooth skin." She knew that he was black, through a mutual friend, the poet and Blake scholar Milton Klonsky. (Years later, in a sort of epiphany, she recognized Anatole's loping walk as an African-American cultural style: "It was almost as if this were inside him dying to get out and express itself, but he felt he couldn't do it.")

After graduation, she got a job as an editor at the literary semiannual *Discovery*. She persuaded Broyard to submit his work, and in 1954 the magazine ran a short story entitled "What the Cystoscope Said"—an extraordinary account of his father's terminal illness:

> I didn't recognize him at first, he was so bad. His mouth was open and his breathing was hungry. They had removed his false teeth, and his cheeks were so thin that his mouth looked like a keyhole. I leaned over his bed and brought my face before his eyes. "Hello darlin'," he whispered, and he smiled. His voice, faint as it was, was full of love, and it bristled the hairs on the nape of my neck and raised goose flesh on my forearms. I couldn't speak, so I kissed him. His cheek smelled like wax.

Overnight, Broyard's renown was raised to a higher level. "Broyard knocked people flat with 'What the Cystoscope Said,'" Lish recalls. One of those people was Burt Britton, a bookseller who later co-founded Books & Co. In the fifties, he says, he read the works of young American writers religiously: "Now, if writing were a horse race, which God knows it's not, I would have gone out and put my two bucks down on Broyard." In "Advertisements for Myself," Norman Mailer wrote that he'd buy a novel by Broyard the day it appeared. Indeed, Bernays recalls, on the basis of that story the Atlantic Monthly Press, offered Broyard a twenty-thousand-dollar advance—then a staggeringly large sum for a literary work by an unknown—for a novel of which "Cystoscope" would be a chapter. "The whole literary world was waiting with bated breath for this great novelist who was about to arrive," Michael Vincent Miller, a friend of Broyard's since the late fifties, recalls. "Some feelings of expectation lasted for years."

Rumor surrounded Broyard like a gentle murmur, and sometimes it became a din. Being an orphan of the avant-garde was hard work. Among the black literati, certainly, his ancestry was a topic of speculation, and when a picture of Broyard accompanied a 1958 *Time* review of a Beat anthology it was closely scrutinized. Arna Bontemps wrote to Langston Hughes, "His picture . . . makes him look Negroid. If so, he is the only spade among the Beat Generation." Charlie Parker spied Broyard in Washington Square Park one day and told a companion, "He's one of us, but he doesn't want to admit he's one of us." Richard Gilman recalls an awkwardness that ensued when he stumbled across Anatole with his dark-skinned wife and child: "I just happened to come upon them in a restaurant that was not near our usual stomping grounds. He introduced me, and it was fine, but my sense was that he would rather not have had anyone he knew meet them." He adds, "I remember thinking at the time that he had the look of an octoroon or a quadroon, one of those—which he strenuously denied. He got into very great disputes with people."

One of those disputes was with Chandler Brossard, who had been a close friend: Broyard was the best man at Brossard's wedding. There was a falling out, and Brossard produced an unflattering portrait of Broyard as the hustler and opportunist Henry Porter in his 1952 novel, "Who Walk in Darkness." Brossard knew just where Broyard was most vulnerable, and he pushed hard. His novel originally began, "People said Henry Porter was a Negro," and the version published in France still does. Apparently fearing legal action, however, Brossard's American publisher, New Directions, sent it to Broyard in galley form before it was published.

Anne Bernays was with Broyard when the galleys arrived. Broyard explained to her, "They asked me to read it because they are afraid I am going to sue." But why would he sue, she wanted to know. "Because it says I'm a Negro," he replied grimly. "Then," Bernays recalls, "I said, 'What are you going to do?' He said, 'I am going to make them change it.' And he did."

The novel went on to be celebrated as a ground-breaking chronicle of Village hipsters; it also—as a result of the legal redactions—reads rather oddly in places. Henry Porter, the Broyard character, is rumored to be not a Negro but merely "an illegitimate":

> I suspect [the rumor] was supposed to explain the difference between the way he behaved and the way the rest of us behaved. Porter did not show that he knew people were talking about him this way. I must give him credit for maintaining a front of indifference that was really remarkable.
>
> Someone both Porter and I knew quite well once told me the next time he saw Porter he was going to ask him if he was or was not an illegitimate. He said it was the only way to clear the air. Maybe so. But I said I would not think of doing it. . . . I felt that if Porter ever wanted the stories about himself cleared up, publicly, he would one day do so. I was willing to wait.

And that, after all, is the nature of such secrets: they are not what cannot be known but what cannot be acknowledged.

Another trip wire seems to have landed Broyard in one of the masterpieces of twentieth-century American fiction, William Gaddis's "The Recognitions." Livelli explains, "Now, around 1947 or '48, William Gaddis and Anatole were in love with the same gal, Sheri Martinelli. They were rivals, almost at each other's throats. And Willie was such a sweetheart that he had a mild approach to everything, and Anatole was sort of a stabber: he injected words like poison into conversations." When "The Recognitions" came out, in 1955, "Anatole caught on to it right away, and he was kind of angry over it." The Broyard character is named Max, and Gaddis wrote that he "always looked the same, always the same age, his hair always the same short length," seemingly "a parody on the moment, as his clothes caricatured a past at eastern colleges where he had never been." Worse is his "unconscionable smile," which intimates "that the wearer knew all of the dismal secrets of some evil jungle whence he had just come."

Broyard's own account of these years—published in 1993 as "Kafka Was the Rage"—is fueled by the intertwined themes of writing and women. Gaddis says, "His eyes were these great pools—soft, gentle pools. It was girls, girls, girls: a kind of intoxication of its own. I always thought, frankly, that that's where his career went, his creative energies."

Anne Bernays maintains, "If you leave the sex part out, you're only telling half the story. With women, he was just like an alcoholic with booze." She stopped seeing him in 1952, at her therapist's urging. "It was like going cold turkey off a drug," she says, remembering how crushing the experience was, and she adds, "I think most women have an Anatole in their lives."

Indeed, not a few of them had Anatole. "He was a pussy gangster, really," Lucas, a former professor of comparative literature, says with Bed-Stuy bluntness. Gilman recalls being in Bergdorf Goodman and coming across Broyard putting the moves on a salesgirl. "I hid behind a pillar—otherwise he'd know that I'd seen him—and watched him go through every stage of seduction: 'What do you think? Can I put this against you? Oh, it looks great against your skin. You have the most wonderful skin.' And then he quoted Baudelaire."

Quoting Baudelaire turns out to be key. Broyard's great friend Ernest van den Haag recalls trolling the Village with Broyard in those days: "We obviously quite often compared our modus operandi, and what I observed about Anatole is that when he liked a girl he could speak to her brilliantly about all kinds of things which the girl didn't in the least understand, because Anatole was really vastly erudite. The girl had no idea what he was talking about, but she loved it, because she was under the impression, rightly so, that she was listening to something very interesting and important. His was a solipsistic discourse, in some ways." Indeed, the narrator of "What the Cystoscope Said" tells of seducing his ailing father's young and ingenuous nurse in a similar manner:

> "Listen," I said, borrowing a tone of urgency from another source, "I want to give you a book. A book that was written for you, a book that belongs to you as much as your diary, that's dedicated to you like your nurse's certificate." . . . My apartment was four blocks away, so I bridged the distance with

talk, raving about *Journey to the End of the Night*, the book she needed like she needed a hole in her head.

Broyard recognized that seduction was a matter not only of talking but of listening, too, and he knew how to pay attention with an engulfing level of concentration. The writer Ellen Schwamm, who met Broyard in the late fifties, says, "You show me a man who talks, and I'll show you a thousand women who hurl themselves at his feet. I don't mean just talk, I mean dialogues. He *listened*, and he was willing to speak of things that most men are not interested in: literature and its effect on life." But she also saw another side to Broyard's relentless need to seduce. She invokes a formulation made by her husband, the late Harold Brodkey: "Harold used to say that a lot of men steal from women. They steal bits of their souls, bits of their personalities, to construct an emotional life, which many men don't have. And I think that Anatole needed something of that sort."

It's an image of self-assemblage which is very much in keeping with Broyard's own accounts of himself. Starting in 1946, and continuing at intervals for the rest of his life, he underwent analysis. Yet the word "analysis" is misleading: what he wanted was to be refashioned—or, as he told his first analyst, to be *transfigured*. "When I came out with the word, I was like someone who sneezes into a handkerchief and finds it full of blood," he wrote in the 1993 memoir. "I wanted to discuss my life with him not as a patient talking to an analyst but as if we were two literary critics discussing a novel. . . . I had a literature rather than a personality, a set of fictions about myself." He lived a lie because he didn't want to live a larger lie: and Anatole Broyard, Negro writer, was that larger lie.

Alexandra Nelson, known as Sandy, met Broyard in January of 1961. Broyard was forty, teaching the odd course at the New School and supporting himself by freelancing: promotional copy for publishers, liner notes for Columbia jazz records, blurbs for the Book-of-the-Month Club. Sandy was twenty-three and a dancer, and Broyard had always loved dancers. Of Norwegian descent, she was strikingly beautiful, and strikingly intelligent. Michael Miller recalls, "She represented a certain kind of blonde, a certain kind of sophisticated carriage and a way of moving through the world with a sense of the good things. They both had marvelous taste."

It was as if a sorcerer had made a list of everything Broyard loved and had given it life. At long last, the conqueror was conquered: in less than a year, Broyard and Sandy were married. Sandy remembers his aura in those days: "Anatole was very hip. It wasn't a pose—it was in his sinew, in his bones. And, when he was talking to you, you just felt that you were receiving all this radiance from him." (Van den Haag says, "I do think it's not without significance that Anatole married a blonde, and about as white as you can get. He may have feared a little bit that the children might turn out black. He must have been pleased that they didn't.")

While they were still dating, two of Broyard's friends told Sandy that he was black, in what seemed to be a clumsy attempt to scare her off. "I think they really weren't happy to lose him, to see him get into a serious relationship," she says. "They were losing a playmate, in a way." Whatever the cultural sanctions, she was unfazed. But she says that when she asked Broyard about it he proved evasive: "He claimed that he wasn't black, but he talked about 'island influences,' or said that he had a grandmother who used to live in a tree on some island in the Caribbean. Anatole was like that—he was very slippery." Sandy didn't force the issue, and the succeeding years only fortified his sense of reserve. "Anatole was very strong," she says. "And he said about certain things, 'Just keep out. This is the deal if you get mixed up with me.'" The life that Broyard chose to live meant that the children did not meet their Aunt Shirley until after his death—nor, except for a couple of brief visits in the sixties, was there any contact even with Broyard's light-skinned mother and older sister. It was a matter of respecting the ground rules. "I would try to poke in those areas, but the message was very direct and strong," Sandy explains. "Oh, when I got angry at him, you know, one always pushes the tender points. But over time you grow up about these things and realize you do what you can do and there are certain things you can't."

In 1963, just before their first child, Todd, was born, Anatole shocked his friends by another big move—to Connecticut. Not only was he moving to Connecticut but he was going to be commuting to work: for the first time in his life, he would be a company man. "I think one of his claims to fame was that he hadn't had an office job—somehow, he'd escaped that," Sandy says. "There had been no real need for him to grow up." But after Todd was born—a daughter, Bliss, followed in 1966—Anatole spent seven years working full-time as a copywriter at the Manhattan advertising agency Wunderman Ricotta & Kline.

Over the next quarter century, the family lived in a series of eighteenth-century houses, sometimes bought on impulse, in places like Fairfield, Redding, Greens Farms, and Southport. Here, in a land of leaf-blowers and lawnmowers, Bed-Stuy must have seemed almost comically remote. Many of Broyard's intimates from the late forties knew about his family; the intimates he acquired in the sixties did not, or else had heard only rumors. Each year, the number of people who knew Buddy from Bed-Stuy dwindled; each year, the rumors grew more nebulous; each year, he left his past further behind. Miller says, "Anatole was a master at what Erving Goffman calls 'impression management.'" The writer Evelyn Toynton says, "I remember once going to a party with Sandy and him in Connecticut. There were these rather dull people there, stockbrokers and the usual sorts of people, and Anatole just knocked himself out to charm every single person in the room. I said to him, 'Anatole, can't you ever *not* be charming?'" Miller observes, "He was a wonderful host. He could take people from different walks of life—the president of Stanley Tools or a vice-president of Merrill Lynch, say, and some bohemian type from the Village—and keep the whole scene flowing beautifully. He had perfect pitch for the social encounter, like Jay Gatsby."

It was as if, wedded to an ideal of American self-fashioning, he sought to put himself to the ultimate test. It was one thing to be accepted in the Village, amid the Beats and hipsters and émigrés, but to gain acceptance in Cheever territory was an achievement of a higher order. "Anatole, when he left the Village and went to Connecticut, was able not only to pass but even to be a kind of influential presence in that world of rich white Wasps," Miller says. "Maybe that was a shallower part of the passing—to be accepted by Connecticut gentry."

Broyard's feat raised eyebrows among some of his literary admirers: something borrowed, something new. Daphne Merkin, another longtime friend, detected "a 'country–squire' tendency—a complicated tendency to want to establish a sort of safety through bourgeoisness. It was like a Galsworthy quality."

Even in Arcadia, however, there could be no relaxation of vigilance: in his most intimate relationships, there were guardrails. Broyard once wrote that Michael Miller was one of the people he liked best in the world, and Miller is candid about Broyard's profound influence on him. Today, Miller is a psycho-therapist, based in Cambridge, and the author, most recently, of "Intimate Terrorism." From the time they met until his death, Broyard read to him the first draft of almost every piece he wrote. Yet a thirty-year friendship of unusual intimacy was circumscribed by a subject that they never discussed. "First of all, I didn't *know*," Miller says. "I just had intuitions and had heard intimations. It was some years before I'd even put together some intuition and little rumblings—nothing ever emerged clearly. There was a certain tacit understanding between us to accept certain pathways as our best selves, and not challenge that too much." It was perhaps, he says a little sadly, a limitation on the relationship.

In the late sixties, Broyard wrote several front-page reviews for the *Times Book Review*. "They were brilliant, absolutely sensational," the novelist Charles Simmons, who was then an assistant editor there, says. In 1971, the

Times was casting about for a new daily reviewer, and Simmons was among those who suggested Anatole Broyard. It wasn't a tough sell. Arthur Gelb, at the time the paper's cultural editor, recalls, "Anatole was among the first critics I brought to the paper. He was very funny, and he also had that special knack for penetrating hypocrisy. I don't think he was capable of uttering a boring sentence."

You could say that his arrival was a sign of the times. Imagine: Anatole Broyard, downtown flaneur and apostle of sex and high modernism, ensconced in what was, literarily speaking, the ultimate establishment perch. "There had been an awful lot of very tame, very conventional people at the *Times*, and Broyard came in as a sort of ambassador from the Village and Village sophistication," Alfred Kazin recalls. Broyard had a highly developed appreciation of the paper's institutional power, and he even managed to use it to avenge wrongs done him in his Village days. Just before he started his job at the daily, he published a review in the *Times Book Review* of a new novel by one Chandler Brossard. The review began, "Here's a book so transcendently bad it makes us fear not only for the condition of the novel in this country, but for the country itself."

Broyard's reviews were published in alternation with those of Christopher Lehmann-Haupt, who has now been a daily reviewer at the *Times* for more than a quarter century, and who readily admits that Broyard's appointment did not gladden his heart. They hadn't got along particularly well when Lehmann-Haupt was an editor at the *Times Book Review*, nor did Lehmann-Haupt entirely approve of Broyard's status as a fabled libertine. So when A. M. Rosenthal, the paper's managing editor, was considering hiring him, Lehmann-Haupt expressed reservations. He recalls, "Rosenthal was saying, 'Give me five reasons why not.' And I thoughtlessly blurted out, 'Well, first of all, he is the biggest ass man in town.' And Rosenthal rose up from his desk and said, 'If that were a disqualification for working for the New York *Times*'—and he waved—'this place would be empty!'"

Broyard got off to an impressive start. Lehmann-Haupt says, "He had a wonderful way of setting a tone, and a wonderful way of talking himself through a review. He had good, tough instincts when it came to fiction. He had taste." And the jovial Herbert Mitgang, who served a stint as a daily reviewer himself, says, "I always thought he was the most literary of the reviewers. There would be something like a little essay in his daily reviews."

Occasionally, his acerbic opinions got him in trouble. There was, for example, the storm that attended an uncharitable review of a novel by Christy Brown, an Irish writer who was born with severe cerebral palsy. The review concluded:

It is unfortunate that the author of "A Shadow on Summer" is an almost total spastic—he is said to have typed his highly regarded first novel, "Down All the Days," with his left foot—but I don't see how the badness of his second novel can be blamed on that. Any man who can learn to type with his left foot can learn to write better than he has here.

Then, there was the controversial review of James Baldwin's piously sentimental novel of black suffering, "If Beale Street Could Talk." Broyard wrote:

> If I have to read one more description of the garbage piled up in the streets of Harlem, I may just throw protocol to the winds and ask whose garbage is it? I would like to remind Mr. Baldwin that the City Health Code stipulates that garbage must be put out in proper containers, not indiscriminately "piled."

No one could accuse Broyard of proselytizing for progressive causes. Jason Epstein, for one, was quick to detect a neoconservative air in his reviews, and Broyard's old friend Ernest van den Haag, a longtime contributing editor at *National Review*, volunteers that he was available to set Broyard straight on the issues when the need arose. Broyard could be mischievous, and he could be tendentious. It did not escape notice that he was consistently hostile to feminist writers. "Perhaps it's naïve of me to expect people to write reasonable books about emotionally charged subjects," one such review began, irritably. "But when you have to read and review two or three books each week, you do get tired of 'understanding' so much personal bias. You reach a point where it no longer matters that the author's mistakes are well meant. You don't care that he or she is on the side of the angels: you just want them to tell the truth."

Nor did relations between the two daily reviewers ever become altogether cordial. Lehmann-Haupt tells of a time in 1974 when Broyard said that he was sick and couldn't deliver a review. Lehmann-Haupt had to write an extra review in less than a day, so that he could get to the Ali-Frazier fight the next night, where he had ringside seats. Later, when they discussed the match, Broyard seemed suspiciously knowledgeable about its particulars; he claimed that a friend of his had been invited by a television executive to watch it on closed-circuit TV. "I waited about six months, because one of the charming things about Anatole was that he never remembered his lies," Lehmann-Haupt says, laughing. "And I said, 'Did you see that fight?' And he said, 'Oh, yeah—I was there as a guest of this television executive.' *That's* why he couldn't write the review!"

Broyard had been teaching off and on at the New School since the late fifties, and now his reputation as a writing teacher began to soar. Certainly his fluent prose style, with its combination of grace and clarity, was a considerable recommendation. He was charismatic and magisterial, and, because he was sometimes brutal about students' work, they found it all the more gratifying when he was complimentary. Among his students were Paul Breslow, Robert Olen Butler, Daphne Merkin, and Hilma Wolitzer. Ellen Schwamm, who took a workshop with him in the early seventies, says, "He had a gourmet's taste for literature and for language, and he was really able to convey that: it was a very sensual experience."

These were years of heady success and, at the same time, of a rising sense of failure. An arbiter of American writing, Broyard was racked by his inability to write his own magnum opus. In the fifties, the Atlantic Monthly Press had contracted for an autobiographical novel—the novel that was supposed to secure Broyard's fame, his place in contemporary literature—but, all these years later, he had made no progress. It wasn't for lack of trying. Lehmann-Haupt recalls his taking a lengthy vacation in order to get the book written. "I remember talking to him—he was up in Vermont, where somebody had lent him a house—and he was in agony. He banished himself from the Vineyard, was clearly suffering, and he just couldn't do it." John Updike, who knew Broyard slightly from the Vineyard, was reminded of the anticipation surrounding Ellison's second novel: "The most famous non-book around was the one that Broyard was not writing." (The two non-book writers were in fact quite friendly: Broyard admired Ellison not only as a writer but as a dancer—a high tribute from such an adept as Broyard.)

Surrounded by analysts and psychotherapists—Sandy Broyard had become a therapist herself by this time—Broyard had no shortage of explanations for his inability to write his book. "He did have a total writer's block," van den Haag says, "and he was analyzed by various persons, but it didn't fully overcome the writer's block. I couldn't prevent him from going back to 'The Cystoscope' and trying to improve it. He made it, of course, not better but worse." Broyard's fluency as an essayist and a reviewer wasn't quite compensation. Charles Simmons says, "He had produced all this charming criticism, but the one thing that mattered to him was the one thing he hadn't managed to do."

As the seventies wore on, Miller discussed the matter of blockage with his best friend in relatively abstract terms: he suggested that there might be something in Broyard's relationship to his family background that was holding him back. In the eighties, he referred Broyard to his own chief mentor in gestalt therapy, Isador From, and From became perhaps Broyard's most important therapist in his later years. "In gestalt therapy, we talk a lot about 'unfinished business': anything that's incomplete, unfinished, haunts the whole personality and tends, at some level, to create inhibition or blockage," Miller says. "You're stuck there at a certain point. It's like living with a partly full bladder all your life."

Some people speculated that the reason Broyard couldn't write his novel was that he was living it—that race loomed larger in his life because it was unacknowledged, that he couldn't put it behind him because he had put it beneath him. If he had been a different sort of writer, it might not have mattered so much. But Merkin points out, "Anatole's subject, even in fiction, was essentially himself. I think that ultimately he would have had to deal with more than he wanted to deal with."

Broyard may have been the picture of serene self-mastery, but there was one subject that could reliably fluster him. Gordon Lish recalls an occasion in the mid-seventies when Burt Britton (who was married to a black woman) alluded to Anatole's racial ancestry. Lish says, "Anatole became inflamed, and he left the room. He snapped, like a dog snapping—he *barked* at Britton. It was an ugly moment." To people who knew nothing about the matter, Broyard's sensitivities were at times simply perplexing. The critic Judith Dunford used to go to lunch with Broyard in the eighties. One day, Broyard mentioned his sister Shirley, and Dunford, idly making conversation, asked him what she looked like. Suddenly, she saw an extremely worried expression on his face. Very carefully, he replied, "Darker than me."

There was, finally, no sanctuary. "When the children were older, I began, every eighteen months or so, to bring up the issue of how they needed to know at some point," Sandy Broyard says. "And then he would totally shut down and go into a rage. He'd say that at some point he would tell them, but he would not tell them now." He was the Scheherazade of racial imposture, seeking and securing one deferral after another. It must have made things not easier but harder. In the modern era, children are supposed to come out to their parents: it works better that way around. For children, we know, can judge their parents harshly—above all, for what they understand as failures of candor. His children would see the world in terms of authenticity; he saw the world in terms of self-creation. Would they think that he had made a Faustian bargain? Would they speculate about what else he had not told them—about the limits of self-invention? Broyard's resistance is not hard to fathom. He must have wondered when the past would learn its place, and stay past.

Anatole Broyard had confessed enough in his time to know that confession did nothing for the soul. He preferred to communicate his truths on higher frequencies. As if in exorcism, Broyard's personal essays deal regularly with the necessary, guilt-ridden endeavor of escaping family history: and yet the feelings involved are well-nigh universal. The thematic elements of passing—fragmentation, alienation, liminality, self-fashioning—echo the great themes of modernism. As a result, he could prepare the way for exposure without ever risking it. Miller observes, "If you look at the writing closely enough, and listen to the intonations, there's something there that is like no writer from the completely white world. Freud talked about the repetition compulsion. With Anatole, it's interesting that he was constantly hiding it and in some ways constantly revealing it."

Sandy speaks of these matters in calmly analytic tones; perhaps because she is a therapist, her love is tempered by an almost professional dispassion. She says, "I think his own personal history continued to be painful to him," and she adds, "In passing, you cause your family great anguish, but I also think, conversely, do we look at the anguish it causes the person who is passing? Or the anguish that it was born out of?"

It may be tempting to describe Broyard's self-positioning as arising from a tortured allegiance to some liberal-humanist creed. In fact, the liberal pieties of the day were not much to his taste. "It wasn't about an ideal of racelessness but something much more complex and interesting," Miller says. "He was actually quite anti-black," Evelyn Toynton says. She tells of a time when she was walking with him on a street in New York and a drunken black man came up to him and asked for a dollar. Broyard seethed. Afterward, he remarked to her, "I look around New York, and I think to myself, If there were no blacks in New York, would it really be any loss?"

No doubt this is a calculation that whites, even white liberals, sometimes find themselves idly working out: How many black muggers is one Thelonious Monk worth? How many Willie Hortons does Gwendolyn Brooks redeem? In 1970, Ellison published his classic essay "What America Would Be Like Without Blacks," in *Time*; and one reason it is a classic essay is that it addresses a question that lingers in the American political unconscious. Commanding as Ellison's arguments are, there remains a whit of defensiveness in the very exercise. It's a burdensome thing to refute a fantasy.

And a burdensome thing to be privy to it. Ellen Schwamm recalls that one of the houses Broyard had in Connecticut had a black jockey on the lawn, and that "he used to tell me that Jimmy Baldwin had said to him, 'I can't come and see you with this crap on your lawn.'" (Sandy remembers the lawn jockey—an antique—as having come with the house; she also recalls that it was stolen one day.) Charles Simmons says that the writer Herbert Gold, before introducing him to Broyard, warned him that Broyard was prone to make comments about "spades," and Broyard did make a few such comments. "He personally, on a deeper level, was not enamored of blacks," van den Haag says. "He avoided blacks. There is no question he did." Sandy is gingerly in alluding to this subject. "He was very short-tempered with the behavior of black people, the sort of behavior that was shown in the news. He had paid the price to be at liberty to say things that, if you didn't know he was black, you would misunderstand. I think it made him ironical."

Every once in a while, however, Broyard's irony would slacken, and he would speak of the thing with an unaccustomed and halting forthrightness. Toynton says that after they'd known each other for several years he told her there was a "C" (actually, "col," for "colored") on his birth certificate. "And then another time he told me that his sister was black and that she was married to a black man." The circumlocutions are striking: not that *he* was black but that his birth certificate was; not that *he* was black but that his family was. Perhaps this was a matter less of evasiveness than of precision.

"Some shrink had said to him that the reason he didn't like brown-haired women or dark women was that he was afraid of his own shit," Toynton continues. "And I said, 'Anatole, it's as plain as plain can be that it has to do with being black.' And he just stopped and said, 'You don't know what it was like. It was horrible.' He told me once that he didn't like to see his sisters, because they reminded him of his unhappy childhood." (Shirley's account suggests that this unhappy childhood may have had more to do with the child than with the hood.)

Ellen Schwamm remembers one occasion when Broyard visited her and Harold Brodkey at their apartment, and read them part of the memoir he was working on. She says that the passages seemed stilted and distant, and that Brodkey said to him, "You're not telling the truth, and if you try to write lies or evade the truth this is what you get. What's the real story?" She says, "Anatole took a deep breath and said, 'The real story is that I'm not who I seem. I'm a black.' I said, 'Well, Anatole, it's no great shock, because this rumor has been around for years and years and years, and everyone assumes there's a small percentage of you that's black, if that's what you're trying to say.' And he said, 'No, that's not what I'm trying to say. My father could pass, but in fact my mother's black, too. We're black as far back as I know.' We never said a word of it to anybody, because he asked us not to."

Schwamm also says that she begged him to write about his history: it seemed to her excellent material for a book. But he explained that he didn't want notoriety based on his race—on his revealing himself to be black—rather than on his talent. As Toynton puts it, Broyard felt that he had to make a choice between being an aesthete and being a Negro. "He felt that

once he said, 'I'm a Negro writer,' he would have to write about black issues, and Anatole was such an aesthete."

All the same, Schwamm was impressed by a paradox: the man wanted
to be appreciated not for being black but for being a writer, even though
his pretending not to be black was stopping him from writing. It was one
of the very few ironies that Broyard, the master ironist, was ill equipped to
appreciate.

Besides, there was always his day job to attend to. Broyard might suffer
through a midnight of the soul in Vermont; but he was also a working journalist, and when it came to filing his copy he nearly always met his dead-
lines. In the late seventies, he also began publishing brief personal essays in
the *Times*. They are among the finest work he did—easeful, witty, perfectly
poised between surface and depth. In them he perfected the feat of being
self-revelatory without revealing anything. He wrote about his current life, in
Connecticut: "People in New York City have psychotherapists, and people in
the suburbs have handymen. While anxiety in the city is existential, in the
country it is structural." And he wrote about his earlier life, in the city:
"There was a kind of jazz in my father's movements, a rhythm compounded
of economy and flourishes, functional and decorative. He had a blues song
in his blood, a wistful jauntiness he brought with him from New Orleans."
(Wistful, and even worrisome: "I half-expected him to break into the Camel
Walk, the Shimmy Shewobble, the Black Bottom or the Mess Around.") In a
1979 essay he wrote about how much he dreaded family excursions:

> To me, they were like a suicide pact. Didn't my parents know that the world
> was just waiting for a chance to come between us?
>
> Inside, we were a family, but outside we were immigrants, bizarre in our
> differences. I thought that people stared at us, and my face grew hot. At any
> moment, I expected my father and mother to expose their tribal rites, their
> eccentric anthropology, to the gape of strangers.
>
> Anyone who saw me with my family knew too much about me.

These were the themes he returned to in many of his personal essays,
seemingly marking out the threshold he would not cross. And if some of his
colleagues at the *Times* knew too much about him, or had heard the rumors,
they wouldn't have dreamed of saying anything. Abe Rosenthal (who did
know about him) says that the subject never arose. "What was there to talk
about? I didn't really consider it my business. I didn't think it was proper or
polite, nor did I want him to think I was prejudiced, or anything."

But most people knew nothing about it. C. Gerald Fraser, a reporter and an editor at the *Times* from 1967 until 1991, was friendly with Broyard's brother-in-law Ambassador Franklin Williams. Fraser, who is black, recalls that one day Williams asked him how many black journalists there were at the *Times.* "I listed them," he says, "and he said, 'You forgot one.' I went over the list again, and I said, 'What do you mean?' He said, 'Shirley's brother, Anatole Broyard.' I was dumbstruck, because I'd never heard it mentioned at the *Times* that he was black, or that the paper had a black critic."

In any event, Broyard's colleagues did not have to know *what* he was to have reservations about *who* he was. He cultivated his image as a trickster—someone who would bend the rules, finesse the system—and that image only intensified his detractors' ire. "A good book review is an act of seduction, and when he did it there was nobody better," John Leonard says, but he feels that Broyard's best was not always offered. "I considered him to be one of the laziest book reviewers to come down the pike." Soon a running joke was that Broyard would review only novels shorter than two hundred pages. In the introduction to "Aroused by Books," a collection of the reviews he published in the early seventies, Broyard wrote that he tried to choose books for review that were "closest to [his] feelings." Lehmann-Haupt says dryly, "We began to suspect that he often picked the books according to the attractiveness of the young female novelists who had written them." Rosenthal had shamed him for voicing his disquiet about Broyard's reputation as a Don Juan, but before long Rosenthal himself changed his tune. "Maybe five or six years later," Lehmann-Haupt recalls, "Rosenthal comes up to me, jabbing me in the chest with a stiffened index finger and saying, 'The trouble with Broyard is that he writes with his cock!' I bit my tongue."

Gradually, a measure of discontent with Broyard's reviews began to make itself felt among the paper's cultural commissars. Harvey Shapiro, the editor of the *Book Review* from 1975 to 1983, recalls conversations with Rosenthal in which "he would tell me that all his friends hated Anatole's essays, and I would tell him that all my friends loved Anatole's essays, and that would be the end of the conversation." In 1984, Broyard was removed from the daily *Times* and given a column in the *Book Review.*

Mitchel Levitas, the editor of the *Book Review* from 1983 to 1989, edited Broyard's column himself. He says, "It was a tough time for him, you see, because he had come off the daily book review, where he was out there in the public eye twice a week. That was a major change in his public role." In addition to writing his column, he was put to work as an editor at the *Book Review.* The office environment was perhaps not altogether congenial to a man of his temperament. Kazin recalls, "He complained to me constantly about being on the *Book Review*, because he had to check people's quotations and such. I think he thought that he was superior to the job."

Then, too, it was an era in which the very notion of passing was beginning to seem less plangent than preposterous. Certainly Broyard's skittishness around the subject wasn't to everyone's liking. Brent Staples, who is black, was an editor at the *Book Review* at the time Broyard was there. "Anatole had it both ways," Staples says. "He would give you a kind of burlesque wink that seemed to indicate he was ready to accept the fact of your knowing that he was a black person. It was a real ambiguity, tacit and sort of recessed. He jived around and played with it a lot, but never made it express the fact that he was black." It was a game that tried Staples' patience. "When Anatole came anywhere near me, for example, his whole style, demeanor, and tone would change," he recalls. "I took that as him conveying to me, 'Yes, I am like you. But I'm relating this to you on a kind of recondite channel.' Over all, it made me angry. Here was a guy who was, for a long period of time, probably one of the two or three most important critical voices on literature in the United States. How could you, actively or passively, have this fact hidden?"

Staples pauses, then says, "You know, he turned it into a joke. And when you change something basic about yourself into a joke, it spreads, it metastasizes, and so his whole presentation of self became completely ironic. *Everything* about him was ironic."

There were some people who came to have a professional interest in achieving a measure of clarity on the topic. Not long before Broyard retired from the *Times*, in 1989, Daphne Merkin, as an editor at Harcourt Brace Jovanovich, gave him an advance of a hundred thousand dollars for his memoirs. (The completed portion was ultimately published, as "Kafka Was the Rage," by Crown.) Merkin learned that "he was, in some ways, opaque to himself," and her disquiet grew when the early chapters arrived. "I said, 'Anatole, there's something odd here. Within the memoir, you have your family moving to a black neighborhood in Brooklyn. I find that strange—unless they're black.' I said, 'You can do many things if you're writing a memoir. But if you squelch stuff that seems to be crucial about you, and pretend it doesn't exist.' . . ." She observes that he was much attached to aspects of his childhood, but "in a clouded way."

When Broyard retired from the *Times*, he was nearly sixty-nine. To Sandy, it was a source of some anguish that their children still did not know the truth about him. Yet what was that truth? Broyard was a critic—a critic who specialized in European and American fiction. And what was race but a European and American fiction? If he was passing for white, perhaps he understood that the alternative was passing for black. "But if some people are light enough to live like white, mother, why should there be such a fuss?" a girl asks her mother in "Near-White," a 1931 story by the Harlem Renaissance author Claude McKay. "Why should they live colored when they could be happier living white?" Why, indeed? One could concede that the passing of Anatole Broyard involved dishonesty; but is it so very clear that the dishonesty was mostly Broyard's?

To pass is to sin against authenticity, and "authenticity" is among the founding lies of the modern age. The philosopher Charles Taylor summarizes its ideology thus: "There is a certain way of being human that is *my* way. I am called upon to live my life in this way, and not in imitation of anyone else's life. But this notion gives a new importance to being true to myself. If I am not, I miss the point of my life; I miss what being human is for *me*." And Romantic fallacy of authenticity is only compounded when it is collectivized: when the putative real me gives way to the real us. You can say that Anatole Broyard was (by any juridical reckoning) "really" a Negro, without conceding that a Negro is a thing you can really be. The vagaries of racial identity were increased by what anthropologists call the rule of "hypodescent"—the one-drop rule. When those of mixed ancestry—and the majority of blacks are of mixed ancestry—disappear into the white majority, they are traditionally accused of running from their "blackness." Yet why isn't the alternative a matter of running from their "whiteness"? To emphasize these perversities, however, is a distraction from a larger perversity. You can't get race "right" by refining the boundary conditions.

The act of razoring out your contributor's note may be quixotic, but it is not mad. The mistake is to assume that birth certificates and biographical sketches and all the other documents generated by the modern bureaucratic state reveal an anterior truth—that they are merely signs of an independently existing identity. But in fact they constitute it. The social meaning of race is established by these identity papers—by tracts and treatises and certificates and pamphlets and all the other verbal artifacts that proclaim race to be real and, by that proclamation, make it so.

So here is a man who passed for white because he wanted to be a writer, and he did not want to be a Negro writer. It is a crass disjunction, but it is not his crassness or his disjunction. His perception was perfectly correct. He *would* have had to be a Negro writer, which was something he did not want to be. In his terms, he did not want to write about black love, black passion, black suffering, black joy; he wanted to write about love and passion and suffering and joy. We give lip service to the idea of the writer who happens to be black, but had anyone, in the postwar era, ever seen such a thing?

Broyard's friend Richard A. Shweder, an anthropologist and a theorist of culture, says, "I think he believed that reality is constituted by style," and ascribes to Broyard a "deeply romantic view of the intimate connection be-tween style and reality." Broyard passed not because he thought that race wasn't important but because he knew that it was. The durable social facts of race were beyond reason, and, like Paul Broyard's furniture, their strength came at the expense of style. Anatole Broyard lived in a world where race had, indeed, become a trope for indelibility, for permanence. "All I *have* to do," a black folk saying has it, "is stay black and die."

Broyard was a connoisseur of the liminal—of crossing over and, in the fa-miliar phrase, getting over. But the ideologies of modernity have a kicker, which is that they permit no exit. Racial recusal is a forlorn hope. In a sys-tem where whiteness is the default, racelessness is never a possibility. You cannot opt out; you can only opt in. In a scathing review of a now forgotten black author, Broyard announced that it was time to reconsider the assump-tion of many black writers that "'whitey' will never let you forget you're black." For his part, he wasn't taking any chances. At a certain point, he seems to have decided that all he had to do was stay white and die.

In 1989, Broyard resolved that he and his wife would change their life once more. With both their children grown, they could do what they pleased. And what they pleased—what he pleased, anyway—was to move to Cam-bridge, Massachusetts. They would be near Harvard, and so part of an intel-lectual community. He had a vision of walking through Harvard Square, bumping into people like the sociologist Daniel Bell, and having conver-sations about ideas in the street. Besides, his close friend Michael Miller was living in the area. Anne Bernays, also a Cambridge resident, says, "I re-member his calling several times and asking me about neighborhoods. It was important for him to get that right. I think he was a little disappointed when he moved that it wasn't to a fancy neighborhood like Brattle or Chan-ning Street. He was on Wendell Street, where there's a tennis court across the street and an apartment building and the houses are fairly close to-gether." It wasn't a matter of passing so much as of positioning.

Sandy says that they had another the-children-must-be-told conversation shortly before the move. "We were driving to Michael's fiftieth-birthday party—I used to plan to bring up the subject in a place where he couldn't walk out. I brought it up then because at that point our son was out of college and our daughter had just graduated, and my feeling was that they just absolutely needed to know, as adults." She pauses. "And we had words. He would just bring down this gate." Sandy surmises, again, that he may have wanted to protect them from what he had experienced as a child. "Also," she says, "I think he needed still to protect himself." The day after they moved into their house on Wendell Street, Broyard learned that he had prostate cancer, and that it was inoperable.

Broyard spent much of the time before his death, fourteen months later, making a study of the literature of illness and death, and publishing a number of essays on the subject. Despite the occasion, they were imbued with an almost dandyish, even jokey sense of incongruity: "My urologist, who is quite famous, wanted to cut off my testicles. . . . Speaking as a surgeon, he said that it was the surest, quickest, neatest solution. Too neat, I said, picturing myself with no balls. I knew that such a solution would depress me, and I was sure that depression is bad medicine." He had attracted notice in 1954 with the account of his father's death from a similar cancer; now he recharged his writing career as a chronicler of his own progress toward death. He thought about calling his collection of writings on the subject "Critically Ill." It was a pun he delighted in.

Soon after the diagnosis was made, he was told that he might have "in the neighborhood of years." Eight months later, it became clear that this prognosis was too optimistic. Richard Shweder, the anthropologist, talks about a trip to France that he and his wife made with Anatole and Sandy not long before Anatole's death. One day, the two men were left alone. Shweder says, "And what did he want to do? He wanted to throw a ball. The two of us just played catch, back and forth." The moment, he believes, captures Broyard's athleticism, his love of physical grace.

Broyard spent the last five weeks of his life at the Dana Farber Cancer Institute, in Boston. In therapy sessions, the need to set things straight before the end had come up again—the need to deal with unfinished business and, most of all, with his secret. He appeared willing, if reluctant, to do so. But by now he was in almost constant pain, and the two children lived in different places, so the opportunities to have the discussion as a family were limited. "Anatole was in such physical pain that I don't think he had the wherewithal," Sandy says. "So he missed the opportunity to tell the children himself." She speaks of the expense of spirit, of psychic energy, that would have been required. The challenge would have been to explain why it had remained a secret. And no doubt the old anxieties were not easily dispelled: would it have been condemned as a Faustian bargain or understood as a case of personality over-spilling, or rebelling against, the reign of category?

It pains Sandy even now that the children never had the chance to have an open discussion with their father. In the event, she felt that they needed to know before he died, and, for the first time, she took it upon herself to declare what her husband could not. It was an early afternoon, ten days before his death, when she sat down with her two children on a patch of grass across the street from the institute. "They knew there was a family secret, and they wanted to know what their father had to tell them. And I told them."

The stillness of the afternoon was undisturbed. She says carefully, "Their first reaction was relief that it was only this, and not an event or circumstance of larger proportions. Only following their father's death did they begin to feel the loss of not having known. And of having to reformulate who it was that they understood their father—and themselves—to be."

At this stage of his illness, Anatole was moving in and out of lucidity, but in his room Sandy and the children talked with humor and irony about secrets and about this particular secret. Even if Anatole could not participate in the conversation, he could at least listen to it. "The nurses said that hearing was the last sense to go," Sandy says.

It was not as she would have planned it. She says, gently, "Anatole always found his own way through things."

The writer Leslie Garis, a friend of the Broyards' from Connecticut, was in Broyard's room during the last weekend of September, 1990, and recorded much of what he said on his last day of something like sentience. He weighed perhaps seventy pounds, she guessed, and she describes his jaundice-clouded eyes as having the permanently startled look born of emaciation. He was partly lucid, mostly not. There are glimpses of his usual wit, but in a mode more aleatoric than logical. He spoke of Robert Graves, of Sheri Martinelli, of John Hawkes interpreting Miles Davis. He told Sandy that he needed to find a place to go where he could "protect his irony." As if, having been protected by irony throughout his life, it was now time to return the favor.

"I think friends are coming, so I think we ought to order some food," he announced hours before he lapsed into his final coma. "We'll want cheese and crackers, and Faust."

"Faust?" Sandy asked.

Anatole explained, "He's the kind of guy who makes the Faustian bargain, and who can be happy only when the thing is revealed."

A memorial service, held at a Congregationalist church in Connecticut, featured august figures from literary New York, colleagues from the *Times*, and neighbors and friends from the Village and the Vineyard. Charles Simmons told me that he was surprised at how hard he took Broyard's death. "You felt that you were going to have him forever, the way you feel about your own child," he said. "There was something wrong about his dying, and that was the reason." Speaking of the memorial service, he says, marveling, "You think that you're the close friend, you know? And then I realized that there were twenty people ahead of me. And that his genius was for close friends."

Indeed, six years after Broyard's death many of his friends seem to be still mourning his loss. For them he was plainly a vital principle, a dancer and romancer, a seducer of men and women. (He considered seduction, he wrote, "the most heartfelt literature of the self.") Sandy tells me, simply, "You felt more alive in his presence," and I've heard almost precisely the same words from a great many others. They felt that he lived more intensely than other men. They loved him—perhaps his male friends especially, or, anyway, more volubly—and they admired him. They speak of a limber beauty, of age-lessness, of a radiance. They also speak of his excesses and his penchant for poses. Perhaps, as the bard has it, Broyard was "much more the better for being a little bad."

And if his presence in American fiction was pretty much limited to other people's novels, that is no small tribute to his personal vibrancy. You find him reflected and refracted in the books of his peers, like Anne Bernays (she says there is a Broyard character in every novel she's written) and Brossard and Gaddis, of course, but also in those of his students. His own great gift was as a feuilletonist. The personal essays collected in "Men, Women and Other Anticlimaxes" can put you in mind of "The Autocrat of the Breakfast-Table," by Oliver Wendell Holmes, Sr. They are brief impromptus, tonally flawless. To read them is to feel that you are in the company of someone who is thinking things through. The essays are often urbane and sophisti-cated, but not unbearably so, and they can be unexpectedly moving. Liter-ary culture still fetishizes the novel, and there he was perhaps out of step with his times. Sandy says, "In the seventies and eighties, the trend, in litera-ture and film, was to get sparer, and the flourish of Anatole's voice was de-pendent on the luxuriance of his language." Richard Shweder says, "It does seem that Anatole's strength was the brief, witty remark. It was aphoristic. It was the critical review. He was brilliant in a thousand or two thousand words." Perhaps he wasn't destined to be a novelist, but what of it? Broyard was a Negro who wanted to be something other than a Negro, a critic who wanted to be something other than a critic. Broyard, you might say, wanted to be something other than Broyard. He very nearly succeeded.

Shirley Broyard Williams came to his memorial service, and many of his friends—including Alfred Kazin, who delivered one of the eulogies—remember being puzzled and then astonished as they realized that Anatole Broyard was black. For Todd and Bliss, however, meeting Aunt Shirley was, at last, a flesh-and-blood confirmation of what they had been told. Shirley is sorry that they didn't meet sooner, and she remains baffled about her brother's decision. But she isn't bitter about it; her attitude is that she has had a full and eventful life of her own—husband, kids, friends—and that if her brother wanted to keep himself aloof she respected his decision. She describes the conversations they had when they did speak: "They always had to be focused on something, like a movie, because you couldn't afford to be very intimate. There had to be something that would get in the way of the intimacy." And when she phoned him during his illness it was the same way. "He never gave that up," she says, sounding more wistful than reproachful. "He never learned how to be comfortable with me." So it has been a trying set of circumstances all around. "The hypocrisy that surrounds this issue is so thick you could chew it," Shirley says wearily.

Shirley's husband died several months before Anatole, and I think she must have found it cheering to be able to meet family members who had been sequestered from her. She says that she wants to get to know her nephew and her niece—that there's a lot of time to make up. "I've been encouraging Bliss to come and talk, and we had lunch, and she calls me on the phone. She's really responded very well. Considering that it's sort of last-minute."

Years earlier, in an essay entitled "Growing Up Irrational," Anatole Broyard wrote, "I *descended* from my mother and father. I was *extracted* from them." His parents were "a conspiracy, a plot against society," as he saw it, but also a source of profound embarrassment. "Like every great tradition, my family had to die before I could understand how much I missed them and what they meant to me. When they went into the flames at the crematorium, all my letters of introduction went with them." Now that he had a wife and family of his own, he had started to worry about whether his children's feelings about him would reprise his feelings about his parents: "Am I an embarrassment to them, or an accepted part of the human comedy? Have they joined my conspiracy, or are they just pretending? Do they understand that, after all those years of running away from home, I am still trying to get back?"

SOURCE: *The New Yorker*, June 17, 1996, pp. 66–81.

BLISS BROYARD

WHEN I BEGAN this project, there was one person whose family history interested me perhaps more than any other: Anatole Broyard, the black writer and longtime literary critic for the *New York Times* who passed as a white man for most of his life. My interest was simple and highly personal: I had researched Anatole in great detail for an essay that I wrote about him more than a decade ago—and his story still haunts me today. And it haunts me because of its typicality, as complex as it is, toward what Kwame Anthony Appiah calls "cosmopolitanism." And cosmopolitanism in the black tradition has many forms.

Anatole Broyard was born on July 16, 1920, in New Orleans to Paul Broyard and Edna Miller. He and his parents were black people with light complexions. Anatole was their only son. He had two sisters: One shared his complexion—that is, was not discernibly black—while the other was much darker (the inheritance of melanin is imprecise). In all records and by all accounts, the family was identified as Negro and identified itself as Negro. But when Anatole was still a child, the Broyards moved north to the Bedford-Stuyvesant area of Brooklyn, thus joining the Great Migration that took hundreds of thousands of southern blacks to northern cities and that took the ancestors of so many people in this book to the North as well.

In the French Quarter, Anatole's father, Paul, had been a legendary dancer, beau, and *galant*. Brooklyn was a less welcoming environment. Though Paul Broyard arrived there a master carpenter, he soon discovered that the carpenters' union was not favorably inclined toward colored applicants. A stranger in a strange city, Paul decided to pass as white in order to join the union and get work. It was strictly a professional decision, which affected his career and nothing else. But his son, Anatole, would make the same decision and expand on it, passing for white in every area of his life—working at the *Times*, living in Southport, Connecticut; and raising two children who believed he was white, in the process alienating himself from his mother and his siblings and countless others from his black past. He died in 1990, having kept his secret from all but a few friends and associates for more than five decades.

I never met Anatole Broyard. I read him regularly in the *New York Times* for years—and admired his writing while troubling myself over his secret, which, unlike the vast majority of his readers, I knew. I knew. I was told that Anatole was black in 1975, when I was twenty-five years old, by my mentor, Charles T. Davis, the first African American to be tenured in the Yale English department. Charles and his wife, Jean Curtis Davis, were friends with Broyard's sister and brother-in-law, the former ambassador Franklin Williams and his wife, Shirley. Because they knew Shirley so well, they knew all about Anatole's family's past. They were highly amused that the *Times* was unwittingly employing someone who was passing for a white man. I was fascinated and disturbed by this fact. And when Broyard died, I decided to explore it. I interviewed many people who knew him, used a genealogist to track down his family's records in the Louisiana state archives, then published an essay about his life in the *New Yorker*.

In the process of writing my essay, I called Anatole's daughter, Bliss Broyard. We talked a few times on the phone, as I was deciding whether or not to write about her father's story. Finally, after talking to my editors at the *New Yorker*, Tina Brown and Henry Finder, I decided to plunge ahead. I tried to tell Bliss in person, when I thought I would be visiting the campus of the University of Virginia at Charlottesville, where she was a student. But that trip was canceled. So I told her on the phone. Anatole had a close circle of friends who knew his secret. His wife, Alexandra Nelson, a white woman of Norwegian ancestry, knew it as well. But it was entirely hidden from Bliss and her brother, Todd, almost up until the moment Anatole died. When I told her that I planned to write about her father, Bliss became quite angry with me. I was outing him in a way, and that upset her. But as the years have passed, Bliss's feelings seemed to have softened somewhat. I was delighted this past summer when she left me a copy of her book about her father, *One Drop*, at the house we lease on Martha's Vineyard. When I read her book, I discovered that she was *still* pretty angry at me! Nevertheless, when I began this project, I decided to ask her to participate, precisely because she was so angry and did not, I believe, fully understand how culturally black her father and his father truly had been. I wanted to see how Bliss had been affected, an entire decade after I published my essay, by her father's secret and its revelation, and I wanted to learn what, if anything, DNA testing could add to the story. She was surprised, I believe, but she eagerly agreed.

"When I first met you," Bliss said, "I thought this step of outing him myself would allow me to regain control over my identity. But what I have come to realize is that I am not in control of the way that people see me or my dad. It's always going to be a compromise between how I see myself and how the world sees me. Between how the world sees my dad and how I do."

Bliss took for the title of her book the redolent phrase "one drop"—it refers to one drop of blood, which is the way that blackness was defined legally throughout the United States (if you had one traceable black ancestor—one single drop of black blood—you had the legal standing of a Negro, which, of course, was not a good thing). Her book is fascinating and helped me to understand her father better, yet the essence of his life—his decision to pass as a white man—remains something of a mystery, at least to me. And that mystery, I think, is not his desire to break through the glass ceiling of race but the repudiation of his visibly black sister, Shirley, in the lives of his children.

Bliss and I began our discussion by talking about her memories of her father, whom she loved and admired profoundly. Flipping through Bliss's photos—past pictures of Anatole walking on the beach in Martha's Vineyard, standing stock-still as an army officer, holding his young daughter—he almost looks like a white man. It is only in his high-school yearbook photo that he looks, at least to my eyes, unmistakably black. This was, curiously, before he started identifying himself as a white man. According to Bliss, that happened when he filled out an application form for a Social Security card the following year, in 1938. He was seventeen years old. He needed a Social Security number to get a job. In that same year, that same summer, his sister Shirley, who was a couple of years younger, went to the same state office to see if there were any summer jobs. She was told there were no jobs for colored girls.

Looking at Anatole's application, the eye is immediately drawn to question number twelve—the question about color. On Anatole's form there is a check next to "Negro" that has been crossed out, and then there's a check next to "White." The letter C has been handwritten as well, which could stand for "Creole" or "colored." There's no way to know. The form is astonishing to behold because of the way that he erased his identity, agonizing over his decision to pass, right there on the form.

"He was confused," Bliss said sadly.

I asked her how she learned her father's secret. Her mother, Sandy, had told me the story, but I wanted to hear it from Bliss's point of view. She told me that for the first twenty-five years of her life she was, for all intents and purposes, a white person. Though her father was "legally" black Bliss was raised white in the whitest of white towns—Southport, Connecticut—and she looked white and believed herself to be white. She did not learn that her father was black until just months before he died of prostate cancer. "My mom said that she and Dad wanted to have a family meeting, which was very out of character for us," she recalled. "And Dad was quite ill at this point. I remember I had to bring a beach chair for him to sit in while we waited for my brother to come. The cancer had metastasized, and the doctors had let us know that there wasn't really anything else they could do."

"I think my mother had been kind of encouraging him to figure out how to finish up his life. And telling my brother and me this secret was one of those things that he needed to do. So we sat down in the living room, and my mom said, 'Anatole, is there anything that you'd like to tell your children?' And he said, 'Oh, I don't want to get into that today.' My brother and I kind of caught eyes and were like, 'Get into what?' And then my mother explained over my father's protesting that there was some secret from my father's childhood that would explain a lot. And she said that the secret was even more painful than this pain of cancer. But he didn't want to talk about it that day. He said that he would tell us eventually—that he needed to think about how to present things, that he wanted to order his vulnerabilities so they didn't get magnified during the discussion. That's a quote. He wanted to 'order his vulnerabilities.' And I remember this because it was so distinctly him."

Ultimately it was her mother, not her father, who revealed the family secret. "What ended up happening," said Bliss, "is my father went back in the hospital after that meeting, with another medical emergency. His bladder burst, and he had to go into emergency surgery, and my mother took it upon herself to tell us then—as my father was about to face the surgery. At that point we had just been watching my father screaming for help as if he were literally drowning, because he was in such terrible pain. So my mom simply said, 'I think I better tell you what the secret is.' And she said, 'Your father is part black.' That was her language. Then she sort of talked a little more, and she said that he was mixed and that his parents were Creoles from New Orleans, where there had been a lot of race mixing at one point, and that when he was growing up, his parents had had to pass in order to get work, and it had confused him about what the family was supposed to be. And she told us that his two sisters, Lorraine and Shirley, had stayed in the black community and they both lived as black and that's why we never saw them."

Bliss's mother also said that when Anatole was growing up, he was a victim of frequent abuse due to his color—and Bliss believes that this in many ways shaped his decisions in later life. "My mother," said Bliss, "told us that when he was child, my father used to come home with his jacket torn from getting into fights, that the black kids would pick on him because he looked white, and the white kids would pick on him because he looked black, and his parents would just ignore it. They wouldn't ask what happened. And he didn't want his own kids to go through the same thing he did."

Bliss says that she had no inkling that her father had been concealing his race, but she also recalls feeling no shock upon learning this secret. Her father was dying—and *would* die in just a few days—and her thoughts were focused on his health. The fact that he was part black was immaterial. "We laughed," said Bliss. "I thought the secret was going to be something. And it was just, like, he's part black. You know? This is the terrible secret from his childhood that's caused so much pain? We didn't get it. In fact, it seemed kind of cool, like, I remember saying to my mother, 'Oh, that means that we're part black, too!' Because I had always bought into this idea of the American melting pot, and here I was an example of it."

While Bliss does not seem the least bit concerned about the content of her father's secret—and the realization that she is part black—she remains deeply concerned over why he felt the need to keep the secret from her, his daughter. Indeed, in talking with her it is palpably clear that she still struggles with this—and still wonders why her father concealed so much from one of the people in the world who was closest to him. In the end she believes that he did so for a variety of complex reasons, all deeply intertwined with our nation's tortured past. "I think," she said, "that a big part of it was just that he didn't want us to have to struggle with our racial identity the way that he had. He just thought that he'd saved us from having that struggle. I think that, you know, he didn't want us to be black, that for him, growing up in Bed-Stuy in the forties, being black wasn't a good thing. And he always was sort of encouraging us to meet the kind of people who could help us later. I think that's what we were supposed to do in Connecticut. He was always telling us that we should learn how to play squash, because, you know, those are the kinds of people who can give you jobs. For him there was a kind of social cachet."

There are, of course, overwhelming advantages to being white in America. When Anatole surveyed the racial landscape and decided that his children would have an easier time of it if they were white, he knew what he was doing. And about this he was, without a doubt, correct. Being white, in general, in America, has had enormous historical and economic advantages. The cost, however, could be enormous as well. Anatole's life and virtually all his personal relationships were contorted by his decision. Bliss has great sympathy for him but also clearly recognizes the consequences of his decision—the internal chaos that it may have spawned.

"I think he wanted to spare us from a lot of pain that he had as a child," said Bliss. "But I don't know that he wanted to be white, either. He just wanted to be a kind of outsider to both these racial labels and expectations and prejudices that went with them, 'cause, you know, he was kind of a cool cat. He didn't want to be some white guy. He held black people up on a pedestal and was always making these comments about black athletes being better than white athletes, always the stereotypes, or black musicians being better than white musicians. At the same time, though, he also had some prejudicial feelings about blacks himself, and I think that my dad looked down on black people. I mean, I heard him saying prejudiced things when I was growing up sometimes. There was this time he was trying to sell our house in Cambridge. It was a very nice house, but down the block there was some low-income housing. And these buyers were coming back to look at the house for the third time, and even though he was sick, he walked up and down the street, picked up all the trash so it would look nicer. And then he came back fuming. I said, 'what's wrong?' He said, 'There are some black kids playing down the street. And these people are never going to want to buy this house if they see that.' And I was shocked. I remember saying, 'Dad, you sound like a goddamn racist.' And then he got up and left the table."

In this regard Anatole was acting like many black people, meaning that we make comments of this sort all the time. Nonetheless, the comment is startling—and as Bliss and I explored the implications of her father's decision to keep his race secret, similarly ironic contradictions arose. When I think about Bliss's father, I am reminded of how hard it is to be black and successful. His story is among the saddest I know, not because of its abstract implications but because of the costs to his mother and sisters. Anatole gained a world; they lost a son and brother. And how does one measure the comparative costs of that trade-off?

Bliss believes that her father liked to pretend that he had put his family in the past, but in reality she thinks he lived with the guilt or struggle of his decision on a daily basis.

"He was a family man," said Bliss, shaking her head. "He loved our family, and I think that he loved his family, and I think he had terrible guilt about it. I remember in 1979, when I was twelve, it was Mother's Day, and my father had decided to get my mom these really fancy earrings from Tiffany's, a kind of much nicer present than he usually did. He told me all about it, and I picked them out in the catalog with him, and then when he came down to give her the present, she was making dinner, even though it was Mother's Day, and she didn't sort of turn around and sit down quickly enough to accept the present. He abruptly lost his temper and threw the Tiffany box across the room. And I couldn't believe it. It was just so irrational. Then, later that night, I just went to bed, and my parents were kind of fighting, and then my mom woke me up in the middle of a deep sleep. She was looking for the bologna. She wanted to know where I had put the bologna when I had helped her unpack the groceries earlier that day. Because every night my dad had a bologna and cheese sandwich. Every night—with a single beer. So I told her, you know, 'It's in the meat drawer, I think.' And she went running back downstairs. I followed her, because I couldn't figure out what was going on."

When Bliss arrived in her family's kitchen, she was confronted by a scene of utter chaos. "My mother was kneeling in front of the refrigerator," she said, "and there were all these broken mayonnaise jars and things all over the floor. Because my dad had ransacked the refrigerator. I couldn't believe it. I said, 'What has got into him? It's Mother's Day. He got you this nice gift.' And my mother said, 'Well, his mother died, and I think he's feeling guilty.' This was the first I had heard that she was dead—and she had died nine months earlier."

Bliss can remember meeting her grandmother Edna Broyard only once in her life. "I had just turned seven," she recalled, "and my grandmother came out for the day to Connecticut where we were living and sat in a lawn chair in the backyard for a while, and then we went to the local country club and all had dinner, and then she went back home with my Aunt Lorraine. Then later, when I was going through my father's letters—he kept every letter he had ever received—I found a letter from my grandmother, who was living in a nursing home, dated a few weeks prior to this visit saying, 'Dear Anatole, I am not that young anymore. I am just going to be seventy-six. I want to meet my grandchildren for once in my life.' So she had requested this visit. And then she had her one visit."

Bliss says that her requests to see her grandmother again were always met with excuses. To me this story encapsulates what would be the unimaginably painful consequences of Anatole Broyard's decision to pass.

Turning to her family tree, Bliss told me that before she began writing her book, she had no knowledge of her family history as it related to her father's line beyond the fact that they came from New Orleans. Her research on her book revealed much more. Bliss was able to trace her family back to the middle of the eighteenth century, to her great-great-great-great-great-great-grandfather, a white Frenchman named Étienne Broyard who was born in 1729 and arrived in New Orleans in 1753, when it was part of New France. I wondered how her father would have felt about that. No doubt he would have been pleased; it certainly wouldn't have threatened his sense of the black identity that he had fled. It would have confirmed what was written right on his face: that he had a long, mixed racial heritage. Indeed, it probably would have impressed him, just as Bliss's research skills impressed me.

Bliss and I then began to explore the part of her heritage that had so tormented her father: her African ancestry—which, as it turns out, is filled with remarkably fascinating and quite unusual stories. It can be traced back to the marriage of her great-great-grandparents, Henry Antoine Broyard, a white man born on July 18, 1829, and Marie Pauline Bonnet, a free woman of color. They married in 1855. Marie's family came from the French colony of Saint-Dominque, now Haiti, as refugees of Toussaint Louverture's revolution, the only successful slave revolt in the Western Hemisphere. The Bonnets were expelled from Haiti along with thousands of other free people of color, because the new government feared they might still be loyal to France. And like many of their fellow refugees, they came to New Orleans because of the French culture there and its relatively large mulatto, elite population.

The fact that Henry and Marie formed a mixed-race couple is not surprising. Marie Pauline's parents were educated. Her father was a carpenter, and in fact he may even have worked with her future husband, who was also a carpenter. They all lived in the New Orleans neighborhood known as Treme, which has been called the oldest black neighborhood in America, though in fact it was quite mixed, even back in the 1850s—as was all of New Orleans, much more so than anywhere else in the South at that time. So to some extent Henry and Marie were mimicking the behaviors and mores of their city when they joined together. There were other factors as well. Records show that Henry's father had had children with a black woman—and so Henry had half siblings living as free people of color. Moreover, there is evidence that Henry himself had a child with another free woman of color before he married Marie. So Henry and Marie were surrounded by interracial couples.

Nonetheless, these two people did something very unusual: They got married. It was illegal for blacks and whites to get married in 1855 Louisiana. Even though Marie was free, she was visibly and officially black, and in the years leading up to the Civil War anti-black feelings in the South were rising and free people of color were being viewed with ever-mounting suspicion as possible instigators of slave revolts. Yet Marie and Henry were able to marry. How was this possible? Bliss's novel theory is that it was facilitated by the same means that Anatole Broyard would use a century later—only in reverse: She believes that Henry Broyard passed as black! His race, on his marriage license, is listed as "Negro." He even volunteered for the army in the Civil War as a colored man, serving in the famous Louisiana Native Guard, one of the first all-black regiments in the war.

Tellingly, after black-and-white marriages were legalized again in 1870, Henry Broyard indicated that he was white on the census, and his family indicated the same on his death certificate. If Bliss is indeed right about her ancestor's origins, it would seem that following the Civil War he stopped passing, although his wife and all their children continued to list themselves as mulattoes.

Bliss is struck by the irony of this. "I thought, how could it be that my great-great-grandfather passed from white to black?" Passing, it would seem, has a long history in her family.

I have consulted with many scholars about Bliss's ancestor, and I am convinced that Henry Broyard could possibly have decided to pass for black, although for obvious reasons this was extraordinarily rare. On the other hand, he could have been a mulatto himself. Race is such a tenuous thing, especially in New Orleans.

"I come from a very illustrious line," said Bliss, laughing. "I like to think of it as a little bit of a love story. It was important for me to find that moment of mixing, and I thought it was rape in a slave cabin. I mean, that was the sort of image you always have, right? But I think this was a love relationship. It's quite unusual."

Henry and Marie Pauline's oldest son was Nat Broyard. He is Bliss's paternal great-grandfather, and according to her research, he was a carpenter who built some of the biggest buildings in New Orleans in the 1890s. He was also, according to Bliss, very active in Republican politics at that time and may have been friends with Homer Plessy and the group of Creoles in Louisiana who pressed one of the most important civil-rights lawsuits in American history—an early and unsuccessful challenge to segregation that ended up in the infamous 1896 Supreme Court decision *Plessy v. Ferguson.* The failure of Plessy's case cemented the "separate but equal" doctrine and helped institutionalize Jim Crow racism in this country for another six decades. If Nat Broyard knew and helped Homer Plessy, he has my deepest admiration. Plessy and his friends stood up for racial justice in the worst of times.

In this life of passing, Anatole Broyard was a virtuoso of ambiguity and equivocation. People who learned about his secret generally heard rumors about "distant" black ancestry—perhaps a great-grandfather. Anatole wanted things vague. He rarely spoke directly to anyone about his racial background.

"My father," recalled Bliss, "never said anything about it to me, but he said it to, I guess, my mother and some other friends who had asked. He'd say, 'Oh, you know, my great-grandfather found his wife under a coconut tree.' That was his way of saying that she was from the islands. Or he would say that there were some 'Caribbean influences' in his past. But he'd never come out and say 'black.'"

The truth, of course, was very different. Nat Broyard, Anatole's paternal grandfather, was half black, and he married a half-black woman named Rosa Cousin. Her father was a white man named Anatole Cousin (the source of Anatole Broyard's name), and her mother was Marie Evalina Xavier, whose family was also part of this Haitian refugee community in early-nineteenth-century New Orleans.

Nat and Rosa Broyard's son was Paul Broyard, Anatole's father. Paul followed in his father's footsteps, working as a carpenter and builder in New Orleans. His wife was Edna Miller. She was from a colored Creole family in New Orleans, and in her photographs she looks like an elegant African American woman of her day. There is simply no doubt, based on Bliss's book and my own research, that Anatole Broyard was at best confused if he did in fact believe that he had only one black ancestor. He had many black ancestors, just as he had white ancestors, and in the United States when he was born—and in the United States today—he would be defined as an African American. And so would Bliss.

Our DNA testing further confirmed this. Bliss's admixture test revealed that she is 17.2 percent sub-Saharan African, 78 percent European, and 4.7 percent East Asian. Her African results indicate that 37 percent of her African ancestry came from Upper Guinea and 63 percent comes from Congo Angola, which is where more than a quarter of all the slaves brought to America came from.

"I'm an octoroon," she said. "My daughter is a steeth—she's a sixteenth black. My dad was a quadroon. A quarter black."

I asked Bliss if she saw race as a matter of choice. "I'm in a very unusual situation," she said. "I can decide how much I want this to be a part of who I am. In a lot of people, their race is so apparent that they don't have any control over how they are seen. I think race is the sum of experience and a state of mind. When I went to New Orleans and did my genealogy and learned about my family history, that made me feel like a different person. When I look in the mirror, I see a different person now. But without having grown up as black and without looking black, it's hard for me to feel that I am black, you know? I don't feel that I have earned the right to call myself black, since I wasn't raised that way and I don't look black. But, you know, at the same time, my father was black. I'm black. There's just a lot of explaining to do."

I told Bliss that based on her DNA she most certainly has a significant amount of African ancestry. And she was fascinated to hear that her results indicate that her first enslaved maternal ancestor on her father's side (we tested her father's sister) was most likely shipped from what is now Angola to the New World sometime between 1750 and 1808. The slaves shipped from Angola were generally handled by Portuguese slave traders—which triggered an interesting memory in Bliss.

"Edna Miller," she said, "my father's mother. When they moved to New York in 1930, the census taker came around, and she said that her family was Portuguese. And Portuguese keeps cropping up in her family line, and I always suspected that somebody in her family had been a slave in the

United States, and maybe they came over with a Portuguese slave trader or something."

Before we said good-bye, I told Bliss once again how powerfully her father's story had affected me. I still remember when I learned that Anatole was black. I was stunned. And I remember thinking, "He's reviewer for the *New York Times*, but he's passing." And I had very mixed emotions about that. I was proud of him, but I wanted him to have fought the battle as a black man and not as a black man passing as a white man. I wanted him to have made it as a daily reviewer at the *New York Times* with everyone knowing his race. And I have often wondered whether he ever felt this, too—could he have achieved so much if he had identified himself as a black man? And would it have made him happier?

Bliss does not know any better than I do. "He believed in that kind of modernist notion of self-invention," she said. "He thought that he could create himself and be who he wanted to be and that the only authority on his identity was himself. And he was ahead of his time in that way."

The irony, of course, is that he should have been able to define himself. I deeply believe that. But Anatole was trapped in a system of racist class values—deeply American racist class values. And he couldn't recreate his conscience. He couldn't obliterate this sense of rejecting actual people with whom he had grown up. But what kind of person could? And that was naïve on his part.

"It's also naïve," Bliss said, nodding her head, "that he believed that people who looked like himself, who didn't look visibly black, could make race not matter. I think that he wildly underestimated the level of racism and prejudice that people experience every day. It was very easy for him to say, 'Forget your race.' But some people don't want to forget their race."

This is very true. And it is also true that there is probably no way in the world her father could have achieved what he did had he identified himself as black rather than white. "He never could have gotten that job at the *Times*," Bliss said. "If he had been openly black at that time? There was no other black critic on staff of a daily major paper in the United States. And one of the reasons he couldn't have gotten the job is that if he had been openly black, he would have been expected to write only about, to know only about black subjects."

Nonetheless, I believe that Anatole Broyard made a terrible mistake. And I've had people pass in my own family. My cousin Pat Carpenter was black, divorced his first wife, and married a white woman, and he didn't want anybody in the family to contact him. My father's Uncle Roscoe married a white woman and passed. When my great-grandmother died, my grandpa, my father's father, wouldn't tell his own brother that their mother had died, because he was so angry at him for having passed. I was raised with these stories. I know firsthand that the black experience has always been multicolored. But Anatole's decision will always, on some level, be a puzzle to me—especially the fact that he couldn't talk to his children about it.

In parting, I told Bliss that I wish I could have met her father just to console him, just to encourage him to talk to the people who loved him. Hearing this, Bliss smiled knowingly. "If I could say something to him now, it would be something simple," she told me. "I'd just say, 'I can understand why you were trying to protect yourself and protect your family, but you don't have to anymore. Times have changed, and being black can be a wonderful thing. There are so many great aspects of the culture and your own family history that should not be buried, and we'd like to know. I'd like to know.'"

I am very sorry she never got the chance to say this. I think it would have unburdened him in some way to hear it.

SOURCE: Henry Louis Gates, Jr., *In Search of Our Roots: How 19 Extraordinary African Americans Reclaimed Their Past* (New York: Crown, 2009).

ELIZABETH ALEXANDER

DR. ELIZABETH ALEXANDER is a poet, professor, and chair of the African American Studies Department at Yale University. She is the author of five books of poems (including *American Sublime*, a finalist for the Pulitzer Prize) and two collections of essays. Among her many honors, she has been awarded a National Endowment for the Arts Fellowship, two Pushcart Prizes, a Guggenheim Fellowship, and the inaugural Alphonse Fletcher, Sr. Fellowship for work that "contributes to improving race relations in American society." In 2008, Barack Obama selected her to compose and read a poem at his inauguration as president of the United States.

Elizabeth was my student at Yale and since then has become a dear friend, someone whom I have relied on for advice and inspiration time and time again. I asked her to be in the series *Faces of America* for the same reason that I asked Malcolm Gladwell: because both can trace their ancestry, in part, to the West Indies. I also invited her because over the years I thought I had come to know part of her family story, and I was fascinated by the way in which it embodies the complex nature of racial identity in America. She and her parents, like countless other African Americans, forged strong identities for themselves despite knowing very little about their deep ancestors. Her mother has written two excellent books on her family's past, but there are profound questions that she has been unable to answer. I wanted to take a try at these questions myself. And I must say, the results truly surprised her and me. Elizabeth, as we shall see, has one of the largest documented family trees of any African American on record—with ancestors whose lives, it turns out, stretch from Jamaica to Wales, from the heart of Africa to the heart of Europe.

Her story begins in one of my favorite places on earth: New York City. Elizabeth Alexander was born on May 30, 1962, in Harlem. Her parents were Clifford Leopold Alexander, Jr., and Adele Logan, both also born in New York, he on September 21, 1933, and she on January 26, 1938. Theirs was an exceptionally close family with a clear sense of what it meant to be black and what it took to succeed in 1960s America. Elizabeth's father was a pioneer in the civil rights movement and a very significant person in African American history. A trailblazer in the truest sense, Clifford attended Harvard University in the 1950s, where he was elected the first African American student-body president. He graduated with an A.B. in government and then went on to study law at Yale, one of the first black people to earn degrees from both those universities. Among his many accomplishments, he was one of President Lyndon Johnson's closest advisers on civil rights, and he played a major role in the passage of the Civil Rights Act of 1964. He was also, under President Carter, the first African American secretary of the army. In this capacity, he promoted Colin Powell to the rank of brigadier general.

Elizabeth says that even as a very young child she was aware that her father was engaged in something important—and that it was deeply related to race. "We had a sense of being in the midst of a historical time," she told me. "We were race people—that was always plain and clear. That was part of the language. It was the primary lens. I wouldn't say that my parents were race obsessed in any way, but they saw the world in large part along the lines of those struggles."

The Alexanders moved from Harlem to Washington, DC, when Elizabeth was two years old, because her father was offered a job in the Johnson administration. So Elizabeth grew up in the nation's capital, during one of the most tumultuous times in our history, immersed in the civil rights movement. "One of my most powerful memories," she said, "was when Martin Luther King was killed, and Washington erupted in riots and fires. I remember my father couldn't come home. I'm not sure what President Johnson sent him to do to help, but as the city was burning maybe ten blocks away from our house, I knew that Daddy was doing something helpful—but also that he wasn't there, and we were waiting for him to come back. And then when he came back, he told us about flying over the city and watching it burning. We knew at that point already who Dr. King was and what he was trying to do. We knew about Medgar Evers. Somehow it all seemed tied together."

As we began to explore her genealogy, Elizabeth told me that she knew much more about the great sociopolitical events of her youth than she did about her ancestry. Politics, culture, and race, she said, were constant subjects in the Alexander home. The past was not. "I had my whole childhood with my maternal grandmother and my paternal grandfather," Elizabeth said. "Both of my grandparents were only children. We spent a great deal of time with these grandparents. But they didn't tell us much of anything about where they came from."

Her paternal grandfather, Clifford Alexander, Sr., was particularly reticent. He had immigrated to America from Jamaica as a young man, leaving behind a mother whom he never saw again and rumors that he was the illegitimate son of a Jewish merchant. Perhaps unsurprisingly, he rarely discussed these matters. "He gave a few tantalizing details," said Elizabeth. "He told me that his father died in the great earthquake in Jamaica in 1907, but that was about it. When he was a few days away from passing, in the middle of the night I realized we don't know his parents' names. And so I asked him and received no last names, just Emma and James, and that was pretty much all that we knew."

This is a rather sad story, and the telling of it clearly gripped Elizabeth. She said to me that she was especially eager to learn more about her grandfather and that, indeed, she had peppered him with questions as a child. Everything about his life was interesting to her. "I remember," she said, "I asked my grandfather once, 'Did you know anybody in America when you came?' And he said no. I couldn't imagine going somewhere and not being met, so I asked, 'What happened when you got off the boat?' 'Well,' he said, 'there were always people there. There were chaps.' That was the way he talked: he was from Jamaica, his English was different. His vocabulary was not the same as ours. So he said, 'There were chaps who would show you where you could live and where you could work.' And you needed these chaps, because this was a segregated country that he was coming into. He said these chaps took him to Harlem and showed him a boarding house and where you could get a job."

Harlem, at the time, was a melting pot of comparatively well-educated West Indian immigrants and many more poor, less-educated African American migrants from the South who transformed Harlem from a community that was 67 percent white in 1920 to a community that was 70 percent black just ten years later. Class tension, racial tension, and cultural tension between the groups abounded. But Elizabeth does not recall that her grandfather suffered from these things. They certainly did not limit his career. Clifford ended up overseeing a YMCA and managing the branch of a bank. He was a community leader in every sense of the term and an enduring inspiration to his activist son.

"The sense that I got from my grandfather was of an incredibly vibrant Harlem," Elizabeth said, "with a whole lot of different kinds of black people in it. That was always my sense of that world. And he became someone who was a very helpful figure in Harlem. When he passed away, I can't tell you how many people at his funeral came up and said, 'Your grandfather gave me advice about starting a patty stand,' 'Your grandfather gave me help with this.' He really was a community person in the present, and he just didn't talk about the past. Maybe there are sadnesses, too. You leave your mother, and you never see her again. So who knows if that was part of it? Maybe he just didn't want to discuss that."

I asked Elizabeth if she thought her grandfather was embarrassed about his immigrant status. I kept thinking of him getting off that boat and looking around for a "chap" to show him where to stay. I can imagine African Americans making fun of a Jamaican like that.

Elizabeth told me that she didn't think so. Her grandfather, she believed, was simply someone who had reinvented himself and did not want to look backward. As evidence, she told me that she had once asked him to tell her the story of his journey from Jamaica to New York. He turned the whole thing into a kind of shaggy-dog story for his grandchildren.

She remembered him chuckling as he spun his yarn: "He started out by saying that he was born on the road between Spanishtown and Kingston, and we loved that, because we were these urban children, and we couldn't imagine being born on the road. And then he said he stowed away on a banana boat, and I didn't know what to think. But when I cleaned out his apartment after he died I found sort of a passage document from a United Fruit Company boat. So maybe he stowed away, but with papers? He chuckled when he told us the stowaway part, so I don't know if he was trying to give us an adventure tale, but that's all we ever knew. We knew that there was something funny but couldn't quite discern what it was."

It turns out that Elizabeth's grandfather's story about being a stowaway on a banana boat was a riddle of sorts. We found the actual records of her grandfather's immigration to America. They show that his story was an interesting mix of fantasy and fact—leaning heavily toward the side of fantasy. The *SS Turrialba*—owned by the United Fruit Company (in a way, a "banana boat")—arrived at Ellis Island, New York, from Jamaica on August 31, 1918, and its manifest lists twenty-one-year-old Clifford Alexander not only as a paying passenger but as a first-class passenger as well. His race is listed as "West Indian," and his home is Kingston, Jamaica.

We were also able to find his birth certificate in Jamaica. It indicates that Clifford was born in Kingston to a woman named Emma Honeywell, a seamstress living at 4 Wildman Street. No father is named on the birth certificate, but Emma's address gave us a starting point for some theorizing. Wildman Street is in the oldest part of Kingston, a very poor neighborhood. Number 4, where Clifford was born, is today an alley running behind the street. Some of the oldest residents of the neighborhood told us that, for the past century at least, the alley has been filled with one-room rental apartments. So Clifford Alexander was born into intense poverty.

The fact that no father is named on Clifford's birth certificate indicates that the family legend about his being illegitimate is almost certainly correct. I wanted to find out if the stories about his Jewish father were also true. According to Elizabeth, Clifford had told her, at the end of his life, that his parents were named Emma and James. The Emma part had checked out. What about the James part? Could we locate a Jewish merchant named James Alexander?

If you do enough genealogical research, you will be forced to face the sad fact that family stories are often pure invention. In my own family, we cherished the idea that we were all related to Horatio Gates, the Revolutionary War general. Research showed there wasn't a shred of truth to the story. For many African Americans, whose ancestry is hidden by slavery, myths of Native American roots or Igbo princesses from Africa abound. Very few are true. Another, less common but nonetheless persistent mythology in some West Indian families is the existence of a male Jewish ancestor; Malcolm Gladwell's family, as we shall see, shared the same belief. (As a matter of fact, about 35 percent of all African American males are descended from a white male ancestor, according to their Y-DNA.) Of course, there are often kernels of truth in family lore, and sometimes family stories turn out to be true. From our research, it seems that it might be possible that Clifford Alexander's father was a Jewish merchant. We don't know for certain, but there is significant evidence to support it.

First is the surname: Alexander. Alexander in Jamaica is thought of as a "Jewish" name, and it's not uncommon for a woman to give her illegitimate child the father's name to create a connection to the father, even if they're not legally associated. This was, indeed, quite a common practice at the time when Elizabeth's grandfather was born. There are other factors that led us to think that he might have been Jewish as well. Jamaica in the nineteenth century was a very complex society with regard to race and class. Everyone had a place, everyone knew that place, and that place was signified by color. The white ruling elite, of course, was at the top. Jewish people and free people of color were at the same social level one tier down (and both groups, curiously enough, won the right to vote in the same year, 1831). Below them was the bulk of the population: black slaves of all different skin tones but predominantly pure, unmixed black people. So in spite of the second-class status of Jews, claiming a Jewish ancestor for a black person meant that you had white ancestry. And in Jamaica that was a very good thing. For a black woman, slave or free, a relationship with a white man, even a Jewish man, could be a dramatic step up in the world. Emma may have been willing to engage in a relationship for this reason alone.

Unfortunately, this is all speculation. With the records available to us we were not able either to prove or to disprove the existence of a Jewish merchant in Elizabeth's family or to document a connection between Emma Honeywell and any man who might have been the father of her son Clifford. There are no records of a man named James Alexander living in Jamaica at that time, nor is there any evidence that a man fitting his description might have died in the 1907 earthquake, as Elizabeth's family story says. (DNA, however, has something to say about this story, as we later found out.)

Our research, however, was not entirely fruitless. It did yield more information about Elizabeth's great-grandmother Emma Honeywell. We found her baptismal record, dated May 6, 1859. It shows that she was born in Kingston, in the parish of St. Elizabeth, sometime in March 1859. Her parents are listed as Edward and Esther Honeywell, and her mother's occupation is listed as "servant." We also found the marriage certificate of Edward Honeywell and Esther Elisabeth Powell. They were married on July 15, 1857, by the Reverend R. D. Lynch in St. Elizabeth Parish. We wanted to see if Esther Powell was related to Colin Powell, whose family is also from Jamaica, but unfortunately we found no connection at all.

Further searching uncovered Emma's father's baptismal record. It shows that Edward Honeywell, "a Domestic of Northampton," aged twenty-one years old, was baptized on September 17, 1852. This record also contains a very telling omission. It does not state Edward's complexion, which in the Jamaica of this era means that he was black (white people and those with mixed blood made this known because it was a badge of honor). So, based on his profession as a "domestic" and the absence of recorded information about his race, I told Elizabeth that it was almost certain that her great-great-grandfather was black and a former slave.

"That's amazing," said Elizabeth. "It doesn't surprise me, but I also never even allowed myself to speculate beyond the one person that we knew. We had heard of Emma, but I never thought about her parents."

Elizabeth and I were both intrigued by the fact that Edward was baptized at age twenty-one. This means that he was born about 1831. And although the British act abolishing slavery in Jamaica passed in 1833, and became effective in 1834, slaves were still held in apprenticeships until 1838. So Edward most likely spent the first years of his childhood as a slave and then, when he was about seven, received his freedom. But he was free for fourteen years before he was baptized. Why did he wait so long? There's no way of knowing. It is possible that he came under the sway of religion at this point—possibly through another person such as his wife, Esther, or via the influence of a preacher. Records show that he was baptized on the same day as many of his neighbors, so it seems entirely possible that some kind of a hell-fire preacher came into his community distributing the fear of God en masse. There is no way to know for sure, but it seems a very likely explanation.

Elizabeth and I both wanted to know more about Edward's slave past. His baptismal record notes that he was a domestic servant and that he lived in Northampton. This was not a familiar place name to us, so our researchers began searching and found hand-drawn maps from the early nineteenth century of St. Elizabeth Parish. They showed that the parish contained something called "Northampton Pen." The word *pen* was the Jamaican term at that time for a cattle farm, and Northampton Pen was one of the largest pens in the country—including a plantation house and an estate of over fifteen hundred acres. This is where Elizabeth's great-great-grandfather and most likely his parents were slaves.

The farm is a ruin today, just some walls, the bare remains of some kind of entrance gate, open fields crossed by a single road, and lots of goats. But in the first decades of the 1800s, it was a very significant operation, owned by an Englishman named John Chambers. Records show that in 1826 Chambers owned 299 slaves. That's a large number of slaves for Jamaica and is much larger than most plantations in the United States held, even at the height of slavery here. When Chambers died in 1832, the inventory of his estate listed all his slaves. On the list is a boy named Edward, age two and a half years, valued at forty pounds (which would be about forty-five hundred dollars today). Incredibly, this two-and-a-half-year-old boy is Elizabeth's great-great-grandfather.

"My God," said Elizabeth, looking at the record. "When you see in black and white what it is to be valued as property when you're a toddler—I'm sorry, but these are all babies. That's hard to take."

This inventory told us more about the lives of Edward and the other slaves. It appears that Chambers did not treat his property as badly as many Jamaican slave owners did. Jamaica, like the rest of the Caribbean islands and much of South and Latin America, was a death camp for African slaves, a far worse place to be than the United States in terms of life expectancy. As a matter of fact, of a total of about 10.8 million slaves who survived the Middle Passage, only 450,000 or so Africans arrived in the United States between 1619 and 1865. The common practice in many parts of the Caribbean and South America was for owners simply to work their slaves until they died and then replace them, devoting little or no effort to maintaining their health or adequately feeding them. In America, by contrast, the importation of Africans was abolished in 1808, so slaves could not be easily replaced through importation. They were thus bred for generations of work and, while clearly mistreated, were not primarily viewed as replaceable parts. As a result, although there were only 450,000 Africans brought to the United

States in the slave trade, the African American population today numbers over thirty-five million people. Far more slaves went to the Caribbean and to South America—and the vast majority of them died, leaving no descendants. But the Northampton Pen was an exception. Chambers's records show a large number of births on his estate and many slaves who seem to have lived into their seventies and eighties—which in the 1830s was a very long time. So they must have been fed decently and received some kind of medical care. This, of course, does not make Edward and his family's slavery acceptable in any way. Elizabeth and I simply find it interesting to know that it could have been much worse.

Unfortunately, we could learn nothing more about Edward—and nothing at all about his parents. But, as I told Elizabeth, I think this scarcity of detail in itself tells us something about the Honeywells and illuminates her grand-father's silence about his past. Genealogies reflect a family's history in many different ways. They are so much more than a list of names. And when you find lives as elusive as these, it is because, for whatever reasons, our ances-tors could not, or did not, record key facts about their existence. They were too poor to have access to records or for records to have access to them; they didn't own property or pay taxes on property. Often, births of the poor were not recorded; some churches kept records of baptisms, marriages, and funerals; others did not. And even when these sorts of records were kept, sometimes they have been lost, destroyed, or discarded. Frankly, if you think about it, most of our ancestors, on any branch of our family trees, were regu-lar people who lived on the lower levels of society, most often beneath liter-acy. The only records that we were able to locate across two generations of Honeywells were a baptismal certificate, a marriage license, and the estate records of the white man who owned them. These were not prosperous people. I am always astonished by how much we can find out about any-one's ancestors, to tell you the truth, given the small percentages of literacy in Europe and America and in any country until very recently and given that the overwhelming percentage of our ancestors were, at best, members of the working poor.

"But there they are," said Elizabeth, pointing to her great-great-grandparents' marriage license. "It's hard to imagine. I mean, what you can know is that the kind of work they had to do wouldn't have left much time for imagination, but what we also know about people under all kinds of diffi-cult conditions and what we know about black people is that creativity and beauty comes out of that privation. So we have the spirituals, and we have folk tales, and we have aphorisms—we have so much production that comes out of people under very, very extreme circumstances. And I imagine in that regard they were like so many others. But it's all imagining, isn't it? Even with what we know as scholars about the sorrow songs—we have some records, but really, really trying to understand the circumstances from which those arise you have to use imagination."

Elizabeth is right, of course. It's a stirring fact that our slave ancestors left behind not documents or property but an incredible amount of cultural wealth. It is a tragedy that we are only able to imagine their individual contributions to that collective wealth—and the worlds they might have made had they been free.

Moving back down Elizabeth's paternal line, we looked at the ancestry of Clifford Alexander's wife, Elizabeth's grandmother, Edith MacAlister. Edith was born in 1902, in Yonkers, New York, just a few miles north of the Harlem neighborhood where she spent most of her adult life. She died when Elizabeth was a baby, and Elizabeth has no memory of her. Fortunately, her life is well documented. Her mother was a woman named Harriet, who was born sometime around 1880 in Pennsylvania, and her father was Walter Nathan MacAlister, born in July 1880 in Cumberland County, North Carolina. Harriet and Walter were almost certainly the children of freed slaves. And though we could not identify Harriet's last name or the identity of her parents, we were able to trace Walter back two generations into slavery using plantation records and census data. His parents were Nathan MacAlister, born in 1840 in Cumberland County, and a woman named Margaret, who was born a slave in Virginia in January 1854 and died a free woman sometime in 1900. We even found Nathan MacAlister's mother: a woman named Maryanne MacAlister who was born in 1816 in North Carolina.

This meant that on Elizabeth's father's side, we were able to trace her ancestry into slavery back to 1816 in America and 1831 in Jamaica—which is quite extraordinary for any African American.

Turning to Elizabeth's maternal line, we started with her mother, Adele Logan, born in 1938 in New York City. She has an impressive family as well. Adele's mother was Wenonah Bond, born in Birmingham, Alabama, on December 18, 1906. Her father, Elizabeth's great-grandfather, was Robert Percy Bond, born on June 18, 1868, in Norfolk, Virginia. His father was a remarkable man named John Robert Bond, born on May 24, 1843, in Mold, a town in Wales. John is Elizabeth's immigrant ancestor on her maternal line. According to her family's lore—and to some very impressive research done by her mother, a highly regarded historian—John was the son of a white woman from England and a black ship's cook named Robert Bond. According to the family, John came to America as a young man to join the fight against slavery. It's a wild story, more like a Hollywood movie than what we tend to find in the historical record, and I was eager to see what portion of it might be true. Much to my surprise, records suggest that the family account is substantially true, but with a few surprising twists.

Census records from Liverpool, England (which is about twenty miles from Mold) show that in 1851, an eight-year-old boy named John Robert Bond was living with his thirty-five-year-old father, Robert Bond, and his thirty-year-old mother, Ann Evans. In our records, Robert Bond lists his occupation as "cook on a ship" and states that he was from Bermuda. These are, undoubtedly, Elizabeth's ancestors.

"That's a total shock," said Elizabeth, ecstatic. "It was a big unknown, and again I didn't know enough about the history to be able to even speculate on whether he would have been in Liverpool for some time, for another generation, or come from Africa as a slave or come from the West Indies. That's fascinating. Bermuda was never in the equation."

Records also show that John Robert Bond left England and journeyed to New Bedford, Massachusetts, around the time of the Civil War (we could not identify the precise date of his arrival, but records definitely place him there by 1863). In that era, New Bedford was a center of the shipping and whaling industries, the latter of which was perhaps the most open occupation in the entire American economy for black men. Shortly after escaping to freedom in the North, Frederick Douglass had moved there for this very reason. We don't know exactly what drew Elizabeth's ancestor to New Bedford or what he did there, but we do know that John made a very unusual decision for a foreign-born black person. In May 1863, as the Civil War entered its third long year, he enlisted in the Union navy. He was twenty-one years old and had lived almost all his life in England. But he clearly believed in the Union cause, and he served with honor. On February 1, 1864, he was wounded in action when a bullet pierced his chest. It could have been a fatal wound, but he survived, was honorably discharged, and was granted an invalid's pension of eight dollars a month. He was just twenty-two years old. And around this time, he met an African American woman named Emma Thomas. We weren't able to track down records of where Emma was born or who her parents were, but she and John Robert Bond married in June 1865, just weeks after the end of the Civil War. They eventually headed north to New England and settled in Hyde Park, Massachusetts, where they raised a family of four children, one of whom was Elizabeth's great-grandfather Robert Percy Bond.

John Robert Bond died peacefully in Hyde Park in 1905, never returning to England. I wanted to find out more about the family that produced this remarkable individual. Unfortunately, this proved very difficult. We knew that his mother, Ann Evans, had moved from her home town of Mold to the nearby city of Liverpool sometime in the late 1840s or early 1850s. The 1851 census records for Mold list her father, John's maternal grandfather, as a man named John Evans. At the time, John was sixty-eight years old, and according to the census, he was a former farmer turned pauper. We were able to trace John Evans back three more generations to Elizabeth's seventh-great-grandfather Edward Evans, born in nearby Northop, Wales, in January 1706. But we couldn't find out much about any of the people along this line. They most likely lived in the same region for generations, earning a subsistence living as farmers and miners like virtually everyone around them.

We were also unable to determine why Ann Evans left Mold for Liverpool. Maybe her reasons were economic; maybe there was some kind of conflict with her family. There is no way to tell. But in Liverpool, she met and married the ship's cook from Bermuda, Robert Bond, and this may have made it impossible to return to her family. Neither Elizabeth nor I can imagine this white girl from a small village coming to the big city and marrying this mulatto, then returning to her hometown.

"That's a story," said Elizabeth. "Even a hundred years later that story is seen as a novelty. Think about that confrontation. Even now when people talk about our president's parents, that's seen as a novelty. Of course, we know these comings together aren't so novel after all. But it had to be traumatic—it couldn't have been just 'Oh, a negro; come, sit down, take tea.'"

We then tried to learn more about the ship's cook, Robert Bond. This search proved frustrating as well. Census data indicated that he and Ann lived on Leeds Street, in the dock area of Liverpool, one of the busiest ports in the world at that time, with a well-established black community. The census indicated Robert had come from Bermuda—and this conforms to what we know of nineteenth-century Liverpool. Many sailors from the Caribbean settled there because of the shipping industry and married local women and had families. But we could learn nothing more about Robert or his ancestors. We could not even figure out what happened to Robert and Ann after 1851. They simply disappear from the historical record. The fact that Robert was a cook on a ship offers a clue as to why there's no further trace of him or his family. Perhaps he and Ann died, or perhaps they went back to Robert's home in Bermuda. But we just don't know. We do know that their son did not disappear. John Robert Bond made his mark on history. He was a half-English, half-Caribbean freedom fighter. I wish we could have learned more about him—but the little glimpse we have is nonetheless wonderful and inspiring.

I asked Elizabeth how she felt knowing that so much of her ancestry—on both her parents' lines—was white or at least racially mixed. "Well, you know," she replied, "blackness is not a monolith. It never has been. We were always already mixed in a million different ways. Even as our family stories and our family trees differ, things are much less black and white, if you will, than rigid categorizations would have us think. At the same time, that doesn't mean that our social identities are not very defining in many ways. I care about all my ancestry, but I'm still black—always have been. I just have always seen it as something that's a complicated weave."

Moving back down Elizabeth's maternal family tree, we traced the ancestors of her mother's father, Arthur Courtney Logan. Arthur was born in 1909 in Tuskegee, Alabama. His mother, Adella Hunt, was born in 1863 in Sparta, Georgia, and her ancestors stretch back six generations to a man named John Batte, who was born in 1606 in Yorkshire, England. He is Elizabeth's eighth-great-grandfather. He is also her oldest immigrant ancestor—and he was a wealthy white Englishman. It is unclear when the African and Anglo populations mixed in Elizabeth's maternal line, but there is no question about John Batte's ethnicity. He was as English as can be. His former home in England, Oakwell, is today a museum, and he lived the life of a gentleman of his time and class.

The story of John Batte's journey to the New World illuminates the diverse economic and cultural systems that shaped early America. Virginia was settled with a very different attitude and ethic than New England was. The original settlers of New England were fleeing religious persecution; the people who went to Virginia, primarily, were there to make money. In 1606, the year when John Batte was born in Yorkshire, King James I of England gave a charter to what was known as the Virginia Company of London which allowed its shareholders to establish a colony on the coast of America. Almost as soon as the first settlers arrived, they realized that there was money to be made in farming and land development, the colony's most basic resource and the major resource that Europe lacked (Europe's poor and middle classes had almost no access to land ownership—it was all controlled by the nobility). But while there was plenty of land in Virginia, there was a shortage of people to clear it and work it. So the Virginia Company came up with a plan which they called the "head rights system." Businessmen would pay the cost of transporting indentured servants from Europe to Virginia. The servants would arrive and work off their indenture for a fixed period of time (usually seven years) and then become freemen, qualified to own land. This plan supplied the colony with labor. The reward for the businessmen who paid for the transport was significant: for every individual they brought over they received fifty acres.

Elizabeth's ancestor John Batte saw a pot of gold in this system. In the year 1628, when he was just twenty-two years old, he set sail for Virginia with a business partner and thirteen indentured servants. In exchange, he received a land grant of 750 acres in Charles River County, Virginia. John, however, did not remain long in America. Records show that he returned to England and then, for more than a decade, traveled back and forth from the colony to his homeland for business. In the year 1643, he received a second grant of 526 acres in James City County, Virginia, for transporting another eleven people from England to the colony. This meant that he and his business partners owned more than a thousand acres of land in Virginia in 1643, all farmed by indentured servants and, possibly, by African slaves (the first slaves came to Virginia in 1619, but the slave system did not come to dominate the colony's economy until almost a century later). In 1651, John moved his family to the colony, after fighting on the losing side in the English Civil War. He died sometime around the year 1653, a founding settler of Virginia and a wealthy man.

"He was entrepreneurial," said Elizabeth, looking at the many records we had of her eighth-great-grandfather's business deals. "But it also makes me think about what enables you to make your mark as a person like this. Well, one thing is that a whole lot of other people have to do the laboring for you. I think about all of those indentured servants and eventually the slaves who did that work. That's a question mark. He exploited people. And it's impossible for me to not read that against all that it takes for non-white people to make their way."

I then told Elizabeth that however she felt about him, John Batte was by no means the end of this line of her family. He was from the English upper class, and his well-documented roots stretch back generations to John I, King of England, and his titled mistress, Clemence. John I was born in 1167 and is a crucial figure in world history. The youngest son of Henry II and Eleanor of Aquitaine, he engaged in a long power struggle with his brother, King Richard II, also known as Richard the Lionhearted. The rivalry between these brothers is a focal point of the Robin Hood legend, and it has been treated, with varying degrees of accuracy, in countless films, poems, and novels. As a child, I remember thinking it was just a fairy tale. But it was, in fact, a very real rivalry, and when Richard died childless in 1199, John inherited the crown—and a divided nation. From the beginning of his rule, the barons of England and Scotland blamed him for a multitude of social problems as well as for heavy taxes, the loss of English territories in France, and abuse of power. After years of conflict, the barons finally drew up a list of demands and threatened civil war if John didn't agree to meet them. This led to one of the most significant events of the past two thousand years: in June 1215, John and the barons met at Runnymede, outside London, and drew up a document which came to be known as Magna Carta.

Magna Carta was a milestone in the history of world government. It limited the king's powers and led to what we now call English common law—and it forms the basis of the constitutions of many countries, including our own. It was, in essence, the first document to declare that no man is above the law.

Elizabeth's ancestor John was forced to sign Magna Carta, which is not exactly inspiring. But among the barons who forced him to do it was another relative of Elizabeth's: her twenty-second-great-grandfather Saher De Quincy, the Earl of Winchester.

"That is completely mind-blowing," said Elizabeth. "How about that? It stretches me completely beyond anything I could have imagined. I thought I had some English ancestry, but I just wouldn't have thought to take it there. It never occurred to me—again, in part because of my own devotion to African American history and culture and bringing out the voices that haven't been heard—to think that there are volumes and volumes about these people. I could spend years in the library reading about them. It's amazing."

Moving back even further from King John, I showed Elizabeth that her family is deeply intertwined with the royalty of almost every medieval European nation—from France to Italy to Germany, including a figure even more important than John: Charlemagne, Emperor of the Holy Roman Empire. Born in the year 742, Charlemagne is called "the Father of Europe" and was the greatest ruler of his age—a legendary warrior and statesman who was one of the people who wrested Europe out of the Dark Ages. The power base and center of his court was in Aachen, in the western part of Germany, on the border of Belgium and the Netherlands. In the year 770, Charlemagne inherited the title King of the Franks and went on to accumulate titles and territory by waging war all over the continent. He ventured as far east as Hungary and south to Lombardy in northern Italy. In 774, he became King of Lombardy and, in 800, Holy Roman Emperor—crowned by Pope Leo III himself.

Charlemagne was a man of war and conquest, of course, but he was also respected as a man of learning. His reign ushered in what is known as the Carolingian Renaissance, which included a revival of art, religion, and culture—in an era when almost all these things were on the verge of being lost to Western civilization. Most of the surviving works of classical Latin were copied and preserved by Carolingian scholars. And through internal reforms and foreign conquests, Charlemagne helped to define what we now think of as Europe. We also know what he looked like. His biographer, who was his servant, described his appearance: "Charles was large and strong, and lofty of stature, though not disproportionately tall, his height is well known to have been seven times the length of his foot; the upper part of his head was round, his eyes very large and animated, nose a little long, hair fair, and face laughing and merry."

Charlemagne is Elizabeth's thirty-seventh-great-grandfather. He had good reason to be smiling all the time, to be laughing and merry. He had twenty children that we know about, thirteen with his five wives and seven others with his five acknowledged mistresses. Elizabeth is descended from his second wife, Hildegard, born sometime around the year 757 in what was then called Rhineland.

I told Elizabeth that her family tree is more radically mixed than any African American I have ever studied. She laughed, but we both know this kind of knowledge can be somewhat confusing. Most African Americans have some white ancestry; according to geneticists, 58 percent of the African American people have at least 12.5 percent European ancestry, the equivalent of one great-grandparent. And we have already discussed the fact that fully three out of ten black men trace their ancestry to a white male, most probably during slavery. At some point in our lives, we almost all realize that one side of our family profited enormously by exploiting the labor of another side. Elizabeth is unusual, in my experience, in that she can put names and faces for quite a distance in time on both sides. I have white ancestors whom I cannot name, starting with my great-great-grandfather on my father's side. Elizabeth, on the other hand, can point to John Batte and say, "I descend from this man who owned a manor in England in 1640, a man who helped settle Virginia." And Elizabeth, like Quincy Jones, who was profiled in the first *African American Lives* series, can point much further back than that—to legendary kings and queens of Europe. Very few African Americans can do that. And it is, I think, a very complicated thing to know about oneself.

Asked how she feels about these people, she replied, "I have ambivalence about them, not because they're white but because of how they built what they had. All of this stops when it gets to the black people—that generationally amassed wealth doesn't make it all the way down. It's hard to feel that connection. And I can't look at the aristocrats on the European side without thinking about that moment where they start to mix in the United States with people of African descent. What happens to those lines? I keep going back to the case of Captain Batte. What is privilege if it's tied to exploitation? Unto itself, it's not just a beautiful coat, right? This is a complicated, thorny history that's not just about beautiful things but also about the human cost of beautiful things."

I reminded her that one of the most important facts about African American history is that our ancestors who came to this country as slaves almost invariably came because they were captured, in Africa, by their fellow Africans, carried to a port, and sold to Europeans. Africans were not innocent in the slave trade. Our African ancestors fought and captured and sold other Africans into the slave trade to the New World. And if we could trace our roots back to African nobility, as someone like Elizabeth can do directly to European nobility, we would most probably realize that we are related to dark-skinned kings and queens whose privilege was built on the same kind of exploitation that white men like Captain Batte employed. It's just a fact. There are no innocents on our family trees. The sad truth is that the only reason most of our poor ancestors didn't exploit other people is that they couldn't.

"That's true," said Elizabeth. "And in a funny way, you know, it takes me back to my little teeny-tiny nuclear family and the two grandparents that I knew. I've made a life for myself essentially knowing about only two generations, drawing on what I respected and was proud of in those generations. I'm so proud of the grounding and sense of self that my parents and grandparents gave me. That sense of identity wasn't so much about being able to go far back but about connecting to a history of struggle and commitment to issues of justice—the ethics with which you live your life. So the micro matters—that's what's important, that's what you can get your teeth into. But then what do you do with the centuries?"

I told her I had no answer to this question. She has millennia of documented ancestors, stretching back farther than any African American I know. But only she can decide what they mean to her, how the knowledge of their names and stories will shape her identity over time.

Turning to our DNA testing, I told Elizabeth that her admixture results revealed that she is 66 percent European, 27 percent African, and 7 percent Native American. She told me that she had more or less expected this result, given what she knew from the genealogy. She had even heard stories, she said, that her maternal grandmother, Edith MacAlister, was part Native American—and though we could not verify these stories, they could well be true. She certainly does have a fairly significant amount of Native American ancestry, unlike most African Americans.

We then began to look at some of the most interesting DNA results that I have ever seen. Elizabeth's mitochondrial DNA belongs to a haplogroup called L0a. This is a subgroup of the most ancient haplogroup of all, L0, which arose about 150,000 years ago in Africa, probably in what is now Ethiopia. Over the millennia, offshoots of L0 arose in many different parts of the African continent. Elizabeth's originated about 55,000 years ago, and, ultimately, its members were very likely part of the Bantu migration just a few thousand years ago, one of the greatest migrations in human history. Between three and four thousand years ago, a small group of Bantu-speaking Africans migrated out of a core area in what we think is southern Cameroon and basically peopled a huge percentage of the rest of central and southern Africa, bringing a totally new genetic mixture to African populations. They carried their language and their genes west and then to the southeast, all the way to Mozambique.

When geneticists compared Elizabeth's mitochondrial DNA with everyone in the Family Tree DNA database, they found that she shares a genetic signature with thirteen people living today in Guinea-Bissau, eight in Gabon, seventeen in Cameroon, five in Ethiopia, and four in Angola. These are her genetic cousins. They all share a common ancestor in the past few thousand years. Another testing company, Roots for Real, which is based in Cambridge, England, also ran the results through their database, and they found that Elizabeth matched people living today in Nubia, Angola, and Guinea-Bissau. The vast geographic spread in the distribution of these findings—she has matches all over Africa through her maternal line—shows just how far the Bantu migration went, how radically it changed Africa just a few thousand years ago.

I showed Elizabeth's results to two prominent slavery historians at Boston University, John Thornton and Linda Heywood. They worked with me on *African American Lives*, and I asked them to review Elizabeth's data to see if they could narrow down the African origins of the first slave ancestor on her maternal line—the woman in her family who was first brought to the New World. They were able to rule out her matches in Nubia, Ethiopia, and Gabon because none of these countries was involved in the slave trade to Jamaica or to the United States. There was some slave trade with Cameroon, but it was insignificant. So that left us with either Angola or Guinea-Bissau. Elizabeth has more exact matches in Guinea-Bissau, but her haplogroup tends to be more common in Angola. Also, her oldest known ancestor on her maternal grandmother's line was from Virginia, which, along with other southern states, received a high percentage of slaves from Angola. So based on our genealogical research on her mother's side and her genetic analysis, Thornton and Heywood concluded that Elizabeth's original female African ancestor most probably came from Angola, along with 24 percent of the ancestors of all the African American people. In addition, based on the history of the slave trade, Thornton and Heywood also concluded that Elizabeth's ancestors probably lived near the Angolan coast, in part of what was known as the Lunda Empire, which sold large numbers of slaves, captured in wars with neighboring African tribes, to the Dutch and Portuguese.

Through DNA, we had therefore unlocked a crucial piece of Elizabeth's heritage. Despite all the white Europeans in her family tree, her mitochondrial DNA goes straight back to Africa.

It was now time for us to solve a few mysteries. Our genealogical research had been able to identify Elizabeth's third-great-grandfather on her mother's line, Robert Bond, the ship's cook from Bermuda who settled in Liverpool. He disappears from the documentary record sometime after 1851, perhaps returning to his home in Bermuda. We had been unable to trace his line back any further using available records. So we turned to DNA in the hope of learning more. But to study Elizabeth's maternal great-great-grandfather's DNA, we needed to test a male directly descended from him in her mother's family, because as a woman, Elizabeth does not carry any Y-DNA at all. One of her male cousins agreed to let us test him, and the results indicated that Elizabeth's maternal grandfather's Y-DNA belonged to the haplogroup called E1b1a. This haplogroup dominates the region south of the Sahara. It's most common among Bantu-speaking Africans, and it reaches levels of up to 90 percent among the Mandinka and the Yoruba people. Its distribution throughout Africa is often used to chart the expansion of the great Bantu migration throughout sub-Saharan Africa. It is also the most common haplogroup among African American males. About 60 percent of African American men can trace their ancestry to this branch of the family tree.

According to John Thornton and Linda Heywood, many of the Bantu speakers who share the E1b1a haplogroup come from Mozambique. But only 2 percent of the slaves who arrived in the New World came from that region of Africa. And none went to Bermuda. So John and Linda focused on another area where this haplogroup is common, one that did contribute greatly to the Bermuda slave trade. And they concluded that the male line of the Bond family hails from the Senegambia region, in the country that is today known as Sierra Leone, which is dominated by the Mende people. Our consultants' databases added credence to this theory when they revealed that Elizabeth's male cousin matches haplogroups with two people living today in Sierra Leone, both of whom are Mende.

There was one further mystery to try and solve. We wanted to see if DNA could tell us anything about the identity of Elizabeth's paternal great-grandfather—Clifford Alexander, Sr.'s father—the man who, according to family lore, was a Jewish merchant named James residing in Jamaica at the turn of the twentieth century. To map the Y-DNA of Elizabeth's paternal ancestors, we collected a sample from her father. It shows that her paternal line belongs to the haplogroup called J1e, which is a subgroup of the haplogroup J, which originated in the Near East about twenty thousand years ago, during the Ice Age. Of special significance, J1 is the most common haplogroup among Ashkenazi Jews. About 40 percent of Ashkenazi men have chromosomes in J1.

Looking at the Family Tree DNA database, we found people matching this Y-DNA in many places today: there were single matches in Spain, Hungary, Poland, Romania, Slovakia, and the Syrian Arab Republic. And all these matches identified themselves as Ashkenazi Jews. This is very strong evidence that Elizabeth's great-grandfather was in fact an Ashkenazi Jew.

Elizabeth was not surprised at this discovery. She had long believed the family stories about her grandfather's being the illegitimate child of a Jewish merchant, and as indicated earlier, there had been some circumstantial evidence to support these stories. Elizabeth was very surprised, however, by what else we learned from her father's DNA. Her father's Y-DNA, I told her, pointed to an Ashkenazi Jewish background, and his mitochondrial DNA also pointed to Europe. This, as Elizabeth and I both knew, was highly unusual. Almost 95 percent of the African American people can trace their mitochondrial DNA straight back to Africa because it is comparatively rare to be descended from a white woman who had children with a black man. Elizabeth's own mitochondrial DNA, for example, show that her mother's line goes to Angola. But her father's DNA reveals that his maternal line doesn't go to Africa at all. He belongs to the haplogroup called U6a, which is European, just like his father's line. And he has exact mitochondrial matches with people living today in the United Kingdom and the Netherlands. There is no doubt he is descended from a white woman. We don't know her name, we don't know the story, but we have incontrovertible genetic evidence that there *is* a story. Clifford Alexander, civil rights pioneer, is descended on both sides from white people. This is true for about 1 percent of the African American people. Anybody who looked solely at his Y-DNA and his mtDNA, in fact, would think he was a European man.

"Well, it just gets curiouser and curiouser," said Elizabeth. "But of course, if all of us were known only by our DNA, we'd have a whole different American history." I told her that truer words were never spoken.

The autosomal DNA testing conducted by the Broad Institute revealed that Elizabeth is a distant cousin of Stephen Colbert, the television host and satirist who was also profiled in *Faces of America*. They share eight million identical base pairs on chromosome 2, pairs 160 to 168. Elizabeth was delighted with this news and excitedly told me that she had once been on Stephen's show and felt a connection with him (that he is also extraordinarily well read and profoundly insightful is another link they share). But she and I, I think, were both still reeling from the amount of information we had gathered and processed together. We had been able to show her that some of her most treasured family stories were true. Some we had verified with a paper trail, some with DNA. And we had uncovered new stories—some wilder than anybody in her family ever could have fantasized.

"I think there's something wonderful about having certain sureties disrupted," she said, looking at her father's DNA test results. "Especially in the middle of one's life, to learn that certain things that you always thought were in place actually are much more entangled and complex and deeper than you ever could have known—that's completely fascinating. I just wish I knew all of the pieces. We happen to know a tremendous amount about Europe in my particular case, but there are still pieces that we don't know. And what does it mean if you grow up not knowing any of this—a culture that teaches you not necessarily to identify with any of that, not to dream that any of that could mean anything, could have any connection to you? There's something fabulously disruptive that shakes up the orders of things, when you draw the line in a different way than others might expect."

She considered further: "But what does that change for me? Well, it gives me a lot more to wonder about and to think about. And it gives me a more complicated way of thinking, not just about black people and blackness but about human questions, human communities, human families—and very, very tangled and fascinating human histories.

"I find myself thinking about Charlemagne," she said, as I rose to leave her home in New Haven. "He was a learned man, able perhaps to prognosticate about the direction of human history. Could he have imagined me, in his wildest, wildest, wildest imaginings into the future?"

My guess, I said, is no.

SOURCE: Henry Louis Gates, Jr., *Faces of America: How 12 Extraordinary People Discovered Their Pasts* (New York: New York University Press, 2010).

OPRAH WINFREY

OPRAH WINFREY IS one of the most famous people on earth. I wanted to involve her in this project from the moment I conceived it, because she fascinates me, as she apparently does just about everyone else. I admire her tremendously for what she's accomplished, who she is, and what she represents to African Americans. There's never been anybody in our history quite like her. This fuels my curiosity at its most basic level. I am dying to know how this woman, a descendant of illiterate slaves in Mississippi, dirt-poor scratchers of the soil, became the inimitable "Oprah," a cultural icon wherever human beings watch TV or film.

I'm also, I must admit, quite curious about the possible sources of certain aspects of her character. I think that Oprah somehow is as close to an Everyperson as any human being has ever been—she appeals to white people and black people and just about every other shade of people, males as well as females. She has an uncanny capacity to name the zeitgeist, the spirit of the time, to identify the key issues that most concern us as human beings at any given moment. And I want to know where that capacity comes from—what her family tree might tell us, if anything, about the source of this extraordinarily rare capacity for empathy and communication. Of course, there's no way to know for sure. There never is. There are tens of thousands of biographies of famous people, and none of them explain their subject fully. Yet each can teach us something, bringing us perhaps just a little closer to an explanation that makes sense. And that's what I set out to do here: get a little closer to an understanding of what makes Oprah tick by looking at her ancestors. I got a lot more than I bargained for.

Oprah Gail Winfrey was born January 29, 1954, in Kosciusko, Mississippi, a rural town just north of Jackson. Her parents were poor, young, and unmarried. Her father, Vernon Winfrey, was twenty-one years old when he fathered Oprah. Her mother, Vernita Lee, was just nineteen. Both came from families that had been in this area in Mississippi since the days of slavery. And like many African Americans of their day, they both fled the rural South—part of the Great Migration of blacks looking for better economic opportunities in northern cities. But their journeys took very different paths.

Vernon Winfrey served in the army, got an honorable discharge, and moved to Nashville, Tennessee, taking with him the work ethic that he had learned on his father's farm. By the late 1950s, he was reaping the benefits of his decision to go north. He ran his own barbershop in Nashville—which he still does and at which he works every day—and his own house.

By contrast, Vernita moved to Milwaukee in 1954 and felt compelled to leave her infant behind for several years, to be raised by her maternal grandparents, Hattie Mae and Earlist Lee. Oprah had little understanding of why her family had been torn apart. She was told that her mother had moved to Milwaukee to have "a better life" there. She grew up confused about basic aspects of her family. But she has vivid, formative memories of those years she spent with her grandmother, Hattie Mae Lee. And it seems that right from the start she knew she would grow up to achieve more than the Jim Crow South was allowing her family to achieve.

"I remember," Oprah said, "standing on the back porch and looking through the screen door, and my grandmother was boiling clothes in a big black pot. And she said, 'Oprah Gail, I want you to pay attention to me now. I want you to watch me, because one day you're gonna have to learn how to do this for yourself.' And I watched and looked like I was paying attention but distinctly recall a feeling that 'No, I'm not. This will not be my life.' She worked for a white family and used to always say to me, 'What you want to do is grow up and get yourself some good white folks. You want to get good white folks, like me.' Because her white folks let her bring clothes home, and many of the things that we had came from her good white folks. And I think her idea of good white folks was just that they give you things and you get to bring food home. But I also think it meant for her that you at least got to keep a piece of your dignity—a piece—and that's the best you could do. And so she'd say, 'I want you to grow up and get some good white folks.' And, you know, I regret that she didn't live to see that I did get some good white folks workin' for me, yeah. She couldn't imagine this life."

Oprah was observing firsthand the rural poverty that drove so many African Americans northward and the forces of racism that permeated every aspect of life in the Jim Crow South. But Kosciusko was also the only place she'd ever called home, and before she was old enough fully to understand its limitations, her mother insisted that she join her in the North. And so the six-year-old Oprah moved to Milwaukee. The difference between life in Mississippi and life in Milwaukee was profound, and the experience was deeply traumatic for her.

Prior to the move, Oprah says she had no relationship with or memory of her mother. "I'd only been raised by my grandmother," she said. "I knew I had a mother, but all those years my primary relationship was with my grandmother, and all of a sudden just one day I'm packed up and put in a car and told, 'You're gonna go live with your mother now.' It was horrible. But something inside me clicked. I knew that I was going to have to take care of myself—that I didn't have my grandmother anymore."

In Milwaukee, Oprah's mother was collecting welfare, working as a maid to earn a bit of extra money—and starting a new family. "My mother had another child," remembered Oprah. "And she was living in the home of a woman named Ms. Miller. And Ms. Miller was a colored lady, but a very light-skinned colored lady who did not like colored people."

Oprah began to cry at the memory of that household. "I instantly knew that Ms. Miller did not like me because of the color of my skin," she said. "I was too dark, and Ms. Miller would say it. My half sister Pat was five years younger than me, and she was light-skinned, and my mother was staying there because Ms. Miller loved my half sister. And I was put out on the porch to sleep. I wasn't even allowed in the house to sleep, and it was because I was brown-skinned, which didn't compute for me because my mother was brown-skinned, too. But I realized she was okay to Ms. Miller because she had Pat."

I found this story very moving—and deeply illustrative of the horrible ways that African Americans have internalized racism, the ways we've visited pain on each other. It is an unfortunate but vital part of our collective history, an experience that, sadly, is shared by thousands and thousands of people. Our people have long been color-struck. I know because I experienced those feelings myself. I remember, as a kid, being proud that my father was visibly mixed—that his whole side of the Gates family was light. Many of them even looked white; some could—and did—"pass," and they had "good hair," straight hair. And I thought that was wonderful. You didn't want to look like Nat King Cole, even with his beautiful process, his glistening chemically straightened hair. You didn't want to be too "dark."

Oprah recalls sensing this situation the minute she walked into the house where her mother was living. Nevertheless, she was powerless to change things—and her life began to spin out of control. Between the ages of six and fourteen, she moved back and forth between Milwaukee and Nashville, alternating between the homes of her mother and father, growing ever more isolated until disaster struck.

"I was nine years old," she said, her voice trembling. "And I got sent back to Milwaukee for the summer and ended up staying there, because my mother had said that she was going to marry her boyfriend and we were going to be a family. But the summer of my ninth year, things changed immensely for me, because I was raped by the boyfriend of my mother's cousin, who my mother was also living with. He became a constant sexual molester of mine. I thought it was my fault. I thought I was the only person that had ever happened to, that it would not be safe for me to tell. And so I was sexually molested from the time I was ten to the time I was fourteen in that house."

This monster abused Oprah publicly and openly, leaving unimaginable scars. "He practically told everybody," she recalled. "He'd say, 'I'm in love with Oprah. I'm gonna marry her, she's smarter than all of you.' He would say it, and we'd go off to places together. Everybody knew it. And they just chose to look the other way. They were in denial."

Alone, with no one to trust or confide in, Oprah saw her adolescence become a living hell. She wouldn't fully understand the profound trauma of these events for many years. Indeed, there was a time in the black community when the sexual molestation of children was considered to be something alien to the black experience, something that happened only in white families, like suicide, supposedly. "I was about forty when I stopped thinking it was my fault," she says. "I got all my therapy on *The Oprah Winfrey Show.*"

School was Oprah's only respite, a place where she could feel safe and in control. Her grandmother, Hattie Lee, had taught her to read at an early age, and this gave her a great advantage. "I'd grown up reading," Oprah recalled, "and when I went to my kindergarten class, on the first day of kindergarten I was so bored. I thought, I'm gonna lose my mind with these kids sitting there with their ABC blocks. So I wrote my kindergarten teacher a letter. I sat down and I wrote, 'Dear Miss New.' And I wrote down all the words that I knew. I said, 'I know words.' I knew 'Mississippi,' 'hippopotamus,' 'Nicodemus.' I wrote down all the big words I knew. And so she said, 'Who did this?' And I got marched off to the principal's office, and I got put in the first grade the next day. And then they skipped me to second because I was such a good reader."

This was an integrated school. Oprah never went to a segregated school. But Miss New was a black teacher. And the fact that Oprah's first teacher in kindergarten was a black teacher deeply impressed her. "If she had been white," Oprah wondered, "would I have had the courage to write that letter? I don't know. I remember going home and saying, 'I have a colored teacher.' And she was colored like me. She was brown-skinned. So I felt like I could connect to her and that she would understand me. And so I got myself out of that kindergarten class."

Hearing Oprah talk about her early schooling, I was particularly struck by the contrast between the reinforcing climate she discovered in her school and the alienation she experienced within her home, especially hearing the horrific stories of her sexual abuse. The very idea of education transformed her—school had clearly given her an enormous amount of gratification and self-assurance. At the same time, school could not protect her from the trauma of daily life in her mother's house.

By the time she was fourteen, Oprah was living on the streets of Milwaukee. "I became a sexually promiscuous teenager," she recalled. "I ran away from home. I was going to be put into a detention center and ended up being sent to my father instead. I was out of control."

Oprah's father, Vernon Winfrey, provided a lifeline. The authority that emanated from him, the order and financial security of his Nashville home, and the role model offered by his new wife combined to give Oprah discipline and stability—and a chance to save herself. All of this would eventually lead to a profound transformation. What's more, Vernon provided a renewed focus on education, reinforcing Oprah's earlier passion for learning, which the abuse had served to obscure.

"On the Winfrey side of my family," Oprah recalled, "education was everything. I remember coming home once, and I had a C and my father said, 'C's are not allowed in this house.' And we were sitting in the kitchen, and he opened the door and said, 'You can stay out there with those people if you're gonna bring a C because you are not a C student! If you were a C student, I would let you get C's, but you're not a C student, so you can't bring 'em in this house.'"

However, before any transformation could occur, Oprah was forced to endure another terrible ordeal. When she moved back to Nashville, her father struggled to instill order and discipline in her life. He didn't know the deep, dark secrets of her abuse. He knew only that she was troubled, and he tried to respond. But her father could not imagine the true depths of her problems, or their origin. "He said to me that there would be no association with boys. He didn't know there had already been an association. Because I was pregnant when I came to my father, and my father didn't know it. So he sat down and said to me that he would rather see a daughter of his dead, floating down the Cumberland River, than to bring shame on the Winfrey name. And I knew I was pregnant. I thought about killing myself."

The stress caused Oprah to go into premature labor. Her legs started to swell, and her father sent her to see a doctor—accompanied by her stepmother, Zelma Winfrey. "We went to the pediatrician," Oprah recalled. "And the pediatrician says, 'Either this is the biggest tumor I've ever seen in my whole life or you're pregnant. Are you pregnant?' My stepmother was there in the room. So I said, 'No.' And so he asked my stepmother to leave the room, and then I broke down and cried, and oh, my God, it was bad."

Oprah then had to go back home and tell her father. She doesn't recall what he did or said, only that he was devastated by the news and that she was overwhelmed with shame, falling further into a deep depression, consumed by thoughts of suicide. The story is harrowing—and its ending was tragic. Oprah went into labor shortly after seeing the doctor and delivered a baby who would die a few months later. With that, her father took full control.

"My father," she recalled, "came in and said to me, 'This is your second chance.' He said, 'We were prepared to take this baby and let you continue your schooling, but God has chosen to take this baby, and so I think God is giving you a second chance. If I were you, I would use it.'"

With this second chance, Oprah transformed her life. Thanks to her father's discipline—and with her stepmother's encouragement—Oprah focused on her studies, won a scholarship to study speech, drama, and English at Tennessee State University, where she excelled, realizing all of her enormous intellectual potential. At the age of nineteen, she began co-anchoring the news at Nashville's CBS affiliate. And by 1977 she had moved to Baltimore's ABC affiliate, before taking a new job in Chicago seven years later, which would catapult her to the unimaginable heights she has since attained.

Hearing Oprah tell me the story of her early life enabled me to begin to see how she had been shaped, positively and negatively, by her family. And I wanted to find out more about these various family members, about who had raised them, where and how, under what circumstances. I found ample material on both her father's and her mother's sides. Oprah's maternal grandparents were Earlist Lee, born in 1887 in Hinds County, Mississippi, and Hattie Mae Presley, born around 1900. Oprah lived with them for the first six years of her life. They had a tremendous impact on shaping her childhood, even more than was usual for someone of Oprah's generation. Indeed, Oprah is able to describe her grandparents' daily life in vivid, eloquent detail.

"I slept with my grandmother in a big poster bed in the living room," she said. "We had a hearth, and the living room had the bed in it. There was just one big room with the hearth, the bed. People would come to visit, and there'd be the chairs in front of the bed. We called it the front room. Behind the front room was the kitchen. There was no running water. To the side was another room where my grandfather slept. My job in the morning was to go to the well and bring water, then to take the one cow out to pasture. Then my job was to do whatever my grandmother wanted me to do—get the eggs from the chicken without breaking the eggs. When it was hog-killing time, I was the one picking up all the intestines, and I would flick things off here and there. I had all the worst jobs."

Oprah remembers her grandmother making lye soap and homemade shoes and sewing their clothes. "It was a really big deal to get store-bought clothes or patent-leather shoes," she marveled. "It was a rural life. There was no indoor plumbing, no bathrooms. I bathed only on Saturdays. And it was my job to empty the slop jar in the morning. We had the slop jar under the bed. It was my job to keep the irons clean—because we had these irons for ironing clothes, and so when you used starch, they'd have to be washed off and scraped. It was my job to do that. I was a busy little girl."

Hearing her recount the basic level of her family's existence, the amount of grinding labor it took merely to provide the most fundamental features of daily existence, one can't help but be amazed at how far Oprah has come— she is almost like a character in a fairy tale. Yet her memory is absolutely correct: The rural poverty she describes was typical, indeed pervasive, among black people in the South. Oprah grew up in a community of sharecroppers, people bound to the soil by a system that was intended to replace slavery with its mirror image, a system of peonage to which most blacks were chained economically, as surely as they had been chained in slavery. The vast majority of former slaves became sharecroppers, almost as soon as slavery ended, and very few were able to break out of this system and own their own land.

Oprah's father, Vernon, recognized this and encouraged the education of his children as strongly as he could. Unfortunately, Hattie Lee, Oprah's maternal grandmother, had a different imaginative horizon, a horizon delimited in scope by the confines of the sharecropping system, Jim Crow segregation, and its various complex legacies. No doubt because of this set of experiences, she could not imagine encouraging her granddaughter to dream of getting an education so that she could become a doctor or some other kind of professional. Instead Hattie Mae wanted Oprah to grow up and "work for good white folks." And, given the severe limits of her own options, this was a noble and loving enough goal to which to aspire for her granddaughter.

But curiously, one generation back, Hattie Mae's family had taken a very different approach to the harsh system in which they found themselves. Hattie's mother was Amanda Winters, born around 1874 in Kosciusko, Mississippi. Amanda was the daughter of Pearce and Henrietta Winters, both former slaves in Mississippi. All these people seemed to have prized education. Amanda attended a freedmen's school, and for their time she and her siblings were quite accomplished individuals. Her brother, Jesse Winters, attended Wilberforce University, and her sister, Matilda, was a math teacher. Amanda herself taught public school English to black children in the 1890s and 1900s. She seems to have risen high in the community as well. She married Nelson Alexander Presley in 1893. They had eight children together, including Hattie Mae. What's more, after Nelson died (sometime around 1907), Amanda married Charles Bullocks, also widowed and seemingly well-to-do for a black man of his time.

Digging deeper, we discovered something most unusual about Amanda. When the NAACP was founded in 1909, one of its biggest supporters was a visionary philanthropist named Julius Rosenwald. Rosenwald had made a fortune with Sears, Roebuck and Company, and he was really passionate about what we would have called back then "Negro-white relations." Starting in 1912, he gave millions of dollars to help rural black communities set up elementary schools. Remarkably, in 1929, Oprah's great-grandmother Amanda became a trustee of one of these schools—a very rare feat for a woman of her day, white or black. We do not know exactly why she was appointed, but it is probably a sign of how respected she was in her community. Amanda was clearly a very accomplished, able woman. According to our research, she organized not only the school but also the Methodist church in Kosciusko.

How did Amanda's daughter Hattie Mae end up in such difficult straits just one generation later? The answer is illustrative of the precarious status of all African Americans in the Jim Crow South. Whatever gains they made were inevitably fragile, sometimes including even the ownership of land, the crucial variable for the accumulation of wealth in this country.

Records show that Amanda and her second husband, Charles Bullocks, borrowed money from the Federal Land Bank. After Bullocks died, Amanda defaulted on payments, and the bank seized their land. Amanda offered to pay her debts with money from her children, but the banks wanted the land. According to Katherine Esters, who is Oprah's cousin and the family's unofficial historian, they wanted it because they didn't think it was right that a black man—and now a black woman—had owned so much land. So the bank seized it all, along with all of Amanda's belongings. She then moved to her first husband's property and lived in a shanty for the rest of her life, dying sometime around 1940. Thus she was unable to preserve her briefly held prosperity, much less pass it on to her children, although her first husband's land did remain in the family as a more lasting form of wealth.

This story is tragic, of course, but Oprah was thrilled to learn that at the height of segregation her great-grandmother was working to educate African Americans. "It feels like I've carried it on," she said. "It feels like she would be the kind of person you would've had to have been to be able to stand up in a room. I mean, I feel it myself now when I go into a corporate room and I'm the only black face in that room and I'm the only female. I often say that

'I go forth alone, and I stand as ten thousand,' which is a line from one of Maya's poems."

I nodded in agreement. Oprah's maternal ancestors clearly shared her willpower and her passion for education and the ownership of property.

Oprah now wanted to learn more about these people from whom she descended, and I did my best to oblige her, even though the chasm of slavery began to make things very difficult. Amanda Winters's parents were the eldest generation on her maternal line that we could find. Their names were Henrietta and Pearce Winters. The 1870 census tells us that Pearce was born a slave around 1849, and the 1880 census tells us that his wife, Henrietta, was born a slave in Mississippi around 1854 (Henrietta's last name is not recorded). This census also tells us that by 1880, Pearce and Henrietta were living in Attala County, Mississippi, with their five children, including Oprah's great-grandmother Amanda. Sadly, we know nothing more about these people.

Oprah was disappointed to hear that we could not with certainty trace Amanda's line any further than this. But by going back a branch along Oprah's maternal line, we were able to learn more about the ancestry of her maternal grandfather, Earlist Lee. Earlist's parents were Harold and Elizabeth Lee. According to the 1870 census, Harold was born a slave around 1855 in Hines County, Mississippi, whereas Elizabeth was born in freedom, also in Mississippi, sometime around 1875. The same census data revealed that Harold's parents—Oprah's great-great-grandparents—were named Grace and John Lee. They both were born slaves in Mississippi in 1833, which means they spent the first thirty-two years of their lives as a white man's property.

It is very difficult to find any records documenting the lives of our slave ancestors during the years that they were held in bondage. As we have seen, the slave system stripped them by design of the last names that they created for themselves, as part of a larger process of officially and legally denying their humanity. Indeed, names, records, language, family structures—all were intentionally repressed by the slave owners.

In Oprah's case, by searching over the records of slave owners in Mississippi, we were extremely lucky. We found an 1860 slave schedule for someone called S. E. Lee, who owned a female slave, age twenty-six, which is how old Oprah's great-great-grandmother Grace would have been in 1860. S. E. Lee also owned a male slave, age twenty-six, which is how old her great-great-grandfather John would have been in 1860. Moreover—and this is very important—he owned a male slave, age five, which is how old Oprah's great-grandfather Harry Lee would've been in 1860. No other slaves in the county match these three ages and relationships of proximity to a white person named Lee. You don't exactly have to be Sherlock Holmes to deduce that these people are most probably Oprah's ancestors, even though they stand nameless in their slave owner's records.

Of course, matching ages and genders of slaves listed in the 1850 or 1860 slave schedules with freedmen and -women listed in the 1870 census is not absolute proof of identity, but it is overwhelmingly likely that these three people are Oprah's ancestors on this side of her family, her direct ancestors who were born into slavery and remained in slavery until the end of the Civil War. We were especially fortunate in that this is the only slave owner named Lee in the state of Mississippi whose slaves' ages matched that of her ancestors. And we looked at every Lee in the entire state.

Oprah was deeply moved when I showed her S. E. Lee's slave schedule. This seemingly simple document, almost 150 years old, listing human beings as objects of property, bore evidence of her ancestors' existence. There were her great-great-grandparents, written down as possessions, their ages and color recorded, but not their names. Oprah began to cry. And she cried, I think, because she was shocked to see two human beings from whom she is directly descended listed merely as nameless objects along with "the chickens and the cows," as she put it.

I asked her whether her family ever talked about slavery when she was growing up. She said no, absolutely not. "When you grow up poor and on welfare," she continued, "you don't have time to think about what came before." This is true, of course, but then I suggested that there might be another reason as well—a reason I've contemplated many times regarding the lives of all black Americans, be they rich, poor, or somewhere in between. For years and years, we were embarrassed about slavery. We were embarrassed about our slave past. That's why I think it's so extraordinary that our generation is embracing our slave heritage so very enthusiastically—slavery, the proverbial skeleton in America's historical closet. Some African Americans were so embarrassed by the fact of slavery that they would claim that their family members never had been slaves, a historical impossibility! Slavery has traditionally been difficult for all Americans to deal with honestly and openly. But this has changed with a new generation of African Americans hungry for all the details of their family's past, even the most painful and humiliating ones. We now realize that ultimately these are tales of survival and triumph.

Oprah agrees. "When I did the movie *Beloved*," she said, "it was not as successful at the box office as any of us would have wanted it to be, and I was asked by so many press people, 'Why would you want to tell this story?' I wanted to tell the story because I find such pride in the story. My strength comes from their strength. That's one of the reasons I work so hard. And I feel like I have not even the right to be tired, ever, because I know I come from this. I didn't know names and backgrounds, but I know I come from this." Indeed, and so do we all.

At this point we had traced Oprah's maternal lineage as far back as the written record would allow. So we turned to her paternal line—and found another wealth of fascinating stories. Oprah's paternal grandfather, Elmore Winfrey, was born in 1901 in Poplar Creek, Mississippi. Her paternal grandmother was Beatrice Woods, born in 1903 in Carroll County. Oprah knew Elmore and Beatrice. Though she saw them rarely after she left Mississippi, she heard plenty of stories about them from her father, and these stories accord with the records that we were able to find.

In some ways the Winfreys were archetypal citizens of the Jim Crow South, where economic opportunities for African Americans were exceedingly scarce. Like the vast majority of their peers, they were sharecroppers, and their lives were brutally harsh. However, in one crucial way they were different. Most sharecroppers were illiterate, because whites wanted them that way. If black farmers couldn't read or count, then they couldn't manage their own transactions. That made them vulnerable, and they could be taken advantage of. (Indeed, if you look at contracts written in the Jim Crow years between blacks and whites, blacks were often paid less than their fair share.) There were exceptions, though. By all accounts, Elmore and Beatrice Winfrey were two of them. Elmore could read and write and understand math. He was reportedly a good businessman who successfully managed his own farm. We found a land deed revealing that in 1942 Elmore spent $3,425 on a 104-acre piece of land, ten miles southwest of Poplar Creek. This is truly remarkable for a black person who lived at his time, either in the North or in the South, but especially in the South.

Oprah was not at all surprised by this news. "I've heard great stories," she said, "about my grandfather being the businessman that he was." She also heard all about the vicious racism that surrounded the lives of her grandparents and their neighbors—and how education offered the only way out of this morass. "My father," she said, "often tells this story about my grandfather not wanting his wife and daughters to have to go and work for the white man or work in the white man's kitchen, because he understood, many times, that, you know, Mr. White Man would be abusing those women and that there would be nothing that he could do about it. What he always wanted to do was to be able to be the provider in such a way for his family that he would never have to put the women in the family in that position. He understood that education was the open door to freedom for them. So thanks to him, all my father's siblings were well-educated, and every time I went to their house, that's all anybody ever talked about. 'So-and-So was in school, So-and-So's finishing school and graduating, So-and-So's going to college.' It was where I got that belief system. It came from that part of the family."

Talking to Oprah's father, Vernon, we learned another remarkable thing about his parents. Vernon told us that whenever his father encountered white people, Elmore would tip his hat and say "Yes, sir" and "No, sir." Vernon believes that his father felt compelled to do this, and Vernon had trouble accepting that. He feared that his father, however much he may have loved him, was just another Uncle Tom. But years later Vernon was shocked to learn that Elmore was quite the opposite—and that in fact in 1965 he and Beatrice housed two civil-rights workers in a back bedroom of their home. Vernon couldn't believe what his father had done, how much of his economic stability and security he was willing to risk to further this political cause, to which he had seemingly been oblivious for decades.

According to Vernon, the sheriff came to Elmore—a white sheriff, of course—and said to him, "You're one of the most respected Negras in this area. Now, other black people think that you're sending the message that it's okay to support the civil-rights movement." And Elmore replied, "Well, if you want to know what message I'm sending, go to that civil-rights march on Sunday, because I'll be sitting in the front row, sending my message—it's time for a change!"

Oprah had never heard this story before I told it to her. And it surprised her, the same way it astonished her father when he first heard it. It was as if her grandfather, a mild-mannered man, conservative in his habits, had become a fiery black militant, seemingly overnight.

We could not confirm Vernon's account of his father's conversation with the sheriff, but we were able to track down the two civil-rights workers whom Elmore housed—Luther Mallett, an African American from Kosciusko, and Matthew Rinaldi, a white college student from Long Island. Both testify to the role Elmore played in the movement in Mississippi. Indeed, they said that both Elmore and Beatrice were strong supporters of the civil-rights movement and that they had placed themselves in great danger by housing them. They recall that the couple was subjected to violent threats and that there was a cross burning on the lawn of the Winfrey home. They also told us that after a freedom house in nearby McCool, Mississippi, had been burned down by local whites, Elmore used his carpentry skills to help rebuild it, making the dangerous trip between Kosciusko and McCool even as armed Klansmen were traveling the same roads.

Oprah was pleased to hear these stories. They ultimately reduced her to tears of pride. And going back another generation on her paternal line, we found even more remarkable ancestors. Elmore's parents were Sanford Winfrey, born in 1872 in Poplar Creek, and Ella Staples, born in 1874 in Choctaw County, Mississippi. Ella's family can be traced forward to the Staple Singers, who are Oprah's distant cousins. Her husband, Sanford, was a farmer and may have been a teacher as well. Many towns in rural Mississippi had a one-room schoolhouse for black children. Vernon claimed that Sanford was the head teacher and that he taught all subjects through all ages. Friends and neighbors even called him "the professor."

We couldn't find a record of Sanford's being paid to teach, so we cannot confirm Vernon's claim. But Vernon was able to evoke a sense of the importance that education played in his family's life. He says that his father, Elmore, often spoke of how Vernon's grandfather Sanford insisted that his children learn to read and write—and that Elmore had two sisters who became schoolteachers.

Going back one more generation on Oprah's paternal line, we come to Sanford Winfrey's parents, Oprah's great-great-grandparents, Constantine and Violet Winfrey. And here Oprah's deep roots grow even more fascinating to me. In fact, the story of Constantine Winfrey is one of the most remarkable stories about a former slave that I have ever encountered.

Constantine Winfrey was born in October 1836 in Georgia and was married to a woman named Violet, who was born in North Carolina in 1839. She didn't have a last name, or if she did, it was never recorded. It seems that Violet was acquired in North Carolina, where she is listed as having been born, and then shipped somehow to Mississippi, no doubt because of the cotton boom. Constantine and Violet were married around 1859. They had eight children together.

Oprah knew that the Winfrey name came from this man, Constantine—she had heard of him in her family's lore, and she knew him to be the highest branch on the family tree—but she'd never heard anything more about him. And she had no idea where his last name came from. I think we found out. Constantine Winfrey probably took his name because he was a slave owned by a man named Absalom F. Winfrey. There is no concrete proof that Constantine was owned by Absalom or that he took his name, but in the 1870 census Constantine is listed as living three houses down from Absalom, and Absalom, like Constantine, also moved to Mississippi from Georgia. Furthermore, an 1850 slave schedule indicates that Absalom had seven slaves, the profile of one of whom fits Constantine exactly.

As for who Constantine was, the 1870 census indicates that at that time he and his wife were living with their five children and that both Constantine and Violet were illiterate. This is of course to be expected, since almost no slaves could read. But I learned something remarkable about Constantine, something that would prove to be consistent among later generations of Winfreys, including Oprah. Ten years later, in the 1880 census, Constantine and Violet are listed again, but now Constantine can read. And he can write.

Oprah and I were dumbfounded. At thirty-five, as a newly freed slave, he couldn't read and he couldn't write. At forty-five, just ten years later, he could do both. In ten years he had mastered literacy as an ex-slave. And that's while he was still having to work as a farmer every day, pick cotton, earn a living, raise and take care of a growing family. What's more, Oprah's great-great-grandfather not only embraced education himself—he emphasized education to his children and to the rest of the colored section in his hometown. We located a report from the Montgomery County School Board dated 1906 indicating that Constantine Winfrey moved an entire schoolhouse to his property so that the black children in his town could get an education.

Why did people on both sides of Oprah's family care so deeply about literacy and education? We don't have a simple answer. Even Oprah didn't know. But she was affected strongly by the revelation. "I can't even begin to explain what that is," she said, "but I think it's deep that that is where I've come from. I mean, I've always sort of understood on the periphery how important education is, and also inside myself, but I didn't know that that was the root of where I came from."

Indeed, as we have seen, through several of her ancestral lines, Oprah is at the tail end of a long chain of people who loved education. While I cannot prove this scientifically, I happen to believe that this is why she is who she is. Or rather, it is deeply reflective of who she is. But there's another side to the story of her roots, another element that has defined her family since Constantine. And that element is the ownership of land, a factor as crucial to the shaping of her family as education was.

I wanted to discover how Constantine supported himself after slavery. Where did he get this land that he used to feed his family for generations, the land to which he moved this schoolhouse? How did an illiterate slave in 1870 eventually come to own acres and acres of prime farmland within just a couple of decades? As it turns out, Constantine had purchased the land in two different parcels. And the story of those purchases, contained in the land deeds and mortgage agreements, is not only remarkable, it is the only story of its kind that many other historians of this period and I have ever encountered.

Constantine bought the first parcel in 1876 from a white man by the name of John R. Watson. It was obtained through a highly unusual means of payment. According to the deed, Constantine agreed to give Watson eight bales of "lint," or cleaned cotton, in exchange for eighty acres of land. But there was a catch: Constantine didn't have any cotton. To get his land, he had to grow it and pick it first. The deed stipulates that Watson give Constantine usage rights on the eighty acres with the understanding that in two years Constantine would produce his eight bales. Each bale of lint cotton had to weigh four hundred pounds. So that's thirty-two hundred pounds of cotton. To get this much clean cotton, Constantine probably had to grow and harvest about four times as much, because of the debris and detritus contained in harvested cotton. In other words, Constantine had to grow and pick and clean more than six tons of cotton, and do so in two years!

Now, remember: John Watson is a white man, and this is 1876, the year Reconstruction ended and the Old South really started rising again. Needless to say, this was a very bad time for blacks. Moreover, throughout the 1870s the entire country was in terrible economic shape. There was essentially a depression that lasted the whole decade. So white people were poor, and black people were poorer. And these are the circumstances under which Constantine signs this agreement, promising that he would harvest this monster load of cotton in just two years. In addition, the agreement stated that if he could not deliver the eight bales of cotton in the allotted time period, he would be forced to vacate the land and lose all the cotton he had picked. In effect, Constantine Winfrey signed a two-year mortgage, with full payment due at the end of the agreed-upon time. It was all or nothing by the end of those two years. To me this sounds like an absolutely impossible set of tasks to fulfill.

But somehow Constantine pulled it off. And we know that because we found two deeds, both dated 1881, indicating that Constantine Winfrey had satisfied his obligation and owned his land free and clear. What's more, we also found a third deed, from 1882, indicating that Constantine had purchased a second plot of land, another eighty acres adjacent to the Watson plot. He paid $250 for this plot, which was a lot of money in 1882, and which indicates that he must have been doing very well developing his first eighty acres.

So Constantine managed to be a thrifty, productive farmer at a time when the status and power of black people were falling apart in the South. Constantine Winfrey somehow, through sheer grit and energy and determination, managed to thrive. Not only was his land deed unusual, it was possibly unique. I could find no other instance in which a black man used cotton as the payment of a mortgage in the former slaveholding South.

Oprah rightly sees this land as the heroic monument it surely is, for this was the very first property that any member of her family ever owned. It was this farm that sustained and supported her family for generations. Just as important, it was this farm that played a crucial role in furthering the progress of Poplar Creek's black community, by becoming the literal foundation for their education. This is fascinating to a historian like myself, because it's a patent

reminder that the black community never consisted of one economic or social class. It had parts, or economic subdivisions. Even in the earliest years
following slavery, the black community had a very distinct class structure, a
structure that was sometimes based on color, sometimes based on education,
sometimes based on property ownership. Among the slaves freed following
the Civil War, this was really the start of the black middle class. And of all
these factors contributing to class status, property ownership was most important, because it had the potential of being the longest-lasting.

Stories such as those of Constantine Winfrey are all too rare in our textbooks. If we encountered this story in a film, either Watson would abscond
with the eight bales of cotton or the Klan would burn Constantine out shortly
after he had constructed his new home! Tragically, we know that such betray-
als did occur all too frequently. But such success stories like Constantine's, no
matter how rare, reveal how truly complex and variegated was the multi-
layered set of economic and social relationships between black people and
white people in the postbellum southern United States. Stories such as these
are no doubt far more common than previously imagined, and they wait to
be discovered in the historical records of our individual ancestors, hidden under the lush foliage of the branches of our family trees.

Constantine Winfrey's remarkable story is also where the paper trail of
Oprah Gail Winfrey's family tree ends. Constantine and his wife outlived
slavery and made their respective marks on history. Prior to them, however,
there's no written record of any of Oprah's ancestors, at least none we've
yet been able to find. The slave system obliterated any vestige of them. So
now it was time to turn to DNA in the hopes of tracing her family all the
way back to Africa.

Before we conducted her DNA analysis, I asked Oprah how she'd felt
about Africa when she was growing up—was it somewhere to which she
wanted to be connected? Or was she embarrassed about the images of
Africans she saw on television and in films? Today she is deeply connected
to Africa, devoting large amounts of her time and resources to humanitarian
causes there, but she freely admits that when growing up she was embarrassed by her African roots, just as many of us in our generation were. "I
was ashamed," she responded. "If anybody asked, 'You from Africa?' in
school, I didn't want anybody to talk about it. And if it was ever discussed
in any classroom I was in, it was always about the Pygmies and the, you
know, primitive and barbaric behavior of Africans. And so I remember
wanting to get over that period really quickly. The bare-breasted *National
Geographic* pictures? I was embarrassed by all of it. I was one of those
people who felt, 'I'm not African, I'm American.' They were primitive."

Oprah's honesty was quite refreshing. And I daresay her views were held by most African Americans until very recently. As a preadolescent I recoiled just as Oprah did. But also like Oprah, when I saw positive images of Africa during the Black Power era, and then when I started to study Africa in college and in graduate school, as I began to understand more, I began to feel a deep connection to the place and its people. Today, like most African Americans, Oprah sees Africa as it really is—a vast continent, full of diverse cultures, ancient civilizations, and boundless beauty. After centuries of separation, we're eager to reconnect on many levels—spiritually, economically, and politically.

I asked Oprah what she most hoped DNA would answer about her African ancestry. She told me that she's often been told she was a Zulu—a descendant of that great South African nation who fought so hard and so effectively against the British for so many years. She said, "When I'm in Africa, I always feel that I look Zulu. I feel connected to the Zulu tribe." The Zulus are legendary, and Oprah has talked about her possible Zulu connection more than once on her television program. She said to me that it would be a great shock if it turned out she was not a Zulu. I hoped, for her sake, that the test results would verify her instincts.

But Oprah's DNA told a different story. Our analysis of her mitochondrial DNA, which bears evidence of her maternal line's lineage, revealed that Oprah shares genetic traits with people in three parts of Africa: the Kpelle people in Liberia, the Bamileke people in Cameroon, and a Bantu-speaking tribe in Zambia. We also found identical matches to her among the Gullah people in South Carolina.

These results meant she could not be descended from a Zulu. Indeed, as it turns out, none of the Africans brought to America as slaves had Zulu heritage. The Zulu homeland in southern Africa was simply too far away from the main centers of the trade for any Zulu person to have been captured and sold into the transatlantic slave trade.

Oprah needed a moment to process this information. She still feels that spiritually she is a Zulu—which is a very healthy way to think about our putative African or European ancestry. And despite not being of Zulu descent, Oprah has a very rich African genetic heritage nonetheless: Zambia, Cameroon, Liberia—her genes are spread all over the continent. Indeed, as I explained to her, Oprah's DNA shows up in so many different places because of the history of Africa. She is herself living proof of how, over centuries, even millennia, tribes migrated great distances, and people were taken away as captives in wars, or sold into slavery, or married into other tribes.

Discussing her results with the historians John Thornton and Linda Heywood, I tried to find out where Oprah's first enslaved ancestor might have come from. The Bantu in Zambia, according to Thornton and Heywood, were generally not victims of the transatlantic slave trade. They were simply too isolated, and so, for the most part, were Oprah's Bamileke ancestors, who lived in the interior of modern Cameroon. This means that Oprah's other exact match—her DNA hit among the Kpelle people in Liberia—most likely points toward the origin of her first enslaved matrilineal ancestor.

Indeed, this result, combined with her DNA match among the Gullah people in South Carolina, squares nicely with the history of the slave trade, according to Thornton and Heywood.

The Gullah were a very unusual group of enslaved Africans. During the eighteenth century, they were brought to islands off South Carolina and Georgia from an African region that encompassed modern-day Senegal, Liberia, and Angola. Prized for their skills in harvesting rice, these people were able to remain on these isolated islands for generations, largely sheltered from direct contact with whites, who preferred to live away from the pestilential coast—and thus they were able to develop their own unique language and culture, which have been handed down from generation to generation along with their own distinctive DNA signatures.

According to Thornton and Heywood, the fact that Oprah's DNA has been found among the Gullah people suggests that her first matrilineal ancestor came to the United States through South Carolina and that that woman's owner later moved down to Mississippi, leading eventually to the birth of Oprah's oldest known female ancestor, Henrietta Winters, born in Mississippi around 1850. From South Carolina we can trace a path back across the Atlantic to the region of Africa now called Liberia. We don't know who owned Oprah's first enslaved matrilineal ancestor in America, nor do we know her name. But taking the genetic evidence and this historical evidence together, both Thornton and Heywood agreed that it is highly likely that Oprah was descended from the Kpelle people in Liberia and that her ancestor most likely either was captured in a battle or became a slave as the result of a marital dispute, as was custom in this region. Thus I felt very confident telling Oprah that she shares ancestry with the three hundred thousand Kpelle people who still live in the rain forests of central Liberia.

Oprah was stunned by the news. "That's me," she said wistfully, looking at the charts of her DNA that I had handed her. "I'm Kpelle. I feel empowered by this." And no doubt the Kpelle will welcome Oprah as a long-lost sister, just as warmly as the Zulu have done.

Oprah's admixture results were just as surprising. As we have seen throughout this book, many African Americans claim a considerable degree of Native American ancestry, but most have little or none. Oprah defies this trend; her admixture results are 8 percent Native American and 3 percent Asian. Since these two results can code for each other, we can conclude that Oprah has 11 percent Native American ancestry, placing her among the 5 percent of African Americans who have a significant amount of this genetic heritage. And this is probably the result of the proximity of blacks and Indians in her ancestors' home in Mississippi in the early nineteenth century, before the Trail of Tears in the 1830s.

This concluded our research. When it had begun, Oprah had lived for the past two decades as one of the most famous people on earth, but also as someone who was unable to name her great-great-grandmother, much less assert the identity of her maternal ancestor's original African tribe. By the time we said good-bye, all that had changed. She shared an exact genetic match with an African human being who identifies herself as a Kpelle today. She was the heir of Constantine, a remarkable entrepreneur; of Amanda, a devoted educator; of Elmore and Beatrice, who risked all they had for civil rights. Taken together, the recovery of these ancestors—even the bare-bones stories that we've been able to piece together—help to explain why it would perhaps not surprise some of these ancestors that their descendant had become the most famous African American in the world.

SOURCE: Henry Louis Gates, Jr., *In Search of Our Roots: How 19 Extraordinary African Americans Reclaimed Their Past* (New York: Crown, 2009).

PART VI
READING PLACES

THE IDEA EXPLORED in the previous section, that black identity is not a monolith, extends to every corner of the world, wherever the African Diaspora has taken its descendants. Many years before Gates ventured into Latin America to make his documentary, *Black in Latin America*, he had traveled extensively in Europe and Africa, recording what he found in essays, books, and films.

One idea that recurs frequently in these pieces is that homes have to be built; they do not come ready-made. He goes to Africa, expecting to fall naturally into an ancestral home, but his daughters are quick to remind him of the foreignness of the place. He tracks his different impressions of the West Indian population of London over the course of twenty years: a group that had seemed ill at ease and unrooted during his first visit in the 1970s is very much settled, at home, two decades later. Even Harlem, which has been mythologized as "organically" black, had to be cultivated to become the nurturing artistic environment that it was for so many years (and is again). South America and the Caribbean, which, having received far more Africans as slaves than did North America, reflect black influences throughout their cultures—even as Afrodescendants are disproportionately on the bottom rungs of society.

The African Diaspora is a history of dislocation and relocation. In these selections, Gates looks at the ways in which people of African descent have transformed and been transformed by their diverse locations the world over.

Abby Wolf

AFRICA, TO ME

I go to set an example to the youth of my race. I go to encourage the young. They can never be elevated here. I have tried it sixty years—in vain. Could I by my example lead them to set sail, if I die the next day, I should be satisfied.

—NEWPORT GARDNER, ON THE EVE OF
HIS EMIGRATION TO LIBERIA IN 1826

One three centuries removed
From the scenes his fathers loved,
Spicy grove, cinnamon tree,
What is Africa to me?

—COUNTEE CULLEN, "HERITAGE"

In view of the present world catastrophe, I want to recall the history of Africa. I want to retell its story so far as distorted science has not concealed and lost it. I want to appeal to the past in order to explain the present. I know how unpopular this method is. What have we moderns, we wisest of the wise, to do with the dead past: Yet, "All that tread the globe, are but a handful to the tribes that slumber in its bosom," and who are we, stupid blunderers at the tasks these brothers sought to do—who are we to forget them? So now I ask you to turn with me back five thousand years and more and ask, what is Africa and who are Negroes?

—W. E. B. DU BOIS, *THE WORLD AND AFRICA*

By almost common consent, the modern world seems determined to pilfer Africa of glory. It was not enough that her children have been scattered over the globe, clothed in garments of shame—humiliated and oppressed—but her merciless foes weary themselves in plundering the tombs of our revered sires, and in obliterating their worthy deeds, which were inscribed by fame, upon the pages of ancient history.

—HENRY HIGHLAND GARNET

"So, DADDY, WHAT in the world am I supposed to have in common with *them*?" my younger daughter, Liza, shouted at me within the confines of our suffocating train cabin, furnished by the BBC and Zambia National Railways. It was more a cry of frustration than anger. In 1994, we were on a 3,000-mile train trip, filming an episode of *Great Railway Journeys* for the BBC and PBS.

"Nothing!" her older sister, Maggie, responded on my behalf, hoping to preempt any possible response premised on our commonality of ancestors, of black skin, thick lips, or kinky hair. "They live in mud huts," she continued, "they are covered with dust, their clothes are ragged . . . they don't even wear shoes!"

What *do* we have in common? I allowed myself to wonder in silence, seeking to avoid the smug intensity of my daughters' gaze as they dared me to try to think of a convincing response, even while some part of them might have been desperately hoping that I could.

As, I sat there, amused at my daughters' honesty, despairing to think of a clever one-liner that would deflect the enormous challenge of their question, these couplets from Countee Cullen's "Heritage," standard in black literary anthologies, kept dancing through my mind:

What is Africa to me:
Copper sun or scarlet sea, . . .

Africa? A book one thumbs
Listlessly, till slumber comes.

And then that curiously ridiculous refrain:

Spicy grove, cinnamon tree,
What is Africa to me?

I had never really appreciated Countee Cullen's poem before. I had never actually liked the sentiments it expresses about our African heritage—the emotions ranging from ambivalence, at best, to revulsion, at worst—shared all too frequently by my American Negro ancestors and my contemporaries, their African American descendants, in the privacy of their families and in ritual settings like the church, beauty parlors or barber shops, sororities or fraternal orders. The African American's relationship to Africa has long been ambivalent, at least since the early nineteenth century, when 3,000 black men crowded into Bishop Richard Allen's African Methodist Episcopal Church in Philadelphia to protest noisily a plan to recolonize free blacks in Africa. Inexplicably, I suddenly thought of my father, who proudly received the "I ain't left nuthin' in Africa" award every year at my mother's family reunion, and I burst into laughter.

"It's *not* funny," one of my unrepentantly American daughters, now exasperated, shouted at me as I reflected on our standing family joke about my father's aversion to Afros, dashikis, and most things "African."

"I know, I know," I halfheartedly pretended to apologize through tears of laughter and sadness. Truth be told, I wasn't sure that I could answer that question honestly without resorting to platitudes or appeals to sentimentality.

Four years later, I found myself in the Sudan, in the village of Q'ab, an oasis in the heart of the Nubian Desert long believed to hold the key to a miracle cure for rheumatism. In a run-down schoolroom, the elderly headmaster, Mohammed Ali Hammeto, carefully explained in Arabic that the cure had proven to come from the village sand dune and that each year hundreds of people flock to receive it. They are buried up to their necks in the scorching sand for twenty minutes a day over the course of a week, covered by a little awning to keep the sun off their heads. As their bodies sweat, the mineral deposits in the sand are believed to work miracles. The headmaster said he has seen crippled men walk strong from the village. Throughout the Sudan, this dune at Q'ab is renowned: many have sought its curative powers at other dunes, but to no avail. Q'ab alone holds the secret.

As I prepared to be buried, I addressed the assembled schoolchildren and the villagers, explaining that I was an American, a descendant of slaves, and that I had come to make a film so that Americans and Europeans would know more about the glories of ancient Nubia. A brief silence followed the translation of my speech into Arabic, broken suddenly by a woman who shouted at the top of her voice: "Africa is on your face!" Everyone applauded and laughed. As I looked at the crowd of these multicolored people of Q'ab— their skin medium brown to the silkiest ebony, their hair kinky and tight and soft and straight—it suddenly occurred to me that there are many ways of wearing Africa on our faces, that my daughters wear the great continent's stunning variety in their own ways, while I wear it in still another.

My father and his father, both of whom I knew, and his father's father, whom I did not, were legendary in our family for scorning any sort of wistful romance with Africa. My family and our neighbors and friends thought of Africa and its Africans as extensions of the stereotyped characters that we saw in movies and on television in films such as *Tarzan* and in programs such as *Ramar of the Jungle* and *Sheena, Queen of the Jungle.* Cullen's lamentation of being "three centuries removed from the scenes his fathers loved" was not in all honesty shared by my father and his father, and practically all of the American Negroes I ever met in the fifties or early sixties.

For as long as I can remember, I have been passionately intrigued by "Africa," by the word itself, by its flora and fauna, its topographical diversity and grandeur; but above all else, by the sheer variety of the colors of its people, from tan and sepia to jet and ebony. I turned ten in 1960, the great year of African independence. Without prompting from my teachers or, Lord knows, from my father, I memorized the names of each independent African country and its new leader, learning to pronounce these polysyllables just as our evening news commentator did on television each night. By the time I was twelve, I had become obsessed with Stanley and Livingstone, with Cecil Rhodes's unfulfilled quest to create a republic from the Cape to Cairo (suitable, he was quick to add, for the comfortable existence of any white man, a part I chose to ignore), and the painstaking persistence of the Leakeys in looking for evidence of the origins of the human family among fragments of bone and tools and utensils sifted from the East African soil. Could I have been the only black person who wanted to throw a party every time the Leakeys identified still another toe bone that lent credence to their claim that *all* of humanity had its birth in darkest Africa? Peking Man and Cro-Magnon be damned! Such was my passion for "Africa," a place I knew primarily through the words and pictures of my geography books.

My father's feeling—shared, I feared, by my two daughters on that sweltering afternoon on the Zambian train—of complete and apparently unambivalent disconnection from Africa has a painfully long history among "African Americans" (many of whom, if truth be told, have never grown comfortable with calling ourselves "black," let alone "African"). Phillis Wheatley, the very first African to publish poetry in the English language, gave voice to this anxiety as early as 1773, even before it occurred to her to use her powerful pen to indict slavery and European racism: "Twas mercy brought me from my *Pagan* land," she wrote, a land, most probably in Gambia or Senegal, from which she was abducted when she was six or seven. In an earlier poem, Wheatley had called Africa "The land of errors and Egyptian gloom," thanking the "Father of mercy" for bringing "me in safety from those dark abodes" that were the Africa not of her memory but of the Enlightenment imagination of eighteenth-century Europe and America.[1]

"Thank God for slavery," Richard Pryor would outrageously exclaim more than 200 years later, at the end of a devastatingly humorous account of his first visit to Africa. He unwittingly summarized one persistent view among African Americans that no amount of wishful thinking or "political correctness" can seem to wash away entirely, perhaps because its pedigree includes far too many distinguished black intellectuals. Even the redoubtable Frederick Douglass, who as early as 1854 ventured that the liberation of the American Negro slave was inextricably intertwined with the "liberation" of knowledge about ancient African civilization, especially the sub-Saharan "Negroid" origins of Egyptian civilization and what he called the fundamental unity of all Negro peoples—even he preferred to embrace "Africa" more as an imaginative construct than as an actual place, full of tens of millions of black human beings. In fact, in 1872, Douglass wondered aloud "why anyone should leave this land of progress and enlightenment and seek a home amid the death-dealing malaria of a barbarous continent."[2] The Western stereotype of Africa and its black citizens as devoid of reason and, therefore, subhuman was often shared by white master and black ex-slave alike. Writing early in the nineteenth century, a group of free blacks in Philadelphia adopted the following resolution:

> Resolved that, without art, without science, without a proper knowledge of government, to cast into the savage wilds of Africa the free people of color seems to us the circuitous route through which they must return to perpetual bondage.[3]

Douglass would give voice to still another cause for anxiety among African Americans toward their ancestral kinsmen: slavery, and its complex historical causes, including black African complicity in its origins. "Depend upon it," Douglass wrote,

> the savage chiefs of the western coasts of Africa, who for ages have been accustomed to selling their captives into bondage, and pocketing the ready cash for them will not more readily accept our moral and economical ideas than the slave traders of Maryland and Virginia. We are, therefore, less inclined to go to Africa to work against the slave-trade than to stay here to work against it.[4]

The relation between the descendants of the slaves and their African forebears, Douglass argues, had long been severed by the latter's willing participation in the commodification of their own brothers and sisters. The Negro American was sui generis, not an extension of a noble past filled with black gods and kings, but a new being, shaped on the American continent just as surely as his neighbors of European descent had been. He was urged to forget his putative African past and create a future as an American; as Cullen would put it in "Heritage,"

> *What is last year's snow to me,*
> *Last year's anything? The tree*
> *Budding yearly must forget*
> *How its past arose or set—*

To acknowledge that attitudes such as these run deep and wide in African American culture (assuring my father and my daughters a vast and distinguished company) is not to deny the contrary view, of Africa's and Africans' long and distinguished traditions. The 3,000 black men who crowded into Bishop Allen's church in Philadelphia in 1817 felt compelled to protest colonization because several black leaders such as Paul Cuffe, James Forten, and Allen himself were quite enthusiastic about it. However, Douglass contemporaries Martin R. Delany, Henry Highland Garnet, Alexander Crummell, and Edward Wilmot Blyden, among many others, celebrated the connections they believed to exist between American Negroes and the African continent. For Blyden, Africa was "the negro's home." "Your place," Blyden advised his fellow American Negroes, "has been assigned you in the universe as African, and there is no room for you as anything else." Nor was there a geographical locale in the world more appropriate and suitable for the Negro than Africa:

> Africa is his, if he will. He may ignore it. He may consider that he is divested of any right to it; but this will not alter his relations to that country, or impair the integrity of his title. He may be content to fight against the fearful odds in this country; but he is the proprietor of a vast domain. He is entitled to a whole continent by his constitution and antecedents.[5]

For Blyden, the future itself belonged to Africa and the Africans, because "Africa may yet prove to be the spiritual conservatory of the world . . . it may be that [Europeans] may have to resort to Africa to recover some of the simple elements of faith."[6] In a gesture that must have struck his colleagues as quite bold if not outrageous, Blyden declared that the Dark Continent, with its millions of supposedly benighted Africans, would be the salvation of a decaying and decadent Western civilization.

Like his friend and colleague Alexander Crummell, Blyden believed that it was incumbent upon the American Negro, perhaps out of reciprocity, to serve as the vanguard in the reclamation of "the continent" and "the race"; Crummell maintained that "both our positions and our circumstances make us the guardians, the protectors, and the teachers of our heathen tribes."[7] It is, however, worth noting that even Pan-African nationalism was sometimes infected with a certain ambivalence and condescension toward its African brothers and sisters, the very same condescension felt by those who longed to leave Africa far, far behind in the historical past. As James McCune Smith, a black American physician educated at Edinburgh and friend of Frederick Douglass put it in the middle of the nineteenth century, the American Negroes' identification with Africa, and their habit of calling themselves "African," waned as the Civil War approached:

> The terms by which orators addressed their leaders on [the day the African Slave Trade was abolished in 1808] was universally "Beloved Africans!" The people in those days rejoiced in their nationality and hesitated not to call each other "Africans" or "descendants of Africa." In after years the term "Africa" fell into disuse and finally discredit.[8]

Still, the ardent desire to honor and reclaim the Negro's link to Africa—by color, by history, by culture, by "blood"—never entirely disappeared, even among those who refused to romanticize the American Negro's return to the Continent. Instead, for those so inclined, Africa became a metaphor for an ancestral greatness, for roots, for spirituality, in which American Negroes could share. Mary McLeod Bethune, the great black activist and educator, identified herself as "my Mother's daughter," and claimed that the "drums of Africa still beat in my heart."[9] Frederick Douglass, echoing a belief voiced by John Stuart Mill in 1850, railed in 1854 against "the fashion of American writers to deny the Egyptians were Negroes and claim that they are the same race as themselves. This has . . . been largely due to a wish to deprive the Negro of the moral support of the Ancient greatness and to appropriate the same to the white man."[10] Alain Locke confessed in 1925 that Negro Americans had shared a "missionary condescension . . . in their attitudes toward Africa," which was "a pious but sad mistake. In taking it, we have fallen into the snare of our enemies and have given offense to our brothers." Locke went on to say that "Africa is not only our mother, but in light of most recent science is beginning to appear as the mother of civilization."[11]

Among black scholars, then, the role of Africa was hotly disputed. As the historian Carter G. Woodson put it: "[T]he contemporary school of thought which taught that the American Negro had been torn completely from his African roots in the process of enslavement had done incalculable harm, especially in the education and training of younger Negro scholars."[12]

In part, this dispute stemmed from the absence of "African Civilization" in the college curriculum. W. E. B. Du Bois himself—the greatest American Negro intellectual in the twentieth century and an ardent Pan-Africanist who would emigrate to Ghana, where he died in 1963 editing the *Encyclopedia Africana*—even he once confessed that he had no idea of the depth of the history of African civilization until the German-born anthropologist Franz Boas revealed this to him in a lecture at Atlanta University in 1906. Moreover, Paul Robeson had to attend the School of Oriental and African Studies in London in the early thirties to learn "that along with the towering achievements of the cultures of ancient Greece and China there stood the culture of Africa, unseen and denied by the looters of Africa's material wealth." "I am a Negro with every drop of blood and every stir of my soul," Robeson declared. "I want to be more African."[13] The effect of the West's systematic ignorance of African history was to treat it as if it had slept for millennia, even as the rest of the world's civilizations erupted. Marcus Garvey, for example, the most passionate Pan-Africanist of his generation (the one preceding Robeson's) and the father of the modern "Back to Africa" migration movement, argued that "when Europe was inhabited by a race of cannibals, a race of savage men, heathens and pagans, Africa was peopled with a race of cultured black men who were masters in art, science, and literature." Nevertheless, "You do not know Africa," precisely because "Africa has been sleeping for centuries—not dead, only sleeping." Garvey demanded that Africans take charge of their own destiny: "Wake up, Ethiopia! Wake up, Africa! Let us work towards the one glorious end of a free, redeemed, and mighty nation. Let Africa be a bright star among the constellation of nations. Africa for the Africans at home and abroad."[14]

Garvey's popular movement, which struck a certain spiritual chord with working-class blacks in Harlem in the late teens and early twenties, resonated powerfully, if sometimes ironically, with American Negro intellectuals as well, in the form of a primitivistic embrace of "Africa" that was just as unrelated to African reality, in its way, as its opposite—racist stereotyping. The literary movement of the twenties known as the Harlem Renaissance, along with its cousin, the Francophone movement known as "Négritude" (born in Paris in 1934), were based in large part on a primitivistic romance with an "Africa" that never was. These lines from the Senegalese poet Leopold Senghor could be the epigraph of the Négritude movement: "Bare woman, black woman / clad in your color which is life, in your form which is beauty."[15] A poem by the Jamaican Claude McKay, who moved to Harlem and was a pivotal figure in the Harlem Renaissance, is typical of one American version of the romantic re-creation of a misty African past. Its title, "Outcast," reveals the sense of alienation and loss the poet feels, isolated from the haven against racism that Mother Africa once was to black people:

> *For the dim regions whence my fathers came*
> *My spirit, bondaged by the body, longs.*
> *Words felt, but never heard, my lips would frame;*
> *My soul would sing forgotten jungle songs,*
> *I would go back to darkness and to peace,*
> *But the great western world holds me in fee,*
> *And I may never hope for full release*
> *While to its alien gods, I bend my knee.*
> *Something in me is lost, forever lost,*
> *Some vital thing has gone out of my heart,*
> *And I must walk the way of life a ghost*
> *Among the sons of earth, a thing apart.*
> *For I was born, far from my native clime,*
> *Under the white man's menace, out of time.*[16]

Africa, the ultimate source of our identity, Africa, the paradise lost by slavery, is the home for which we are destined to search, yet never retrieve:

> *Subdued and time-lost*
> *Are the drums—and yet*
> *Through some vast mist of race*
> *There comes this song*
> *I do not understand,*
> *This song of atavistic land,*
> *Of bitter yearnings lose*
> *Without a place—*
> *So long,*
> *So far away*
> *Is Africa's*
> *Dark face.*[17]

Africa, for these poets, is the proverbial grail, the definitive sign of identity and authenticity desperately sought, yet never to be recovered. This seeking, without ever finding, is the mark of the American Negro's alienation, the fate of black people living in a majority white culture far removed from Africa's maternal embrace.

Despite the popularity of Marcus Garvey's "Back to Africa" movement and the romantic yearnings of the Harlem Renaissance in the twenties, many African American intellectuals remained ambivalent, at best, about their putative relation to Africa throughout most of the twentieth century—at least until the advent of the Black Power and the Black Studies movements in the late sixties. The novelist Richard Wright's attitude is typical: "I could not feel anything African about myself," in part because Africans "had sold their people into slavery," he wrote in 1954. After a sojourn in Ghana in the early fifties, he concluded, "I had understood nothing. I was black and they were black, but my blackness did not help me."[18] European slavery and colonialism, in the end, had been good for Africa, he argued outrageously, because their vengeance had forced Africans to sever themselves from "irrational ties of religion and custom and tradition"—in other words, all of the hallmarks of traditional African civilization. Sounding a still all-too-familiar note, he told a conference in Paris two years later, "I do say 'Bravo!' to the consequences of Western plundering, a plundering that created the conditions of the possible rise of rational societies for the greater majority of mankind. . . ."[19] So much for the Harlem Renaissance writer's attempt to transform Africa's image for American Negroes through primitivism. As Alain Locke had warned at the time, "Even with all our scientific revaluation, all our 'New Negro' compensation, all our anti-Nordic polemics, a certain disrespect for Africa still persists widely."[20]

One could write a dissertation about the range of African American emotions about Africa, as several scholars have. My point in rehearsing these disparate attitudes, from romantic black nationalism to the disgust and anxiety articulated most clearly by black apologists for slavery and colonization, is that the question that my daughters dared me to answer in 1994 on our 3,000-mile train trip through Zimbabwe, Zambia, and Tanzania has in one form or another vexed fully three centuries of African Americans. In (virtually) dragging them, at the ages of fourteen and twelve, to Africa, I was arranging for them to experience this conundrum of cultural continuity and discontinuity for themselves.

My own initial encounter with Africa had come much later in life than theirs. While an undergraduate at Yale, I spent half a year working in an Anglican mission hospital in the village of Kilimatinde in the center of Tanzania. Toward the end of my stint, I hitchhiked, with a recent Harvard graduate, Lawrence Biddle Weeks, across the equator: We began in Dar es Salaam, went north to Mombasa, on to Nairobi, and from there into Kampala, Uganda, a day following Idi Amin's 1971 coup. At the Congolese border we were denied entry—we were too green to offer the expected "dash," or a small bribe—so it was on down to Kigali, the capital of Rwanda, to get new visas, then back up to Goma on Lake Kivu. On the back of a truck full of empty beer bottles, driven by a kindly Lebanese merchant, Larry and I spent six days slowly making our way through tropical rain forests and the bush before arriving in the city of Kisangani, the major port of the indomitable Congo River, just in time to catch the riverboat as it started its five-day journey to Kinshasha, near that great river's mouth. In two months' time, we traveled from the Indian Ocean to the Atlantic without ever leaving the ground.

My attitudes when I first came to the African Continent in 1970 were as romantic as any; in my sophomore year I had read Du Bois's account of his own first visit to the Continent in 1923, and it certainly had shaped my own expectations:

> When shall I forget the night I set foot on African soil? I am the sixth generation in descent from forefathers who left this land. The moon was at the full and the waters of the Atlantic lay like a lake. All the long slow afternoon as the sun robed herself in her western scarlet with veils of misty cloud, I had seen Africa afar . . . The spell of Africa is upon me. The ancient witchery of her medicine is burning my drowsy, dreamy blood. This is not a country, it is a world, a universe of itself and for itself, a thing Different, Immense, Menacing, Alluring. It is a great black bosom where the spirit longs to die. It is life so burning, so fire encircled that one bursts with terrible soul inflaming life. One longs to leap against the sun and then calls, like some great hand of fate, the slow, silent, crushing power of almighty sleep—of Silence, of immovable Power beyond, within, around. Then comes the calm. The dreamless boat of midday stillness at dusk, at dawn, at noon, always. Things move—black shiny bodies, perfect bodies, bodies of sleek unearthly poise and beauty. Eyes languish, black eyes—slow eyes, lovely and tender eyes in great formless faces. . . .[21]

Upon arriving in the village, I had written to a black classmate back at Yale, "I am nursing at the breast of Mother Africa." Six weeks or so later, his reply arrived: "Dear Skip—I have been nursing at a few breasts myself. Get a grip, my brother!" By then, I was quite embarrassed by and already disabused of my romantic pretensions. My very first night was spent in tears, wondering what could have possessed me to pledge to live in a village of 500 people, with no electricity, telephones, television, or running water, and where the "express" bus (which delivered both telegrams and the mail); passed through just twice each week. *Please* write to me, I begged my friends, because I *love* to read. After half a year assisting the delivery of anesthesia alongside a band of Australian missionaries, my most naive fantasies about the immediacy of my African heritage were cured. The Wagogo villagers and surrounding peasant farmers and the neighboring Masai herdsmen were not simple extensions of my putative African family but peoples with their own discrete histories and their own unique cultures.

I would return to Africa many times after that first extended stay in 1970–1971, but it was on the trip I made, in the company of my reluctant family, to film the episode of the *Great Railway Journeys* series that I got the idea for a film series and book about ancient African civilizations and its lost wonders, which I thought of as an African version of "The Seven Wonders of the World."

To compile a list of these wonders, I invited the suggestions of several scholars of African Studies, from Africa, Europe, and America. I collated their responses and arrived at two dozen, including the familiar and less familiar: the Nile, Niger, and Congo Rivers; the Sphinx; the Great Pyramid of Cheops and the Valley of the Kings: the Asante Kingdom and Yorubaland; Dahomey and the slave castles in West Africa; Great Zimbabwe; the Great Mosque at Djenne; the Sankoré Mosque at Timbuktu; the Dogon people; and several others. Since the items on this list conveniently, mercifully, clustered (no fewer than four—the Niger, Djenne, Timbuktu, and the Dogon—are in Mali, for example), I realized that I could encompass most of them in six journeys. My quest to encounter the glories of Africa's past would be a journey of discovery, for the readers and viewers, of course, but for me as well.

Traveling by Land Cruiser, camel, and dhow, interviewing kings and peasants, priests and prophets, renowned archaeologists and local taxi drivers, market women and Imams, I sought in these travels, not so much to answer directly my daughters' questions about what African Americans today bore in common with their African ancestors, but to discover who, indeed, "the African people" were and what, in fact, they had contributed to civilization—especially before the Europeans arrived to enslave many of them, colonize their land, and exploit its natural resources. I knew that any meaningful explanation of what Africa was to me would depend on discovering what Africa was, and is, both to Africans and to all of us, to the world's great family of questing peoples. What was the legacy of art and cultures to which they gave birth? I sought to answer these questions not only on behalf of my own children, but on behalf of all of us who believe that the world's collective civilization cannot be fully understood without our awareness of its historically suppressed or discarded parts. Through this book and its accompanying film series I hope to contribute in a small way to restoring those parts to their full glory for a shared appreciation, critique, and understanding.

Why do I believe this to be necessary? Are the achievements of Africa really so fully suppressed? Let's face it squarely: When most of us think of Africa, the images that come to mind are of poverty, flies, famine, war, disease, and limitless acres of savanna inhabited only by majestic game. How many culturally literate Americans know anything at all about the truly great ancient civilizations of Africa, which in their day were just as complex and just as splendid as any on the face of the earth? Who among us is uninfluenced by the images of Africa perpetuated early in this century by the stories of Tarzan: twenty-three novels, sixteen movies, and a syndicated comic strip, each depicting the inevitable, natural dominance of the scion of a titled English family over Africa's flora, fauna, and its half-witted denizens? (So popular had Tarzan become by 1929 that the New Orleans *Times-Picayune* only half-jokingly suggested that if Tarzan were to run for president in 1929, he would receive as many votes as incumbent president Herbert Hoover!)[22]

Europeans have since the early days of their own civilization been fascinated, if not obsessed, with both Africans and the African continent; but the West has been content more often to use Africa for the projection of fantasies from its collective unconscious than to acknowledge it as an actual place to be encountered and analyzed dispassionately, where human beings have forged their own individual identities and collective histories. While this huge continent is the birthplace of humankind, its history of systematic victimization mocks its numerous contributions to the development of civilization. From the very beginnings of documented contact with Europeans, Africa and its peoples have often been misinterpreted to justify one European interest or another. The very name Africa, Ali Mazrui asserts, illustrates how Europe and Western ideology began to shape attitudes about African culture and history.

The etymology of the word "Africa" is uncertain. Adrian Room maintains, "The name derives directly from Latin *Africa* or Greek *Aphrike*, and was applied not to the whole continent but to a region that originally corresponded to modern Tunisia."[23] Valentin Mudimbe points out that "Aethiops" was "the proper name of Vulcan's son in Greek mythology," and "is the generic qualification of any dark-skinned person." By the time of Isidorus, "Aethiopia" "qualifies the continent": "the land or the continent is called Aethiopia because of . . . the heat (*calore*) or the color (*colore*) of the people living near the sun that burns them." By the first century AD, Africa had been subdivided by geographers into three regions: Egypt, Libya, and Aethiopia, "the last corresponding more or less to sub-Saharan Africa."[24] Indeed, many scholars believe that "Ethiopia" in ancient Greek writings more often than not refers to the civilizations of Kush and Meroë in present-day Sudan; a word—like "Zanzibar," "Ghana," and "Abyssinia" (derived from Arabic roots)—that refers to the black or brown colors of its inhabitants.

So, the word "Africa" has Greco-Roman origins: "*Africa*" in Latin means "sunny," and "*Aphrike*" in Greek means "without cold." But what the Greeks and Romans used to designate its northern regions, Europeans would soon use to refer to the entire continent. And by declaring the whole region to be Africa, Europe defined a homogeneous population, understood to be black. Thus, the term "African" came to hold racial as well as geographical meanings. Ali Mazrui maintains that consequently, academics, in an effort to reclaim African history as *valuable* and "*African*," have endlessly attempted to prove that our African ancestors were all "negroid." Mazrui argues that "[t]o insist that nothing is African unless it is Black is to fall into the white man's fallacy." Likewise, to make overgenerous claims about the African past has been a pronounced tendency of scholars and commentators eager to refute racist claims about Africa's supposed "primitivism" and "barbarity." The result is that much of African history has been suffocated between two extremes of ideological interpretation.[25]

Scholars such as Frank Snowden, Jr., have observed that the earliest recorded contacts between Europeans and black Africans were not informed by the sort of Western chauvinism that would finally define this relationship. For example, Ethiopia, as the ancients called all of black Africa, occupies a prominent place in Homeric poems, and Ethiopians are mentioned with more kindness than Homer's kindred tribesmen. In the *Iliad*, the poet locates Ethiopia near the warm rim of the inhabited earth—"On the warm limits of the farthest main"—and in the *Odyssey*, he divides the people and the land into two parts, one toward the sunrise and the other toward the sunset. The Ethiopians were Homer's "blameless race," and Memnon was held to be amongst the noblest of men: "to Troy no hero came of nobler line / or if nobler Memnon it was thine."[26] According to Mudimbe, Memnon was "the black son of Eos and a descendent of Tros and Dardanos," and "an ancestor of Ethiopian Kings." Hesiod called him the "King of Ethiopians." And again in characterizing the black-skinned and frizzy-haired Eurybates, who was both Odysseus's herald and close companion, Homer likened him to the great wanderer himself: "For it was in Eurybates['s] large soul alone, Odysseus viewed an image of his own." Emphasis was placed on the justice and magnanimity of these individual Ethiopians, and, by extension, of their entire people. Diodorus Siculus, a first-century BC Roman historian, said that "Memnon led to Troy, 2000 soldiers and 200 chariots and signaled his valor and reputation with the death and destruction of many Greeks till he was slain by an ambush lain for him by the Thessalonians."[27]

Moreover, Greek dramatists made Ethiopians central figures in some of their plays: Sophocles and Euripides each wrote a drama entitled *Andromeda,* though neither version survives. These plays were constructed around the experiences of the Ethiopian princess Andromeda, the beloved daughter of Cepheus and his queen Cassiopea. Homeric traditions also associated Olympian divinities with Ethiopian religious festivals. The poet tells us that on the occasion of a meeting of the council of divinities held in the interest of the long-suffering Odysseus, Poseidon was absent, having gone to receive a sacrifice of bulls and rams from the Ethiopians.

> *But now Poseidon had gone to visit the Ethiopians worlds away.*
> *Ethiopians off at the farthest limits of mankind,*
> *a people split in two, one part where the Sungod sets*
> *and part where the Sungod rises. There Poseidon went*
> *to receive an offering, bulls and rams by the hundred—*
> *far away at the feast the Sea-lord sat and took his pleasure.*[28]

Likewise, when Iris, goddess of the rainbow, went as messenger to Boreas and Zephyrus "to ask for their assistance in the funeral rites of Patroclus, she was invited by the denizens of the wind to join them in a feast they were celebrating." Iris refused by saying:

> *not now; for I must again make my way*
> *over the ocean currents to the land*
> *Where dwell the Ethiopians, who adore*
> *The Gods with hectacombs, to take my share of sacrifice.*[29]

Diodorus relates that when he went to Egypt, the priests told him of the Greeks who had been there and included Homer. They also told him that each year Egyptians carried tabernacles of certain of their gods to Ethiopia and after certain celebrations there, brought the shrines back to Egypt—"as if the Gods had returned out of Ethiopia: The Ethiopians say that the Egyptians are settlers from among themselves. . . . The customs of the Egyptians, they say, are for the most part Ethiopian, the settlers having preserved their old traditions. Considering the kings gods, paying the great attention to funeral rites . . . these are Ethiopian practices; also the style of their statues and the form of their writing are Ethiopian." With the conquest of Egypt by Alexander in 332 BC and the Roman occupation soon after, firsthand accounts of sub-Saharan Africa accumulated dramatically.

No doubt in part because of these occupations, it was not long before contrary attitudes toward Africa begin to find expression in classical literature.

Long before this, however, Herodotus, for example, had written that Africans had "speech that resembles the shrieking of a Bat rather than the Language of Men," lacked "individual names," were "dog-headed humans," and even "headless beings."[30] In the first century AD, even after direct Roman contact with black Africans, the Roman scholar Pliny the Elder would confirm that "by report [Africans] have no heads but mouth and eies in their breasts." As Mudimbe observes:

> Pliny's geography of monstrosity faithfully mirrors Herodotus's description, albeit in a more detailed way. To Herodotus's general geographic frame of monsters—dog-headed and headless peoples (IV, 191)—living in the eastern region of Libya, Pliny opposes a curious table of "tribes" inhabiting a vague area around the *Nigri fluvio eadem natura quae Nilo* ["the river Black which has the same nature as the Nile"]: the Atlas peoples, who have no names; the cave-dwellers, who have no language and live on the flesh of snakes; the Garamantes, who do not practice marriage; the Blemmyae, who are headless and, as already indicated by Herodotus, have their mouths and eyes attached to their chests; the Satyrs; and the Strapfoots.[31]

What is important about the coexistence of the negative and positive descriptions of black Africans by the ancient Greeks is that by the fifth century BC "Africa" was already a veritable tabula rasa on which Europeans would inscribe their deepest fears and anxieties about the human condition, as well as their most ardent and highest aspirations for human civilization. And, despite even more frequent contact through the first century AD, these attitudes persisted. To recall Sir Thomas Browne's pregnant observation: "[W]e carry within us the wonders we seek without us: there is all Africa and her prodigies in us."[32] But it was the centuries of the European slave trade, and the subsequent "scramble for Africa" at the turn of the century, that led to Africa's almost total demonization as the opposite of all that humanity aspired to be.

The twentieth century both inherited, and contributed to, the generally shared opinion that Africa is a benighted place completely lacking in civilization. The view that Africa lacks "history" (and therefore memory and reason) is most closely associated with the Enlightenment. The claim was standardized by Hegel's *The Philosophy of History*, published in 1790, according to which the peoples of the world are divided into those who have an active historical presence and influence and those who do not, who are passive, without creative powers, and therefore condemned to be conquered and led. Hegel states that Africa "is not a historical continent: it shows neither change nor development." Its people are "capable of neither development nor education. As we see them today, so they have always been," ignorant, static, deracinated. And whatever good Hegel could find in Africa, he attributed it to other peoples.

> Historical movement in [Africa]—that is in its Northern part belongs to the Asiatic or European world. Carthage displayed there an important transitory phase of civilization, but as a Phoenician colony, it belongs to Asia. Egypt will be considered in reference to the passage of the human mind from the Eastern to the Western phase, but it does not belong to African Spirit. What we properly understand by Africa is the Unhistorical and Underdeveloped spirit, still involved in the conditions of mere nature, and which had to be presented here only as the threshold of World's History.[33]

The European custom of crediting non-Africans with African achievements has remained remarkably vigorous since Hegel's day. In 1930, C. G. Seligman, a famous English historian, articulated the Hamite theory, which holds that whites were responsible for African civilization. He writes bluntly: "The civilizations of Africa are the civilizations of the Hamites, its history the record of these peoples and of their interaction with the two other African stocks, the Negro and the Bushman." He then asserts that the two other "stocks" are inferior, and any advances in civilization they have made are due to the extent to which they have been subject to "Hamitic" influence.[34] Seligman's work typified the imperialist and racist assumptions that have structured and infected the formal study of African history. As Basil Davidson asserts: "Time and again the achievement of men in Africa—men of Africa—have been laid at the door of some mysterious but otherwise unexplained 'people outside of Africa' . . . over the past fifty years or so, whenever anything remarkable or inexplicable has turned up in Africa, a whole galaxy of non-African peoples are dragged in to explain it."[35] Even as late as the sixties, the Oxford historian Hugh Trevor-Roper was arguing that the African past was nothing more than the "unrewarding gyrations of barbarous tribes in picturesque but irrelevant corners of the globe. . . . History is essentially a form of movement, and purposive movement too. . . . Perhaps, in the future, there will be some African history . . . but at present there is none. There is only the history of Europeans in Africa."[36]

If theorists such as Seligman proved especially useful in justifying the systematic exploitation of a continent and its inhabitants during the Age of Imperialism, the same sort of thinking, in a more contemporary guise, has come to serve those who would deny the persuasive archaeological evidence that Africa is the birthplace of humankind.

The discovery in the seventies in Hadar, Ethiopia, of the skeleton of "Lucy," the hominid who lived approximately 3.2 million years ago and who has been identified as the human family's common ancestor; along with the discovery in 1979, in the Kibish region of Laetoli, Tanzania, of a 165-foot-long trail of the earliest hominid footprints, have left little doubt that, in the words of paleontologist Christopher Stringer, "what unites us is far more significant than what divides us. Our variable forms mask an essential truth—that under our skins, we are all Africans, the metaphorical sons and daughters of the man from Kibish."[37] The idea that the ancestors of human beings had evolved in Africa was first suggested by Darwin; but despite his authority, and despite the major archaeological findings of scientists such as Raymond Dart and Mary and Louis Leakey (as well as popularizations of their work such as *African Genesis* by Robert Ardrey), many people in the West find this idea shocking and have been passionately resistant to it. There can be little doubt that centuries of representations of Africa as a continent peopled by barbarous savages have contributed enormously to this resistance. When a *Time* magazine cover featuring an artist's depiction of a reconstructed Lucy announced that she was the Ur-mother, the "Eve," of the human family, its readers were incredulous, judging by the letters to the editor and the resulting commentary on television talk shows. It may be some time before a general acceptance of Sir Thomas Browne's inspired speculation that "there is all Africa and her prodigies in us."

Can scientific evidence, and popularizations of the history of African civilizations, help to erase racist depictions of Africans, depictions at least two and a half millennia old? "Africa is at war," Ali Mazrui has written, "It is a war between indigenous Africa and the forces of Western civilization."[38] But the war, in fact, is one over defining and preserving the heritage of African civilizations in the face of systematic denials of the nature and extent of that very heritage. It is, in other words, a war over interpretation and representation. For far too many of us in the West, Africa remains—even at the dawn of the twenty-first century—the vast, unchanging, irredeemable Dark Continent.

Recent historiography has made remarkable progress in defeating the long tradition of pernicious and misleading accounts of African civilization: staple works such as the *Cambridge History of Africa, The UNESCO History of Africa, The Encyclopedia of Africa South of the Sahara, Encarta Africana,* and *Africana: The Encyclopedia of the African and African American Experience* are solid scholarly contributions to establishing the range and the complexity of the African past. More speculative work has forced us to see the historical reconstruction of the past as ideologically tainted. In 1987, for example, a radical view was put forth by Martin Bernal in his controversial work *Black Athena,* in which he asserts that the Greco-Roman past was distorted by Western historians who altered it to fit an "Aryan model," denying its African and Asiatic roots. Bernal, like many scholars, now contends that the growth of Western civilization owes a great deal to Asiatic and African worlds, and that assimilation and influence occurred in both directions, not merely the one traditionally supposed.

While correcting the errors of two millennia of history is critically important, that corrective impulse is not without its own perils. As the historian Caroline Neale shows, reactions to histories such as Trevor-Roper's gave rise to a generation of apologists and cheerleaders for black Africa, who ignored anything that might reflect poorly upon Africa; that is, any history that would even inadvertently reinforce images of, say, illiteracy or lack of technological development. Neale has argued that by doing this, this generation of apologists played into the hands of racist Western historians by implicitly accepting their views of "civilization." So, historically, scholars have challenged the idea of social evolution—that is, a picture of stagnation in precolonial Africa—instead of also critiquing Western ideas of progress. She contends that historians felt pressured to show "not that whatever Africa had had was somehow humanly worthwhile, but that Africans deserved the respect of others, and could respect themselves, [only] because they had had in their past the things that Europeans valued!"[39]

Finding a way to let the African past speak on its own terms, in its own multiplicity of voices, to an audience of Westerners both black and white is the challenge I faced in writing this book and the series it accompanies. I have tried to do this, always acutely aware of the vast record of both racist and romantic depictions of Africa, of my desire to redress that grievous imbalance, and of the fact that each of us speaks from a specific place in the world, replete with biases and prejudices—and, in my own case, a great deal of wishful thinking on behalf of my African ancestral past. In my heart, I want all of the pharaohs to have been "black." (They were not.) I want the lost Ark of the Covenant to be located in St. Mary's Church in Axum. (Not likely, but the jury is still out.) I want there to have been a great collection of black scholars at the Sankoré Mosque in Timbuktu between the fourteenth and the sixteenth centuries. (There were.) I want so much for the African past and future . . . a past that has been denigrated for so very long, and a future that often seems in danger of being stillborn. I want all this—but not at the expense of scholarly evidence and reliable data. To elevate Africa above what height of achievement can be supported by dependable evidence would, in fact, be to demean the heritage that I claim to love so deeply.

It is difficult for most of us even to begin to comprehend the sheer size of the African continent, the second largest in the world. The United States would barely cover the Sahara Desert alone! "In fact," as the writer John Reader notes, "the United States, China, India, and New Zealand could all fit within the African coastline, together with Europe from the Atlantic to

Moscow and much of South America."[40] And yet, despite its vast geographical size, the continent's population of 748 million is only slightly larger than Europe's. One hundred thousand years ago, our human ancestors, possibly no more than one hundred, first migrated from the African continent and colonized the remainder of the world, Reader argues, only to return 500 years ago "behaving as though they owned the place." Modern Africa consists of fifty-one countries. Its people speak some 1,500 languages (not counting dialects), yet we often speak about "Africa" as if it were a single country in which people speak one indigenous language. "Say something in African to me," Americans often ask African visitors, not realizing that fully "*one-quarter* of the world's languages are spoken only in Africa," as the Pulitzer Prize–winning scholar Jared Diamond has shown.[41]

In ten months, I visited twelve African countries, and traveled tens of thousands of miles, in run-down trucks and Land Cruisers; dugout canoes, dhows, and diesel barges; by camel and by foot; camped my way across the Sudan's Nubian Desert from Khartoum to Delgo; and navigated the treacherous terrain of the magnificent Ethiopian Highlands in search of the lost Ark of the Covenant. Despite the extent of these travels, Africa remains as endlessly mysterious and fascinating to me as it was when I, at that age of ten, devoted my evenings to memorizing the name of the leader of each new African nation—when Africa was indeed still only a book—and a nightly newscast—to me.

My own attitudes about Africa and my African heritage can best be summed up in an anecdote that Ghanaians like to tell about their African American cousins. In 1957, Kwame Nkrumah became the first president of a newly independent Ghana. Himself a graduate of the historically black Lincoln University, Nkrumah issued a call to black Americans to come to Ghana, claim their patrimony, and help to build the new nation. The first group of black Americans who heeded Nkrumah's call solemnly collected themselves at Labadi Beach in Accra, where they participated under a full moon in a ritual of denunciation of American racism and of their American citizenship. Then they flung their passports as far out to sea as they could.

Late one moonlit night, about a month later, African residents at Labadi Beach noticed strange shadows at the ocean's edge. Curious, they went with their torches to investigate. To their enormous surprise, they discovered that the shadows were those same black Americans, now searching furiously in the low tide for their passports! I'm afraid this anecdote—apocryphal as it may be—defines the arc of my own experience: I love arriving in Africa, almost as much as I love returning home to America.

What else have I learned from my own African journey? I have learned that, contrary to conventional wisdom, the great natural expanses of the Indian and Atlantic Ocean, the Congo, Niger, Limpopo, and Nile Rivers, the

Ethiopian Highlands and the Sahara Desert, were not insurmountable barriers for the Africans who lived near to them. Like all civilized peoples, Africans saw such natural wonders as highways, through which to connect with other human beings and civilizations. If trade is the enemy of distance, it is also the godfather of movements among societies that result in the exchange of ideas, languages, and genetic materials, as well as in the barbarity of enslavement. It is the result of one instance of that barbarous practice in the eighteenth century—the enslavement of a woman who came to be called Jane Gates—that I am an American. I have learned that I am neither Fon nor Beninian, Asante nor Ghanaian, Swahili nor Kenyan, Nubian nor Sudanese. Though not a member of any one of these great peoples in particular, I am as a descendant of a West African slave and of ex-slaves, the product of a truly Pan-African new world culture forged out of the crucible of slavery. However deep and abiding my love of the African continent and its people, I am an American, albeit an African American, destined to call this place, and not that unimaginably varied massive continent, my home.

Finally, I have come to understand a truth that may be the only meaningful answer to the daunting question put to me by my daughters on that suffocating train ride through Zimbabwe seven years ago. Africa is not only the cradle of the human community, it is the mother of Civilization itself. All human civilization wears Africa on its face, just as surely as my daughters and I do, as their children's children will, as do we all. And until the West—and the rest of us—knows Africa, we can never truly know ourselves.

NOTES

1. Phillis Wheatley, "On Being Brought from Africa to America," in *The Norton Anthology of African American Literature*, ed. Henry Louis Gates, Jr., and Nellie Y. McKay (New York: W. W. Norton & Co., 1997).

2. See *The Life and Writings of Frederick Douglass*, Philip S. Foner, ed., vol. 1 (New York: International Publishers, 1950), 351.

3. Marion Berghahn, *Images of Africa in Black American Literature* (Totowa, N.J.: Rowman and Littlefield, 1977), 40. Bradford Chambers, ed., *Chronicles of Black Protest* (New York: New American Library: 1969), 52.

4. Frederick Douglass referring to the African Civilization Society, *Apropos of Africa: Sentiments of Negro American leaders on Africa from the 1800s to the 1950s*, compiled and edited by Adelaide Cromwell Hill and Martin Kilson (London: Cass, 1969), 164.

5. Edward Wilmot Blyden, in Marion Berghahn, *Images of Africa in Black American Literature* (Totowa, N.J.: Rowman and Littlefield, 1977), 51.

6. Henry S. Wilson, *Origins of West African Nationalism* (London: Macmillan, 1969), 242, 246.

7. Ibid.

8. Dorothy Sterling, ed., *Speak Out in Thunder Tones: Letters and Other Writings by Black Northerners, 1787–1865* (Garden City, N.Y.: Doubleday 1973), 1.

9. Richard Newman, *African American Quotations* (Phoenix, Ariz.: Oryx Press, 1998), 13.

10. Frederick Douglass, "The Claims of the Negro Ethnologically Considered." An address before the Literary Societies of Western Reserve College at Commencement, July 12, 1854 (Rochester, N.Y.: Lee, Mann and Co., Daily American Office, 1854).

11. Alain Locke, ed.; with an introduction by Arnold Rampersad, *The New Negro* (New York: Maxwell Macmillan International, 1992).

12. Ulysees Lee, *The ASNLH, The Journal of Negro History, and American Scholarly Interest in Africa*, in *Africa Seen by American Negroes* (Paris: Présence Africaine, 1958), 409.

13. Newman, *African American*, 17.

14. Ibid., 15.

15. Leopold Sedar Senghor, *Selected Poems* (London: Rex Collings, 1976), 33.

16. Berghahn, *Images*, 128–129.

17. Ibid., 130–131.

18. Richard Wright, *Black Power: A Record of Reactions in a Land of Pathos* (New York: Harper Perennial, 1995).

19. Ibid., xxvi.

20. Newman, *African American*, 16.

21. W. E. B. Du Bois, *Dusk of Dawn: An Essay Toward an Autobiography of a Race Concept* (New York: Schocken Books, 1969), 117, 123.

22. See Edward H. McKinley, *The Lure of Africa: American Interests in Tropical Africa, 1919–1939* (Indianapolis, Ind.: Bobbs-Merrill, 1974), 68.

23. Adrian Room, *African Placenames* (Jefferson, N.C.: 1994), 13.

24. Valentin Y. Mudimbe, *The Idea of Africa* (Bloomington, Ind.: Indiana University Press, 1994), 26–27.

25. Ali Mazrui, *The Africans: A Triple Heritage* (Boston: Little, Brown, and Co., 1986), 23.

26. Joseph E. Harris, ed., *Africa and Africans as Seen by Classical Writers. The William Leo Hansberry African History Notebook* (Washington, D.C.: Howard University Press, 1977), 82.

27. Ibid.

28. Homer, *Odyssey*, Book 1; translated by Robert Fagles; Introduction and Notes by Bernard Knox (New York: Viking, 1996), 25–30.

29. *Odyssey*, Book 5, 309–320.

30. Diodorus Siculus 3, 1–5.

31. Mudimbe, *The Idea of Africa*, 78.

32. Ibid., 78.

33. Georg Wilhem Friedrich Hegel, *The Philosophy of History* (New York: Dover Publications, Inc., 1956), 99.

34. C. G. Seligman, *Races of Africa* (London: T. Butterworth, Ltd., 1930), 96.

35. Basil Davidson, *Old Africa Rediscovered* (London: Gollancz, 1964), 29, 37.

36. Hugh Trevor-Roper, *The Rise of Christian Europe* (New York: Harcourt, Brace Jovanovich, 1965), 9, and also see opening remarks of the first lecture of a series by Hugh Trevor-Roper by the same name in *The Listener Magazine* (Nov. 28, 1963), 71.

37. Christopher Stringer and Robin McKie, *African Exodus: The Origins of Modern Humanity* (New York: Henry Holt, 1997).

38. Mazrui, *The Africans*, 12.

39. Caroline Neale, "The Idea of Progress in the Revision of African History" in *Writing Independent History: African Historiography* (Westport, Conn.: Greenwood Press, 1985), 112–117.

40. John Reader, *Biography of a Continent* (New York: Alfred A. Knopf, 1997), 4.

41. Jared Diamond, *Guns and Germs: The Fates of Human Societies* (New York: W. W. Norton, 1997), 377.

SOURCE: Henry Louis Gates, Jr., *Wonders of the African World* (New York: Knopf, 1999).

BLACK LONDON

ABOUT TWENTY-FIVE years ago, I took a job at the London bureau of *Time*. New in town, I had set out on foot from Bayswater Road for the Time-Life Building, on New Bond Street. Soon I was desperately lost and desperately trying not to show my desperation. It was that time of the morning when the only people around were those who actually worked on the street, and they all seemed to speak an alien tongue. This was my first time in England, where I was to live for the next few years, but I might as well have been in Vladivostok: I couldn't understand a word anyone was saying. Then I saw a black face and, out of habit, eagerly approached: at last, in this strange land, a *brother*. The man was cleaning the sidewalk outside a men's clothier's, dousing the concrete with soapy water and sweeping it over the curb. I gave him a prayerful look: Could he possibly tell me how to find New Bond Street? The man stared at me quizzically, and when he opened his mouth he sounded exactly like every other workman I'd encountered.

I was dumbstruck; it was as if the voice were the work of an unseen ventriloquist. Though I must have known better, I had, on some level, always assumed that my black compatriots *sounded* black because they *were* black: I'd assumed (I cringe to relate now) that the shape of our African lips had something to do with our characteristic consonants and vowels. Black comedians like Godfrey Cambridge could "do" a white voice—they delighted in it—but you didn't think they could really keep it up for very long. I spent the next weeks studying first generation English blacks as they spoke, mesmerized by the sight of protuberant lips forming sounds—whether plummily R.P. or blurry and filled with glottal stops—that were indistinguishable from those of their white counterparts. It took a while for the novelty to wear off. My initial travels through black London, then, were for me a succession of spit-takes: black people who sounded English without even trying.

What bliss it was to be black and living in London! How free you felt from the mundane prejudices of race-obsessed America! Here was a country where the boundaries between the races had been erased. Or so, for a time,

I could imagine. I eagerly sought out London's island immigrants: the Trinidadians in Ladbroke Grove; the Barbadians in Finsbury Park, Notting Hill Gate, and Shepherd's Bush; and the Jamaicans (who then made up—as they continue to do—more than two thirds of the West Indian population) concentrated in Brixton. As I soon learned, the history of Britain's West Indians—as a substantial presence, rather than the occasional anomaly—went back only to 1948, when a boatload of nearly five hundred Jamaicans docked at Liverpool. Postwar England had a pressing need for manual labor, and the West Indians provided a convenient source. There had, of course, been people of African descent in England for centuries; the National Portrait Gallery currently has an exhibition devoted to Ignatius Sancho, who corresponded with Sterne and was painted by Gainsborough; and, long before Enoch Powell, Queen Elizabeth I demanded that all the blacks in England pick up and leave. But this was the first time they had established themselves as a collective presence, in numbers that grew to two hundred thousand within a decade and a half. Black London—and it was in London that the great majority of them pooled—was born. The Jamaican poet Louise Bennett called the process "colonization in reverse."

The presence of the black *Gastarbeiter* inevitably caused a certain unease among the natives. You wanted to be good hosts, of course, but you were hard pressed to know what to do when the guests forgot that they *were* guests. And that was the trouble with those postwar West Indians. You'd welcomed them into your home (*so* nice they could stop by), but now the hour was getting late. And, though you'd turned up the lights, noisily switched on the Hoover, even asked if you could call them a cab—done everything you politely could—they still didn't get the message: *You can all go home now.* That's when the sense of panic began to rise.

The blacks arrived at a time of "overemployment," but, as the sixties wore on, overemployment turned to underemployment, and a new and newly disaffected generation found itself out of luck and out of place. If many of them had no jobs, though, they did have their folkways; and in the contest of cultures bangers-and-mash was no match for curry goat. That sense of cultural difference was itself the cause of further unease. Britain had always had its own internal ethnic clashes, but they were familiar and, for the most part, unthreatening, the stuff of music-hall caricatures—"When Ah take a couple o' drinks on a Sa'day night, Glasgow belongs tae me!"

Gradually, my enthusiasm for the Afro-Saxon diaspora soured into frustration at its marginality and powerlessness. I'd arrived from a land where James Brown and Jimi Hendrix—and Miles Davis and John Coltrane—ruled; where an entire generation, so it seemed, had with pen and brush taken up the task of self-representation. In London, the only cultural vitality appeared to come from forms that were borrowed, essentially unmodified, from the Caribbean. I would visit London's leading black bookstore, the New Beacon, and find that nearly everything on the shelves was from the West Indies or America. "How can they be English?" John La Rose, the poet and publisher who ran the store, used to say to me about his fellow-expatriates. "Their entire culture is West Indian."

On Saturday, the younger generation of Britain's recent immigrants would gather at some vacant house that had recently been "liberated" for the occasion, the electricity and gas reconnected for an evening's bacchanalia. It was called "goin' blues," and although the site changed from week to week, you rarely had to ask where it was being held: you could hear it half a block away, as the reggae thudded through the adjoining council housing. You paid your twenty pence at the door and entered into sweltering, Caribbean heat. The floors trembled from the enormous bass loud-speakers. Upstairs, people queued for hot food and for Johnnie Walker served in Coke cans. Everybody was smoking ganja; you could get high just from breathing. But what always struck me was how joyless it all seemed: nobody spoke or even laughed. Expressions were hard, affectless. The only white man I ever saw at a blues party was the one who distributed cocaine and ganja. "Him not white," an acquaintance told me. "Him da *pusher* mon, dat all." Otherwise, the only words you'd hear spoken all night were in the imperative mood. "Pass da ganja" and (if you accidentally brushed by someone in the crowded room) "Don't touch me, mon." Not jubilation but escape was the order of the night. And their language itself was another means of escape. "Da rotted kayan" were the police; "da monkeys" or "da natives" were the English; "Babylon," with a pleasing semantic symmetry, could refer either to England or to Jamaica. There was even a peculiar nomenclature for cognition: a Jamaican friend used to tell me, "Da monkey understands. But da black mon overstands." The one thing they could all overstand was that, no matter how many drinks on a Saturday night, London did not belong to them.

Twenty-five years later, a culture that is distinctively black *and* British can be said to be in full flower, both on the streets and in the galleries. "What we had before was the Afro-Caribbean presence in Britain," says Stuart Hall, a professor of sociology at the Open University, who is, among other things, black Britain's leading theorist of black Britain. "But the emergence of a black British culture can now be seen. For the first time, being black is a way of being British."

This development is partly a reflection of social engineering: in the aftermath of the riots that swept Brixton and other black neighborhoods in 1981,

employment measures like Section 11 were adopted, accelerating the placement of blacks in public sector jobs and helping to create something of a
black middle class, however tiny. It's partly a reflection of the entrepreneurial ethos of Thatcherism itself. And it's partly a reflection of the liminal status of a new generation that was always looking both ahead and behind.
"You know that if you go into a smart boutique on Oxford Street," Hall
says, "one of the things you will find is a very smart, good-looking black
woman. Blacks become objects of desire in curious ways, with some secret
umbilical connection to what's cool or exotic or sexy, or to the body or to
music—all the things that Puritan English culture both reviled and desired.
They've turned marginality into a very creative art form—life form, really—
and they've done so at the level of youth culture, of music, of dress. They've
styled their way into British culture. Which isn't hard, of course—it's one of
the most unstylish places in the world."

Among those who have styled their way into British culture is Ozwald
Boateng, the first black tailor, he says, to hang out his own shingle on Savile
Row, and, at thirty, the youngest. His parents came from the Ashanti region
of Ghana, and he has a West African's dark-chocolate skin, though at six feet
three he's tall for a Ghanaian. More than Boateng's blackness, his brashness
makes him an anomaly on the street: Slick Rick meets Paul Stuart. Even the
shop's décor—the mustard-yellow walls, the purple carpet, the cerise velvet
that drapes the freestanding dressing room—seems a deliberate affront to the
staid establishments that surround it. But what makes him so subversive, sar-
torially speaking, is his conservatism. "Balance" is Boateng's rallying cry as a
maker of men's suits, and I'm impressed, too, by his ability to strike a balance between bland assimilation and strident racial self-assertion. He tells
me that he's "a big believer in being Ashanti," but he also declares, "I love
the whole pompous cast of English tradition." He recounts an annual occasion when the tailors from Savile Row have a formal, sit-down dinner. "And
all the Lords, and everyone—it's a men's club. Really a staunch British organization. And every so often there would be a toast to the Queen, so you'd
stand up: 'The Queen, the Queen!' It's like totally fantastic." You sense in
Boateng a deliciously camp devotion to the ways of little England: he finds
them—well, fetching. And how, I inquire, did he dress at this congregation of
the sartorial centurions, the last guardians of tradition? Did he wear gray
flannel? Boateng appears to be aghast at the possibility. "Actually," he says,
squaring his shoulders, "I wore a black velvet suit with a *slight* glitter in it."

To see what's new here, it helps to talk to someone who has succeeded under the terms of the older covenant, and can remind you that in the more rarefied circles of London society you're still unlikely to encounter a black face.
The dress designer Bruce Oldfield, whose clients include the Princess of

Wales, was adopted as a child by a white woman who lived in rural England. "I don't think I really saw black people en masse until I was about twenty-one, when I came to London and lived in Brixton," he says. At any rate, the visible signs of Oldfield's Jamaican heritage are pretty discreet. "I have a great rapport with Arabs, because they think *I'm* an Arab," he tells me, with a low, mischievous chuckle, "Which is handy, because they've got a lot of money, and they like buying flashy frocks." These days, Oldfield has left Brixton for behind, and the London he inhabits is essentially color-free. "I mean, if I go into a trendy restaurant, like the Caprice or the Ivy, I don't see many black people," he says. "I just don't see black people where I go. I'm rarely in a house where there's another black person, socially." He speaks of all this matter-of-factly, and yet it's clear that he sees himself, finally, as an interloper in the circles he moves through. "English society is very compartmentalized," he says. "There are black people who cross over, obviously—there'll be an interior decorator, a designer, people like me." Yet there's all the difference in the world between thinking that you belong and thinking that you've crossed over. Oldfield doesn't quite manage a smile when he tells me, "I cross over because I'm amusing and witty and charming."

As you'd expect, a lot of the recent cultural ferment associated with black London happens much closer to street level. You feel that energy when you page through some of the black newspapers, like the weekly *Voice* (which claims to have two hundred thousand readers) and the more bourgie *New Nation* (which has been publishing only since November and hopes to reach thirty thousand). And you feel it even in the crudely satiric *Skank*, which is produced by and addressed to younger blacks. *Skank* has a less than reverential attitude toward black celebrities (devoting an entire page to the splayed nostrils of the Birmingham-based black boxer Chris Eubank, which it likens to King Kong's); and it spoofs such historic episodes of black resistance as the 1981 Brixton riots, by offering "the Brixton Riots '95 role playing game." ("Feel the tension as you try to light that petrol bomb! Feel your pulse race as you try to find a hiding place for that brand new 48 inch Dolby stereo, laser color TV and video you happily found lying in Dixons!") Then, there was a scabrous cartoon sequence entitled "Lunch Box Christie," which focused on the runner Linford Christie's supposedly outsized endowment. (Christie sued the magazine, but only because the cartoon also implied that he took drugs to increase his athletic performance.)

Skank is published by the X Press, which is otherwise exclusively a book-publishing house. The press's founder, Dotun Adebayo, was born in Nigeria and came to the U.K. when he was six; his father taught physics at the University of London, though he has since retired and returned to Nigeria. The Adebayos are a textbook story of upward mobility: during one period, Dr.

Adebayo had five children at university in England at the same time. Dotun Adebayo himself studied philosophy at the University of Essex; his brother Diran, a successful novelist, attended Oxford. Dotun Adebayo, like others of his generation, has a strong sense of mission—the familiar first-generation drive to fulfill the longings of the immigrant parents. "I drive a very old car, but it happens to be a Jaguar," he told me. "The reason I have it is my father, and his dream. He always wanted a Jaguar XJ-6. My father came back over to this country recently, and I didn't even tell him I had this car, I just told him I'd pick him up. He was so proud. He said, 'Ah Dotun. When I lived in England, I always wanted this car.' It didn't matter that he'd spent thirty years here without achieving what he wanted to achieve—he had actually achieved it for the next generation. So that the onus is now on us to do something."

Adebayo's first big score as a book publisher was Victor Headley's "Yardie"—pulp fiction about Jamaican gangster life. "Basically, we postered the whole of Brixton," he recalls. "You woke up one morning and everywhere you looked in Brixton it said 'Yardie.' Within a few weeks, we'd sold thousands and thousands of copies." The X Press has now published fifty-one titles, most by black British authors, and most delightfully lurid and action-packed. (The titles include "Rude Gal," "Curvy Love-box," and "The Ragga and the Royal.") The success of these books shows that there is a black reading public—though Adebayo would argue that black London is something that is in the process of being created. "You need to go outside London and see the other inner cities, and then you will realize there is a black London," he told me. "The black people in Manchester are Mancunians first. Black people second. There's no link point over there. In the circles I move in—and I move in circles from ragamuffin kids to intellectuals, or what have you—there is definitely an urge to create a black London."

In the main, the black London that existed in the sixties and seventies was bound by what Stuart Hall calls a "transistor culture"—by certain kinds of music and the radio stations that played them. Though blacks in Britain have always been known for the music they brought with them from the islands (like ska and reggae and its rougher offspring, ragga), it is only relatively recently that these musical styles have evolved beyond their precursors. Today, the mores of the black British club scene have drifted far from those island moorings.

You can get a sense of just how far at Rampage, a movable feast held one recent Friday at the S.W.1 Club, near Victoria Station. By a quarter past ten, there's already a line of young working-class blacks all the way down the block and around the corner. They queue relatively quietly, chatting in small groups. Inside the small foyer, everyone is halted for a serious security check, scanned by metal detectors and thoroughly patted down by bouncers with headsets. Then they pay their eight pounds cover charge and proceed up a flight of steps and into a large rectangular room. It is furnished sparely, with just a few tables and chairs—nowhere near enough to accommodate a crowd that will grow to a thousand or more by midnight, but by then everybody will be bumping and grinding to Garage and House, hip-hop, Jungle, and even some R & B. At first, men face each other, dancing, but in postures that are menacing rather than erotic. It's as if they were shadowboxing to the heavy bass beat. Few couples dance together; instead, the genders divide and watch each other, with the men engaged in active display. A man moves in and out of another man's space, mimicking and exaggerating the other's moves. Again, it's pretend sparring; occasionally a shoulder knocks a shoulder.

The hair stylist Daniel ("Er, I still use 'Daniel X,'" he says sheepishly, "but my friends tell me it's *such* a cliché") fluently explains the vitality of the popular music scene to me. "I was really disturbed when I first heard Jungle, because they took some of my favorite reggae tunes and just speeded them up," he says. "The vocals sounded like Mickey Mouse. I was like 'That tune's sacred! How dare you play it at that speed?' They'd double the speed, sample stuff, then put a chant over it, like 'I'll kill your mother.' It took me a little while to come around." Now Daniel speaks of Jungle music with the zeal of a convert. He distinguishes with scholastic precision between Jungle (the drum-and-bass kind of thing that has crossed over, to the point where fifty-year-old David Bowie has a couple of Jungle tracks on his new album) and *Jungle* Jungle, which remains hard-core and all black. But that's not the point. The point is that Daniel himself is about to put out a Jungle track in a couple of months, on his label, Ticking Time Records. Daniel sees a musical world rife with possibility; and should he fail there are multitudes behind him.

In no small measure, black culture simply *is* youth culture in London today. Bizarre as it first seems, speaking with a Jamaican inflection has become hip among working-class white kids. If blacks are only 1.6 per cent of the population, the percentage of wiggers—white wannabes—seems considerably higher. It would be a mistake, though, to come to any hasty conclusions. Imitation and enmity have an uncanny ability to coexist. Paul Gilroy, a leading theorist of black British culture, and a professor at Goldsmiths' College, at the University of London, tells me about white skinheads who beat up blacks and then go home and listen to the rap group Public Enemy. It's as if they can't decide whether they want to bash blacks or be blacks.

And there you have the central contradictions of post-Thatcherite England: the growing cultural prominence of black culture there doesn't mean that racism itself has much abated. The police recently bugged the apartment of the young white thugs suspected of killing a seventeen-year-old black student, Steven Lawrence, and found them hashing over various ways of killing blacks—even demonstrating the right moves with their kitchen knives. Just last week, a report by the Office for Public Management found that the Royal Navy has "a level of awareness of cultural diversity which is 10 or 20 years behind that of society at large and which can reasonably be said to constitute institutional racism." The same investigation concluded that in the R.A.F. blacks are routinely excluded from honor-guard or V.I.P. details: "An unwritten rule summarized as 'no blacks, Pakis, spots or specs' governed basic assumptions about how things should 'really' or 'normally' be."

Nor are the better-off necessarily better disposed. At a dinner party at a Suffolk manor house, a group of fairly well-to-do Englishmen discuss their hopes and fears for postelection Britain while a fly-on-the-wall documentary-maker named Paul Watson films the group he has convened. The guests—a sales director at a real-estate company, a Lloyds insurance broker, a restaurant owner, and so forth—talk spiritedly about, inter alia, the disagreeableness of blacks. ("I would encourage the black minorities to move back to their country of origin," one says.) Controversy ensues when the documentary is shown on Channel 4, but the participants have few regrets: one of them, a baronet's son named Henry Erskine-Hill, says, "I would think our opinions are representative of the views of a great many people." Erskine-Hill was asked by a newspaper if he was a racist. "It depends what you mean by racism," he sagely replied.

What's clear is that British identity itself remains, as Stuart Hall would say, a contested space. A few years ago, Norman Beresford Tebbit, who was one of Margaret Thatcher's ministers and a onetime chairman of the Tory Party, complained that when Britain's cricket team played one of the West Indian teams "our blacks" tended to root for the wrong side. How could they be truly British if they weren't rooting for the British team? And it's perfectly true that most black Brits fail the so-called Tebbit test; collective allegiances don't always align themselves altogether neatly. In Britain, the challenge is to figure out a vocabulary for addressing the intersections of racial and national identities.

"The trouble is, all of our language on race and race relations has always been borrowed from the United States, and there are reasons why that's wrong," Trevor Phillips, a longtime television broadcaster and producer, complains to me, in crisp Oxford English with just the faintest lilt to it. (He spent his childhood between Guyana and North London.) "Effectively, Caribbean Americans behave in the United States as classical immigrants do and succeed as classical immigrants do—Koreans, say. Here we behave like black Americans in northern cities. Our experience is just the same as that of the blacks who migrated from the South to Chicago—all the way down to welfare dependency, and so forth."

The statistics *are* pretty dire. The unemployment rate among Afro-Caribbeans in Britain is around twenty-five per cent, and in some parts of London it's closer to fifty per cent. The fraction that belongs to the professional class is only two per cent. Despite the fact that Afro-Caribbeans make up only 1.2 per cent of the population, moreover, a recent survey indicated that there may be as many as sixty-one thousand racially motivated assaults against Afro-Caribbeans over the course of a year.

Phillips, a man whose velvety burnt-sienna skin is accented by copper-framed glasses, is the chairman of the Runnymede Trust, and is regarded by many black Brits as a leading cultural broker. As influential as he is at present, he is likely to become more so in the near future. For one thing, he's a friend of Tony Blair's and is said to be in line for a position of some importance. Rumor has him as the chairman of the London Arts Board—or even, once the city's council system of governance is overhauled, as mayor. The possibility of his being raised to a peerage has also been mentioned. Perhaps not surprisingly for such an insider, he doesn't see how separatist ideologies will ever prosper among English blacks. "I think most black people in this country are embarrassed by the idea of being separate," he says. "Our neighbors don't come to lynch us, by and large. And, you know, we go out with their daughters, for Christ's sake." The saving grace of a class-bound society, after all, is that the right class credentials can often override other obstacles.

"The one thing that saves me on the street with the police," Dotun Adebayo tells me, "is they hear my accent and then they think, Hang on, this isn't your typical black bus driver or minicab driver, and take you a bit more seriously. And class is distinguished more by the way you speak than by anything else. In fact, the most tangible racism you'll find here is from the working classes. They're the ones who are going to fight you on the street. Whereas with the middle classes it can be 'Oh, gosh, you went to Oxford as well? Oh, jolly good.'" The novelist Caryl Phillips, who grew up between St. Kitts and England, where he studied at Cambridge, tidily describes the relationship between sociolect and skin color: "In the States, until I open my mouth I look as if I fit in. In Britain, it's only when I open my mouth that I fit in."

That situation can lead to some cultural contortions. Yvonne Brewster, the artistic director of the black theatre company Talawa and a recent O.B.E. ("for services in the arts"), tells me about what she dubs "the raffia ceiling." She says, "Linford Christie will say to you, 'I cannot drive my Porsche.' The man is a millionaire, but he could get arrested for stealing the car. That's why someone like the boxer Chris Eubank dresses up like a kind of antediluvian English toff, with plus fours and a monocle, so he is easily identifiable. You know, there's method to his madness. Even if they stop him with his Mercedes-Benz, they say, 'Ah, it's Chris Eubank—drive on.' In this country, there's absolutely no chance of burning that raffia ceiling. If you put your head above the parapet, you're likely to get it cut off."

For Yvonne Brewster, a member of Jamaica's "mulatto élite," there was never anything abstract about the vagaries of race and class in her new country. "My father had two farms, one in Portland and one in St. Thomas, and there was a man who used to do the horses in St. Thomas," she recalls. "He used to call me Miss Yvonne. Anyway, he came over here as a migrant, because there was no future for him in Jamaica and he didn't have any education. I was over here studying, and I was at Tottenham Court Road underground station and he saw me and came up and hugged and kissed me." That the laborer should have presumed on the solidarity of color and acquaintance horrified her, and, in her vulnerable state, she recoiled. "I suppose what flashed through my mind was that in Jamaica this man wouldn't even come within six feet of me," she says. "Anyway, I never saw the man again." She breaks off, and I notice that there are tears in her eyes.

Yet if the barriers of class seem higher in England, those of race seem far more permeable. I'm always struck by the social ease between most blacks and whites on London streets. I was recently near the Brixton market, across the street from the entrance to its open air section, and two men—tall, coal-black, muscle-bound—came loping toward a small young white woman who was walking by herself in the opposite direction. What happened then was—well, nothing. The needle on the anxiety meter didn't so much as quiver. Throughout the area, blacks and whites seemed comfortable with one another in a way that most American urbanites simply aren't and never have been. "The advantage we have here in England is that you are more likely to be accepted for who you are," one black Londoner tells me. "People don't judge you by who your partner is or who your friends are. I have this white girlfriend who lives in Brixton. We were going shopping in a market, and I met some Lisson Grovers"—the "ruffneck" denizens of a large housing project—"who had never seen me with a white woman. They took it really well. They were like 'Yeah, O.K.'" Annie Stewart, the editor of the *Voice*, says, "I think something like forty per cent of our men have a relationship with a white woman. You find a second generation of blacks here who are more integrated than the first generation."

Some of this sense of belonging is simply a result of racial dispersion. The Labour M.P. Bernie Grant points out, "Even in my area, Tottenham, housing is mixed among the various races—blacks are mixed with whites and Asians and people from Cyprus, and it's all one big cosmopolitan bundle." Americans who imagine Brixton to be analogous to Harlem are always surprised to see how large its white population is. London is where seventy per cent of Britain's blacks reside, but its blackest neighborhoods are almost never more than two-thirds black, and usually they're substantially less.

All this sounds like a good thing, and yet blacks in London often speak enviously of the salience of race in America. "I love going to New York, because I can walk down the street and the place is full of black people," says Ekow Eshun, who is the twenty-eight-year-old editor of *Arena*—a sort of English *Details.* "A lot of the identity of the city is forged on the basis of that. The whole young black generation—the whole hip-hop thing—is very, very alive in New York, and it has a marked effect on the character of the city." So part of the romance with America that you find in black Britain has to do with a sense that America has, racially speaking, a critical mass.

The allure of America isn't just that of indelible blackness, though. It's also the allure of class mobility. Of all the black Londoners I've spoken to, Trevor Phillips delivers the most impassioned homage to America, and it's in precisely these terms: "I think the thing about the West Indians in the United States—and I know it's probably not fashionable to say this—is the openness of American society. There is, I think, genuine social mobility if you're ready for it." He's convinced of this because of his father's fortunes. His father left school at thirteen and had never learned to write other than in block capitals; in England, he worked in the post office. Trevor remembered visiting his father at work one day, in a large sorting office manned largely by blacks. "They were all wearing Post Office uniforms, blue jackets with red piping, and then across the floor comes a white man wearing a suit, a gray suit, and my father said to me simply, 'That's one of the guv'nors,' meaning that it signified two things: that this man is completely separate from us, and that no matter what I, George Phillips, do—no matter how much people respect me, no matter how well I know my job—I will never be one of them." Then his father came to New York, got a job as a security guard at Columbia University, and decided, for some reason, to go to night school and learn bookkeeping. "In a year, I think, he had become the treasurer of a little think tank at Columbia called the American Assembly. This guy goes to the United States, he gets some education at the age of fifty-seven, gets his qualifications, and he ends up signing for Henry Kissinger's expenses." Phillips is practically swelling in the recitation—there's a nearly evangelical fervor to his voice now—and he looks at me as if to say, How can you not love a country like that?

Like many other British blacks, it must be said, he has a slightly romantic view of black America. "The idea that my children could grow up in a place where all kinds of rich people, the people who call the shots, who feel comfortable in their skins, are black—that's the greatest advantage I could give them," he says. It's a seductive image, this land where blacks call the shots, and one I often hear yearningly invoked by black Brits. They'd disavow it, of course, but I detect an implicit fantasy of black America as a Cotswolds village populated by Oprah Winfrey, Bill Cosby, Michael Jordan, Terry McMillan, Spike Lee, Michael Jackson, Quincy Jones, Vernon Jordan, and dozens more of their ilk. ("Yo, Trev—sorry this is kind of last minute, but Oprah, Cos, and Colin were thinking about snagging a bite at Georgia Brown's and then maybe popping over to the Senate to try and talk some sense into them about the new education bill. Care to join us?") *That's* their American fantasy, and it seems unsporting to demur.

What's curious is that, while black Londoners look yearningly across the Atlantic, their American counterparts in the arts increasingly turn to them for inspiration. Thelma Golden, a curator of contemporary art at the Whitney Museum, in New York, is voluble on the subject of how much more vibrant—how much more advanced—the new black arts scene in London is compared with its New York equivalent. "In a way, I'd much rather be a black curator in London than in New York, because the excitement and sophistication there is extraordinary, way ahead of what's happening here in New York," she told me.

"Most thinking people don't know that there is a huge creative upsurge going on in the young black generation," Stuart Hall says. Hall was born and educated in Jamaica, came to England in 1951, as a Rhodes Scholar, and has watched three successive generations learn what it means to be black and British. But clearly the word is getting out, in part because of people like Hall himself. A soft-spoken man in his early sixties, with warm light-brown skin, a close-cropped gray beard, and gentle manner, he is a tutelary figure for dozens of artists who constitute, in a free-form way, a postmodern black arts scene. He himself has played a central role in this development; indeed, for some he has nearly guru-like status. The black photographer David A. Bailey says of him, "People will say, 'Tell us your stories, Obi Wan Kenobi.'" But Hall's characteristic tone is far from oracular. What he brings to London's black arts scene is really a set of emphases; for him, identities are things we make up, but not just out of any old thing. As he puts it, "identities are the names we give to the different ways we are positioned by, and position ourselves in, the narratives of the past."

Today, Hall and his wife, Catherine, live on Mowbray Road, in Kilburn, in a three-story yellow brick Victorian house. Hall has a high-ceilinged, book-lined study on the second floor; on the way to it you pass by a patrician-looking portrait of his nearly white grandfather. Amid the Jane Austen and Henry James are books with titles like "The Photographs of Rotimi Fani-Kayode" and "Race and the Education of Desire." There's a poster for Isaac Julien's 1986 film "Looking for Langston," and another for the fiftieth-anniversary staging of a C. L. R. James play, produced by Yvonne Brewster. Hall's movements are cautious, and he uses a cane to get around—he's in chronic pain—yet he grows animated when he talks about the coalescence of the new artistic vanguard in black London, one that's devoted to reinventing the very idea of British identity.

He shows me some photographs of the late Rotimi Fani-Kayode, who belonged to a prominent Yoruba family in Nigeria and settled in London, and, Hall says, managed "to use all the elements of his cultural heritage with a kind of equal weight and yet at the same time to transform each by the presence of the other." Still, it isn't insignificant that Fani-Kayode's principal subject was the black body. "What's happened with the new generation is that they've begun to acknowledge their own blackness," Hall argues. "They've begun to paint and photograph their own bodies. They can live with their own bodies—this is a very important turning point." This inward turn has meant leaving behind a "progressive" convention of the eighties: using "black" to refer indifferently to all nonwhites, including South Asians. "People don't use 'black' in quite that way any longer, because they want to identify more precisely where they come from, culturally," Hall says. That moment of self-reflexivity plays out in all sorts of ways: Sonia Boyce's four-panel drawing "Lay Back, Keep Quiet, and Think of What Made Britain So Great" (1986) positions her own brown visage in a wallpaper pattern that was designed to mark the fiftieth year of Victoria's reign; filmmakers like Isaac Julien and John Akomfrah produce visual meditations on memory and migration; multimedia artists like Keith Piper use computer-abetted installations to reflect on the politics of image. All these artists acknowledge their indebtedness to Hall, and yet for him the real significance of the new black arts scene is that it isn't, any longer, a black arts scene. "It's reached the point where a lot of artists who began by identifying themselves with ethnic minority groups have fought off the 'burden of representation'—the idea that they have to speak on behalf of their entire race. They're moving outward into engaging in a more culturally diverse mainstream. They're questioning and diversifying that mainstream."

The challenge of questioning and diversifying the mainstream is something that Lord Taylor of Warwick knows intimately, and, as we sat in the Peers'

Guest Room of the House of Lords, he told me about the contrast between his own career and that of his father, Derief Taylor. His father was a champion cricket player from Jamaica who went on to play for Warwick; he was also a qualified accountant. When he retired from the playing field, however, he could only find work doing menial labor. "He was always striving to improve himself," Lord Taylor says, "and then he reached a kind of ceiling and began to sort of see his ambitions through me." Taylor, for his part, went on to become the first black to be head pupil at Moseley Grammar School, in Birmingham, and the first black to win the Gray's Inn Advocacy Prize, and—when the Criminal Evidence (Amendment) Bill is enacted—he will be the first black to create British law.

"Some tea, milord?" a florid faced servant murmurs. Lord Taylor—England's only, though not its first, black Lord—graciously murmurs assent.

And yet the story of his ennoblement—he has enjoyed this salutation for less than six months—isn't an altogether edifying one. It seems that when the Tory Party put him up for a vacant seat in Cheltenham, vociferous protests came from the Party locals—retired colonels and other stalwarts, who had a hard time seeing themselves represented by the son of a Jamaican cricketer and laborer. He was forced to stand aside. That episode embarrassed the national Party, and Prime Minister John Major sought to make the best of things by arranging for him to receive a peerage. "None of the parties have a good record on race, one has to be honest about that," Lord Taylor admits.

Ultimately, though, he believes that black Britain's destiny belongs to black Britain—something that does give him pause. "Trevor's right—I think the aspirational thing is part of Asian culture, but it certainly is not part of the Afro-Caribbean culture here," he says. "If you read the Afro-Caribbean newspapers, week by week it tends to be gloom and doom—deaths in police custody, unemployment, some black person taking her company to the industrial tribunal because of being sacked or not getting the right job, and all that sort of thing. And we all identify with it. Just because we're professionals, we all identify with it."

As is true of so many of black London's illuminati, Lord Taylor has a corresponding fascination with the global preeminence of America's black superstars. "We have media and show-biz people who have made it, but they're few in number—no more than ten or eleven—and they don't have the global standing of their American counterparts," Lord Taylor says. He goes on to tell me that as a child in England he took inspiration from a magazine for American blacks. "Many of my positive black role models came from *Ebony*—people like Muhammad Ali, Martin Luther King, Jesse Jackson, Quincy Jones. You know, it was always the elitism, but that encouraged me, because I could see that there were and are successful black people.

That was the sweet part of it. The sad part of it was they were all American. They were untouchable in that sense." Having long cherished a fantasy of appearing in *Ebony* himself, Lord Taylor says he was jubilant to learn recently that *Ebony* would be featuring him and his family in its May edition.

There are moments—for me, this was one—when an American visitor to black London feels caught in a time warp. Their number are small, their achievements still, somehow, measurable. "Just a few weeks ago," Lord Taylor recalls, "an editor at *Ebony* calls me and says, 'Lord Taylor, could you fax me a list of the fifty top black chairmen of companies in England?' I just fell about laughing, and he couldn't understand what the joke was, and I said, 'I can try to get you five,' because they just don't exist. The big companies do not have black directors. That's the whole point." Ekow Eshun says, "The frustrating thing about Britain is that the black presence in this country is decades behind America, especially in terms of high culture." I see what he means, and yet that isn't my reaction. So I'm left struggling to understand why black Britain seems to me at once twenty years behind the times and twenty years ahead, somehow both pre- and post-nationalist. No doubt both temporal impressions are illusory. Yet perhaps what is most heartening about black London is cultural rather than racial—that has the capacity to acknowledge difference without fetishizing it, the freedom to represent without having to be representative. In the unending Kulturkampf between irony and solidarity, irony seems to be ahead in black London, at least on points.

As Lord Taylor of Warwick could attest, many things have changed since the nineteen-sixties, when a Tory parliamentary candidate could triumph with the slogan "If you want a nigger neighbor, vote Labour." And many things haven't. "I'm also going into business," Lord Taylor had told me when we spoke. "I'm going to be a sort of corporate headhunter, joining one of the top firms in the world." He was girding himself for the challenge, which he discussed with Dale Carnegie gumption: "A lot of it will be networking— meeting the right people." Even after being raised to the peerage, he'd had more than his share of meeting the wrong people. He recalled an encounter with a woman at a formal cocktail party a few months ago. "So you're Lord Taylor," she said, studying him coolly. "I'll bet you do a good limbo." Today, Taylor's entry in the latest edition of Dod's parliamentary guide appears directly above that of another life baron, one Norman Beresford Tebbit. Make of that what you will.

SOURCE: *The New Yorker*, April 28, 1997.

HARLEM ON OUR MINDS

The real fever of love for the place will begin to take hold upon him. The subtle, insidious wine of New York will begin to intoxicate him. Then, if he is wise, he will go away, any place—yes, he will even go over to Jersey. But if he be a fool, he will stay and stay on until the town becomes all in all to him; until the very streets are his chums and certain buildings and corners his best friends. Then he is hopeless, and to live elsewhere would be death. The Bowery will be his romance, Broadway his lyric, and the Park his pastoral, the river and the glory of it all his epic, and he will look down pityingly on all the rest of humanity.

—PAUL LAURENCE DUNBAR

It was loving the City that distracted me and gave me ideas. Made me think I could speak its loud voice and make the sound human. I missed the people altogether.

—TONI MORRISON

THE IDEA OF a black renaissance has a long and curious history in American culture.

Writing in *Lippincott's Magazine* in 1889, an anonymous reviewer, lamenting the absence of the Great American Novel, predicted that a truly sublime American literature would be created not by a man but by a woman, and an African American woman at that:

Fate keeps revenge in store. It was a woman who, taking the wrongs of the African as her theme, wrote the novel that awakened the world to their reality, and why should not the coming novelist be a woman as well as an African? She—the woman of that race—has some claims on Fate which are not yet paid up.

451

This artist, the reviewer went on to predict, would emerge at the fore-front of a bold new movement in the arts, a veritable renaissance in black-face. With Toni Morrison's receipt of the 1993 Nobel Prize in literature and the unprecedented number of black artists at work in so many genres today, it is difficult not to recognize the signs that African Americans are in the midst of a cultural renaissance.

Today's African American renaissance is the fourth such movement in the arts in this century. It is also the most successful and the most sustained. The first occurred at the turn of the century. In 1901, the black Bostonian William Stanley Braithwaite, a distinguished critic and poet, argued that "we are at the commencement of a 'negroid' renaissance . . . that will have as much importance in literary history as the much spoken of and much praised Celtic and Canadian renaissance." At the end of a full decade of un-precedented literary productions by black women—who published a dozen novels and edited their own literary journal between 1890 and 1900—and precisely when the poet Paul Laurence Dunbar, the novelists Pauline Hop-kins and Charles Chesnutt, and the essayists W. E. B. Du Bois and Anna Julia Cooper were at the height of their creative powers, a critic in *The A. M. E. Church Review* in 1904 declared the birth of "The New Negro Liter-ary Movement," likening it, as had Braithwaite, to the Celtic renaissance.

It was Booker T. Washington who first hoped to institutionalize the cul-tural and political force of this New Negro. In 1900 Washington enlisted several of his fellows (including his nemesis, Du Bois) to construct an image unfettered by the racist burdens of the past, a past characterized by two-and-a-half centuries of slavery and nearly half a century of disenfranchise-ment, peonage, black codes, and legalized Jim Crow—not to mention the vicious assault on negro freedom and political rights enacted in literature, in theater and on the vaudeville stage, and throughout the popular visual arts, in the form of a blanket of demeaning stereotypes of deracinated, ugly, treacherous, hauntingly evil Sambo images. At the beginning of the century, families could encounter these images throughout their homes from the time they turned off their alarm clocks in the morning and sat down to their egg cups or tea cosies, napkin rings or place mats at breakfast, to the time they spent in the evenings playing parlor games, reading advertisements in magazines, or addressing U.S. government postcards. Such an onslaught of stereotypes, reinforced subliminally in advertisements and on trading cards, in pulpits on Sundays, and even in the law, demanded resistance and an organized response. "We must turn away from the memories of the slave past," Washington demanded, no doubt with this proliferation of negations of black humanity in mind. "A New Negro for a New Century," he argued, would be the answer.

This New Negro movement, which took at least three forms before Alain Locke enshrined it in the Harlem Renaissance in 1925, drew its artistic inspiration from across the Atlantic in Europe. First, Anton Dvorak in the early 1890s declared spirituals America's first authentic contribution to world culture and urged classical composers to draw upon them to create *sui generis* symphonies. A decade later, Pablo Picasso stumbled onto "dusky Manikins" at an ethnographic museum and forever transformed European art, as well as Europe's official appreciation of the art from the African continent. Picasso's *Les Demoiselles d'Avignon* (1906–7) the signature event in the creation of cubism—stands as a testament to the shaping influence of African sculpture and to the central role that African art played in the creation of modernism. The cubist mask of modernism covers a black Bantu face. African art—ugly, primitive, debased in 1900; sublime, complex, valorized by 1910— was transformed so dramatically in the cultural imagination of the West, in such an astonishingly short period, that the potential for the political uses of black art and literature in America could not escape the notice of African American intellectuals, especially Du Bois, himself educated in Europe and cosmopolitan to the core, and Locke, the Harvard-trained philosopher, who went to Oxford as a Rhodes scholar in 1907, the year after Picasso stumbled uncannily onto the African sublime, and who studied aesthetics in Germany in the heady years of the modernist explosion. If European modernism was truly mulatto, the argument went, then African Americans could save themselves politically through the creation of the arts. This renaissance, the second and most famous in black history, would fully liberate the Negro—at least its advanced guard.

The Harlem or New Negro Renaissance was born through the midwifery of Locke, who edited a special issue of *Survey Graphic* magazine entitled "Harlem: Mecca of the New Negro" in March of 1925, which was followed by the 446-page anthology *The New Negro: An Interpretation,* replete with illustrations by the German expressionist Winold Reiss and the African American Aaron Douglas. Writers such as Langston Hughes, Jean Toomer, Countee Cullen, Jessie Fauset, and Zora Neale Hurston—the fundaments of the black canon today—came of age at this time, leading the *New York Herald Tribune* to announce that America was "on the edge, if not already in the midst, of what might not improperly be called a Negro renaissance." Locke liked the term, too: part 1 of his anthology is called "The Negro Renaissance." Locke even urged young black visual artists to imitate the European modernist, so heavily influenced by sub-Saharan African art. "By being modern," Locke declared, with no hint of irony, "we are being African."

For Locke and his fellow authors, the function of a cultural renaissance was inherently political: the production of great artworks, by blacks, in sufficient numbers, would lead to the Negro's "reevaluation by white and black alike." And this reevaluation would facilitate the Negro's demand for civil rights and for social and economic equality. Stopped short by the 1929 stock market crash, which hurt the white patrons upon whom the Renaissance was so dependent, the Renaissance writers (a tiny group, numbering perhaps fifty), whom Locke thought of as "the Negro's cultural adolescence," were never able to nurture black art to its formal adulthood, nor were they able to usher in the new world of civil rights through art.

The third renaissance was the Black Arts movement, which lasted from 1965 to the early seventies. Defining themselves against the Harlem Renaissance and deeply rooted in black cultural nationalism, the Black Arts writers saw themselves as the artistic wing of the Black Power movement. Writers such as Amiri Baraka, Larry Neal, and Sonia Sanchez saw black art as fulfilling a function, primarily the political liberation of black people from white racism. Constructed on a fragile foundation of the overtly political, this renaissance was the most short-lived of all. Yet many of the artists who have come of age in the decades since were shaped or deeply influenced by this period. By 1975, with the Black Arts movement dead (Baraka had become a Marxist in 1973), Black Studies departments in peril, and a homogenized disco music on the rise, many of us wondered if black culture were not undergoing some sort of profound identity crisis. A decade later, however, black writers, visual artists, musicians, dancers, and actors would enter a period of creativity unrivaled in American history.

Critics date the current renaissance variously, some tracing its origins to the resurgence of black women's literature and criticism in the early eighties, especially in the works of Ntozake Shange, Michele Wallace, Alice Walker, and Toni Morrison. These women and their successors were able, simultaneously, to reach a large, traditionally middle-class, white female readership plus a new black female audience that had been largely untapped. The growth of this community of readers has resulted in an unrivalled number of novels by and about black women since 1980, as well as an unprecedentedly large African American market for books about every aspect of the black experience. While it is always arbitrary to try to date a cultural movement, it seems reasonable to note an upsurge in black creativity in 1987, the year in which August Wilson's *Fences* premiered on Broadway and Toni Morrison published her masterpiece, *Beloved*. Both would receive Pulitzer Prizes. In that same year, PBS aired Henry Hampton's *Eyes on the Prize*, the six-part documentary of the civil rights era; Cornell scholar Martin Bernal published *Black Athena*, a bold revisionist history that locates the origins of classical Greek civilization in Africa. As Nelson George says in his *Buppies, B-boys, Baps, and Bohos: Notes on Post-Soul Black Culture*, T-shirts with slogans such as

"Black By Popular Demand" and "It's A Black Thing, You Wouldn't Understand" spread across the nation from predominately black colleges. Moreover, the rap revolution was well under way at about this time. Meanwhile, Spike Lee and Wynton Marsalis were establishing themselves as masters of film and jazz. Since that year, the production of cultural artifacts in virtually every field and genre has been astonishing.

The grandchildren of Du Bois's "Talented Tenth," those who were able to profit from the affirmative action programs implemented in the late sixties that are facing such a harsh onslaught today, have thus for the past decade been in the midst of a great period of artistic productivity, much of it centered in New York. The signs of cultural vibrancy are unmistakable: in dance, Bill T. Jones and Judith Jamison; in literature, Toni Morrison and Terry McMillan, Walter Mosley and John Edgar Wideman; in drama, August Wilson; in poetry, Rita Dove; in opera, Anthony Davis and Thulani Davis; in jazz, Wynton Marsalis and Cassandra Wilson; public intellectuals such as Cornel West and bell hooks, Greg Tate and Lisa Jones; the visual artists Martin Puryear and Lorna Simpson; the rap musicians Public Enemy and Queen Latifah; the filmmakers Spike Lee, Julie Dash, and John Singleton—the list is stunningly long. From television to op-ed pages, from the academy to hip-hop, never before have so many black artists and intellectuals achieved so much success in so very many fields. Do their efforts amount to a renaissance?

"It depends on how you define 'renaissance,'" Cornel West has argued. "The rebirth by means of a recovery of classical heritage, I wouldn't call it that. What we do have, however, is a high-quality ferment, a proliferation of a variety of new voices that are transgressing the boundaries in place. These artists exhibit a certain kind of self-confidence, a refusal to accept the belief that they have to prove themselves. Artists such as Wright and Baldwin clearly wrestled on a different terrain."

A different terrain, indeed. Since 1968, when the civil rights movement, a century old, ended so abruptly with the murder of Dr. King, affirmative action and entitlement programs have *dramatically* affected the black community's collective economic health. Not only has the size of its middle class quadrupled since 1968 but, according to the 1990 census, almost as many blacks between the ages of 25 and 44 are college graduates as are high school dropouts, whereas "just twenty years ago, there were five times as many black high school dropouts as college graduates in the workforce," as Sam Roberts reported in the *New York Times* on 18 June 1995. Between 1970 and 1990, moreover, the percentage of blacks who had attended some college increased from 9.1 percent to 33.2 percent, of those graduating from college from 5.1 percent to 11 percent, the highest in history, and of those with some postgraduate work from 1.2 percent to 4.1 percent. By 1989, 1 in 7 black families were middle class (earning $50,000 or more), compared to 1 in 3 white families. "Just a generation ago," Roberts writes, "only 1 in 17 black families" could claim middle-class status; the increase is clearly the result of governmental "prodding." For African Americans, however, it is the best of times and the worst of times. While part of the black community has experienced two decades of unprecedented growth, another part lags dramatically behind. Black America has simultaneously the largest middle class *and* the largest underclass in its history. And the current renaissance of black art and culture—with its inherent schisms and tensions—is unfolding against this conflicted socioeconomic backdrop. Let us pursue this paradox.

Despite their remarkable gains, a certain sense of precariousness haunts the new black middle class and the art that it consumes. Its own economic uplift remains perilously novel. An ambivalent romance with the street and b-boy culture—an intimacy, a freshness, but also a sense that one could go back "there" at any time—haunts much contemporary black literature, film, and hip-hop. The partition between the classes, in the minds of many blacks, is as thin as rice paper.

But because the shtetl memory, as it were, is still so very recent, the romanticization of the ghetto is accompanied by its demonization. The movement to censor gangsta rap, for instance, can be seen as part of the black bourgeoisie's anxiety, its deep-seated fear that it, too, is just one or two paychecks away from the fate of the underclass. The black middle class defines itself by consumption, but it is never free from the past and presence of racism. In fact, it often defines itself *against* this very history.

The nature and size of the new black middle class is significant here because of what it implies about patronage and the economics of black art: whereas the Harlem Renaissance writers were almost totally dependent upon the whims of white patrons who marketed their works to a predominately white readership, the sales of some of the most phenomenally successful black authors, such as Terry McMillan, the Delaney sisters, Toni Morrison, and Alice Walker, are being sustained to an unprecedented degree by black consumers. The same is true, if to a lesser extent, in the other arts. Thelma Golden's "Black Male" exhibit, for instance, dramatically lifted annual attendance figures at the Whitney Museum by attracting a large number of new black patrons. The rise of the black middle class is, thus, simultaneous with the rise of black art, especially the black novel. And black novelists—black women novelists in particular—seem to owe a large part of their appeal to their capacity to express the desires and anxieties of this new middle class more freely from the *inside* than any previous generation could possibly have done. (In this way, McMillan's role within black culture is similar to that of Defoe and Richardson in the eighteenth century.) Quite often, too, these black writers have black editors and black agents, and their books are reviewed by other black authors, assigned by black teachers, and sold in black bookstores.

This new presence and authority of blacks in cultural institutions, largely a result of affirmative action programs and the active recruitment of minorities, is unprecedented in American history. And signs of the cultural flowering that define a renaissance are everywhere. On two occasions in the past two years, no less than three black authors appeared *simultaneously* on the *New York Times* best seller list (one author, Toni Morrison, appeared in both the fiction and nonfiction categories). "All black books these days are trade books," commented Erroll McDonald, a Yale graduate and vice president at Pantheon Books. "The 'one-nigger syndrome' is dead." Black authors have won an unprecedented number of prizes in the last decade, including Pulitzer Prizes, National Book Critics' Circle Awards, National Book Awards, and PEN/Faulkner Awards. The culmination of these achievements, of course, was Toni Morrison's Nobel Prize.

In addition, traditionally white cultural institutions such as the Whitney Museum, the Museum of Modern Art, the Guggenheim Museum, and the Lincoln Center Theater have integrated their boards of directors, and jazz has become a part of the canon of American music as defined by both the Lincoln Center and the Smithsonian Institution. Black Studies departments have never had larger enrollments or a stronger, more solid presence at America's premier research institutions. Public intellectuals representing a wide array of ideologies, such as Gerald Early, Cornel West, Stephen Carter, Derrick Bell, Lani Guinier, Stanley Crouch, Michele Wallace, bell hooks, Trey Ellis, Shelby Steele, Randall Kennedy, and Patricia Williams, publish their opinions regularly in a variety of national journals. George Wolfe's appointment as the director of the New York Public Theater is symptomatic of the growing "crossover" authority that blacks increasingly have come to possess within broader American cultural organizations. And, perhaps most dramatically of all, black filmmakers, following the lead of Spike Lee, have never been more numerous or better funded than they are today. If we add television shows such as *The Cosby Show, A Different World, The Fresh Prince of Bel Air,* and *The Oprah Winfrey Show* to the mix, it is clear that the black presence in American society has never been more prevalent and more widely consumed.

One reason for the newest renaissance is that the generation that integrated historically white institutions in the late sixties and early seventies has now, two decades later, returned to those very institutions to occupy positions of power and authority. Never before have so many black creative artists produced so much art, in so many genres, for such a diversified, integrated audience. Case in point: hip-hop, once the marching music of a defiant oppositional culture, is now the music of the white suburbs, the *American Bandstand* of the 1990s, the premier American music.

The current renaissance is characterized by a specific awareness of previous black traditions, which these artists echo, imitate, parody, and revise, self-consciously, in acts of riffing or signifying or sampling. As the jazz and opera composer Anthony Davis puts it, "There are three different strains in the black music revolution today—classical jazz (such as Wynton Marsalis), avant jazz (such as Anthony Braxton), and the fusion of hip-hop and jazz (such as the compositions of Steve Coleman). What each shares, however," he continues, "is a common attempt to rediscover the past." Davis's opera *X, The Life and Times of Malcolm X* (1986) is a prime example. "What this is, is a renaissance of postmodernism, and postmodernism, in America, is quintessentially black," he concludes.

This concern with the black cultural past and the self-conscious grounding of a black postmodernism in a black nationalist tradition are accompanied by a kind of nostalgia for the Black Power cultural politics of the sixties and the blaxploitation films of the early seventies. Unlike the earlier periods, however, the current movement defines itself by a certain openness, a belated glasnost that allows for parodies such as George Wolfe's play *The Colored Museum* (1986); Robert Townsend's *Hollywood Shuffle* (1987); Keenen Ivory Wayans's blaxploitation parody, *I'm Gonna Git You Sucka* (1988); and, more recently, Rusty Cundieff's *Fear of a Black Hat* (1994), a satire about the hip-hop generation.

The art of this period is also characterized by its deep self-confidence in the range and depth of the black experience as a source for art. Richard Wright once predicted that if "the Negro merges into the mainstream of American life, there might result actually a disappearance of Negro literature—as such." As a Negro, he continued, he was "a rootless man." Few black writers today would agree with Wright on either point. In fact, the opposite seems to have occurred: black writers and artists seem to have become *more* conscious of the specificities of their cultural traditions rather than *less* conscious. Toni Morrison has frequently stated that she is a black writer first, a writer second, effectively reversing decades of attempts by black writers to make their work "universal" by writing about whites. These artists *presume* that black experiences are universal experiences. If, as Wright once put it, "the Negro is America's metaphor," this generation seems to maintain that the experiences of African Americans are metaphors for the entire human condition, with America itself standing as a metaphor for much that has been liberating as well as horrendous in black and human history.

"What defines this renaissance, unlike the others," says the novelist Jamaica Kincaid, "is that people like us are just getting started. Somebody told me recently that literature is dead. But it's not that *literature* is dead; it is that *English literature* is dead. It is as if someone has removed the hands from over our mouths, and you hear this long, piercing scream. There really isn't much that is new to say about being a white person." This art, she continues, is appealing not just because of its content but because of its forms, "its ways of looking at the world, the way the world has forced us to look at it. And what we, as artists, are saying is: 'this is what it looks like.'"

Traditionally, black art has fallen into two large schools of representation. One we might think of as a lyrical, quasi-autobiographical modernism (as found, say, in Zora Neale Hurston's *Their Eyes Were Watching God* or Ralph Ellison's *Invisible Man),* in which a questing protagonist succeeds against oppressive racist odds. The other we can call realism or naturalism (as found, for instance, in Richard Wright's *Native Son* or Ann Petry's *The Street*), in which a protagonist's life choices, and hence fate, are determined by forces, such as racism or capitalism, which are insurmountable—that is, unless the entire system is transformed by violent and dramatic revolution.

In black postmodernist writing, much of the fiction being created by black women in particular consists of coming-of-age tales in which racial politics takes a secondary role to the unfolding of a sensitive, gendered consciousness. Today, a politicized naturalism is more likely to be found in black film, such as John Singleton's *Boyz N the Hood,* and, of course, in gangsta rap, such as the dada vorticism of Public Enemy's *It Takes a Nation of Millions to Hold Us Back,* or in the rap-meets-poetry movement. The most subtle and sophisticated of this art, however, such as Toni Morrison's masterpiece *Beloved,* or Spike Lee's *Do the Right Thing,* brings both tendencies together, creating a new form, which we might think of as a lyrical super-naturalism.

All renaissances are acts of cultural construction, attempting to satisfy larger social and political needs. And the African American postmodern renaissance is no exception. In their openness, their variety, their playfulness with forms, their refusal to follow preordained ideological lines, their sustained engagements with the black artistic past, the artists of this renaissance seem as determined to define their work freely within a black tradition as they are to consolidate a black presence within America's corporate cultural institutions. "There are many neighborhoods in what we might think of as a larger cultural community," Anthony Davis muses. Given the sophistication of so much of this art, and given its demonstrated power to turn a profit, it is highly likely that the achievements of this renaissance will be the deepest, the longest-lasting, and the most appreciated by the larger American society. "Today the white people want to be colored," Jamaica

Kincaid asserts. "There is no longer such a thing as an 'American' culture. It's all black culture."

What lessons from the Harlem Renaissance can we draw upon to critique our own?

Many critiques have been made of the Harlem Renaissance's putative faults and purported limitations, which range from overdependence on white patronage to pandering to debased white taste in the form of primitivistic depictions of black sensuality and hedonism in the literature, art, music, and dance of the period. We can debate these claims and even accept some, with enormous qualifications, as true, despite the fact that *all* artists are dependent upon patronage (and all renaissances especially so) and despite the fact that the literature created during the Harlem Renaissance—especially the poetry of James Weldon Johnson, Langston Hughes, and Sterling Brown, and the fictions of Jean Toomer and Zora Neale Hurston—drew upon African American vernacular musical and oral traditions to create *sui generis* African American modernist forms that today, three-quarters of a century later, are judged to be canonical even by the most conservative keepers of the American canon. What's more, the literature created by these fifty-odd brave souls, black inscriptions on a near tabula rasa, proved to be the fertile ground out of which emerged writers such as Richard Wright, Ann Petry, Ralph Ellison, James Baldwin, Gwendolyn Brooks, Amiri Baraka, Alice Walker, and Toni Morrison, to list just a few artists who use the Renaissance writers as their silent second texts.

Harlem as a site of the black cultural sublime was invented by those writers and artists at the turn of the century determined to transform the stereotypical image of Negro Americans as ex-slaves, members of an inherently inferior race—biologically and environmentally unfit for mechanized modernity and its cosmopolitan forms of fluid identity—into an image of a race of culture-bearers. To effect this transformation, the New Negro would need a nation over which to preside. And that nation's capital would be Harlem, that realm north of Central Park, centered between 130th and 145th Streets.

Since the earliest decades of this century, then, the lure of Harlem has captivated the imagination of writers, artists, intellectuals, and politicians around the world. Stories are legion of African American and African pilgrims progressing to Manhattan, then plunging headlong into the ultimate symbolic black cultural space—the city within a city, the "Mecca of the New Negro" (as Alain Locke put it)—that Harlem became in the first quarter of the twentieth century. Fidel Castro's recent journey uptown, recalling his famous sojourn at the Hotel Teresa thirty-five years ago, is only the most recent of a long line of such pilgrimages into America's very own heart of darkness. The list of pilgrims is long and distinguished, including Max Weber and Carl Jung, Federico García Lorca and Octavio Paz, Zora Neale Hurston and Langston Hughes, Kwame Nkrumah and Wole Soyinka, Marcus Garvey and Malcom X, Ezekiel Mphaphlele and Nelson Mandela, and so forth. "Harlem was like a great magnet for the Negro intellectual," Hughes wrote, "pulling him from everywhere. Once in New York, he had to live in Harlem." Harlem was not so much a *place* as it was a state of mind, the cultural metaphor for black America itself.

What *does* seem curious to me about the Harlem Renaissance—and relevant to us here—is that its creation occurred precisely as Harlem was turning into the great American slum. The death rate was 42 percent higher than in other parts of the city. The infant mortality rate in 1928 was twice as high as in the rest of New York. Four times as many people died from tuberculosis as in the white population. The unemployment rate, according to Adam Clayton Powell, Jr., was 50 percent. There was no way to romanticize these conditions, but Locke and his fellows valiantly attempted to do so. Even James Weldon Johnson, one of the most politically engaged of all the Renaissance writers in his capacity as the first black secretary of the NAACP, wrote *Black Manhattan* to create the fiction of Harlem as a model of civility and black bourgeois respectability, rather than as an example of the most heinous effects of urban economic exploitation and residential segregation. For Johnson, Harlem was "exotic, colorful, sensuous; a place of laughing, singing, and dancing; a place where life wakes up at night." Moreover, he continued, "Harlem is not merely a Negro colony or community, it is a city within a city, the greatest Negro city in the world. It is not a slum or a fringe, it is located in the heart of Manhattan and occupies one of the most beautiful and healthful sections of the city." Locke, always an optimist, whom Charles Johnson called "the press agent of the New Negro," declared Harlem the cultural capital of the black world: "Without pretense to their political significance, Harlem has the same role to play for the New Negro as Dublin had for the New Ireland or Prague for the New Czechoslovakia. Harlem, I grant you, isn't typical—but it is significant, it is prophetic." The "Harlem" of literature and the Harlem of socioeconomic reality were as far apart as Bessie Smith was from Paul Whiteman. The valorization of black rhythm, spontaneity, laughter, sensuality—all keywords of depictions of blacks by blacks at the time—contrasted starkly with Harlem's squalor and the environmental or structural limitations upon individual choices such as those finally depicted in Wright's *Native Son* (1940) in part as a reaction *against* what he felt to be the Renaissance writers' bohemian decadence.

The Renaissance's fascination with primitivism, one could argue, has today found a counterpart in three arenas of representation: the reconstruction of the institution of slavery; the valorization of vernacular cultural forms as a basis for a postmodern art; and the use of a lyrical voice-of-becoming in fictions that depict the emergence of black female protagonists with strong, resonant voices and self-fashioned identities. Subjects heretofore to be avoided—such as slavery and the female tale of the transcendence and emergence of the self—and vernacular linguistic forms have all emerged like the return of the repressed as dominant themes in African American literature. What remains to be explored, however, in the written arts of *this* renaissance, are the lives and times of the grandchildren of the Bigger Thomases and Bessie Mearses of *Native Son,* which by and large have been of interest primarily to young black filmmakers, who far too often seem to be caught in the embrace of a romantic primitivism, navigating us through the inner city more for sexual titillation than for social critique. Given the stark statistics that we all know so well describing the nightmare reality of black inner-city life—one in three black men between the ages of 20 and 29 in prison, on probation, or on parole; 46 percent of all black children born at or beneath the poverty line—one is forced to wonder where *this* generation's Bigger Thomas is. Until *this* subject matter finds a voice as eloquent as that voice of the newly emergent and aspiring middle-class black self, today's renaissance runs the risk of suffering the sorts of critique that we level against the Harlem Renaissance seven full decades later. For there are two nations in America, and these two nations, one hopeless, one full of hope, are both black. African Americans live a hyphenated life in America. Morrison's *Beloved* explores what the hyphenation of race costs. It is incumbent upon our artists now to explore what the hyphenation of *class* costs.

Perhaps it is no accident that the most interesting rendering of the tension between the myth of Harlem and its social reality is to be found *not* in a text produced in that period but in Morrison's *Jazz,* which is set in Harlem in 1926. In this novel Morrison succeeds in creating a protagonist whose fate is as shaped by her environment as by her actions, in a curious kind of stasis or equilibrium that seeks to resolve the tension between the naturalism of Richard Wright and Ann Petry on the one hand, and the lyrical modernism of Jean Toomer, Zora Neale Hurston, and Ralph Ellison on the other. "Word was," Morrison's narrator tells us, "that underneath the good times and the easy money something evil ran the streets and nothing was safe—not even the dead." It is in this novel that the Harlem Renaissance finally finds its most sophisticated voice *and* its most pointed critique, the newest renaissance grounding itself in the mirror of the old, bridging that gap between the shadow and the act, the myth and the reality, the fiction and the fact. Morrison's ultimate message would seem to be a warning, a warning that it is only when our artists today speak the city's "loud voice and make that sound human," avoiding "miss[ing] the people altogether," in all their complexity, that *this* renaissance can claim to be the renaissance to end all renaissances. Much depends on whether we get it.

SOURCE: *Critical Inquiry* 24, no. 1 (Autumn 1997).

INTRODUCTION, *BLACK IN LATIN AMERICA*

I FIRST LEARNED that there were black people living someplace in the Western Hemisphere other than the United States when my father told me the first thing that he had wanted to be when he grew up. When he was a boy about my age, he said, he had wanted to be an Episcopal priest, because he so admired his priest at St. Philip's Episcopal Church in Cumberland, Maryland, a black man from someplace called Haiti. I knew by this time that there were black people in Africa, of course, because of movies such as *Tarzan* and TV shows such as *Sheena, Queen of the Jungle* and *Ramar of the Jungle*. And then, in 1960, when I was ten years old, our fifth-grade class studied "Current Affairs," and we learned about the seventeen African nations that gained their independence that year. I did my best to memorize the names of these countries and their leaders, though I wasn't quite sure why I found these facts so very appealing. But my father's revelation about his earliest childhood ambition introduced me to the fact that there were black people living in other parts of the New World, a fact that I found quite surprising.

It wasn't until my sophomore year at Yale, as a student auditing Robert Farris Thompson's art history class "The Trans-Atlantic Tradition: From Africa to the Black Americas," that I began to understand how "black" the New World really was. Professor Thompson used a methodology that he called the "Tri-Continental Approach"—complete with three slide projectors—to trace visual leitmotifs that recurred among African, African American, and Afro-descended artistic traditions and artifacts in the Caribbean and Latin America, to show, a la Melville Herskovits, the retention of what he called "Africanisms" in the New World. So in a very real sense, I would have to say, my fascination with Afro-descendants in this hemisphere, south of the United States, began in 1969, in Professor Thompson's very popular, and extremely entertaining and rich, art history lecture course. In addition, Sidney Mintz's anthropology courses and his brilliant scholarly work on the history of the role of sugar in plantation slavery in the Caribbean and Latin America also

464

served to awaken my curiosity about another black world, a world both similar to and different from ours, south of our borders. And Roy Bryce-Laporte, the courageous first chair of the Program in Afro-American Studies, introduced me to black culture from his native Panama. I owe so much of what I know about African American culture in the New World to these three wise and generous professors.

But the full weight of the African presence in the Caribbean and Latin America didn't hit me until I became familiar with the Trans-Atlantic Slave Trade Database, conceived by the historians David Eltis and David Richardson and based now at Emory University. Between 1502 and 1866, 11.2 million Africans survived the dreadful Middle Passage and landed as slaves in the New World. And here is where these statistics became riveting to me: of these 11.2 million Africans, according to Eltis and Richardson, only 450,000 arrived in the United States. That is the mind-boggling part to me, and I think to most Americans. All the rest arrived in places south of our border. About 4.8 million Africans went to Brazil alone. So, in one sense, the major "African American Experience," as it were, unfolded not in the United States, as those of us caught in the embrace of what we might think of as "African American Exceptionalism" might have thought, but throughout the Caribbean and South America, if we are thinking of this phenomenon in terms of sheer numbers alone.

About a decade ago, I decided that I would try to make a documentary series about these Afro-descendants, a four-hour series about race and black culture in the Western Hemisphere outside of the United States and Canada. And I filmed this series this past summer, focusing on six countries—Brazil, Cuba, the Dominican Republic, Haiti, Mexico, and Peru—choosing each country as representative of a larger phenomenon. This series is the third in a trilogy that began with *Wonders of the African World,* a six-part series that aired in 1998. That series was followed by *America Behind the Color Line,* a four-part series that aired in 2004. In a sense, I wanted to replicate Robert Farris Thompson's "Tri-Continental" methodology to make, through documentary film, a comparative analysis of these cardinal points of the Black World. Another way to think of it is that I wanted to replicate the points of the Atlantic triangular trade: Africa, the European colonies of the Caribbean and South America, and black America. *Black in Latin America,* another four-hour series, is the third part of this trilogy, and this book expands considerably on what I was able to include in that series. You might say that I have been fortunate enough to find myself over the past decade in a most curious position: to be able to make films about subjects about which I am curious and about which I initially knew very little, with the generous assistance of many scholars in these fields and many more informants I interview in these countries.

The most important question that this book attempts to explore is this: what does it mean to be "black" in these countries? Who is considered "black" and under what circumstances and by whom in these societies? The answers to these questions vary widely across Latin America in ways that will surprise most people in the United States, just as they surprised me. My former colleague, the Duke anthropologist J. Lorand Matory, recently explained the complexity of these matters to me in a long and thoughtful email: "Are words for various shades of African descent in Brazil, such as *mulattoes, cafusos, pardos, morenos, pretos, negros,* etc., types of 'black people,' or are *pretos* and *negros* just the most African-looking people in a multidirectional cline of skin color–facial feature–hair texture combinations?" And how do social variables enter the picture? Matory asks: "Suppose two people with highly similar phenotypes are classified differently according to how wealthy and educated they are, or the same person is described differently depending upon how polite, how intimate, or how nationalistic the speaker wants to be? In what contexts does the same word have a pejorative connotation, justifying the translation of *nigger,* and in another context connote affection, such as the word *negrito?*"

How important is the relation of race and class? As Matory told me, "Debates about 'race' are almost always also about class. We debate the relative worth of these *two* terms in describing the structure and history of hierarchy in our two societies. North Americans," he concluded quite pungently, "tend to be as blind about the centrality of class in our society and vigilant about the centrality of race as Latin Americans are vigilant about the reality of class and blind about the reality of race." And what about the term *Latin America?* Though this term lumps together speakers of the Romance languages and ignores the fact that there are millions of speakers of English, Dutch, and various creole languages throughout the Caribbean and South America, for convenience's sake, it seemed to be the most suitable and economical term that we could agree on to refer to this huge and richly various set of societies, each with its own unique history of slavery, genetic admixture, and race relations.

The more I learn about the trans-Atlantic slave trade, the more I realize how complex and extensive the cultural contacts among the three points of Robert Farris Thompson's "Tri-Continental" triangle could be, even—or especially—at the individual level, both those of slaves and of black elites, with Europeans and Americans and with other black people. Most of us were taught the history of slavery in school (if we were taught at all) through simple stereotypes of kidnappings by white men, dispersal of related tribal members on the auction block to prevent communication and hence rebellion, and the total separation of New World black communities from each other and from their African origins. The idea that some members of the African elite were active players in the commerce of the slave trade or that they traveled to the New World and to Europe and home again for commercial, diplomatic, or educational purposes is both surprising and can be quite disturbing.

While some scholars of slavery and of African American Studies (and I include myself in this group) may have come late to an understanding of the remarkable extent of contact between Africans on the continent with Africans in Europe and throughout the Americas (as well as, for our purposes in this book, the similarities and differences in the historical experiences and social and cultural institutions Afro-descendants created throughout the Western Hemisphere), intellectuals, writers, musicians, and elites of color have long been keenly aware of each other, starting as early as the seventeenth and eighteenth centuries, if not before. For example, exchanges between African rulers and the courts of Europe started very early in the modern era. We know from the visual archival record, for instance, that emissaries from the monarchs of Ethiopia and the kingdom of Kongo came to the Vatican as early as the fifteenth and sixteenth centuries, respectively, and established formal diplomatic embassies there. An Ethiopian embassy before Pope Eugenius IV at the Council of Florence in 1439 is depicted in bronze at the entrance to St. Peter's. And Antonio Emanuele Funta (or Ne Vunda) was ambassador to the Vatican from Kongo, sent by King Alvaro II to Pope Paul V in 1604, via Brazil and Spain, arriving in 1608, when he died. The role of African elites in the trans-Atlantic slave trade after the early 1500s led to diplomatic and commercial negotiations back and forth between Europe and Africa and Africa and Brazil, for example. And this is a logical development, once we allow Africans the same degree of agency that we presume for Europeans in the exercise of the slave trade, which was, all too often, I am sad to say, first and last, a business. But these commercial contacts were followed by those between scholars and intellectuals as well. "El negro Juan Latino," a former slave who wore his blackness in his name, became the first African professor of grammar at the University of Granada and the first African to publish a book of poetry in Latin, in 1573. Latino is mentioned in the opening section of Cervantes's *Don Quixote* and was sometimes cited in biographical dictionaries in the eighteenth century as evidence of the African's "improvability." The Abbas Gregorius, from Ethiopia, collaborated with a German scholar to create the first grammar of the Amharic language less than a century after Juan Latino thrived. We recall him both through his grammar and through a striking image of him that has survived. But black men and women of letters from across the black world seem to have shared a certain fascination with each other as well and seem to have taken inspiration from the accomplishments of each other, if only through works such as the Abbé Henri Grégoire's *De la littérature des nègres* (The Literature of Negroes), published in 1808. In 1814, the Haitian Emperor Henri Christophe ordered fifty copies of Grégoire's book and invited him to visit his kingdom.

Perhaps in the same way that Latin and the Roman Catholic Church gave men and women of letters in the late Middle Ages—say, in what is now Italy or what is now Germany or France—a certain degree of common culture, even if workers or serfs in those societies did not share access to that common identity, so, too, black writers in Boston and New York, London and Paris, Jamaica and the Gold Coast throughout the eighteenth century could be aware of each other, sometimes commented on each other's existence, read and revised or troped each other's books, sometimes even corresponded about each other, and traveled back and forth either between Africa and Europe, America and Europe, or among Africa, Latin America, America, and Europe. I am thinking of Jacobus Capitein and Anton Wilhelm Amo from the Gold Coast, both of whom attended universities in Europe before returning to Africa; the Jamaican Francis Williams, one of the first black persons to read law at Lincoln's Inn in London (whose writing Hume disparaged in his influential essay "Of National Characters" of 1754), and who returned to Jamaica following his studies to establish a school, just as Capitein did in the Gold Coast; the widely read and commented on poet Phillis Wheatley, the first person of African descent to publish a book of poetry in English, who sailed to London to publish her book and served as inspiration to some of the black abolitionists there; the master of the epistle, Ignatius Sancho, who corresponded with Sterne and who wrote about Wheatley's enormous significance; and the first five authors of a new literary genre called the slave narratives, who revised what I call "the trope of the talking book" in each of their memoirs of their enslavement. One of these, the best-selling author Olaudah Equiano (Gustavus Vassa), who was born in Africa, visited fourteen islands in the West Indies as a slave (including the Bahamas, Barbados, Jamaica, Montserrat, St. Kitts, and the Mosquite Shore) and the United States, before ultimately settling in England as a free man. Many of these people were cited by foes of slavery as prima facie evidence that the African was at least potentially the intellectual equal of Europeans and was therefore an argument for the abolition of slavery. Indeed, Grégoire dedicated his book to Amo, Sancho, Vassa, his friend Cugoano, and Wheatley, among others.

As the free African American community grew in the United States, contacts with the Caribbean and Latin America increased dramatically in the nineteenth century. The black abolitionists Henry Highland Garnet and Frederick Douglass offer two salient examples. Garnet, a militant abolitionist, the first black minister to preach to the House of Representatives and a pioneering figure in the black colonization movement, traveled to Cuba as a cabin boy before he was ten and in 1849 founded the African Civilization Society to advocate for the emigration of free black people to Mexico and the West Indies, as well as to Liberia. Garnet served as a missionary for three years in Jamaica. In 1881, he became the United States minister to Liberia, where he died two months later and where he is buried. Frederick Douglass, between January 24 and March 26, 1871, served by appointment of President Ulysses S. Grant as the assistant secretary to the commission to Santo Domingo, exploring the possibility of annexing the Dominican Republic as a state, the nation's first black state, according to Douglass, who passionately supported this plan for this reason. Between 1889 and 1891, Douglass served as the US consul general to Haiti and chargé d'affaires to the Dominican Republic. During this period, Douglass wrote several essays and speeches about the Haitian Revolution and Toussaint Louverture and the importance of Haiti as "among the foremost civilized nations of the earth," as a speech delivered on January 2, 1893, was entitled. Even in nineteenth-century African American literature, Cuba was a fictive presence, for example, in Martin R. Delany's novel *Blake* (serialized in 1859 and in 1861–1862) and in a short story published by Thomas Detter in 1871 entitled "The Octoroon Slave of Cuba."

In the twentieth century, as we might expect, the contacts only increased in degree and number. Booker T. Washington, as the historian Frank Andre Guridy notes, had extensive interchanges at the beginning of the century with black Cuban intellectuals such as Juan Gualberto Gómez, whose son studied at Tuskegee. His autobiography was published in Spanish in its first Cuban edition in 1903, just two years after it was published in the States. Washington developed programs that trained black Cuban students at his Tuskegee Institute in the vocations and industrial arts and trades. Washington's educational program also influenced the thinking of the black Brazilian intellectual Manuel Querino.

Marcus Garvey's United Negro Improvement Association (UNIA) in the early decades of the twentieth century had more of a presence throughout the Caribbean and Latin America than most of us have realized, again thanks to Frank Guridy's research. Garvey named the ships of his Black Star Line after black heroes such as Phillis Wheatley and Frederick Douglass, as we might expect, but also after Antonio Maceo, the "Bronze Titan," one of the leading generals in the Cuban War of Independence and one of Cuba's founding fathers. The first stop of the *Frederick Douglass,* in fact, on its 1919 Caribbean tour was Cuba; the Cuban branch of the UNIA was founded that year, and Garvey visited Cuba two years later in March 1921, a trip that was covered in the *Heraldo de Cuba* newspaper in Havana. It turns out that Cuba had more branches of the UNIA than did any country other than the United States. The UNIA operated in Cuba until 1929, when it was closed down under the Machado government, using the same law, the Morua law, that had been used to ban the all-black Independent Party of Color and the organization of political parties along racial lines in 1912.

Du Bois—himself of Haitian descent, through his father, who was born in Haiti in 1826—proudly boasted of the many Afro-Latin Americans who attended the Pan-African Conference in London in 1900 and the first Pan-African Congress in Paris in 1919. At the 1900 conference, representatives from St. Kitts, Trinidad, St. Lucia, Jamaica, Antigua, and Haiti attended. In the pages of the *Crisis,* Du Bois reported that thirteen representatives from the French West Indies attended the 1919 congress (just three less than came from the United States), seven from Haiti, two from the Spanish colonies, one from the Portuguese colonies, and one from Santo Domingo. He tells us that Tertullian Guilbaud came from Havana, "Candace" and "Boisneuf" came from Guadeloupe, "Lagrosil" from the French West Indies, and "Grossillere" from Martinique. Du Bois also tells us that Edmund Fitzgerald Fredericks, a "full-blooded Negro," attended from British Guiana.

The historian Rebecca Scott discovered that the Cubans Antonio Maceo and Máximo Gómez not only visited the United States but rented a house together in New Orleans, in the Faubourg Tremé district in 1884. The pivotal role of black officers such as Maceo and black soldiers in the Cuban-Spanish-American War attracted the attention, as you might suspect, of black journalists, intellectuals, and activists throughout the United States. Du Bois, of course, regularly covered events germane to the black communities throughout the Caribbean and South America as well as Africa in the pages of the *Crisis,* and published Arturo Schomburg's (himself a Puerto Rican) account of the massacre of three thousand followers of the Independent Party of Color in Cuba in 1912.

James Weldon Johnson, perhaps truly the Renaissance man of the Harlem Renaissance, had extensive contacts with Afro-Latin America. In 1906, he was made consul to Venezuela; in 1909, he transferred to Nicaragua. In 1920, the NAACP sent Johnson to investigate allegations of abuse by occupying US Marines. He blasted the imperialist intentions of the US occupation of Haiti in a three-part series published in the twenties in the *Nation* magazine, a series he published as the book entitled *Self-Determining Haiti.* In his autobiography, *Along This Way,* Johnson relates the curious and amusing story that, just as he and a companion traveling on a train are about to be booted from a "first-class car," or a white car, and removed to the Jim Crow car, they talk to each other in Spanish. This is what happens when they do:

As soon as the conductor heard us speaking in a foreign language, his attitude changed; he punched our tickets and gave them back, and treated us just as he did the other passengers in the car. . . . This was my first impact against race prejudice as a concrete fact. Fifteen years later, an incident similar to the experience with this conductor drove home to me the conclusion that in such situations any kind of a Negro will do; provided he is not one who is an American citizen.

These levels of contact not only occurred between intellectuals and writers and at the diplomatic level. Stories about black baseball players pretending to be Cuban were part of the lore of black popular culture when I was growing up; teams in the Negro Baseball Leagues played teams in Cuba and even took "Cuban" names as early as the late nineteenth century, names such as the Cuban Giants, the Cuban X-Giants, the Genuine Cuban Giants (one team was named the Columbia Giants). And several "Cuban" teams, which purportedly included white and black Cubans and some African Americans, played in the United States under these rubrics in defiance of the color line, including the All Cubans, the Cuban Stars (West), the Cuban Stars (East), and the New York Cubans. So what we might think of as "transnational black consciousness" has unfolded at many levels of culture, high and low, between African Americans and black people in the Caribbean and Latin America, as extensively in the arts and letters as in popular cultural forms such as sports.

Of course, several musical collaborations come to mind, including "Cubana Be, Cubana Bop," recorded in 1948 as a single by Dizzy Gillespie, Chano Pozo, and George Russell; and the albums *Orgy in Rhythm,* recorded by Art Blakey, Sabu Martinez, and Carlos "Patato" Valdes in 1957, and *Uhuru Afrika,* recorded by Randy Weston and Candido Camero in 1960, to list just a few early notable examples.

Intricate relations obtained among black writers and critics of the Harlem Renaissance, especially Langston Hughes, who lived for a total equivalent of a year and a half with his father in Mexico and who translated the works of Caribbean writers, such as Nicolás Guillén and Jacques Roumain, from Spanish and French into English. Hughes and his colleagues who created the Harlem Renaissance were pivotal as role models in the birth of the Négritude movement in Paris in 1934, for its founders, Aimé Césaire and Leopold Sédar Senghor. Both movements were directly influenced by Jean Price-Mars's pioneering scholarship of black vernacular traditions and the Vodou religion in works such as *So Spoke the Uncle.*

In all, it is clear that, for well over 250 years, in various degrees and at several levels, there has existed a Pan-African intellectual community keenly aware of one another, looking to one another for support and inspiration to combat anti-black racism in Africa, Latin America, the Caribbean, and the United States, in the northern and southern hemispheres. And you might say that now it is the scholars of diaspora studies who are catching up with the creative writers, artists, activists, athletes, and intellectuals who have long seen themselves as sharing a certain special sort of transcontinental New World "black" subject position.

In spite of the unique histories of slavery and persons of African descent in each of the six countries discussed in this book, certain themes recur. In a sense, this book is a study of the growth and demise of the sugar economy in many of these countries, along with that of coffee and tobacco. In most of these societies, a great deal of miscegenation and genetic admixture occurred between masters and their slaves, very early on in the history of slavery there. Several of these countries sponsored official immigration policies of "whitening," aiming to dilute the numbers of its citizens who were black or darker shades of brown by encouraging Europeans to migrate there.

And speaking of skin color, each of these countries had (and continues to have) many categories of color and skin tone, ranging from as few as 12 in the Dominican Republic and 16 in Mexico to 134 in Brazil, making our use of *octoroon* and *quadroon* and *mulatto* pale by comparison. Latin American color categories can seem to an American as if they are on steroids. I realized as I encountered people who still employ these categories in everyday discussions about race in their society that it is extremely difficult for those of us in the United States to see the use of these categories as what they are, the social deconstruction of the binary opposition between "black" and "white," outside of the filter of the "one-drop rule," which we Americans have inherited from racist laws designed to retain the offspring of a white man and a black female slave as property of the slave's owner. Far too many of us as African Americans see the use of these terms as an attempt to "pass" for anything other than "black" rather than as historically and socially specific terms that people of color have invented and continue to employ to describe a complex reality larger than the terms *black, white,* and *mulatto* allow for.

After extended periods of "whitening," many of these same societies then began periods of "browning," as I think of them, celebrating and embracing their transcultural or multicultural roots, declaring themselves unique precisely because of the extent of racial admixture among their citizens. (The abolition of "race" as an official category in the federal censuses of some of the countries I visited has made it extremely difficult for black minorities to demand their rights, as in Mexico and Peru.) The work of Jose Vasconcelos in Mexico, Jean Price-Mars in Haiti, Gilberto Freyre in Brazil, and Fernando Ortiz in Cuba compose a sort of multicultural quartet, though each approached the subject from different, if related, vantage points. The theories of "browning" espoused by Vasconcelos, Freyre, and Ortiz, however, could be double-edged swords, both valorizing the black roots of their societies yet sometimes implicitly seeming to denigrate the status of black cultural artifacts and practices outside of an ideology of *mestizaje,* or hybridity.

What did all of these societies ultimately share in common? The unfortunate fact that persons of the seemingly "purest" or "unadulterated" African descent disproportionately occupy the very bottom of the economic scale in each of these countries. In other words, the people with the darkest skin, the kinkiest hair, and the thickest lips tend to be overrepresented among the poorest members of society. Poverty in each of these countries, in other words, all too often has been socially constructed around degrees of obvious African ancestry. Whether—or how—this economic fact is a legacy of slavery, and of long, specific histories of anti-black racism, even in societies that proudly boast themselves to be "racial democracies," "racism free," or "postracial," is one of the most important themes explored in this book and cries out to be explored and acted on in the social policies of each of these six countries.

SOURCE: Henry Louis Gates, Jr., *Black in Latin America* (New York: New York University Press, 2011).

BRAZIL: "MAY EXÚ GIVE ME THE POWER OF SPEECH"

Black in Latin America

> *On the whole emancipation [in Brazil] was peaceful, and whites, Negroes, and Indians are to-day amalgamating into a new race.*
>
> —W. E. B. Du Bois, 1915

> *In South America we have long pretended to see a possible solution in the gradual amalgamation of whites, Indians and Blacks. But this amalgamation does not envisage any decrease of power and prestige among whites as compared with Indians, Negroes, and mixed bloods; but rather an inclusion within the so called white group of a considerable infiltration of dark blood, while at the same time maintaining the social bar, economic exploitation and political disfranchisement of dark blood as such. . . . And despite facts, no Brazilian nor Venezuelan dare boast of his black fathers. Thus, racial amalgamation in Latin-America does not always or even usually carry with it social uplift and planned effort to raise the mulatto and mestizoes to freedom in a democratic polity.*
>
> —W. E. B. Du Bois, 1942

FOR A VERY long time, whenever I heard the word *race,* only images of black people in the United States came to mind. As silly as it might sound now, to me, then, *race* was a code word for black people, and for their relations with white people in this country. I think that this is probably some sort of African American exceptionalism for people my age, people who came of age in the Civil Rights Movement of the late fifties and sixties. Even today, in our era of multiculturalism, I still find it necessary sometimes to remember that *race* is not just a black thing, that *race* (by which most of us mean ethnicity) signifies a lot of different kinds of people, representing a full range of ethnicities, in a lot of different places, and that African Americans in this country don't have a patent on the term or the social conditions that have resulted either from slavery or the vexed history of racial relations that followed slavery in the United States.

I should say that African Americans don't have a patent *especially* on slavery, as I much later came to realize, throughout the New World. When I was growing up, I simply assumed that the slave experience in the New World was dominated by our ancestors who came to the United States between 1619 and the Civil War. And I think that many Americans still assume this. But it turns out that the slave ancestors of the African American people were only a tiny fraction—less than 5 percent—of all the Africans imported to the Western Hemisphere to serve as slaves. Over eleven million Africans survived the Middle Passage and disembarked in the New World; and of these, incredibly, only about 450,000 Africans came to the United States. The "real" African American experience, based on numbers alone, then, unfolded in places south of our long southern border, south of Key West, south of Texas, south of California, in the Caribbean islands and throughout Latin America. And no place in our hemisphere received more Africans than Brazil did.

I think that probably the first time that I ever thought about race, integration, segregation, or miscegenation outside of the context of the United States, Jim Crow, and the Civil Rights Movement was the night that I saw the film *Black Orpheus*. I had thought about Africa quite a lot, and the black people who lived in Africa, from the time I was in the fifth grade, in 1960, the great year of African independence, the year that seventeen African nations were born. But thinking about black people and Africa is not the same as thinking about race. No, that came, for the first time, when I was a sophomore at Yale, assigned to watch *Black Orpheus* in the class called "From Africa to the Black Americas," the art history class taught by the great scholar Robert Farris Thompson.

Black Orpheus, directed by Marcel Camus and shot in Brazil, was released in 1959, to rave reviews. In fact, it won the Palme d'Or at the Cannes Film Festival that year and an Academy Award for Best Foreign Language Film and a Golden Globe for Best Foreign Film in 1960. Based on a play written by Vinicius de Moraes entitled *Orfeu da Conceição*, the film adapts the legend of Orpheus and Eurydice. Set mostly in the Morro da Babilônia favela in the Leme neighborhood in Rio de Janeiro, the film is stunning, even fifty years later, for the fact that it seamlessly transforms a classical Greek tale in black or brown face, as it were, without preaching about race or class and without protest or propaganda. It just assumes its propositions, as it were. The key Greek characters are here, including Hermes, the messenger of the gods, and Cerberus, the three-headed dog that guards the gates of Hades, as well as Orpheus and Eurydice, of course, played by an athletic Breno Mello and the irresistibly beautiful Marpessa Dawn, the goddess of black Brazilian cinema, who turned out to have been born in Pittsburgh of Filipino and African American descent.

Three things grabbed me when I saw the film. First, as I have mentioned, was the seamless translation of the Greek myth to a Brazilian context, with the race of the characters taken for granted and not trumpeted or strained in any way. Second was the use of Umbanda and Candomblé, which some people have called Brazil's national African religions. When Orpheus descends (down a spiral staircase at, cleverly, the Office of Missing Persons) into Hades to find and retrieve Eurydice, "Hades" turns out to be an Umbanda ritual, complete with female worshipers dressed in white and the pivotal Yoruba god Ogun. Eurydice's spirit speaks to Orpheus, in fact, through one of these female worshipers, now possessed by her spirit. Most striking sociologically, perhaps, is the fact that virtually everyone in the film is black or brown; very few "white" people appear in the film, and none appears in a significant role, similar, as I later discovered, to Zora Neale Hurston's novel *Their Eyes Were Watching God*. Watching the film, my friends and I thought that Brazil was that most remarkable of places: a democracy in brown. Brazil, judging from the film, was a mulatto. For us, *Black Orpheus* seemed to be a sort of cinematic analogue to Gilberto Freyre's theory of Brazil as a unique racial democracy. And all that made me want to visit there, but not as much, to be honest, as the vain hope that I'd spot one of the daughters of the beautiful Marpessa Dawn.

I thought about all of this, in flight, high above the Amazon, I supposed, on my way to Brazil for the first time, heading to Carnaval in February 2010. Between 1561 and 1860, Brazil (as we have seen) was the final destination of almost five million African slaves—some of them, perhaps, my distant cousins. But that wasn't where my mind was taking me. Try as I might, I couldn't help dwelling on the Brazil of my imagination: the pageantry and ecstasy of Carnaval; its syncretic mixtures of indigenous, African, and European cultural elements; the dancing to music and song born in Africa; the Yoruba, Fon, and Angolan-based religions blended into Candomblé and Umbanda; the many regional expressions of Afro-Brazilian religions such as Xangô, Batuque, Tambor de Mina. All of these forms of culture were signal aspects of an irresistibly vibrant national culture synthesized from so many strands contributed by its multiethnic people—a sea of beautiful brown faces with brilliant white smiles, at least as shaped in my mind by Carnaval scenes from *Black Orpheus.*

So much of Brazil's syncretic culture manifests itself at Carnaval. And the most "African" of the various manifestations of Carnaval traditions in the country occurs each year in Bahia. As I boarded the packed connecting flight from São Paulo to Salvador—full of Brazilian tourists from other parts of the country, tourists from other countries, and even a few other African Americans, some of whom I learned were regulars—I began to wonder what exactly I would find when my plane touched down. Because about 43 percent of all slaves brought to the Americas ended up in Brazil, today over 97 million Brazilians in a total population of 190 million people have a significant amount of African genetic ancestry, self-identifying as either Brown (*parda*) or Black (*preta*) in the federal census (among five categories, including White (*branca*), Yellow (*amarela*), and Indígenous, Brown, and Black). This makes Brazil in effect the second-largest black country in the world, after Nigeria, if we use definitions of blackness employed in the United States. (Brazil, one might say, is genetically brown, though there are some areas of the country, such as Porto Alegre, that are overwhelmingly white.) And a third of Brazil's slaves—about a million and a half people—landed in Brazil through the port here, in Bahia.

Thanks to the Trans-Atlantic Slave Trade Database, we now know that about 70 percent of them came from Angola, and much of black Brazilian religion is based on two sources: the Yoruba orishas from western Nigeria and Benin and also what the historians Linda Heywood and John Thornton call "Angolan Catholicism," whose roots were in Angola and which the slaves brought with them to Brazil. Angolan Catholicism was born out of King Afonso's skillful and deliberate blending of Christianity and Central African religions promoted by "Xinguillas" (as the Portuguese called them), a process that was well advanced by 1516, even before there was any significant African presence in Brazil. And Angolan Catholicism was every bit as much an African religion as was the Yoruba religion of the orishas. When many slaves from other parts of Africa arrived in Brazil, they were converted to Catholicism not as practiced in Portugal but as practiced in Angola, and indeed many were in fact catechized by Angolans informally, if not formally. And this syncretic combination manifests itself in the religion called Candomblé, one of the most compelling cultural products of Pan-African culture in the New World. Candomblé is at the heart of black Brazilian culture. And if Brazil's black culture has a capital, it is Bahia, without a doubt.

Brazil, I knew, was also a place of contradictions. It was the last country in the Western Hemisphere to abolish slavery, in 1888, just after Cuba abolished slavery in 1886. But it was also the first to claim it was free of anti-black racism, as Gilberto Freyre's doctrine of "racial democracy" became associated with Brazil's official identity. When I studied Brazil in college, at the end of the sixties, it was still generally thought to be a model society of a postracial world—a far cry from the rigidly segregated United States that the Civil Rights Movement was attempting to dismantle—although its racial-democracy ideology had come under fire (Du Bois critiqued it in 1942) and its military dictatorship had forbidden debate about race and racism in the country. And, indeed, Brazil remains one of the most racially mixed countries on earth—a hybrid nation descended from Africans, Europeans, and its original indigenous inhabitants. In the United States, people with African ancestry are all categorized as black; in Brazil, racial categories are on steroids, including at least 134 categories of "blackness." Brazilians, or so I'd been told, believe that color is in the eye of the beholder. But who are the Afro-Brazilians? And what do they think of their history—of their own relation to Africa and to blackness? I wanted to know their story.

Bahia had especially fired my imagination, since so much of the literature about African retentions in the New World refers to rites and cultural practices developed there. Five hundred years ago, the Portuguese established a sugar cane empire in this region, in the present-day states of Bahia and Pernambuco—one of the largest plantation economies on earth. Initially, the Indians were used as field workers, but their numbers proved inadequate. The Portuguese needed slave labor to meet the demand, and so Africans were poured into the region. The first Africans came from the Portuguese Atlantic islands as specialized workers employed in the sugar-making process proper. As the demand for sugar increased, the number of slaves imported to Brazil exploded. Angola was the central source of these slaves.

By 1600, Brazil produced half the world's sugar, and that sugar was produced through the labor of African slaves. I was extremely keen to see this place that so many Africans had first looked on when they disembarked from the slave ships, no doubt terrified and miserably disoriented, awaiting their fates in the New World, some even convinced that they were about to be eaten by white cannibals! But nothing I had dreamed or imagined, nothing I had read or even researched, prepared me for what I experienced in Bahia. I stepped out of my car on a busy street and looked around, and I thought, "My God, I am back *in Africa!*" Seriously. Everywhere I looked, I saw Brazilians with Africa inscribed on their faces and just as deeply on their culture. Across the street, I spotted a woman's headdress I had seen just a few years before in Nigeria. Because of the long history of cultural trade between Bahia and West Africa, going back to the nineteenth century,

West African cloths and other cultural objects were part of the trade, along with slaves.

Few of us realize that the traffic of the Yoruba between Brazil and Nigeria has been a two-way street at least since the early nineteenth century, when some freed slaves returned to the mother land in growing numbers after the defeat of the 1835 Muslim rebellion there, creating cross-pollination in Yoruba religious practices, among other things. Today, I learned, there is a great attempt of some culturally conscious black Brazilians to be "authentic," and items such as cloth are still imported, though Brazilian-manufactured cloths make up the majority percentage of those used by Candomblé devotees and middle-class blacks, since imported cloth is very expensive. Bahia celebrates its African roots, its African heritage, and never more so than during Carnaval. The people here are more "African," genetically, than in any other concentrated part of Brazil. The smells in the air, the gait of men in the streets, the way women move, their ways of worshiping and their religious beliefs, the dishes they eat—all remind me so much of things I had seen and smelled and heard in Nigeria and Angola, but transplanted across an ocean, similar and familiar but distinct: Africa, yes, but with a New World difference, Africa with decided twists.

Mesmerized, avidly on the lookout for those daughters of Marpessa Dawn, I walked the streets for hours before heading off to my first meeting, with João Reis, professor of history at the University of Bahia. I wanted to understand what had happened here, and so I wanted to start with Professor Reis, who has spent his entire professional life studying the history of slavery in Brazil. Straight off, he told me that ten times more Africans had come to Brazil as slaves than had gone to the United States. The reasons, he said, were both economic and geographic. Brazil was closer to Africa than was any other major destination in the New World (far closer than were the Caribbean or the English colonies in North America); in fact, though it is counterintuitive, it was quicker and easier to sail to Europe from certain African ports through Brazil, as it were. Moreover, the land surrounding the magnificent Bay of All Saints, where Salvador, Bahia's capital, was founded in 1549, was a fertile growing ground for one of the era's most desirable and extraordinarily profitable products: sugar. As a result, by the beginning of the seventeenth century, the words *sugar* and *Brazil* were synonyms. And virtually all of it was produced with slave labor. Sugar is a leitmotif of this book; as the center of sugar production shifted, so did the size of the slave trade and the slave population, over a two-hundred-year period from Brazil to Haiti to Cuba. While both Mexico and Peru had sugar mills, and these were worked by slaves, most Afro-Mexicans and Afro-Peruvians labored in urban areas, many worked in the textile industry and still others produced foodstuffs in towns. In Colombia, or "New Granada" (outside the scope of this book), they worked primarily in mines and not in sugar.

"Salvador, Bahia, was one of the most important Atlantic cities in the sixteenth, seventeenth, and through the eighteenth century," Reis explained to me, with the patience of a great lecturer used to teaching hopelessly unprepared US undergraduates. "In the nineteenth century, it was full of foreigners from Europe, from the United States, from the Caribbean, and from Africa. It was a multicultural society, a cosmopolitan society, maybe even more cosmopolitan than the way we live here today." Reis explained that Brazil was a prime destination for adventurers, and accordingly, many Europeans who came to Bahia were single men. In the British colonies of North America, entire families often emigrated to set up new lives. But in Bahia's early history, Portuguese bachelors were the norm; and they found sexual conquest where they could—brutally, or coercively, and sometimes willingly—first among native women and then among African slaves. The racial blending that later came to define Brazil began.

I asked Professor Reis how these slaves were treated, especially in comparison to the treatment of slaves in the United States. Were they treated better, more humanely, than were their counterparts in the United States? That they were, of course, is part of Freyre's explanation of the origins of Brazil's "racial democracy" and is now part of its national mythology. The national story Brazil likes to tell today about its slave past is highly unusual. According to this story, the country made a more or less seamless transition from slavery to tolerance, from a terribly informal yet terribly effective racism (Brazil had no laws prohibiting blacks from occupying any post in society or politics) to racial democracy, because of the intimacy—specifically, sexual intimacy—between master and slave. How did this come about? And could any country make such a shift? Was slavery in Brazil somehow fundamentally different than it was in the United States? The answers I got were complex.

Reis told me that the people of Bahia often freed their slaves or allowed them to buy their own freedom. Indeed, citizens of Bahia granted manumission—emancipation—to more slaves than did any other region in the Americas. You'd think that made it a lucky destination, if a slave could ever be considered lucky. But it belied a deeper, more disturbing reality. There were many more slaves in Bahia at a certain point in the slave trade than there were almost anywhere else—and for most of those who had been born in Africa, life in their new country was short and unbearably harsh. (As slavery matured in southern Brazil thanks to mining and, later, coffee, Minas, Rio, and São Paulo came to have larger slave populations. The city of Rio, for example, became in the mid-nineteenth century the largest slave city in the hemisphere ever, with close to one hundred thousand slaves.) Bahia's steady supply of human labor caused many slaves to suffer especially bad treatment, just because they were so easily replaceable, like spare parts for a car. Working conditions were often brutal beyond description.

"American planters did not have such easy access to the source of slave production in Africa," Reis explained to me, "so slaves were treated much better in the US than they were in Brazil. There, they had better housing, better clothes; they were better fed. And from very early in the slave trade, the slave population was self-reproductive there. Nothing of this sort happened in Brazil."

In Brazil, Reis continued, slave owners could always replace dead Africans with living Africans, at minimal cost. Most of us don't realize how close Brazil is to the west coast of Africa, so importing new slaves could be cheaper than the costs of food, medicine, or decent shelter for older slaves. This wasn't the case in the United States, where the transportation costs of slavery were material and the life of an individual slave was, in a perverse way, accordingly highly valued. In Brazil, the Portuguese often effectively worked the slaves to death because it was cheaper to replace them than to care for them.

The slaves who received their freedom were the exceptions, not the rule, given the huge numbers of slaves imported into Brazil. According to Reis, many of those slaves who managed to be manumitted were the offspring—or descendants—of sexual liaisons between female African slaves and their masters, often the result of rapes. In these cases, the Brazilian-born, mixed-race children fared much better in gaining their freedom than did their African-born mothers, or than most of their female contemporaries and virtually all of their male contemporaries. In this way, different classes of black people emerged under slavery and perpetuated their class position, with "class" being signified by color, by degrees of mixture—hence, the birth of the browning of Brazil. But most of the slaves would not have mixed with white Brazilians, of course; if they propagated, they did so with one another.

"I'm not saying that there was no mixing, no reproduction," said Reis quietly. "There was. But that was on the margins. And the slaves who were born in Brazil received manumission much faster and easier than the African-born person, because they could develop relationships with masters which were more intimate, which were easier to manage—completely different to the Africans who came over without knowing the language, who were sent directly to the labor fields. Most domestic slaves, for example, were born in Brazil. They were in the big house. They were closer to the master's family. And so they could get manumission easier. There are statistics showing precisely that in the competition for manumission, the Brazilian-born slave, especially the mixed race, was much more successful than African-born slaves. It was not humane."

After saying goodbye to Reis, I wanted to examine for myself evidence of Bahia's African roots, having read so much about them. So I visited Pai (Portuguese for "Father," in the religious sense) João Luiz at his nearby Candomblé temple. As we have seen, Candomblé is the religion created in Brazil by slaves looking for a way to stay in contact with their ancestral gods from Angola, Nigeria, and Dahomey (now the Republic of Benin). Brazil nursed, nurtured, re-created, and embraced the rituals of Candomblé. But Africa birthed them.

Father João's temple is one of more than eleven hundred Candomblé shrines in Salvador. I love learning about the Yoruba gods and reading stories about them—stories as rich as the stories we cherish about the Greek and Roman gods—in their various manifestations on both sides of the Atlantic. Whereas Zeus and Jupiter and their compadres live in Western culture through literature, here the gods live through ritual and worship, generally alongside the Holy Trinity and the Christian saints, though the literature of Umbanda and Candomblé, written by initiates, is also very popular in Brazil, as it is in Cuba. I admire Father João, and told him so, for keeping the African gods alive in the New World.

"It's very important to me," he told me, as we sat down to chat, just outside his temple, in a favela, as we waited for his devotees to arrive for a ceremony. "I was born into a religious family. When I was seven years old, the spirit became a part of me. At fourteen it came to me again, and by the age of sixteen I was in charge of a temple. I'm now forty-nine years old, and I never think about stopping. I just think about evolving and growing. We raise our sons in order for them to take over this vivid and true religion from me, when I am no longer able."

Father João explained how Candomblé combined African traditions with certain tenets of Roman Catholicism—teachings that some Africans had come across first in Angola, because the Portuguese often baptized captured slaves before shipping them to Brazil, and that others encountered only after they arrived in Brazil. But Thornton and Heywood pointed out to me, however, Candomblé's African origins are far more complex: "The Portuguese did capture and then baptize African slaves," they explained to me. "In fact, they usually did, but this misses the point. Christianity was indigenous to West Central Africa, not only in the Kingdom of Kongo where it had been the 'national' religion since the early sixteenth century, and where people took immense pride in being Catholic, but in Angola, too, where the colonized population was also Christian and even in places like Matamba and among the Dembos people that weren't under Portuguese control but accepted the religion anyway." Though the roots of Candomblé are multiple, then, its foundation is solidly in Angolan Catholicism, as we have seen, and in the Yoruba and Fon religions of the orishas and voduns, as imported from Nigeria and Dahomey. These religions organized around worship of the Orishas are still actively practiced in West Africa today and, in various forms, throughout the New World, as Candomblé in Brazil; Santería in Cuba, and Vodou (also known as *Sevi Lwa* in Creole) in Haiti. (*Orişa* is the Yoruba word, *orixá* is Portuguese, *oricha* is Spanish, and *orisha* is English. The gods of Vodou are called *iwa,* rather than *orishas.*)

The spread of these religions, and their commonalities, throughout the larger Latin American slave community is one of the great mysteries in the history of religion and one of the most fascinating aspects of the history of African slavery in the New World. How and why the Yoruba gods became the foundation for this truly Pan-African religion is another great mystery, since the Yoruba were not a dominant ethnic group among the slaves. There are many theories about this, including the relative lateness of the influx of Yoruba slaves in certain parts of Latin America, namely, Bahia and Cuba. Despite the considerable geographic, national, and linguistic barriers of Africans living in Brazil, Cuba, and Haiti, for instance, all of the Yoruba-affiliated religions that they created are cousins, as it were, with their gods bearing the same names (save for linguistic differences among French, Spanish, English, and Portuguese) and similar functions and characteristics as deities. It is also true that Candomblé's precedents among the Ewe-Gen-Aja-Fon ethnic cluster are "just about as rich as its precedents among the ancestors of the Yoruba," as the anthropologist J. Lorand Matory pointed out to me. Followers of Candomblé, the Brazilian version of this larger panreligion, pray to the orixás, deities that are different expressions of the complex human experience and the natural world. The supreme god, Olodumaré, does not have a place in the rituals, being too distant from humans. He is not even considered an orixá, properly speaking. The orixás form a pantheon of gods that help their devotees to survive and live fulfilling lives; the orixás belong to a problem-solving religion. Somewhat like the Greek and Roman gods and somewhat, perhaps, like Catholic saints, orixás keep lines of communication open between mortals and the divine—existing in a state of being somewhere between man and God.

Father João described to me his theory of how the slaves' desperation for relief from the horrendous conditions of their enslavement led to their invocation of the orixás and gave birth to Candomblé. "When the slaves arrived here, they arrived like animals," he said. "They had no value. People just wanted work from them. If it wasn't for the orixás that they brought to Brazil in their hearts and in their minds . . . ," his voice trailed off, and he shook his head, seeming to imagine their despair. "I believe that black people here survived, or managed to carry on, because they had a lot of faith in the orixás. The churches could never have replaced African gods. It was a way they had to worship because they didn't have the liberty to express their religion. The Catholic religion did not provide a path for them. So they used Candomblé in order to communicate with the orixás and ask for protection. This was how they survived."

I asked Father João how this unique mixture of faiths had changed over the centuries—and what he saw in its future. "There was a time when Candomblé faced much discrimination," he said, beaming, referring to opposition from Brazil's white, elite establishment. "But today the people of Brazil are beginning to give it the respect it's due. Back then, Candomblé had no way of evolving because black people were not allowed to study. They were oppressed. Today we live in a more civilized society, where people try to understand the religion. I believe Candomblé has everything in its power to grow." He went on, though, to say that devotees of Candomblé are increasingly subjected to vicious verbal attacks and even physical violence by members of evangelical Christian churches today.

Following a religious ceremony, which struck me as very similar to ceremonies I had seen in Nigeria and ones I was to see in Cuba and Haiti, I left Father João's temple reflecting on the fact that as much as the people of Africa were oppressed under slavery, their culture, their energy, and their ways of life and worship could not be extinguished. They took powerful new forms that still endure across Brazil (and, indeed, wherever slaves were taken in the New World). Candomblé is one manifestation of this process. The next stop on my journey was designed to consider another of these Pan-African cultural forms: capoeira.

Like many art forms, capoeira can be hard to describe in words. It is an extraordinary physical discipline, combining martial arts, dance, and rhythms. Today, its elegance and power can be seen all over the world. But its roots are believed to be traced to urban, nineteenth-century Rio de Janeiro. In the neighborhood of Vale das Pedrinhas, I sat down with renowned capoeira master Mestre Boa Gente, to be interviewed live on his community radio program. He began to talk about how slaves developed capoeira. "The masters of the house, the barons and the colonels, did not want the black people to organize themselves," he said, his eyes bright, his entire body engaged in his story. "On coffee plantations, on sugar plantations, weapons were not allowed. But the black people were being tortured. They discovered, in capoeira, a way to strengthen and defend themselves."

According to Mestre Boa Gente, slaves began conditioning their bodies through movements and exercises that became capoeira in preparation for self-defense or rebellion (though there's no evidence that it was ever used for any actual fighting). They couldn't be caught readying for battle, he said, so they disguised their regimen as a kind of ceremonial, even celebratory, dancing, consisting of well-coordinated and syncopated, almost balletic movements and movements characteristic of the martial arts.

"They would be there, training," he explained, "and then they'd hear the cavalry coming. There would be a lookout, a capoeirista, watching, and when he saw them, he'd start playing to the sound of the cavalry. And everything would change from a fight to a dance." Scholars believe that capoeira has its roots in different African martial arts traditions, but no one knows for sure. One version of capoeira is called "Capoeira Angola," but it originated in Brazil; the reference to Angola no doubt stems from the fact that so very many of the slaves in Brazil hailed from Angola. Capoeira Angola is less popular than Capoeira Regional. As Africans' lives were transformed by slavery, they transformed African traditions and created entirely new ones. They created a new culture in their new world, and capoeira is one such form.

"The cavalry would turn up, and they would see all the black people doing their samba," Mestre Boa Gente went on, laughing. "And the cavalry would say, 'Oh, the blacks, they are playing around, they are dancing.' And they'd start clapping. When the cavalry left, they'd continue training." Today, Mestre Boa Gente helps to keep Bahia's young people off the dangerous streets of the favela by teaching them capoeira. He gives them a proud black tradition to carry forward—an energy and passion that cannot be denied (indeed, he has more energy than any sixty-five-year-old I've ever met).

Not every historian agrees with Mestre Boa Gente's story of how capoeira was born. In 1890, two years after the abolition of slavery in 1888, the Republican criminal code introduced capoeira as a specific crime and repressed, persecuted, and exiled its practitioners in Rio. Gradually, capoeira—always vibrantly alive underground—came out of the shadows and was performed as a ceremonial dance in parades and marches. Its military applications, however, are believed by many scholars to be folklore. Still it is hard, in this vibrant man's presence, not to respect the authority of Brazil's black oral traditions and accept every word he says. Capoeira certainly has no greater champion. "If everyone did capoeira, there would be no wars," he proclaimed. "Capoeira is not a sport. It's something that enters you. With every practice, with every day, you get stronger and stronger."

Having caught some of Mestre Boa Gente's seemingly boundless energy, I hit the streets once again, eager to learn about Bahia's famous version of Carnaval. Like so many public celebrations, Carnaval combines a great number of traditions. The ancient Greeks staged Saturnalias and Bacchanalias, wild parties that included masters and slaves alike. The Catholic Church later absorbed these sorts of celebrations to create what we now recognize as Carnaval, even before the slave trade to the New World began. In Mardi Gras celebrations in New Orleans—and in the liturgical traditions of Catholic, Episcopal, and a few other churches—Fat Tuesday (or Shrove Tuesday) is the culmination of these celebrations, the day before Ash Wednesday, which marks the beginning of Lent.

Carnaval, like its cousin Mardi Gras, is essentially a joyous annual festival marking the beginning of Lent—one last chance to live it up before embarking on the forty days of this somber fasting period, ending with the feast of Easter. Traditionally, many Catholics and other Christians give up meat or other indulgences for forty days. (In fact, the word *carnival* derives from the Old Italian *carnelevare,* "to remove meat.") In Brazil, Africans added their own traditions to the European traditions. The parades for Carnaval in Rio and São Paulo consist of various samba schools and Blocos Afro and other groups with their respective costumes, bands, and floats. These are akin to "krewes" in New Orleans's Mardi Gras. At the start of the processions of one of the leading Blocos Afro, Ile Aiye, a figure called the "Mãe de Santo" (the mother of the saints) tosses popcorn to the crowds as a symbolic propitiation to the lord of pestilence, Omolu, asking him to intervene to ensure a peaceful celebration.

For a long time, what we might think of as Afro-Carnaval, though joyously celebrated, was a relatively simple street party in Bahia, heavily influenced by Yoruba traditions, compared to the national and well-orchestrated event it is today. Indeed, black brotherhoods were banned from participating in the official Rio Carnaval at the turn of the twentieth century because they were so "African," or "primitive." In the earliest colonial periods, these brotherhoods played a key role in promoting Afro-Brazilian participation in all of Brazil's religious festivals, well before the Yoruba became a significant presence in the slave trade there. Though they weren't banned at this point, there were complaints made that some of their practices were "heathenish." This ban occurred when Brazil was engaging in an official policy of "whitening," by encouraging the immigration of millions of European migrants. (In fact, between 1872 and 1975, just over 5.4 million Europeans and Middle Eastern immigrants came to Brazil.) But in the latter half of the twentieth century, black samba groups were welcomed back into official celebrations; later, in the seventies, influenced by the Black Power movement in the United States, reggae, and Pan-African movements on the continent, a variation of these samba groups called Blocos Afro came into being, a testament to black pride and consciousness.

I traveled to meet with João Jorge, founder of Olodum, one of several principal Blocos Afro. While some of these Afro-Brazilian cultural organizations have a strong cultural-nationalist and activist bent, Olodum is more multicultural than nationalist or traditionally African, as is the Blocos Afro called Ile Aiye ("the world is my house," in the Yoruba language), headed by the magisterial leader named Antônio Carlos Vovo, a man strikingly regal, with a noble bearing reminiscent of a Benin bronze bust *(vovo* means "grandfather"). He explained to me that Ile Aiye is dedicated to preserving the traditional forms of Candomblé and is restricted to black members. When I asked him how in the world one determines who is "black" among the rainbow of browns and blacks that is the face of Brazil, he laughed and said that it is up to prospective members to self-identify.

J. Lorand Matory informed me that "the original entry test in Ile Aiye involved scratching the applicant's skin with a fingernail. Only if it blanched with 'ash' would the applicant be admitted." With good humor, Vovo added, "We know the difference." I got the feeling that Vovo's was a most cosmopolitan definition of blackness: if you say you are black, then you are black. And in Brazil, a huge percentage of the population, through its DNA, would most probably satisfy the US law of hypodescent, reaffirmed by the Supreme Court as recently as 1986 (as James Davis points out in a fascinating book about color classification in the United States entitled *Who Is Black? One Nation's Definition*).

I marched along behind Ile Aiye's remarkably stunning procession, starting from its headquarters in Curuzu, a section of the Libertade district, or barrio, at about 9:00 p.m. and converging on the Campo Grande in the center of the city at about 3:00 a.m. The members were all dressed in crisp white, red, and yellow dresses and robes (the official colors of Ile Aiye) and singing hauntingly beautiful songs. I could just as easily have been in Yorubaland, it seemed. Vovo's Ile Aiye represents one stream in the politics of culture of the Blocos Afro; João Jorge's Olodum represents another. Both understand full well the enormous political potential of black culture in Brazil; they just pursue their goals in different ways.

"Olodum was founded as a Carnaval group, to create art and culture from the black-consciousness movement," João Jorge explained. "Before, Carnaval was a celebration, purely and simply for fun. The black population participated, but without a black *consciousness*. The change—the rupture—came when Olodum and other organizations affirmed themselves as black, affirmed that these identities serve political roles. Today, Carnaval in Bahia is an instrument of the black population, a means of social promotion—entertainment through raising awareness."

This is a street party and an expertly choreographed parade with a purpose, I thought. But I also recognized the tension between the Carnaval of yesterday and the Carnaval of today. While African religions, ideas, art, and exuberance had found ways to persist and flourish, it was clear that the stamp of "slave" had never quite disappeared from the Afro-Brazilian experience, and connotations of inferiority associated with slavery shadowed the darkest and "most African" of the Brazilian people. Ile Aiye and Olodum and the other Blocos Afro had to be born, I recognized, as part of a larger effort to restore the legacy of Africa to a place of honor from which it had fallen during Brazil's period of whitening, the long period following the abolition of slavery in which it was in denial about its black roots.

As much as I hated to leave this magical center of African culture in the New World, I now felt that it was time for me to travel beyond Bahia. I knew that further inland an even greater genetic mixing of Africans, indigenous peoples, and Europeans had been common. And understanding the many complexities of this mix, I realized, was the only way to begin to understand the complexities of race and racism in contemporary Brazil.

As I drove into the hills of the interior, watching the landscape steadily elevate as we approached the mining region, it occurred to me that this was the journey many slaves had taken in the eighteenth century. The sugar empire in Brazil was fading then, as global prices fell. But gold and diamonds were discovered in the high sierra. Portuguese investors brought slaves to perform more labor there, in a place called Minas Gerais, meaning "general mines."

I soon arrived in the town of Diamantina, where Júnia Furtado, a professor of history, had agreed to meet with me. I was immediately struck by my new surroundings. Diamantina was a Portuguese colonial town, built in 1710, and is preserved to near perfection. You can see drawings of it from three hundred years ago that look almost exactly the same as it does today (though back in the eighteenth century the place would have been buzzing, whereas now it is a rural university town and a tourist destination).

Anyone could tell Diamantina was different from Bahia—and a long way from Africa—just by looking at it for a moment. But Professor Furtado told me something right off the bat that set the two of them even further apart. In Diamantina, she said, blacks and whites had lived together, side by side, throughout the age of slavery. Indeed, she said, many freed slaves owned property, just as they did in Bahia, Pernambuco, and São Paulo. (Bahia also had a class of urban slaves who could move about freely, earn a living, and pay the owner a regular fee; they were called *negros de ganho*.) Furtado explained to me, "Sometimes they even came to own their own slaves. We know that white people, freed black people, and freed mulattoes lived on the same streets, all over the city," she continued. "There were freed black people living on the larger streets in nice houses, with two stories."

After hearing about the brutal working conditions of Bahia's sugar plantations and Minas's plantations and mining fields, this was rather surprising to me. I asked Furtado how this could have occurred at a time when Europeans considered Africans barbaric, uncivilized, and inferior. In the United States, after all, we had communities of free blacks in both the North and the South; about 10 percent of the black population in 1860 was free. But they generally didn't live in integrated communities with whites.

"This place was very distant from everywhere else," she explained, referring to the urban context in contrast to the life of a slave on a plantation or in a mine. "In the eighteenth century, it took months to travel here, so these people were pretty much apart from the rest of the world." In other words, in Diamantina, blacks and whites could live outside social norms. What happened in Diamantina, it seemed, stayed in Diamantina. And quite a lot happened, especially at night. I asked Furtado how free blacks came to be free in the first place. She explained that many of these freed blacks were women, that white men in Diamantina frequently took African women as concubines and then freed them in their wills or on their deathbeds, while others allowed the women to work in the mines or as prostitutes, saving their money to buy their own freedom. "They had to live amongst themselves," Furtado explained. "White men were the majority of the free population, and they needed women to have sex."

The bachelor factor again, I thought, realizing that while, in some ways, Diamantina sounded downright progressive, hadn't slave women always been forced to be concubines for white men throughout the slave trade and across continents in the New World? I asked Furtado what made the women of Diamantina so different.

"Women really achieved a superior social status here," she asserted. "In 1774, around 50 percent of the houses were owned by black women. They possessed slaves. They were able to have a status very similar to the men they were living with."

I found it hard to believe the church would put up with any of this. Furtado nodded with a mischievous smile. "Of course the church disapproved completely of this situation," she chuckled, "but what we saw here was a kind of silence from the church. There were some visits from bishops, and all this sin was denounced. People would pay some amount of money and say, 'I won't do it anymore.' But when the bishop left the city, everybody started living together again!"

The line, according to Furtado, was drawn at marriage. While couples could live together and trust everyone around them to look the other way, only "equals" received the sanctification of the church to marry. "White married white, freed people married freed people, black people married black people," she stated flatly.

Furtado then offered to take me to the house once owned by the most famous black woman in Brazilian history, a woman named Chica da Silva, one of Diamantina's most successful women in the eighteenth century. She's an icon in Brazil. In the 1970s, her story was even made into a film starring the country's first black female superstar, Zezé Motta. Few slaves in the history of the United States could imagine a life as complex as Chica's. And the difference between slavery in Brazil and slavery in the United States lay in the essence of her story: Chica da Silva could *almost* escape her blackness.

Furtado told me that Chica da Silva was born in Brazil and came to Diamantina as a slave. Her master, a white diamond merchant, fell in love with her. "When he met her," said Furtado, "he'd just arrived from Portugal. She had already one small boy with her former owner, a doctor, and he bought her from him. And I think it was a case of love—an immediate case of love, because he arrived in August, in December she already belonged to him, and he freed her on Christmas Day."

"They stayed together for fifteen years," Furtado continued, as we wandered through Chica's impressive home. "They had thirteen children together, one after another. And she was buried in Sao Francisco Church, a very exclusive church for the white brotherhood."

The thought of an African woman rising to such a height within a slave-owning culture seemed miraculous. But Furtado explained that this ascendance did not come without cost. Chica da Silva was black, yet her rise to power within the community was part of a conscious "whitening" effort. "She acted like she was a white woman," Furtado explained. "She dressed like one; she was buried in the white church. What can I say? It was a way of integration."

The consequences of Chica's choice—the shedding of most vestiges of her black identity—echoed for generations in the lives of her children and grandchildren. "They really embraced the white," Furtado said. "Because it was the way of social climbing in this society. The goal was to become white people." Indeed, Furtado's research shows that many of Chica's sons moved with their father to his homeland of Portugal, settling in Lisbon and presenting themselves as whites in Portuguese society. There are even records that suggest that some of Chica's descendants in Lisbon paid money to the Crown officially to erase their black heritage.

"We have the registers," said Furtado, "of investigations of her blood because her sons and grandsons who wanted to take any position in the Portuguese society had to have their lineage investigated, their genealogy. Because having someone who was black or Moor or Jewish—they're all problems. It was forbidden for them to enter in the Order of Christ or to enter in the university to apply for a job or a position. So they had to apply this way in Lisbon and then they had to ask for forgiveness to the queen for having a grandmother or a mother who was black. They had to pay money. And because of the money they had, in fact these children got good positions, good jobs, good places, even in Portugal." They managed to erase their blackness bureaucratically.

This points to something crucial in Chica's story. We shouldn't think of hers as a case of a mixed person "passing" which is the analogy that we, as Americans, generally come to right away. It was much more complicated than that. Chica was definitely African descended, and no amount of European clothing or mimicked behavior could change that. But she wasn't simply trying to hide that. Rather, she was doing something fundamentally different: she was advancing by class. After all, lower-class Portuguese who achieved wealth did much the same thing: they abandoned their country customs and took on the airs of the aristocracy, if they were able to. In the United States, in contrast, no amount of wealth or behavior would ever make a black-skinned person "white," and that is a fundamental difference between the two societies. Class was fluid in Brazil, in a way that it was not for black people in the United States. The process, in other words, was always about class status first and much less about race per se, something very difficult for us to grasp in the United States.

I thought about this as we left the house. Chica da Silva's transformation from a slave to a wealthy matriarch included a whitening process. Her star wouldn't have risen if she had practiced Candomblé, worn traditional garments, and, well, stayed black. And her decision had an effect on her family for generations. I found this capacity of a female slave for social mobility fascinating, since it was so unlike the experience that this same person would have had in the United States, but I also have to say that I found it somewhat disturbing. And the more I thought about it, the more confusing the story seemed to me. I realized, with a start, that I was thinking about Chica da Silva in terms of "passing" for white in the United States, not in the way race was socially constructed in Brazil. Everyone in Brazil knew that Chica was black; money and manners "whitened" her socially only. In the United States, a drop of blood is all it takes to make a person "black"— and the history of passing is replete with tragedy, from the descendants of the abolitionist writer and physician James McCune Smith to the Harlem Renaissance novelist Jean Toomer to the *New York Times* book critic Anatole Broyard. But could blacks in Brazil choose a more nuanced racial identity than we can in the United States? Were the scores of racial classifications that Brazilians of color used to describe themselves neutral descriptors; or were these ways to separate from the darkest, most "Negroid" aspects of the African experience in Brazil, and their connotations as base, inferior, and degenerate? Was I imposing a US interpretive framework on the subtleties of a society I was ill prepared to understand? Had Brazil's long history of miscegenation created a complexly shaded social structure, from white, on one end, to black, on the other, which had managed, somehow, to escape the negrophobia that remains so much a part of US society? In other words, should we be celebrating the social fluidity that Chica da Silva enacted for herself and her progeny, rather than critiquing it? If so, should we, in the era of multiculturalism and mixed-race identities, look at Chica and people like her as prophets of the social construction of race, as harbingers of a new era in race relations?

Questions like this can quickly become abstract, academic, and impossible to answer. I've often found that the place to go for a reality check is the barbershop or the beauty shop. After all, black hair is a big deal—whether you embrace it, tame it, or straighten it with a hot comb or chemicals. I wanted to know how Brazil's mixed-race culture dealt with black hair; I wanted to know what was hiding in "the kitchen."

I headed to Belo Horizonte, capital of the state of Minas Gerais. I knew there were concentrated Afro-Brazilian communities in the favelas there— the poorest areas. And that's where, in the blackest part of Minas Gerais, I stepped into the beauty shop of Dora Álves to find out just how beautiful black is in Brazil. Álves does hair, but she also does politics, as a cultural activist. She told me that her customers often ask her to make their hair look straighter, less frizzy, less kinky . . . more white. Álves teaches them to take pride in their black hair and their black heritage.

"Sometimes, we'll have someone arriving at the salon," she told me, "and she is so depressed, with such low self-esteem. She thinks her hair is ugly, that her hair is terrible. Sometimes the mother still has her baby in a stroller, and she arrives asking me, 'Oh, my God, is there any way to solve this hair?' Sometimes we go into schools, and the teacher will come up with a child—he'll whisper, just like this, into my ear, 'Do you think there's anything that can be done?'"

I shook my head, astonished at the idea of exposing the skull of a baby in a stroller to the torture of hair-straightening chemicals.

"I'll say, 'No, let's have a chat!'" Álves went on, emphatically. "I sit down, I put the child on my knee, and I say, 'Your hair is beautiful. You are beautiful. I'm organizing a fashion show, and you can be in it.' And the child starts to relax, and the next thing you know, the child is strutting around. She's all happy, all joyful, walking around like Gisele," referring to Brazilian Gisele Bündchen, whom *Forbes* magazine recently said was the highest-paid model in the world.

Álves wants to reach kids early, so she regularly visits schools and community centers to promote black pride. It's a big commitment, especially for a woman who runs her own business. But it drives her to distraction to see Afro-Brazilians trying to leave their blackness behind the way Chica da Silva did.

"Why do so many black women have low self-esteem here in Brazil if they have Afro hair?" I asked. Why would black people be so alarmed at having black hair in the world's second-largest black nation?

"It's a question of history," Álves explained, shaking her head. "It's also a question of the media, too. You see it in the advertisements, in magazines, on TV—you see that most of the women are white. If you go and count, there might be one black girl, just one. And the rest are white, with their hair straightened out. So black women can't see themselves at all."

They can't see themselves at all, I thought, stepping out of the shop. I turned back to wave at Álves and thank her again. But my mind was spinning with questions. Black people were everywhere, but had they absorbed Brazil's urge to whiten itself? And their history included characters like Chica da Silva, who had walked away from her blackness—and been idolized for it. In the United States, everyone just sees me as black, and that's how I think of myself. But in Brazil, racial mixing had made things far more complicated, more graduated, more nuanced, perhaps?

So what is blackness in Brazil? And just how beautiful is white? As someone with a mixed-race heritage myself, I decided to ask passersby on the street what they thought of me. And I learned, quickly, that my color was in the eye of the beholder.

"If I lived in Brazil," I asked one man, "what color would I be?"

"*Caboclo*," he answered.

I asked another man, "What race am I, what color?"

"*Pardo*," he said.

The answers kept coming, all different. "Light *moreno*." "*Mulatto*." "*Cafuso*." Each was specific, as if describing a different color of the rainbow. It seemed objective—to a point.

"We're all black, even though we're different colors," one man argued.

"I'm black," another piped in. "He's light *moreno.*"

"Black. He'd be black," a woman said. "I'm not a racist, no."

Her answer rung in my head. I couldn't help noticing that those who called themselves black and identified me as black did so with a certain defiance, or apologetically. Many people wanted to be one of Brazil's seemingly endless shades of brown, not black, and to assure me that I was brown, too. Were these categories, these many names for degrees of blackness, a shield against blackness? The mixing in Bahia, Minas Gerais, and other areas in slavery times and replicating itself since had produced Brazilians of a brown blend. But these many shades of black and brown clearly weren't equal.

I called my friend Professor Reis and described my experience to him. He reminded me that there are in fact well over a hundred different words to describe degrees of blackness in Brazil: 134, in fact—a word for every shade. Very dark blacks are *preto* or *negro azul* (blue black). Medium-dark blacks are *escuro. Preto desbotado* refers to light-skinned blacks. If you're light enough to pass for white and you seem to be trying, then you're *mulatto disfarçado. Sarará* means white-skinned with kinky hair. The country's focus on color, it struck me, bordered on obsession. The list went on, and on, and on, dizzyingly.

I decided to return to Salvador, Brazil's black capital, to find out what in this country's past made attitudes toward blackness so problematic—to learn more about Brazil after slavery, when degrees of blackness were already spread across the country. I met with Wlamyra Albuquerque, another historian who teaches at the Federal University of Bahia. We settled in the library at the Geographical and Historical Institute, carefully drinking cool glasses of water so as not to damage the fragile works in the archives. I asked her what the white ruling class had thought about African culture in Brazil after the abolition of slavery in 1888. "The elite reacted very badly to the end of slavery," she replied. "What bothered them was how to deal with the large population of color. Various ministers who were a part of the government believed that in order for Brazil to become a civilized country, it had to undergo a process of whitening. The government invested a great deal in European immigration to the country."

Abolition may have ended slavery, Albuquerque said, but it didn't transform Brazil into the tolerant multicultural nation that so many blacks and white abolitionists must have hoped it would become. Between about 1884 and 1939, four million Europeans and 185,000 Japanese were subsidized to immigrate to Brazil and work as indentured servants. The process, a formal government program, was called *branqueamento*—which translates, literally, as "whitening." Obviously, the white elite hoped to increase the number of whites reproducing among blacks to lighten the national complexion. But the effort was also aimed sharply at eradicating vestiges of African culture.

"The government told Brazilians that to be black was something close to savagery," Albuquerque explained. "From that moment, they began to persecute practices that were seen as black—like Candomblé and capoeira—trying to convince people that these practices were barbarous and that it was a civilizing act to stop them."

As I silently cheered for Candomblé and capoeira—African creations that survived the era of *branqueamento*—Albuquerque began to tell me about one black man, a pioneering intellectual, who had taken a bold, brave stand against the government's racist ideologies. His name was Manuel Querino. He's still little known even inside Brazil. His story is rarely taught in universities, much less in high schools. But he is an important figure nonetheless: a historian, artist, labor unionist, and black activist who deserves to be better known. You might think of Querino as a Brazilian mixture of Booker T. Washington and W. E. B. Du Bois: he pushed for technical education for blacks and was a teacher at a trade institute, like Washington; but at the same time, he was a member of the exclusive Instituto Geográfico e Histórico (where I was talking to Albuquerque), as Du Bois would have been. But unlike Washington and Du Bois, he was also involved in trade unionism and local politics (he was an alderman), and he often allied himself with oligarchical politicians. Querino, in other words, was a rather complex man.

"Querino emphasized the role of the African as a civilizer," Albuquerque told me. "He thought there was no need for the white immigrants, as Brazil had already been civilized by the Africans. He said the Brazilian worker was much more capable than the foreign worker of dealing with the challenges of Brazilian society."

"Querino was also an artist and spoke about this population's artistic abilities," she continued. "He was concerned with showing African customs and traditions in Bahia. So he was a dissonant voice when everyone else was saying that those who came over as slaves were not capable of a more sophisticated style of work."

I was stunned that I had never heard of this man. (I later learned that the hero of the novel *Tent of Miracles,* by Jorge Amado, is partially based on Querino. Amado can be thought of as the Gilberto Freyre of Brazilian literature.) Slaves were acknowledged as essential in many quarters. But Querino had argued that Africans were integral to Brazil's cultural identity. For me, hearing about his life was like learning for the first time about W. E. B. Du Bois or Carter G. Woodson—two of my great personal heroes in African American history. I was absolutely riveted as Albuquerque began searching the archives' copy of one of Querino's essays for her favorite passages.

"Here it is," she said, thumbing through a journal. "'Whoever rereads history will see the way in which the nation always has glory in the African that it imported.' It's about how we should have pride in being the descendants of these Africans. Querino is the father of black history here—and also of black mobilization and of racial positivity within the black movement."

Querino was a seminal figure in the black intellectual history of Brazil. And yet, as I learned from Professor Albuquerque, Querino's pioneering ideas about race and racism largely died with him in 1923. Instead, the creation of Brazil's official identity—as one of the world's few truly mixed, supposedly racist-free nations—is credited to the work of one man: Gilberto Freyre.

Unlike his unsung counterpart Querino, Freyre is taught widely in schools, even in the United States, and is celebrated for recognizing the value and significance of Africans within Brazilian culture (I read his work when I was in college). But also unlike Querino, Freyre was white. He was born into a middle-class family in 1900, only twelve years after abolition. His father was a public employee, and his mother's family owned a sugar plantation. Freyre spent his youth on plantations owned by his mother's relatives. And plantation life served as the inspiration for Freyre's most celebrated work, published in 1933: *Casa Grande e Senzala* (*The Masters and the Slaves;* a better translation would be "The Big House and the Slave Quarters"). In that book, he argued that race relations in Brazil were quite fluid during slavery, in spite of the violence at the heart of the system. But slavery, he argued, was not solely defined by violence. He described Brazil, the last country in the Western Hemisphere to abolish slavery, as the first place most likely to eliminate racism, because it was not a mainstream mentality of normal Brazilian citizens. Racial democracy was in process of being constructed.

Freyre argued that because blacks, whites, and indigenous peoples were all having sexual relationships and reproducing with each other—a mixing traditionally called *miscegenation,* a term of some baggage and controversy today—race relations were better in Brazil than they were in slave-owning cultures that were more rigidly segregated. I'd brought my copy of Freyre's book with me and, as I traveled across Brazil, frequently looked over some of the key passages that had stuck with me all these years later. I found that they still troubled me, like this one:

> The truth is that in Brazil, contrary to what is to be observed in other American countries and in those parts of Africa that have been recently colonized by Europeans, the primitive culture—the Amerindian as well as the African— has not been isolated into hard, dry, indigestible lumps incapable of being assimilated by the European social system. . . . Neither did the social relations between the two races, the conquering and the indigenous one, ever reach that point of sharp antipathy or hatred, the grating sound of which reaches our ears from all the countries that have been colonized by Anglo-

Saxon Protestants. The friction here was smoothed by the lubricating oil of a deep-going miscegenation.

Freyre claimed that whites and blacks not only had sex but sometimes married, with the church's blessing (though live-in arrangements were suitably "damned by the clergy"). He argued that this racial mixing constituted the core of Brazil's identity. Like Querino, he maintained that Brazil wasn't Brazil without Africans and their culture. But his work lacks any real sympathy or understanding of what it actually means to be a Brazilian of African descent.

I realized then that Freyre had, in many ways, taken Querino's place in Brazilian history. He's credited with the first view of Brazil as a nation that should take pride in its mixed-race heritage. But did he articulate anything beyond an essentially primitivist or romantic view of race relations during slavery?

> Every Brazilian, even the light-skinned fair-haired one, carries out in him on his soul, when not on soul and body alike . . . the shadow, or at least the birthmark, of the aborigine or the Negro. . . . In our affections, our excessive mimicry, our Catholicism, which so delights the senses, our music, our gait, our speech, our cradle songs—in everything that is a sincere expression of our lives, we almost all of us bear the mark of that influence.

When Freyre wrote these words, in 1933, US blacks were under the boot of Jim Crow. Segregation was the order of the day, and many whites in the United States were fighting to keep it permanent. And yet Freyre asserted that black Brazilians and white Brazilians were bound together by blood and destiny. He argued that they had created each other, that they mutually constituted each other. Many people who read Freyre in the United States—he was actually educated at Baylor and at Columbia—during these years of Jim Crow must have thought he was either dangerously radical or else insane. Who alive here then would ever have dared claim that the United States could be the world's model racial democracy?

When I first read Freyre, I remember faulting him for being overly romantic, even naïve. Masters raped slaves. Many long-term sexual relationships were the result of coercion at best. Respect between peoples comes with social equality. And, obviously, when one person owns another, there can be no equality. Period. But I had to acknowledge the impact that Freyre's writing is said to have had on Brazil. Some scholars argue that it changed the way whites looked at blacks, and it also changed the way blacks thought about themselves, though it is difficult to imagine a work of scholarship having this much social impact. Freyre, drawing on mid-nineteenth-century Brazil legend, was nevertheless one of the first scholars to argue more or less cogently that Brazil—its culture and its identity—was created by the blending of three equal races: Europeans, indigenous peoples, and Africans. We cannot overestimate how novel this idea was in its time, or how eagerly liberal and progressive academics, such as W. E. B. Du Bois, seized on it—at least for a time—in their attempt to undermine de jure segregation in the United States.

Traveling north from Salvador, I was greeted warmly by Gilberto Freyre Neto, the grandson of the writer, at the writer's home in Recife, the capital of the state of Pernambuco and the fourth-largest metropolitan area in Brazil. After Bahia, Pernambuco was Brazil's second-largest center of sugar-plantation slavery in colonial Brazil. Recife's airport is named for Freyre, surely a first, or at least one of the very few times that an airport has been named for an intellectual! I told him I was honored to meet him after having studied his grandfather at Yale. And I relished my personal tour of Freyre's house, where he lived from 1940 until his death in 1987. Neto showed me his grandfather's medals of honor, the desk at which he sat and wrote his books, and even a first-edition copy of *Casa Grande e Senzala*.

Neto's life is dedicated to keeping his grandfather's work alive, so he was happy to sit with me and dig into Freyre's writings. I started by asking him how attitudes toward black people changed after his grandfather's 1933 masterpiece was published.

"I think the book was a real turning point in the 1930s," he told me. "Gilberto raised the Brazilian blacks to the same cultural standing as the Portuguese. He equated them. He said Brazil only became Brazil when African culture, which was often superior to Portuguese, became culturally miscegenated. From that moment on, we had a 'complementariness.' We became an ideal meta-race."

At the time *Casa Grande e Senzala* was published, Germans were rallying behind Hitler and his calls for Aryan purity. Freyre took the completely opposite view, arguing that its racial mix was essential to bringing Brazil to the height of its cultural and societal potential. Whitening had been a mistake.

"His studies were based very heavily on experiences that my grandfather lived through and information that he was able to gather from sources that were curiously trivial," Neto explained. "A lot of the time, they were not even considered academic. He drew from newspaper cuttings, interviews with elderly people, knowledge that was gathered mostly from interactions. So my grandfather inhabits the dichotomy of either 'Love Gilberto Freyre' or 'Hate Gilberto Freyre.' Some academics think of him as a novelist, while others think of him as one of the most profound analyzers of Brazilian society."

Novelist, sociologist, neither, or both, Freyre's impact really can't be over-stated. His writings changed attitudes about race across the entire nation. Many of Brazil's leaders, no matter what their politics were, sooner or later embraced his ideas. They overturned institutionalized policies that overtly discriminated against blacks. Brazil's official whitening process came to an end. And Freyre fixed, in its place, the concept of "racial democracy"—the idea that Brazil was so racially mixed that it was beyond racism.

Beyond racism. I sat back for a moment. I was beginning to feel some-thing romantic toward Brazil—as Freyre had always felt. Even today, Brazil boasts of its racial harmony and its multicultural identity. And I could al-most see it. While the United States was busy policing the racial boundaries with Jim Crow, Freyre was arguing, Brazilians were busy embracing one an-other! The joyous celebration of Carnaval became a globally recognized symbol of Brazilian brotherhood across racial lines. Racial democracy cer-tainly seemed to lie at the heart of Brazilian identity.

But could it be real? What about Brazil's extensive poverty, especially among blacks? What about Ile Aiye and Olodum, which rose in the seven-ties from a need to reassure blacks (and to educate whites) that it is glorious to be descended from Africa? Like any reasonable person—black or white—I want to believe we live in a world where a society beyond racism can ex-ist, not just in theory. But I need to see evidence of this progress to believe it. And in the restaurants where I ate and in the hotels where I stayed, in upper-class residential neighborhoods, on the covers of magazines at city newsstands—virtually everyone in a position of power looked white.

Neto was adamant in response to my questions. If racial democracy isn't real already, he assured me, it is becoming real. He read once more from his grandfather's works: "I think we are more advanced in solving the racial question," he quoted, "than any other community in the world that I know."

I left Neto with as many questions as answers and headed south to Rio de Janeiro, Brazil's most famous city—and its cultural and intellectual capi-tal. I'd managed to secure a meeting with Zezé Motta, the actress who played Chica da Silva in Brazil's famous film, which premiered in 1976. As a black actress, I thought, she must have had strong feelings about playing this character, and I was hoping she could help me clarify my feelings about this so-called racial democracy.

What I didn't expect—and what I got—was a meeting with a most thoughtful, articulate artist. Chica da Silva may have personified racial de-mocracy, but life for Zezé Motta has been quite different. "Before I became successful," she said, "I took pictures for advertisements, and the client did not approve them, saying, 'This client is middle class and wouldn't take suggestions from a black woman.' And on TV, I played various roles which were actually always the same one: the maid."

"I was always defending Chica da Silva," she explained. "I would say, 'Chica da Silva did what she had to do. Don't demand Angela Davis attitude from her.' Her merit lies in the fact that she was born a slave, but she could not accept this. She turned the game around and became a queen."

Perhaps paradoxically, at the same time she defended Chica da Silva for being complicit in her own whitening, Motta discovered how connected she was to her own blackness.

"It's very hard for a black person in Brazil to have a career as an actress," she confided, "but in the case of Chica da Silva, it had to be a black woman. The producer didn't want me because I was too ugly— until very recently, in Brazil, the black people were considered ugly. The producer preferred her to be a mulatta, a lighter actress. But the director didn't budge. It had to be a black woman."

Who wouldn't want Chica da Silva—a black woman—played by this great, and stunningly beautiful, black actress? I kept listening.

"After the film, I was considered a Brazilian sex symbol," she laughed, "because the character became very present in the male imagination. At that time, there would never be a black person on the cover of the big magazines, because they'd say, 'The cover sells.' But as I had become the queen, the sex symbol, an important magazine put me on the cover. And someone high up in the magazine said that if it didn't sell, the person who signed off on it would be fired!"

Motta's portrayal of Chica da Silva made her a star, overnight. She enjoyed the recognition that came with her fame, and she was certainly proud of her work. But her new status brought her new experiences along Brazil's ever-moving color line. And those experiences revealed to her Brazil's anti-black racism—a racism that her country claimed did not exist.

"I traveled to sixteen countries promoting the film, including the United States," Motta continued. "And I started to think, 'There are so few black actors in the Brazil media. Where is everybody?' This country has a debt toward its black people."

I thought about Motta's words as I traveled to my next meeting. I'd arranged to sit down with one of my heroes, a truly great man who has spent his life advocating for Afro-Brazilians: Abdias do Nascimento. I had wanted to meet him for a very long time; Nascimento is one of the gods of the international black-intellectual tradition. He is now ninety-six years old, but the grip of his handshake is still firm and his mind razor sharp. He's been fighting the good fight for three-quarters of a century, as a senator, a university professor, and a writer. Nominated for the Nobel Peace Prize, he founded the Institute of Afro-Brazilian Studies in Rio and is widely recognized as the country's greatest black activist. Some people even call him the Nelson Mandela of Brazil.

I was honored to be in his presence, and I told him so. He accepted me graciously, with the calm and dignity of a leader naturally born. An exquisite gold statue of Exú, the messenger of the gods, stood on a china cabinet near Nascimento's dining table. I asked him about the status of black people, politically and socially, in all aspects of contemporary Brazil. Was racial democracy an ideal or a reality? Had it ever existed? Could it ever blossom?

"This is a joke, which has been built up since Brazil was discovered," Nascimento replied with conviction. "And Brazil likes to spread this around the world. But it's a huge lie. And the black people know that. The black people feel in their flesh the lie that is racial democracy. You just have to look at the black families. Where do they live? The black children—how are they educated? You'll see that it's all a lie."

He listened patiently while I recounted my recent visit with Gilberto Freyre's grandson. Nascimento didn't buy plantation life as whites and blacks holding hands in the sunshine, either. He told me he found the idea "sentimental." And if you don't accept that picture, he pointed out, you can't accept racial democracy. Interestingly enough, in the late forties, Nascimento published a short-lived magazine called *Quilombo,* in which Freyre and other white intellectuals published essays in a column entitled "Racial Democracy."

"There is the myth that slavery in Brazil was very gentle, very friendly, even," he said. "These are all fabrications. Slavery here was violent, bloody. Please understand, I am saying this with profound hatred, profound bitterness for the way black people are treated in Brazil—because it's shameful that Brazil has a majority of blacks, a majority that built this country, that remain second-class citizens to this day."

He spoke so passionately but without bombast, his convictions firm, well considered, strong. In his eloquence, he reminded me of the Nigerian Nobel laureate for literature, Wole Soyinka. As I continued to listen, somewhat in awe, Nascimento explained how formal racism in Brazil had been replaced by an equally dangerous informal racism. Racial democracy was a mask, a public face that Brazil put on for the world, he explained. Day-to-day, real-life Brazil was still hostile to blacks, still trying to "whiten away" vestiges of African culture.

"My parents never talked about African gods," he lamented. "I researched them, but the African gods were hidden. The only gods that appeared in public were the Christian gods, the Catholic ones. But the gods of those who lived in little huts, who were ashamed or afraid to reveal their true beliefs?"

He shrugged his shoulders and held out empty hands. "It was not a law. It was an unwritten law that one shouldn't really talk about African gods. It's only now that African gods are talked about openly."

"I was the first black senator who was conscious of being black," he said, proudly. "And I ripped the fantasy of the Senate apart. Every single session, I would start by declaring, 'I invoke the orixás! I invoke Olorum! I call Exú! May Exú give me the power of speech! Give me the right words to get at these racists who have been in power for five hundred years! The right words to tell Brazil, to tell the world that the black people are aware, that the black people are awake!'" I could only imagine that scene, the horror on the faces of his fellow senators as he declaimed about the Yoruba gods, invoking my favorite of the lot, Exú, messenger of the gods, the god of interpretation, rather like Hermes in Greek mythology. I glanced at his statue. It was almost as if the lovely, nine-inch gold statue of the trickster broke into a smile. We both burst into laughter.

I asked him what he saw in Brazil's future. Was he optimistic that the situation might improve? I was curious to see how he'd respond to the question. I was expecting, I think, some kind of visceral explosion. Instead, Nascimento was very calm and seemed to have long ago formed his answer.

"If I weren't an optimist, I would have hung myself," he told me. "This action is so repetitive—this thing that has been going on for five hundred years. So if I weren't an optimist, I would have hung myself."

Everything Nascimento said made me more eager to see more of Brazil as it truly is. The Brazil of my imagination had its place. Brazil's vision of itself has its own life. But for this journey to have meaning, I needed to witness the Brazil of the real world. And there could be no better place than Rio de Janeiro. I roamed widely through the wealthy neighborhoods, Copacabana and Ipanema, walking the beaches and driving around the lovely homes. I began to recognize the wisdom in Nascimento's words. There were very few black people anywhere. I stopped at a newsstand and looked at the magazine covers, slowly taking in what I was seeing: rows upon rows of white faces, white models, a white Brazil. I could have been in Switzerland. As I looked for even one brown face among these pictures, I thought of Zezé Motta's story. If someone asked me for proof that we were standing in a majority-black country, I couldn't have produced it at that newsstand.

I asked myself what black Brazilian I could remember having seen consistently in the media in the United States. Pele, the Albert Einstein of soccer, came to mind first, but then so did Ronaldo, Robinho, Ronaldinho, Neymar, and other soccer players. Maybe a musician or two, such as Milton Nascimento, and a model or two. That was it.

I went on, looking for black Brazil. And I found it—not at Ipanema or Copacabana but in Rio's famous slums, the favelas. I arrived in the particularly infamous neighborhood called the City of God, one of Brazil's most famous favelas, if only because it was the title of a very popular and well-made film released in 2002. Here, among some of the world's worst slums, Afro-Brazilian life was vibrant, visible, omnipresent, and distressfully poor.

The City of God is where Brazil's most famous rapper, MV Bill, was born and raised. I knew he still lived there—even though his fame made it more than possible to leave. He was happy to talk to me about what life is really like for Afro-Brazilians. I started by asking him why he still lives in the same poverty-stricken favela. In the United States, hip-hop stars tend to move to Beverly Hills or a comparable neighborhood when they make it, no matter where they came from.

"I don't condemn those who make money, leave the ghetto, and go to live somewhere else," he replied. "But my thing with the City of God is different, independent of whatever money I make. Living here is part of my identity."

The City of God looked like the opposite of wealthy Rio—here, all the faces were different shades of the darker browns. I asked MV Bill if everyone in the neighborhood is black.

"The majority," he answered, nodding his head. "The City of God is considered one of the blackest neighborhoods in Rio de Janeiro. But even here in a black neighborhood, it is the smaller population of lighter people that have the best opportunities in life."

The remains of whitening, I thought immediately. Those who appear to fit the European dream of *branqueamento* are doing better than their darker neighbors, even after all this time.

"But in Brazil, we're not allowed to talk like this," MV Bill said, interrupting my thoughts. "We have to live in a racial democracy that doesn't exist. There is no equality."

I told MV Bill that my own experience had reflected that. During any travels, I was fortunate to stay in nice hotels and to eat at good restaurants, but I had often been the only black person who was not serving. MV Bill only seemed surprised to hear I'd been treated so well.

"It's because of your social standing," he explained. "But there will be many places where you'd be the only black man and you'd still be treated badly."

I had assumed that MV Bill would be treated well wherever he went. After all, the man is a star. But now I asked him if he had ever suffered poor treatment just for being black.

"Of course," he answered readily, "before, during, and after my fame."

"Why is Brazil so racist?" I finally said, for the first time on my journey. "It's the second-largest black nation in the world."

MV Bill nodded. He knew what I was asking, even if he didn't have an answer. "We have lived under the myth of racial democracy," he replied. "But this is exposed as a lie when we look at the color of the people who live in favelas, the color of the people who are in prison, the color of the people who survive by committing crimes. People will tell you that our problem in Brazil is an economic problem or a social problem, anything but a racial problem—it can never be racial. But it is."

His words struck an emotional chord. In the United States, too, blacks are often accused of being at fault for their own poverty.

"There are a lot of people who don't have jobs because they have not had access to education," he went on. "And without access to education, they have not been able to get any professional qualifications. And without any qualifications—on top of all the prejudices against those who live in a place like this—it is very hard to get good jobs. We have a lot of people who are not criminals, who are not drug addicts, but who don't have an occupation, who are not doing anything."

I sat back, trying to process his comments. While it is true that racial segregation was outlawed in Brazil, the legacies of slavery—so recently abolished, relatively speaking—persist, as does color prejudice. Although segregation had never been legal, as it had been in the United States, it manifests itself throughout Brazilian society. As I would find to be true throughout Latin America, the darkest people in these societies tend to be at the bottom of the social scale. Racial democracy was a beautiful and alluring ideal, but had it ever been more than a romantic white worldview, designed to keep Afro-Brazilians in their place? After all, a black-pride movement is not needed, is it, in a society in which racial democracy obtains? As Abdias do Nascimento explained to me quite perceptively, because of this ideology of the country as blessedly free of racism, Brazil never had a civil rights movement, like the one we had in the United States, because it did not have de jure segregation to rail against. Brazil's racism was informal—devastatingly effective, but informal nonetheless. And this meant that blacker Brazilians never have had a chance to demand redress for the racism that they still feel they suffer.

I turned to watch children playing in the street, young lives full of potential. I asked MV Bill if he thought any of these children might one day become the Barack Obama of Brazil.

"I think so, yes," he said, smiling. "But there is only one way: through education. And education in Brazil is a luxury item. I think our greatest revolution will be to have young people like these becoming lawyers, having political power, influencing the judicial system. Those are the signs we hope for."

I left MV Bill and his inspiring spirit of hope, in the City of God. But our conversation lingered in my mind. The cycle of poverty is inevitably vicious—no money means no education, no education means no job, no job means no money And the cause for this cycle, most scholars and activists agree, is the legacy of slavery and a function of the lingering remnants of anti-black racism. What was Brazil doing to right this wrong, to begin, systematically, to put an end to the inequality that slavery visited on persons of African descent and their descendants?

The answer won't surprise Americans, but it has taken hold only recently in Brazil: affirmative action. The future, the hopes, and the very lifeblood of Afro-Brazilians lie in the hands of the country's university system. But unlike affirmative-action programs in the United States, Brazil has embarked on a most radical, and extremely controversial, form, one destined to stir even more controversy in many quarters of Brazilian society than affirmative action has done in the United States.

The first program designed to offer poor blacks a road out of poverty was launched in 2003 at the State University of Rio de Janeiro. It set aside 20 percent of the university's admissions for black students, and it was the only program of its kind anywhere in the country. Now, similar programs have spread through Brazil, leading to often fierce debates. The goal? To help achieve the dreams articulated so eloquently by MV Bill and Abdias do Nascimento: to integrate the middle class, in the same way that affirmative-action programs did in the United States starting in the late sixties, so that black children could grow up to become engineers, lawyers, and doctors in relative proportion to their percentage in the population.

I knew the introduction of affirmative action had been very controversial in Brazil. So I scheduled an appointment to hold a debate with a class taught by Professor Marilene Rosa at the State University of Rio de Janeiro. She offered to speak with me about what affirmative action means for her country and how both blacks and whites feel about it.

"I started teaching at this university in 1995," she told me. "There was already a debate surrounding affirmative action at that time, although it took until 2003 for any laws to be passed."

But then, virtually overnight, the student body at this traditionally white university began to reflect the cultural diversity of Brazil as a nation. I asked her what happened when the program went into effect and what the reaction of the community had been. Rosa shook her head.

"It suffered criticism from all sides," she said, "criticism that said the level would fall, saying the university would fall behind other universities, and it didn't happen. On the contrary, at present I'm coordinating a study group, and my best students are the quota students."

Supporters argued that without affirmative action, Afro-Brazilian children had no chance to achieve equality, much less become leaders who could represent their communities in society and government. Slavery and racism left blacks at a disadvantage, keeping generation after generation of black youth trapped in poverty. Only through affirmative action, and through quotas, they argued, could blacks succeed in numbers proportionate to their share of the population. And then, perhaps, social equality could follow.

Critics of the policy were just as vocal. They argued that affirmative action would only increase interracial friction—by forcing Brazilians to focus on race rather than to dismiss it as irrelevant. Brazil's many categories of blackness didn't help soothe any tensions. After all, who was "black"? Rosa spent a fair amount of time directing students toward different resources that they needed to thrive. Defining blackness, she explained, was defining who got into the university.

"There was even a debate at one point between the students, who created a sort of court to determine who the quota students would be by looking at them," she explained. Ultimately, however, who was "black" was left to self-identification—a very good thing, too, since I couldn't imagine the judgments of such a court dictating young people's futures! But Rosa laughed at my indignation. She saw young people fighting for their blackness, their identity, and it gave her hope for the future.

"I used to say, 'How good when someone declares themselves black to get somewhere,'" she said, smiling broadly. "The idea of declaring yourself black is already a victory."

Many public universities followed the lead of Rosa's school, and some have put even higher quotas in place. (The Federal University of Bahia, perhaps fittingly, reserves 40 percent of its spaces for poor and black students.) But these were wrenching changes, she stressed to me, and her students continue to argue about affirmative action among themselves, to this day. As a professor, I know that a debate among students can be quite enlightening. So I asked her to set up a debate, and she graciously obliged. What I saw did not disappoint.

"Are we not perhaps camouflaging a much deeper problem?" one student asked urgently. "If the aim is to end racism, aren't we just reinforcing it in reverse?"

"It's not a way of camouflaging racism," another answered. "It's a way of showing that we're trying to readdress it. Because for four hundred years, blacks were enslaved, and when it was abolished, they were excluded."

"What we are doing is attacking the consequence," a young woman countered, "and not the cause."

"Whoever benefits from it is in favor, and whoever doesn't is against it," another student said wearily.

"There are 130 million active voters today," said a young, Afro-coiffed man (one of half a dozen students who belonged to the black student union, who had come to the debate wearing identical T-shirts), whose tone and attitude reminded me of black students in the United States in the late sixties. "Out of these 130 million, only 3 percent hold a university diploma. There are 40 million illiterate people in the country today. The university is already an oligarchic space, an aristocratic space. All of us here are in a privileged position. This is a privilege, do you understand? This is not debatable."

"The role of the public university is to educate all parts of society," one young man piped in. "The public university is not there to cater to the elite."

"I'd like him to itemize the privileges he says the elites get," another student shot back, "because I don't see whites being privileged but, instead, blacks or lower-income people being privileged when they're able to opt for the quota system."

This is getting good, I thought.

"You don't know what the privileges are?" another student asked, incredulous. "In higher education, 1 percent of professors are black. In the health system, black women get less anesthesia in labor than whites. This is official data. Black people with the same education as white people get paid 35 percent less while doing the same job."

I watched these passionate young people, the black nationalists among them growing ever more vocal, more adamant, taking pride in displaying contempt for foes of affirmative action, and thought about scenes like this from the late sixties back at Yale, when ours was the first affirmative-action generation and many of us acted out our political convictions and our anxieties in similarly offensive, impatient ways. I also thought about the privileges of my own life, privileges enabled by my inclusion among that pioneering generation. In 1966, Yale University graduated six black men. The class of 1973, which entered three years later, consisted of ninety-six black men and women.

I wanted to let these students speak and argue and hash it out for themselves, but I also wanted them to know that I would never have gone to Yale without affirmative action. Barack Obama would not have attended Columbia University, and it's likely he would not have attended Harvard Law School. Affirmative action—by which I mean taking into account ethnicity, class, religion, and gender as criteria for college admission—is not a perfect remedy for a history of discrimination, by any means; but it is the best system we have in the United States to address a past that can't be altered. "Not even God can change the past," Shimon Peres is fond of saying. But equal access to elite college education can help to change the effects of structural inequities we inherit from the past. And ultimately, I believe, in Brazil or in the United States, education will be the only way to redress the most pernicious effects of centuries of race-based slavery and a century of anti-black racism, formal and informal. Diversifying the middle class—changing the ratio of black Brazilians to white Brazilians in the upper economic classes, aiming for some sort of curve of class more reflective of Brazil's ethnic composition—is the only way to achieve the "racial democracy" of which Brazil so proudly boasts. Even with the quite drastic form of affirmative action that some of its universities have decided to implement (and Brazil's Supreme Court is soon to weigh in on the legality of these rigid quotas, just as the US Supreme Court did in our country), this sort of class redistribution among Brazil's large black population is going to take a very long time.

I have to say that I found myself somewhat sad to learn from the black people I interviewed that "racial democracy" was at best a philosophical concept, perhaps a dream or a goal, and at worst an often bandied about slogan, rather than a revolutionary anomaly that had been piercing itself across centuries of racial discrimination in Brazil. I remember my excitement when I first encountered this idea in the late sixties, hoping that someplace existed in the Western Hemisphere in which black people in a mixed-race society had been accorded their due as full and equal citizens—a place in which white people didn't discriminate against black people because they were black. There is so much that I love about Brazil, the largest African outpost in the whole of the New World: Candomblé, Carnaval, capoeira; its astonishing menagerie of classifications of brown skin; languidly sensual music forms such as samba and bossa nova; films such as *Black Orpheus* and *City of God* that startle with their bold innovations in the representation of blackness; *feijoada,* its national comfort food of pork and beans; the enticing sensuality more or less openly on display on its beaches; the seamless manner in which practitioners of Roman Catholicism marry this religion to Candomblé; and, always, its soccer teams, among many other things.

Nevertheless, Gilberto Freyre's "racial democracy" is a very long way from being realized—so far away today, it occurs to me, that I wonder if he meant it to be a sort of call to arms, a rallying cry, an ideal to which Brazilians should aspire. How much farther away must it have been in 1933, when he formulated it? I had expected to find an immense, beautiful, rich landscape, occupied by one of the world's most ethnically diverse people, whose identity has been informed over half a millennium by a rich and intimate interplay among indigenous peoples, Africans, and Portuguese. I certainly found those things. I discovered an Afro-Brazilian experience that is vibrantly alive, evolving, impatient, engaged—right now, today.

At the same time, I encountered a social and economic reality that is deeply troubled, deeply conflicted, by race, a reality in which race codes for class. Perhaps Nascimento is right that for decades, Afro-Brazilians of every hue have lived, and perhaps suffered, in the shadow of a myth. Their country told them that racial democracy had made, or would make, everything racial all right and that there was no need to fight for equal rights. But today's Brazil is a very long way from becoming a racial paradise, and any sensible black Brazilian—and white Brazilian—knows that. Half a millennium of slavery and anti-black racism can't be wiped away with a slogan, no matter how eloquently wrought that slogan is. Nevertheless, I had seen a great deal that made me hopeful, most notably the fact that black consciousness is clearly establishing itself as a political force throughout the society in various ways, ways that compel the larger society to listen. And perhaps Brazil's experiment with affirmative action in higher education—no matter how it is modified, as it will be—will begin to accomplish in the twenty-first century the sort of equality of opportunity that has proved to be so elusive in Brazil for so very long, a Brazil richly and impressively "African" and black in its cultural diversity yet always already economically dominated by the white descendants of the masters and the descendants of post-emancipation white immigrants. I hoped, as my plane took off, that I was witnessing the realization of Abdias do Nascimento's invocation to the god Exú that Brazil's black community at long last find its political voice as forcefully and as resonantly as it had long before found its artistic voice and that, in so doing, Brazil might experience a new kind of social revolution, a revolution that could lead to the creation of the world's first racial democracy.

SOURCE: Henry Louis Gates, Jr., *Black in Latin America* (New York: New York University Press, 2011).

PART VII
CULTURE AND POLITICS

THIS SECTION BEGINS with the essay that put Gates on the cultural map. "2 Live Crew, Decoded" is a defense of a rap group whose lyrics were deemed obscene. Gates wrote in favor of singer Luther Campbell's first amendment rights, of course, but not just in favor of those rights; he also wrote a careful explication of the black vernacular and of black forms of conversation that, to untrained white ears, sounded simply obscene. But for Gates, it is always necessary to go back to the culture from which a writer takes his language and his diction, and this reaching back has remained a constant in Gates's own writing.

There are amusing details within these pieces (the placement of "hip-hop" in quotes shows precisely where that musical form was, or was not, on the mainstream radar in 1990), and there are some hard pronouncements ("Ending the Slavery Blame-Game" continues to attract heated reactions for its calling out of African slave traders). In all of these selections, published in the mainstream media, we see Gates's capacity to distill complex academic concepts into highly readable prose, a skill that has kept him at the fore of public intellectual life for more than two decades.

Abby Wolf

2 LIVE CREW, DECODED

THE RAP GROUP 2 Live Crew and their controversial hit recording "As Nasty As They Wanna Be" may well earn a signal place in the history of First Amendment rights. But just as important is how these lyrics will be interpreted and by whom.

For centuries, African-Americans have been forced to develop coded ways of communicating to protect themselves from danger. Allegories and double meanings, words redefined to mean their opposites ("bad" meaning "good," for instance), even neologisms (bodacious) have enabled blacks to share messages only the initiated understood.

HEAVY-HANDED PARODY

Many blacks were amused by the transcripts of Marion Barry's sting operation, which reveal that he used the traditional black expression: one's "nose being opened." This referred to a love affair and not, as Mr. Barry's prosecutors have suggested, to the inhalation of drugs. Understanding this phrase could very well spell the difference (for the mayor) between prison and freedom.

2 Live Crew is engaged in heavy-handed parody, turning the stereotypes of black and white American culture on their heads. These young artists are acting out, to lively dance music, a parodic exaggeration of the age-old stereotypes of the oversexed black female and male. Their exuberant use of hyperbole (phantasmagoric sexual organs, for example) undermines—for anyone fluent in black cultural codes—a too literal-minded hearing of the lyrics.

This is the street tradition called "signifying" or "playing the dozens," which has generally been risqué, and where the best signifier or "rapper" is the one who invents the most extravagant images, the biggest "lies," as the culture says. (H. "Rap" Brown earned his nickname in just this way.) In the face of racist stereotypes about black sexuality, you can do one of two things: disavow them or explode them with exaggeration.

2 Live Crew, like many "hip-hop" groups, is engaged in sexual carnival-esque. Parody reigns supreme, from a takeoff of standard blues to a spoof of the black power movement; their off-color nursery rhymes are part of a venerable Western tradition. The group even satirizes the culture of commerce when it appropriates popular advertising slogans ("Tastes great!" "Less filling!") and puts them in a bawdy context.

2 Live Crew must be interpreted within the context of black culture generally and of signifying specifically. Their novelty, and that of other adventuresome rap groups, is that their defiant rejection of euphemism now voices for the mainstream what before existed largely in the "race record" market.

Rock songs have always been about sex but have used elaborate subterfuges to convey that fact. 2 Live Crew uses Anglo-Saxon words and is self-conscious about it: A parody of a white voice in one song refers to "private personal parts," as a coy counterpart to the group's bluntness.

Much more troubling than its so-called obscenity is the group's overt sexism. Their sexism is so flagrant, however, that it almost cancels itself out in a hyperbolic war between the sexes. In this, it recalls the intersexual jousting in Zora Neale Hurston's novels. Still, many of us look toward the emergence of more female rappers to redress sexual stereotypes. And we must not allow ourselves to sentimentalize street culture: The appreciation of verbal virtuosity does not lessen one's obligation to critique bigotry in all of its pernicious forms.

Must First Understand

Is 2 Live Crew more "obscene" than, say, the comic Andrew Dice Clay?

Clearly, this rap group is seen as more threatening than others that are just as sexually explicit. Can this be completely unrelated to the specter of the young black male as a figure of sexual and social disruption, the very stereotypes 2 Live Crew seems determined to undermine?

This question—and the very large question of obscenity and the First Amendment—cannot even be addressed until those who would answer them become literate in the vernacular traditions of African-Americans. To do less is to censor through the equivalent of intellectual prior restraint—and censorship is to art what lynching is to justice.

Source: *The New York Times,* June 19, 1990.

"AUTHENTICITY," OR THE
LESSON OF LITTLE TREE

IT'S A PERENNIAL question: Can you really tell? The great black jazz trumpeter Roy Eldridge once made a wager with the critic Leonard Feather that he could distinguish white musicians from black ones—blindfolded. Mr. Feather duly dropped the needle onto a variety of record albums whose titles and soloists were concealed from the trumpeter. More than half the time, Eldridge guessed wrong.

Mr. Feather's blindfold test is one that literary critics would do well to ponder, for the belief that we can "read" a person's racial or ethnic identity from his or her writing runs surprisingly deep. There is an assumption that we could fill a room with the world's great literature, train a Martian to analyze these books, and then expect that Martian to categorize each by the citizenship or ethnicity or gender of its author. "Passing" and "impersonation" may sound like quaint terms of a bygone era, but they continue to inform the way we read. Our literary judgments, in short, remain hostage to the ideology of authenticity.

And while black Americans have long boasted of their ability to spot "one of our own," no matter how fair the skin, straight the hair, or aquiline the nose—and while the nineteenth-century legal system in this country went to absurd lengths to demarcate even octoroons and demioctoroons from their white sisters and brothers—authentic racial and ethnic differences have always been difficult to define. It's not just a black thing, either.

The very idea of a literary tradition is itself bound up in suppositions—dating back at least to an eighteenth-century theorist of nationalism, Johann Gottfried Herder—that ethnic or national identity finds unique expression in literary forms. Such assumptions hold sway even after we think we have discarded them. After the much ballyhooed "death of the author" pronounced by two decades of literary theory, the author is very much back in the saddle. As the literary historian John Guillory observes, today's "battle of the books" is really not so much about books as it is about authors, authors

515

who can be categorized according to race, gender, ethnicity, and so on, standing in as delegates of a social constituency.

And the assumption that the works they create transparently convey the authentic, unmediated experience of their social identities—though officially renounced—has crept quietly in through the back door. Like any dispensation, it raises some works and buries others. Thus Zora Neale Hurston's *Their Eyes Were Watching God* has prospered, while her *Seraph on the Suwanee,* a novel whose main characters are white, remains in limbo. *Our Nig,* recently identified as the work of a black woman, almost immediately went from obscurity to required reading in black and women's literature courses.

The case of Forrest Carter, the author of the best-selling *The Education of Little Tree,* provided yet another occasion to reflect on the troublesome role of authenticity. Billed as a true story, Carter's book was written as the autobiography of Little Tree, orphaned at the age of ten, who learns the ways of Indians from his Cherokee grandparents in Tennessee. *The Education of Little Tree,* which has sold more than 600,000 copies, received an award from the American Booksellers Association as the title booksellers most enjoyed selling. It was sold on the gift tables of Indian reservations and assigned as supplementary reading for courses on Native American literature. Major studios vied for movie rights.

And the critics loved it. *Booklist* praised its "natural approach to life." A reviewer for the *Chattanooga Times* pronounced it "deeply felt." One poet and storyteller of Abenaki descent hailed it as a masterpiece—"one of the finest American autobiographies ever written"—that captured the unique vision of Native American culture. It was, he wrote blissfully, "like a Cherokee basket, woven out of the materials given by nature, simple and strong in its design, capable of carrying a great deal." A critic in *The (Santa Fe) New Mexican* told his readers: "I have come on something that is good, so good I want to shout 'Read this! It's beautiful. It's real.'"

Or was it?

To the embarrassment of the book's admirers, Dan T. Carter, a history professor at Emory University, unmasked "Forrest Carter" as a pseudonym for the late Asa Earl Carter, whom he described as "a Ku Klux Klan terrorist, right wing radio announcer, home grown American fascist and anti-Semite, rabble-rousing demagogue and secret author of the famous 1963 speech by Gov. George Wallace of Alabama: 'Segregation now . . . Segregation tomorrow . . . Segregation forever.'" Forget Pee-wee Herman—try explaining this one to the kids.

This is only the latest embarrassment to beset the literary ideologues of authenticity, and its political stakes are relatively trivial. It was not always such. The authorship of slave narratives published between 1760 and 1865 was also fraught with controversy. To give credence to their claims about the horrors of slavery, American abolitionists urgently needed a cadre of ex-slaves who could compellingly indict their masters with first-person accounts of their bondage. For this tactic to succeed, the ex-slaves had to be authentic, their narratives full of convincing, painstaking verisimilitude.

So popular did these become, however, that two forms of imitators soon arose: white writers, adopting a first-person black narrative persona, gave birth to the pseudoslave narrative; and black authors, some of whom had never even seen the South, a plantation or a whipping post, became literary lions virtually overnight.

Generic confusion was rife in those days. The 1836 slave narrative of Archy Moore turned out to have been a novel written by a white historian, Richard Hildreth; and the gripping *Autobiography of a Female Slave* (1857) was also a novel, written by a white woman, Mattie Griffith. Perhaps the most embarrassing of these publishing events, however, involved one James Williams, an American slave—the subtitle of his narrative asserts—"who was for several years a driver on a cotton plantation in Alabama." Having escaped to the North (or so he claimed), Williams sought out members of the Anti-Slavery Society, and told a remarkably well-structured story about the brutal treatment of the slaves in the South and of his own miraculous escape, using the literacy he had secretly acquired to forge the necessary documents.

So compelling, so gripping, so *useful* was his tale that the abolitionists decided to publish it immediately. Williams arrived in New York on New Year's Day, 1838. By January 24, he had dictated his complete narrative to John Greenleaf Whittier. By February 15, it was in print, and was also being serialized in the abolitionist newspaper *The Anti-Slavery Examiner.* Even before Williams's book was published, rumors spread in New York that slave catchers were on his heels, and so his new friends shipped him off to Liverpool—where, it seems, he was never heard from again. Once the book was published, the abolitionists distributed it widely, sending copies to every state and to every Congressman.

Alas, Williams's stirring narrative was not authentic at all, as outraged Southern slaveholders were quick to charge and as his abolitionist friends reluctantly had to concede. It was a work of fiction, the production, one commentator put it, "purely of the Negro imagination"—as, no doubt, were the slave catchers who were in hot pursuit, and whose purported existence earned Williams a free trip to England and a new life.

Ersatz slave narratives had an even rougher time of it a century later, and one has to wonder how William Styron's *The Confessions of Nat Turner*—a novel that aroused the strenuous ire of much of the black intelligentsia when it was published in 1976—might have been received had it been published by James Baldwin. "Hands off our history," we roared at Mr. Styron, the white Southern interloper, as we shopped around our list of literary demands. It was the real thing we wanted, and we wouldn't be taken in by imitators.

The real black writer, accordingly, could claim the full authority of experience denied Mr. Styron. Indeed, the late .1960s and early '70s were a time in which the notion of ethnic literature began to be consolidated and, in some measure, institutionalized. That meant policing the boundaries, telling true from false. But it was hard to play this game without a cheat sheet. When Dan McCall published *The Man Says Yes* in 1969, a novel about a young black teacher who comes up against the eccentric president of a black college, many critics assumed the author was black, too. The reviewer for *The Amsterdam News,* for example, referred to him throughout as "Brother McCall." Similar assumptions were occasionally made about Shane Stevens when he published the gritty bildungsroman *Way Uptown in Another World* in 1971, which detailed the brutal misadventures of its hero from Harlem, Marcus Garvey Black. In this case, the new voice from the ghetto belonged to a white graduate student at Columbia.

But the ethnic claim to its own experience cut two ways. For if many of their readers imagined a black face behind the prose, many avid readers of Frank Yerby's historical romances or Samuel R. Delany's science fiction novels are taken aback when they learn that these authors are black. And James Baldwin's *Giovanni's Room,* arguably his most accomplished novel, is seldom taught in black literature courses because its characters are white *and* gay.

Cultural commentators have talked about the "cult of ethnicity" in postwar America. You could dismiss it as a version of what Freud called "the narcissism of small differences." But you also see it as a salutary reaction to a regional Anglo-American culture that has declared itself as universal. For too long, "race" was something that blacks had, "ethnicity" was what "ethnics" had. In mid-century America, Norman Podhoretz reflected in *Making It,* his literary memoirs, "to write fiction out of the experience of big-city immigrant Jewish life was to feel oneself, and to be felt by others, to be writing exotica at best; nor did there exist a respectably certified narrative style in English which was anything but facsimile-WASP. Writing was hard enough but to have to write with *only* that part of one's being which had been formed by the acculturation-minded public schools and by the blindly ethnicizing English departments of the colleges was like being asked to compete in a race with a leg cut off at the thigh."

All this changed with the novelistic triumphs of Saul Bellow and Philip Roth—and yet a correlative disability was entered in the ledger, too. In the same year that Mr. Styron published *The Confessions of Nat Turner,* Philip Roth published *When She Was Good,* a novel set in the rural heartland of gentile middle America and infused with the chilly humorlessness of its small-town inhabitants. This was, to say the least, a departure. Would critics who admired Mr. Roth as the author of *Goodbye, Columbus* accept him as a chronicler of the Protestant Corn Belt?

Richard Gilman, in *The New Republic,* compared Mr. Roth to a "naturalist on safari to a region unfamiliar to him" and declared himself unable to "account for the novel's existence, so lacking is it in any true literary interest." Maureen Howard in *Partisan Review* said she felt "the presence of a persona rather than a personal voice." To Jonathan Baumbach, writing in *Commonweal,* the book suggested "Zero Mostel doing an extended imitation of Jimmy Stewart." "He captures the rhythms of his characters' speech," Mr. Baumbach says of Mr. Roth, "but not, I feel, what makes them human." If the book was written partly in defiance of the strictures of ethnic literature, those very strictures were undoubtedly what made the book anathema to so many reviewers.

And what if *When She Was Good* had been published under the name Philip McGrath? Would the same reviewers still have denounced it as an artistic imposture? Does anyone imagine that Zero Mostel would have come to mind? Yet there is a twist in the tale. Even a counterfeit can be praised for its craft. For some, the novel's worth was enhanced precisely because of its "inauthenticity"—because it was seen as an act of imagination unassisted by memory.

Under any name, Kazuo Ishiguro's *Remains of the Day*—a novel narrated by an aging and veddy English butler—would be a tour de force; but wasn't the acclaim that greeted it heightened by a kind of critical double take at the youthful Japanese face on the dust jacket? To take another example, no one is surprised that admirers of Norman Rush's novel *Mating* would commend the author on the voice of its female narrator. Subtract from the reality column, add to the art column. Thus Doris Grumbach, who commended Mr. Roth's novel for its careful observation, concludes her own review with an assessment of technique: "To bring off this verisimilitude is, to my mind, an enormous accomplishment." Would she have been so impressed with the virtuosity of a Philip McGrath?

Sometimes, however, a writer's identity is in fact integral to a work's artifice. Such is the case with John Updike's *Bech: A Book,* the first of two collections of short stories featuring Mr. Updike's Jewish novelist, Henry Bech. The 1970 book opens with a letter from the protagonist, Henry, to his creator,

John, fussing about the literary components from which he was apparently jury-rigged. At first blush (Bech muses), he sounds like "some gentlemanly Norman Mailer; then that London glimpse of *silver* hair glints more of gallant, glamorous Bellow. . . . My childhood seems out of Alex Portnoy and my ancestral past out of I. B. Singer. I get a whiff of Malamud in your city breezes, and am I paranoid to feel my 'block' an ignoble version of the more or less noble renunciations of H. Roth, D. Fuchs and J. Salinger? Withal, something Waspish, theological, scared and insultingly ironical that derives, my wild surmise is, from you."

What is clear is that part of the point of John Updike's Bech is that he is *John Updike's* Bech: an act Cynthia Ozick has described as "cultural impersonation." The contrast between Bech and Updike, then, far from being irrelevant, is itself staged within the fictional edifice. You could publish *Bech* under a pseudonym, but, I maintain, it would be a different book.

Conversely—but for similar reasons—one might argue that exposing the true author of *Famous All Over Town,* a colorful picaresque novel set in a Los Angeles barrio, was a form of violence against the book itself. Published in 1983 under the nom de plume Danny Santiago, the book was hailed by Latino critics for its vibrancy and authenticity, and received the Richard and Hinda Rosenthal Foundation Award from the American Academy of Arts and Letters for an outstanding work of fiction. But Santiago, assumed to be a young Chicano talent, turned out to be Daniel L. James, a septuagenarian WASP educated at Andover and Yale, a playwright, screenwriter and, in his later years, a social worker. And yet Danny Santiago was much more than a literary conceit to his creator, who had for twenty years lost faith in his own ability to write; Danny was the only voice available to him. Judging from the testimony of his confidant, John Gregory Dunne, Mr. James may well have felt that the attribution was the only just one; that *Famous All Over Town* belonged to Danny Santiago before it quite belonged to Daniel James.

Death-of-the-author types cannot come to grips with the fact that a book is a cultural event; authorial identity, mystified or not, can be part of that event. What the ideologues of authenticity cannot quite come to grips with is that fact and fiction have always exerted a reciprocal effect on each other. However truthful you set out to be, your autobiography is never unmediated by literary structures of expression. Many authentic slave narratives were influenced by Harriet Beecher Stowe; on the other hand, authentic slave narratives were among Stowe's primary sources for her own imaginative work, *Uncle Tom's Cabin.* By the same token, to recognize the slave narrative as a genre is to recognize that, for example, Frederick Douglass's mode of expression was informed by the conventions of antecedent narratives, some of which were (like James Williams's) whole-cloth inventions.

So it is not just a matter of the outsider boning up while the genuine article just writes what he or she knows. If Shane Stevens was deeply influenced by Richard Wright, so too were black protest novelists like John O. Killens and John A. Williams. And if John Updike can manipulate the tonalities of writers like Saul Bellow, Bernard Malamud, and Philip Roth, must we assume that a Bruce Jay Friedman, say, is wholly unaffected by such models?

The distasteful truth is that like it or not, all writers are "cultural impersonators."

Even real people, moreover, are never quite real. My own favorite (fictional) commentary on the incursion of fiction upon a so-called real life is provided by Nabokov's Humbert Humbert as he reflects upon the bothersome task of swapping life stories with a new and unwanted wife. Her confessions were marked by "sincerity and artlessness," his were "glib compositions"; and yet, he muses, "technically the two sets were congeneric since both were affected by the same stuff (soap operas, psychoanalysis, and cheap novelettes) upon which I drew for my characters and she for her mode of expression."

Start interrogating the notion of cultural authenticity and our most trusted critical categories come into question. Maybe Danny Santiago's *Famous All Over Town* can usefully be considered a work of Chicano literature; maybe Shane Stevens's *Way Uptown in Another World* can usefully be considered within the genre of black protest novels. In his own version of the blindfold test, the mathematician Alan Turing famously proposed that we credit a computer with intelligence if we can conduct a dialogue with it and not know whether a person or machine has been composing the responses. Should we allow ethnic literatures a similar procedure for claiming this title?

At this point, it is important to go slow. Consider the interviewer's chestnut: are you a woman writer or a writer who happens to be a woman? A black writer or a writer who happens to be a black? Alas, these are deadly disjunctions. After struggling to gain the recognition that a woman or a black (or, exemplarily, a black woman) writer is, in the first instance, a writer, many authors yet find themselves uneasy with the supposedly universalizing description. How can ethnic or sexual identity be reduced to a mere contingency when it is so profoundly a part of who a writer is?

And yet if, for example, black critics claim special authority as interpreters of black literature, and black writers claim special authority as interpreters of black reality, are we not obliged to cede an equivalent dollop of authority to our white counterparts?

We easily become entrapped by what the feminist critic Nancy K. Miller has called "as a" criticism: where we always speak "as a" white middle-class woman, a person of color, a gay man, and so on. And that, too, is a confinement—in the republic of letters as in the larger policy. "Segregation today . . . Segregation tomorrow . . . Segregation forever": that line, which Asa Earl Carter wrote for George Wallace's inauguration speech as Governor, may still prove his true passport to immortality. And yet segregation—as Carter himself would demonstrate—is as difficult to maintain in the literary realm as it is in the civic one.

The lesson of the literary blindfold test is not that our social identities don't matter. They do matter. And our histories, individual and collective, do affect what we wish to write and what we are able to write. But that relation is never one of fixed determinism. No human culture is inaccessible to someone who makes the effort to understand, to learn, to inhabit another world.

Yes, Virginia, there is a Danny Santiago. And—if you like that sort of thing—there is a Little Tree, too, just as treacly now as he ever was. And as long as there are writers who combine some measure of imagination and curiosity, there will continue to be such interlopers of the literary imagination. What, then, of the vexed concept of authenticity? To borrow from Samuel Goldwyn's theory of sincerity, authenticity remains essential: once you can fake that, you've got it made.

SOURCE: Originally published in *The New York Times Book Review*, 1991. Reprinted in *Stories Matter: The Complexity of Cultural Authenticity in Children's Literature*, edited by Dana L. Fox and Kathy G. Short (Urbana, IL: National Council of Teachers of English, 2003).

THE CHITLIN CIRCUIT

THE SETTING WAS the McCarter Theatre, a brick-and-stone edifice on the outskirts of the Princeton University campus. On a hot, sticky evening last June, five hundred members of the Theatre Communications Group—all representatives of serious, which is to say nonprofit, theatre—had gathered for their eleventh biennial national conference. The keynote speech was being delivered by August Wilson, who, at fifty-one, is probably the most celebrated American playwright now writing and is certainly the most accomplished black playwright in this nation's history. Before he said a word, the largely white audience greeted him with a standing ovation.

That was the conference's last moment of unanimity. For here, at this gathering of saints, the dean of American dramatists had come to deliver an unexpected and disturbing polemic. American theatre, Wilson declared, was an instrument of white cultural hegemony, and the recent campaign to integrate and diversify it only made things worse. The spiritual and moral survival of black Americans demanded that they be given a stage of their own. They needed their very own theatres the way they needed sunlight and oxygen. They needed integration the way they needed acid rain.

"There are and have always been two distinct and parallel traditions in black art: that is, art that is conceived and designed to entertain white society, and art that feeds the spirit and celebrates the life of black America," Wilson told his Princeton audience, in a quietly impassioned voice. "The second tradition occurred when the African in the confines of the slave quarters sought to invest his spirit with the strength of his ancestors by conceiving in his art, in his song and dance, a world in which he was the spiritual center." That was the tradition Wilson found to be exemplified by the Black Power movement of the sixties and its cultural arm, the Black Arts scene. Revolutionary Black Arts dramatists such as Ed Bullins and Amiri Baraka were models for authentic black creativity, Wilson maintained, and he placed himself in their direct line of descent.

"His speech was shocking and it was thrilling," recalled Ricardo Khan, the president of the Theatre Communications Group and the artistic director of the country's premier black repertory company, the Crossroads Theatre, in New Brunswick. Wilson is light-skinned, with sparse hair and a close-cropped beard: to some in the audience, he brought to mind Maulana Karenga ("Black art must expose the enemy, praise the people and support the revolution"); to others, Ernst Blofeld ("Hot enough for you, Mr. Bond?"). The black members of the audience started glancing at one another: heads bobbed, a black-power sign was flashed, encouragement was murmured— "Go ahead, brother," "Tell it." Many white audience members, meanwhile, began to shift uneasily, gradually acquiring an expression compounded of pain and puzzlement: *After all we've done for him, this is how he thanks us?* The world of nonprofit theatre is tiny but intense, and, as soon became clear, Wilson's oration was its version of the Simpson verdict.

In the conversational ferment that ensued, almost every conceivable question was given a full airing: Did Wilson's call for an autonomous black theatre amount to separatism? Did race matter to culture, and if so, how much? Was Wilson's salvific notion of the theatre—and his dream of a theatre that would address ordinary black folk—mere romantic delusion? In the course of much high-minded hand-wringing, practically the only possibility not broached was that a black theatre for the masses *already* existed—just not of an order that anybody in the world of serious theatre had in mind.

What attracted the greatest immediate attention was Wilson's unqualified denunciation of color-blind casting. To cast black actors in "white" plays was, he said, "to cast us in the role of mimics." Worse, for a black actor to walk the stage of Western drama was to collaborate with the culture of racism, "to be in league with a thousand naysayers who wish to corrupt the vigor and spirit of his heart." An all-black production of "Death of a Salesman," say, would "deny us our own humanity."

Not surprisingly, Wilson's stand on this issue has found little acceptance among working black actors, dramatists, and directors. Lloyd Richards— Wilson's long-time director and creative partner—has never thought twice about casting James Earl Jones as Timon of Athens or as Judge Brack in "Hedda Gabler." Wole Soyinka, the Nigerian playwright and Nobel Laureate, staunchly declares, "I can assure you that if 'Death of a Salesman' were performed in Nigeria by an all-Eskimo cast it would have resonances totally outside the mediation of color." What's more surprising is that many stars of the Black Arts firmament are equally dismissive. "If O.J. can play a black man, I don't see any problem with Olivier playing Othello," Amiri Baraka says, with a mordant laugh. And the legendary black playwright and director Douglas Turner Ward claims that many of Sean O'Casey's plays, with their ethos of alienation, actually work better with black actors.

But the dissent on color-blind casting was almost something of a footnote to Wilson's larger brief—that of encouraging the creation of an authentic black theatre. As he saw it, the stakes couldn't be greater. Black theatre could help change the world: it could be "the spearhead of a movement to reignite and reunite our people's positive energy for a political and social change that is reflective of our spiritual truths rather than economic fallacies." The urgency of this creed led to a seemingly self-divided rhetoric. On the one hand, Wilson maintained that "we cannot depend on others," that we must be a "self-determining, self-respecting people." On the other hand, this self-sufficiency was to be subsidized by foundations and government agencies.

If Wilson's rhetoric struck many of his listeners as contradictory—seeming to alternate the balled fist and the outstretched palm—the contradictions only multiplied upon further investigation. August Wilson, born Frederick August Kittel, is in some respects an unlikely spokesman for a new Black Arts movement. He neither looks nor sounds typically black—had he the desire, he could easily pass—and that makes him black first and foremost by self-identification. (His father was a German-American baker in Pittsburgh, where he grew up.) Some see significance in this. The estimable black playwright OyamO, né Charles Gordon, says, "Within our history, many people who are lighter—including the very lightest of us, who can really pass—are sometimes the most angry."

Nor has it escaped comment that Wilson failed to acknowledge his own power and stature within the world of mainstream theatre: his works début at major Broadway theatres, and the white critical establishment has honored them with a cascade of Pulitzer, Drama Desk, and Tony awards. The experimental black playwright Suzan-Lori Parks, whose works include "Venus" and "The Death of the Last Black Man in the Whole Entire World," says, "August can start by having his own acclaimed plays première in black theatres, instead of where they première now. I'm sorry, but he should examine his own house." One historical luminary of black theatre charges that Wilson himself is the problem of which he purports to hold the solution: "Once the white mainstream theatre found a black artistic spokesman, the one playwright who could do no wrong, the money that used to go to autonomous black theatre started to dry up."

And yet, on closer examination, sharply drawn lines of battle begin to blur. Wilson's oration provoked a swinging rebuttal in *American Theatre* by Robert

Brustein, who is the artistic director of the American Repertory Theatre, the drama critic for *The New Republic*, and a long-time sparring partner of Wilson's. Brustein charged Wilson with promoting subsidized separatism: "What next?" he asked. "Separate schools? Separate washrooms? Separate drinking fountains?" With Anna Deavere Smith—herself a paradigm of casting beyond color—serving as the moderator, the men are to continue their debate this Monday, in New York's Town Hall. The critic Paul Goldberger, writing in the *Times* last week, went so far as to declare that "this is shaping up to be the sharpest cultural debate" since the Mapplethorpe controversy. You'd never guess that Brustein and Wilson are in complete agreement on the one subject that agitates them most: the disastrous nature of the donor-driven trend to diversify regional theatres. Brustein dislikes the trend because he believes that it supplants aesthetic considerations with sociological ones. Wilson dislikes it because, as is true of all movement toward integration, it undermines the integrity and strength of autonomous black institutions.

He has a point. George Wolfe, the producer of the Public Theatre, singles out the Lila Wallace–Reader's Digest Fund as having been "incredibly irresponsible" in this regard. He goes on to explain, "It has created a peculiar dynamic where, you know, there was a struggling black theatre that had been nurturing a series of artists and all of a sudden this predominantly white theatre next door is getting a couple of million dollars to invite artists of color into its fold." (To be sure, the officials at the Lila Wallace Fund have also given money to black companies like the Crossroads.) But Wilson wants to take things another step, and create black theatres where they do not currently exist. He believes that any theatre situated in a city with a black population of more than sixty percent should be converted into a black theatre. White board members and staff would be largely retired in order to insure what he believes to be a cultural and moral imperative: art by, of, and for black people.

Unquestionably, Wilson remains in the grip of a sentimental separatism. (I'll own that it has an emotional grip on me, too, just a rather attenuated one.) He says he has a lot of respect for the "do for self" philosophy of the Nation of Islam; in the early seventies, he was briefly a convert, though mostly in order to keep his Muslim wife company. He's a man who views integration primarily as a destructive force—one that ruined once vital black institutions. He thinks back fondly to an era when we had our own dress shops and businesses, our own Negro Baseball League. This segregated, pre–*Brown v. Board of Education* era was, he'll tell you, "black America at its strongest and most culturally self-sufficient." From his perspective, separate-but-equal, far from being a perversion of social justice, is an ideal that we should aspire to.

Now, it's one thing to hear this view espoused by Minister Louis Far-rakhan and quite another to hear it advanced by August Wilson, a man as lionized as any writer of his generation. It represents a romantic attempt to retrieve an imaginary community in the wake of what seems to be a disinte-gration of the real one. One of the functions of literature is to bring back the dead, the absent, the train gone by; you might say that cultural nationalism is what happens when the genre of the elegy devolves into ideology, the way furniture might be kilned into charcoal.

Certainly the brutal reductionism of August Wilson's polemics is in stark contrast to his richly textured dramatic oeuvre. Wilson first came to promi-nence in the mid-eighties, with his fourth play, "Ma Rainey's Black Bottom," which the director Lloyd Richards was able to move from the Yale Reper-tory Theatre to the Cort Theatre on Broadway. There, his dramatic and ver-bal imagination galvanized critics, who heralded a major new presence on the American stage. With "Ma Rainey," an ambitious, and still ongoing, cy-cle of plays came to public notice. Wilson's aim is to explore black Ameri-can life through plays set during each of the decades of the century; most are situated in a black working-class neighborhood of Pittsburgh. "Joe Turner's Come and Gone" (1986), for example, takes place in 1911, and deals with the sense of cultural loss that accompanied the Great Migration; "The Piano Lesson" (which received the Pulitzer in 1987), set during the De-pression, uses a dispute over an inherited piano—once the possession of a slave owner—to show that the past is never quite past. In "Fences" (a 1990 Pulitzer), which opens in the year 1957, the grandiloquently embittered Troy Maxson is a former Negro League baseball player who now works as a gar-bage man; the trajectory of his own life has made a mockery of the sup-posed glories of integration.

Wilson's 1990 play "Two Trains Running" takes place in a Pittsburgh luncheonette in the late sixties:

Wolf: I thought [the jukebox] was just fixed. Memphis, I thought you was gonna get you a new jukebox.
Memphis: I told Zanelli to bring me a new one. That what he say he gonna do. He been saying that for the last year.

If you're black, you can't rely on the Zanellis of the world, as the charac-ters in the play learn to their detriment. But a great deal more than race pol-itics is going on here. An unruly luxuriance of language—an ability to ease between trash talk and near-choral transport—is Wilson's great gift; some-times you wish he were less generous with that gift, for it can come at the expense of conventional dramaturgic virtues like pacing and the sense of closure. Even when he falters, however, Wilson's work is demanding and complex—at the furthest remove from a cultural manifesto.

But if Wilson's avowed cultural politics is difficult to square with his art, it comes with a venerable history of its own. In 1926, W. E. B. Du Bois, writing in his magazine *The Crisis*, took a dim view of "colored" productions of mainstream plays (they "miss the real path," he warned) and called for a new Negro theatre, for which he laid down "four fundamental principles":

> The plays of a real Negro theatre must be: 1. *About us.* That is, they must have plots which reveal Negro life as it is. 2. *By us.* That is, they must be written by Negro authors who understand from birth and continual association just what it means to be a Negro today. 3. *For us.* That is, the theatre must cater primarily to Negro audiences and be supported and sustained by their entertainment and approval. 4. *Near us.* The theatre must be in a Negro neighborhood near the mass of ordinary Negro people.

What would such a theatre look like? Wilson, of course, directs us to what may seem the most plausible candidate: the dramatic art of the Black Power era. That moment and milieu bring to mind a radicalized, leather-clad generation forging its art in the streets, writing plays fueled by the masses' righteous rage: revolutionary art by the people and for the people. That's certainly how the illuminati liked to represent their project. Baraka's manifesto for "The Revolutionary Theatre" provides a representative précis: "What we show must cause the blood to rush, so that pre-revolutionary temperaments will be bathed in this blood, and it will cause their deepest souls to move, and they will find themselves tensed and clenched, even ready to die. . . . We will scream and cry, murder, run through the streets in agony, if it means some soul will be moved."

Theatre, precisely because of its supposed potential to mobilize the masses, was always at the forefront of the Black Arts movement. Still, it's a funny thing about cultural movements: as a rule, they consist of a handful of people. (The Aesthetic, the Constructivist, the Futurist movements were devoted largely to declaring themselves, self-consciously, to *be* movements.) And by the late sixties, it was clear that the vitality of Black Arts drama had come to center upon two New York–based theatres: the Negro Ensemble Company (N.E.C.), based downtown, under the direction of Douglas Turner Ward; and the New Lafayette Theatre, based in Harlem, under the direction of Robert Macbeth. Here was the full flowering of genuine black theatre in this country—the kind that would raise consciousness and temperatures, that promised to make us whole.

"Populist modernism," in a phrase coined by the literary scholar Werner Sollors, characterized the regnant ethos of that time and place—its aspiration to an art of high seriousness that would engage the energies of the masses. But between the ideals of modernism and those of populism, one or the other had to give. OyamO—who, like many more senior luminaries of the Black Arts scene (Baraka and Ed Bullins among them), was affiliated with the blacker and artier New Lafayette—recalls that the Harlem theatre's high-flown airs were accompanied by paltry audiences. "There was a condescending attitude toward this community, buttressed by the fact that it was getting five hundred grand from the Ford Foundation every year," he recalls. And the N.E.C. was similarly provided for. This isn't to say that worthy and important work wasn't created in these theatres; it was. But these companies do provide a textbook example of how quickly beneficence becomes entitlement, and patronage a paycheck.

And so the dirty little secret of the Black Arts movement was that it was a project promoted and sustained largely by the Ford Foundation. Liberal-minded Medicis made it; in the fullness of time, they left it to unmake itself. Ed Bullins, one of the principals of the New Lafayette, remembers how that particular temple—a magnificent structure on 137th Street, which the Ford had converted from a movie house with the help of some tony theatrical architects—was destroyed. He describes a meeting between a visiting program officer from the Ford Foundation and the theatre's board. The visitor noticed that there were no women on the board, and he asked about their absence. Bullins both laughs and groans when he recalls, "And then some great mind from Harlem, an actor, spoke up and said, 'Oh, no, we don't need any women on the board, because every thirty days women go through their period and they get evil.' Then and there, I saw one million dollars start sprouting wings and flapping away through the door."

These days, of course, *all* nonprofit theatre is starved for cash. And yet black theatres are already out there, as someone like Larry Leon Hamlin could tell you. Hamlin is the artistic director for the National Black Theatre Festival, and by his count there are perhaps two hundred and fifty regional black theatres in this country, about forty of which are reasonably active. Of course, most of Wilson's own plays gestated at places like the Huntington Theatre Company or the Yale Rep before they were launched on the Great White Way. I asked Wilson about this apparent contradiction. He explained that the Negro Ensemble Company had fallen into decline by the early eighties: "It was not doing work of the quality that we deserve, and there's no theatre that's since stepped into the breach." Wilson can sound as if he were boycotting black theatres for artistic reasons, which is why some people in the black-theatre world can't decide whether he's their savior or their slayer. "I do good work," he says, his point being that his plays deserve the best conditions he can secure for them. And among white theatres, he says, "the rush is now on to do anything that's black. Largely through my plays, what the theatres have found out is that they had this white audience that was starving to get a little understanding of what was happening with the black population, because they very seldom come into contact with them, so they're curious. The white theatres have discovered that there is a market for that."

The fact that part of Wilson's success owes to the appeal of ethnography is precisely what disturbs some black critics: they suspect that Wilson's work is systematically overrated along those lines. "August is genuinely very gifted," Margo Jefferson, one of those critics, says. "Whites who don't know the world whereof he writes get a sense of vast, existential melodramas, sweeping pageants, and it's very exciting, with his insistence always that these people onstage are the real and genuine black people. What happens with whites is that the race element is signaling them every minute, 'You know nothing about this, you're lucky to be here.'"

So if you're looking for a theatre of black folk, by black folk, and for black folk—a genuinely sequestered cultural preserve—you'll have to cross the extraordinary dramas of August Wilson off your list. Nor would the Black Arts scene, for all its grand aspirations, qualify: the revolution, it's safe to say, will not be subsidized. You could be forgiven for wondering whether such a black popular theatre really exists. But it does, and, if populist modernism is your creed, it will probably turn your stomach. It's called the Chitlin Circuit, and nobody says you have to like it. But everything in God's creation has a reason, and the Chitlin Circuit is no exception. Perhaps OyamO brings us closest to comprehension when he despairingly observes an uncomfortable truth: "A lot of what they call highbrow, progressive, avant-garde theatre is *boring the shit out of people.*" Not to put too fine a point on it.

The setting now is the Sarah Vaughan Concert Hall—built in 1925 as a Masonic temple—on Broad Street, in downtown Newark. It's a chilly, overcast Sunday afternoon, closing in on three o'clock, which is when the matinée performance of Adrian Williamson's play "My Grandmother Prayed for Me" is supposed to begin. In every sense, we're a long way from the Princeton campus, the site of the despond-drenched T.C.G. conference. On the sidewalk, patrons are eating grilled sausages and hot dogs. Older people make their way inside with the assistance of wheelchairs or walkers; younger ones strut about and survey one another appraisingly. There is much to appraise.

These people are styling out, many of them having come from church: you see cloudlike tulle, hat-bands of the finest grosgrain ribbon, wool suits and pants in neon shades. Women have taken care to match their shoes and handbags; men sport Stetson and Dobbs hats, Kente-cloth cummerbunds and scarves. There's a blue velvet fedora here, electric-blue trousers there, a Super-fly hat and overcoat on a man escorting his magenta-clad wife. Bodies are gleaming, moisturized and fragrant; cheeks are lightly powdered, eyes mascaraed. Broad Street is a poor substitute for a models' runway, but it will have to do until the theatre doors open and swallow up this impromptu village. There are nearly three thousand seats in the hall; within several minutes, most of them are occupied.

The Chitlin Circuit dates back to the nineteen-twenties, when the Theater Owners Booking Association brought plays and other forms of entertainment to black audiences throughout the South and the Midwest. Though it had a reputation for lousy pay and demanding scheduling—its acronym, TOBA, was sometimes said to stand for "Tough on Black Asses"—it was the spawning ground for a good number of accomplished black actors, comics, and musicians. TOBA proper had gone into eclipse by the decade's end, yet the tradition it began—that disparagingly named Chitlin Circuit—never entirely died out. Touring black companies would play anywhere—in a theatre if there was one (sometimes they booked space on weekends or late at night, when the boards would otherwise be vacant) or in a school auditorium if there wasn't. Crisscrossing black America, the circuit established an empire of comedy and pathos, the sublime and the ridiculous: a movable feast that enabled blacks to patronize black entertainers. On the whole, these productions were for the moment, not for the ages. They were the kind of melodrama or farce—or as often both—in which nothing succeeded like excess. But the productions were for, by, and about black folks; and their audience wasn't much inclined to check them against their Stanislavsky anyway.

You don't expect anything very fancy from something called the Chitlin Circuit. Wilson—by way of emphasizing the irreducible differences between blacks and whites—had told the T.C.G. members that "in our culinary history we had to make do with the . . . intestines of the pig rather than the loin and the ham and the bacon." The intestines of the pig are the source of the delicacy known as chitlins; it's a good example of how something that was originally eaten of necessity became, as is the way with acquired tastes, a thing actively enjoyed. The same might be said of the Chitlin Circuit, for the circuit is back in full flush, and has been for several years. Black audiences throughout the country flock to halls like the Beacon Theatre in New York, the Strand Theatre in Boston, and the Fox Theatre in Atlanta. Those audiences are basically blue-collar and pink-collar, and not the type to attend traditional theatre, Larry Leon Hamlin adjudges. But, as the saying has it, they know what they like.

The people behind the shows tend not to vaporize about the "emancipatory potentialities" of their work, or about "forging organic links to the community": they'd be out of business if black folks stopped turning up. Instead, they like to talk numbers. Terryl Calloway, who has worked as a New England promoter for some Chitlin Circuit productions, tells me about plays that have grossed twenty million dollars or more. "It's no joke," he says gravely.

"Good afternoon! Are you ready to have a good time?" This is the master of ceremonies warming up the Newark crowd. The play that ensues is a now standard combination of elements; that is, it's basically a melodrama, with abundant comic relief and a handful of gospel songs interspersed.

So what have we turned out to see? It seems that Grandmother—stout of body and of spirit—is doing her best to raise her two grandsons; their mother, Samantha, having fallen into crack addiction and prostitution. (When we first see Samantha, she is trying to steal her mother's television in order to pay for her habit.) The elder boy, Rashad, is devout and studious, but the younger one, Ein, has taken up with bad company; in fact, today is the day that he and his best friend, Stickey, are to be inducted into the Big Guns, a local gang headed by Slow Pimp. When Stickey is killed on the street by a member of a rival gang, Ein sets out, gun in hand, to avenge his death. What's a grandmother to do? Well, pray, for one thing.

Artistically speaking, "My Grandmother Prayed for Me" makes "Good Times" look like Strindberg. The performances are loud and large; most of the gospel is blared by said grandmother with all the interpretative nuance of a car horn. So broad, so coarse, so over-the-top is this production that to render an aesthetic evaluation would seem a sort of category mistake, like asking Julia Child to taste-test chewing tobacco. But it deals with matters that are of immediate concern to the Newark audience, working-class and middle-class alike: gang violence, crack addiction, teen-age pregnancy, deadbeat dads. For this audience, these issues are not *Times* Op-Ed-page fodder; they're the problems of everyday life, as real and close at hand as parking tickets and head colds. It's also true that black America remains disproportionately religious. (Count on a black rap artist—"gangsta" or no—to thank Jesus in his liner notes.) So that's part of it, too.

On my way to the Sarah Vaughan Concert Hall, I bumped into Amiri Baraka, who, when he learned my destination, gave me a gleaming smile and some brotherly advice: "You're about to step into some deep doo-doo."

Maybe he's right, and yet I find myself enjoying the spectacle as much as everybody else here. "You lost faith in the church, abandoned your kids, and I even heard you were prostituting," the grandmother tells her daughter. "Let me tell you something. Them drugs ain't nothing but a demon." Samantha's response: "Well, if they a demon, then I'm gon' love hell." People laugh, but they recognize the sound of a lost soul. So the two fabled institutions of the inner city, the pusher and the preacher, must battle for Samantha's soul. There's a similar exchange between the good son and the one going to the bad:

Rashad: Those boys you hang with ain't nothing but a bunch of punks. All y'all do is run around these streets beating up on people, robbing people, our black folks at that. . . .

Ein: If we so-called punks, why we got everybody scared of us? I'll tell you why—because we hardcore. We'll smoke anybody that get in our way.

Rashad: Hardcore? . . . Ain't a thing you out there doing hardcore. Let me tell you what hardcore is: hardcore is going to school, putting your nose in a book getting an education. Hardcore is going to church trying to live your life right for the Lord. Hardcore is going to work every day, busting your behind providing for a family. Look around you. Grandma provided all of this for us, and she pray for us every day. Now *that's* hardcore.

This doubtless isn't what Wilson has in mind when he speaks of the spiritual fortification and survival that black drama can provide. All the same, the audience is audibly stirred by Rashad's peroration, crying out "Hallelujah!" and "Testify!" The subject of racism—or, for that matter, white people—simply never arises: in the all-black world depicted onstage, the risks and remedies are all much closer to hand.

That's one puzzle. Here's another: If theatre is dying, what do we make of these nearly three thousand black folks gathered in downtown Newark? The phenomenon I'm witnessing has nothing in common with "Tony n' Tina's Wedding," say, or dinner theatre in Westchester, offering "Damn Yankees" over a steak and two veg. It's true that black audiences have always had a predilection for talking back at performances. But more than that is going on in this theatre: the intensity of engagement is palpable. During some of the gospel numbers, there are members of the audience who stand up and do the Holy Dance by their seats. However crude the script and the production, they're generating the kind of audience communion that most playwrights can only dream of.

In "My Grandmother Prayed for Me," the deus ex machina is pretty literal. When Ein sets off to seek vengeance, his grandma and brother go in search of him, joined by Samantha, who–having been visited by an angel in the shape of a little boy–has seen the light. ("It was this voice, Mama, this voice from Heaven. It told me that Ein and Rashad need a good mama.") The curtain rises on a gang-infested project. It appears that Ein, too, has seen the light and laid down his gun. "I know I haven't had the best things in life," he tells Slow Pimp defiantly, "but God gave me the best grand-mother in the world." Slow Pimp doesn't take his defection well, but it's Rashad who catches the first bullet. Next, Slow Pimp turns his gat on the meddling grandmother. She prays for divine intervention and gets it: the gun jams; Slow Pimp is struck by lightning; the angel raises Rashad from the ground. The audience goes wild.

Nobody said it was high culture, but historically this is what a lot of American theatre, particularly before the First World War, was like. Other "ghettoized" theatres, for all their vibrancy, also ignored many of the crite-ria for serious art–not least the Yiddish theatre, a center of immigrant Jew-ish life in New York at the end of the nineteenth century and the beginning of the twentieth. The former *Times* theatre critic Frank Rich says, "What we think of as the Yiddish theatre today was essentially popular entertainment for immigrants. There were what we'd now think of as hilarious versions of, say, 'King Lear,' in which King Lear lives. Or there were fairy tales, about an impoverished family arriving on the Lower East Side and ending up on Riverside Drive living high on the hog." (There was also, as he notes, an avant-garde Yiddish theatre, based largely in the Bronx, but that's a differ-ent, and more elevated, story.)

The fact that the audience at the Sarah Vaughan Concert Hall is entirely black creates an essential dynamic. I mentioned elements of comic relief: they include a black preacher greedy for Grandma's chicken wings; a randy old man trailing toilet paper from a split seam in the back of his pants; the grandmother herself, whose churchiness is outlandishly caricatured; endless references to Stickey's lapses of personal hygiene. All the very worst stereo-types of the race are on display, larger than life. Here, in this racially se-questered space, a black audience laughs uninhibitedly, whereas the presence of white folks would have engendered a familiar anxiety. *Will they think that's what we're really like?* If this drama were shown on television–on any inte-grated forum–Jesse Jackson would probably denounce it, the N.A.A.C.P. would demand a boycott, and every soul here would swap his or her finery for sandwich boards in order to picket it. You don't want white people to see this kind of spectacle; you want them to see the noble dramas of August Wil-son, where the injuries and injustices perpetrated by the white man are never far from our consciousness. (It should be mentioned that there are far more respectable and well-groomed versions of gospel drama—most notably Vy Higgenson's "Mama I Want to Sing" and its progeny—that have achieved a measure of crossover success, serving mainly as vehicles for some very impressive singing. But they're better regarded as pageants, or revues, than stage plays.) By contrast, these Chitlin Circuit plays carry an invisible racial warning sticker: For domestic consumption only—export strictly prohibited.

For the creators of this theatre, there are other gratifications to be had. "I've never made so much money in my life as I made when I did the forty or so cities we did on the Chitlin Circuit," James Chapmyn, one veteran of the circuit, tells me. And Chapmyn wasn't even one of the top grossers. "The guy that did 'Beauty Shop' probably grossed fifteen to twenty-five million dollars in the Chitlin Circuit," he says. "These plays make enormous money."

Chapmyn is a blunt-featured, odd-shaped man, with a bullet head and a Buddha belly. He's thirty-six, and he grew up in Kansas, the son of a Baptist minister. He tells me that he fell out with his father in his early twenties. "He was adamant in teaching us to stand up for who we are, and who I am happens to be a black gay man. He taught me to tell the truth," Chapmyn says, but adds that his father changed his mind when his son came out. "I just wish you had lied," the minister told his son. A resulting disaffection with the church—and a spell as a homeless person—impelled him to write a play for which he has become widely known: "Our Young Black Men Are Dying and Nobody Seems to Care." His experience with the Chitlin Circuit was decidedly mixed but still memorable.

Chapmyn, like everyone else who has succeeded on the Chitlin Circuit, had to master the dark arts of marketing and promotion; and to do so while bypassing the major media. He genially explains the ground rules: "What has happened in America is that you have a very active African-American theatre audience that doesn't get their information from the arts section in the newspaper; that doesn't read reviews but listens to the radio, gets things stuffed in their bulletins in church, has flyers put on their car when they're night-clubbing. That's how people get to know about black theatre. Buying the arts section ain't going to cut it for us. That audience is not interested in the 'black theatre,' and the black-theatre audience is not interested in reading that information. We use radio quite extensively, because in our community and places we've gone African-Americans listen to radio. In fact, there's kind of an unspoken rule on the Chitlin Circuit: if a city doesn't have a black radio station, then the Chitlin Circuit won't perform there."

But the Chitlin Circuit has a less amiable side; indeed, to judge from some of the tales you hear, many of its most dramatic events occur offstage.

The inner-city version of foundation program officers are drug dealers with money to burn, and their influence is unmistakable. "They do everything in cash," Chapmyn says. "At our highest point, I know that after we all got our money, we were still collecting in the neighborhood of a hundred thousand dollars a week. That was cash being given to us, usually in envelopes, by people we didn't know. It was scary." He continues, "When I was in that circuit, I dealt with a lot of people who didn't have anything but beeper numbers, who would call me with hotel numbers, who operated through post-office boxes, who would show up at the time of the show—and most of the time take care of me and my people very well."

Not always, though. "In one city, I think we did three shows, and the receipts after expenses were a hundred and forty thousand dollars," Chapmyn recounts. "My percentage of that was to be sixty-five thousand dollars. I remember the people gave me five thousand and told me that if I wanted the rest I'd have to sue them." He ended up spending the night in jail. "I was so mad I was ready to hurt somebody," he explains. "Somebody is going to tell me that they got my sixty thousand dollars and they ain't going to give it to me? I think I flipped a table over and hit somebody in the face."

Larry Leon Hamlin, too, becomes animated when he talks about the sleazy world of popular theatre. "Contracts have been put out on people," he tells me. "If you are a big-time drug dealer, it's like, 'These plays are making money, and I've got money. I'm going to put out a play.' That drug dealer will write a play who has never written a play before, will direct the play, who has never directed a play before. They get deep with guns." James Chapmyn says he dropped out of the circuit because of the criminal element: "Here I am doing a play about all the things killing African-American men, chief among those things being the violence and the drugs, and I'm doing business with people who are probably using the money they make from drugs to promote my play. I had a fundamental problem with that." Chapmyn, plainly, is a man with a mission of uplift. By contrast, many other stars of the Chitlin Circuit have the more single-minded intent of pleasing an audience: they stoop to conquer.

That might be said, certainly, of the most successful impresario of the Chitlin Circuit, a man named Shelly Garrett. Garrett maintains that his play "Beauty Shop" has been seen by more than twenty million people; that it's the most successful black stage play in American history; and that he himself is "America's No. 1 black theatrical producer, director, and playwright." Shelly Garrett has never met August Wilson; August Wilson has never heard of Shelly Garrett. They are as unacquainted with each other as art and commerce are said to be. (Except for "Fences" and "The Piano Lesson," both of which were profitable, all of August Wilson's plays have lost money.)

Garrett is a handsome man in his early fifties, given to bright-colored sports coats and heavy gold jewelry, and there is about him the unquiet air of a gambler. He was born in Dallas, worked there as a disk jockey, and later moved to Los Angeles to begin an acting career; he didn't make his début as a dramatist until 1986, with "Snuff and Miniskirts." It played in the Ebony Showcase Theatre, in Los Angeles, for about six weeks. The following year, he staged "Beauty Shop." After running on and off in Los Angeles, that show went on tour, and, as Garrett likes to say, "the rest is history." Garrett had his audience in the palm of his hand and his formula at his fingertips; all that was left was for him to repeat it with slight variation, in plays like "Beauty Shop Part 2," "Living Room," "Barber Shop," and "Laundromat."

"It reminds you of the old commedia-dell'arte stuff," OyamO says of Garrett's approach to theatre. "But it's black, and it's today, and it's loud." He also makes the obvious remark that "if a white man was producing 'Beauty Shop,' they would be lynching it." Still, what Shelly Garrett does has a far better claim to be "community theatre" than what we normally refer to by that name.

Garrett's dramatis personae are as uniform as restaurant place settings: the parts invariably include a mouthy fat woman, a beautiful vamp, a sharp-tongued and swishy gay man, and a handsome black stud, who will ultimately be coupled with the fat woman. Much of the dialogue consists of insults and trash talk. Other options and accessories may be added, to taste; but typically there's a striptease scene, and lots of Teddy Pendergrass on the mixing board. The gay man and the fat woman swap gibes—"play the dozens"—during lulls in the action.

Although Garrett's plays adhere to pretty much the same institutional and narrative template, they are not dashed off. "I take so much time in rehearsals and writing these shows," Garrett tells me. "I might rewrite a show forty times, and I take so much time with them and the rehearsals and the delivery of the lines that I just run actors crazy. I run them nuts. But then, at the end, when they get their standing ovation, they love me." A strained chuckle: "Takes them a long time to love me, but finally they do." Garrett prides himself on his professionalism, which lifts him far above the cheesier theatrical realm where drug-pusher auteurs and shakedown artists might freelance. And there's something disarming about his buoyant, show-me-the-money brand of dramaturgy.

Garrett is not the product of anyone's drama workshop; he comes from a world in which the Method refers to a birth-control technique. He has seen almost no "legitimate" theatre, even in its low-end form: "I'm embarrassed to tell people that I've never even seen 'The Wiz.' On Broadway, I've seen 'Les Miz,' 'Cats,' and—What was that black show that had Gregory Hines in it?" His shows play to ordinary black people—the "people on the avenue," as Wilson wistfully puts it—and if these shows are essentially invisible to the white mainstream, so much the better. "But I have things in my show that black people can relate to," Garrett declares. "If you're sitting in that audience and something is happening on that stage that you can absolutely not relate to, why are you even there?"

In "Beauty Shop," Terry (conservative, pretty) is the proprietor of the hair salon; Sylvia (sexy), Margaret (fat), and Chris (gay) are stylists; and Rachel (tall, well dressed) is a customer.

Terry: Barbara Dell! Is that man still beating on her?
Sylvia: Punching her lights out! It must have been a humdinger 'cause her glasses were *real* dark!
Terry: Well, if she's stupid enough to stay there with him, she deserves it!
Rachel: I have never understood why a woman just takes that kind of stuff off of a man.
Margaret: I can't understand a man raising his hand to *hit* a woman!
Chris: I guess you wouldn't. What man would be *brave* enough to hit *you*?

Despite outrageous caricature, it doesn't seem quite right to call these plays homophobic. The gay characters may be stereotyped, but the bigots aren't treated charitably, either; the queen is always given the last word. "You are an embarrassment to the male gender, to the Y.M.C.A., the Cub Scouts, Boy Scouts, U.S. Army, and . . . Old Spice!" a customer tells Chris in the course of a steadily escalating argument. Chris replies, "Now what you *need* to do is go home and have a little talk with you *mother*! I wasn't *always* gay, I *might* be your *daddy*!" Politically correct it isn't, but neither is it mean-spirited. At the end, the fat woman is rewarded with a desirable man. And occasionally there are even monologues with morals, in which philandering males are put in their place by right-on women.

First and foremost, though, Garrett is a businessman. His production company moves along with him; he refuses to fly, but has a bus that's fully equipped with fax and phone. He's known for his skill in saturating the black press and radio stations. He's also known for the money he makes selling merchandise like T-shirts and programs. He can tell you that his average ticket price is twenty-seven dollars and fifty cents, that he rarely plays a venue with fewer than two thousand seats, that a show he did in Atlanta net-

ted about six hundred thousand dollars a week. (For purposes of comparison, the weekly net of hit "straight" plays—like "Master Class," "Taking
Sides," and so forth—is typically between one and two hundred thousand
dollars; the weekly net of hit musicals like "Miss Saigon," "Les Misérables,"
and "Sunset Boulevard" is usually in the neighborhood of five hundred thousand.) In New York, Garrett's "Beauty Shop" had weekly revenues of more
than eight hundred thousand, and that was for an eleven-week run, during
which the show sold out every week but one. Garrett remembers the time
fondly: "They put me up at the Plaza in New York. First black to ever stay at
the penthouse of the Plaza. And I was there for three weeks—the penthouse
of the Plaza!"

To most people who both take the theatrical arts seriously and aspire to
an "organic connection" with the black community, Garrett is a cultural
candy man, and his plays the equivalent of caries. Woodie King, Jr., of New
York's New Federal Theatre (which has had unusual success in attracting
black audiences for black theatre), expresses a widespread sentiment in the
world of political theatre when he describes Garrett as "an individual going
after our personal riches." He says, "It's not doing anything for any kind of
black community. It's not like he's going to make money, then find five deserving women writers and put on their work. It's always going to be about
him." It's clear that for dramatists who view themselves as producing work
for their community, but depend for their existence on foundation and government support, Garrett is an embarrassment in more ways than one.

"Artistically, I think they're horrible," the Crossroads' Ricardo Khan says
of the Chitlin Circuit's carnivalesque productions. "I don't think the acting is
good, I don't think the direction is good, I don't think the level of production
is good. But I don't put them down for being able to speak to something that
people are feeling. I think the reason it's working is that it's making people
laugh at themselves, making them feel good, and they're tired of heavy
stuff." But his political consciousness rebels at the easy anodyne, the theatre-
goer's opiate. His own work, he says, aspires to raise consciousness and
transform society. He sounds almost discouraged when he adds, "But people
don't always want that. Sometimes they just want to have fun."

Nobody wants to see the Chitlin Circuit and the Crossroads converge. But
there's something heartening about the spectacle of black drama that pays
its own way—even if aficionados of serious theatre find something disheartening about the nature of that drama. So maybe we shouldn't worry so
much about those Du Boisian yardsticks of blackness. That way lies heart-
break, or confusion. Wilson and his supporters, to listen to them, would

divvy up American culture along the color line, sorting out possessions like an amicably divorcing couple. But, as I insist, Wilson's polemics disserve his poetics.

Indeed, his work is a tribute to a hybrid vigor, as an amalgam of black vernacular, American naturalism, and high modernist influences. (In the history of black drama, perhaps only Baraka's 1964 play "Dutchman" represents as formidable an achievement, and that was explicitly a drama of interracial conflict. By contrast, one of Wilson's accomplishments is to register the ambiguous presence of white folks in a segregated black world—the way you see them nowhere and feel them everywhere.) There's no contradiction in the fact that Wilson revels in the black cadences of the barbershop and the barbecue, on the one hand, and pledges fealty to Aristotle's Poetics, on the other. Wilson may talk about cultural autarky, but, to his credit, he doesn't practice it. Inevitably, the audience for serious plays in this mostly white country is mostly white. Wilson writes serious plays. His audience is mostly white. What's to apologize for?

By all means, let there be "political" art and formalist art, populism and modernism, Baraka and Beckett, but let them jostle and collide in the cultural agora. There will be theatres that are black, and also Latino and Asian, and what you will; but, all told, it's better that they not arise from the edicts of cultural commissioners. Despite all the rhetoric about inclusion, I was struck by the fact that many black playwrights told me they felt that their kind of work—usually more "experimental" than realist—was distinctly unwelcome in most black regional theatres. Suzan-Lori Parks reminds me that she didn't grow up in the 'hood: "I'm not black according to a nationalist definition of black womanhood. . . . We discriminate in our own family." As a working dramatist and director, George Wolfe—who, in the spirit of pluralism, says he welcomes all kinds of theatres, ethnically specific and otherwise—admits unease about the neatly color-coded cultural landscape that Wilson conjures up. "I don't live in the world of absolutes," Wolfe says. "I don't think it's a matter of a black theatre versus an American theatre, a black theatre versus a white theatre. I think we need an American theatre that is of, for, and by us—*all* of us."

You may wonder, then, what happens to that self-divided creed of populist modernism: the dream of an art that combines aesthetic vanguardism with popular engagement—which is to say the elevated black theatre for which Wilson seeks patronage. "People are not busting their ass to go and see this stuff," OyamO says bluntly, "and I keep thinking, if this stuff is so significant, why can't it touch ordinary people?" There's reason to believe that such impatience is beginning to spread. Indeed, maybe the most transgressive move for such black theatre would be to explore that sordid, sullying world of the truly demotic. Ed Bullins, the doyen of black revolutionary theatre, regales me with stories he's heard about Chitlin Circuit entrepreneurs "rolling away at night with suitcases of money"—about the shadowy realm of cash-only transactions. But the challenge appeals to him, all the same.

So brace yourself: the Ed Bullins to whom Wilson paid tribute—as one whose dramatic art was hallowed with the blood of proud black warriors— now tells me he's been thinking about entering the Chitlin Circuit himself. Call it populist postmodernism. Somehow, he relishes the idea of a theatre that would be self-supporting, one that didn't just glorify the masses but actually appealed to them. Naturally, though, he'd try to do it a little better. "The idea is to upgrade the production a bit, but go after the same market," he says eagerly. Now, that's a radical thought.

SOURCE: *The New Yorker*, February 3, 1997.

CHANGING PLACES

"HOW DO YOU spell 'rat,'" my father would ask me during a lull in one of his many bid whist card games with his buddies from the paper mill. "R-a-t," I'd respond dutifully, with all of the preschool pride that I could muster. "Not that mousy kind of a rat," he'd say. "I mean like 'rat now.'" His buddies would howl as my perplexity grew.

Like many black people who came of age in the '60s, I've always delighted in the mind-bending playfulness of the black vernacular. And jokes turning on malaprops and double-entendres are among the most vital aspects of black culture. The Kingfish's quip, on "Amos 'n' Andy," that he and Andy should "simonize our watches" is nearly canonical in many black households.

But all of us have our favorites. It's said that Tim Moore, the actor who played Kingfish, once had to appear in court as a defendant. "Yo' honor," he told the judge, "not only does I resents the allegation, but I resents the alligator!"

Still, I have to confess that the use of "ax" for "ask" has always been, for me, the linguistic equivalent of fingernails' scraping down a blackboard. The first time I heard the word "ask" pronounced that way was on a Bill Cosby album in the 60's.

"I'm-o, I'm-o ax you a question," his character stammers, and in my Appalachian hamlet we'd laugh at that, certain that nobody would really be foolish enough to say "ax" for "ask."

Don't get me wrong: it's not as if the black citizens of Piedmont, W.Va., spoke the king's English, but axing was something we did in the woods.

It was when I first visited Bermuda, where just about everyone I met says "ax," that I began to suspect that this usage had deeper origins than I'd known. Sure enough, as William Labov, a linguist at the University of Pennsylvania, explained to me, "aks" is traceable to the Old English "acsian," a nonstandard form of "ascian," the root of "ask."

Professor Labov argues that black Americans have become more monolingual since the 60's—that fewer of them have a mastery of standard English.

That's the result of residential segregation, the fact that poor blacks tend to live with poor blacks. But it's also compounded by desegregation, which ended up separating the black poor and the black middle class.

Because of these two factors, there's now a large group of poor black people whose face-to-face conversations are almost entirely with people like themselves. As the cultural critic Greg Tate told me, black people are "segregated, landlocked and institutionalized between prison, the project and public institutions." He added that "there's a certain tribal caste to segregated African-American communities for that reason," and that's reflected in their increased monolingualism.

Writing in *The Times* 25 years ago, James Baldwin ventured that the black vernacular was one of self-defense. "There was a moment, in time, in this place," he recalled, "when my brother, or my mother, or my father, or my sister, had to convey to me, for example, the danger in which I was standing from the white man standing just behind me, and to convey this with a speed and in a language, that the white man could not possibly understand, and that, indeed, he cannot understand, until today."

Is that still true? The black vernacular seems to be everywhere these days, from Dave Chappelle's show to Boost Mobile's "Where you at?" ad campaign.

"It becomes part of the mainstream in a minute," the poet Amiri Baraka told me, referring to the black vernacular. "We hear the rappers say, 'I'm outta here'—the next thing you know, Clinton's saying, 'I'm outta here.'" And both Senator John Kerry and President Bush are calling out, "Bring it on," like dueling mike-masters at a hip-hop slam.

Talk about changing places. Even as large numbers of black children struggle with standard English, hip-hop has become the recreational lingua franca of white suburban youth. Baldwin's notion of using black English to encode messages seems almost romantic now.

Is it possible, after all these years, that white folk have come to speak "black" far better than blacks speak "white"? Just axing.

SOURCE: *The New York Times*, September 30, 2004.

FORTY ACRES AND A GAP IN WEALTH

LAST WEEK, THE Pew Research Center published the astonishing finding that 37 percent of African-Americans polled felt that "blacks today can no longer be thought of as a single race" because of a widening class divide. From Frederick Douglass to the Rev. Dr. Martin Luther King Jr., perhaps the most fundamental assumption in the history of the black community has been that Americans of African descent, the descendants of the slaves, either because of shared culture or shared oppression, constitute "a mighty race," as Marcus Garvey often put it.

"By a ratio of 2 to 1," the report says, "blacks say that the values of poor and middle-class blacks have grown more dissimilar over the past decade. In contrast, most blacks say that the values of blacks and whites have grown more alike."

The message here is that it is time to examine the differences between black families on either side of the divide for clues about how to address an increasingly entrenched inequality. We can't afford to wait any longer to address the causes of persistent poverty among most black families.

This class divide was predicted long ago, and nobody wanted to listen. At a conference marking the 40th anniversary of Daniel Patrick Moynihan's infamous report on the problems of the black family, I asked the conservative scholar James Q. Wilson and the liberal scholar William Julius Wilson if ours was the generation presiding over an irreversible, self-perpetuating class divide within the African-American community.

"I have to believe that this is not the case," the liberal Wilson responded with willed optimism. "Why go on with this work otherwise?" The conservative Wilson nodded. Yet, no one could imagine how to close the gap.

In 1965, when Moynihan published his report, suggesting that the out-of-wedlock birthrate and the number of families headed by single mothers, both about 24 percent, pointed to dissolution of the social fabric of the black community, black scholars and liberals dismissed it. They attacked its author as a right-wing bigot. Now we'd give just about anything to have those statis-

544

tics back. Today, 69 percent of black babies are born out of wedlock, while 45 percent of black households with children are headed by women.

How did this happen? As many theories flourish as pundits—from slavery and segregation to the decline of factory jobs, crack cocaine, draconian drug laws and outsourcing. But nobody knows for sure.

I have been studying the family trees of 20 successful African-Americans, people in fields ranging from entertainment and sports (Oprah Winfrey, the track star Jackie Joyner-Kersee) to space travel and medicine (the astronaut Mae Jemison and Ben Carson, a pediatric neurosurgeon). And I've seen an astonishing pattern: 15 of the 20 descend from at least one line of former slaves who managed to obtain property by 1920—a time when only 25 percent of all African-American families owned property.

Ten years after slavery ended, Constantine Winfrey, Oprah's great-grandfather, bartered eight bales of cleaned cotton (4,000 pounds) that he picked on his own time for 80 acres of prime bottomland in Mississippi. (He also learned to read and write while picking all that cotton.)

Sometimes the government helped: Whoopi Goldberg's great-great-grandparents received their land through the Southern Homestead Act. "So my family got its 40 acres and a mule," she exclaimed when I showed her the deed, referring to the rumor that freed slaves would receive land that had been owned by their masters.

Well, perhaps not the mule, but 104 acres in Florida. If there is a meaningful correlation between the success of accomplished African-Americans today and their ancestors' property ownership, we can only imagine how different black-white relations would be had "40 acres and a mule" really been official government policy in the Reconstruction South.

The historical basis for the gap between the black middle class and underclass shows that ending discrimination, by itself, would not eradicate black poverty and dysfunction. We also need intervention to promulgate a middle-class ethic of success among the poor, while expanding opportunities for economic betterment.

Perhaps Margaret Thatcher, of all people, suggested a program that might help. In the 1980s, she turned 1.5 million residents of public housing projects in Britain into homeowners. It was certainly the most liberal thing Mrs. Thatcher did, and perhaps progressives should borrow a leaf from her playbook.

The telltale fact is that the biggest gap in black prosperity isn't in income, but in wealth. According to a study by the economist Edward N. Wolff, the median net worth of non-Hispanic black households in 2004 was only $11,800—less than 10 percent that of non-Hispanic white households,

$118,300. Perhaps a bold and innovative approach to the problem of black poverty—one floated during the Civil War but never fully put into practice—would be to look at ways to turn tenants into homeowners. Sadly, in the wake of the subprime mortgage debacle, an enormous number of houses are being repossessed. But for the black poor, real progress may come only once they have an ownership stake in American society.

People who own property feel a sense of ownership in their future and their society. They study, save, work, strive and vote. And people trapped in a culture of tenancy do not.

The sad truth is that the civil rights movement cannot be reborn until we identify the causes of black suffering, some of them self-inflicted. Why can't black leaders organize rallies around responsible sexuality, birth within marriage, parents reading to their children and students staying in school and doing homework? Imagine Al Sharpton and Jesse Jackson distributing free copies of Virginia Hamilton's collection of folktales "The People Could Fly" or Dr. Seuss, and demanding that black parents sign pledges to read to their children. What would it take to make inner-city schools havens of learning?

John Kenneth Galbraith once told me that the first step in reversing the economic inequalities that blacks face is greater voter participation, and I think he was right. Politicians will not put forth programs aimed at the problems of poor blacks while their turnout remains so low.

If the correlation between land ownership and success of African-Americans argues that the chasm between classes in the black community is partly the result of social forces set in motion by the dismal failure of 40 acres and a mule, then we must act decisively. If we do not, ours will be remembered as the generation that presided over a permanent class divide, a slow but inevitable process that began with the failure to give property to the people who had once been defined as property.

SOURCE: *The New York Times*, November 18, 2007.

ENDING THE SLAVERY BLAME-GAME

THANKS TO AN unlikely confluence of history and genetics—the fact that he is African-American and president—Barack Obama has a unique opportunity to reshape the debate over one of the most contentious issues of America's racial legacy: reparations, the idea that the descendants of American slaves should receive compensation for their ancestors' unpaid labor and bondage.

There are many thorny issues to resolve before we can arrive at a judicious (if symbolic) gesture to match such a sustained, heinous crime. Perhaps the most vexing is how to parcel out blame to those directly involved in the capture and sale of human beings for immense economic gain.

While we are all familiar with the role played by the United States and the European colonial powers like Britain, France, Holland, Portugal and Spain, there is very little discussion of the role Africans themselves played. And that role, it turns out, was a considerable one, especially for the slave-trading kingdoms of western and central Africa. These included the Akan of the kingdom of Asante in what is now Ghana, the Fon of Dahomey (now Benin), the Mbundu of Ndongo in modern Angola and the Kongo of today's Congo, among several others.

For centuries, Europeans in Africa kept close to their military and trading posts on the coast. Exploration of the interior, home to the bulk of Africans sold into bondage at the height of the slave trade, came only during the colonial conquests, which is why Henry Morton Stanley's pursuit of Dr. David Livingstone in 1871 made for such compelling press: he was going where no (white) man had gone before.

How did slaves make it to these coastal forts? The historians John Thornton and Linda Heywood of Boston University estimate that 90 percent of those shipped to the New World were enslaved by Africans and then sold to European traders. The sad truth is that without complex business partnerships between African elites and European traders and commercial agents, the slave trade to the New World would have been impossible, at least on the scale it occurred.

Advocates of reparations for the descendants of those slaves generally ignore this untidy problem of the significant role that Africans played in the trade, choosing to believe the romanticized version that our ancestors were all kidnapped unawares by evil white men, like Kunta Kinte was in "Roots." The truth, however, is much more complex: slavery was a business, highly organized and lucrative for European buyers and African sellers alike.

The African role in the slave trade was fully understood and openly acknowledged by many African-Americans even before the Civil War. For Frederick Douglass, it was an argument against repatriation schemes for the freed slaves. "The savage chiefs of the western coasts of Africa, who for ages have been accustomed to selling their captives into bondage and pocketing the ready cash for them, will not more readily accept our moral and economical ideas than the slave traders of Maryland and Virginia," he warned, "We are, therefore, less inclined to go to Africa to work against the slave trade than to stay here to work against it."

To be sure, the African role in the slave trade was greatly reduced after 1807, when abolitionists, first in Britain and then, a year later, in the United States, succeeded in banning the importation of slaves. Meanwhile, slaves continued to be bought and sold within the United States, and slavery as an institution would not be abolished until 1865. But the culpability of American plantation owners neither erases nor supplants that of the African slavers. In recent years, some African leaders have become more comfortable discussing this complicated past than African-Americans tend to be.

In 1999, for instance, President Mathieu Kerekou of Benin astonished an all-black congregation in Baltimore by falling to his knees and begging African-Americans' forgiveness for the "shameful" and "abominable" role Africans played in the trade. Other African leaders, including Jerry Rawlings of Ghana, followed Mr. Kerekou's bold example.

Our new understanding of the scope of African involvement in the slave trade is not historical guesswork. Thanks to the Trans-Atlantic Slave Trade Database, directed by the historian David Eltis of Emory University, we now know the ports from which more than 450,000 of our African ancestors were shipped out to what is now the United States (the database has records of 12.5 million people shipped to all parts of the New World from 1514 to 1866). About 16 percent of United States slaves came from eastern Nigeria, while 24 percent came from the Congo and Angola.

Through the work of Professors Thornton and Heywood, we also know that the victims of the slave trade were predominantly members of as few as 50 ethnic groups. This data, along with the tracing of blacks' ancestry through

DNA tests, is giving us a fuller understanding of the identities of both the victims and the facilitators of the African slave trade.

For many African-Americans, these facts can be difficult to accept. Excuses run the gamut, from "Africans didn't know how harsh slavery in America was" and "Slavery in Africa was, by comparison, humane" or, in a bizarre version of "The devil made me do it," "Africans were driven to this only by the unprecedented profits offered by greedy European countries."

But the sad truth is that the conquest and capture of Africans and their sale to Europeans was one of the main sources of foreign exchange for several African kingdoms for a very long time. Slaves were the main export of the kingdom of Kongo; the Asante Empire in Ghana exported slaves and used the profits to import gold. Queen Njinga, the brilliant 17th-century monarch of the Mbundu, waged wars of resistance against the Portuguese but also conquered polities as far as 500 miles inland and sold her captives to the Portuguese. When Njinga converted to Christianity, she sold African traditional religious leaders into slavery, claiming they had violated her new Christian precepts.

Did these Africans know how harsh slavery was in the New World? Actually, many elite Africans visited Europe in that era, and they did so on slave ships following the prevailing winds through the New World. For example, when Antonio Manuel, Kongo's ambassador to the Vatican, went to Europe in 1604, he first stopped in Bahia, Brazil, where he arranged to free a countryman who had been wrongfully enslaved.

African monarchs also sent their children along these same slave routes to be educated in Europe. And there were thousands of former slaves who returned to settle Liberia and Sierra Leone. The Middle Passage, in other words, was sometimes a two-way street. Under these circumstances, it is difficult to claim that Africans were ignorant or innocent.

Given this remarkably messy history, the problem with reparations may not be so much whether they are a good idea or deciding who would get them; the larger question just might be from whom they would be extracted.

So how could President Obama untangle the knot? In David Remnick's new book "The Bridge: The Life and Rise of Barack Obama," one of the president's former students at the University of Chicago comments on Mr. Obama's mixed feelings about the reparations movement: "He told us what he thought about reparations. He agreed entirely with the theory of reparations. But in practice he didn't think it was really workable."

About the practicalities, Professor Obama may have been more right than he knew. Fortunately, in President Obama, the child of an African and an American, we finally have a leader who is uniquely positioned to bridge the great reparations divide. He is uniquely placed to publicly attribute responsibility and culpability where they truly belong, to white people and black people, on both sides of the Atlantic, complicit alike in one of the greatest evils in the history of civilization. And reaching that understanding is a vital precursor to any just and lasting agreement on the divisive issue of slavery reparations.

SOURCE: *The New York Times*, April 23, 2010.

IS HE A RACIST?

James Watson's Errant, Perilous Theories

Is Dr. James Watson racist? After the controversy that erupted last fall when the father of DNA suggested that there are inherent, unalterable biological differences in intelligence between black people and everyone else, I wrote to Watson and requested an interview in which he could explain his remarks. Our conversation this spring underscores how America's battles with race and racism will play out in the era of the genome.

Watson and his British colleague, Francis Crick, are remembered popularly for identifying the "double helix" structure of DNA. Watson's contribution was to define how the four nucleotide bases that make up deoxyribonucleic acid combine in pairs; these base pairs are the key to the structure of DNA and its various functions. In other words, Watson identified the language and the code by which we understand and talk about our genetic makeup.

Watson was just 25 when he and Crick published their findings and 34 when he won the Nobel Prize. His youth and a certain absent-minded professorial quirkiness made him a national hero, the symbol of American enterprise and intelligence. In 1989, he was named head of the Human Genome Project at the National Institutes of Health. In 1994, he became president of Cold Spring Harbor Laboratory, a lavishly funded center for the advanced study of genomics and cancer.

On Oct. 14, a former Watson assistant, Charlotte Hunt-Grubbe, wrote an article suggesting that Watson believes nature has created a primal distinction in intelligence and innate mental capacity between blacks and everyone else that no amount of social intervention could ever change. She quoted him as saying that he was "inherently gloomy about the prospect of Africa," since "all of our social policies are based on the fact that their intelligence is the same as ours—whereas all the testing says not really" and that "people who have to deal with black employees find that [the belief that everyone is equal] is not true."

His words caused a tidal wave of shock and disgust. The father of DNA seemingly supported the most ardent fantasy of white racists (David Duke waxed poetic on his Web site that the truth had at last been revealed). One of the smartest white men in the world seemed to confirm that the gap between blacks and whites in, say, SAT results has a biological basis and that environmental factors such as centuries of slavery, colonization, Jim Crow segregation and race-based discrimination—all of which contributed to uneven economic development—are not very significant. Nature has given us an extra basketball gene, as it were, in lieu of intelligence.

On Oct. 19, Watson profusely apologized; on Oct. 25, he retired from Cold Spring Harbor.

When I read about Watson's remarks, I was astonished and saddened. Since we had met before, as alumni of Clare College at the University of Cambridge, I sent him a letter; as editor of TheRoot.com, I offered him a platform in the black world through which he could explain, defend and perhaps clarify the remarks attributed to him. He accepted, and on March 17 we spoke for well over an hour, with no holds barred.

"Well?" one of my friends asked. "Is he a racist?"

Not really. But I think that Watson is what W.E.B. Du Bois called a "racialist"—that is, he believes that certain observable traits or forms of behavior among groups of people might indeed have a biological basis in the code that scientists, eventually, may be able to ascertain; that, in the search for the basis of behaviors, we can move from correlation to causation (that genetic sequencing patterns can be correlated to intelligence); and that racial differences between ethnic groups in behavior and ability reflect immutable genetic traits rather than environmental factors.

The distinction between "racist" and "racialist" is crucial. James Watson is not a garden-variety racist, as he has been caricatured, the sort epitomized by David Duke. He also seemed embarrassed and remorseful that Duke and his ilk had claimed him as one of their own. Not surprisingly, he apologized profusely, contending that he had been misquoted, at worst, and taken out of context, at best.

But Watson does seem to believe that many forms of behavior—such as "Jewish intelligence" (his phrase) and the basketball prowess of black men in the NBA (his example)—could, possibly, be traced to genetic differences among groups, although no such connection has been made on any firm scientific basis. Girded by his conviction that everyone should be judged as individuals, he blithely asserted that if a genetic basis for "Jewish intelligence" was found, it wouldn't affect anyone in the slightest: "no one should be judged by a term like 'black.'" But a phrase such as "Jewish intelligence" contradicts this claim.

Precisely because of the misuses of science and pseudo-science since the 18th century, which put in place fixed categories of "races" to justify an economic order dependent on the exploitation of people of color as cheap sources of labor, it has never been possible for a person of African descent to function in American society simply as an "individual."

Watson's error is that he is too eager to map individual genetic differences (which do exist) with ethnic variation (which is sociocultural and highly malleable), and to provide a genetic explanation for ethnic differences. Watson said he was gloomy about the prospects of Africans as a group but later insisted that people shouldn't be judged as groups. Doesn't this illustrate the persistence of race categories, of "kind-mindedness," despite his declared intention?

Abilities and behaviors, such as intelligence or basketball skills, that are popularly attributed to groups and are defined as "genetic" will continue to limit or determine the treatment of individuals who fall into those "racial" categories, regardless of an individual's propensities and achievements. In the end, visions that are racialist may end up doing the same work of those that are racist.

Having spent the past three decades studying racist discourse about the degree of reason that people of African descent possess, I know that such conclusions—say, about an entity called "Jewish intelligence"—could deleteriously affect me as a black person because it could reinforce stereotypes about Jewish people being genetically superior and black people being inherently less intelligent than other groups. If such differences in intelligence were purported to have a genetic basis, all of the social intervention in the world could have only so much effect. Why bother with costly compensatory education programs if, after all, nature is fundamentally to blame, severely limiting what these programs can achieve? Sooner or later, members of these supposedly "lesser" ethnic groups or genetic populations could find their life possibilities limited and perhaps even regulated.

I worry even more that Watson confessed to me that "we shouldn't expect that [ethnically] different persons have equal intelligence, because we don't know that. And people say that these should be the same [that is, all ethnic groups] . . . I think the answer is we don't know." Later, he remarked that "we're not all the same," by which he meant genetically, across ethnic groups. Soon, some scientist somewhere will claim to have proved this, and that claim could be deeply problematic for the future of black people in this society, even if my rights to equal treatment under the law are not predicated upon the hypothesis that all human groups have the same genetic endowments. Watson's tendency to theorize about groups—a very human tendency— undermines his declared belief that humans should be judged as individuals.

Afterward, I realized what fear my conversation with Watson had confirmed: that the idea of innate group inferiority is still on the table, despite all the progress blacks have made in this society, and that the last great battle over racism will not be fought over access to a lunch counter, or the right to vote, or even the right to occupy the White House; it will be fought in a laboratory, under a microscope, on the battleground of our DNA. That is where we, as a society, will resolve the contentious claim that groups are, by nature, differently advantaged in the most important way: over the degree of reason or intelligence that they ostensibly possess.

SOURCE: *The Washington Post*, July 11, 2008.

PART VIII
INTERVIEWS

As a contributor to *The New York Times* and *The New Yorker*, as editor-in-chief of *The Root*, as publisher of the *Du Bois Review* and *Transition*, Gates has a number of public platforms for his writing. Over many years, Gates has used these public platforms to conduct interviews with world leaders and thought leaders, artists, writers, filmmakers, and politicians.

The two interviews that frame this section are both about migration, about black people opening one door when race has seemed to close another. Although the two interviews were conducted forty years apart (he spoke with James Baldwin and Josephine Baker in the early 1970s and with Isabel Wilkerson in 2010) and with figures who in time and profession were far removed from each other, similar themes emerge about the migrant experience of blacks. For both the expatriates and the Great Migration travelers, America holds great promise—unrealized and sometimes corrupted, but promise nonetheless. The interviews that come in between these two—with Wole Soyinka, Condoleezza Rice, and William Julius Wilson—all pick up similar themes of self-determination, collective action, and potential—and the paths to fulfill them.

In the *Henry Louis Gates, Jr. Reader*, perhaps it is an odd choice to end with the voices of others. But what Gates elicits from each of his interlocutors is the same thing that has guided his writing over the years: each subject, like Gates himself, creates a narrative to help make sense of the world around us, to understand institutions and the individuals within them, and to create an environment for the free and ferocious exchange of ideas.

Abby Wolf

AN INTERVIEW WITH
JOSEPHINE BAKER AND JAMES BALDWIN

In 1973, Henry Louis Gates, Jr., was in Paris interviewing black American expatriates. He sought to know why, after the "gains" of the sixties, so many black Americans still found it necessary to live abroad. In addition to interviewing Leroy Haynes, proprietor of a Parisian Soul Food restaurant, Beauford Delaney, painter, and Bob Reid, musician, Gates interviewed Josephine Baker and James Baldwin. Although some twelve years have passed since these interviews, the observations and comments of Baker and Baldwin offer us insights into the expatriate experience then, and America now.

The interview with Josephine Baker began in her home, "Villa Maryvonne," in Monte Carlo. Later, while she and Gates were dinner guests at James Baldwin's home in St. Paul-de-Vence in the south of France, Gates concluded his interview with Baker and interviewed Baldwin. Although all of the conversation over dinner that night was not preserved, Baker's and Baldwin's responses to Gates's questions were. The individual interviews I have edited to read as a single conversation so that the genial ambience of that evening in St. Paul could be captured. Gates speaks of that evening and the events that led up to it in his own introduction to this piece.—Anthony Barthelemy

SO MANY QUESTIONS that I should have asked that night, but did not! I was so captivated by the moment: under the widest star-filled evening sky that I can remember, in the backyard of Baldwin's villa at St. Paul, drunk on conversation, burgundy, and a peasant stew, drunk on the fact that James Baldwin and Josephine Baker were seated on my right and left. It was my twenty-second summer; a sublime awe, later that evening, led me to tears.

Those few days in the south of France probably had more to do with my subsequent career as a literary critic than any other single event. At the time, I was a correspondent at the London bureau of *Time* magazine, a training that is, probably, largely responsible for the quantity of my later critical writing, and for its anecdotal opening paragraphs. I had just graduated from Yale College in June, as a Scholar of the House in History. *Time*, to even my great surprise, had hired me to work as a correspondent during the six month collective vacations at the University of Cambridge. I figured that I would "read" philosophy or literature at Cambridge, take the M.A. degree, then join permanently the staff at *Time*.

So, I sailed to Southampton from New York on the *France* in June, 1973. After a week of pure fright and anxiety—after all, what *does* a *Time* correspondent *do*?, and *how*?—I decided to go for my fantasy. I proposed doing a story on "Black Expatriates," perhaps every young Afro-American would-be-intellectual's dream. To my astonishment, the story suggestion was approved. So, off we (Sharon Adams, to whom I am married, and I) went by boat, train, and automobile to Europe, in search of blackness and black people.

In the Paris bureau of *Time*—Paris was the only logical point of departure, after all—I dialed Jo Baker's phone number. (*Time* can get to virtually *anyone*.) She answered her own phone! Stumbling around, interrupting my tortured speech with loads of "uh's" and "um's," I asked her if she would allow me to interview her. On one condition, she responded: "Bring Jimmy Baldwin with you to Monte Carlo." Not missing a beat, I promised that I would bring him with me.

Baldwin agreed to see me, after I had begged one of his companions and told him that I was heading south anyway to see Jo Baker. Cecil Brown, the companion told me, was living there as well, so maybe I could interview him as well? Cecil Brown, I thought. Def-i-nite-ly! (*Jiveass Nigger* had been a cult classic among us younger nationalists in the early seventies.) So, off we went.

Imagine sitting on a train, from Paris to Nice, on the hottest night of August, 1973, wondering how I could drag Baldwin from St. Paul to Monte Carlo, and scared to death of Baldwin in the first place. It was a thoroughly Maalox evening; to top everything else, our train broke down in a tunnel. We must have lost twenty pounds in that tunnel. Finally, just after dawn, we arrived at Nice, rented a car, then drove the short distance to St. Paul.

After the best midday meal that I had ever eaten, before or since, I trekked with great trepidation over to Baldwin's "house." "When I grow up . . . ," I remember thinking as I walked through the gate. I won't bore you with details; suffice it to say that if you ever get the chance to have dinner with Jimmy Baldwin at his house at St. Paul, then *do* it. "Maybe I could write *Notes of a Native Son* if I lived here," I thought.

I am about to confess something that literary critics should not confess: James Baldwin *was* literature for me, especially the essay. No doubt like everyone who is reading these pages, I started reading "black books" avidly, voraciously, at the age of thirteen or fourteen. I read *everything* written by black authors that could be ordered from Red Bowl's paper store in Piedmont, West Virginia. LeRoi Jones's *Home* and *Blues People*, Malcolm's *Autobiography*, and *Invisible Man* moved me beyond words—beyond my own experience, which is even a further piece, I would suppose. But nothing could surpass my love for the Complete Works of James Baldwin. In fact; I have never before written about Baldwin just because I cannot read his words outside of an extremely personal nexus of adolescent sensations and emotions. "Poignancy" only begins to describe those feelings. I learned to love written literature, of any sort, through the language of James Baldwin.

When Baldwin came into the garden to be interviewed, I was so excited that I could not blink back the tears. That probably explains why he suggested that we begin with wine. Well into that first (of several) bottles, I confessed to him my promise to Jo Baker. Not missing a beat, he told me to bring Jo *here*. Did he think that she would drive back from Monte Carlo with me? Just tell her that dinner is served at nine.

And she did, after a warm and loving lunch with her family (we met *eleven* of the legendary twelve children), at her favorite restaurant overlooking Cape Martin. She had recently returned from a pilgrimage to Israel, and was looking forward to her return to the stage, her marvelous comeback. She was tall, as gracious and as warm as she was elegant, sensuous at sixty-five. Pablo this; Robeson that; Salvador so and so: she had been friends with the Western tradition, and its modernists. Everywhere we drove, people waved from the sidewalks or ran over to the car. She was so very *thoughtful*, so intellectual, and so learned of the sort of experience that, perhaps, takes six decades or so to ferment. I cannot drink a glass of Cantenac Brown without recreating her in its bouquet.

How did all of this lead to my present career? *Time* would not print the story, because, they said, "Baldwin is passé, and Baker a memory of the thirties and forties." My narrative remains unpublished, but shall appear in a new essay collection called *With the Flow*. When I went "up" to Cambridge from *Time* and London in October 1973, I was so angered by the idiocy of that decision that I threw myself into the B.A. curriculum for English Language and Literature. A year later, I was admitted into the Ph.D. program, and four years later, I was awarded my degree.

That evening was the very last time that my two heroes saw each other, and the last time that Jo Baker would be interviewed at her home. She would die, on the stage, too soon thereafter. One day I hope to be forced to write about my other hero, James Baldwin.—HLG

Gates: Mrs. Baker, why did you leave the United States?

Baker: I left in 1924, but the roots extend long before that. One of the first things I remember was the East St. Louis Race Riots (1906). I was hanging on to my mother's skirts, I was so little. All the sky was red with people's houses burning. On the bridge, there were running people with their tongues cut out. There was a woman who'd been pregnant with her insides cut out. That was the beginning of my feeling.

One day I realized I was living in a country where I was afraid to be black. It was only a country for white people, not black, so I left. I had been suffocating in the United States. I can't live anywhere that I can't breathe freedom. I must be free. Haven't I that right? I was created free. No chains did I wear when I came here. A lot of us left, not because we wanted to leave, but because we couldn't stand it anymore. Branded, banded, cut off. Canada Lee, Dr. Du Bois, Paul Robeson, Marcus Garvey—all of us, forced to leave.

Gates: Did the French people offer you a respite from race prejudice?

Baker: The French adopted me immediately. They all went to the beaches to get dark like Josephine Baker. They had a contest to see who could be the darkest, like Josephine Baker, they said. The French got sick, trying to get black—café au lait—you weren't anything unless you were café au lait.

I felt liberated in Paris. People didn't stare at me. But when I heard an American accent in the streets of Paris, I became afraid. I would tremble in my stomach. I was afraid they'd humiliate me.

I was afraid to go into prominent restaurants in Paris. Once, I dined in a certain restaurant with friends. An American lady looked at our table and called the waiter. "Tell her to get out," the lady said. "In my country, she is belonging only in the kitchen." The French management asked the American lady to leave. To tell the truth, I was afraid of not being wanted.

Gates: Mr. Baldwin, when did you leave the United States and for what reasons?

Baldwin: It was November, 1948, Armistice Day as a matter of fact. I left because I was a writer. I had discovered writing and I had a family to save. I had only one weapon to save them, my writing. And I couldn't write in the United States.

Gates: But why did you flee to France?

Baldwin: I had to go somewhere where I could learn that it was possible for me to thrive as a writer. The French, you see, didn't see me; on the other hand, they watched me. Some people took care of me. Else I would have died. But the French left me alone.

Gates: Was it important for you to be left alone?

Baldwin: The only thing standing between my writing had to be me: it was I, it was me—I had to see that. Because the French left me alone, I was freed of crutches, the crutches of race. That's a scary thing.

Gates: Did you find any basic differences between Americans and Europeans, since you said that you could at least be left alone in Paris?

Baldwin: There was a difference, but now the difference is a superficial one. When I first came to Paris, it was poor—everybody was broke. Now, Europe thinks it has something again, that it has regained the material things it lost. So Europeans are becoming Americans. The irony, of course, is that Europe began the trend even before America was formed. The price of becoming "American" is beating the hell out of everybody else.

Gates: Mrs. Baker, you said you felt "liberated" in France. Did the freedom you found here in France sour you towards the United States?

Baker: I love the country within which I was born. These people are my people. I don't care what color they are—we are all Americans. We must have the application to stand up again.

Once I fought against the discriminatory laws in America but America was strong then. Now, she is weak. I only want to extend my fingers to pull it out of the quicksand, because that's where it is. I have all the hope· in the world, though. The storm will come; we can't stop it. But that's all right. America will still be—but it will be the America it was intended to be. We were a small train on the track. We fell off. We'll get on again.

Gates: Where do you think the United States is heading, with distrust in government so apparent, with Watergate attracting worldwide attention?

Baker: America was the promised land. I just want to give them my spirit; they've lost the path. That makes me suffer. I was so unhappy in the United States; I saw my brothers and sisters so afraid. The problem is deep—it has long roots. It is basic. The soil must be purified, not only must the root be pruned. It makes me unhappy to think that—I wouldn't be human if I weren't made unhappy by that. Needlessly, people will suffer. They need someone who can give them more than money. Someone to offer his hand, not just his money.

Gates: Mr. Baldwin, do you think that Watergate is a new, a significant departure in American history, or do you think it is the logical extension of policies begun long before Nixon, before this century even?

Baldwin: Simply stated, Watergate was a bunch of incompetent hoods who got caught in the White House in the name of law and order.

Gates: Do you think the public hearings, indictments, and possible convictions could purge America, could allow it to change those things which you do not like about it?

Baldwin: America is my country. Not only am I fond of it, I love it. America would change itself if it could, if that change didn't hurt, but people rarely change. Take the German people, for example. The German experiment during the war was catastrophic. It was a horror not to be believed. But they haven't changed: the German nation is basically the same today as it was before the war.

In a different sense, it is easy to be a rebel at age eighteen; it is harder to be one at age twenty-five. A nation may change when it realizes it has to. But people don't give up things. They have things taken away from them. One does not give up a lover; you lose her.

Gates: What do you see as the significance of Vietnam to America?

Baker: I won't criticize America today. She is weak. I said all this years ago. It all came true. But it is never too late. It can be saved, but we Americans are so proud—false dignity, though. It's nothing to be ashamed about to acknowledge our mistakes; Vietnam was a mistake. All that money for no progress, that turned the whole world against America.

But actually, My Lai happened first with the Indians. We brought on our own enemies—nobody, no matter how powerful, needs enemies.

Gates: Did you ever regret that you had left the United States, or did you ever feel guilty, particularly during the Civil Rights Era, for not being there to participate?

Baker: Some of my own people called me an Uncle Tom; they said I was more French than the French. I've thought often about your question, about running away from the problem. At first, I wondered if it was cowardice, wondered whether I should have stayed to fight. But I couldn't have done anything. I would have been thwarted in ways in which I was free in France. I probably would have been killed.

But really, I belong to the world now. You know, America represented that: people coming from all over to make a nation. But America has forgotten that. I love all people at the same time. Our country is people of all countries. How else could there have been an America? And they made a beautiful nation. Each one depositing a little of his own beauty.

It's a sad thing to leave your country. How very often I've felt like the Wandering Jew with my twelve children on my arms. I've been able to bear it, though. It might be a mistake to love my country where brothers are humiliated, where they kill each other, but I do love it. We are a wealthy people, a cultivated people. I wish people there would love. They can't go on like that. There's going to be a horrible storm. It's going to be a disaster. They'll torture each other through hate. It's ironic: people ran from slavery in Europe to find freedom in America, and now. . . .

Gates: Why don't you return to live in America now; aren't things a lot better for blacks?

Baker: I don't think I could help America. I want to be useful, where I can help. America is desperate. In New York last year, I regretted for the first time not being young again. Young Americans need understanding and love. Children don't want to hear words; they want to see examples, not words—not blah, blah, blah—profound love, without malice, without hate.

Gates: When did you eventually return to the United States and why?

Baker: It was in 1963; I kept reading about the "March on Washington," about preparation for the march. I so much wanted to attend. But I was afraid they wouldn't let me.

You see, for years I was not allowed to enter the United States. They said I was a Communist, during President Eisenhower's administration. They would make a black soldier—to humiliate me—they would make a black soldier lead me from a plane to a private room. It was so terrible, so painful. But I survived.

Then, in 1963, we applied to President Kennedy for permission to go to the March on Washington. He issued me a permanent visa. I wore the uniform I went through the war with, with all its medals. Thank God for John Kennedy for helping me get into America.

They had humiliated me so much; but still, I love them as if nothing happened. They didn't know what they were doing—digging their own grave through their hate. Then came Vietnam.

Gates: So you were actually forbidden to return to the United States between 1924 and 1963?

Baker: Yes. They said I was a Communist because I dared love—thrown out for preferring freedom to riches, feelings to gold. I am not to be sold; no one can buy me. I lost America; I had nothing in my pockets, but I had my soul. I was so rich. For all this, they called me a Communist. America drives some of its most sensitive people away. Take Jimmy Baldwin: he had to leave the States to say what he felt.

Gates: And what were your first impressions of life in "exile"?

Baldwin: I was no longer a captive nigger. I was the exotic attraction of the beast no longer in the cage. People paid attention. Of course you must realize that I am remembering the impression years later.

Gates: Did life abroad give you any particular insight into American society?

Baldwin: I realized that the truth of American history was not and had never been in the White House. The truth is what had happened to black people, since slavery.

Gates: What do you think characterized Europeans to make them more ready to accept you at a time when you felt uncomfortable living in America?

Baker: America has only been around for less than four hundred years; that's not a long time, really. Apparently it takes more than that to realize that a human being is a human being. Europeans are more basic. They see colors of the skin as colors of nature, like the flowers, for example.

Gates: Did you find any difference between the manner in which French men and women viewed you as a black man?

Baldwin: That's a very important question. Before the Algerian war, and that's crucial in this, the black man did not exist in the French imagination; neither did the Algerian. After Dien Bien Phu, and after the "Civil War" as the French persist in calling it, there began to be a discernible difference between the way women and police had treated you before and after the war.

Gates: But were black Americans treated like Algerians were during their quest for independence?

Baldwin: Of course I was removed, but you became a personal threat as a black American. You were a threat because you were visible. The French became conscious of your visibility because of the Algerians. You see, the French did not and don't know what a black man is. They'd like to put the blacks against the Algerians, to divide and rule, but the Arabs and black Americans were both slaves, one group was the slaves in Europe, the other back in America.

Gates: But surely you must believe that social change can come, that great men can effect change?

Baldwin: Change does come, but not when or in the ways we want it to come. George Jackson, Malcolm X—now people all over the world were changed by them. Because they told the secret; now, the secret was out.

Gates: And the secret?

Baldwin: Put it this way. In 1968, along with Lord Caradon (British Delegate to the United Nations then), I addressed an assembly of the World Council of Churches in Switzerland on "white racism or world community?" When Lord Caradon was asked why the West couldn't break relations with South Africa, he brought out charts and figures that showed that the West would be bankrupt if they did that: the prosperity of the

West is standing on the back of the South African miner. When he stands up, the whole thing will be over.

Gates: How do you assess the results of the war in Vietnam on the American people?

Baldwin: Americans are terrified. For the first time they know that they are capable of genocide. History is built on genocide. But they can't face it. And it doesn't make any difference what Americans think that they think—they are terrified.

Gates: From your vantage point, where do you think not only America but Western Civilization is heading?

Baldwin: The old survivals of my generation will be wiped out. Western Civilization is heading for an apocalypse.

SOURCE: Henry Louis Gates, Jr., "An Interview with Josephine Baker and James Baldwin." *The Southern Review* 21, no. 3–4 (1985).

THE FUTURE OF AFRICA:
SOYINKA AND GATES

THIS INTERVIEW WITH Nobel Laureate Wole Soyinka was originally published in 2008 by The Root.com, where Henry Louis Gates, Jr., is editor in chief. This is a transcription of portions of the video interview.

Henry Louis Gates, Jr.: How are Nigerians, and indeed other Africans, reacting to the candidacy of Barack Obama for the presidency of the United States?

Wole Soyinka: The fire, when I was in Nigeria lately, the fire has not caught on within the nation, but I can tell you that Nigerians in this country [the U.S.] are rooting like blazes for Obama. They've set up . . . I know those who contributed campaign funds up to the maximum that individuals are allowed to pay. I know that caucuses are there. They write to the campaign team. And no, no, the enthusiasm is very, very high there, high here [in the U.S.]. And it's beginning to percolate into the mother continent.

Gates: How much of a difference do you think the election of a black president will make to American policy towards Africa, or indeed to anything?

Soyinka: I don't know about American policy towards Africa on its own, but in terms of world politics and the relationship of the United States to the rest of the world, I think that the election of Obama stands a chance of assisting the American nation to recover its prestige and its high regarding it once had, many, many years, many decades ago, so long ago I cannot remember, in the world. The idea of, not the descendant of a slave, but at least a descendant of a slave continent, rising to the pinnacle of power in the United States, it says something to the rest of the world, and even to the leadership of the rest of the world, about America on which many, many nations had given up ages ago. And Americans have been looked at with the kind of—no, it won't be an immediate sense of respect, but there would be a new regarding. And there is the

566

possibility, also, of a change of policies at a very high level in many troubled parts of the world, and I'm referring especially to the Middle East and the Arab World. Of course, there are also, there are some dictators who will be very alarmed by the possibility of an even more, of a liberal attitude towards things like democracy and so on and so forth, now championed, now championed by somebody of African descent. So there are those complexities which are very interesting to study, as it unravels. But I believe that, in the interest of the United States, I hope that, and others of the world, incidentally, that Obama gets the ticket.

Gates: Should [Robert] Mugabe and his generals be subject to war crimes charges?

Soyinka: I believe that a lesson has got to be made to discourage others. It's not enough to put people like Charles Taylor on trial. I mean, his crimes were obvious. There are far more subtle ways of degrading a people, even in this case it wasn't all that subtle. When you take a bulldozer to the homes of your opposition, and you just turn living, teeming areas into deserts overnight, simply because they disagree with your political policy, that is a crime against humanity, and I believe that people like Mugabe should be tried for crimes against humanity, yes.

Gates: South Africa, Russia, China, all voted to block sanctions in the Security Council against Zimbabwe, but sanctions were certainly significant in helping to end apartheid. Why were sanctions OK then and not now?

Soyinka: Well, you must ask Thabo Mbeki that. Maybe he has an answer to that very profound question. Why were sanctions all right then, but not against Mugabe? Is it because Mugabe is black? Shall we then say that we should let Charles Taylor go free, where we put Radovan Karadzic on trial?

Gates: Oh, the doctor with the white beard, Santa Claus. [*laughter*]

Soyinka: What a character. [*laughter*] So we put all those on trial, but somehow African leaders and their government should be subject to double standards. I mean, what are these people talking about? I don't understand it. I find the conduct of China is not as surprising, because China is onto a business trajectory right now and is not looking right or left. [*laughter*] And the Soviet Union doesn't surprise me too much. That's now a dictatorship masquerading under Putin, masquerading as a democracy. The democratic gains, the struggle, the heroism—and it was heroism, of even people like Khrushchev, those who began this mountain before you come to the latter, Gorbachev and the others—the heroism, the courage of those people is being treated like rubbish, being trivialized by characters like Putin. So we now have a dynastic situation, in which one individual puts his clone on the throne and continues to whittle down the freedoms which were gained at such a terrible risk, and in some cases terrible prices.

Gates: How do we end the carnage in Darfur?

Soyinka: The carnage in Darfur and the entire situation in Darfur can be ended by two major groups. We have a situation in Sudan where Sudan is a member of various organizations, the African Union, the Arab League, the United Nations. Primary responsibility rests with the African Union. Sudan is a test case. The African Union says it has a peer mechanism—this is one of its boasts—a peer mechanism for examining and for judging the conduct of members, leaders in that case. They meet in caucus somewhere. They scratch each other on the back. Heaven knows what they say. But they don't do it out in the open. Now, if they brought their peer mechanism processes out in the open, in which the government of Sudan is indicted openly, its conduct is indicted, then, of course, the government is subject to censure by not just the governments of the African Continent, but by the people themselves, because they see what they stand to see on what basis this judgment has been made. And then there becomes, . . . the people will have the right to impose a moral compulsion on the African Union to act against Omar al-Bashir. That's number one. Second, Sudan belongs to the Arab League. The Arab League has a responsibility to call Sudan to order, to actually accuse Sudan openly, to break with Sudan, for everyone to see that even his second tier or family relationship has disowned him, has disowned that government, has disowned and condemned that conduct. And this, then, gives the United Nations an additional fillip for acting, living up to its responsibilities in the Sudan, because the United Nations calls on various nations to act as peace keepers, as peace enforcers in other nations. We have Nigerians who are serving in Lebanon . . .

Gates: Absolutely.

Soyinka: . . . who are serving in the Balkans and so on. Why on Earth is the Sudan being treated like some little backwater kind of third rate, third level member of the United Nations family? So these are three groupings which have a primary responsibility. But the first one is African Union. African Union should expel Sudan. Expel Sudan, and then the Arab League should also expel Sudan. So you turn that state into a pariah, a complete pariah, which becomes fair game and places a mandatory moral responsibility to all the nations, to sanction, to boycott, and in fact to harass militarily where necessary, where possible the forces of the government of Sudan.

Gates: Do you have any thoughts on the war crime indictment of the President of Sudan, Omar al-Bashir?

Soyinka: Well, as you know, well, you might know or not remember, that we did put him on trial. This is Omar al-Bashir. We had a kind of symbolic trial of him in New York. The Genocide Watch organized it, and I was in fact the judge, the principal judge. [*laughter*] I knew you'd laugh at that. But it was a very solemn occasion. And it was staged deliberately in this huge hall just opposite the United Nations, so that, and this was on the third floor, third or fourth floor, and with a background. There was a wide window behind us. So you had all the flags of the nations fluttering in the background. And witnesses were flown directly from Sudan, and some were taken, some were already refugees in this country or in other places. There were victims of torture. There were doctors. You had foreign journalists, some of whom, one of whom, in fact, had been imprisoned by the Sudanese authorities because he went where they did not want him to go. And the charges, in fact . . . Omar al-Bashir was represented by a lawyer, not of his own choosing, but we found a lawyer for him, since he didn't answer our charges. And it was symbolic. It was a ritual, if you like. It was play acting, if you like. But it was dead serious. And in fact, his—Omar al-Bashir's—advocates put up a very strong case for him. In fact, I think they got carried away, because they are professional lawyers, and they didn't want to seem to be playing into the hands of the judgment which everybody expected and wanted. And he was found guilty, of course, on all charges, and the result was sent, the decision was sent to the United Nations, to various governments and to human rights organizations all over the world. So there's already material, even from the amateur section, before we talk about the findings of UN representatives who have been sent to respond. And already there are some sealed indictments against some of his officials. I don't know if these include Omar al-Bashir. But Omar al-Bashir certainly should be declared a war criminal and should be seized wherever he is and put on trial.

Gates: Well, are you proposing a 21st century version of the Congress of Berlin?

Soyinka: What is wrong with having this time an internally organized, quote unquote, Congress of Berlin undertaken by free peoples in their own interest for their own future, recognizing the fact that they've been leading a false life? They've been living an externally donated existence. And I'm talking about political structures, contests of ideologies, all foreign contests. No. We've been playing surrogate to the ideologies of others, economic policies, even down to architectural ideology. I mean, you look at the architectural face of the African continent. What do you see? You could be in New York in many instances. And they move straight from those New York skyscrapers to the most degrading kind of slums you ever encountered.

Gates: Yes.

Soyinka: And so, the idea of starting all over might sound formidable and daunting. But I ask you, what, when you compare it to what is happening in the Congo today, what more or less is coming to an end on the West African coast in formally quiet, democratic Ivory Coast, in Liberia, in Sierra Leone, and when you look at the destruction of Sierra Leone, beautiful Sierra Leone, and the degradation of the youthful generation, the dehumanizing . . . I mean, we've lost generations to this dehumanizing. Can you think of anything worse than that, actually removing, depriving youth of their humanity from the age of eight, nine, ten? And so, when I look at the option, when I look at what seems to be an impossible task, and when I look at what the AU, which succeeded the Organization of African Unity, when I think of what is not happening there, I think that the time may be better occupied with sitting down and saying, OK, let's go back to that moment, and let us see if some of the problems we're having, including civil wars, interminable civil wars, Eritrea, Congo, Kinshasa tomorrow, sections of the one Congo moving into the other, to go and sort them out there. And in turn, they in turn go in through the back door to go and sort the other side out. When you think of internal problems, you think of Niger and Nigeria, the Niger Delta, the oil-producing delta, in which this oil-producing area, which has been absolutely savaged by oil exploration, with the collaboration of the center, with the collaboration of those in power at the center. Is Nigeria a nation? Or is it just something we describe as a nation space? And what these people in the Delta Region are asking for today? They're raising the stakes all the time, from resource control, which is denied for so many decades, moving towards increased autonomy. Many of the more radical are now saying, listen, we want our own nation. We want complete independence. We want to go back to the kind of nation states that existed . . . , I mean, this is a very extreme position, but I'm just telling you what is the thinking in many areas, out of sheer generational frustration. So while on the one hand, yes, I agree, it's a very daunting task, you look at what is on the ground right now. It's an impossibility.

Gates: It's been what seems like, to me as a literary critic, an explosion of brilliant writing by women on the African continent, and more particularly by Nigerian women. I'm thinking mostly recently of Chimamanda

Ngozi Adichie. Do you read their works? And what do you think of them? And how do you explain this boom of energy and insight?

Soyinka: Well, it's very difficult to explain why the mantle of writers has been picked up by the women like Chimamanda Adichie, I'm talking especially fiction, mostly fiction, most competently and vibrantly. It's a phenomenon, which quite literally sociologists should go into. It could be, of course, that, because most of these writers, the more notable of them come from the East, with the experience of the civil war and the impact it made on their reflective temperaments, that they reached a stage now where they can look back on it, and this thing happened in their childhood, and the experiences and the—

Gates: Sometimes before they were born.

Soyinka: In some cases before they were born. But their stories, and their parents went through it, and they learned to understand the impact. And so very often there's a theme, even if the theme is submerged under the study of humanity in general. There's a theme. There's a theme which acts as an impetus for a certain literary surge. And . . . war could have done it in the case of the women in Nigeria. It's just a theory.

Gates: Certainly in Chimamanda Ngozi Adichie's case, that's her great theme. [*Pause.*]

Gates: I've never asked you this, but is there any resentment on the African continent that you've encountered when you see these Western figures galloping into Africa on their white horses offering to solve all the problems of poverty? I mean, people like Bono, for example? I mean, is he seen as a hero? Or is there some element of condescension or neocolonialism or resentment that accompanies those sorts of effort?

Soyinka: Well, I can assure you that there is in many areas a lot of resentment when . . . what you call the St. Georges on white chargers come in with their lances to deal definitively with the dragons of illness, of corruption, of productivity, etc. But that has to do more with attitude. It's because they come as if they have all the solutions. They don't come as prospective partners in a mutual enterprise for the advancement of humanity, in which one side of humanity has obviously been disadvantaged, owing to their various histories. It has to do a lot with attitude. For instance, I can tell you that in many, many far flung areas, there are some unsung heroes of African development. Those go into the remote areas, assess what is needed. It could be very simple things. It could be even wells, bore holes, irrigation system utilizing the sparse benefits of nature, and introducing even new methods of cultivation and so on and so forth, helping to control pests, agricultural pests and so on. And they work side by side with the people. And they are loved, they're accepted as simply partners in progress, if you like, in development. And they go back again and again and again. There's no resentment against those people. It's when people come with aid, A-I-D, organizational aid, in which those, especially those who are somewhat enlightened, see that 60% of the aid which is being offered, which has been announced to the whole world, actually goes to the payment of salaries and ameliorants and privileges of those who come in, who live in a different lifestyle completely from those who they have come to help. Now, one is not suggesting for a single moment that they should go into huts and not have some creature comforts. No, no, no. We're talking about literally what are called bureaucratic aid, which is what you see bureaucracy sitting on top of a minimum resource.

Gates: Mercedes, servants. . . .

Soyinka: You understand. That really is where the problem lies. And the whole attitude is very patronizing, very condescending. It's like, "you people." You know? "You people." You should know that this is what I mean, that "you people" attitude, separating yourself already from those who you've come to assist. [*Pause.*]

Soyinka: Let's take the African American attitude first. When Richburg, that's his name, I think, Richburg?

Gates: Keith Richburg.

Soyinka: When he wrote that book, *Out of America: A Black Man Confronts Africa*, it was a nasty book, because it was nasty not because it told the truth, but because it revealed a very disgusting level of self-hate. If Richburg had left out the self-hate, I would have recommended that book as a primer for African Americans for an introspective look at their own history, and at the history of the country, the nation, the continent, [at those who] collaborated in selling them into the trade basket of the European world. See, African Americans must first of all come to terms with the level of guilt of their own peoples in their transportation across the Atlantic, across the Sahara. They have been turned into nothing but cattle and beasts of burden.

Gates: You're talking about the black African [role in the trans-Atlantic slave trade].

Soyinka: I'm [saying that] African Americans must go back [to this history]. Then, if they confront that history, they will find no surprise whatsoever. They are the same people. Their descendants, their kin, their mental kin, are treating their own people in exactly the same way. Only this time, it's a bit difficult to sell us into slavery to go and join African Americans where they are today. All they have to do is examine that history very,

very carefully, and they would have no problem in recognizing the real nature of the Idi Amins or the Bokassas, Mugabe, Sani Abacha, etc. It's the simplest exercise.

Gates: Black on black oppression, continuous.

Soyinka: Continuous, continuous. And they've just got to come to terms with that and stop. They must mature beyond the point of saying, these are my immediate oppressors. There are no other oppressors. Yes, they must confront their immediate oppressors. They must demand their complete fundamental human rights, economic rights, political rights wherever they happen to be. But they must stop thinking . . . they must move beyond believing that there are no oppressors of humanity outside the ones who are really stepping on their toes in their immediate environment. That's one way of dealing once and for all with this very irritating and sometimes very dispiriting attitude of African Americans towards what we are undergoing on the African continent. We feel a kind of double betrayal when that happens, when, for instance, embassies opened here to support Idi Amin over on that side.

Gates: That's embarrassing.

Soyinka: I mean, it's very embarrassing.

Gates: In the name of black nationalism.

Soyinka: Black nationalism, never mind the color of the boots. That boot is on my neck. I want it off. [*laughter*]

Gates: Let's talk about Africa since 1960. Even I, who was ten years old in 1960, the great year of African independence, even I was infected by the enthusiasm, sense of hope, the optimism that finally our people on the continent were taking over. They were kicking the Europeans out. It was going to be a new day. Almost a new kind of human being. Democracy would come to the continent, both political democracy and economic democracy. What's happened to that dream?

Soyinka: I mean, the reality we have to face is that they never really left. The Europeans, the colonial powers, never really left Africa. We have expressions like neocolonialism, neoimperialism, etc., which, of course, are cultural phrases, but what is the reality? The reality is that in leaving the French, the British, the Portuguese left behind in many cases their surrogates to carry on this time what I call the internal colonial adventure. They left behind those who would continue to execute their own policies, to maintain a relationship, a subservient relationship, even though [it looks] very glitzy on the surface. All the leaders went around with their . . . long limousines, and they were seen in international caucuses sweeping in with their huge entourage. And it looked as if they were receiving egalitarian treatment and relationship. But this was not the truth. Take Nigeria, for instance. Take Nigeria. We have the incredible admission these days, now open, because many of us have known it for quite a while, from colonial officers who admit that when the British left in 1960, before they left, they made sure that they falsified not merely the electoral process that handed over power to that section, the less advanced section of the nation, but they even falsified the census, the national census. And one of these officers used the expression, he said, what are they talking about, Nigerian politicians rigging the election? He said, it was we, the British, who taught them how to rig it. It's there in black and white in his document. He was a colonial officer at the time, giving instructions to rig the elections in favor of the less advanced section of the nation.

Gates: By which you mean the North, the Muslim.

Soyinka: In this particular case, yes, the North, the feudal, I'll use the expression, feudal, the feudal part, the less progressive in political ideological terms, less advanced, even economically, because the productive mechanisms, modern productive mechanisms, which were adopted by many newly independent African countries lagged, shall we say, lagged a little bit behind in those areas. And that's what's happened. And of course, the first comers into these stakes of power, once they were there, they were determined to make sure nobody else feasted at that board. And this, I'm afraid, is a story which has been repeated throughout many countries on the African continent.

SOURCE: The Root.com, October 25, 2008.

A CONVERSATION WITH CONDOLEEZZA RICE

On Leadership

CONDOLEEZZA RICE IS the Thomas and Barbara Stephenson Senior Fellow on Public Policy at the Hoover Institution, professor of political economy in the Stanford Graduate School of Business, and professor of political science at Stanford University. She served as the 66th Secretary of State of the United States from 2005 to 2009 in the administration of President George W. Bush.

Henry Louis Gates, Jr.: Secretary of State Condoleezza Rice, thank you very much for granting me this interview.

Condoleezza Rice: It's a pleasure to be with you.

Gates: How do you define a leader?

Rice: A leader is someone who inspires others toward a common goal. The most important thing about leadership is to remember that you are trying to bring people together to achieve something. And none of us wants to be pushed and shoved in any particular direction, so if you treat the people that you're leading with the same respect with which you would like to be treated, then I think you are a good leader.

Gates: Are leaders chosen or are leaders made?

Rice: I think leaders are made. I have never believed that anyone is born to anything. And leadership is also something that I think you get better at over time. In many experiences, as a younger person trying to lead a university or leading people, you make mistakes because you're young and maybe a little too aggressive. I think leaders are not only made, but they get better at leading over time.

Gates: Let's talk about that idea with regard to your own upbringing. When I looked at your family pictures, I particularly noticed the way your parents looked at you. They seemed to be looking at someone who was going to be a major player, going to be a leader. Is that a self-fulfilling prophecy, do you think, the kind of reinforcement through self-esteem that is part of the air that you breathe?

Rice: There is no doubt that without John and Angelina Rice, I would not have ended up where I did. I grew up in the segregated South where the messages could have been absolutely crushing, but somehow my parents made the messages about empowerment, which is no small trick in and of itself. They also, from a very young age, wanted me to understand that I should want to make decisions. So I was president of the family from age four. I remembered this as I was writing my book and I thought, 'What in the world were they thinking?' I think they were just trying to give me a sense that even in the family context, it was all right for this four-year-old to have real responsibilities and to carry them out.

Gates: Your parents are just extraordinary. Did you find that your friends had a similar relationship of intimacy and equality, given the limits, with their parents? Was it a class thing or was it unique to your parents?

Rice: I suppose it was, in part, a class thing. I think in middle class Birmingham, in the little enclave in which we lived, Titusville, most of the families, fortunately, were two-parent families in which both men and women worked. So girls received early signals that they could have a profession, could have a career. Most of my friends, just like my parents, gave me every opportunity and, in fact, some opportunities you didn't even want—to play in recitals and to stand up and give little speeches. That was all part of the ether in Birmingham. But of course, I was an only child. I've always said it is easier to be an only child than to be a parent of an only child; [*laughter*] when the friends go away and the little one needs somebody to play with, the parent has to stand in. So probably the real difference is that I lived in a more adult world than my friends did. They had siblings. They could go home and play with those siblings. My parents had to be my playmates after dark.

Gates: So this little girl, who was reared on the idea that strength and discipline and leadership were expected of you, grew up to be Provost of Stanford University and U.S. Secretary of State! More than anyone else I know, you have had an opportunity to observe leaders in action. What makes a good leader? Can you give an example of someone who has been a model for you of leadership?

Rice: A good leader has to have a vision of where they are leading people. If you don't know where you're going, then you're not going to be able to bring others around a common goal and a common vision. But that vision has to be, on the one hand, realistic. It can't be pie-in-the-sky or people won't warm to it. They will ridicule it. On the other hand, if the vision is too confined to the world as it is and doesn't have a strong sense of the world as it should be, then it's not inspiring. So I have always found that the best leaders are people who have that vision that pushes people to think about what is possible, but shows them a realistic way to get there. And I have been fortunate to see a lot of great leaders.

One of the strongest leaders I ever encountered was the woman who is currently the president of Liberia, Ellen Johnson Sirleaf. When you talk to her about Liberia, and you are standing in Liberia, you say to yourself 'what is she seeing?' I remember when we first went to Liberia after she had been inaugurated as president. I was there for her inauguration. It was an extraordinary event. But we were going up to her office, which I think was on the fifth floor, and the elevator simply quit. It just stopped because electricity was so rare in Liberia. And she, very proudly, said, 'Oh, don't worry. The next time you come, that'll be fixed.' So this is somebody who, in these very dire circumstances, has painted a vision for the future that I think Liberians are warming to and are inspired by. We sometimes decry vision and we talk about people as being too idealistic, but if you are not an idealist, if you're not an optimist, then you can't lead.

Gates: So one needs to be an idealist sufficient to paint the dream and a pragmatist sufficient to create the pathway to the dream.

Rice: That's right. And very often you will find people who are good at one or the other, but not at both. The best leaders are people who are good at both.

Gates: How long were you trapped in that elevator?

Rice: Well, fortunately, we were able to kind of pry it open. [*laughter*] Then we had to walk five flights of stairs in the Liberian heat. That wasn't much fun either. Because the air conditioning was also long gone.

Gates: If leaders can be made, which you said they can, what are some of the important lessons, from your experience, that you would offer to an aspiring leader, particularly in the Black community?

Rice: Well, I very often encounter young people and they say, 'I want to be a leader.' In my opinion, that is the wrong place to start. The first questions to ask are 'What am I passionate about? What do I care about? What am I going to learn enough about to actually have something to say about it?' And then an aspiring leader should ask him or herself, 'How am I going to acquire that knowledge and that expertise so that I'm not just talking through my hat?' as we might have said where I grew up in Alabama. And once you have started on that path, you can have early leadership experiences by taking on hard jobs. If there is something somebody doesn't want to do, you do it. And do it with a lot of vigor and a lot of enthusiasm. And that is a great leadership experience.

Gates: It's like Booker T. Washington, sweeping the room . . .

Rice: Absolutely. Because I am a professor, I often reflect on how to talk about these issues with young people. I have had students say, 'I don't want an internship where I'm just going to be stuffing envelopes.' And I say 'Well, perhaps when you start that internship, all you are capable of doing is stuffing envelopes. But as you demonstrate that you're more and more capable, you will get greater and greater responsibility.' Those who emerge as leaders are people who have demonstrated that they can take responsibility in the hardest circumstances, mobilize others, and move them forward.

Gates: Let's talk about young people a bit more. I know how deeply troubled you are, as am I, about the fact that seventy percent of Black children are born to a single mother. When you were talking earlier about the nuclear family in your neighborhood, not only did your friends have two parents who lived together, but they both worked. So did I, in West Virginia. How do we translate these lessons for future generations? Particularly, those lessons about entrepreneurial leadership for the large part of the Black community that was not privileged to be raised in the environments in which you and I were raised?

Rice: Well, unfortunately, the nuclear family is still in decline. The data get worse, not better. And we cannot simply sacrifice the kids who find themselves in that condition by saying we really should be trying to build nuclear families. We should be. But for children who are not fortunate enough to have that, some adult—a minister or a teacher—needs to step in and advocate for that child. No ten-, fourteen- or eighteen-year-old is going to be able to navigate the complexities of life in America alone, particularly life in America for a minority kid. In many communities, even when I was growing up, it was a teacher who would step into the role of advocate or mentor. While my community was middle class and we had two-parent families, not every community in Birmingham was middle class. My parents and their friends, as teachers, very often took on responsibilities for helping isolated kids to navigate the world. I tell a story in *Extraordinary, Ordinary People* about my father, a Presbyterian minister, and the youth fellowship at his Black middle-class church. Behind that church was a government project called Loveman Village, where two-parent families were less common and parents were often not educated people. Kids from all over the community came to youth fellowship. I later teased my father that the reason his youth fellowship was so popular was because he was a Presbyterian minister and so he could host dances. The Baptists couldn't. [*laughter*] But in that youth fellowship, my father and the church sent messages: 'Your kid is smart. Your child ought to go to college. I've got a scholarship for your child from Spelman College or Knoxville College. And I want your kid to go to college. Your daughter or your son.' So, it is not ideal if there has to be a substitute for the nuclear family, but in our world, we may have to rely on others to advocate for those children.

Gates: It takes a village.

Rice: It does take a village.

Gates: You have learned a great deal from these different communities you've inhabited: segregated Alabama, the academy, the White House. You must have observed many different leadership styles. Did you deliberately set out to emulate or adopt a particular style of leadership?

Rice: I believe that you learn a lot about leadership as you take on leadership positions. I remember my first year as provost at Stanford. I was pretty tough. I was a thirty-eight-year-old provost. Though I had had tenure for a number of years, I had never been a department chair. Nevertheless, I was promoted to full professor in May, and to provost in June. And so—

Gates: That's amazing.

Rice: Well, the president of Stanford, Gerhard Casper, took this chance. But in those first few months, I really felt I had to assert my authority. And I did it sometimes by not delegating and not letting people do their jobs. And if something wasn't accomplished in three or four days, then there I was trying to do it for them. I had a long talk with my father in the summer after my first year as provost, and he said 'Let me tell you something. If somebody is trying to do their job, but they're not doing very well, your job as a leader is not to go do their job, but to help them figure out why they're not getting it done. Because if you don't do that, pretty soon nobody who is any good is going to work for you because they're going to be tired of you constantly taking over.' I learned a very important lesson from that. When I then became national security advisor and, particularly, secretary of state, where I had a 55,000-person department to run . . .

Gates: It's hard to micromanage that.

Rice: But I had learned that when something isn't getting done, perhaps you can intervene to help that person. That's a very different concept. It's more collaborative and more about working with people to help them remove barriers. So those are the kinds of lessons that I think you learn by having leadership experiences and maybe not doing it as well as you might the first time around.

Gates: You benefited, obviously, from great mentors, starting with your parents. I'm asked to speak in corporations all the time, particularly by minority people, about the secret to success. And I say, from my point of view, it's about finding a great mentor, being adopted by a mentor. But then they say 'Well, how do you do that?' What is your advice for finding a mentor?

Rice: Well, first to recognize that you need one. And that is the first step because the idea that anybody gets there on their own is one of the great fictions in society. Everybody needs somebody to help them navigate their course and advocate for them, to push them ahead. Secondly, you have to be pretty aggressive about finding mentors. And I know that it is ideal if you can find mentors who look like you. But it really may not be possible. Some of my most important mentors—as a matter of fact, all of my early mentors other than my parents and a few teachers—were White men. In fact, they were old White men, because they were the people who dominated the fields in which I was working: International politics, Soviet Studies. I would have been waiting a long time to find a Black female mentor in Soviet Studies. So being comfortable with the fact that they may not look like you is important. And third, trying to seek out people in whom you are interested. I very often say to my students, you know, we're a little bit vain as faculty. If you think this is somebody you're really interested in getting to know, go read something they've written. Then go talk to them about it. And try to establish a relationship. You can't be shy about seeking out mentors. Many people love to be sought out in that way and want to help, but you need to have something in mind that you would like to have them help you do; for instance, get a fellowship or an internship. Ask them 'Can I help you with that project?' I think we have made mentoring too formal a term. What we really mean is finding people who will help you out, who will think about you when a possibility comes along, and who can give you a little advice along the way.

Gates: One crucial mentor for you was Josef Korbel, Madeleine Albright's father. Could you tell us the story of how this relationship came into being?

Rice: It came about because I was a failed piano major. [*laughter*] I started playing piano when I was three years old. I went off to college to be a piano performance major, and at the end of my sophomore year in college, I went to the Aspen Music Festival School. And I met twelve-year-olds at the Aspen Music Festival School who could play from sight what it took me all year to learn. I was seventeen. I thought 'I'm about to end up teaching thirteen-year-olds to murder Beethoven for a living and that's not what I want to do.' So I went back and said to my parents 'I'm changing my major.' They said, 'What are you changing it to?' I said, 'I have no idea.' They said, 'You don't know what you want to do with your life?' I said, 'Right, it's my life.' They said, 'It's our money, find a major.' [*laughter*] And so, after a couple of false starts, one in English literature, which I didn't like, and one in local government, which I liked even less, I literally wandered into a course in international politics just thinking 'Oh, it fits into the right time slot on my schedule.' And it was taught by Josef Korbel. All of a sudden, I knew what I wanted to do. He opened up this world of international affairs and diplomacy and the Soviet Union and Russia, and it was like finding love. All of a sudden, inexplicably, for a Black girl from Birmingham, Alabama, I wanted to be a Soviet specialist. And he continued to nurture that interest. I remember giving a presentation in his class and he said, 'You should be a professor.' I remember thinking, 'Oh, come on, me a professor?' So he was a very good mentor because he kept helping me to define what I wanted to be. He didn't try to impose a view on me. He was a terrific mentor.

Gates: Were your parents supportive or did they say have you bumped your head out there in Denver? A Black Russian . . .

Rice: Exactly. [*laughter*] No, fortunately my parents didn't say 'Why in the world is a Black girl from Birmingham talking about being a Soviet specialist?' They said, 'That's great, honey, go for it.' And they were thrilled. I'm not sure they knew what a Soviet specialist did. But they were happy to support it.

Gates: You were lucky.

Rice: I *was* lucky. I used to say, when I would address parents at Stanford as provost, 'When your kid comes home and says "mom and dad, I've found it. It's Etruscan art." Don't panic. It might in fact turn out all right.' [*laughter*]

Gates: In those early days of your education and career, was there a moment when you realized that you were going to be a leader?

Rice: Oh, I still don't think of it in those terms. I think that I have had special experiences and unique circumstances. I don't think I am a particularly unique person in that regard.

Gates: You are the first Black female secretary of state.

Rice: I know, but I . . .

Gates: In history.

Rice: But it's a combination of preparation and circumstances. I was fortunate to find something I loved doing. International politics. Soviet specialist. I happened to be fortunate that a Soviet specialty was hot property in 1981, 1982, when I came out of college. I am fortunate that I met Brent Scowcroft, who would become George H. W. Bush's national security advisor. I had done my work and I had worked hard. I had learned Russian. I had done the basic research. And I had written articles that identified me as a rising young Soviet specialist. Scowcroft took me to the White House as the special assistant to President Bush for Soviet affairs, and I was fortunate to be in the right place at the right time. I got to be the Soviet specialist at the end of the Cold War, because in 1989, everything broke loose in Europe. Now, some people say serendipity. But I say, some combination of serendipity, good luck, and maybe divine intervention, [*laughter*] but that's how I see what emerged for me.

Gates: Fair enough. Does being a leader necessarily mean that you'll be isolated from those you lead?

Rice: You have to have just a little distance from those that you lead. I don't think that a leader can just be one of the gang. Sometimes you have to make really hard calls that you would not want to make with your friends. Sometimes leaders can bring everybody together around an idea and there's consensus and we can all be very happy, but sometimes a leader has to say 'All right, we've had enough discussion, this is what we're going to do.' And a little distance helps you when you have to do the second.

Gates: I feel the same way about not allowing my students to call me by my first name, which is very unpopular now. Many of my colleagues will insist, but you create this false sense of equality, of intimacy, and then you could flunk them. I think it's unfair. It confuses people.

Rice: I think it is confusing. My students call me Professor. My graduate students call me Professor, and the day that they graduate, they call me Condi.

Gates: But can a leader be loved and respected?

Rice: I think a leader can be respected. I don't know if loved is the right term. You can be admired. And I hope that as a leader, I have been admired. I do think you can be admired as someone who cares a lot about the people who work for them. And maybe that is the closest thing to being loved. You ought to care about what is happening to people, for example, if somebody's family situation is difficult. You ought to care if somebody is having difficult health issues. You ought to care if somebody is not feeling fulfilled in what they're doing. Caring about the people who work with you and for you is a very important part of leadership. And when you think about it, you would like to be cared about. You don't want people to just be cold and uncaring about what's going on in your life.

Gates: It must be very, very painful being in the White House watching the polls and seeing the President or the administration taking flack. How do you bolster a leader, at the worst time, whose feelings are hurt?

Rice: Well, it helps to have a sense of humor. And all of the leaders with whom I have worked—the two presidents with whom I've worked and even the president of Stanford—had great senses of humor about the views of the outside world about them. I was fortunate to work with people who have a firm grounding, a kind of center to themselves, so that they are not thrown off course by every headline; it makes it a lot easier to get through tough times. It is also particularly important to remember, in national and international leadership, that history has a long arc, not a short one. What people think about you today may not be what they think about you tomorrow or, most importantly, what history will think about you. I often think about Harry Truman who was perhaps, in my opinion (and I know many people will be surprised), the greatest president of the twentieth century in the United States.

Gates: Greater than Franklin Roosevelt?

Rice: Even so. Franklin Roosevelt was great for what he took the country through, of course. But from my perspective as somebody who cares about America's role in the world, it was Harry Truman that figured it out. And he did it by taking really tough decisions. When he recognized Israel in 1948, George Marshall, who was his secretary of state, told him (maybe it's apocryphal, but I think it's probably true), 'I will continue to be your secretary of state, but I'll never vote for you again.'

Gates: Really?

Rice: Marshall was furious. He thought that it was going to throw the world into turmoil, and in fact, war broke out in the Middle East the next day. Harry Truman's decision in 1948 to recognize Israel turns out to have been one of the most important decisions of the twentieth century. But he took it because he felt it was right. He was the one, of course, who believed the integration of the armed forces could take place and it was not going to diminish morale as everybody said it was going to do. This was a man who really took tough decisions and when he said 'The buck stops here,' he meant it. When you aren't so focused on today's headlines, you are a better leader.

Gates: And the chaos following Truman's decision on Israel ended up securing the Nobel Prize for Ralph Bunche.

Rice: That's right.

Gates: Ralph Bunche brings me back to an earlier generation of Black leaders. Are we doing all we can to groom leaders within the African American community for the next generation?

Rice: Well, I do think we are seeing the emergence of African American leaders in a broad range of contexts. Clearly, we have a lot of African Americans now in corporate leadership—leading corporations that we would never have dreamed of when you and I were growing up. That there would be a Black man heading American Express; could you have imagined that? So in the corporate world, I think we're doing much, much better. What is concerning to me, and I have sat on corporate boards, is when I look at the next couple of levels, I don't see as many Blacks moving into that pool, where the next set of CEOs are going to come from.

We need to be very concerned about that and, by the way, it is true in academia as well, and in government. We should not only focus on 'Well, somebody got to the top.' But there are pools from which people are chosen to get to the top. We should look at whether we are filling those pools with young Black Americans, and giving them the experiences. The military is terrific at seeing a bright young captain and saying 'That person looks like he's got the potential to be a colonel,' or 'she has the potential to be a general, but needs to have these career experiences in order to do that.' The corporate world is somewhat better at it, too. We are terrible at it in the government. I was stunned when I was secretary of state, to walk into room after room after room. I could go a whole day as secretary of state and never see anybody who looked like me. In the foreign service, it's still not diverse enough. But also, people are not moved in a way that means they're going to become assistant secretary, which is the position of responsibility from which you're going to get the major ambassadors appointed and so on.

Gates: But you were talking earlier about your father's youth group, which is leadership training. You went to Black schools, in which they spotted you. You would be nurtured. Is that happening within the race today?

Rice: I don't see it. Sometimes we old folks sound, you know, the way old folks start to sound. 'Well, back in the day . . . ' And back in the day, of course, we had this peculiar characteristic of being segregated and had, in a certain sense, second class citizenship. On the other hand, our parents had the ability to control the messages that their kids received, the ability in a Black school to demand excellence (as my school always said, 'You have to be twice as good') and to have it and have no racial overtones. What I worry somewhat about is that in integrated environments, you can get a couple of responses that are not very good for

Black kids. One is to assume that they are somehow less capable and therefore to start to engage in noblesse oblige: 'Let's give them a little bit of a break.' Deadly. Secondly, to empower victimhood. I think one of the worst things you can let anybody tell you is that you're a victim of something. Because the minute you are a victim of something, you have completely lost control. And in a more integrated environment, sometimes in trying to recognize the challenges that are associated with being Black in America, it eases over into victimhood and that is a problem.

Gates: And that lets us make excuses for bad behavior.

Rice: That's right.

Gates: Or lacks in performance. I agree with you, and I don't think that it's just us being romantic or sentimental about the past. They demanded performance.

Rice: They sure did. They were caring, and I can remember my mother staying after school to help her science students who weren't doing very well, so they didn't just leave you hanging out there if you didn't perform. But you were expected to perform.

Gates: So should we have segregated schools again?

Rice: Well, of course we aren't going to go and shouldn't go back to segregated schools. But somehow, I do think within these great White institutions or great integrated institutions, it puts a special responsibility on, for instance, Black faculty, to remind Black students that there are no easy ways here. And when I was at Stanford, I started a program called Partners in Academic Excellence. This started when I conducted my first Phi Beta Kappa ceremony as provost. In the three hundred or so Phi Beta Kappas, I think there were two Black kids. I thought, 'Something is really wrong with this picture.' And I started to wonder if maybe something was wrong with the messages about excellence and so forth. We started Partners in Academic Excellence, where we paired Black freshmen with Black graduate students and a Black faculty member once a week. The Black graduate students would read the papers of the Black freshman for their Humanities requirement, and they would say 'That's not an A paper that you just wrote.' So something was going on there, and we started to think about where else might this be the case, perhaps for other minority students, for athletes. There were lower expectations of athletes than there should have been in a place like Stanford. Or women and math.

So I'm a big proponent of really challenging kids. And it's not just minority kids. It's about seeping into our academic environments, our educational environments more broadly, with a kind of self-esteem movement. I was helping my cousin's daughter a few years back when she was about ten years old. She was doing math homework and she had $5 \times 9 = 40$. And I said, 'That's wrong.' And she said, 'There are no wrong answers.' [*laughter*] And I said, 'Oh yes there are, and that's one of them!' So recommitting to excellence and high standards is important because, going back to our theme of leadership, leaders have to have the highest standards for themselves and for the people that they lead. And people appreciate it when you have high standards.

Gates: When you walked into a room with the most powerful leaders in the world, when the door opened, did they see a Black person coming through first or a woman coming through first?

Rice: Well, in most places, they first saw the secretary of state of the United States. [*laughter*] I have often said I really do think role definition might be stronger for women than it is for minorities. I think we are starting to get past role definition for Blacks. I could see it. I'm not a humanist and I'm certainly not a student of popular culture, but I remember thinking a few years back as I was watching a commercial, that it was no longer limiting the Black role. Your insurance agent just might happen to be Black, or your doctor might just happen to be Black. And something was happening where we were starting to divorce role and race. Now it's not complete, but with Colin Powell, people started to consider him as the chairman of the Joint Chiefs of Staff who just happens to be Black.

Gates: They started to, yes, but initially it was a shock. I had people in Latin America tell me about the first time they saw Colin Powell representing the U.S. military on television. They were in a bar, and the whole place stopped.

Rice: But now we take it for granted. Black secretaries of state, oh, well.

Gates: Dime a dozen.

Rice: And then, finally, the Black president of the United States. Now I don't believe we're a race-blind society; when somebody walks in your room, you still see a Black person. But maybe you are less likely, increasingly, to think this way, which is where I think we want to be. For women, particularly in positions of authority and particularly in positions having to do with national security and the like, it is also, finally, starting to break down.

Gates: But why? You would think, I mean there are so many more White women, powerful women, why would it be the way that race boundaries would break down before gender?

Rice: I think we have weird notions about gender. I go to these conferences from time to time and somebody will quite nicely and quite well-meaningly say, 'Well, women lead differently. They're consensus builders.' I say, 'Yeah, like Maggie Thatcher, right?' [*laughter*]

Gates: Or Golda Meir.

Rice: The fact is, when you think about it, it's a pretty ridiculous notion. But there is this concept with gender that somehow, women have the feminine and therefore softer side when they lead, and men are just going to go out there. And you say any good leader, male or female, has to have a range of assets, capabilities, and styles. Some days, it's 'Let's all come together and reason about this and we'll come to a joint conclusion.' And some days, it's 'I've had enough of this, we're just going to do it.'

Gates: Did you ever feel condescended to, even for a second?

Rice: When I was younger, I sometimes felt awfully young in the room. And in some places in the world—Russia, for instance—it's a very patriarchal society. I can remember giving my first big lecture in Russia, in the Soviet Union. It was at the home of the American ambassador and he had invited all these Soviet leaders and generals. And I gave the address in Russian. At the end of it, there was a dinner and I was seated next to a Soviet general and he essentially said, 'Why is a nice girl like you so interested in bombs and bullets?' [*laughter*] I said something about actually being rather fond of military power or something to back him off. But a story appeared the next day in the newspaper saying that I should have been thinking about my suitors, but instead I was thinking about bombs and bullets. But not in many, many years has that been a problem.

Gates: Turning to your book, as a public person, former secretary of state, you could have written an enormous memoir focused mostly on diplomacy, foreign policy, interactions with the world. You could have dropped names, made a million dollars, sold a zillion copies. So why make your first book after leaving office a very personal memoir—what I call your Black book—in which you reflect on family and your life growing up in the Jim Crow South, the dawn of the Civil Rights era?

Rice: With every implausible event and circumstance in which I found myself, whether it was negotiating with Palestinians and Israelis or getting off a plane that says the United States of America, toward the end of my time in government I just got more and more interested in and compelled by the question that so many people ask me: 'How in the world . . .

Gates: Did a girl like you . . . '

Rice: Right, exactly. [*laughter*] And I would look sometimes at a particular picture that you saw, Skip, when you came to my house.

Gates: I love that picture.

Rice: This little five-year-old girl with bows and rolled up bangs. How did she become secretary of state? And I was very attracted to trying to tell the story. I always tell people that in order to know how that happened, you had to know John and Angelina Rice. And I wanted to tell their story, both because it explained my story and because it explains a story, I think, of people that are sometimes a little bit forgotten. There was a striving middle class in the segregated South that was somehow in these bizarre circumstances of Jim Crow, yet still getting educated and educating their children and becoming professionals and doing all of the things that then really set us up to be ready when the Civil Rights Act passed. And I wanted to do it not from the perspective of the great leaders of the movement or certainly not as an historian or as a sociologist. My great friend Clay Carson, an historian at Stanford, gave me very good advice. I talked to him before I wrote the book. And I said, 'You know, Clay, I'm not really an historian of this era.' And he said, 'That's not what you're going to do here. This is how you remember it as a little girl.' And it freed me then to take the perspective of telling the story of these forgotten people as a little girl. I think theirs is a generation to which we owe a lot.

Gates: And if we don't remember them, they will be forgotten.

Rice: They'll be forgotten because of the way that historians, for a lot of very good reasons, often focus on the leaders and the rulers of a particular period. And you know very little about the normal people, the average people, the ordinary people. And yet, these ordinary people—and my parents were ordinary people—were living in extraordinary circumstances and were getting extraordinary results.

Gates: That is why I like doing people's family trees. Because I am discovering and reuniting you with lost ancestors. And they are all extraordinary. Just finding them makes it extraordinary. But you've written a beautiful book.

Rice: Thank you.

After a lengthy exchange on the wars in Iraq and Afghanistan, they return to the subject of leadership and Black America.

Gates: . . . I want to return to where we started the interview: leadership and Black America. Was President George W. Bush misunderstood by Black America? And if so, who bears the greatest responsibility for this misunderstanding? Black leadership or the Bush administration?

Rice: President Bush was fundamentally misunderstood by Black America. And I'll come to the question of responsibility. On the one hand, he's a Republican and I have said very often that part of the problem is the Republican party has a lot to live down for what happened in 1964 when the Civil Rights Act was passed and when some tried to take advantage of that to build a southern strategy to build a base for the party among disaffected segregationists.

Gates: Which they did quite effectively.

Rice: But at a great cost to our soul in the Republican party, which should have been, as most Republican Senators were, most Republican Congressmen were, four-square behind the Civil Rights Act. A young Congressman from Illinois, Donald Rumsfeld, for instance, supported the Civil Rights Act. So there's that history. And a pity that the party of Lincoln would do that. Secondly, for a long time I think that the party didn't speak in a language about issues that are American issues but perhaps have a more fundamental effect on the Black community; for instance, the nature of the public school education system. President Bush tried to speak to those issues. One of my first conversations with him was not about foreign policy. In 1998 we were at Kennebunkport together thinking about what he might do if he ran for president. And he talked about the soft bigotry of low expectations and how people didn't expect enough of Black kids. He talked about the minority achievement gap and how could it be that we had so many Black and Hispanic kids who couldn't read at third grade level six or seven years into their education? He had a desire to do something about that. And even though he didn't want to use quotas in the University of Texas system, he had gone to a top ten percent strategy so that if you were in the top ten percent, which brought many, many more Blacks into the number, you got into the UT system. So he was attuned to these issues from the very beginning. Yes, he cared about minorities and their forward progress.

So whose responsibility was it? Well, I don't know that Black America and a lot of traditional media outlets were willing to listen to that story. But after September 11th, we had no choice. President Bush had no choice but to become a war president. He didn't go to Washington to be a war president. He wanted to redefine in many ways what it meant to be a Republican. When he said compassionate conservatism, he meant caring about education of all children, particularly minority children, and that's why No Child Left Behind was so important to him. He wanted to reform immigration policy. He wanted to think about how we could deal with entitlements in a way that didn't disadvantage the poor, but made them affordable. And September 11th and a war presidency drowned a lot of that out.

Gates: So then whose fault? Is there anything that could have been done?

Rice: I think it's mostly circumstances, but it's possible that everybody including the White House could have been more attuned to how those messages were being heard. There wasn't enough effort to go and speak to people. I remember during and shortly after Katrina was unfolding, I talked to the president and said, 'Mr. President, we have a race problem.' And we reached out to Bruce Gordon, who was president of the NAACP at the time. You know, the White House can be sometimes an isolated place and you have to be constantly sure to be reaching out beyond the boundaries of the people who would normally be a part of your constituency and pull them in. The thing President Bush was really proud of was that he had taken twenty-eight percent of the Black vote in Texas. So those who got to know him best believed in this man as someone who cared about all Americans and I'm sorry it didn't get better communicated.

Gates: I heard him on Leno a couple of weeks ago. And he said the worst moment in his presidency was Kanye West effectively calling him a racist, saying he didn't care about Black people. Help us to understand that. Was that true?

Rice: It was true. I remember he was so hurt—it was a shock to him that anybody would think that he would somehow let people suffer because they were Black. There was nothing worse you could say about him or about the president of the United States than that. And that says something, too, about how he viewed himself.

Gates: It does. I was shocked. I was lying in bed watching and was thinking 'Wow, this may be worse than 9/11.'

Rice: Maybe over time this will get straightened out. But Bush was really, really saddened and angered by it.

Gates: So did you and Colin Powell make Barack Obama president? Did you prepare the way? Were you the John the Baptist for the Jesus?

Rice: [*laughter*] Oh, I see. Well, I don't know about that analogy. But I do think that slowly but surely Americans saw Black Americans, African Americans, in positions that they would never have dreamed of ten years before . . .

Gates: In a million years.

Rice: First, the highest ranking military officer is Black. OK. Now the chief diplomat and the national security advisor at the same time are Black. And then you have another Black secretary of state and OK, well maybe this is all right. And then now you have a Black president. Yes, I think there has been a progression that's been hopeful.

Gates: I think that's absolutely the case. If America is an idea, as you have said numerous times—the idea of a land of freedom and opportunity for all—can you talk a little bit about how we as a country have navigated different parties' conceptions of that idea? We seem to be getting more and more polarized, particularly since President Obama was elected. So it's not always clear to me that that idea means the same thing to all sides in our country anymore. And that's different than when we were growing up.

Rice: I think the American idea still has powerful resonance with almost all Americans. And that idea is that we are a free people who are protected both by and from our government and we are a free people who can have the opportunity to fully express ourselves and fully reach our potential through life, liberty, and the pursuit of happiness. And that is our birthright as Americans. I think most Americans still believe that that is the American idea. Where we're breaking down is in the confidence that it is really true. And we had great confidence—even in segregated Alabama, where you could not go into a restaurant—that the American idea was still for us. Because all we had to do was to get the United States to be what it said it was. We didn't have to make the United States be something different. It just had to be what it said it was. And now, if you are in east Oakland or south-central LA or the poorest parts of Boston, do you really still believe that? When I can look at your zip code and I can tell whether or not you're going to get a good education, is the American idea really alive and well? And that, I think, is what is causing the tension and the friction.

By the way, it's not just poor Americans. Families that always believed that their kids would be better off than they were are now not so sure. And the house that was the great pride of every American family, is now worth half its value. And I think our anxiety and our anger and our desire to want to shake Washington and say 'Listen to me' is driven not by the unraveling of the idea, but the unraveling of the belief that the idea is more than just a myth. It's real. And that's a great danger to us as a country because we are not held together by blood or religion or nationality. We are African Americans and Mexican Americans and Indian Americans and Korean Americans and German Americans and we are Muslims, Jews, Protestants, and Catholics and we're nothing at all, some of us. So if we are not held together by religion or by blood, we are only held together by that idea. And if that idea isn't true, then we will come apart as a society and as a country.

Gates: You are talking about economic scarcity and the class divide in this country. Is it going to get better? Or unfortunately worse?

Rice: We have lost time and we've lost ground to deal with the implications of globalization. The implication of globalization is that the $18-an-hour unskilled job is gone forever. That job, by the way, isn't even in China anymore. It's gone someplace else even for the Chinese. And our skills and our education as a people don't match up well with the jobs that are available. Now ask anybody on Route 128 or in the Silicon Valley, 'Can you find enough engineers?' They will tell you no. Go to some places and ask if they can find enough people who can write well, forget math and science. And they'll tell you no. So somehow we have this divorce between the education and training of our people and the jobs that are available. And the impact of globalization is getting faster and wider and our ability to match up with it is diminishing and we are losing time. So that, I think, is the real economic challenge.

Gates: Can we get our mojo back? I'm talking about all Americans now. Do we have leaders who can energize us? Do we have a community that will work to carry out our leaders' vision?

Rice: Oh, sure. We have to do some really hard things, you know. We've got to get our education policies right immediately. We've got to do something about immigration. Immigrants are not the enemy. Immigrants are the life's blood of the United States. We have to get the economy going again. You know, the private sector has to lead that growth. But I'm a real optimist about America because so many times we have made the impossible seem inevitable. And we are not a people that are given over to wringing our hands. I am an optimist about our ability to deal with the current challenges.

Gates: Thank you, Dr. Rice, for a marvelous interview.

Rice: Thank you.

SOURCE: Henry Louis Gates, Jr., "A Conversation with Condoleezza Rice: On Leadership," *Du Bois Review: Social Science Research on Race*, First View Article (March 2011): 1–16. Copyright © 2011 W. E. B. Du Bois Institute for African and African American Research. Reprinted with permission of Cambridge University Press.

A CONVERSATION WITH
WILLIAM JULIUS WILSON
ON THE ELECTION OF BARACK OBAMA

WILLIAM JULIUS WILSON is Lewis P. and Linda L. Geyser University Professor and Director of the Joblessness and Urban Poverty Research Program at the Malcolm Weiner Center for Social Policy at the John F. Kennedy School of Government at Harvard University. He is the leading figure in the field of urban sociology and is the author of numerous publications, including three field-defining books, The Declining Significance of Race: Blacks and Changing American Institutions *(1978),* The Truly Disadvantaged: The Inner City, the Underclass, and Public Policy *(1987), and* When Work Disappears: The World of the New Urban Poor *(1996). He has served as an adviser to both President Bill Clinton and President Barack Obama.*

Henry Louis Gates, Jr.: Thank you so much, Bill, for doing this interview for the *Du Bois Review*. When did you decide that Barack Obama was a serious, viable candidate for the presidency, and what sealed it for you about him?

William Julius Wilson: What sealed it for me was when he won the Iowa caucuses. After hearing his victory speech afterward, I said to myself, *This guy is on his way. He is really a serious candidate.* Prior to that time, Skip, I was somewhat skeptical. In fact, I had given some consideration to working for Hillary Clinton in the fall because I didn't think Barack was a viable candidate. My view changed following the victory in Iowa.

Gates: I was out at Stanford, and I fell asleep before the election results. And I woke up with CNN on, and it was 2 AM, and it was that speech that was going on. And I jumped out of bed. It was the first time that he had really moved me since the convention speech.

Wilson: Right.

Gates: But I felt like I felt when I used to hear Bobby Kennedy speak. And then I sent Oprah an e-mail immediately, you know: [*laughter*] This guy is here, you know. I'm serious.

Wilson: Absolutely, absolutely.

Gates: What was the lowest moment during the primary season for you?

Wilson: The public's reaction to that video clip of Reverend Wright's incendiary comments. I thought that Obama might not be able to recover from the political fallout. I was very, very worried until he gave that brilliant race speech in response to the uproar over Reverend Wright, which got him back on track.

Gates: What was brilliant about that speech?

Wilson: Well, there are several things that were brilliant about it. First of all, as I point out in my new book, *More Than Just Race*, that speech is a model for what I consider to be effective political framing. Because in appealing to the goodwill of the American people, he emphasized points that I'm sure resonated with them, including points that highlighted the importance of helping people to help themselves. You see, Americans tend to support programs that attempt to develop a level playing field, including programs that enable people to help themselves. For example, as the research of [Lawrence] Bobo [W. E. B. Du Bois Professor of Social Sciences at Harvard University] and his colleagues so clearly demonstrates, although a significant majority of Whites don't support quotas and numerical guidelines, they will support programs that provide scholarships for Black students who get good grades in school. And they support training and education programs to help Black workers improve their chances for employment, programs to help people to help themselves. Obama's speech on race appealed to that kind of sentiment. But even more important, from my point of view, was the comprehensive vision of the factors that contribute to racial inequality in this society, a vision that not only highlighted structural impediments, such as the legacy of slavery and discrimination and the lack of economic opportunities for low-skilled Black males, but also the cultural responses to these structural inequities—responses that actually perpetuate poverty and social disadvantages. So, he integrated both structural and cultural factors, and that's what impressed me a great deal. He did not uncouple the cultural factors from the structural ones like Bill Cosby did. He displayed in this speech a comprehensive understanding of the impact of race in America, and after listening to that speech, I said to myself, *This guy is really sophisticated.*

Gates: Were you surprised at the continuing Black nationalist critiques that he's not Black enough?

Wilson: Yeah, I think those critiques are ridiculous, quite frankly. I mean here is a man who is addressing issues that are central to the Black community. I have listened with some irritation to critiques by Black intellectuals that his stimulus package does not address issues that affect the poor, including poor Blacks. Such critiques show how ill informed these critics are. For example, included in the stimulus package is a "making work pay" credit that even low-income families who don't make enough to pay income tax can claim, an extended period for the receipt of unemployment benefits, health insurance for the jobless whose insurance was covered by previous employers, a temporary increase in the earned-income tax credit, a lowering of the income threshold for the receipt of the child tax credit, and so on. All of these provisions would help poor workers, including poor Black workers. But even more important, President Obama also has focused on what I consider to be some very important race-specific programs. For example, he is going to create what he calls twenty promised neighborhoods patterned after the Harlem Children's Zone, which is an excellent model. Geoffrey Canada's mission, when he created the Harlem Children's Zone, was to flood a number of blocks in Harlem with educational, social, and medical services to create a comprehensive safety net for the children in that area. However, during the campaign, when I was co-chair of Obama's urban policy committee, I was somewhat concerned that he was placing so much emphasis on the Harlem Children's Zone because that program had not been rigorously evaluated.

Gates: Hadn't been scaled up.

Wilson: Well, it hadn't been evaluated more importantly. It had been sort of scaled up in Harlem because it went from twenty-four blocks to one hundred blocks, and the program is now reaching about 4000 parents and 7500 kids, okay. So Canada has scaled up the program in Harlem. Canada was able to get corporate leaders to support him, and he now has an annual budget of roughly $58 million. But the program had not been rigorously evaluated when I was working on the campaign in the primaries, and I was just fearful that a rigorous evaluation could possibly yield trivial results. I no longer have that concern. Roland Fryer, our brilliant young economist here at Harvard, has evaluated this program using a rigorous random assignment design, which includes a control group of students who are not in the program and an experimental, or a treatment, group. And Skip, the preliminary results of this evaluation are absolutely spectacular. They are unbelievable. You see, the Harlem Children's Zone includes two public charter schools that differ from the regular public schools in the sense that the teachers were selected on the basis of their ability to teach students and on their dedication, not on whether they had a degree from a school of education. Moreover, the students are in school 60% longer than those in the regular public schools, including a very short summer vacation. Skip, the results of this evaluation are spectacular. Here we have kids from some of the most impoverished backgrounds, mostly from poor single-parent families, whose scores on the cognitive test far exceed those of kids in the public schools of New York. The math scores are especially dramatic and compare favorably with those of kids who live in upper-middle-class White suburbia. The charter school was one of the last major components of the program, and it was opened in 2004. Of the kids in the third grade, who benefited from entering the program when they were in kindergarten, 100% scored at or above grade level in math in 2007 in one of the charter schools, and 97% in the other school. Moreover, 87% of the kids in the eighth grade scored at or above grade level in math, even though they did not have the benefit of early exposure to the charter school. To repeat, here are kids from some of the most impoverished backgrounds performing as well in math as those kids in upper-middle-class suburbia.

And not only the math scores, but even the verbal scores are quite impressive. As I point out in my book *More Than Just Race*, living in poor segregated neighborhoods for long periods of time has an adverse effect on verbal ability, as measured by the cognitive tests. And these effects linger on even after these kids leave these neighborhoods. So it takes time to overcome the effects of living in chronic economically poor segregated neighborhoods on verbal skills. Nonetheless, even the verbal scores have improved dramatically, especially for the kids who are younger. And now they're talking about selecting these kids for this program from a lottery at the time they're born, when they come out of the womb. And so as this program continues, the scores are going to be even more spectacular.

I am so pleased that Roland Fryer is evaluating this program. You know Roland is not like a typical economist relying solely on mathematical models. He recognizes that in order to come up with a comprehensive explanation of the success of this program, he needs the help of sociologists and others who understand social behavior and group interaction, and that's what he's doing. He's examining both the quantitative data and the qualitative data collected for the evaluation, and I understand that he's going to be asked by Arne Duncan, the new secretary of education, if he hasn't already been asked, to help design the twenty promised neighborhoods for the Obama administration, which as I indicated will be patterned after the Harlem Children's Zone.

Now to get back to your question, here's a Black president addressing issues that fundamentally affect Black people, poor Black people. And it just saddens me to hear these ill-informed Black nationalist critiques.

Gates: What do you think motivates their critique? Did they expect that the first Black president would be Malcolm X and Marcus Garvey, you know?

Wilson: You know, they're so consumed with the traditional views that if he's a Black president, he should be speaking specifically to race-specific issues and so on. If Obama had followed their wishes, he would not be president of the United States.

Gates: He'd be a visiting professor in African American Studies. [*laughter*]

Wilson: And Black people realized that. I was very impressed with Black voters during the primaries and the general election. They didn't jump on the Obama bandwagon initially. They were for Hillary Clinton because they didn't think Obama stood a chance of getting elected. They thought that he was not a viable candidate among White voters. They wanted to get rid of the Republican political control of the White House and the Congress, so they weren't going to waste their vote. However, Obama's stunning victory in the Iowa caucuses in early January and his strong second-place finish in the New Hampshire primary convinced a substantial number of Blacks that many White Americans are prepared to vote for a Black man for president of the United States. African American voters jumped on the Obama bandwagon and displayed a level of political sophistication that was truly extraordinary. Basically, they did not insist that Obama tailor his message to address the needs of Blacks. They gave Obama the slack he needed to navigate the treacherous racial terrain. They did not rally to the defense of the Reverend Jeremiah Wright when Obama had to break with him, and they were critical of some Black leaders and Black intellectuals who maintained that Obama should be talking more about race-specific issues. Ordinary Blacks realized that he had to reach out to Whites, he had to reach out to Hispanics, he had to reach out to Asians, you know. And they recognized he needed to communicate an inclusive message.

Gates: That he had to be president of all the people.

Wilson: Precisely. And this reminds me of an interesting conversation that I had with a Black taxi driver who drove me from the airport in South Bend, Indiana, to the University of Notre Dame, where I was to deliver a lecture in early February 2008. He had just read Jesse Jackson's attack on Obama in the *Chicago Sun Times*. He asked me, "What is wrong with Jesse Jackson?" And I remember him saying, "How is Obama going get elected president in this White society by talking constantly about issues that don't affect White people. Let the man get elected, then we can raise questions about how he plans to deal with the problems of Blacks!"

That's a very sophisticated remark. Much more sophisticated than a lot of these Black intellectuals who have been trashing Obama because his messages were not tailored to Black people.

Gates: Absolutely. When and where did you first meet Obama, and what was it like?

Wilson: Well, I met him in 1996, he was campaigning for the state legislature in Illinois, and a law school professor, friend of mine, a law school professor at the University of Chicago, who's now teaching at Yale University, invited a group of us to come to her house to hear him discuss campaign issues. So we were sitting in her living room listening to him, and I was thinking, during that meeting, wouldn't it be great if this young man could become a national politician? Of course, at that time, I never dreamed he was going to be the president of the United States. I would have just been happy if he had simply become a member of Congress.

Gates: And what was he like?

Wilson: I found him very, very engaging, and I found that his message really resonated with me because he was talking about coalition building, and the need to address issues that would pull people together. And as I listened to him, I was thinking that he fully recognized the political importance of generating a sense of interdependence, where groups come to recognize that they can't achieve their goals without the help of other groups. That's the recipe for successful coalition building. If you can't generate a sense of interdependence, then coalitions collapse, and that's what he talked about. And that is so important, and I thought that this guy has his finger on the pulse.

Gates: What is your greatest hope for Obama's first term, and what is your greatest fear?

Wilson: Well, my greatest hope is that he will, with his policies, effectively deal with this terrible economic crisis. I think if he can do that before the end of his first term, he will definitely be reelected. That's my greatest concern. Obama has selected brilliant people to work with him; he has some great ideas; he's very smart. I think he will help to ease international tensions, but my greatest concern, my greatest hope is that he's able to overcome this economic crisis.

My greatest fear is a terrorist attack. You have Dick Cheney going around saying that Obama's policies will make us less safe. Dick Cheney and George Bush are the ones who have made us less safe. Their policies and actions have increased the possibility of another terrorist attack. Okay, so that's what worries me. If there's a terrorist attack during the time Obama is in office, then they will place the blame on him and try to deflect attention from policies and actions of the previous administration that heightened, not diminished, international tensions and the animosities of terrorists. So that's my greatest fear, a terrorist attack.

Gates: What does the election of Obama mean for the racial divide in America?

Wilson: I think, and some people will say, I'm overly optimistic, but I really do feel that his election has helped to bridge the racial divide somewhat. We still have a long way to go, but I do think his election has helped to bridge the racial divide. I like the way he frames the issues as he attempts to get people to understand the nature of race relations in this society and to appreciate the need to address issues of race in constructive ways. I strongly believe that he will use the bully pulpit to bring races together, not apart. He will create a sense of interdependence, that I just talked about, by getting people to recognize that they have more commonalities than differences and that they cannot accomplish their desired goals without the help of other people. Social psychological research on group interdependence reveals that when groups believe that they need one another, they are more likely to overcome their prejudices and join in programs that foster mutual interaction and cooperation. Moreover, when people from different groups come together, their perceptions and behaviors tend to change. I think that the Obama presidency will create this sense of interdependence. Whether it will last beyond his presidency remains to be seen. But only the most myopic observer would deny that we have made racial progress in this country. The Obama presidency will strengthen the foundation that makes continued progress possible, a foundation that encourages, not discourages, frank and thoughtful discussions of both structural and cultural forces that interact to create or perpetuate racial inequality.

Here's another issue I should raise in this connection. Economic problems tend to generate social tensions. If you have a demagogic leader who does not hesitate to fan or exploit the fears of citizens during hard economic times, things could really get ugly. When people are uptight and worried about their jobs, history has shown that demagogic leaders often seek political gain or media attention by using negative populist messages to shift the focus from the real source of our problems on to Blacks, other people of color, and immigrants, often leading to a demagogic mobilization of racism against these groups. But Obama has been able to very effectively use positive messages to bring people together, not divide them. In terms of race relations, he is the right president during these hard economic times because social tensions are indeed high.

Gates: You know it's a great point. What does Obama's election mean for the class divide in this country? What does it mean for poor Blacks, for the urban poor who've been such a centerpiece of your work?

Wilson: Well, you know, Obama is also very aware of class problems. It reminds me, did you read his first book? *Dreams from My Father?*

Gates: Mm-hmm.

Wilson: Well you may recall he talked about his meeting, first meeting with Reverend Wright, and he talked about the importance of addressing the issue of class inequality. And he was talking about my book *The Declining Significance of Race.* And Reverend Wright wasn't hearing any of this. Wright said, "That Black brother from the University of Chicago talking about the declining significance of race, what country does he [*laughter*] live in?"

Gates: I'd forgotten that, but you remembered it.

Wilson: Yeah, well I remember it because there was a recent article in the *New Yorker,* and the author of the article referred to this exchange between Obama and Wright. See, in *The Declining Significance of Race* I argued that economic class position had become more important than race in determining Black life chances. And Obama was talking about the need to pay more attention to class inequality.

Now what will his election do for the class divide in the Black community? I think that by trying to improve conditions of the Black poor, he will hopefully create programs to address their plight so that they will not continue to slide further and further behind more privileged Blacks, as they have done during previous administrations. Scaling up programs patterned after the Harlem Children's Zone is one example.

Gates: Does the election of Obama mean that we are in a so-called post-racial society, finally done with racism in America?

Wilson: Absolutely not. This whole idea of a post-racial society is ridiculous. Race still is a very important factor, and the reason for this is not only the lingering racism in American society despite Obama's election—and I want to come back to another point that I forgot about White people's reaction to Obama since he's been elected—but as long as you have a disproportionate number of Black people concentrated at the very bottom of the economic ladder, race is going to continue to be a factor in our society. Because economic disadvantage will continue to be associated with negative responses like crime, drug consumption, broken families, and so on. And until we deal effectively with the overwhelming concentration of Blacks in low-paying jobs, and in the jobless ranks—conditions that represent the legacy of previous racial discrimination, segregation, and racism—race will continue to be an important factor in American society. As the late Black economist Vivian Henderson put it, it's as if racism, having put Blacks in their economic place, where you have a disproportionate number of Blacks at the bottom of the economic ladder, stepped aside to watch changes in the economy destroy that place. Now let me just elaborate on the latter point. Because you have so many Blacks in these disadvantaged positions in the changing economy, it makes them extremely vulnerable. Two things are happening. Actually, I'm not talking now about the downturn in the economy, overall that certainly is a major factor, but there have been two ongoing processes that have adversely affected Blacks. Number one is the computer revolution, which rewards skilled workers, including skilled Blacks, and displaces low-skilled workers, including high school dropouts today, and that's a major problem in the Black community.

Gates: 50%.

Wilson: They have absolutely no chance in this society. So, the computer revolution is one thing. The second thing is the growing internationalization of economic activity where low-skilled Blacks are competing not only with other low-skilled workers in this country but also with low-skilled workers around the world. Blacks are very vulnerable to this development. For example, take the apparel industry. Forty percent of the workers in the apparel industry are Black, and the apparel industry has been hard hit by the globalization of the economy. We shipped the jobs off to Bangladesh and these other places.

Gates: 46% of the Black workers?

Wilson: 40% of all workers in the apparel industry are Black. And that industry has been hard hit. Blacks have borne the brunt of the deindustrialization as well. A higher percentage of Black workers have been displaced because of deindustrialization than that of any other group of workers. Manufacturing industries have been relocated not only to the suburbs but to places around the world. So as long as you have Blacks in those vulnerable economic positions, it's ridiculous to talk about a post-race society. Because you have so many Blacks who are vulnerable to these kinds of economic changes, many of them are not going to be able to respond to these changes in ways that are positive. Many of them will turn to drugs, to crime, become estranged from families. And unless we deal with the economic plight of poor Black people, a significant percentage of Black people overall, it's ridiculous to talk about a post-race society.

Gates: But can we target them specifically as a group?

Wilson: Yes, I think it's important to do that. As I pointed out in *More Than Just Race*, the question is not whether the policy should be race neutral or universal, the question is whether the policy is framed to facilitate a frank discussion of the problems that ought to be addressed and to generate broad political support to alleviate them. I now feel that in framing public policy, we should not shy away from an explicit discussion of the specific issues of race and poverty; on the contrary, we should highlight them in our attempt to convince the nation that these problems should be seriously confronted and that there is an urgent need to address them. And the legislation to address the issues of race and poverty should be framed in a way to generate a sense of fairness and justice to combat inequality and to make Americans aware that our country would be better off if these problems were seriously confronted and indeed eradicated.

Let me say one other thing before I forget. You asked me what does the Obama election mean for poor Blacks, and I mentioned that he will create programs to address their plight. Indeed, his new White House Office of Urban Affairs is gearing up to propose a series of new programs to address urban poverty. This office requested and recently received a memo from me on some of my suggestions of ways to combat urban poverty in the inner city. However, I also want to point out that I think that the election of Barack Obama as president of the United States has and will continue to have huge symbolic significance. Blacks feel more proud of themselves, and this may help to undermine the defeatist feeling, especially among young kids who see this powerful symbol of Black progress. I was on a conference call of Black leaders a day before the election, and Barack Obama spoke for about ten minutes, and one of the things he said to us resonated—"Our grandchildren seeing Michelle and the kids roaming around the White House will think differently about themselves."

Gates: Honestly, did you ever think you would live to see an African American president? Does it alter your own sense of the possible?

Wilson: I mentioned before that when I first met Barack Obama and heard him discuss political issues, I thought it would be great if he could become a national politician. But at that time, 1996, it never occurred to me that he could become president of the United States. But to be honest Skip, when he was elected to the Senate in 2004, I did think about the possibility of his being elected president of the United States. Let me tell you why I had that thought. I have always felt that a Black politician's political message could trump the issue of race when he or she ran for political office. Take for example, Deval Patrick's gubernatorial election in Massachusetts. Like Obama, Patrick won because of his great appeal across economic, racial, and ethnic lines, and he dramatically demonstrated that a Black politician can indeed generate widespread support with the right message—an inclusive message. His election reinforced the view, in my mind, that a politician's message, not his or her race, is of primary importance.

I first developed this view when I closely followed Jesse Jackson's campaign in the 1988 Michigan caucuses when he ran against Michael Dukakis. Jackson, who is often viewed as a polarizing figure, transcended the racial divide in a stunning upset of Dukakis. Jackson not only won landslide victories in Detroit, but he also drew a surprising measure of White support in the Upper Peninsula and in cities like Ann Arbor, Kalamazoo, and Saginaw. Like Patrick and Obama, Jackson's popularity was based on the broad appeal of his message, which focused on jobs, a higher minimum wage, education, housing, and day care for working women. Jackson's victory in Michigan made me realize that Black candidates can draw political support from non-Black voters if their political messages address the constituents' basic concerns. However, unlike Obama, Jackson was not always consistent with that message. And in the other primaries that year, his message was far less inclusive. But Obama has always been consistent with his inclusive messages. And I honestly believed back in 2004 that if he ran for president that he would stand a good chance of getting elected. I felt that the strength of Obama's unifying political messages would undercut the importance of race as a defining factor in the success or failure of his presidential campaign.

My belief that his message would ultimately trump race was seriously challenged during the primaries because the color of his skin did seem to be a major drawback. The negative ads and messages with racial undertones were somewhat effective in the primaries because a significant percentage of voters were not paying close attention to the campaign. Sometimes it is necessary to change only a few minds to swing an election. That is why campaigns resort to negative personal attacks when they are behind. To unsophisticated White voters who might have had some doubts about voting for a Black man, all of these negative messages reinforced the view that he was different from them. Race in this instance did indeed matter. However, the negative messages did not get any traction in the general election because people were paying closer attention. You cannot make wise decisions if you don't have good information. People were better informed in the general election. They were able to see Obama in action. They followed his campaign, they watched the debates—they saw how smart and informed he is. They saw his political sophistication, his demeanor, and therefore the efforts to describe him as dangerous, a terrorist, a Muslim, and so on fell flat. Indeed, they seem to have backfired. McCain's favorability ratings plummeted while Obama's increased. To repeat, Obama had to perform brilliantly in the debates and on the campaign trail to render these messages ineffective. You can't make wise decisions if you don't have good information. And people were better informed during the general election because people were paying attention and therefore had more adequate information.

Now people who overemphasize the importance of race are somewhat dumbfounded not only by Obama's popularity since he has become president but by the popularity of Michelle Obama as well. According to the opinion polls, Obama's popularity is higher than that of the previous five incoming presidents at this point in their presidency—almost three months after entering office. And Michelle Obama's popularity, as first lady, is significantly higher at this point than either that of Nancy Reagan, Barbara Bush, Hillary Clinton, or Laura Bush. And the Obamas' popularity cuts across party lines and even includes a notable percentage of voters who voted for John McCain. Having good information matters. Americans are concerned about the economic crisis and therefore they are paying attention and are better informed as a result. And they are indeed impressed with the performances of both Barack and Michelle Obama, regardless of their race.

SOURCE: Henry Louis Gates, Jr., "A Conversation with William Julius Wilson on the Election of Barack Obama," *Du Bois Review: Social Science Research on Race* 6, no. 1 (2009): 15–23. Copyright © 2009 W. E. B. Du Bois Institute for African and African American Research. Reprinted with permission of Cambridge University Press.

A CONVERSATION WITH ISABEL WILKERSON

On America's Great Migration

ISABEL WILKERSON IS the author of The Warmth of Other Suns: The Epic Story of America's Great Migration *(2010), which has won numerous awards, including the 2010 National Book Critics Circle Award for Nonfiction and the NAACP Image Award for best literary debut. Wilkerson won the Pulitzer Prize for her work as Chicago Bureau Chief of* The New York Times *in 1994, becoming the first black woman to win the prize in journalism and the first African American to win for individual reporting. She is Professor of Journalism and Director of Narrative Nonfiction at Boston University.*

Henry Louis Gates, Jr.: Isabel, thanks so much for doing this interview. I love your book. Your book is historic. Congratulations.

Isabel Wilkerson: Thank you so much.

Gates: What is the Great Migration? When did it start, when did it end, how many people were involved, and why is it important?

Wilkerson: The Great Migration was an outpouring of six million African Americans from the South to the North and West. It was, in many ways, what I call a defection from the Jim Crow caste system; the system that ruled the lives of all people—even White people—who were living in the South. This caste system held everyone in a fixed place. And so there was an outpouring of people who left the South for all points North and West from 1915 to 1970, when the initial reasons for the migration were no longer in effect—meaning the caste system essentially came to an end, legally.

Gates: Well, we have all heard various interpretations and explanations for this defection. I love the metaphor of the defection. That's very original and very profound. You interviewed over 1000 people, you spent fifteen years thinking about and writing this book. What do you think the ultimate reasons for this defection were?

Wilkerson: I think one ultimate reason was a kind of seeking of political asylum, which we don't often think about when you look at the North and West and the cities that came to be, and that people just happened to be there. My questions were: How did they get there? Why did they leave? What were the circumstances that propelled them to leave? What was life like for them in the South and what was life like for them, ultimately, in the North and West? And what was it that gave them that drive, that perseverance, that restlessness to make the decision of their lives: to leave the only place that they had ever known for a place that they had never seen and hope that life would be better? I really wanted to understand that. That is the reason why I set out to find three people who would represent the three streams of the Great Migration, and get to know them, hear their stories, and then recount their stories in a narrative that would interweave their experiences with the larger tableau, what was going on around them, from the beginning of their lives until the end of the Migration and beyond.

Gates: When you say "defection," that suggests that you think the prime cause was political. People fleeing Jim Crow and anti-Black racism. When I was an undergraduate, it was the boll weevil. People fled the fact that the cotton crop failed because of the boll weevil epidemic, and so they had to find jobs in the North. Economics caused migration. This was during World War I, you know the drill. But you disagree?

Wilkerson: I think it was too large. We're talking about six million people. So six million different reasons, six million precipitating events for each one of them. The South is huge; it goes from Texas to Virginia and down to Florida. Not all of those states are cotton-producing states. So cotton could not be the reason for all of the people who might have been participating in this migration. Also, even those who might have been from the cotton-producing states might not have been leaving for that reason. There are many, many reasons why people leave.

I did a lot of research on migration itself. I became obsessed with the idea of why people do this. America is made up of people who came from someplace else. I mean, even the Native Americans came over the Bering Strait. So there is a history to this phenomenon; I mean, America is what it is because people came from someplace else. And I love to see the comparisons between what these people did—why they left where they were—and the people who might have come over from Europe or across the Atlantic in steerage, or across the Rio Grande, or the Pacific Ocean. People leave when life becomes untenable wherever they are, for many different reasons. When it comes to the motivation for the Great Migration, I think the overarching desire was to escape a caste system that controlled their lives from the moment that they awoke in the morning to the time that they went to sleep; that determined, for example, that it was illegal for a Black person and a White person to play checkers together. Even for White people who might have wanted to play checkers with somebody who was of a different race, they couldn't do it. That system was controlling of everybody.

Gates: It was ridiculous.

Wilkerson: It was ridiculous. Somebody actually sat down and wrote that as a law. Across the South, in many courtrooms, there was a Black Bible and a White Bible to swear to tell the truth on. That gets to the level of extremism and detail and forethought that went into making sure that there was no opportunity for people to ever cross paths or get to know one another. In South Carolina, it was the custom that Black people and White people could not go up the same staircase in many workplaces. How do you logistically even do that?

Gates: How do you think of it?

Wilkerson: How do you think of it, and how do you make that work? I mean, what happens when a Black person wants to go up the steps and they have to wait for the White person because they can't be on the staircase at the same time? It was that kind of insanity, when you think about it, that they were fleeing.

Gates: And a rational person would flee that.

Wilkerson: A rational person would flee. Everybody, every African American in those states had to make a decision as to whether they would stay or whether they would go. I do not make any judgment as to which was the better decision. The people that left ended up feeling that they could not stay under those circumstances. And I find it really fascinating to know that there is something different about people who leave, in all parts of human migration.

Gates: Let's follow this, because this is one of your several original contributions in this book. You are the first scholar that I know of to treat migrants like immigrants. The immigrant mentality—though we tend to stereotype it with certain ethnic groups—we all know and respect. But the only group of (im)migrants I know of who were not admired in the literature were the Black people from the South. E. Franklin Frazier famously said, these people are uncouth. And many of us don't realize the class tensions that manifested themselves within the Black community as early as the Harlem Renaissance, when the old Negroes, who had been free, descended from free Negroes in the North, saw all of these sharecroppers coming up. They despised them. They wanted to give them, as Booker T. Washington said, a toothbrush and a bar of soap.

Wilkerson: And send them back.

Gates: And send them back. But you say, no. That they had been stereo-typed. And people like E. Franklin Frazier were wrong, that they didn't have a higher immorality rate, they didn't have a higher out-of-wedlock birthrate, that they weren't people who eschewed education. In fact, the fact that they migrated showed that they were motivated.

Wilkerson: At a certain point, I was reading a book a day, and journal arti-cle after journal article after journal article. There is so much data now that disproves the stereotypes and mythologies about those migrants. One statistic is that they were more likely to be married than the people they encountered in the North. They had a lower divorce rate; they were more likely to remain married, in other words. They were more likely to be raising their children in two-parent households, which is what I actually grew up around in my own parents' migration experi-ence. The adults around us, when I was growing up, did all the things that the data show. They were more likely to be making more money than the people in the North that they encountered; not because they were making more per hour, but because they were working longer hours and multiple jobs. This is typical immigrant behavior. They also were more likely to be doubled and tripled-up in housing, which is why you've got this incredible amount of overcrowding that first attracted the scholars that began looking at it. Sociologists were naturally looking at what was going on with overcrowding, with the children, and with the spread of disease. And that is how this migration began to become calcified in our minds as something that was a problem. People were not looking at the migrants and what they were striving to do. Of course there was a transition period, they had come from farms, they had come from small towns, they had very thick accents, they didn't have the citified clothes of the people . . .

Gates: "Call me country" [*laughter*].

Wilkerson: They were country people, country folk. When they got to the North, they stood out; they didn't easily blend in with the people who were already there. But that didn't mean that they didn't come to work hard. That was all they knew, if you think about it. Particularly in the South, when you're talking about World War I, the depression years, World War II—these were sharecroppers who often were merely work-ing for the right to stay on the land that they were farming. So they were used to working very hard and not being paid at all. And even those who were working and had jobs as janitors, maids, domestics, yard boys, whatever they might have been, were underpaid. Even the professionals were being woefully underpaid. Most of the teachers in the South at that time were being paid forty percent of a full salary, openly without apology by the powers that be, for doing the same thing that their White counterparts were doing as teachers. So they were being woefully underpaid for their work, and they came to these cities in order to survive, in order to make it, and make life better for themselves and their children. Many of them were not going to be able to truly benefit from the advantages of being in the North because it was maybe in some ways too late for them. They could not go back and get the education that they hadn't gotten, if they had only completed the eighth grade. Here they were, thirty years old, and they were not going to be able to truly take advantage of all of the culture that they would be exposed to. But their children might. And isn't that what all immigrants are doing this for?

Gates: That's what we're all supposed to be doing it for.

Wilkerson: So much of the mythology does not represent the reality of these people's lives. And my goal was to get a sense of what their lives were really like.

Gates: But why were they demonized this way in the sociological literature?

Wilkerson: Well, I think it also gets to what you were saying about the stratification that they met once they arrived. People who were there before them did not want them there. Industries wanted them there because, actually, they were recruited. They did not just show up out of nowhere. The migration began because the Northern industry needed labor during World War I. World War I cut off, to a great degree, immigration from Europe, which had been providing the labor for Northern industry. Many of the Europeans who were in the United States had to go back to Europe and immigration was cut off. And Northern industry began looking to find where they could get cheap labor to fill the spaces left over by the immigrants. They were looking for the cheapest labor available, and they found African Americans and began recruiting them. But that did not mean that other people there wanted them. That meant that the people who would be competing against them were not welcoming them at all.

Gates: And you're talking about Black people.

Wilkerson: I'm talking about Black people, I'm talking about recent immigrants from other parts of the world, and that was because there was a potential for the new migrants to drive down the wages of everybody else. Many of the black migrants were not permitted to join unions, for example. Many of them were actually brought in as strike-breakers. They had no concept of a union, because unions would not have been accepted in the South at all. That was out of the question. So they had no idea what they were getting themselves into. Think about all the barriers and challenges that they had to face upon arrival. They faced hostility from Black people who were already there. They faced hostility from immigrants who had just arrived themselves from all parts of Europe or other parts of the world, who were scuffling to try to make it themselves—because a migrant or an immigrant cannot fail. As an immigrant, you are far away from home, you have made this great leap of faith, you have left all that you know, and you know the people back home are talking about you, just saying, "I know they're not going to be able to make it."

Gates: "They'll be back."

Wilkerson: So an immigrant cannot fail. Failure is not an option. They have to take whatever challenges and barriers there are. They have to bear up under them. I came to have such great empathy and understanding of what they had to endure.

Gates: As you know, I have spent the last five years being obsessed with genealogy; my genealogy and the genealogy of lots of well-known Americans. In a sense, as I hear you talking, it occurs to me that you're recuperating your own genealogical story.

Wilkerson: When the migration began in 1915, ninety percent of all African Americans were living in the South. By the end of the Great Migration in 1970, forty-seven percent—nearly half—were living outside of the South. Between 1915 and 1970, there was this great arc of migration. People went everywhere, from Washington to New York to Boston, to Chicago, Detroit, to the West Coast. So it was a total redistribution of an entire people. The majority of African Americans that you meet in the North and the West now, even to this day, have roots in the South. When they want to look at their genealogy, ultimately they want to get back to Africa. But to get there, you have to go through the South.

   And that is a beautiful thing, when you think about the connection between North and South. In other words, when this migration occurred, the people were not just carrying themselves and their hopes and dreams, they were carrying the South with them. And as they were carrying the South, they were carrying the folkways, the language, the food, and the values of the South, which often are not recognized and appreciated. In some ways, they were transporting that with their luggage tied with string.

Gates: Culture.

Wilkerson: And when that cultural exchange made it to the North, it created whole new art forms.

Gates: Art forms like classic blues. Like jazz.

Wilkerson: Like jazz, and Motown. Motown would not even exist had there been no Great Migration. And that's because the founder of Motown,

Berry Gordy's parents were born and raised in Georgia. They went to Detroit as part of this Great Migration, raised their son there, he got to be a grown man, looked around, wanted to go into music, but didn't have the money to go scouting all over the country. He looked right around him in the neighborhoods of Detroit. There was Diana Ross, a child of the Migration. Her mother had come up from Alabama, her father from West Virginia, and they met in Detroit. And then you have The Jackson 5; their mother had come from Alabama, their father had come from Arkansas, and they met in the North. They wouldn't have even existed had there not been this Great Migration.

Gates: So Black people cross-pollinated through the migration.

Wilkerson: I call them mixed marriages.

Gates: That's what they were. And that's a really great metaphor. You have a gift for metaphors; it makes your narrative even more powerful. For example, you characterize the Great Migration as "the leaderless revolution." Could you explain what you mean by that?

Wilkerson: I love that idea. When you think of it being a leaderless revolution, it gives power to everyone, whatever their background. No one set a time and a date. Though, yes, Robert S. Abbott, the Editor of the *Chicago Defender*, did encourage people to leave. But there was no one who had to tell all of those six million people that on this day, at this hour, we will leave. It was an unfurling of all of these people over time. And they left on their own. They made individual, private decisions that this was the best thing for them. And in fact, they defied their leaders. Booker T. Washington didn't live to see the migration itself, but of course he would have encouraged people to stay. Frederick Douglass famously said that a defection or a departure from the South would be a "disheartening surrender." There were many ministers in the South who encouraged people to stay. They could see their flock disappearing. One story is the case of a minister who preached from the pulpit in Tampa, Florida. One Sunday, encouraging his flock to stay, he said, "our roots are here, we should stay here, this is where the forefathers are." The next day, he was stabbed for what he said. And then they left. These were church-going people.

Gates: Amazing. But, it was more common for ministers to just pick up and follow the flock.

Wilkerson: Well, actually, they *had* to follow their flock. Barbers had to follow their customers. Teachers went where the students were going. There are clubs that exist to this day in major cities that represent these lost communities. In Los Angeles, for example, there's a Monroe, Louisiana, club. There's a Lake Charles, Louisiana, club. There are multiple clubs representing people from New Orleans and many, many Texas clubs. In other words, they picked up and left but recreated their communities in the new world. And I like the language of "the new world"—the idea of people who left with the same immigrant heart. And the fact that they doubled up once they arrived. There's a case in New York where it go so crowded that people actually had to rent a share of a bed. They rotated use of the bed because it was so overcrowded there weren't even enough places for people to live. So that meant that the night shift would come in the morning and tap the shoulder of the person who was getting ready to go to work and say "It's my turn. You've got to get up. Time for me to go to sleep." It gives a whole new meaning to the idea of timeshare.

Gates: Gives a whole new meaning to the idea of clean sheets [*laughter*].

Wilkerson: I hadn't even thought about that. But you know, there are so many stories about immigrants who sacrifice everything. Double-up and live.

Gates: This experience is so unlike my own family history. I'm from Piedmont, West Virginia, which is halfway between Pittsburgh and Washington DC. All of the branches of my family, for 250 years—all the Black people are within a thirty-mile radius of where I was born.

Wilkerson: They stayed?

Gates: They stayed. A few of us left to go to college. My brother is an oral surgeon in New Jersey. But the family, all branches, they all stayed. So this migration experience is alien to my own family. Was telling your family story the motivation for writing this book?

Wilkerson: In a way it was to answer questions that I had always had growing up. People didn't talk about it. When people left, they left for good, didn't look back. And I found that my parents hadn't really talked about it. My mother in particular didn't talk very much about it. It's almost as if they were starting with a clean slate, as immigrants often do, and they didn't share the difficult things with their children. Maybe they didn't want to burden them with the pain that they had experienced.

Gates: It is the same with the memory of slavery. People didn't want to talk about that.

Wilkerson: There are some parallels between the last slaves who were interviewed in the 1930s and this last group of people who experienced Jim Crow. They truly experienced the worst of Jim Crow and they did not want to talk about it. The Jim Crow caste system didn't end until the 1960s; it was quite firmly in place until then. It was violently enforced to the degree that for the decades leading up to the Great Migration and the early decades of the migration, there was a lynching somewhere in the South every four days. That shows you how very real the fear had to have been for people who were living in those circumstances. It was said by one historian of the era that lynching was so common that almost every Black American in the South would have known someone directly who had been lynched or would have heard of a lynching near them. So they were fleeing something that was quite real: real fear.

I wanted to understand what it was that led to my existence. The majority of African Americans, as I said, wouldn't even be alive had this cross-pollination not occurred, had people not migrated to Detroit, to Chicago, to Cleveland, met people that they never would have met. In my family's case, my mother migrated from Rome, Georgia, to Washington, DC. My father migrated from southern Virginia to Washington, DC, in a different decade. They would never have met otherwise.

Gates: In what years did they migrate?

Wilkerson: My mother in the mid-1940s and my father in the 1950s. They both went and got a second degree at Howard, which is how they ultimately met. My father had been a Tuskegee Airman and my mother was a teacher. My father became a civil engineer. But they would never have met had there been no Great Migration. And that's the story of so many people.

To speak to your story, places like West Virginia, like Washington, DC, are in some ways on the border. It's the beginning of Jim Crow going South.

Gates: That's right. Washington, for us, was so close, but it was the South.

Wilkerson: It was the South for many people. But not if you were from Mississippi, it wasn't. For people familiar with the history of the Confederacy, it would not at all have been considered the South because it was the capital of the Union. So there's a complicated history when it comes to Washington, DC. But there is a sense of longevity when it comes to the border places. The border places allow you a little bit of both so that the drive to leave would not be the same, from my perspective. If you were in Georgia, if you were in Florida, if you were in Mississippi, Alabama, there was this great drive to leave and that's why they did.

Gates: Absolutely. There was no need for slaves in the hills of West Virginia. Many of us who are from that area descend from people who were freed long before the Civil War. This is completely unlike the overwhelming experience for Black people in the South.

Wilkerson: It is an unusual history. It's almost as if you are a protected group there, in an odd kind of way. But for the vast majority of African Americans, the Great Migration is the story that led to the existence of so many people all over the country being spread out as they are.

Gates: There is a special issue of the *North American Review* from 1884 and I love it because all the great thinkers of the race—T. Thomas Fortune,

Frederick Douglass—they all write essays on the future of the Negro. One person said not only will the Negro never leave the South, but if we stay long enough we will have Black states. Like maybe Mississippi, or maybe Alabama, will become a Black state, so it behooves us to stay. And now, as you know, there are more Black people in Chicago than the whole state of Mississippi. So the Great Migration was completely unexpected. The leaders of the race had no idea that these Negroes were going to up and leave over a fifty-five-year period to the tune of six million people.

Wilkerson: I think that W. E. B. Du Bois might have. He spent time in the South. He spent time in Atlanta and was there during the 1906 riots. He was flabbergasted and dismayed, to say the least, by what he experienced. He also had some difficult experiences when he interacted with long-time southerners who were in the South, who were the leadership there. He was not part of the migration, per se, but he went back and forth, back and forth. And I have the sense that he could see that this was not a tenable situation. He might have been one of the few leaders who could have seen that.

Gates: Well, his anguish voiced in his litany for Atlanta, the poem he wrote after the 1906 riots, expresses that. And he couldn't imagine that it would ever change.

Wilkerson: No. And I think that he would have been clearly, as he did himself, ready to leave.

Gates: I would like to talk about your very interesting and effective narrative strategy. You focus on three people. Ida Mae Brandon Gladney, George Swanson Starling, and Robert Joseph Pershing Foster. You have six million people to choose from and you picked these people. Tell me why you decided on this tripartite narrative strategy and why these three people?

Wilkerson: Well, I went out in the beginning with a great sense of urgency because of the people advancing in years; I had to go and hear as many stories as I could before it was too late. I interviewed over 1200 people—I stopped counting after that—in what I might call an audition or casting call for the people who would ultimately be the protagonists in my book.

Gates: You're totally crazy [*laughter*].

Wilkerson: I get obsessed. I went to senior centers, AARP meetings. I went to Baptist churches in New York where everybody is from South Carolina. I went to Catholic mass in Los Angeles where everybody was from New Orleans. I went to all these different places in order to find these people. And that served a really useful purpose because I could get a sense of the overarching themes. What were the concerns? What was the heart's desire of the people as they were preparing to leave? And what happened to them? I had several things that were going to be required of the people that I would end up with. One is that they had to be the people in the front driving the car, not the children in the back seat. And by that I mean that I wanted to have people who had made the decision to leave, not the people who were observing and helpless, basically going along with what their parents had decided. I also needed to have people who were willing to talk about their experiences, because a lot of people did not want to talk. I also needed to have people who were characters unto themselves.

These three people, in many ways, are just interesting, fascinating people apart from the migration. Dr. Foster, for example, was a surgeon who became the private physician to Ray Charles. He was also an inveterate gambler. There were times when I would finish interviewing him and he wanted me [to] drop him off at the casino, or drop him off at the track. They're just fascinating people, in and of themselves.

I needed people with whom readers could identify. I chose not to do famous people because they can tell their own story, and often do write autobiographies. I wanted people to be able to see themselves in these protagonists and to be able to ask themselves "What would I have done if I had been in this caste system? How would I have borne up under that? Would I have stayed or would I have gone? And how would I have made the transition to this other new place that I've never seen before?"

Gates: Because half stayed.

Wilkerson: Yes, half stayed. There was a decision everybody had to make and I wanted to pull the reader into the moment where they had to face the idea of leaving or staying and making a decision that would be life-altering. This is before cell phones and GPS systems and Skype. Sometimes there would be no guarantee that you would ever see your mother again. It is a huge sacrifice, one that many immigrants have made throughout the course of history in the United States. I wanted to show that we have so much more in common than we have been led to believe.

Gates: You have internationalized the migrant experience.

Wilkerson: Yes. I believe that you can look at these individuals and you can imagine, no matter what your background is, that somebody in your experience had to go through something like this. Psychologically, if not even physically, they had to go through the transition of leaving a place— the only place they had ever known for a place they had never seen.

The other thing about the three people I chose is that I wanted each to represent one of the three major streams of the migration. One stream was up the East Coast from Florida, Georgia, the Carolinas up to Washington, DC, New York, Philadelphia, Boston. The middle stream was from Mississippi, Alabama, Tennessee, Arkansas to Chicago, Detroit, Cleveland, the whole Midwest.

Gates: The one that we stereotypically think about as a migration.

Wilkerson: Yes, we hear so much about that one. And generally to Chicago alone, not even the other cities. And then the final stream, which has been written about the least, is the one from Texas and Louisiana to California and the entire West Coast. Each person represents one stream. I also wanted them to represent the three different decades within this three-generational, fifty-five-year period of time.

So to get the breadth and the scope of the migration, each of the three left in a different decade. Ida Mae Gladney was a sharecropper's wife whose family left in the 1930s and they went from Mississippi to Chicago ultimately. In the 1940s, George Starling, who was a citrus picker who had gone to college and was agitating for better wages and working conditions in central Florida, fled for his life and went to Harlem, where he became a railroad porter. Robert Joseph Pershing Foster was a surgeon who had served in the army in the Korean War and he left Monroe, Louisiana, his hometown, where he was not permitted to perform surgery in the hospital. He ended up taking a somewhat perilous journey from Louisiana to California in 1953.

Gates: As a writer what was the principal challenge of pulling off this great achievement?

Wilkerson: I think the main challenge was dealing with the massive amount of material that I was exposed to. For one thing, I have hundreds and hundreds of pages of transcripts on each one of the individuals that I'm writing about. It is really three books in one; three biographies. Then there is a fourth book, which is the biography of the migration itself. So the greatest challenge was just dealing with this massive amount of information.

And then, on a more personal level, the idea that I was reaching out to people who were up in years. Many of them got sick. I might arrive to interview them and I'd have to go to the hospital instead of their home. Then finally, just the perseverance that it took to work on something for fifteen years. This one project for fifteen years meant that I had to maintain the momentum within myself somehow and remain as committed to it in year nine as I was in year one. That was a challenge.

Gates: Why are you the first person to write about the Great Migration between its beginning and true end? All these other books about the Great Migration are about 1910, 1915, 1930, 1940 and then they say

"Oh yeah, it continued." Why do you think this is the first one to see it as the full historic phenomenon that it was?

Wilkerson: I think that having been a national correspondent and a bureau chief for the *New York Times* made a big difference. I had the opportunity to travel all over the country for my job. I was doing all kinds of stories on any number of topics, but when I was doing something that involved African Americans, I would see that there were connections. Every time I would interview someone in LA they would talk about how they needed to go back to Texas for something. In Detroit, people were talking about going back to a family reunion in Alabama or a funeral in Tennessee. So I began to make the connection that this was not just my people in Washington, DC—people coming up from the Carolinas or Georgia. This was huge. Of course I had done a lot of reading but when I was reporting all over the country for the *New York Times*, in every place there was a connection to the South. And that was one of the things that helped me to look at it from a national perspective.

Gates: What is your take on the South today? You have taught at Emory. As you write, the migration ended and now there is reverse migration. The people from the North are moving back.

Wilkerson: I think that it is the same migration.

Gates: But the flow is different.

Wilkerson: The direction is different, but I think it's the same searching. The title of the book, *The Warmth of Other Suns*, comes from an obscure passage in the footnotes to the reprint of Richard Wright's autobiography *Black Boy* on page 496. It talks about how he was taking a part of the South to transplant in alien soil to see if it could grow differently, if it could drink of new and cool rains and bend in strange winds and respond to the warmth of other suns.

Gates: So is it a good thing? Is it exciting? Is it *as* exciting? Fifty years from now will someone be interviewing another scholar saying "six million Black people moved from the North to the South between 1970 and 2030"?

Wilkerson: I'm going on the record, taking a great leap to say I believe it's a sea change that occurred with the Great Migration. I think that the reverse migration is kind of an echo migration of the children. The children, no longer tethered and burdened by all of the pain that their grandparents and parents had experienced, can now return to a world that is made different because there was a Great Migration. This Great Migration is one of the precipitating events, I argue, that helped to create the atmosphere for the Civil Rights Movement.

And the reason I say that is three-fold. One, the Great Migration provided an opportunity for the people who were the lower caste, cheapest labor in the South, and thus the country, to say "it looks like we have options and we're going to take them." That was revolutionary because until the Great Migration, even though there had been an Emancipation Proclamation, people had not left in the same numbers as the Great Migration. They had stayed because they didn't have the option to leave. There was no option in the North at that time. The North had not opened its doors in any way or shown any interest.

Gates: And they were neo-slaves.

Wilkerson: They were neo-slaves so they were still stuck. And the Great Migration was proof that, given the chance to leave, they would be willing to take that chance. And they would leave.

Secondly, once they got to the North, their relatives would come to visit. The people who were in the South had the opportunity to get exposed to freedoms in the North that they might not have known about before. Or they might have known about them and dreamt about them, but now they could actually see them in operation. They could get on a streetcar and sit wherever they wanted. They could go and buy a meal at a restaurant and be served. That exposed them to the possibilities, even when they went home. You are a changed person once you have been exposed to freedoms like that.

Finally, the people in the North were making more money and, as with any immigrant group, they were sending money back home to the people in the South. And they were helping to finance what would become the Civil Rights Movement. So in multiple ways, the Civil Rights Movement was precipitated by the Great Migration. The Great Migration helped to create the atmosphere. It is so interesting to look at what was going on in the beginning of the Great Migration where there were no opportunities to even protest. All the protest marches and movements that took place toward the end of the migration, would not have been possible—for anybody to walk down the streets of Selma. It was barely possible when it did occur, the March on Selma.

Gates: At the turn of the century they would have just been crushed. They would have been killed.

Wilkerson: Right. It was a totalitarian regime that they were living under. My goal would be for people, especially young people, to be able to see how very limited the options were. John Dollard said that when the options are so limited, when there's no other opportunity to do anything, the one thing that you can do is leave. And that's what they did. They did the one thing that they could do.

Gates: Well I think that one reason for the reverse migration, too, is the nostalgia of the grandchildren. Many of my friends from the North, who were descended from migrants, were sent back for a week or two weeks or a month, and what they remember when I ask them what was it like, is that "Oh man, it was great. We'd milk the cow and slop the hogs." But it was life in the South in a romantic way with Grandma eating biscuits every day. They were shielded from some of the harsh experiences. So in a way it is the tail coming around.

Wilkerson: I do believe that it is a circular thing. I think that as African Americans begin looking at the genealogy, as in the work that you are doing, and they want to share that with their own children, where do they have to go in order to find it? Returning to the place of the ancestors is a way to reclaim one's history, one's culture. And it is a more welcoming place than it was at the time. In some ways it is more welcoming and certainly more livable than many parts of the harsher, anonymous northern cities that have become very challenging for people.

Gates: The South was, effectively, the total Black experience. Even in 1860, there were more free Negroes living in the southern states, states in which slavery was legal than free Negroes living in the North. And most of us don't even realize that. So all the slaves were there and more farm or free Negroes lived in the South then than lived in the North. It was quite dramatic when that shifted.

Just a few more questions. Between 1990 and 2000, more Africans came to the New World. More Africans willingly migrated to the United States than came in the entire slave trade. Do you have any plans in your next book to deal with the migration from Africa? It is just as remarkable, in its way, as the Great Migration in a shorter span of time. Do you have any interest in talking about the West Indian and the African migration in subsequent work?

Wilkerson: I do. I feel that it is all one. This whole approach and focus on migration feels like it is one expression of yearning to be free. And I feel a connection with all of them. When you think of people coming in from the Caribbean, who form a significant part of the African American community in the country now, it was an accident of where the boat happened to arrive that determined that your people ended up in South Carolina instead of Cuba. I think that this migration to the United States— how we all came to be here, one way or the other—it is all a similar yearning to be free here in this country, whether you came up from Georgia to get to New York, or you came from the Bahamas to get to New York.

I also think of the Great Migration as helping to precipitate, to create an environment in which things were opening up for people of color who were coming from all over. I really believe that it has been misunderstood as a singular event that happened in a particular year or a particular city. And I wanted to open it up so people can realize how huge and massive it was. In other words, many of the institutions and structures related to African Americans that exist in the northern cities today are there because of this Great Migration.

As you said before, there were more freed slaves in the South than there were in the North. So where is the population in Harlem? In New York? In Detroit? In Chicago? In Boston? In Washington? Where are they coming from? This is because of the Great Migration. Why are they here? It's because of the Great Migration. So when other groups come, there is a pre-existing structure that was the result of the Great Migration.

Gates: You spend a lot of time writing about the effect of the migration on the North. But what was the effect of the Great Migration on the South?

Wilkerson: The Great Migration meant that the South lost some of its most ambitious African Americans, by definition. You had to have great resolve and some level of resources in order to leave. There is something different about migrants in general. Migrants often have less patience for the status quo, so you have people who would likely be agitators for change overall. I think you are losing a certain kind of person when you lose people in a migration experience.

The South still lags the North on so many levels, when it comes to wages, education, values of the land and property, health considerations. So there are many ways that the South is still lagging and part of it would have to be because of the loss of this brain power and the workers—the most ambitious people who went off to do great things.

Look at the people who are the legacies of the Great Migration. The true legacy of any immigrant experience is the children. You're looking at Toni Morrison, August Wilson, Lorraine Hansberry. You're looking at Richard Wright, Louis Armstrong. And jazz. Jazz wouldn't even be what it is if it were not for the Great Migration.

Gates: But on the other hand, we have old established Black middle class, upper-middle class families who stayed in the South. Like the King family. Or the people who founded the Black insurance companies and the Black banks. So it's complicated.

Wilkerson: It is complicated. You could have businesses that were dependent upon, and built their clientele around, the caste system. In other words, they were serving that level of the caste system. But when it came to creativity and the ability to express oneself, the cultural contributions that African Americans have been able to provide to this country, and thus the world, came out of the Great Migration. Toni Morrison's parents migrated from Alabama, where it would have been illegal for African Americans to walk into a library and just take out a library book. How do you become a writer if you don't have access to books? So many modes of expression became possible when people left the South and their children had the opportunity to be able to grow and thrive in the North.

Jazz wouldn't be what it is, just thinking about Miles Davis. His parents migrated from Arkansas to Illinois. How would he ever have had the opportunity? He came from a fairly well-off family. However, would he have had the luxury of going to schools where he could take music, for example? It would not have been as easy. Thelonious Monk's parents migrated from North Carolina to Harlem when he was five years old, where he had the luxury, the ability, to indulge his genius in a way that he would not have been able to in the tobacco country of North Carolina.

Gates: Romare Bearden from North Carolina.

Wilkerson: Jacob Lawrence. I mean how could we even discuss this without mentioning Jacob Lawrence, who grew up in New York? His parents had migrated.

Gates: And he documented the migration in that great series of panels.

Wilkerson: Absolutely. When you think of the Great Migration you think of Jacob Lawrence and his depictions of it. How beautiful they are. And you think of John Coltrane. John Coltrane migrated at age seventeen from North Carolina to Philadelphia where he got his first alto sax. His mother had preceded him up there and she gave him a used one. And there he began to practice. Where would we be, where would music be, where would jazz be, where would culture be? Not just in this country, but internationally, if John Coltrane had not gone to Philadelphia and gotten an alto sax?

Their expressions of creativity were within them, but it was also the transfer of southern culture. Much of their creation was informed by the spirituals and the gospels that they had grown up with. For Toni Morrison, it was the language that she had grown up with. It is a beautiful expression and marriage of the South and the North.

Gates: I thank God for the Great Migration every Sunday as I eat fried chicken after church [*laughter*]. Isabel Wilkerson, thank you so much for this interview. And congratulations on the accomplishment of a brilliant, brilliant book.

Wilkerson: Thank you so much.

SOURCE: Henry Louis Gates, Jr., "A Conversation with Isabel Wilkerson," *Du Bois Review: Social Science Research on Race* 7, no. 2 (2010): 257–269. Copyright © 2010 W. E. B. Du Bois Institute for African and African American Research. Reprinted with permission of Cambridge University Press.

ACKNOWLEDGMENTS

More people than I can name have taught me and supported me along the
way. I owe a tremendous debt to the following:

Debra Abell
Sharon Adams
Jane Ailes
Elizabeth Alexander
Maya Angelou
Bennett Ashley
Anthony Appiah
Isobel Appiah-Endresen
Romare Bearden
Tina Bennett
Kimberly W. Benston
David Bindman
John W. Blassingame, Sr.
John Morton Blum
Lawrence Bobo
Derek Bok
Carl Brandt
Tina Brown
Lawrence Buell
Rudolph Byrd
Gaston Caperton
Albert Carnesale
Johni Cerny
Richard Cohen
Virgis Colbert
Ethelbert Cooper
Karen C. C. Dalton

D. Ronald Daniel
Charles T. Davis
Brenda Kimmel Davy
Angela De Leon
Dominique de Menil
Rachel Dretzin
Driss Elghannaz
James Engell
David Evans
Drew Gilpin Faust
Henry Finder
Laura Fisher
Philip Fisher
William Fitzsimmons
Alphonse Fletcher, Jr.
Bettye Fletcher and
    James Comer
Leon Forrest
John Hope Franklin
Liza Gates
Maggie Gates
Paul and Gemina Gates
Asako Gladsjo
Thelma Golden
Sarabeth Goodwin
Amy Gosdanian
Donald Graham

Vera Ingrid Grant
Casper Grathwohl
Amy Gutmann
Evelynn Hammonds
Angela Harlock
Aaron Hatley
Candace Heinneman
Bernard Hicks
Evelyn Brooks Higginbotham
Arianna Huffington
Charlayne Hunter-Gault
Glenn H. Hutchins
Steven Hyman and Barbara Bier
Marial Iglesias Utset
Barbara Johnson
Quincy Jones
Vernon Jordan
Phyllis Keller
Joanne Kendall
Martin Kilson
Peter Kunhardt
Spike Lee
Sieglinde Lemke
Joanna Lipper
Paul Lucas
Kit Luce
Mark Mamolen
Erroll McDonald
William McFeely
Dyllan McGee
W. J. T. Mitchell
Marcyliena Morgan
Toni Morrison
Albert Murray
Renée Mussai
Lynn Nesbit
Donald and Susan Newhouse
Peter and Gwen Norton

Charles Ogletree
Deborah Wilson Pampinto
Richard Parsons
Martin Payson
Kari Pei
Martin Peretz
Brian Perkins
Richard Plepler
Steven Rattner and
    Maureen White
Ishmael Reed
David Remnick
Condoleezza Rice
Tamara Robinson
Daniel and Joanna Rose
Henry Rosovsky
Daryl Roth
Neil and Angelica Rudenstine
Ingrid Saunders-Jones
Teresa Lupis Savage
Elaine Scarry
Sharmila Sen
Ruth Simmons
Michael Smith
Wole Soyinka
Claude and Dorothy Steele
Carol Thompson
Helen Vendler
LuAnn Walther
Omar Wasow
Cornel West
Duke Anthony Whitmore
William Julius Wilson
Oprah Winfrey
Linden Havemeyer Wise
Abby Wolf
Donald Yacovone

INDEX

Abbott, Edith, 135
Abbott, Robert S., 611
Abel, Elizabeth, 287
Abrahams, Roger D., 259, 263, 273,
    282n10, 283n12
  Signifyin(g) and, 242, 256, 266–267,
    269, 270
Abrams, M. H., 182
Achebe, Chinua, 199
Adams, Harriet E., 49, 50
Adams, John Quincy, 146
Adams, Revels, 139
Adams, Sharon, 108, 558
Adebayo, Diran, 441
Adebayo, Dotun, 440–441, 444
Adger, Robert M., 59
Adichie, Chimamanda Ngozi, 570–571
African American literature, 1, 43, 49,
    83, 121–124, 154, 156, 161, 162,
    169, 170, 171, 175–177
  American literature and, 160
  anthologies of, 182, 183
  institutionalization of, 183, 288
  reconstructing, 184–185
  women's, 72, 123
African American Lives (PBS), 127, 128,
    132, 290, 292, 293, 385, 387
  subjects in, 129–130, 131
African American National Biography, 127
African American Studies, 74, 134, 149,
    172, 183, 291, 467, 597
African Americans, 75, 146–147, 572,
    573, 591
  alienation of, 421–422
  integral character of, 127

role definition for, 586
slavery and, 1, 143
African literature, 169, 170–171, 176, 177,
    180, 224, 271, 287
African Union, 568, 570
Ailes, Jane, 8, 17
Ailey, Alvin, 130
Akintola, Chief, 199
Akomfrah, John, 448
Al-Bashir, Omar, 568, 569
Albright, Madeleine, 580
Albuquerque, Wlamyra, 494,
    495, 496
Alexander, Clifford, Sr., 373, 374,
    375, 388, 389
Alexander, Clifford Leopold, Jr., 371,
    372, 374–375
Alexander, Elizabeth, 301, 324, 330
  ancestry of, 371–383, 384, 385–386,
    387, 388–389
Alexander, James, 373, 375, 376
Algren, Nelson, 191
Ali, Muhammad, 131, 449
Allen, Lin, 276
Allen, Lynn, 34
Allen, Richard, 415, 418
Allen, William G., 156–157
Alvaro II, King, 467
Álves, Dora, 492, 493
Amado, Jorge, 495
*American Dilemma: The Negro Problem
    and Modern Democracy, The*
    (Myrdal), 137
American literature, 154–155, 166, 160,
    174, 288, 300